THE COLLECTED LETTERS OF
JOSEPH CONRAD

GENERAL EDITOR:
FREDERICK R. KARL

CONSULTING EDITOR:
HANS van MARLE (1922–2001)

VOLUME 6

THE COLLECTED LETTERS
OF JOSEPH CONRAD

VOLUME 6
1917–1919

EDITED BY

LAURENCE DAVIES
FREDERICK R. KARL
AND
OWEN KNOWLES

CAMBRIDGE
UNIVERSITY PRESS

PUBLISHED BY THE PRESS SYNDICATE OF THE UNIVERSITY OF CAMBRIDGE
The Pitt Building, Trumpington Street, Cambridge, United Kingdom

CAMBRIDGE UNIVERSITY PRESS
The Edinburgh Building, CambridgeCB2 2RU, UK
40 West 20th Street, New York, NY 10011-4211, USA
477 Williamstown Road, Port Melbourne, VIC 3207, Australia
Ruiz de Alarcón 13, 28014 Madrid, Spain
Dock House, The Waterfront, Cape Town 8001, South Africa

http://www.cambridge.org

First published 2002

Printed in the United Kingdom at the University Press, Cambridge

Typeface Baskerville 10/12 pt   *System* LATEX 2ε   [TB]

A catalogue record for this book is available from the British Library

Library of Congress Cataloguing in Publication data

ISBN 0 521 56195 7 hardback

This volume is dedicated to
Sylvère Monod,
doyen of French Conradians

CONTENTS

PLATES

These illustrations appear by kind permission of: Baker-Berry Library, Dartmouth College (1, 6, 7, 8, 9, 12); Mr Owen Knowles (2); The British Library (3); Cambridge University Library (4, 5, 10); The National Portrait Gallery (11).

ACKNOWLEDGMENTS

As ever, we offer our warm thanks to the individuals and institutions listed as guardians of the letters.

We are especially grateful for the energy and vigilance of our fellow editors Dr Gene Moore and Dr J. H. Stape, and for the help of Dr R. A. Gekoski in gaining access to private collections.

For a wide variety of support, encouragement, and advice, we also thank Dr Richard Ambrosini, Ms Wanda Bachmann, Ms Susan Bibeau, Professor Andrew Busza, Dr Keith Carabine, Mr James Carroll, Mr Brien Chitty, Mr Philip Conrad, Ms Rachael A. Corkill, Mr Stephen Crook, Professor Mario Curreli, Dr Linda Dryden, Mr Benjamin Essery, Dr Gail Fincham, Dr James Fowler, Ms Barbara Gazduk, Professor Robert Hampson, Ms Sarah Hartwell, Professor Marianne Hirsch, Mr John H. B. Irving, Professor Konrad Kenkel, Ms Barbara Krieger, Professor Attie de Lange, Mr Philip Milito, Professor Padmini Mongia, Professor Zdzisław Najder, Ms Pamela Painter, Dr Ermien van Pletzen, Professor S. W. Reid, Professor Donald W. Rude, Mr Joshua Shaw, Dr Allan Simmons, Dr M. Sprenger, Professor Ray Stevens, Mr Wojciech Swiderski, Dr David Thomason, Ms Cornelia B. Wallin, Professor Cedric Watts, Professor Alison Wheatley, Ms Kim Wilson, and Dr Rowland Wymer.

Editing of Volume Six was made possible in part by a grant from the National Endowment for the Humanities, a federal agency.

As presidential scholars at Dartmouth College, Ms Michelle Rosen and Mr Asa Tapley have gone far beyond the bounds of duty. Their enthusiasm for the edition has been a blessing and a delight.

Just as this volume went to press, even as we were taking to heart and mind one last round of characteristically attentive and meticulous comments, we had the news of Hans van Marle's death. Our loss is deep and wide, and he is irreplaceable.

HOLDERS OF LETTERS

Alberta	Bruce Peel Special Collections Library, University of Alberta, Edmonton
Berg	The Berg Collection: Astor, Lenox, and Tilden Foundations, New York Public Library
BL	The British Library
Bodley	The Bodleian Library, Oxford University
Boston	The Boston Public Library, Massachusetts
Bryn Mawr	Bryn Mawr College Library, Bryn Mawr, Pennsylvania
Churchill	Churchill College, Cambridge University
Clifford	Mr Hugo Clifford-Holmes
Colgate	Colgate University Library, Hamilton, New York
Dartmouth	Special Collections, Baker-Berry Library, Dartmouth College, Hanover, New Hampshire
Doheny	The Doheny Memorial Library (collection dispersed)
Doucet	Bibliothèque Littéraire Jacques Doucet, Paris
Duke	William R. Perkins Library, Duke University, Durham, North Carolina
Elstob	Mr Peter Elstob
Fitzwilliam	Fitzwilliam Museum, Cambridge
Forbes	The late Malcolm Forbes, Jr
Free	Rare Book Department, The Free Library of Philadelphia, Pennsylvania
Harmsworth	Lord Harmsworth
Harvard	The Houghton Library, Harvard University, Cambridge, Massachusetts
Haverford	Special Collections, Haverford College Library, Haverford, Pennsylvania
Hofstra	Special Collections, Hofstra University Library, Hempstead, New York
Indiana	Lilly Library, University of Indiana, Bloomington
Karl	Professor Frederick R. Karl (collection dispersed)
Leeds	Brotherton Library, University of Leeds
Lowens	Mr Peter Lowens
Lubbock	Special Collections, Texas Tech University, Lubbock

Morgan	The Pierpont Morgan Library, New York
Nielson	Mr John Nielson
NLA	The National Library of Australia, Canberra
NLS	The National Library of Scotland, Edinburgh
NYPL	Miscellaneous Manuscripts Division, New York Public Library
NYU	The Fales Collection, New York University Libraries
PAN	Biblioteka PAN, Cracow
POSK	The Polish Library, London
Princeton	Special Collections, Firestone Library, Princeton University, New Jersey
PRO	Public Record Office, London
Rosenbach	The Philip H. and A. S. W. Rosenbach Foundation, Philadelphia, Pennsylvania
Rothenstein	The late Mr John Rothenstein
South Australia	Archives Department, Public Library of South Australia, Adelaide
Stanford	Special Collections, Stanford University Libraries, Palo Alto, California
Syracuse	George Arents Research Library for Special Collections, Syracuse University, Syracuse, New York
Taylor	Mrs C. E. Taylor
Texas	Harry Ransom Humanities Research Center, University of Texas at Austin
UNC	The Wilson Library, University of North Carolina Library at Chapel Hill
V&A	National Art Library, Victoria & Albert Museum, London
Virginia	Special Collections, Alderman Library, University of Virginia
Wellington	The Honourable Company of Master Mariners, HQS *Wellington*, London
Wright	Mrs Purd B. Wright III
Yale	The Beinecke Rare Book and Manuscript Library, Yale University, New Haven, Connecticut

PUBLISHED SOURCES OF LETTERS

Barringer	George Martyn Barringer, ed., 'Joseph Conrad and *Nostromo*: Two New Letters', *Thoth*, 10 (1969), 20–4
Blodgett	Harold W. Blodgett, ed., 'Mencken and Conrad', *Menckeniana* (Baltimore), 29 (1969), 1–3
Candler	Edmund Candler, *Youth and the East: An Unconventional Biography*. Edinburgh: Blackwood, 2nd edn, 1932
CEW	Norman Sherry, *Conrad's Eastern World*. Cambridge University Press, 1966
Conrad News	'A Letter of Conrad to Retinger, 22nd June, 1917', *Conrad News* (1978), 19–20
Cox	E. N. H. Cox, comp., *The Library of Edmund Gosse*. Dulau & Co., 1924
Curle	Richard Curle, ed., *Letters: Joseph Conrad to Richard Curle*. New York: Crosby Gaige, 1928
Curreli (1999)	Mario Curreli, ed., *Cecchi e Conrad: Tre lettere inedite*. Viareggio: Pezzini, 1999
Dryden	Linda Dryden, ed., 'Joseph Conrad and William Mathie Parker: Three Unpublished Letters from Conrad', *Notes and Queries*, 243 (June 1998), 227–30
Fletcher	Chris Fletcher, *Joseph Conrad*. British Library, 1999
G.	Edward Garnett, ed., *Letters from Joseph Conrad, 1895–1924*. Nonesuch Press, 1928
G. (B-M)	Edward Garnett, ed., *Letters from Joseph Conrad, 1895–1924*. Indianapolis: Bobbs-Merrill, 1928
Giertych	Jedrzeg Giertych, 'Conrad do Dmowskiego', *Wiadomości* (London), 51–2 (1952), 8
Hunter (1985, 2)	Allan G. Hunter, ed., 'Letters from Joseph Conrad, 2', *Notes and Queries*, 230 (September 1985), 500–5
Hunter (1985, 3)	Allan G. Hunter, ed., 'Some Unpublished Letters by Conrad to Arthur Symons', *Conradiana*, 17 (1985), 183–98
J-A	G. Jean-Aubry, ed., *Joseph Conrad: Life & Letters*. 2 volumes. New York: Doubleday, Page, 1927
JCLW	Jessie Conrad, ed., *Joseph Conrad's Letters to His Wife*. Privately printed, 1927

Jellard   Janet Jellard, ed., 'Joseph Conrad to His Doctor: Nine
                        Unpublished Letters 1909–1921', *Conradiana*, 19 (1987),
                        87–98
Jessie Conrad   Jessie Conrad, *Joseph Conrad and His Circle*. Jarrold's, 1935
Kane   [William Reno Kane, ed.,] 'To My Brethren of the
                        Pen'. Privately printed, 1927
Karl   Frederick R. Karl, ed., 'Three Conrad Letters in the
                        Edith Wharton Papers', *Yale University Library Gazette*,
                        44 (1970), 148–51
Keating   George T. Keating, ed., *A Conrad Memorial Library:*
                        The Collection of George T. Keating. New York: Doubleday,
                        Doran, 1929
Knowles   Owen Knowles and G. W. S. Miskin, eds., 'Unpublished
                        Conrad Letters: The H. Q. S. *Wellington* Collection',
                        Notes and Queries, 230 (September 1985), 370–6
Knowles & Stape   Owen Knowles and J. H. Stape, eds., 'An Unpublished
                        Conrad Letter of 1918', *The Conradian*, 15 (1990), 56–8
Letters   Frederick R. Karl and Laurence Davies, eds.,
                        The Collected Letters of Joseph Conrad. Cambridge
                        University Press, 1983, etc.
L. fr.   G. Jean-Aubry, ed., *Lettres françaises*. Paris: Gallimard,
                        1929
Listy   Zdzisław Najder, ed., Halina Carroll-Najder, trans.,
                        Joseph Conrad: Listy. Warsaw: Państwowy Instytut
                        Wydawniczy, 1968
Lucas   E. V. Lucas, *The Colvins and Their Friends*. New York:
                        Scribner's, 1928
Lowens (1977)   Peter J. Lowens, ed., 'Joseph Conrad to Captain Halsey:
                        An Unpublished Letter', *Conradiana*, 9 (1977), 187–8
Lowens (1986)   Peter J. Lowens, ed., 'The Conrad–Pinker Relationship:
                        An Unpublished Letter', *Conradiana*, 18 (1986), 45–7
Malay Mail   'Joseph Conrad: Singapore Journalist's Reminiscences:
                        Two Interesting Letters', *Malay Mail*, 2 September 1924
                        (reprinted from *Ceylon Observer*, 17 August 1924)
Marrot   H. V. Marrot, ed., *The Life and Letters of John Galsworthy*.
                        New York: Scribner's, 1936
Meynell   Alice Meynell, ed., *Friends of a Lifetime: Letters to Sydney*
                        Carlyle Cockerell. Cape, 1940
MFJC   Borys Conrad, *My Father: Joseph Conrad*. New York:
                        Coward, McCann, 1970

Moore	Gene M. Moore, ed., 'Conrad Items in the Dent Archive in North Carolina', *Notes and Queries*, 241 (1996), 437–9
Najder (1983, 2)	Zdzisław Najder, ed., Halina Carroll-Najder, trans., *Conrad under Familial Eyes*. Cambridge University Press, 1983
New Republic	'Mr Conrad is not a Jew', *New Republic*, 16 (24 August 1918), 109
Osborne	H. J. Osborne, ed., 'At Sea with Conrad', *Sea Breezes*, 23 (1957), 22–5
Pomian	John Pomian, ed., *Joseph Retinger: Memoirs of an Eminence Grise*. Brighton: University of Sussex Press, 1972
Randall	Dale B. J. Randall, ed., *Joseph Conrad and Warrington Dawson: The Record of a Friendship*. Durham, NC: Duke University Press, 1968
Rude	Donald W. Rude, ed., 'Joseph Conrad Letters, Typescripts, and Proofs in the Texas Tech Collection', *The Conradian*, 11 (1986), 136–54
Roberts	Cecil Roberts, 'Joseph Conrad: A Reminiscence', *Bookman*, 69 (1925), 95–9
Summer's Lease	John Rothenstein, *Autobiography I: Summer's Lease*. Hamish Hamilton, 1965
Vidan (1970)	Gabrijela and Ivo Vidan, eds., 'Further Correspondence between Joseph Conrad and André Gide', *Studia Romanica et Anglica Zagrebiensia*, 29–30 (1970–1), 523–36
Watts	C. T. Watts, ed., *Joseph Conrad's Letters to R. B. Cunninghame Graham*. Cambridge University Press, 1969

OTHER FREQUENTLY CITED WORKS

Conrad, John — *Joseph Conrad: Times Remembered.* Cambridge University Press, 1981

Hart-Davis, Rupert — *Hugh Walpole: A Biography.* New York: Macmillan, 1952 (abbreviated as *Walpole*)

Hervouet, Yves — *The French Face of Joseph Conrad.* Cambridge University Press, 1990 (abbreviated as *French Face*)

Hodgson & Co. — *A Catalogue of Books, MSS. and Corrected Typescripts from the Library of the Late Joseph Conrad . . . Sold . . . by Messrs Hodgson & Co . . . March 13th, 1925*

Karl, Frederick R. — *Joseph Conrad: The Three Lives.* New York: Farrar, Straus, Giroux, 1979

Moore, Gene M., ed. — *Conrad on Film.* Cambridge University Press, 1997

Najder, Zdzisław — *Joseph Conrad: A Chronicle.* New Brunswick, NJ: Rutgers University Press, 1983 (abbreviated as *Chronicle*)

Reid, B. L. — *The Man from New York: John Quinn and His Friends.* New York: Oxford University Press, 1968

Sherry, Norman — *Conrad: The Critical Heritage.* Routledge & Kegan Paul, 1973 (abbreviated as *CH*)

Stape, J. H., and Owen Knowles, eds. — *Conrad: A Portrait in Letters.* Amsterdam: Rodopi, 1996 (abbreviated as *Portrait*)

Watts, Cedric, and Laurence Davies — *Cunninghame Graham: A Critical Biography.* Cambridge University Press, 1979

Unless otherwise noted, references to Conrad's work come from the Kent Edition, published by Doubleday, Page in twenty-six volumes (Garden City, NY, 1925). Books cited without place of publication originated in London.

CHRONOLOGY, 1917–1919

Unless otherwise stated, dates are for book publication in Britain rather than the United States; dates and locations for stories and essays in magazines note only the first appearance.

January–June 1917	Afflicted by poor health and war-time gloom, Conrad prepared *The Shadow-Line* for publication during the first part of this period, then occupied himself with theatrical plans for the stage version of *Victory*.
January 1917	Resumed work on *The Arrow of Gold*, still regarded as short story.
15 January 1917	On ten-day leave, Borys celebrated his birthday at home on the 15th.
March 1917	*One Day More* privately published, the first of 26 limited-edition pamphlets brought out by C. K. Shorter and T. J. Wise. 'The Warrior's Soul' in *Land and Water*.
19 March 1917	*The Shadow-Line* published.
9 April 1917	Edward Thomas killed in the Battle of Arras.
7 May 1917	Completed preface to Edward Garnett's *Turgenev: A Study*, published in October.
Late May–early June 1917	Composed Author's Note for second edition of *Lord Jim*.
June 1917	'Flight' in *The Fledgling*.
2 June 1917	Relinquished Civil List pension.
Late June 1917	Second UK edition of *Lord Jim* published by Dent.
September	Second UK edition of *Youth* published by Dent.
Early October 1917	Revised *Nostromo* for second edition and wrote Author's Note.
October 1917	'The Tale' in *Strand Magazine*.
November 1917	The Conrads went to London, for major surgery on Jessie Conrad's leg; at the Norfolk Hotel from the 16th to the 26th, then moving to 4c Hyde Park Mansions.

3 December 1917	Conrad's 60th birthday.
January 1918	First meeting with Hugh Walpole. Second UK edition of *Nostromo* published by Dent.
26 February 1918	Returned to Capel House.
6 March 1918	'Tradition' in *Daily Mail*.
14 March 1918	Became member of Athenaeum Club.
24 March 1918	Contact with Borys restored after ten days of worrying silence during a fierce German offensive.
25 April 1918	Attended preview of William Rothenstein's war pictures at the Goupil Gallery, London.
May 1918	First meeting with G. Jean-Aubry.
4 June 1918	Completed a draft of *The Arrow of Gold*.
c. 21 June– 13 August 1918	The Conrads in London for further surgery on Jessie Conrad. Borys, on leave during mid-July, joined the family.
Late June 1918	Consulted by André Gide, then in London, about French translations of Conrad's works.
July 1918	Made preparations to return to 'The Rescuer' manuscript in the autumn.
August 1918	'First News' in *Reveille*.
22–24 August 1918	'Well Done!' in *Daily Chronicle*.
Early October 1918	The Conrads in London for two weeks, when Jessie underwent further surgery on her leg.
2 October 1918	Sold the first of many items of Conradiana to T. J. Wise, breaking a gentleman's agreement with John Quinn.
16 October 1918	Borys, suffering from shell-shock and 'slightly gassed', sent to hospital in Rouen.
11 November 1918	Armistice Day.
December 1918– February 1920	*The Arrow of Gold* in *Lloyd's Magazine*.
26 December 1918	Completed draft of 'The Crime of Partition'.
January–July 1919	*The Rescue* in *Land and Water*.
15 January 1919	Ill and in bed, Conrad unable to join in Borys's 21st-birthday celebrations.
20 January 1919	Death of the Conrads' long-serving maid Nellie Lyons.
27 January 1919	Finished Author's Note to *An Outcast of the Islands*.
7–13 February 1919	The Conrads in London for surgical consultations.

21 February 1919	Death of Stephen Reynolds.
3 March 1919	Attended a rehearsal of *Victory* at the Globe Theatre, London.
25 March 1919	Moved from Capel House to a temporary home, Spring Grove, Wye, Kent.
26 March 1919	First performance of *Victory* at the Globe Theatre, London.
12 April 1919	*The Arrow of Gold* published in US.
c. 23 April 1919	Finished Author's Note to *Tales of Unrest*.
May 1919	'The Crime of Partition' in the *Fortnightly Review*.
25 May 1919	Finished writing serial of *The Rescue*.
June–September 1919	Prepared volumes and wrote several Author's Notes for collected edition of his work.
16 June 1919	Sold film rights to four of his works to the Laski Film Company for $22,500
30 June 1919	'Confidence' in *Daily Mail*.
6 August 1919	*The Arrow of Gold* published in UK.
c. 8 September 1919	Finished Author's Note to *A Personal Record*.
October–November 1919	Adapted *The Secret Agent* for the stage.
3 October 1919	Began the move to new home, Oswalds, Bishopsbourne, Kent.
30 November 1919	The Conrads arrived in Liverpool, where Jessie would endure yet more surgery on her leg. While there, Conrad made his first public speech (to University Club). 'Stephen Crane: A Note without Dates' in *London Mercury*.
c. 23 December 1919	The Conrads returned to Oswalds.

INTRODUCTION TO VOLUME SIX

Conrad turned sixty in December 1917. In that year, he had published *The Shadow-Line*, a fictional transformation of his experience as master of the *Otago*. Also in 1917, he tried to work on a story rooted in memories of his youthful adventures in Marseilles which eventually became *The Arrow of Gold*. Perhaps reacting to the strains of the war, perhaps conscious of time's rushing by, Conrad was in retrospective mode. When *The Arrow* appeared in the summer of 1919, the regular fiction reviewer for the *Athenaeum* felt 'a tiny flicker of dismay' on realising that both the subject and the workmanship of Conrad's novel were suspiciously callow:

> As we read Mr Conrad's latest published book we find ourselves wishing once again that it were a common practice among authors to let us know the year in which a book is begun and ended...
> It is impossible not to believe that he has had this particular novel in the cellar for a considerable time – this sweet, sparkling, heady mixture in the strange-shaped bottle with the fantastic label. How does it stand being held up to the light, tasted, sipped, and compared with those dark, foreign beverages with which he has made us so familiar? (8 August 1919, p. 720)

The answer, suggested but never spelled out, was 'none too well'. According to Katherine Mansfield, who signed the review with her initials, the plot leads to a 'crisis so fantastical that we cannot but fancy Mr Conrad of to-day smiling at its stage horrors'; the tone is that of a writer in search of himself; the prose lacks the 'fine economy of suggestion' characteristic of Conrad's great achievements. Rita de Lastaola, the centre round which the other characters revolve, is much more rigidly archetypal than is good for her: 'the *femme fatale*, the woman of all times, the Old Enchantress, the idol before whom no man can do aught but worship, the Eternal Feminine, Donna* Rita, woman'.

The spirit of the age, as Mansfield puts it, 'is an uneasy, disintegrating, experimental spirit'. The young New Zealander, herself an experimentalist, terse, unpredictable, impatient with Romantic archetypes, implies that Conrad in 1919 is either a once-great writer lapsed into second adolescence or a once-great writer passing off apprentice work rescued from some musty drawer – either mutton dressed as lamb or lamb dressed as mutton. Had she seen Conrad's description of *The Rescue* as 'the swan song of Romance as a form of literary art' (To Pinker, 15 February 1919), all her suspicions would have been confirmed.

Persuaded of its force or not, anyone who has read modern biographies or critical studies of Conrad will know the theory that at some moment in his literary career – time and occasion being moot – the arc of his achievement began to fall. Mansfield's review suggests that younger writers already had a sense of his decline. Who among such younger writers as Mansfield, Dorothy Richardson, Virginia Woolf, or D. H. Lawrence would have followed the nineteenth-century precedent of serialising a novel in a popular (rather than avant-garde) magazine, let alone anything as domestic as *Lloyd's*, which had just inherited the readership of *Baby: The Mother's Magazine*?

With one foot on the well-trampled turf of serial fiction and the other on the venerable carpets of the Athenaeum, Conrad's literary alignment was distinctive. While he continued to publish wherever Pinker could find him a home, he had become an institution, the novelist that reviewers staider than Mansfield regularly claimed could only be matched by Hardy, who had, of course, abandoned fiction. During the period of this volume, the collector's market for anything Conradian, however slight, was booming. Students and professors from the United States wanted to know his religious and literary opinions. In the United Kingdom, T. J. Wise and Clement Shorter drew Conrad's attention to the rewards of publishing old work in stringently limited-edition pamphlets. In both countries, publishers were assembling collected editions. Meanwhile, Conrad wondered if he might be in the running for the Nobel Prize (To Pinker, 15 February 1919).

From a distance, then, Conrad's professional life between 1917 and 1919 appears to have combined gravitas, nostalgia, and the need to cut the forests of his earlier life and work a second time. Closer in, the landscape looks more varied. Although few people now write about or even read *The Rescue* or *The Arrow of Gold*, and fewer still would turn to them again, *The Shadow-Line* remains a major work, as distinguished by its tautness and economy as the other two novels are by their prolixity, and though 'The Tale' and 'The Warrior's Soul' are much less known than they deserve, they are the work of a moral and artistic imagination that has in no sense lost its way.

One can argue, indeed, that the strains and tensions in Conrad's life during and even after the war were such that the persistence of his artistic energies is more remarkable than the evidence of weariness or decline. When he complains that life is drudgery, he does it vividly. In connection with their work on the staging of *Victory*, for example, he tells Macdonald Hastings:

I hope that materially your expectation will be realised. Ours. I don't pretend to indifference. My dear H, I have been for 20 years performing on a tight rope (without net) and I am still at it, and I am 59 [60] last birthday. One would like to see some prospect of getting down at last – if only on the brink of the grave, just for a moment.
([27 February 1917])

Soon after, not at all discouraged by tangled negotiations over scripts and actors, he suggested another venture on the tightrope:

> If the ultimate result is at all encouraging I will have a proposal to lay before you for real collaboration. That is if you feel eventually that you can stand me in that relation. For it beats even the married state for delicacy and complexity.
>
> (To Hastings, [early March? 1917])

His wit had not been withering away.

The mood of graveside despondency was also a long-lived feature of his life, especially when his writing froze, but during the war years the pressures strengthened as increasingly the private became contingent on the public. 'All one's interior and private life is knocked into a cocked hat every morning by the public news' (To Curle, 2 December 1917). With their son Borys at the front, Jessie and Joseph Conrad faced the daily anguish of the casualty lists, the widely fluctuating gaps between deliveries of postcards or letters home, and the newspaper stories that said everything and nothing. Borys's leaves were infrequent and inevitably poignant:

> Our boy has just left us at the expiration of his leave. My poor wife snatched nine days of fearful joy – and now that he has gone back to his beloved battery (after celebrating his 19th birthday with us) there is a great aching emptiness in this house.
>
> (To Hastings, 25 January 1917)

In the surviving correspondence, the expression 'fearful joy' occurs five times in the first four months of 1917. Conrad normally used this quotation from Gray to describe his wife's feelings, but there can be no doubt he shared them and saw how much she suffered. When the news came through that Borys was in a military hospital in Rouen, Conrad wrote to him about his mother:

> You can't know dearest how much you are to her. No one can know. I can but dimly feel something of the terrible strain under her serene cheerfulness . . . she had a very hard time of it which all my love for her could not make easier to bear.
>
> (21 October 1918)

Many of his friends were in a similar plight:

> I felt for you, seeing Eric off. It's rather awful. One lives in hope but with set teeth all the time. (To Pinker, [7 October 1917])

The Pinkers, the Sandersons, the Cliffords all had sons exposed to danger, as did a throng of more casual acquaintances. The war that had started so oddly for the Conrads with their ill-timed visit to Cracow had later brought them an experience shared with many thousands of other civilians. Borys did survive (unlike, for example, Sir Hugh Clifford's son by his first marriage), but at the price of gassing, shell-shock, and temporary blindness.

The Armistice of 11 November 1918 gave the Conrads some respite from anxieties about Borys, but little peace of mind. What one might expect to be a moment of transition in the correspondence gathered in this volume was nothing of the sort. Unlike the jubilant atmosphere in the streets of London, where soldiers, nurses, sailors, and civilians danced and sang in temporary oblivion, the mood at Capel House was already reflective rather than exultant, pessimistic rather than utopian:

> We are thankful to know that your boy as well as ours is safe out of the fiery furnace. On this day of sober joy one's thoughts turn to the homes where no losses can be made up and one's gratitude [to] the multitude of those who will never return.
> (To the Sandersons, 11 November)
> A word on this great day to take part in the sober joy you must feel. The great sacrifice is consummated – and what will come of it to the nations of the earth the future will show.
> I can not confess to an easy mind. Great and very blind forces are set free catastrophically all over the world.   (To Walpole, 11 November)

Although, like so many of his contemporaries, Conrad used the language of sacrifice, he had no vision of regeneration to offer, no sense that the road from Armageddon led to the millennial kingdom of secular or sacred peace.

His misgivings were in part political. As his comments to Walpole imply, Conrad was not at all sure that humanity would be saved by President Wilson's Fourteen Points. Since the world after the war threatened to be at least as dangerous as the world before it, the plans for a great peace conference and the institution of a League of Nations dedicated to good sense and good will seemed to him naive and grandiose. Although such figures as J. H. Retinger and Roman Dmowski had asked Conrad to back their markedly divergent plans for the future of their country, and he replied to them with the utmost politeness, he continued to suspect that Poland's soon-to-be-restored independence would be no security against encroachments by its neighbours, especially the Bolshevik government in Russia:

> Poland will have to pay the price of some pretty ugly compromises, as you will see. The mangy Russian dog having gone mad is now being invited to sit at the Conference table, on British initiative!   (To Clifford, 25 January 1919)

In this new European order, even establishing the borders of the new state would be challenging. What was Polish and what was German, Russian, or Lithuanian? Conrad's own birthplace was in Ukraine, a vortex of conflicting nationalisms.

During the war, Conrad had given no overt sign of dissent. When writing to friends and colleagues in the United States about the war or the resurgence of militant nationalism in Ireland, Conrad often moved into the first person plural as if to share the views of other citizens:

> I will tell you frankly that we don't think much about Irishmen now. As long as they didn't actually and materially add to the deadly dangers of our situation we were satisfied. I am speaking now of the bulk of the people, not of our politicians.
>
> (To Quinn, 16 October 1918)

He wrote as a loyal Briton (to the extent of ignoring such complexities as the Unionist role in the Irish crisis) but not as a jingoist. When compared with the patriotic insistence of such contemporaries or friends as Bennett, Wells, Galsworthy, and Ford, the mildness and infrequency of Conrad's contributions to war-time propaganda are striking. It is striking, also, that the two short stories written during the war, 'The Warrior's Soul' and 'The Tale', reflect it only on the slant; the first by shifting present-day controversies about the execution of prisoners of war back to the context of Napoleon's retreat from Moscow, the second by relocating another contemporary controversy, the proper response to neutral ships suspected of supplying the enemy, to 'another – some other – world' (p. 61). Hard weather, fog or blizzard, characterises the moral landscape of these stories. Conrad favoured ambivalence in his war-time fiction but expected of public discourse a kind of sharp honesty:

> London is the silliest place in the world. It's* chatter sounds both absurd and heartless very often. The press with its "Enemy defeats" is exasperating too. The people of this country are not *all* infants. And on top of that comes the "back to the wall" proclamation . . . I think that the general in the Peninsular* War who rode up to his part of the line just before the French attack "en masse" and said simply: "Die hard, men" was better inspired. (To Borys Conrad, 27 April 1918)

Even writing to his son, who had just returned to a dangerous position at the Front, Conrad preferred such frankness, and the end of hostilities did not crimp his distaste for what he called 'the democratic bawlings of the virtuous leaders of mankind' (To the Galsworthys, 24 December 1918).

Added to these, for Conrad, infuriating features of current political life was a round of social disturbance, chiefly in the form of strikes by miners and railway workers tired of the wage restraints imposed on them during the war:

> There is not a whistle, a rumble or a clank to be heard in the whole landscape. A profound peace broods over the land. But a dump of high-explosive shells looks a most peaceable thing in the world, too! (To Quinn, 29 September 1919)

Although never as turbulent as those in Liverpool and the Rhondda during the last years of peace, these latest strikes disrupted Conrad's sense of how an orderly society should behave and made him gloomier than ever about the future.

This disquietude can only have been exacerbated by the ill-health of everyone in the family but young John. Despite a series of agonising probes and operations, each of which seemed to promise a surgical solution, the condition of Jessie Conrad's weaker knee worsened, further limiting her ability to get about. This lack of mobility was particularly trying for her during the moves from Capel House to Spring Grove and from there to Oswalds. She did not lack for medical attention; Sir Robert Jones, who soon became a staunch friend of the family, was one of the most prominent orthopaedic surgeons in the English-speaking world, and a man loved both in the army and among civilians throughout Wales and the north of England for his geniality and compassion. Thanks to Sir Robert, their near-neighbour in Kent Major Kenneth Campbell of the Royal Army Medical Corps, and their own physicians, the Conrads had the best professional attention possible, but it was not enough. Meanwhile, as his handwriting frequently attests, Joseph Conrad suffered debilitating attacks of gout, intimations of prostate trouble, and the jabs of neuralgia. More and more he relied on the secretarial services of Miss Hallowes. It was not the wish to imitate Henry James that led him to dictate *The Arrow of Gold*.

Although the effects of gas lingered distressingly, Borys Conrad's problems were less directly those of the body. Like many of his comrades, he found the return to civilian life disquieting rather than joyful or even comforting. In 1919, he was a patient at the Maudsley, the South London hospital that specialised in the treatment of shell-shock. His love of gadgets, motor cars, and engines gave him great solace and the chance of appropriate jobs, but a combination of restlessness, depression, and bad luck with his employers, especially the soon-to-be former friend of the family Robert Duncan Mackintosh, made it hard for him to settle down.

Through all this time of worries and irritations personal or public, Conrad engaged with his profession. This was a period of finishing or framing certain aspects of his work. One of his preoccupations in this regard was to give contemporary reviewers and future biographers some account of the links between his writings and his life. Especially in letters to Sir Sidney Colvin, who would review *The Shadow-Line* for the *Observer*, Conrad insisted on its closeness to actual experience; to the same friend and correspondent, he made similar claims about his adventures in Marseilles and their appearance in *The Arrow of Gold*. Recent scholars suspect the alloy of these links, yet it is significant that Conrad should want to cast them in the first place. Providing a set of Author's Notes for the collected editions gave another opportunity to write on the connections between art and experience; often brief and usually done in haste, they are still eminently quotable, marking not so much a finishing- as a starting-point for understanding such connections. Conrad, moreover, was not only reconsidering his fictions; the Wise and Shorter pamphlets and the gradual assembly of *Notes on Life and Letters* – in the circumstances, a revealing title – gave him more cause to reflect upon the past.

Too great an emphasis on retrospection would give a false impression of the years covered in this volume. Conrad still had a taste for novelty and excitement. His old suspicion of the stage had slipped away. Hastings was rightly credited as the adaptor of *Victory*, but Conrad read his efforts with close attention, and became fascinated by the glamour of costumes, sets, and casting. The play's run was a mixed success. The King and Queen came to see it, the magazines pictured it, and a good few of the reviews were at least respectful, but a review in the *Illustrated London News* suggests what it lacked:

> It was never the plot that gave the tale distinction, but a certain magic in the descriptive writing and the novelist's gift of suggesting souls in torture, and the power of evil wrecking innocent lives . . . Still, perhaps there is enough colour and movement and thrill at the Globe to satisfy those who know little of him.   (5 April 1919, 498)

Conrad himself had felt that thrill, and none of the play's difficulties deterred him from wanting to do more.

His enthusiasms for the cinema will emerge more fully in the next volume, but one should remember that he was already what producers and financiers would call a 'property'. In June 1919, Pinker sold the US movie rights to *Romance, Lord Jim, Chance*, and *Victory* for $22,500. For a man feeling old and wanting to provide for his family, this windfall came most gratefully, but as the correspondence of later years will show, he found the medium itself exhilarating, even artistically stimulating. Indeed, he was considerably more open to its possibilities than some of his younger colleagues, and not quite the aesthetic reactionary he might have seemed.

Between 1917 and 1919, Conrad made a multitude of new contacts, acquaintances, and friends, while, of course, retaining many old ones. A connection that did fray was the one with John Quinn. Friendship, acquaintance, business relationship – it is hard to find the right expression for Conrad's exchanges with Quinn, whom he never met. Quinn sent baskets of apples, lengthy accounts of his busy public and personal life, his thoughts on politics and the arts, word of negotiations with Doubleday, and payment for the manuscripts Jessie Conrad had a talent for retrieving from obscure drawers. By his own standards, if not Quinn's, Conrad replied at length, telling him about his plans, politely sympathising with Quinn's woes, and often challenging his ideas. In December 1918, Conrad broke the agreement to give Quinn first refusal on manuscripts by offering the typescript and some manuscript sheets of *The Arrow of Gold* to Thomas J. Wise. On 19 June 1919, Quinn wrote a restrained letter about this sale; Conrad answered on 29 September. His letter reaches the burning issue circuitously, and could be taken, according to one's sympathies, as a frank apologia or an exercise in resolute casuistry. In any case, the damage had been done.

With Garnett, on the other hand, a friendship rekindled. Once the war was over, the differences of opinion about military and political morality faded away:

I missed you immensely my dear old friend during all these days. The resumption of our intercourse has been very precious to me. It was a great and comforting experience to have your ever trusted and uncompromising soul come forward again from the unforgotten past and look closely at my work with the old old wonderful insight, with unimpaired wisdom and in unalterable friendship. (22 December 1918)

What touched Conrad in particular was Garnett's readiness to scrutinise *The Rescue* just as in the old days he had scrutinised its ancestor 'The Rescuer'. The familiar and affectionate letters to him came from more than twenty years of intermittent closeness.

Many other familiar correspondents appear in these pages: Cunninghame Graham, who was writing hard and running one last time for Parliament; the Colvins, whose library Conrad 'plundered' while in London, and whose increasing physical frailty brought out Conrad's solicitude; Curle, who persisted as Conrad's prophet by appointment; Will Rothenstein, who served in France as a war artist, his wife, Alice, and their son John; André Gide, who was busy organising Conrad translations as well as writing prodigiously himself; and the extended family of Sandersons with their connections round the globe. Conrad's most frequent contacts were with J. B. Pinker, both as professional partner and as confidant. Conrad's metaphors vary: Pinker is his pilot (19 February 1919) or his literary doctor ([2 May 1917]). When Conrad wondered if their correspondence might one day be published, his mind went back to the unhappy days of their quarrel in 1910:

As between you and me I want all the world to know what you have done for me. But there is one period that might be pruned. I do not suggest destruction but a separate packet. If the world were honest and fair-minded, it could be trusted with the whole truth. But it isn't. It will put the worst construction on any given episode and besmirch the real truth established by so many years of your determined belief in me and of my gratitude to you which, believe me my dear friend, has never been obscured for a moment in my heart, no matter what words might have been written on the spur of the moment. (19 February 1919)

Pinker's side of the correspondence we do not have, but Conrad's side is a constant testimony not only to his agent's acumen but to his extraordinary generosity and forbearance. Given this record, even from the worst times of anger and despair, it would indeed be churlish to 'put the worst construction' on their dealings or 'besmirch the real truth'.

Among the new correspondents, a good few linked Conrad with the world outside Britain. Admirers in the United States, such as Lewis Browne, W. T. Howe, Meredith Janvier, and Barrett H. Clark – respectively a rabbinical student, a book collector, a book dealer cum amateur strongman, and a professor – wanted his views on life and letters. W. G. St Clair and A. T. Saunders provoked memories of old times in South Pacific and East Asian waters. Among the authors Conrad encouraged were H. M. Tomlinson, who wrote about the sea and South America, and Edmund Candler, who drew on his experiences in India and the Middle East. Meanwhile, the range of his francophone correspondence broadened to include, among others, Catherine Willard, a young American actress who was winning a strong reputation in Shakespeare, Ibsen, and Congreve, but had trained in Paris. Her mother, Grace Willard, an energetic journalist and interior designer, advised the Conrads on the decoration and the furnishings of Oswalds, the substantial house they had taken outside Canterbury. One especially significant French correspondent was Jean-Frédéric-Émile Aubry, who called himself, as we call him here, G. Jean-Aubry. Aubry was a Frenchman resident in London, where he edited *The Chesterian*, the house journal of a firm of musical-instrument makers. He enjoyed an extensive acquaintance in French literary and musical circles and was an habitué of Mme Alvar's influential salon in London. Conradians now remember him as Conrad's first biographer, but he also figured in Conrad's life as a genial, witty, worldly friend who knew Ravel, Debussy, de Falla, and Roussel and appealed delightfully to Conrad's musical predilections.

Conrad knew of Hugh Walpole's book about him as early as 1916, the year of publication, but he did not read it until 1918, the year in which this friendship grew. The later Hugh Walpole, fussy, prosperous, sleek, at home with dukes and duchesses, a middlebrow darling, stands in the light of the vigorous man whom Conrad knew and liked. He had recently come back from a series of adventures in Russia, where he had mingled with Scriabin,

Sologub, and Merezhkovsky, won the Order of Saint George for his bravery as a Red Cross orderly under fire, directed an office of British propaganda in Petrograd, and witnessed the revolution of March 1917 and the start of the Bolshevik revolution. Conrad greatly admired *The Secret City*, a novel growing from what Walpole had seen and heard in Petrograd. Like the earlier *The Dark Forest*, it has an urgency and vividness that attest to Walpole's never quite fulfilled promise.

Some of Conrad's most engaging letters were written in barely controlled rage. One can point, for instance, to the brace of tirades against Methuen in 1913 (*Letters*, 5, 195, 200). The equivalent in this volume was directed to S. Nevile Foster, editor of *Land and Water*, where *The Rescue* was about to appear as a serial, but the real object of Conrad's scorn was the illustrator Dudley Hardy:

But really in the scene with the two figures drawn by Mr. Hardy the limits of the widest license* are overstepped. It almost amounts to gross contempt and I tell you this plainly because I feel it strongly. What does he mean by sticking a fur cap on the head of Lingard? What is it – a joke? Or is it to display a fine independence in a story whose action takes place in the tropics?   (12 December 1918)

Hardy topped the insult by visiting Capel House and getting drunk:

Hardy is awful! Awful! I believe you've given me the word of the riddle. I couldn't understand. I thought that he was just simply an unspeakable idiot. Well, he certainly does *not* find truth in wine.   (To Colvin [14 or 21? February 1919])

Such letters allow us a glimpse of Conrad's banked-up fires. The war's immense strain took years to slacken and required of him meanwhile a kind of stoicism or, as Marlow would have put it, restraint. A note to Lewis Rose Macleod, literary editor of the *Daily Mail*, expresses Conrad's way precisely. Having been asked for a contribution to the paper's 'Golden Peace Number', he sent them 'Confidence'. It builds upon a single lapidary statement: 'The seamen hold up the Edifice', and, after a judicious survey, goes to insist that the building remains secure. Nevertheless he admitted to Macleod:

You have had "Tradition" before, and "Confidence" will make a pair. The word in itself is not a bad word for a Peace Number.

As to my own confidence in the future I don't mind telling you privately that it isn't the confidence that dwells in one and runs like soothing balsam in one's veins. It is the sort of confidence one holds on to with teeth and claws for dear life. However I don't say that in my article.   (16 April 1919)

Laurence Davies
Dartmouth College

CONRAD'S CORRESPONDENTS
1917–1919

A dagger after a name marks a tentative ascription.

Elbridge Lapham ADAMS (1866–1934), journalist and book collector, brought out a study of *Joseph Conrad: The Man* in 1925; on a lighter note, he was editor of the *Century Anthology of Porcine Poetry* (1924). He became acquainted with Conrad in 1916 and was one of his hosts on the American tour in 1923.

Mme ALVAR: see HARDING

William ARCHER (1856–1924), a Scot, began his career as a drama critic in 1879, with the *London Figaro*. Later, he wrote for the *World, Nation, Tribune, Morning Leader,* and *Manchester Guardian*. An editor and translator of Ibsen, he fought to make the British stage more serious. During the war, he worked for the War Propaganda Bureau.

Jean-Frédéric-Émile AUBRY (1882–1949) wrote as G., Georges, or Gérard Jean-Aubry. Born in Le Havre, he became a friend of many composers, including Debussy and Ravel; both de Falla and Roussel wrote settings of his poems. From 1908 to 1915, he travelled in Europe and Latin America, promoting the cause of contemporary French music. From 1919 to 1930, he edited *The Chesterian*, a music magazine published by a firm of instrument makers. His books on music include *La Musique française d'aujourd'hui* (1916, translated 1919) and *La Musique et les nations* (1922). Conradians know him for *Joseph Conrad in the Congo* (1926), *Joseph Conrad: Life & Letters* (1927), *Lettres françaises* (1929), *The Sea Dreamer: A Definitive Biography* (1947; trans. 1957), and numerous French translations of Conrad's works.

Mr BATTY: Conrad's letter to him of 19 July 1918 implies that he was or had been a sailor, perhaps in the RNR, but his precise identity remains unknown.

Lewis Saul BENJAMIN (1874–1932) and his wife, Helen Mira Benjamin, took the appropriate pseudonyms 'H. and L. Melville' to edit *Full Fathom Five,* published in April 1910; the selection includes one excerpt from 'Youth' and three from *The Nigger*. 'Lewis Melville' wrote the lives and edited the letters of many authors, among them Lady Mary Wortley Montagu, Smollett, Sterne,

xxxv

Beckford, and Cobbett. His two-volume biography of Thackeray appeared in 1899.

When Rollo Walter BROWN (1880–1956) wrote to Conrad, he was Professor of Rhetoric at Wabash College, Indiana; later he moved to Carleton College, Minnesota, and on to Harvard. In 1924 he gave up teaching in order to write full-time. Brown's works include *The Art of Writing English: A Book for College Classes* (1913) and *How the French Boy Learns to Write: A Study in the Teaching of the Mother Tongue* (1915); for Harvard University Press he edited *The Writer's Art by Those Who Have Practiced It* (1921), which includes the Preface to *The Nigger*.

London-born, Lewis BROWNE (1897–1949) emigrated to the USA when he was fourteen. At the time he wrote to Conrad, he was studying for the rabbinate at Hebrew Union College and a bachelor's degree at the University of Cincinnati. When his vigorously socialist views cost him his first appointment as a rabbi, he became a professional writer and lecturer on religion; among his popular successes were *Stranger Than Fiction: A Short History of the Jews* (1925), *Since Calvary: An Interpretation of Christian History* (1931), and *How Odd of God* (1934).

Major Kenneth CAMPBELL had been an officer in the Royal Army Medical Corps and chief ophthalmic surgeon, Southern Command. He had a practice in London and a country house in Wittersham, Kent. Although not Conrad's general practitioner, Dr Campbell gave him informal advice. Campbell died in 1943.

Edmund CANDLER (1874–1926) read classics at Cambridge. From 1896 to 1903, he taught in Indian schools and colleges, and from 1906 to 1914 he was Principal of Mohindra College in Patiala. He wrote about his extensive travels in Asia for the *Outlook*, *Blackwood's*, and the *Allahabad Pioneer*; in 1904, he was gravely wounded while covering the Younghusband Mission to Tibet for the London *Daily Mail*. He served as an official correspondent with the Indian Expeditionary Force in Mesopotamia, 1917–18, and as a roving reporter for *The Times* in the Transcaucasian Republics, 1918–19. After a spell as Director of Publicity for the Punjab, 1919–21, he retired to Southern France. In addition to his accounts of war and wandering, he published novels, short stories, and *Youth and the East: An Unconventional Autobiography* (1924).

As one of T. Fisher Unwin's readers, Wilfrid Hugh CHESSON (1870–1952) was among the first to see the MS of *Almayer* and was swift to appreciate its promise. As a reviewer for the newspapers, Chesson later contributed several perceptive appraisals of Conrad's fiction.

A publisher, editor, and author, Barrett H. CLARK (1890–1953) devoted his life to the theatre. He was literary editor for Samuel French, New York, from 1918 to 1936; in the latter year he became executive director of Dramatists' Play Service; his own books included *British and American Drama of Today* (1915), *Contemporary French Dramatists* (1915), and *Eugene O'Neill* (1926); his labours as an anthologist included the 58-volume series World's Best Plays (1915–26).

Sir Hugh Charles CLIFFORD (1866–1941; knighted 1909), a colonial administrator, was serving as British Resident in Pahang, Malaya, when he wrote one of the earliest general appreciations of Conrad's work. Later, he was appointed to the governorships of Labuan and North Borneo, the Gold Coast, Nigeria, Ceylon, and the Straits Settlements. He published many volumes of stories and sketches, collaborated on a Malay dictionary, and produced a Malay translation of the colonial penal code.

After three years of selling coal, Sydney Carlyle COCKERELL (1867–1962; knighted 1934) went to work for William Morris and the Kelmscott Press in 1892; thereafter, Cockerell's love of books and fine typography never waned. From 1908 to to 1937, he directed Cambridge University's Fitzwilliam Museum.

Lady Frances COLVIN (née Fetherstonhaugh, 1839–1924), after separation from her first husband, the Revd A. H. Sitwell, made a living as an essayist; when she married Sidney Colvin in 1903, she had known him for more than thirty years. Their friend Robert Louis Stevenson venerated her as his 'madonna'.

Sir Sidney COLVIN (1845–1927, knighted 1911) became a good friend to Conrad, as he had been to Stevenson. Colvin had been Slade Professor of Fine Arts at Cambridge and director of the Fitzwilliam Museum; from 1884 to 1912, he was Keeper of Prints and Drawings at the British Museum. Among his literary works were editions of Stevenson's letters and biographies of Landor and Keats.

Alfred Borys CONRAD (1898–1978), the Conrads' elder son, was educated at private schools and in HMS *Worcester*. He showed an early interest in cars and engineering which helped to earn him a commission in the 'Mechanical

Transport' section of the Royal Army Service Corps at the age of 17½. He never entirely recovered from his war experiences which included being gassed on one occasion and temporarily blinded on another. After the war, his occasionally erratic behaviour strained relations with his father (but not his mother).

Jessie Emmeline CONRAD (née George, 1873–1936) probably met her future husband in 1894. One of nine children, she was working as a typist and living with her widowed mother. The Conrads married in March 1896. Both biographers and those who knew her disagree about her personality: some disparage her stolidity or patronise her want of formal education, others admire her fortitude and her shrewd management of a somewhat cantankerous family. An accident to her knees in 1904 exacerbated a previous injury, leaving her lame and in pain for the rest of her life. She wrote two books about her husband, *Joseph Conrad as I Knew Him* (1926) and *Joseph Conrad and His Circle* (1935); her *Handbook of Cookery for a Small House*, accepted by a publisher in 1906, did not appear until 1923.

H. F. T. COOPER was one of Conrad's British admirers. The copy of *The Shadow-Line* that accompanies the letter to him is inscribed 'H. F. T. Cooper with compliments and thanks from Joseph Conrad June 1917'.

John CROMWELL (1887–1979), born Elwood Dager Cromwell in Toledo, Ohio, made his professional début in 1907; as a stage actor, director, and producer, he had considerable success on Broadway. In 1928, he moved to Hollywood, where he directed such films as *Of Human Bondage* (1934), *Little Lord Fauntleroy* (1936), *The Prisoner of Zenda* (1937), and *Anna and the King of Siam* (1946). A few months after the disastrous try-out in Syracuse, Cromwell was conscripted and had to abandon further plans for the stage version of *Victory*, but in 1940 he directed a film version for Paramount Studios.

Gerald CUMBERLAND was the pseudonym of Charles Frederick Kenyon (1881–1926), an author and musician who made his living as a dramatic and musical critic in Manchester and London. *Set Down in Malice*, a volume of reminiscences, appeared in 1918, and *Tales of a Cruel Country*, a collection depicting war-time Greece, in 1919.

Richard Henry Parnell CURLE (1883–1968) was Scots by birth but English by residence and education. His passion for travel appears in such books as *Into the East: Notes on Burma and Malaya* (1923) and *Caravansary and Conversation* (1937);

his psychological curiosity in *Women: An Analytical Study* (1947). He published many studies of other writers, including Browning, Hudson, Hardy, and Dostoevsky; his first book was *Aspects of George Meredith* (1908). In his relations with Conrad, about whom he wrote three books and many articles and pamphlets, Curle became both protégé and protector – a combination of sympathetic critic, bibliographer, collector, acolyte, entrepreneur, and friend.

After a career as an actor, Henry DANA (1855–1921) became business manager of His Majesty's Theatre, then general manager of the Globe Theatre, Saint Martin's Lane; as such, he worked with the producer Marie Löhr on the staging of *Victory*.

Francis Warrington DAWSON (1878–1962) came from Charleston, South Carolina; his father was a newspaper publisher, and his mother, who followed her son to Paris when he made it his headquarters, belonged to a family of faded plantation-owners. Throughout his life Dawson wrote prolifically: fiction, essays, newspaper stories. He covered strikes, wars, peace conferences, the French Senate and Chamber of Deputies. 'Furthermore', to quote Randall, 'he had a special taste and talent for conversing with the great and near-great' (p. 4). In 1909, while on safari in East Africa with Theodore Roosevelt, Dawson met Conrad's old friends the Sandersons. When Dawson came to England in May 1910, intending to report the funeral of Edward VII, he carried an introduction to Conrad.

Hugh Railton DENT (1874–1938) joined his father's firm in 1888 and became an editor of the Everyman's Library series in 1909; when J. M. Dent died in 1926, Hugh succeeded him as chairman of the board, a position he held until his own death.

Joseph Mallaby DENT (1849–1926) set up in business as a bookbinder in 1872 and turned to publishing in 1888. Among his great successes were the Temple Classics, the Temple Shakespeare, and Everyman's Library. In Conrad's lifetime, Dent published *'Twixt Land and Sea* (1912), *Within the Tides* (1915), *The Shadow-Line* (1917), *The Rescue* (1920), *Notes on Life and Letters* (1921), and most of the Uniform Edition. The rest of that edition appeared posthumously as did *Suspense* (1925) and *Last Essays* (1926).

Roman DMOWSKI (1864–1939), a prominent Polish nationalist writer and politician, had just contributed a chapter to *Russian Realities and Problems*, ed. J. D. Duff (1917); his brief, privately printed discussion of *Problems of*

Central and Eastern Europe also appeared in 1917. His first book, published in 1903, was *Myśli nowoczesnego Polaka* (*Thoughts of a Modern Pole*). The modern Pole, according to Dmowksi, while embracing Polish tradition, should be suspicious of inherited privilege – and of such Polish 'outsiders' as Jews and Orthodox Ukrainians. Before the war, Dmowski led the National Democratic Party in the Russian Duma, where he argued for Polish independence within a Pan-Slavic context; in Warsaw, he organised boycotts of Jewish businesses. Converting to the cause of full independence during the war, he founded the Polish National Committee, which moved from Lausanne to Paris in 1917. Along with Paderewski, Dmowski represented Poland at the Paris Peace Conference and thus was a signatory to the Treaty of Versailles. He was briefly Foreign Minister in 1923.

Marguerite Augusta Ashley DODD (née Edwards, 1851–1930) married George Ashley Dodd, a landowner and barrister, later High Sheriff of Kent, in 1870; they lived at Swinford Old Manor, near Ashford, formerly the residence of the Poet Laureate Alfred Austin.

Frank Nelson DOUBLEDAY (1862–1934) was born in Brooklyn. He began his career in publishing at Charles Scribner's Sons (1877–95); he allied himself with S. S. McClure from 1897 to 1900 before going into partnership with Walter Hines Page as president of Doubleday, Page; in 1927, the firm became Doubleday, Doran. He numbered among his authors Frank Norris, Ellen Glasgow, Stephen Crane, O. Henry, Jack London, Booth Tarkington, and Rudyard Kipling, with whom he maintained a close friendship. Between 1912 and 1914, initially at Alfred Knopf's urging, Doubleday's interest in Conrad changed from casual to serious, and Doubleday started to plan a collected edition. The North American publication of *Chance* was Conrad's first financial success; for the rest of his life his association with Doubleday was rewarding and often cordial. When Conrad made his exhausting journey to the USA in 1923, he made Effendi Hill, the Doubledays' Long Island home, his headquarters.

John DRINKWATER (1882–1937) was a prolific dramatist, essayist, and poet. His plays included *Abraham Lincoln* (1918), *Oliver Cromwell* (1921), and the comedy *Bird-in-Hand* (1928). For many years he worked with the Birmingham Repertory Theatre, originally The Pilgrim Players.

Elizabeth 'Toppie' DUMMETT (née Miéville, 1868–1940) was widowed in 1891. A fine horsewoman and a lively talker, she held court for gatherings of writers, painters, and musicians at her home in Brompton, West London. Her close friendship with Cunninghame Graham lasted until his death.

Samuel Alexander EVERITT (1871–1953): after graduating from Yale in 1895, he began a career in publishing. He became treasurer and executive vice-president of Doubleday, Page, retiring in 1930.

S. Nevile FOSTER was editor and managing director of *Land and Water*, the forerunner of *Country Life*. For the duration of the war he abandoned the magazine's usual fascination with the pursuit of fish and game in favour of covering the war's strategic and political aspects. He continued to publish fiction, however, considered taking *The Shadow-Line*, and published *The Rescue* as a serial.

Ada Nemesis GALSWORTHY, born Ada Pearson (1864–1956), was adopted by Ernest Cooper, a Norwich doctor. As a teenager she studied the piano in Dresden, and later she composed songs. Conrad wrote a preface to her translations from Maupassant, *Yvette and Other Stories* (1904). Although long involved with John, she had been officially and unhappily married to his cousin Arthur until 1904, when the death of John, Senior, eased the threat of family sanctions.

John GALSWORTHY (1867–1933) met Conrad in the *Torrens* in 1893. His early work was tentative, but in 1932 he won a Nobel Prize (an honour denied his friend) for his fiction and his plays. Like the Forsytes, his family was well supplied with money, and he helped Conrad with many gifts and loans as well as constant encouragement.

An Aberdonian, Theodore James Gordon GARDINER (1874–1937) was a major in the Border Regiment seconded to Scottish Command as an intelligence officer; his duties included spy-hunting and the surveillance of enemy aliens. Before the war, although often troubled by ill health, he had been a civil servant in South Africa (where he went through the siege of Kimberley), a tea-planter in Ceylon, and a student at Harvard. After the war, he worked as an arbitrator of industrial disputes and as secretary to the National Club, London. The posthumous *Notes of a Prison Visitor* (1938) record some of his experiences of befriending convicts. His novels include *The Reconnaissance* (1914), *At the House of Dree* (1928), and *The Man with a Weak Heart* (1932); at his death, he was working on a study of Napoleon. One obituarist recalled that 'the richness of his immensely wide experience and knowledge of life was always a generous source from which his friends derived infinite amusement, comfort, and stimulation'. Conrad's friendship with Gardiner, begun during visits to Scotland in 1916, strengthened over the years.

Edward William GARNETT (1868–1937), a publisher's reader and critic, was the husband of Constance, the translator. Constance lived at the Cearne, a woodland house near Limpsfield, Surrey, which became a meeting-place for writers, artists, anarchists, socialists, and Russian refugees; Edward divided his time between the Cearne and London, where he presided over regular literary gatherings at the Mont Blanc restaurant. His encouragement of Conrad in the 1890s was typical of his generous and continuing attention to new writers, for example Edward Thomas, Robert Frost, D. H. Lawrence, and Dorothy Richardson. During the First World War, Garnett served in the Friends' Ambulance Unit; although Conrad disapproved of his pacifism and Russophilia, their friendship endured.

Walter Lionel GEORGE (1882–1926) was born in Paris to British parents, studied at the Sorbonne, and served in the French army. When he moved to London, he worked as a journalist and (during the war) a civil servant. A self-described 'conservative English radical' and feminist, he published books on social and political topics such as *France in the Twentieth Century* (1909), *The Intelligence of Women* (1916), and *The Story of Woman* (1925); his numerous works of fiction such as *A Bed of Roses* (1911) often reflect his involvement in the controversies of the day.

Of all the literary friends of Conrad's later years, André-Paul-Guillaume GIDE (1869–1951) was the most distinguished, the most artistically remarkable. He received the Nobel Prize for literature in 1947. A born-again pagan and a recidivist puritan, his strengths lay both in intimate autobiography and in ironic fictions. Among his works are *Les Nourritures terrestres* (1897), *L'Immoraliste* (1902), *La Porte étroite* (1909), *Les Caves du Vatican* (1912), and *Les Faux-monnayeurs* (1926). His writings, his creation of the *Nouvelle Revue Française*, and his vast network of friends and correspondents placed him at the centre of French literary life. He first met Conrad in July 1911 and dedicated *Voyage au Congo* (1927) to his memory.

The son of a French officer and a Greek princess, Taglioni's grandson, and Hérédia's son-in-law, Comte Auguste GILBERT DE VOISINS (1877–1939) enjoyed a large fortune which enabled him to collect and travel as he pleased; he featured as a rider in Buffalo Bill's circus and made two expeditions to remote parts of China. He also wrote poetry and fiction; Conrad owned four of his books, including *Le Bar de la Fourche* (1909), a novel about prospecting for gold in California.

For almost forty years, Louis GILLET (1876–1943) contributed regularly to the *Revue des Deux Mondes*; it was there that he reviewed *Suspense* as well as *The Arrow of Gold*. An art historian and student of English and German literature, he became curator of the Jacquemart-André collection at the Abbaye de Châalis, near Paris, in 1912, and a member of the Académie française in 1935. His close friendship with Romain Rolland (who portrayed him in his fiction as 'Olivier') was interrupted by a quarrel about the First World War, in which Gillet fought and suffered wounds; other friends included Monet, Péguy, Claudel, and Joyce.

Edmund GOSSE (1849–1928; knighted 1925), poet, literary historian, biographer, and reviewer, exercised a powerful influence on the later Victorian and Edwardian literary world. The autobiographical *Father and Son* appeared in 1907; his critical enthusiasms ranged from Ibsen to Donne. In 1894 he read the MS of *Almayer's Folly*, and in 1902 he procured Conrad's grant from the Royal Literary Fund.

Robert Bontine Cunninghame GRAHAM (1852–1936) began a lasting friendship with Conrad in 1897, the result of a letter praising 'An Outpost of Progress'. A socialist, Scottish nationalist, and (according to some scholars) rightful King of Scotland, Graham had worked and travelled widely in the Americas. He drew on his experiences in many volumes of tales, sketches, and essays and also in his unorthodox histories of the Spanish conquest. From 1886 to 1892 he represented North-West Lanarkshire in Parliament and spent four-and-a-half weeks in gaol for his part in the 'Bloody Sunday' demonstration of 1887. During the First World War he returned twice to Latin America in search of beef and remounts for the British army.

HACHETTE et Cie: French publishers and booksellers, with a branch in London.

Captain Anthony HALSEY owned Spring Grove, the house where the Conrads lived for six months in 1919. As a second lieutenant in the *Philomel* during the Anglo-Boer War, he was twice mentioned in dispatches. From 1910 to 1912, when he retired, he was an inspecting officer in the Coastguard Division.

Louise ('Loulette') Victoria Alvar Woods HARDING (1883–1965) sang professionally as a soprano under the name Louise Alvar, touring with Maurice Ravel, among others. She was the daughter of Ernest Beckman, a writer and member of the Swedish Parliament, and a granddaughter of Anders Fredrik Beckman, Bishop of Skara. She and her husband, a wealthy English barrister, held a literary and musical salon at their house in Holland Park, Kensington; her circle included Manuel de Falla, Camille Saint-Saëns, Gian Francesco Malipiero, Albert Roussel, Salvador de Madariaga, T. S. Eliot, Hugo von Hofmannsthal, and Paul Valéry.

HARMSWORTH: see NORTHCLIFFE

Basil Macdonald HASTINGS (1881–1928) had already written several plays and collaborated on two others with Eden Phillpotts. Having originally joined the army, he applied for transfer to the Royal Flying Corps. While an officer-cadet, he began a magazine, *The Fledgling*, which carried Conrad's essay 'Never Any More' ('Flight'). The dramatisation of *Victory* had a successful run at the Globe Theatre in 1919. After the war, Hastings worked as a journalist, becoming drama critic of the *Daily Express* in 1924. *Ladies Half-Way*, his autobiography, came out in 1927.

John Edmund HODGSON (1875–1952), director of the long-established London firm of auctioneers, dealer in fine books and manuscripts, and scholar, was a past president of the Johnsonian Society and would become the historian of British aviation in its pioneering years. His father had been Master of the Stationers Company. Hodgson's widow Norma (née Lewis, later Lady Dalrymple-Champneys), an authority on eighteenth-century English poetry, became Librarian of Somerville College, Oxford.

William Thomas Hildrup HOWE (1874–1939) managed the Cincinnati branch of the American Book Company, which specialised in text-books, eventually becoming its president. A keen purchaser of literary first editions, he also built up a famous collection of McGuffey's Eclectic Readers.

Lawyer, photographer, book dealer, amateur strong man, Meredith JANVIER (1872–1936) lived in Baltimore. A contributor to the *Baltimore Evening Sun*, he collected some of his essays in *Baltimore in the Eighties and Nineties* (1933) and *Baltimore Yesterdays* (1937), the latter with a preface by H. L. Mencken. Mencken once observed that 'Janvier reveled in buying books as a cat revels in catnip.'

G. JEAN-AUBRY: see AUBRY

Sir Robert Armstrong JONES (1857–1933; knighted 1917, baronetcy 1926), an orthopaedic surgeon, was widely honoured at home and overseas. A native of North Wales, he practised in Liverpool, where he was consulting surgeon to all the large hospitals. He was also a consultant at St Thomas's Hospital, London, and a member of the War Office's Medical Advisory Board. During the war, he held the rank of Major-General and took on the immense task of organising reconstructive surgery at home and in the field. From 1921 to 1925, he served as President of the British Orthopaedic Association. His monographs and textbooks on the surgery of joints, military orthopaedics, and general orthopaedics were widely used.

William Reno KANE (1885–1971) conducted *The Editor: The Journal of Information for Literary Workers*, which continued on and off until 1941. From his office in Ridgewood, New Jersey, Kane was also the publisher of *1001 Places to Sell Manuscripts: The American Writer's Yearbook and Directory to Publications*.

Gladys LANGHAM[†] was a friend of Jessie Conrad's.

Reginald Herbert LEON (1882–1960), a member of the London Stock Exchange, collected books, porcelain, and tapestries, ancient and modern. The volumes from his collection auctioned at Sotheby's in 1922 included the First, Second, and Fourth Folio editions of Shakespeare's plays.

Robert Duncan MACKINTOSH (1865–1934) practised medicine in Barnes, South West London. From 1909 to 1921, when they had a falling out, Conrad valued the company and the advice of this Scottish doctor, an amateur playwright and inventor described by his great-niece as 'an unpractical enthusiast and dreamer'.

Born in New Zealand to Scottish parents, Lewis Rose MACLEOD (1875–1941) began his journalistic career in New South Wales; in 1905 he moved to South Africa, where he became editor of the *Johannesburg Sunday Times*. From 1916 to 1924 he was literary editor of the London *Daily Mail*, where several of Conrad's essays first appeared. Macleod returned to Johannesburg in 1924 to edit the *Rand Daily Mail*.

Caroline MARWOOD (née Cranswick, 1868–1952) married Conrad's friend-to-be Arthur Marwood in 1903; Conrad often visited their Kentish farmhouse about ten miles from Capel House. Arthur died in 1916, and in 1918 she married Walter Pilcher.

Henry Louis MENCKEN (1880–1956) worked for an array of newspapers in his native Baltimore. With George Jean Nathan he founded the *American Mercury* in 1924, remaining as editor until 1933. Often considered the most brilliant – and the most cantankerous – polemicist of his lengthy day, Mencken revivified the American language. A shrewd literary as well as social critic, he published many books, some compiled from his fugitive pieces and some written from scratch; among his works are *George Bernard Shaw – His Plays* (1905), *In Defense of Women* (1917), *The American Language* (1918), and the six series of aptly named *Prejudices* (1919–27). In the Fifth Series (New York: Knopf, 1926), pp. 34–41, Mencken describes the stories in *Youth* as the century's finest. True to form, the Conrad he admires is a sardonic absurdist whose God is not 'a loving papa in carpet slippers, but a comedian'.

Lady Mary St Lawrence MILLAIS (née Hope-Vere, 1861–1948), a Scotswoman, was the Conrads' neighbour at Leacon Hall, near Capel House, and Jessie Conrad's close friend. Widowed in 1897, she was the daughter-in-law of the painter Sir John Everett Millais; her son was Sir John Millais, a naval officer. In later years, she served as a Justice of the Peace.

The original Press Lord, Alfred Charles William Harmsworth (1865–1922) became Baron in 1905 and in 1917 VISCOUNT NORTHCLIFFE. Prepared by life as a teenage reporter and copy-boy, he started the popular magazine *Answers to Correspondents* in 1888. With his younger brother Harold (later Lord Rothermere) Harmsworth went on to buy the London *Evening News* in 1894, give the world the first halfpenny morning paper, the *Daily Mail*, in 1896, and found the *Daily Mirror* in 1903. Like Hearst in the United States, the Harmsworth brothers used the latest publishing techniques to cater to a rapidly expanding readership eager for simple, vivid writing and aggressively presented opinions. In 1908, the Harmsworths acquired a controlling interest in *The Times*. There and in his more popular newspapers, Northcliffe promoted his often alarmist political ideas. During the war, his strident criticisms of Kitchener and of Asquith's Liberal and Coalition governments were heard variously as patriotic or self-seeking, malicious or urgently necessary.

Lieutenant Henry Joseph OSBORNE (born 1891), a temporary lieutenant in the Royal Naval Reserve since March 1915, was serving in HMS *Ready* (a decoy vessel) when Conrad sailed in her in 1916. In 1917, Osborne won the Distinguished Service Cross, and in 1918, after engaging two

German submarines and sinking one, the Croix de Guerre. During his later career, he was stranded in the Gulf of Corinth, 1921, and made voyages to Australia, North America, and South Africa.

Glasgow-born, William Mathie PARKER (1891–1973) published many books on Scottish literature; he also contributed frequently to the *Fortnightly Review*, *Glasgow Herald*, and *John O' London's* and wrote assiduously to well-known authors such as Conrad and Hardy in the hope of being granted 'personal sidelights'.

Upon leaving school, Eric Seabrooke PINKER (1891–1973) went to work for his father. During the war, he won the Military Cross for bravery under fire. When J. B. Pinker died in 1922, 'Mr Eric' became the firm's senior partner and thus Conrad's principal agent. In 1926, he moved to New York and in 1939 was sent to Sing Sing prison for appropriating $139,000 of his clients' funds.

James Brand PINKER (1863–1922) began his working life as a clerk at Tilbury Docks. After three years in Constantinople on the staff of the *Levant Herald*, he returned to England as assistant editor of *Black and White*, a magazine known for its fiction and jaunty drawings. In January 1896, he went into business as a literary agent – one of the first in London. Over the years his clients included Ford, James, Crane, Wells, Bennett, and D. H. Lawrence. He began acting for Conrad in 1900 and helped him through many financial crises, but a serious quarrel in 1910 suspended their relationship for several months and strained it for many more. By the spring of 1912, however, they were closer than ever.

Mary Elizabeth PINKER (née Seabrooke, 1862–1945) married J. B. while he was working in Turkey.

John QUINN (1870–1924), the son of Irish immigrants, came from Ohio. As a New York lawyer, he had a highly lucrative practice in commercial and financial law, particularly the law of tariffs. As a supporter of the arts, he won an exemption for artists from sales taxes and built up a great collection of modern painting and sculpture; he was the chief private buyer at the Armory show in 1913. He also amassed modern literary manuscripts; among the writers he collected on a large scale were Yeats, Pound, Eliot, Joyce, and Conrad. When Quinn auctioned off his Conradiana in 1923, several years after relations between patron and author had chilled, manuscripts and inscribed volumes bought for a total of $10,000 fetched $110,000.

Józef Hieronim RETINGER (1888–1960), a native of Cracow, wrote in French and English as well as Polish. He capped his law degree from Cracow with a doctorate from the Sorbonne; his dissertation appeared as *Le Conte fantastique dans le romantisme français* (Paris, 1909). Political urgencies frustrated his hopes of taking yet another degree from the London School of Economics. During the war, he devoted his energies to polemics in the Polish cause, becoming as a consequence the victim of slanders and intrigues that led the French government to deport him to Spain; he advanced his ideas about the future of Poland in *La Pologne et l'équilibre européen* (1916). In the 1920s, a sympathiser with the revolution, he worked as an agent of the Mexican government. Later, he became a courtly advocate of European unity. He and his first wife, Otylia, came to know the Conrads well; it was Otylia Retinger's mother who invited them to Poland in 1914. Retinger wrote his memoir of the friendship, *Conrad and His Contemporaries* (1941; US edition 1943) with panache; the details, such as the claim of a first meeting in 1909, call for scepticism.

Edric Cecil Mornington ROBERTS (1892–1976) was to become a best-selling novelist, acclaimed playwright, and cosmpolitan *bon vivant*. Among his books were *Pilgrim Cottage* (1933) and *Victoria Four Thirty* (1937). During the First World War, he was a correspondent with the Dover Patrol, the RAF, and the Allied armies in France while doubling as literary editor of the *Liverpool Post*. Between 1920 and 1925, he edited the *Nottingham Journal*. Grace Willard arranged his introduction to Conrad.

Mr ROBERTS: apparently an editor or employee of a US periodical – see the letter of 26 June 1919.

Alexander ROBINSON (1873–1948?) was indentured in Glasgow in 1888 and served as an apprentice in the *Loch Etive* from 16 November 1889 to 27 June 1891; he also sailed in the *Loch Carron*. When he wrote to Conrad in July 1919, he was living in Woodford, Essex. As far as is known, he never obtained a mate's certificate.

Alexander Galt ROSS[†] (1860–1927) was the author of *Religion and the Modern Mind: Lectures Delivered before the Glasgow University Society of St Ninian* (1908).

Alice Mary ROTHENSTEIN (née Knewstub, stage name Alice Kingsley, 1867–1957), an actress, married Will in 1899. Her family had ties with the Pre-Raphaelites.

John Knewstub Maurice ROTHENSTEIN (1902–92; knighted 1952), the son of Alice and Will, was one of Borys Conrad's boyhood friends. Rothenstein became an authority on modern British painting and was Director of the Tate Gallery from 1938 to 1964. His publications include the three-volume *Modern English Painters* (1952–73) and an autobiography in three parts: *Summer's Lease* (1965), *Brave Day, Hideous Night* (1966), *Time's Thievish Progress* (1970).

William ROTHENSTEIN (1872–1945; knighted 1931) was notable for his portrait graphics, paintings, and drawings. Max Beerbohm described him as a young phenomenon in 'Enoch Soames' (*Seven Men*): 'He wore spectacles that flashed more than any other pair ever seen. He was a wit. He was brimful of ideas . . . He knew everyone in Paris.'

André RUYTERS (originally Ruijters, 1876–1952), the Belgian novelist and poet, was a friend of Gide and one of the founders of the *Nouvelle Revue Française*. His translation of 'Heart of Darkness' was serialised in the *NRF* (1924–5).

William Graeme ST CLAIR (1849–1930), born and educated in Scotland, taught in Burma and then moved to Malaya in 1887 to edit the *Singapore Free Press*. He was also conductor of the Singapore Philharmonic Society and a major in the Singapore Voluntary Artillery. When he retired in 1916, he moved to Colombo, but was visiting Britain in 1917.

Rather than follow the family tradition of making port and sherry, Christopher or 'Kit' SANDEMAN (1882–1951) became a journalist, lecturer, and author. Opera, politics, poetry, history, and botany all fascinated him. Between the wars he led several expeditions to Peru and Brazil, rafting on the headwaters of the Amazon and the Huallaga, and collecting orchids for British herbaria. From 1914 to 1918, he served in the Intelligence Corps.

Edward Lancelot ('Ted') SANDERSON (1867–1939) took passage in the *Torrens* in 1893; on that voyage, Conrad read him a draft of *Almayer's Folly*. Sanderson taught at Elstree, his family's preparatory school in Hertfordshire. After service in the Boer War he and his wife, Helen, remained in Africa, first in Johannesburg then in Nairobi, where he served as Town Clerk; he returned in 1910 to be Headmaster of Elstree.

Helen Mary SANDERSON (née Watson, 1874–1967) married Ted in 1898. She was a Scotswoman from Galloway, full of moral and intellectual vigour.

As 'Janet Allardyce', she contributed sketches of East African life to *Scribner's Magazine*.

Katherine SANDERSON (born 1899, married name Mrs C. E. Taylor), the Sandersons' eldest child, a long-time resident of Kenya and latterly of Devonshire. She is named after her grandmother, a great admirer of Conrad's works and the dedicatee of *The Mirror of the Sea*.

Born in Queensland in 1885, Alfred Thomas SAUNDERS lived in Adelaide, South Australia; he was an accountant and amateur historian who often published the results of his researches in the *Adelaide Mail*. He was fascinated by the career of the South Seas pirate 'Bully' Hayes (1829–77). He had been a clerk for Henry Simpson & Co., owners of the *Otago*, during the period when Conrad commanded her.

Eugene Taylor SAWYER (1846–1924), an American, began writing sensational fiction in the 1870s; although he claimed to have originated the Nick Carter detective series, his former collaborators disputed the assertion. When he wrote to Conrad, he was living in San Jose, California.

Edward Richard Buxton SHANKS (1892–1953), the poet, novelist, editor, and critic, went to war in 1914 after a distinguished undergraduate career at Cambridge; in 1915 he was invalided out of the army and transferred to the War Office; from 1919 to 1922, he was assistant editor of the recently founded *London Mercury*; later he became a lecturer at the University of Liverpool and chief leader-writer for the London *Evening Standard*. His abundant bibliography includes *Queen of China and Other Poems* (1919), *Collected Poems* (1926), *Tom Tiddler's Ground* (1934), *Edgar Allan Poe* (1937), and *Rudyard Kipling* (1940).

Clement King SHORTER (1857–1926) edited the *Illustrated London News* from 1891, the *Sketch* and the *English Illustrated Magazine* from 1893 to 1900; he then gave up all three editorships to begin the *Tatler* and the *Sphere*. His critical works include books on the Brontës. Between 1917 and 1919 he published a series of Conrad's works, among them *One Day More*, 'The Tale', and several articles, in pamphlet editions limited to 25 copies each.

John Collings SQUIRE (1884–1958; knighted 1933), acting editor of the *New Statesman*, 1917–18, founded the *London Mercury* in 1919; he edited this literary magazine, loved and loathed for its traditional tastes, until 1934. He was also editor of the English Men of Letters Series and published a prodigious amount of his own poetry and essays.

Yeats's friend Arthur William SYMONS (1865–1945) wrote poetry, essays, and fiction. As a critic, he showed broad tastes in literature, music, and painting, and spoke up for such then-neglected or misread figures as Baudelaire and Blake. In 1896, Symons took 'The Idiots', the first short story Conrad ever sold, for *The Savoy*. Symons underwent a severe mental breakdown in 1908 and could not return to his Kentish home until 1910. In 1925, he published *Notes on Joseph Conrad*.

Richard TANNER, of Lenhall Farm, Bishopsbourne, was estate agent to Colonel Matthew Gerald Edward Bell, lord of the manor of Bishopsbourne and owner of Oswalds, the Conrads' final residence.

Jenny Doris or Dora THORNE (née Jones, 1888–1947) was the daughter of the playwright Sir Henry Arthur Jones, whose *Life and Letters* she published in 1930. She moved in theatrical and literary circles when not in Cyprus, Morocco, Egypt, or Greece with her husband, a civil servant and judge. After her divorce in 1923, she wrote sketches for dailies and magazines and did volunteer work. Her autobiography, *What a Life!*, appeared in 1932.

Graham TILS was a Chicago collector of whom we know nothing beyond his irritation with Conrad, Shorter, and Wise.

Born in Poplar, East London, Henry Major TOMLINSON (1873–1958) grew up in dockland. In 1904, he left a miserably paid job in a shipping-office to write for the *Morning Leader* (later merged with the *Daily News*). He first made a name for his articles about trawlermen; a voyage to the Amazon as a ship's purser gave him the material for his first book, *The Sea and the Jungle* (1912). During the war he worked as a correspondent, first for the *Daily News*, then for GHQ France. Later, he published many volumes of essays, such as *Old Junk* (1918) and *London River* (1921), and novels such as *Gallion's Reach* (1927) and *All Our Yesterdays* (1930). His fiction often has a Conradian tang.

Thomas Fisher UNWIN (1848–1935) published *Almayer's Folly*, *An Outcast of the Islands*, and *Tales of Unrest* at the beginning of Conrad's career, *The Arrow of Gold* and *The Rover* towards its end, and *Tales of Hearsay* posthumously. Neither his business practices nor his adherence to the Liberal party endeared him to Conrad.

Major Frank VERNON (1875–1940; until 1899, Frank Spicer), producer, author, and translator, was born in Bombay. After four years in the army, he returned in 1919 to the West End and resumed his collaboration with J. E. Vedrenne; later, he also produced plays in Paris.

Allan WADE (1881–1955), a theatrical manager and producer, began his career with Frank Benson's Shakespeare company. Wade was frequently associated with companies that fell foul of, or had to circumvent the Censor of Plays: from 1906 to 1915, he was Harley Granville-Barker's assistant and script-reader; from 1912 to 1916 he was secretary of the Incorporated Stage Society; in 1919, after a stint in Paris, he helped found the Phoenix Society and produced nearly all their plays. When Conrad wrote to him in 1918, he was business manager at the Royalty Theatre. Later, Wade translated Cocteau and Giradoux, edited Henry James's dramatic criticism (1948), and compiled a bibliography of W. B. Yeats (1951).

Hugh Seymour WALPOLE (1884–1941; knighted 1937) was born in New Zealand, but his parents soon returned to England, where his father became Bishop of Durham. As a young man, he admired and was admired by Henry James. As a novelist, Walpole first met recognition with *Mr Perrin and Mr Traill* (1911) and *The Duchess of Wrexe* (1914). In *The Dark Forest* (1916), he drew on his experience of working for the Russian Red Cross. Among the most popular of his later novels were the Herries Chronicle series, set in the Lake District, and the Jeremy series, set in various schools. Before meeting Conrad, who was to treat him as a protégé, Walpole had already published his critical appreciation *Joseph Conrad* (1916; revised edition, 1924).

Elliot Lovegood Grant WATSON (1885–1970) took a first in Natural Sciences at Cambridge. In 1910–11, he joined a scientific expedition to north-western Australia. Thereafter he devoted himself to writing essays, fiction, and studies of natural history.

Conrad met Iris Veronica WEDGWOOD (née Pawson, 1886–1982) through Richard Curle. She and her husband, Ralph, were the dedicatees of *Within the Tides* (1915). In the 1920s she published several novels (*The Iron Age*, *The Fairway*, *The Livelong Day*, *Perilous Seas*), and in the 1930s, topographical studies (*Northumberland and Durham*, *Fenland Rivers*).

Among the novels already published by Edith Newbold WHARTON (née Jones, 1862–1937) were *The House of Mirth* (1905) and *Ethan Frome* (1911); when Conrad wrote to her in 1912, *Scribner's Magazine* was serialising *The Custom of the Country*. Among the work to come would be *The Age of Innocence* (1920) and her autobiography, *A Backward Glance* (1934). In 1910, she had gone to live in France for good. During the war, she worked on behalf of refugees; she included 'Poland Revisited' in her fund-raising anthology *The Book of the Homeless* (1915).

Catherine (or Catharine) Livingstone WILLARD (1895?–1954), an actress, was born in Dayton, Ohio; her mother was Grace Robinson Willard, an interior designer, journalist, and friend of the Conrads. Catherine Willard trained in Paris and in 1915 made her British début in *The Taming of the Shrew* with F. R. Benson's Company. From 1918 to 1920, she was a leading player at the Old Vic, where her parts included Olivia, Hermione, Lady Macbeth, and Beatrice – her favourite. In 1921 she returned to the United States, where she took many roles in Boston and New York. She was married from 1925 to 1931 to William E. Barry and from 1931 to 1945 to Ralph Bellamy; both marriages ended in divorce. Her obituary in the *New York Times* gives 1900 as her date of birth; theatrical reference books give 1895. In November 1919, Conrad told Frank Vernon she was twenty.

Thomas James WISE (1859–1937) was a collector – and creator – of bibliographical rarities, particularly those of the Jacobean, Romantic, and Victorian periods. Having prospered as a dealer in lavender and other essential oils, he built up a considerable collection of books and manuscripts, many of which are now in the British Library's Ashley Collection, and enjoyed a solid reputation as a scholar and enthusiast. Meanwhile he was forging, and selling at high prices, spurious early editions of such authors as Wordsworth, Tennyson, Swinburne, Shelley, George Eliot, Charlotte Brontë, and the Brownings. His fakery was first exposed by John Carter and Graham Pollard in 1934. Since then, David Foxon has shown that Wise enriched his own holdings by stealing leaves from books in the British Museum. In 1918, Wise came to replace John Quinn as the preferred purchaser of Conrad's MSS, TSS, and corrected proofs; he was also of service by reprinting individual Conrad essays in small and therefore costly limited editions. In 1920 he published *A Bibliography of the Writings of Joseph Conrad*, and in 1928, *A Conrad Library: A Catalogue of Printed Books, Manuscripts and Autograph Letters by Joseph Conrad*.

EDITORIAL PROCEDURES

Hoping to balance the comfort of the reader against the requirements of the scholar, we have adopted the following conventions:

1. The texts stay faithful to Conrad's spelling, accentuation, and punctuation, but letters omitted from words by accident are supplied in square brackets. We also use square brackets to expand potentially confusing abbreviations but eliminate the stops with which Conrad signalled contractions. Rather than using *sic*, we mark words that might be construed as misprints with an asterisk. Asterisks are not normally used for misplaced apostrophes; missing ones are supplied only when letters are missing too.

2. Where absolutely necessary for the sense, missing pronouns, prepositions, and auxiliary verbs are also supplied in brackets. Gaps in the text, such as those caused by damage to the MS, appear thus: [. . .]. [?] indicates a doubtful reading.

3. Again when sense dictates, full stops and, very occasionally, commas or dashes are tacitly provided; forgotten quotation marks and brackets, inserted. Accidental repetitions do not appear but are recorded in the list of silent emendations at the end of the volume together with a list of corrected typing errors.

4. Especially in pronouns, Conrad used capitals more profusely than other English writers of his time. We preserve his usage, but distinguishing between upper and lower case must often be a matter of judgment rather than certainty. The same is true of locating paragraph breaks.

5. For the letters in French we observe the same conventions, but use square brackets and asterisks more sparingly. Conrad's erratic accentuation we leave as it is, except in texts from *Letters françaises*, where some presumed misprints or misreadings have been altered.

6. For the convenience of those who do not read the letters in sequence, information in footnotes may appear more than once.

7. Although he kept the surname Hueffer until 1919, Conrad's collaborator is called Ford Madox Ford throughout the edition. His wife (who never granted him a divorce) appears as Elsie Hueffer.

8. American readers should note that Conrad used the British system of abbreviating dates; thus 3.6 would mean 3 June, not 6 March.

9. In this volume the Nonesuch rather than the less reliable Bobbs-Merrill edition of the letters to Garnett normally provides the copy-text when no manuscript is available. In similar circumstances, we use the American rather than the British edition of the letters to Curle because the former has fewer censored names.

10. Texts from G. Jean-Aubry's *Joseph Conrad: Life & Letters* always lack farewell and signature.

11. This edition collects all available letters, but only the more interesting telegrams; references to most others appear in the notes.

12. In the provenance headings, letters that have appeared only in microfilmed dissertations or as disjointed fragments in books or articles are described as unpublished. Letters appearing in fuller but still incomplete form are described as published in part.

13. The heading 'TS/MS' denotes a typed letter in which passages other than the salutation or farewell are handwritten.

In January 1912, the Conrads had a new die made for the Capel House letterhead. Instead of the bracketed address for trains and telegrams, the left-hand side now read in two lines:

TELEGRAMS:- CONRAD, HAMSTREET.
STATION:- HAMSTREET, S. E. R. & C. R.^y

This wording appears on letter-cards and sheets for the rest of the Conrads' time at Capel House; until May 1917, the sheets bore no watermark. Thereafter, Capel House stationery was watermarked with a picture of a fortified city gate and the name CRIPPLEGATE.

When the Conrads moved in late March 1919 to temporary quarters they used stationery embossed with the address:

SPRING GROVE.
WYE.
KENT.

This letterhead occurs both on fresh stationery and on unused stock from Capel House and, being uninked, is usually invisible on photocopies.

There are two versions of the Oswalds letterhead. The first dated appearance of Type One is 14 October 1919, and the last, 10 May 1922. In this version, reproduced here in Plate 1, the telegraphic address reads:

TELEGRAMS:- CONRAD, BISHOPSBOURNE

In the second version, BISHOPSBOURNE has changed to BRIDGE. Throughout the period of Letterhead One, full sheets carry the watermark CHARTA SCRIPTORUM above a picture of a mediaeval scholar; half-sheets, used for notes, carry the watermark ROYAL LANCASTER PARCHMENT on one side of the fold and J. S. & CO. LONDON together with the Rose of Lancaster on the other.

1917

To B. Macdonald Hastings
Text MS Colgate; Unpublished

[Capel House]
Friday. [September 1916–February 1917][1]

My dear Hastings.[2]

This is V. G.

Let Jones sleep-walk. It's hardly worth while to exercise our ingenuity in discovering another method of getting psychology into this thing. I was much struck with a remark you made in the dressing room: – that "if this is worth doing at all it's for the money in it". Just so. And from that point of view Irving[3] must be looked after first, last, and all the time.

Am interested to see how you use my speeches in the play. My idea of adap^{on} was quite different: Preserve frame, shape, intention, quite intact – but use other words adapted for scene and conveying also things which in novel pertain to narr[ati]^{ve} and comment. You go the other way: make short work of the frame but preserve the words.

The Lena-Jones (dying) scene would be hardly "adaptation". It's something "out of the record" altogether. You see what I mean? But this is no protest. Merely a remark. No doubt it would be "Grateful and comforting" (you remember Epps' adver[tisem]^{ents}) to the audience and, if they *must* have cocoa . . . Yes. This is a cocoa age, in art.[4] Only pray remember that one can't say what an audience *will* stand (or swallow) till you try them.

---

[1] The stationery (ruled MS paper) is undateable. This text could fit anywhere between September 1916, when the correspondence shows a similar preoccupation with Jones's misogyny, and February 1917, when Hastings delivered a completely revised script; in March 1917 it became clear that Irving wished to play Heyst rather than Jones. This letter apparently concerns a sample scene or fragment of scenario. The original meeting with Irving took place at the Garrick Club. The meeting in Irving's dressing-room mentioned here may have occurred while Conrad was passing through London on Admiralty business; he also refers to this meeting in the letter to Hastings of 22 January.

[2] Basil Macdonald Hastings (1881–1928) had already written several plays and collaborated on two others with Eden Phillpotts. Having originally joined the army, he applied for transfer to the Royal Flying Corps. While an officer-cadet, he began a magazine, *The Fledgling*, which carried Conrad's essay 'Never Any More' ('Flight'). The dramatisation of *Victory* had a successful run at London's Globe Theatre in 1919. After the war, Hastings worked as a journalist, becoming drama critic of the *Daily Express* in 1924. *Ladies Half-Way* (1927), his autobiography, gives further details of his collaboration with Conrad and throws light on the latter's habitual attitudes to the theatre and actors.

[3] The actor–manager Henry Brodribb Irving (1870–1919), lessee of the Savoy Theatre, had made the original connection between Hastings and Conrad: see *Letters*, 5, pp. 573, 623–4. By the end of 1917, he had lost interest in the play.

[4] An age which offered artistic cocoa instead of headier beverages. 'Temperance' advocates, who were especially vocal during the war, promoted alcohol-free 'cocoa-taverns'. During the intervals in theatrical performances, advertisements for Epps's Cocoa and other products were projected onto the safety curtain.

3

And if you only make Jones Big enough (for Irving) they will swallow a lot. As to his dislike of women I am damned if I know what to say. They have spoiled so many of his little games before perhaps? Don't forget however that there is a strain of peculiar craziness about the gentleman. The novel only faintly suggests it. On stage it may pay if Irving will try honestly. Something temperamental rather than mental. He's in fact an unusual sort of crank. Voyez-Vous ça?

> Yours sincerely
>
> J. C.

To J. B. Pinker
Text MS Berg; Unpublished

[Capel House]
Tuesday. [2 January 1917][1]

My dear Pinker [2]

The Eng: Rev: has I believe changed its address so I must ask you to request A[ustin] H[arrison] to send me proofs of the VI inst*mt*.[3]

The secretary thinks she has sent them to me some time ago. But I am certain (after a careful search) that they are not in the house. Assure also A. H. that I never meant disrespect to the Review by letting 2 instal*ts* go in uncorrected. I am very sorry. As to the IVth I went to sea in a hurry.[4] With the Vth the fault lies with my muddle-headedness as after looking for it here I finally allowed myself to be overtaken by time. Very stupid of me.

I am carrying on the Ad[miral]ty art: and the story abreast.[5] I have been however somewhat gouty for a couple of days. However the article will be

---

[1] According to the letter of 'Wednesday evg.' [3 January], Borys last wrote on 20 December; the first Tuesday in January would be eleven or so days after the arrival of Borys's postcard.
[2] James Brand Pinker (1863–1922) began his working life as a clerk at Tilbury Docks. After three years in Constantinople on the staff of the *Levant Herald*, he returned to England as assistant editor of *Black and White*, a magazine known for its fiction and jaunty drawings. In January 1896, he went into business as a literary agent – one of the first in London. Over the years his clients included Ford, James, Crane, Wells, Bennett, and D. H. Lawrence. He began acting for Conrad in 1900 and helped him through many financial crises, but a serious quarrel in 1910 suspended their relationship for several months and strained it for many more. By the spring of 1912, however, they were closer than ever.
[3] Austin Harrison (1873–1928), editor of the *English Review*, where *The Shadow-Line* was appearing at the time.
[4] Having been offered the chance of a North Sea voyage in the *Ready*, a submarine decoy camouflaged as a merchant ship, in November 1916.
[5] Presumably the article was 'The Unlighted Coast', published posthumously in *The Times*, 18 August 1925, and in *Last Essays*. The Admiralty had commissioned this and other, never-written, pieces to depict the work of the Royal Naval Reserve. The story would become *The Arrow of Gold*, which, like most of his novels, Conrad first envisaged on a small scale. On

with you soon. I am anxious also to unload the story but that will take a little longer.

Ever Yours affc^ly

J. Conrad.

PS Strange! We haven't heard from Borys for eleven days now.[1] Jessie's holding herself in, but it isn't good for her. As to me I don't know what to think.

To R. B. Cunninghame Graham

Text MS Dartmouth; J-A, 2, 181; Watts 185

[letterhead: Capel House]
3^d Jan '17

Très cher ami[2]

I thought I could run up to say goodbye[3] – but my swollen foot does not improve and I can just crawl across a room and no more. So these lines go to you – avec mon coeur – to wish you a safe journey and the success of the "entreprise" the forestalling of the yanks and fine galloping days in the Sta Marta valley.

Your protégé Borys[4] is expected on leave about the 15th. We haven't heard from him for more than 10 days which is unusual – but I don't suppose it means anything. Still Jessie is worried. She sends you her love and best wishes for your journey.

I can't say I've been very much bucked-up by the change of the government.[5] The age of miracles is past – and the Yahudi God (Who rules us)

---

3 February 1915 he had called it a 'Carlist war episode from my *very* young days' (*Letters*, 5, p. 441). The references here and in the letter of [15 February] show that, however falteringly, Conrad worked on *The Arrow* well before the date given in some biographies.

[1] Borys, Conrad's elder son, was serving at the Front, in northern France and Belgium; at present, he was in France, near Saint-Quentin.

[2] Robert Bontine Cunninghame Graham (1852–1936) began his lasting friendship with Conrad in 1897, the result of a letter praising 'An Outpost of Progress'. A socialist, a Scottish nationalist, and (according to some scholars) rightful King of Scotland, Graham had worked and travelled widely in the Americas. He drew on his experiences in many volumes of tales, sketches, and essays and also in his unorthodox histories of the Spanish conquest. From 1886 to 1892 he represented North-West Lanarkshire in Parliament; he spent four-and-a-half weeks in gaol for his part in the 'Bloody Sunday' demonstration of 1887. During the First World War he returned twice to Latin America in search of beef and remounts for the British army.

[3] Before Graham sailed for Colombia.

[4] Graham had helped Borys obtain his commission in the Army Service Corps (*Letters*, 5, p. 508).

[5] In December, David Lloyd George (1863–1945) had replaced H. H. Asquith (1852–1928) as Prime Minister. Conrad was never fond of the new man (see, e.g., *Letters*, 5, p. 319).

seems to develop Central European affinities. He's played out as a patron.[1] Why not turn over the whole Establishment and the Non-Conf[st] organisations[2] to the Devil and see what'll happen. Nothing short of that will put this pretty business we're engaged on right. Et encore!

Ever affect[ly] yours

Joseph Conrad.

To J. B. Pinker
Text MS Berg; Unpublished

[letterhead: Capel House]

Wednesday evg. [3 January 1917][3]

My dear Pinker.

As there's nothing from B[orys] and J[essie] is getting awfully jumpy – it occurred to me that you may have a friend amongst the correspondents at the front whom you could ask to look young Conrad up. B has dined twice on Reg's invitation with the correspondents[4] and so is not an utter stranger to them.

By his last letter (12th Dec or thereabouts) he has been shifted for duty at the *III[d] corps' Siege Artillery Park*. His last pc is dated the 20th. Dec. Since then he has not acknowledged his Xmas pudding and other parcels or the 3 letters J[essie] has written him in the last fortnight.

Is my idea possible? I don't like to wire to him for there may be no answer to that too.

Yours ever

J. Conrad.

---

[1] 'Yahudi': Arabic for Jewish; 'Central European affinities': favouring the Central Powers, Austria and Germany; 'patron' in the French sense of proprietor or boss. These sentences play on Graham's scorn for theocentric views.

[2] The Liberal Party abounded in Nonconformists (Protestants not in communion with the state-established Anglican Church, such as Methodists and Presbyterians).

[3] Following immediately on the letter of [2 January].

[4] 'Reg' was Conrad's good friend Reginald Percival Gibbon (1879–1926), a war correspondent with the *Daily Chronicle* currently based in Amiens. Gibbon wrote to Conrad on 27 February, with his impressions of Borys: 'And by God, hasn't this business made a man of him! You ought to see him by a muddy roadside with his wagons and his sergeant, and his calm competence and appetite, and his infantile bad language, and his little half-conscious swagger when he invites his uncle to come and have a drink' (*Portrait*, p. 116). Borys remembered the mess's hospitality as 'so lavish that it affected me to a certain extent, and also wrought havoc among a number of my hosts . . . Those few who were still able to stand insisted upon helping Reggie – who, as always on such occasions, seemed perfectly normal – to plant me on the saddle of my motor-cycle, point me in the general direction of the Front Line, and give a good hearty shove' (*MFJC*, pp. 116–17).

To C. K. Shorter

Text MS BL Ashley 2922; Unpublished

[letterhead: Capel House]

[early January 1917][1]

Dear M[r] Shorter[2]

Ecco! I only regret the specimen is not of fresher complexion; but I don't know whether I could get a better one if I tried.

A very "young" piece of writing. Very young. I was 37 when I wrote it, about the time of our meeting.[3] But at 37 I *was* young. I have matured more rapidly since then. Still, sobered down as I am by years of effort, I can't dismiss it as [a] piece of mere rhetoric. There was genuine conviction at the back of those lines of which much survives in me to this day.

Yours

J. C.

To J. B. Pinker

Text MS Berg; Unpublished

[Capel House]

[early January 1917][4]

Dearest Pinker.

This is the Ad[miral][ty] paper.[5] Had yesterday wire from Sir Douglas Brownrigg.[6] Please phone him that you have MS. and it is coming along.

I can't write the regulation 3 papers. I send this one and he shall have others as I write them. One at end Febr[y.] perhaps. I will write as many as I can.

---

[1] This is a sequel to Conrad's letter of 31 December in which he had promised Shorter a copy of the 'suppressed' Preface to *The Nigger*. This copy, preserved in the British Library, is inscribed 'To Clement Shorter from J. C. 1917'. In the first paragraph, Conrad corrected the misprint 'prjudices'.

[2] Clement King Shorter (1857–1926) edited the *Illustrated London News* from 1891, the *Sketch* and the *English Illustrated Magazine* from 1893 to 1900; he then gave up all three editorships to begin *Tatler* and the *Sphere*. His critical works include books on the Brontës. Between 1917 and 1919 he published a series of Conrad's works in pamphlet editions limited to 25 copies each, among them *One Day More*, 'The Tale', and several articles.

[3] Conrad wrote the Preface in August 1897, when he was 39. A year later, Shorter acquired rights to *The Rescue*, hoping to publish it in the *Illustrated London News*.

[4] The letter of [2 January] had promised the article 'soon'. Letters and telegrams from later in the month imply that Conrad kept his promise.

[5] This was to be the only 'Admiralty paper' Conrad wrote, but 'Flight' (first published in June 1917 as 'Never Any More') also developed from his experiences in the autumn of 1916. See also the letter of [11? April 1917].

[6] As Chief Censor, Royal Navy, a post he had held since 1914, Vice-Admiral Sir Douglas Egremont Robert Brownrigg (1867–1939) was responsible for recruiting prominent authors willing to write about the naval contribution to the war effort.

But you know that I must now finish the story.[1] Must. Join a covering letter in which you tell Sir D that he would have [had] this before New Year if I had not been so gouty in the last half of Dec.

I am always unloading work on you – but then you see I *am* in your hands.

Your[s] affct[ly]

JC

To J. B. Pinker
Text Telegram Berg; Unpublished

[Ashford, Kent
12 January 1917
11. 48 a.m.]

Bookishly London

Boy arrived please send me five pound note today probably in town Tuesday[2]

Conrad

To J. B. Pinker
Text MS Berg; Unpublished

[Capel House]
[15 January 1917][3]

My dear Pinker.

Borys will call on you to-morrow (Tuesday) about noon. He and Jessie are going up for 24 hours by the 10. 17 to-morrow.

If you are engaged about noon give him an app[oin]t[ent] as he feels he must see you if only for 5 minutes before going back.

I am staying at home with John & Rob[t4] to look after these young devils and incidentally to try to get on with the story.

Ever Yours

J. C.

---

[1] Probably a reference to what would become *The Arrow of Gold*, but on 4 December, Conrad had told Dent of his plans to finish *The Rescue* (*Letters*, 5, p. 682). He did not, however, return to serious work on this novel until the autumn of 1918.
[2] The 16th.
[3] Written the day before 16 January, which was the only Tuesday within the period of Borys's leave.
[4] Conrad's younger son John and Robert ('Robin') Sholto Douglas. After his arrest in November 1916 on a charge of indecently assaulting a teen-age boy, Norman Douglas had fled overseas and, as they had often done before, the Conrads were looking after his younger son, who was now a cadet in HMS *Worcester*.

To J. B. Pinker
Text MS Berg; Unpublished

[letterhead: Capel House]
Tuesday [16 January 1917][1]

My dear Pinker

Please let Jessie have what she wants for her expenses in town. She returns home tomorrow evening. She has to pay for a surgical appliance for her good knee which shows signs of the whole strain it had to bear for more than 10 years now.[2]

The kid[3] discloses himself a good fellow and a really fine officer. It's like a dream to see him and hear him talk.

Ever Yours

J Conrad.

To J. B. Pinker
Text MS Berg; Unpublished

[Capel House]
Tuesday evg. [16 January 1917][4]

My dear friend.

Please send the proof to Harrison right off – I want the E. R. text to be correct in last ins*t*. I presume the book is arranged for. If you want the end to "set up" you can demand a revise from Harr: In any case I should like to see proof of book form.

The story the title of which may be: *R. T Fragments.*[5] Will come along before many days. Of course while B[orys] is here I am not likely to do much. But I've worked today and shall push on a bit more tomorrow, till the truant Mother returns with the prodigal Son.

The prodigal is not very bad. Before leaving Eng*d* he had to make up a cash deficiency in the pay chest caused by an officer (a professional gambler with a decoy-wife in Portsmouth) whom he and Bevan[6] had (very improperly) trusted to pay the C*o*. He told them a cock-and-bull story and it ended in Bevan paying £30 and B 25. For this and other reasons poor B left his native shore without a penny in his pocket and the gua[rantee]*d.* overdraft exhausted

[1] Dated by Jessie and Borys Conrad's visit to London.
[2] Since the operation on the other knee in November 1904.
[3] Borys, who had turned nineteen the previous day.
[4] Borys is in London, therefore the second letter of this date.
[5] The 'R' may stand for Rita, the central female character in *The Arrow of Gold*; in the published version, her family name is Lastaola.
[6] Borys's comrade Desmond Russell Bevan (1882–1931) whose father, fortunately, sat on the board of Barclay's Bank.

up to the last pound. Now he has paid it back and has 20 to his credit after spending another 20 between Arras and Capel House. When you consider that he had 3 days in Havre and a day in London – and that he had no break of *any sort* for fully a year this does not seem so *very* outrageous. Please pay him £5 from me – good conduct money.

Ever Yours
J Conrad.

To R. B. Cunninghame Graham
Text MS Dartmouth; Watts 186

[letterhead: Capel House]
17. Jan '17

Cher Ami

Thanks for Your good letter and enclosure for the officer – of your creation, really.[1]

I am glad and more than glad to hear that he has produced a good impression on you. I've heard he has "the respect of his seniors". His friends amongst his Contemporaries are not a few. There is a sort of quiet enthusiasm about him – et il a naturellement des idées de gentilhomme, combined with a deep democratic feeling as to values in mankind. Indeed he might have sat at your feet except for Your divine indignation which is a gift of the gods to You especially – and which in any case is not of his age – and certainly not in his mentality. Car il n'est pas brilliant.* – All good luck go with you très cher ami and whatever happens pray believe in my inalterable* and admiring affection.

Yours
J Conrad.

To B. Macdonald Hastings
Text MS Colgate; Unpublished

[Capel House]
17 Jan 17

Dear Hastings.

This is great news.[2] Do devote your talents to extracting some leave from the stern military men.

Yours all expectation
J. Conrad

---

[1] Another reference to Graham's intervention at the War Office on Borys's behalf.
[2] Hastings had finished a clean draft of *Victory*.

To J. B. Pinker
Text Telegram Berg; Unpublished

[Hamstreet, Kent]
[19 January 1917]
2. 53 pm

Bookishly London
Please cable metropole magazine as follows will you print conrad article sea warfare earliest date 2000 words no payment[1] but admiralty reserving power publish same in english and colonial press any time ends this is my suggestion adopted by Sir Douglas Brownrigg give it your help if you approve

Conrad

To Iris Wedgwood
Text MS Private collection; Unpublished

[letterhead: Capel House]
21 Jan 1917.

Dear Mrs Wedgwood.[2]
Jessie and Borys were so sorry. Your wire did not reach them till they were back here. You see as I could not leave home they did not stay any time in town in order not to deprive me of the boy's company too long. The wire must have been delivered at the hotel directly after they left for the Station.

Speaking soberly I am pleased with him. He has been in his year in France all along the front from Ypres-Arm[enti]ères Vimy ridge to the Somme offensive which he saw well, being always well to front with his battery of Howitzers.[3] The same one he joined in Portsmouth – an unlicked cub,

---

[1] The *Metropolitan Magazine* of New York had been a good market for Conrad's stories. As with other writers who described the Navy at war, the Admiralty paid Conrad's travelling expenses on the understanding that he would not accept payment for his articles.

[2] Conrad met Iris Veronica Wedgwood (née Pawson, 1886–1982) through Richard Curle. She and her husband, Ralph, were the dedicatees of *Within the Tides* (1915). In the 1920s she published several novels (*The Iron Age, The Fairway, The Livelong Day, Perilous Seas*), and in the 1930s, topographical studies (*Northumberland and Durham, Fenland Rivers*).

[3] Short-barrelled artillery pieces firing shells on a flatter trajectory than that of a mortar; Borys was working with lightweight howitzers designed for easy mobility in the field.

18 months ago. He has been gassed a little, has flown in action, has been knocked down by shell concussion (once in the distinguished company of General Gough[1]) has squatted in observation posts, had a joy ride in one of the first tanks[2] – unfortunately the one which had its hind wheels shot away in the first half-hour. So he didn't go very far. He has been doing lieut's work since he went out, and, since last Nov:, he has a captain's job: C[ommanding] O[fficer] of the advanced post of the S[iege] A[rtillery] P[ark], where he lives in a sandbagged cottage and is strafed by Fritz every day. He expects to be promoted soon. He celebrated his 19th birthday here. He said to me: "I am a veteran. When we were first appointed to batteries the M[echanical] T[ransport] for guns was a perfectly new thing. We didn't know what it was we had to do and there was no one to tell us. We had to learn our work under shellfire and sometimes under machine-gunfire. One of my lorries is riddled with M[achine] G[un] bullets." He gave me every minute of his leave and we had many long talks. He was absolutely serene.

I am telling you all this because I can't forget how good and kind to him you were at his emergence from early boyhood. He left us yesterday at 4 o'clock and there is a great emptiness in the house. My wife has been very good. She sends you her love. Pray remember us to the General[3] and believe me always,

Your very faithful and obedient servant
Joseph Conrad.

---

[1] General Sir Hubert de la Poer Gough (1870–1963) commanded the Fifth Army, first mustered for the Battle of the Somme and designed to be a flexible mobile force. He had a name for being the most visible general at the Front, taking more risks than other staff officers, and was far more popular among soldiers than among politicians and editors. In *The Fifth Army* (Hodder & Stoughton, 1931), he describes conditions in early January 1917: 'rain, sleet and snow, piercing winds, a bitter and penetrating dampness' (p. 176); Borys, however, would be returning to what Gough described as 'seven weeks of the hardest frost that I had ever experienced in Europe' (*ibid.*).

[2] Tanks could cross trenches, break through barbed wire, and resist small arms fire or shrapnel. They were first used on 15 September 1916, during the Battle of the Somme. The first major penetration of enemy lines, however, did not occur until November 1917, during the Battle of Cambrai.

[3] From 1916 to 1919, Honorary Brigadier-General Ralph Lewis Wedgwood put his civilian experience with the London and North-Eastern Railway to work as Director of Docks for GHQ, France.

To F. N. Doubleday

Text MS Princeton; Unpublished

[letterhead: Capel House]

22 Jan 17.

Dear Mr Doubleday.[1]

I regret not having thanked you before for the books you have been good enough to send me. I have been specially interested by the Mount Vernon monograph.[2]

We had our boy here for a ten day's leave after a year's continuous service in France. He has been all along the front with his battery, which during the Somme advance was well forward all the time. He has been gassed a little (to begin with) he has flown in action, he had a joy-ride in a tank the first day they went over the German lines. He saw Fritz run for dear life. Unluckily the tank in which he was got its hind wheels shot off – so they didn't get very far. He was also knocked down twice by shell concussion – the last time in the distinguished company of general Gough. He celebrated his 19th birthday with us. We found him greatly matured. But what struck me most was a curious serenity of manner and thought as though nothing on earth could startle him now. And though he gave us every minute of his leave he confessed to me that he was anxious to get back to the battery and to his beloved men. He commands the M[echanical] T[ransport] section and through deaths and changes is the second senior officer of his battery.

He wishes me to remember him kindly to you, and to tell you that the glasses you have been good enough to send to him are the object of general envy and have done some excellent good work at more than one forward observation post of the artillery of the III^d corps.[3] He says he often thought gratefully of you while using them.

---

[1] Frank Nelson Doubleday (1862–1934) was born in Brooklyn. He began his career in publishing at Charles Scribner's Sons (1877–95); he allied himself with S. S. McClure from 1897 to 1900 before going into partnership with Walter Hines Page as president of Doubleday, Page; in 1927, the firm became Doubleday, Doran. He numbered among his authors Frank Norris, Ellen Glasgow, Stephen Crane, O. Henry, Jack London, Booth Tarkington, and Rudyard Kipling, with whom he maintained a close friendship. Between 1912 and 1914, initially at Alfred Knopf's urging, Doubleday's interest in Conrad changed from casual to serious, and Doubleday started to plan a collected edition. The North American publication of *Chance* was Conrad's first financial success; for the rest of his life his association with Doubleday was rewarding and often cordial. When Conrad made his exhausting journey to the USA in 1923, he made Effendi Hill, the Doubledays' Long Island home, his headquarters.

[2] Given Doubleday's tastes and what he would have suspected of Conrad's, this is more likely to have been an example of fine printing from the press of William Edwin Rudge of Mount Vernon, NY, than a monograph on George Washington's estate.

[3] Field-glasses were in high demand at the Front; Conrad had presented Ford with a pair in 1916.

My health has been fair lately. But mentally I am without much grip on my work. We are all feeling the strain more and more, but the national determination to see this thing through hardens as the cruel days go by. It's a pity better use is not made of it. But leaders of genius are rare.

My wife (who has need of all her fortitude) joins me in kindest regards to Mrs Doubleday and yourself and hopes that we will have the great pleasure of seeing You under our roof in better days.

Believe me always

very sincerely Yours

Joseph Conrad.

To B. Macdonald Hastings
Text MS Colgate; Unpublished

[letterhead: Capel House]

22^{d} Jan '17.

My dear Hastings.

My respect for your "cleverness" is greatly increased. In an adaptation that's what counts. I remember your saying (in Irving's dressing room) – "This thing if it's worth doing at all then it's for the money in it." And from that point of view my wife (who represents marvellously the "general public" audience) anticipates the happiest results.

Let us "accept the omen."

I haven't touched the play. Unless we read it together: and follow the inspiration of the moment, that sort of meddling can do no good. The devil of it is that I have no influential friend about the W[ar] O[ffice] – and anyhow you don't send me the name of your corps or of your CO *nor* Nothing. Suppose you do? There is always a "perhaps – !"

The mere detail remarks I venture to offer. *Imprimis* Instead of Hans (?!!) Let the Javanese waiter be called Saridan[?]. If he must have a name. Nobody would address him otherwise than Boy! Speaking to Sch[omberg]: he had better say – Yes Master – No Master – instead of *Sir*. 2do People must [not] speak of *South Sea Islands*. It's no more south-sea than Norway is Italy. There they say Archipelago as eas[il]y as you would say Lancashire. Or simply: the Islands. 3° No Italian-led orchestra would dream of playing God Save the King – and in a Dutch possession too! 4° The speech contrasting Sourabaya with a desert island detonates. ("Sourabaya is bad enough but Samburan etc etc") Sourabaya is let me tell you a bigger, older and much more amusing town than Winchester.[1] And in its own island quite as important. However an audience probably would see nothing funny in the phrase. But why name it at

---

[1] The venerable Wessex city where Hastings was currently based. Surabaya is a large port in eastern Java; Samburan is the fictional island setting of *Victory*.

all? *5°* Heyst would never say "we shall travel on his ship." He has wandered too much to use tourist phrases. He would say "he (i.e. Davids[on]:) will give us a passage in his ship." *6°* Heyst wouldn't remark (to Davids) like an indulgent clergyman or jovial shopkeeper "Sailors! Sailors" H is very much homme du monde. Davids is his inferior – if a chum. That thing grates – and is so objectless. You can find a telling phrase instead something in accord with his state of mind. – All trifles as you see.

Lena's costume My wife points out to me that L wears a body sarong all the time – which is practically a night dress. No malay girl would do that let alone a white woman. If you want L in Malay costume we can concoct a complete one: sarong at waist, belt, scarf, open jacket. Of course that requires warm brown skin for effect but still in the artificial light – The other an actress would feel awkward in. And I am afraid that with sarong under the arms she would look grotesque. I speak of some "fumbling". I didn't notice any. Now we ought to know what Irving will think of it.

Yours cordially

J. Conrad.

To J. B. Pinker
Text MS Berg; Unpublished

[Capel House]
Tuesday. 7. 15 AM. [23 January 1917][1]

My dear Pinker.

I believe you are perfectly right. But I have *given* per agreement this sort of copy to the Ad^lty. No question me keeping money. Please tele^ph to Brownr[i]^gg about 11 o'clock to whom your letter goes by this train

JC.

To J. B. Pinker
Text MS Berg; Unpublished

[Capel House]
Wednesday [24 January 1917][2]

My dear Pinker.

Thanks for your letter. I am sure you don't mind me having opened the matter with Sir D. B[rownrigg] direct; but I am afraid I have given you trouble for nothing that will be much good. I am curious to hear how you have settled the matter. I suppose there can be no doubt in Sir D B's

---

[1] The reference to the 'Admiralty article' indicates a place between the telegram to Pinker of [19 January] and the letter of [24 January].

[2] Conrad has read and returned the script of *Victory*. A telegram to Pinker of [22 January] reads: 'Of course if you say so but should like to see your letter first and after it* looking over Hastings adaptation prevented me writing verily believe it will do well' (Berg).

mind that I am *not* after money in this connection. The copy *belongs* to the Admiralty.

We don't remember receiving the MS of the Shad-Line. But it must be here, somewhere. Jessie's much distressed at the failure of her memory but the boy's visit seems to have driven everything out of her mind for a time. Search-party will be organised this afternoon. But pray my dear friend try to get balance of proof from E. R. You see the text as given to ER. is so different from the MS. *Brain wave*! If I can find the N° of the Met. Mag: with the last instal^t I will send it to you.[1] That will be nearer the final text than the MS.

I creep on with the story.

Hastings' adaptation is horribly efficient. You know what I mean. As he says himself "That sort of thing is done for money". I have sent it back to him. The worst is that he can't get leave to come here and talk over a point or two of importance. I want Irving to see the play as soon as possible.

Yours ever

J. C.

To B. Macdonald Hastings

Text MS Colgate; Unpublished

[Capel House]
25 Jan '17.

My dear Hastings

I am afraid I have given You a wrong impression. Forgive me for being so inexpressive. I am aware under what cramping conditions you've had to work, and I admire – I really do – your skill and your fidelity. My *enthusiasm* I keep for your own plays. They do command it. And you can't very well be angry with me for that.

You can have no conception of my ignorance in theatrical art. I can't even *imagine* a scenic effect. But reading your adaptation I, even I, felt something, what I imagine to be the scenic emotion, come through to me – get home. And also remember that I was trammeled by my knowledge of the book, where I had visualised everything in my own way even as I wrote. Think my dear Hastings – it's no joke to have to adjust one's artistic focus to the swift movement of dramatic presentation.

---

[1] The American *Metropolitan Magazine* began serialising *The Shadow-Line* in September 1916.

Well – enough of this. Only don't imagine for a moment that I fail to appreciate your labour and your gift of loyal rendering.

My note on Lena's dress was but a warning. If I weren't afraid of you charging me with irreverence I would say that I don't mind her coming on in a bath-towel. I know that in the book (here and there) she's by no means overdressed. But then consider the heat of Samburan – whereas the stage of a London theatre! . . . I shiver at the mere thought! You must drill and dress your Lena exactly as you think fit – of course. But first you must catch your Lena. Have you got her? Is she anywhere in sight? I confess *this* is my great anxiety. For – granting Irving – the success must depend on Lena. And speaking very seriously it strikes [me] that it isn't her garments that will be [the] difficulty its what she will bring to us within her very skin.

Our boy has just left us at the expiration of his leave. My poor wife snatched nine days of fearful joy[1] – and now that he has gone back to his beloved battery (after celebrating his 19th birthday with us) there is a great aching emptiness in this house.

Always yours Cordially

J. Conrad.

To J. B. Pinker
Text MS Berg; Unpublished

[Capel House]
[c. 25 January 1917][2]

Dear Pinker

We have found type-copy of Sh-Line, which will do. Please ask the revered Dent[3] to let me have slip-proofs of the last 20pp at least – if possible. And soon I am thinking of motto and dedication.

Your

J. C.

Enc[l] 3 small bills for household furnitures.

---

[1] 'They hear a voice in every wind / And snatch a fearful joy': Thomas Gray (1716–71), 'Ode on a Distant Prospect of Eton College'.
[2] Soon after the letter of [24 January] which refers to hunting for a text of *The Shadow-Line*.
[3] J. M. Dent, publisher of *The Shadow-Line*.

To A. T. Saunders

Text MS South Australia; Unpublished

[letterhead: Capel House]

26 Jan 17.

Dear Sir[1]

Many thanks for your very interesting letter and the curious Hayes pamphlet.[2]

Yes. M[r] Jacques came back with us in the *Torrens*.[3] He was laid up all the passage and I hardly ever saw him. This will partly account for my extraordinary mistake in the Personal Record.[†4] Strange lapse of memory! E. L. Sanderson (also a passenger that time) pointed it out to me a long time ago.

The J. Galsworthy is *the* John of course.[5] Our intimate friendship dates from that passage. He left us in C[ape] Town but sought me out in London afterwards.

I did serve in the *Loch Etive* with Capt Steward* (at one time of the famous *Tweed*). I was 3[d] off[ic][er] and kept my first *Officer's watch* in that ship.[††] Steward died at sea, but I don't remember the year.[6] Capt Cope[7] lives now in Herne Bay, but I haven't seen him for many years. Of the Angels[8] I know nothing.

† Some Reminiscences title has been altered since first Eng edition was published.[9]

†† I mean as a British certificated officer of the Merchant Service.

[1] Born in Queensland in 1885, Alfred Thomas Saunders of Adelaide, South Australia, was an accountant and amateur historian who often published the results of his researches in the *Adelaide Mail*. In 1888, when Conrad commanded the *Otago*, Saunders had been working as a clerk for her owners, Henry Simpson & Co. Saunders was fascinated by the career of the South Seas pirate 'Bully' Hayes (1829–77). In Chapter 38 of *Lord Jim*, Marlow cites Hayes as one of the ruffians who were not as vile as Gentleman Brown.

[2] Either *Bully Hayes: Barrator, Bigamist, Buccaneer, Blackbirder, and Pirate* ('For Private Circulation', Perth, 1915) or *Bully Hayes, Louis Becke and the Earl of Pembroke*, a reprint of columns from the *Adelaide Mail* (1915).

[3] William Henry Jacques (1869–1893) made the voyage in the hope of easing his tuberculosis.

[4] The first section of *A Personal Record* has a vivid and circumstantial reminiscence of Conrad's asking Jacques to read a portion of *Almayer's Folly*. Conrad was mistaken in his assumptions about Jacques's end. Rather than catching 'a fatal cold' and dying either in Australia or homeward bound in another ship, Jacques returned in the *Torrens* and died of consumption two months after reaching England.

[5] He had been travelling with Sanderson in Australia and the South Seas. Conrad's first mention of Galsworthy in surviving correspondence comes in a letter of January 1897 (*Letters*, 1, p. 335).

[6] Conrad served in the *Loch Etive*, an iron-built wool clipper, from August 1880 to April 1881; Captain William Stuart, who died in 1896 while still in command of the *Loch Etive*, was accustomed to the speed and light handling of wooden-built ships such as the *Tweed*, whose master he had been from 1863 to 1874. The *Tweed* was famous not only for fast passages but for her improbable conversion from the *Punjaub*, a paddle-wheeler built to carry troops. Conrad remembers Captain Stuart in 'Cobwebs and Gossamer' (*The Mirror of the Sea*).

[7] W. H. Cope had been Conrad's captain in the *Torrens*.

[8] The famous sea-going brothers, H. R. and W. H. Angel: the latter commanded the *Torrens* before Captain Cope.

[9] To *A Personal Record*.

If the firm of Messrs: H Simpson & Sons still exists in Adelaide please tell them that J. C will never forget the generosity, the courtesy and indeed the kindness of the head of the firm in '88–'89 when he commanded their barque *Otago*.[1]

Pray believe me, with great regard

Yours faithfully

Joseph Conrad.

PS I saw L. Becke once in 1895 or six in a publisher's office and I must say I wasn't favourably impressed then. I haven't read many of his books. Reef & Palm was the last I looked at I think.[2]

To John Quinn

Text MS NYPL; Unpublished

[letterhead: Capel House]

[late January 1917][3]

My dear Quinn.[4]

My wife wanted to write herself the letter of thanks for the lovely apples; but our boy has just left us after his first leave from France and she does not feel equal to talk about him on paper – and yet she feels that she would have to write of him. So I am deputed to tell you how much we have appreciated your gift and then to tell you something of the boy.

He celebrated his 19th birthday with us. He said to me: "I am a veteran. When we, the first batch of youngsters, were appointed to the heavy batteries as Mechanical Transport Officers it was an altogether new thing. Nobody

---

[1] The Adelaide firm of Simpson's, owners of the Black Diamond Line, had long gone out of business.

[2] The Australian fiction-writer Louis Becke (1855–1913) was known for his tales of adventure in the South Pacific, often drawn from his own experiences. These included being tried for piracy with Bully Hayes. Conrad, whom early reviewers often compared to Becke, read *By Reef and Palm* 'again' in 1896: see *Letters*, 1, p. 298. They would have met at the office of T. Fisher Unwin while he was publishing both authors.

[3] After Borys's return to the Front, so probably during the last week in January: the envelope was stamped by the US censor: 'Received February 12, 1917'. Typically, letters to New York were taking about fifteen days. The time could have been several days longer if a mail had just been missed.

[4] John Quinn (1870–1924), the son of Irish immigrants, came from Ohio. As a New York lawyer, he had a highly lucrative practice in commercial and financial law, particularly the law of tariffs. As a supporter of the arts, he won an exemption for artists from sales taxes and built up a great collection of modern painting and sculpture; he was the chief private buyer at the Armory show in 1913. He also amassed modern literary manuscripts; among the writers he collected on a large scale were Yeats, Pound, Eliot, Joyce, and Conrad. When Quinn auctioned off his Conradiana in 1923, several years after relations between patron and author had chilled, manuscripts and inscribed volumes bought for a total of $10,000 fetched $110,000.

could teach us then because nobody knew the practical conditions and the way to go about that work. We had to learn all this by ourselves under shell-fire and sometimes under machine-gun fire. And we have all done pretty well."

One could see he was fairly pleased with himself and extremely proud of his men. He had a year of continuous duty all along the line right from Ypres to the Somme. He has been gassed a little in the early days – a sort of welcome from Fritz. He managed to get in as many side-shows as possible – has flown in action, has squatted in observation posts; went sniper-hunting, had a joy ride in a tank the first time they went over the German lines. But what seems to afford him the greatest satisfaction is having been knocked down by the same shell-concussion with General Gough. The boy had just put the last gun of the battery in position, then got his lorry back on the road and was waiting for a bit because the landscape ahead was full of German shells. He saw a general's car come along from the direction of Pozières. It pulled up opposite him and the general got out, apparently to speak to him. Just at that moment a H.Z. shell[1] landed on the car's forewheel blew the whole thing to smithereens and flung the general covered with his drivers blood and shreds of flesh under B's lorry. B had been flung there too; the lorry (an American-Peerless) was half demolished and of the two men with B one was killed and the other had his hand blown off. B and the general crawled from under the wreck together. The Gen: was a horrible sight. He said to B: "For Goodness' sake lets get out of this". And B said: "Certainly Sir" and pointed out to him an enormous shell-crater quite near the road. So they crawled along over there taking the wounded man with them. In that crater there were a good many people some dead and some alive and luckily two stretcher-bearers who bandaged the man's arm. Meantime B wiped the general down with some rags he found lying about, the best way he could; and then they both sat in that hole for an hour and a half shivering and shaking from the shock. Later the Gen. got away down a trench and B went back to his battery where he helped around generally till the evening, when his junior off[ic]er arrived with an ammunition convoy with which B returned to the replenishing station. But before daybreak he was back with the batt^y with another ammunition convoy. And now said B "whenever the Gen: sees me on the roads he waves his hand to me, though I am certain he doesn't know my name".

We found B matured very much. What struck me most was a sort of good-tempered imperturbable serenity in his manner, speech and thoughts – as if nothing in the world could startle or annoy him any more. He looks

---

[1] A shell from a howitzer.

wonderfully robust and has developed a respectable moustache. He gave us every minute of his leave; wouldn't hear of going to town except for a day and a half with his mother to call on the more intimate of our circle of friends. We got on extremely well together. We talked not only of War but of the other two W's* also. Where the fellow got his taste for wine I can't imagine. As to Women, Cunninghame Graham who went on purpose to meet him in the salon of a very distinguished lady (the world says that she is his last flame. About time. C. G. is sixty-five if a day) wrote to me with great glee that he found the boy "très dégourdi"[1] and that he thought he "will be un homme a femmes like You and I, for he has a way with them". My wife who gave a lunch party has also observed that aptitude and was very much amused. She has indeed snatched a fearful joy during these 10 days. Her fortitude is admirable but I am anxious about her health. She sends you her most friendly regards. What a war-letter I have written!

Believe me always

Yours

Joseph Conrad.

To J. B. Pinker
Text MS Berg; Unpublished

[Capel House]
[late January 1917][2]

My dear Pinker

Will you transmit the three scraps enclosed to Dent. They relate to the Sh-Line. – Title p[age] – Dedication – Motto.[3] Just look at them please as the book is very much your affair. It's you who said: "Let there be a volume". So you ought to control the details.

The enclosed off[ici]^{al} paper belongs to the usual poisonous crop at this time of the year.[4]

Thanks for your letter rec^d this morning. It's all in your hands. I suppose the cable went all the same.[5] Or have you and Sir D B[rownrigg] given it up?

Affct^{ly} yours

J. C.

---

[1] 'Very sharp' – resourceful and alert. Graham would be 65 in May.
[2] Between the 19th, when Conrad asked Pinker to wire the *Metropolitan Magazine*, and the 31st, when Conrad thanked Dent for a mock-up of the three pages; he commented on their appearance the following day.
[3] The dedication to Borys, and the motto taken from the text.
[4] A crop grown by tax collectors?   [5] To the *Metropolitan Magazine*?

To J. M. Dent
Text MS Berg; Unpublished

[letterhead: Capel House]
31 Jany 17.

Dear Mr Dent[1]
  Many thanks.[2]
I hope the book will come out end March.
I am just now held up by gout.

Yours sincerely

J. Conrad

To J. M. Dent
Text MS Berg; Unpublished

[letterhead: Capel House]
1st Febr^y 17.

Dear Mr Dent
  I return here the sp[ecimen] pages with my thanks. The only suggestions I venture to offer is that perhaps the heavy-leaded (inner) lines round the author's name might be removed. I can't very well judge how the t[itle] p[age] will look without them but the effect now is strangely funereal. I would propose also a slightly smaller type for the words *A Confession*.

  This said I leave it all to you. It's rather absurd of me talking typography and "get up" to Aldine House.[3] The sp. p. of the text seems to me perfect.

  I am laid up with a severe attack. This joke has lasted 22 years[4] and I am beginning to be tired of it.

Yours faithfully

J Conrad.

---

[1] Joseph Mallaby Dent (1849–1926) set up in business as a bookbinder in 1872, and turned to publishing in 1888. Among his great successes were the Temple Classics, the Temple Shakespeare, and Everyman's Library. In Conrad's lifetime, Dent published '*Twixt Land and Sea* (1912), *Within the Tides* (1915), *The Shadow-Line* (1917), *The Rescue* (1920), *Notes on Life and Letters* (1921), and most of the Uniform Edition. The rest of that edition appeared posthumously, as did *Suspense* (1925) and *Last Essays* (1926).
[2] For sample text of *The Shadow-Line*.
[3] Dent's London headquarters.
[4] On [21 March], he writes of suffering for 'more than 24 years'.

To J. B. Pinker
Text MS Berg; Unpublished

[Capel House]
[1 February 1917][1]

My dear Pinker

I forward you Dent's letter and the specimen pages. Also my reply to Dent as to matters of typography.

A sentence in his letter is the cause of my starting to worry you again. Personally I have too felt the shortness of the vol.[2]

Well – once more I suggest Prince Roman[3] and in order to make the combination acceptable I've written a Foreword the rough draft of which is enclosed. The title page needn't be changed.

After running your eye over the preface you will decide whether to open the matter to Dent or keep it to yourself. But please send him the pages.

Am laid up with gout in knee.[4] Horrid.

Yours ever

J. C.

To J. B. Pinker
Text MS Berg; Unpublished

[Capel House]
[c. 2 February 1917][5]

My dear Pinker

Will you please put that right by paying in about £10 to my credit. This is my acct for local subsc[ripti]^{ons} and I am being struck by VAD hospitals,[6] one in Ashford and the other in Woodchurch.

Can you send also £30 to Jessie's acc*^t*.

In the matter of *the* loan. I havent the slightest idea how I stand. But there will be the story now in hand worth 500 cert[ainly] (say end this month,

---

[1] Accompanying the specimen pages so that Pinker could see them before they went back to the publisher. 'Dent's letter' is missing: in his reply of 3 February, Dent reassured Conrad that he would 'attend to what you wish about the titlepage and make your book as nice as I can' (TS carbon, Berg).

[2] Evidently Dent was uneasy about the brevity of *The Shadow-Line*; he reiterated his concern that it was too short to stand alone as a volume in a letter of 13 February.

[3] First published in 1911, 'Prince Roman' finally appeared in book form as one of the *Tales of Hearsay*.

[4] The attack must have come on very recently; at 9.42 a.m. on the 30th, Conrad proposed to call on Pinker at 12.40 (telegram, Berg).

[5] Written on the verso of a letter from the London County and Westminster Bank, 1 February, asking Conrad to adjust his overdraft.

[6] Hospitals staffed by nurses of the Voluntary Aid Detachment.

about) and if you could get me a £100 to invest in advance of proceeds I would be glad.

Yours

J. C.

To J. B. Pinker

Text MS Berg; Unpublished

[Capel House]

[early February 1917][1]

Dear Pinker

Herewith agreement with D'day, and many thanks for this of Your many negociations*.

Am glad to hear you generally approve of my instr[ucti]^{ons} to the revered Dent.

The official doc[umen]^t is what had to be.

Story still crawls.

R. T.
Selected Passages
from
Letters

Rotten title. Eh? But I am sick of short ones.

Ever Yours

J. Conrad.

To J. B. Pinker

Text MS Berg; J–A, 2, 181[2]

[Capel House]

Sunday [4 February 1917][3]

My Dear Pinker.

I enclose here a cutting. To have my work held up as an example of the E. R's taste for the morbid[4] has upset me very much. Harr[ison]'s proceedings have been exasperating me all along but I said nothing to you. It would have been no good as we couldn't've done anything. Strangely enough I expected adverse comment (as the story was being noticed) tho' not in that precise

---

[1] Soon after the letters of 1 February about the layout of the title-page.
[2] Omitting the sentence about 'Dent's groan'.
[3] On [1 February], Conrad suggested adding 'Prince Roman' to *The Shadow-Line* to make a larger volume; a reference to the dedication on [7 February] implies that Pinker now knew of the plan to drop it.
[4] This hostile notice is untraced, but more conservative journals such as the *Spectator* often deplored the *English Review*'s moral and aesthetic taste.

shape. He has been doling it out in drops, as if it were poison. No wonder he spoiled its taste altogether.

So you see that a story may get a nasty rap on mere "publication" grounds. I confess I have grown awfully nervous about that piece of work – which is not a story really but exact autobiography. So of course is Prince R. And I suggested P. R. mainly because its incl[usi]^{on} would give me an occasion to say that distinctly in a Preface.[1] If you imagined I was touched by the revered Dent's groan You were never more mistaken in your life. I really felt I would like it very much to be done. And it seemed suitable as in the *de luxe* edition those two pieces will have to go together – with the preface the draft of which you've seen. So another de luxe *vol* would have been settled by a 1st edition. The most, I think, satisfactory way of arranging a *de luxe* edition.

I am really quite jumpy about this thing, and I think I'll cancel the dedication as I don't want the boy's name to be connected with a work of which some imbecile is likely to say: that it is a "good enough" sort of story in the Conrad manner but not a work to be put out by itself with all that pomp etc, etc and to be charged such a price for.[2]

As two auto^{cal} episodes I would have less fear – the preface explaining why they appear by themselves: as they would be out of place amongst collected tales.

What do you think from *this* point of view?

Yours ever

J. Conrad.

To J. B. Pinker
Text MS Berg; Unpublished

[letterhead: Capel House]
Wednesday. [7 February 1917][3]

My dear Pinker

I return the play at once because I am very anxious you should read it at the earliest possible moment.[4]

---

[1] The roughly drafted Foreword to the proposed joint publication of 'Prince Roman' and *The Shadow-Line*; this draft has not survived, and the volume never appeared. The 1920 Author's Note to *The Shadow-Line* describes that work as 'personal experience seen in perspective with the eye of the mind'. 'Prince Roman' appeared posthumously in *Tales of Hearsay*, and thus lacks any authorial marking as autobiography; in any case, it is autobiographical only in the sense of reproducing Conrad's recollections of meeting Prince Roman Sanguszko and of hearing his story from those who had known him.

[2] The dedication to Borys 'and all others who like himself have crossed in early youth the shadow-line of their generation' did appear in book form. Three years later, in the Author's Note, Conrad wrote that 'before the supreme trial of a whole generation I had an acute consciousness of the minute and insignificant character of my own obscure experience'.

[3] Conrad actually returned the proofs of *The Shadow-Line* on the 11th.

[4] A dramatisation of *Almayer's Folly* by the Lancashire playwright Harold Brighouse (1882–1958), best known for the domestic comedy *Hobson's Choice* (1915). See *Letters*, 5, pp. 685–8.

For myself I simply don't know what to say. I always thought that the novel could *not* be adapted for the stage. And B[righouse]'s performance proves it to my mind. But taking it as it stands I must confess that I am surprised at the feebleness of many passages (as scenic effects) and a curious commonplaceness of the general conception and dialogue. But it may be *good stage work* – for all I know.

I must leave that to your experienced judgment. As you, I imagine, haven't seen the book for many years now you will be able to bring also a more detached mind to the task. B has done what he liked with the novel and I suppose the only question for us is:– Is it worth while? Please answer him in both our names and drop me a line when you have done so. I am not moved but I am interested – I mean interested to know what your decision will be.

I've had a large batch of proofs (all the First Part) of Sh-Line from Dent and shall return them to him tonight. Jessie who has seen my last letter to you thinks I am worrying you unduly. *Am* I worrying you? Those things are our common concern in their entirety, not only on their material side; and that being so I can do nothing – not even in such a detail as a dedication – behind your back. And I can't think that my practice – indeed the necessity – of laying my mind open to you strikes you as a nuisance. Am I right?

Ever Yours

J Conrad.

PS I expect to hear from you by our noon post.

To J. B. Pinker
Text MS Berg; Unpublished

[letterhead: Capel House]
Wednesday Night [7 February 1917][1]

My dear Pinker.

You are very good and patient and I feel remorseful at extracting a long letter from you. But to confess the truth I was very glad to get it. Of course all you say is absolutely truth and your good opinion of the piece of work stated so plainly re-assures me. But, you know, to speak openly I feel at times that I am not quite myself. A point of view that in a normal process of considering a given situation would have had its proper place seems now to run away with me. And the annoying thing is that I am half-conscious of it and yet can't pull up when I want to.

---

[1] The day of the comments on Brighouse's script: Conrad has received the letter expected 'by our noon post'.

There are reasons (not excuses) for this temporary lack of balance. I'll have to get over them.

I hope my letter about Alm: Folly was reasonable. I need hardly tell you that leaving that decision to you I do it without any mental reserves or even doubt. I am beautifully resigned and sane. So you needn't fear I'll treat you to a fit of jumps over *that* business. The writing of that letter my dear Pinker has been the finest piece of self-control I've achieved for years and years.

Yours ever

J Conrad.

PS I am glad you think it justified to invest the lot. But pray remember that of the amount only £400 is to go to my credit with you. I mean the Am: proceeds of the story.

PPS I shall [be] busy all tomorrow working a fully elaborated plan of sea-convoys which I am going to send to Sir D Brownrigg. I must out with it to relieve myself.

To W. T. H. Howe

Text MS Berg; *Listy* 363; Original unpublished

[letterhead: Capel House]

10 Febr 17

Dear Mr Howe[1]

Many thanks for your charming letter. I am very proud of those early appreciations which it seems I have managed not to forfeit in the course of my literary life. That, you see, is a haunting fear of many writers, I dare say.

A man changes in the course of 20 years. However my ideas were settled and my character formed long before I began to write. On the other hand the road still before me begins to look very short and lies overshadowed by many anxieties. Our eldest boy has just been here on a 10 days' leave after 13 months at the front. A fearful joy. His contemporaries (he celebrated his 19th birthday here) are falling like cornstalks under the scythe.

May you and America be spared such anxieties.

Yours sincerely

Joseph Conrad.

[1] William Thomas Hildrup Howe (1874–1939) managed the Cincinnati branch of the American Book Company, which specialised in text-books, eventually becoming its president. A keen purchaser of literary first editions, he also built up a famous collection of McGuffey's Eclectic Readers.

To J. M. Dent
Text MS Berg; Unpublished

[letterhead: Capel House]

11 Febr. 17.

Dear Mr Dent.

I am returning you the corrected slips by rail to save a day. I have kept them a long time.

I dare hope the text will be without blemish of any sort. But one can never tell. After going over it innumerable times I've discovered at the last moment the word *broad* repeated three times in a paragraph of five lines. Enough this to shake one's confidence for ever.

Pray send me a revise (2 sets if possible) which I promise to return in 24 hours.

Have you settled yet how the book is going to be dressed? Generally I am not so inquisitive but this small thing is very much my own – you know.

In haste

Yours

J. Conrad.

To J. B. Pinker
Text MS Berg; Unpublished

[letterhead: Capel House]

[c. 12 February 1917][1]

My dear Pinker

I have your letters. Your point of view on the Brighouse achievement is exactly mine. The only consideration worthy of regard is: whether the production of that thing (supposing it came off) wouldn't damage the prospects of Victory towards which I feel quite differently. Not only the prospects but its (possibly successful) career – I mean.

I go into it because theatrical prospects begin to interest me. B is negligible for me, Hastings isn't. He is curiously prosaic and tending to the obvious – but as a workman he's all there. And I rather fancy that I can deal with him. I have been reading my Western Eyes while laid up. A dead frost[2] – like Nostromo was – but there's an enormous play in it. Not at all on nihilist lines. The struggle of two "tendencies" for the possession of the girl – Revolt and Reaction – and for the intermediary the man who betrayed her brother. By taking the audience into confidence from the first there will be no end

---

[1] Pinker had now read Brighouse's dramatisation, which Conrad sent to him on the seventh; by the fourteenth, Pinker had responded to the plan for *Under Western Eyes*.

[2] The English equivalent of the French *un four noir*, by which Conrad usually means a commercial failure.

of great effects. And what a crowd of people – grotesque, amusing tragic, sympathetic: Mme de S – and Peter Ivanovitch – Laspara and his daughters – Sophia – then Natalia and Razumov himself. And no one need die at the end.

I feel a great longing to *collaborate* on that with H. Let him plan the frame-work acceptable to me – then take my words. In France it would take well, I am certain. And in Russia too eventually where the book did make a sensa-tion. (I don't think it's worth my while to translate Victory into French. But the other *would be* worth while).

This was going to be [a] long letter for you to read at leisure – a whole programme of work:- but this moment I receive this from the very Hastings.

It's damnable in a way. Do you think Irving wants to slip out of it in that way?[1] I[t] doesn't look *that* at first glance – but one doesn't feel confident as to the intention.

Ever Yours in haste.

J. C.

To J. B. Pinker
Text MS Berg; Unpublished

[Capel House]
[c. 12 February 1917][2]

Dear Pinker

Will You give the permission in my name if Dent agrees?

Your

JC.

To J. M. Dent
Text MS Berg; Unpublished

[letterhead: Capel House]
Wednesday [14 February 1917][3]

Dear Mr Dent

Shadow Line

As to chapters: The Story is now divided into six chap. numbered I to VI. Also in *two parts*.

---

[1] The letter of [28 February] implies that Irving had raised objections to the script.
[2] Written on the verso of a letter from Lady Sybil Cutting (née Sybil Marjorie Cuffe, 1879–1943) dated 11 February. She was collecting material for *A Book of the Sea* (Clarendon Press, 1918). Her anthology includes extracts from 'Youth' and 'Heart of Darkness'. By the time it appeared, she had remarried and become Lady Sybil Scott. Twice widowed, she became Lady Sybil Lubbock by her third marriage (1926). Her autobiography, *The Child in the Crystal*, came out in 1939.
[3] A reply to Dent's letter of the 13th, in which he had asked Conrad to disguise the brevity of *The Shadow-Line* by splitting it 'into something like chapters' (TS carbon, Berg).

Pray *cancel* division into parts, (I omitted to do so on the slips) then insert blank page if you like between each division from I to VI. Only please *don't* use the word Chapter just simply I. II. III. IV. V. VI.

As to portrait: Do let me see it before you decide. I'll return it at once. The Cadbys have some 8 or 10 negatives of me (about 3 years old)[1] and we could perhaps select one of them – unpublished one – of course for some small payment.

Yours in haste

J Conrad

What about the enclosed portrait?

To J. B. Pinker

Text MS Berg; Unpublished

[letterhead: Capel House]

Wednesday [14 February 1917][2]

My dear Pinker

Thanks for your letter. I shall write you at length to-morrow.

Will you please send ch: A. A. Farrar for 5. 5 John's tuition and another to Miss N. Lyons. 5.[3]

Yours ever

JC

Glad you like the Western Eyes notion. Russia will be a matter of interest for some years to come.[4] And the thing would be Russia presented to Western Eyes.

PS Dent wishes [to] publish portrait in one of B'woods old books. I've consented.

---

[1] Probably those made in September 1913 (*Letters*, 5, p. 284). Will and Carine Cadby, cobblers and photographers, had a studio in Borough Green, Kent. Carine was a formal innovator as well as a portraitist. Her recollections of Conrad as a sitter are reprinted in Martin Ray's *Joseph Conrad: Interviews and Recollections* (Macmillan, 1990), pp. 147–8. Dent had asked for 'a good portrait of you' to insert in one of the new editions.

[2] Dated by references to the 'Western Eyes notion' and Dent's request on the 13th for a picture.

[3] Arthur A. Farrar, John Conrad's tutor, was headmaster of the elementary school in Orlestone, near Capel House; Nellie Lyons had been in service with the Conrads since 1898; she often suffered from ill health and died in 1919.

[4] Military reverses, mutinies, food shortages, and street demonstrations were shaking the foundations of the old régime; within a month of Conrad's writing this letter, the Petrograd Soviet took control of St Petersburg, the Tsar abdicated, and the Provisional Government promised elections for a Constituent Assembly.

To J. B. Pinker

Text MS Berg; Unpublished

[letterhead: Capel House]

Thursday. [15 February 1917][1]

My dear Pinker.

I expect I'll get a revise of the Sh-Line in a day or two and then *that* will be off my sick mind. For *it*, the mind, isn't exactly right. Dam' flighty, restless, all over the place. Of course thats better than being paralysed —

I sent my convoy scheme to Sir D B[rownrigg] because he's in touch with the Chief of the Staff. He made to it the tactical objection which I expected. But my point was that in that way in sending say 100 grain, meat or cotton ships I would expect 80% to get home at 10 knots.[2] Whereas if strung up singly over the ocean even at 12 or 14 knots it's doubtful (as things are) whether 50% would get there.

If I felt better than I do I should dearly love a turn of patrol duty just now.[3] And I dare say I would be allowed without difficulty.

Continuing my interrupted letter on theatrical matters (which you will read at your leisure) I think that after putting in some practice with Hastings I would launch myself out single-handed. The subject is in that very story I am writing now.[4] Of course I am keeping the story within the limitations of Magazine fiction. And its rather a nuisance to have perceived its dramatic possibilities of which the greater part must be kept out, as much too good for the Met. Mag. And the play won't be easy. To put a femme galante (not exactly in that character but as an ardent Royalist) and her peasant sister very hard headed, very religious, and very mercenary on the stage will not be an easy matter. But it's nothing to what your job will be to persuade an actress to take it up (it will be an actress'[s] play) and to find an experienced actor capable to make up as an ingenuous youth of barely twenty. It will take you all your skill, diplomacy, patience, persuasiveness and also all your faith in me to carry the business through.

Don't think I am doing nothing but dreaming of what I may do. I am telling you those things because I have litterally* not a single soul in the world to whom I could talk like this. I am not neglecting the substance for shadows. I will be done with the story before very long and then I shall take

---

[1] A continuation of the 'interrupted letter on theatrical matters' of [c. 12 February]. In his letter of the 13th, Dent promised revises in a couple of days.

[2] Conrad's now-lost plan apparently anticipated the tactics of North Atlantic convoys in the Second World War.

[3] Recapitulating his experience of naval patrol duty the previous autumn.

[4] The incipient *Arrow of Gold*. The focus on the dramatic potential of the sisters suggests a link to both the third section of the finished novel and the fragment 'The Sisters' abandoned in 1896 and not published in Conrad's lifetime.

up the Rescue.[1] Of that, however, I will talk to you in my next. I really begin to
think that I must have a thorough change. Get into another house. Theres one
offering now, situated in a Rich Man's park. The late Laureated Austin used to
live there. The R. M wants me to go there. He has asked me to lunch with him.
His name is Ashley Dodd.[2] I shall certainly get a lunch out of him if I am well
enough to get out on Saturday. Jessie sends her love. She has an awful cough.

Ever Yours

J. Conrad.

P[S] We had ½ doz p[ost] cards from B[orys]. Have you heard from Eric
lately?[3]

To Sir Sidney Colvin

Text MS Fitzwilliam; Unpublished

[letterhead: Capel House]

21 Febr '17.

My dear Colvin[4]

I promised you that you should see the *complete* text of my little book before
everybody else. I could not send it to you before, but here is at last a set of
the revise which I can venture to offer to your eyes, tho' I didn't transpose
on it the corrections (a good many of them too) on the "marked" set which
I had to return at once to Dent.

You may take it that anything which is obviously shocking in wording or
punctuation has been put right.

The *stylisation* is pretty well what I wanted it to be. Anyway I can do no
more to it.

Yours as ever

J Conrad.

Our dear love to Lady Colvin[5] and yourself. We expect you to signal your
arrival at the first spell of good weather.

---

[1] The novel begun in 1896, taken up in the autumn of 1918, and finished in May 1919.

[2] George Ashley Dodd, landowner and barrister, formerly High Sheriff of Kent, lived at
Swinford Old Manor, Ashford, previously the home of Alfred Austin (1835–1913), the much-
derided Poet Laureate.

[3] Pinker's son Eric, who was serving in France.

[4] Sir Sidney Colvin (1845–1927, knighted 1911) became a good friend to Conrad, as he had been
to R. L. Stevenson. Colvin had been Slade Professor of Fine Arts at Cambridge and director
of the Fitzwilliam Museum; from 1884 to 1912, he was Keeper of Prints and Drawings at the
British Museum. Among his literary works were editions of Stevenson's letters and biographies
of Landor and Keats.

[5] For Lady Colvin, see the letter to her of [9 August 1918].

To J. M. Dent
Text MS Berg; Unpublished

[Capel House]

Thursday. [22 February 1917][1]

Dear Mr Dent

I am laid up again.

I really don't want to raise objections. I am putting to you my point of view. For instance as to the house. It isn't mine. I hope to be soon out of it. It isn't the house in which either Lord Jim or Youth were written. That sort of thing is good enough for the ill[ustrat]*ed* press but why give it durability which it does not deserve? At least to my view.

However I am sending you a set of photographs which includes one good one of the house. I also like the photo of myself in the study.

But pray do what you like.

Yours

J. C.

To R. H. Leon
Text MS Berg; Unpublished

[letterhead: Capel House]

22[d] Febry '17

Dear Sir[2]

The play *One Day More* is the dramatisation done more than 10 years ago of the short story *To-morrow* the last in the volume called *Typhoon* pub[d] by M[r] Heinemann in 1902 or 3.

One Day More was never published as a play; but the English Review printed the whole text in one of its issues for the year 1912 or 13.[3]

Sorry can't be more precise.

I have heard that a second-hand bookseller H. Danielson 16 Camden St NW. has been offering the pamphlet preface to the Nigger last year.[4]

---

[1] Received in Dent's office on the 23rd.

[2] Reginald Herbert Leon (1882–1960), a member of the London Stock Exchange, collected books, porcelain, and tapestries, ancient and modern. The volumes from his collection auctioned at Sotheby's in 1922 included the First, Second, and Fourth Folio editions of Shakespeare's plays.

[3] *One Day More*: finished February 1904, performed 1905, published *English Review*, August 1913. Leon must have caught wind of Shorter's imminent publication of a tiny limited edition. *Typhoon, and Other Stories* appeared in 1903.

[4] This was the pamphlet *The Art of Fiction* privately printed for Conrad in a hundred copies, 1902. For Conrad's dealings with Danielson, which were more direct than this letter implies, see *Letters*, 5, pp. 622–3.

There are about 40 copies in existence in Eng^d and the US in all. I regret that I have only two which I must keep for the 1st editions sets for my two boys.

What you say of *Chance* editions in 1913 is very curious. I know nothing of it. Some publishing muddle.[1] Once I have done with the proofs the book's fate is out of my hands. The only edition in which I take interest is the Collected Edition (limited to 1000 sets in Eng^d & in the US) which Doubleday, Page in New York and Mr Heinemann here are going to publish after the war. I've settled the format, the bindings, the fount and the paper. For the text it will be exactly the text of the English 1st editions freed from misprints and with, perhaps, a few (very few) verbal alterations. Of course both the *Nigger* preface and the dramatic form of *To-morrow* will have their places there.

Pardon this scrawl. I am laid up with gout and am writing this in bed.

Believe me

yours faithfully

Joseph Conrad.

To J. B. Pinker
Text MS Berg; Unpublished

[Capel House]
Thursday. [22 February 1917][2]

My dear Pinker

I am laid up again in more pain than I had for a long time.

Pray settle the enclosed bill and send me a ch for £10. I represent our parish at the V[oluntary] A[id] D[etachment] meeting and tho' I wont be able to go, I fear I must send my contribution.

I was done on Monday with Sh-Line proofs, at last.

How are you? And what news of Eric?

Ever Your

J. C.

---

[1] Copies of *Chance* dated 1913 are considerable rarities; because of a strike at the bindery, publication in Britain was delayed until January 1914.
[2] The first Thursday after finishing the proofs.

To J. B. Pinker
Text MS Berg; Unpublished

[letterhead: Capel House]
Saturday [24 February 1917][1]

My dear Pinker

A funny thing has happened. Two men wrote to me on the same day making inquiries about an *Ode on the Titanic* which I am supposed to have published in the xix Century mag!

As you know I never published an *Ode* anywhere; and I dare say you are convinced that I couldn't write a line of verse to save my life. Anyhow it is a fact. I couldn't. I am totally devoid of a metrical faculty. As one of these men is Clement Shorter and the other Reginald H. Leon (a collector of books) the thing deserves investigation. It is Clement Shorter who definitely names the xix Century.[2] The other man simply says "published in a magazine".

Both are familiar with E[nglish] R[eview] to which they allude in connection with *One day more*. So there doesn't seem to be any confusion in their minds.

I am having a hell of a time –

Ever Yours

J. C.

PS Glad to hear good news of Eric. Thanks for the cheques.

To R. H. Leon
Text MS Private collection; Unpublished

[letterhead: Capel House]
Saturday. [24 February 1917][3]

Dear Sir

I haven't the consolation to have gained my infirmities on active service. I have been subject to this wretched gout for 20 years and am beginning to find it monotonous. I hope with all my heart that you'll be able to shake off your trouble before very long.

Sorry your sanity has become suspect to your friends on account of your liking for my work.

---

[1] This and the 'Saturday' letters to Leon and Shorter share topics and the likelihood of being written on the same day. The letter to Pinker must come soon after that of 22 February with its request for news of Eric Pinker.
[2] Shorter was wrong about the magazine as well as the author.
[3] As for the 'Saturday' letter to Pinker.

And in this connection: I've never written an *ode*!!! I couldn't write a line of verse to save my life. I am totally devoid of all metrical faculty. I have directed my agent to make inquiries for if there is such a thing in existence I must disown it at once.

The Coll^d Limited Edition will be also de Luxe. And my aim is to make it absolutely complete. Every scrap of my writing will be eventually embodied in it. But there will be no Ode there. That Ode is a myth.

I am still laid up and feeling abominably seedy.

Yours faithfully

J. Conrad

To C. K. Shorter

Text MS BL Ashley 2923; Unpublished

[letterhead: Capel House]
Saturday [24 February 1917][1]

Dear Mr Shorter.

I am much flattered at your proposal to print *One Day More* and am delighted by your promise to send me five copies.[2]

What is the *Ode on the Titanic* you mention? I am devoid of all metrical faculty. I couldn't write a line of verse to save my life. Really!

Yours very sincerely

Joseph Conrad.

PS All I wrote a propos of the loss of the Titanic were two articles for the ER.[3] Pardon this scrawl. Am in bed with gout and having a fiendish time.

To Sir Sidney Colvin

Text MS Yale; J-A, 2, 182

[letterhead: Capel House]
27 Febry 1917

My dear Colvin.

We were much concerned to hear of your nasty fall on the stone steps outside your house. I hope You have got over the after effects completely by now.

---

[1] As for the 'Saturday' letter to Pinker.
[2] This would be the first of six Conrad pamphlets printed by Shorter in limited editions, nominally of 25 copies each; T. J. Wise produced a further 20 titles in a similar manner. J. H. Stape discusses the whole phenomenon in 'Conrad "Privately Printed": The Shorter and Wise Limited Edition Pamphlets', *Papers of the Bibliographical Society of America*, 77 (1983), 317–32.
[3] 'Some Reflexions Seamanlike and Otherwise' in May 1912, 'Certain Aspects of the Admirable Inquiry' in July; they appear in *Notes on Life and Letters*.

Very dear of you to write so appreciatively about the little book. But I don't agree that a local-knowledge man would be the right reviewer for it. The locality doesn't matter; and if it is the Gulf of Siam it's simply because the whole thing is exact autobiography. I always meant to do it, and on our return from Austria, when I had to write something, I discovered that this was what I could write in my then moral and intellectual condition; tho' even *that* cost me an effort which I remember with a shudder. To sit down and invent fairy tales was impossible then. It isn't very possible even now. I was writing that thing in Dec 1914 and Jan to March 1915.[1] The very speeches are (I won't say authentic – they are that absolutely) I believe verbally accurate. And all this happened in Mch-April 1887.[2] Giles is a Capt Patterson, a very well known person there. It's the only name I changed. Mr Burns' craziness being the pivot is perhaps a little accentuated. My last scene with Ransome is only indicated. There are things, moments, that are not to be tossed to the public's incomprehension, for journalists to gloat over. No. It was not an experience to be exhibited "in the street". — I am sorry you have received an impression of horror. I tried to keep the mere horror out. It would have been easy to pile it on. You may believe me. J'ai vécu tout cela.[3] However I will tell you a little more about all that when we meet. Here I'll only say that experience is transposed into spiritual terms – in art a perfectly legitimate thing to do, as long as one preserves the exact truth enshrined therein. That's why I consented to this piece being pub^d by itself. I did not like the idea of it being associated with fiction in a vol of stories. And this is also the reason I've inscribed it to Borys – and the others.

   Our love to your house.

Yours ever

J Conrad.

[1] The family returned from Austrian Poland in November 1914; Conrad finished his draft of *The Shadow-Line* in December 1915.

[2] 1888. In his 'little book', Conrad drew on his first voyage as Master of the *Otago*; he took command on 24 January, left Bangkok 9 February, and docked in Singapore for medical advice on the evening of 1 March, several of the crew being afflicted with malaria. Subsequently, Conrad sailed the *Otago* to New South Wales, Victoria, Mauritius, and South Australia, relinquishing command at the very end of March 1889. For a description of Captain Patterson, see the letter to W. G. St Clair of 31 March 1917; the mate of the *Otago* was Charles Born, rather than Burns (the name also used in 'Falk' and 'A Smile of Fortune'); the model for the tenacious figure of Ransome may have been Pat Conroy, an able seaman rather than the cook, but Najder's comments are apposite: 'Ransome strikes me not as a character based on recollections but as a fictional partner of the protagonist, whom he complements' (*Chronicle*, p. 521, n. 68). Sherry's is the most comprehensive treatment of the whole episode: *CEW*, pp. 211–49.

[3] 'I have lived through all that.'

PS Re-reading your letter and going over the story I see that the places Bankok and Singapore are distinctly named – but obviously they are not named in the right way or in proper context since the mind of an "experienced reader" like yourself is left in doubt. And I must confess that the matter seemed to me of such slight importance in comparison with the subject treated that I really did not consider it at all while writing. *Don't* refuse Garvin's request[1] if your heart is at all that way inclined.

To B. Macdonald Hastings
Text MS Colgate; Unpublished

[Capel House]
Tuesday evening [27 February 1917][2]

My dear Hastings
    My sincere congratulations.
    No doubt my dear fellow it can be looked upon as done for the sake of pelf (and let him who's without sin throw stones at us[3]) but in truth I am positively touched by all the *devotion* you have put into the task.
    The Epilogue leaves my withers (whatever they are) unwrung.[4] As a matter of fact I think it's a great notion. You see it is as it were outside the drama – just as the Davidson-Excellency interview is outside the story. My wife is perfectly delighted with the new version – if you care to know.
    How you had the pluck to tackle the thing again is a marvel to me. I would have seen the whole Strand-full of Actor Managers damned first.[5]
    I hope that materially your expectation will be realised. Ours. I don't pretend to indifference. My dear H, I have been for 20 years performing on a tight rope (without net) and I am still at it, and I am 59 last birthday.[6] One would like to see some prospect of getting down at last – if only on the brink of the grave, just for a moment.

Yours

J. C.

---

[1] J. L. Garvin (1868–1947) edited the *Observer*, where Colvin's review of *The Shadow-Line* would appear.
[2] The day before the letter to Pinker announcing arrival of the revised script.
[3] From St John's Gospel (7.8): 'He that is without sin among you, let him first cast a stone at her.'
[4] 'We that have free souls, it touches us not: let the galled jade wince, our withers are unwrung': *Hamlet* 3.1.255. The withers can be found between a horse's shoulder-blades.
[5] The Strand being the location of the Savoy Theatre, Irving's domain.
[6] Corrected in MS from '58'.

To J. B. Pinker

Text MS Berg; Unpublished

[Capel House]
Wednesday. [28 February 1917][1]

My dear Pinker.

Hastings has sent me his altered version of Victory. I've returned it to him at once. It is really an improvement from the scenic point of view, and generally a stronger play – apart from embodying Irving's wishes. I don't think that he can raise further trouble. Heyst is to the front all the time, which is what he wanted done. H is a worker. It must have been an awful grind.

Did you make any inquiry (at the xixth Century) as to the alleged Conrad Ode?

I am better. Hope you are well.

Ever Yours

J. C.

To Sir Sidney Colvin

Text MS Yale; J-A, 2, 184

[letterhead Capel House]
1st Mch 17.[2]

My dear Colvin.

I answer your card at once – first to tell you how glad I am to hear you have consented to Garvin's request, next to say that there can be no possible objection to your recognising the autobiographical character of that – piece of writing, let us call it. It is so much so that I shrink from calling it a Tale. If you will notice I call it A Confession on the title page. For, from a certain point of view, it is that – and essentially as sincere as any confession can be. The more perfectly so, perhaps, because its object is not the usual one of self-revelation. My object was to show all the others and the situation through the medium of my own emotions. The most heavily tried (because the most selfconscious) the least "worthy" perhaps, there was no other way in which I could render justice to all these souls "worthy of my undying regard".[3]

---

[1] Here Conrad returns to the mystery of the ode, first mentioned on the 24th.
[2] Mistakenly dated by Jean-Aubry, who read '1st' as '18'.
[3] A quotation from the story itself which Conrad also had placed on the title-page. In the Author's Note (1920) he celebrates 'the men of that ship's company: complete strangers to their new captain and who yet stood by him so well during those twenty days that seemed to have been passed on the brink of a slow and agonizing destruction'.

Perhaps you won't find it presumptuous if after 22 years of work I may say that I have not been very well understood. I have been called a writer of the sea, of the tropics, a descriptive writer, a romantic writer – and also a realist. But as a matter of fact all my concern has been with the "ideal" values of things, events and people. That and nothing else. The humourous*, the pathetic, the passionate, the sentimental *aspects* came in of themselves – mais en vérité c'est les valeurs idéales des faits et gestes humains qui se sont *imposé[e]s* a mon activité artistique.[1]

Whatever dramatic and narrative gifts I may have are always, instinctively, used with that object – to get at, to bring forth les valeurs idéales.

Of course this is a very general statement – but roughly I believe it is true.

Dent proposes to publish in the last week of March; but I shouldn't be surprised if there was some delay. Our most affectionate regards.

Yours ever

J. Conrad.

To B. Macdonald Hastings
Text MS Colgate; Unpublished

[Capel House]

[early March? 1917][2]

My dear Hastings,

I felt all the time that H. B. [Irving] ought to tackle Heyst. That he has seen it himself is a tribute to your dramatisation. Sorry for the grind you have to undergo in consequence.

Pink[er] sent me the American terms. They seem all right.

I hope my dear fellow your plucky labours won't be wasted.

If the ultimate result is at all encouraging I will have a proposal to lay before you for real collaboration.[3] That is if you feel eventually that you can stand me in that relation. For it beats even the married state for delicacy and complexity. For both the only safe basis is the existence of some deepseated

---

[1] 'But the truth is that the ideal values of things and human events have imposed themselves on my artistic activities'. Yves Hervouet traces the contrast made here to Flaubert's distinction between 'la vérité *réelle*' and 'la vérité artistique, idéale': 'real' truth lacks form and purpose; 'ideal' truth shapes and generalises (*French Face*, pp. 178–9).

[2] Despite the implication of future toil in 'the grind you have to undergo', this letter apparently concerns 'plucky labours' already undertaken: the revision of *Victory* in order to make the part of Heyst fit for H. B. Irving. Hastings sent off the revised version in late February and saw Irving for his formal blessing on the 17th. The letter to Pinker of the 19th takes up the possibility of a run in the USA.

[3] Letters to Pinker of [c.12] and [14 February] discuss a possible dramatisation of *Under Western Eyes*; on [15 February] Conrad mooted a 'single-handed' stage version of what became *The Arrow of Gold*.

temperamental accord. I think that in our case it exists and I draw the inference from the fact that my books appeal to you and your plays to me – though indeed we are different enough outwardly.

I think you may trust Pinker's prudence in negotiation. For me his loyalty and skill have been tested through 14 years of successful work.[1] I give him a free hand so that in your conversations with him You may take it for certain that whatever engagements he enters into I'll carry them through in letter and spirit.

> Yours,
>
> J. Conrad

To Sir Sidney Colvin
Text MS Yale; *Listy* 365; Original unpublished

[letterhead: Capel House]
Wednesday. [7 or 14 March 1917][2]

My dear Colvin.

Thanks for your good letter. I feel absolutely safe in your hands and I never meant to say that *You* didn't understand. C'est toūt le contraire. You do.

The Indo-China sheet in any usual Atlas will satisfy your Geographical longings. You will find there Bankok, Cape Liant, and most likely Koh-ring.[3] From the latter the general direction of the ship was towards the tip of the Malay Peninsula where Singapore is.

No. I don't really want that little piece to be recognised *formally* as autobiographical. It's* *tone* is not. But as to the underlying *feeling* I think there can be no mistake. Some reviewers are sure to note that. Others perhaps won't.

I shall try to find the doctor's letter, the agreement, and the Admiralty sheet on which I navigate[d] the ship during those days.[4] I haven't seen these

---

[1] By then more than 16 years.

[2] A Wednesday between 1 March, when Conrad hailed Colvin's readiness to write a review, and the 25th, when it appeared; since Colvin, a punctual man, would have finished writing by then, the 21st seems less likely than the earlier dates.

[3] In *The Shadow-Line*, this mountainous island off the Cambodian coast, 'a great, black, upheaved ridge . . . lying upon the glassy water like a triton amongst minnows . . . seemed impossible to get away from' (p. 84); it also looms over the final pages of 'The Secret Sharer'. In 'Topography in "The Secret Sharer"', *The Conradian*, 26 (2001), 1–16, J. H. Stape cites references to the island as Koh Ryn in Lucien Fournerau, *Bangkok in 1892* (Bangkok: White Lotus Press, 1998), p. 5, a translation by Walter E. J. Tips of an article in *Le Tour du Monde*, 68 (July 1894), 1–64. Cape Liant lies south-south-east of Bangkok.

[4] Some of the charts Conrad used in the *Otago*, including those covering the Gulf of Siam, are preserved at Yale. For the letter from Dr William Willis attesting to the crew's miserable state of health, see J-A, 1, p. 109.

things for years but they must be somewhere in the house. You shall see them, these pièces de conviction,[1] when you come down.

Yours always

J. C.

To J. B. Pinker
Text MS Berg; Unpublished

[Capel House]
Friday [9? March 1917][2]

My dear Pinker

C Graham is in Sth America but his London address is 39 Chester Sq. His Mother would forward your letter.[3]

I had a fairly cheerful letter from Reg. We've heard that Maisie intended to return to Switzerland at once. Is that so? And would that mean a final crisis in their relations?[4]

Yours ever

J. C.

To J. B. Pinker
Text MS Berg; J-A, 2, 185

[Capel House]
Thursday. [March? 1917][5]

My Dear Pinker.

Many thanks for the book where indeed the article on J. C. is wonderful in sympathy and insight. I know you have no time for correspondence or I

---

[1] 'Exhibits'.

[2] Soon after Gibbon's letter to Conrad of 27 February – this letter, first published by Borys Conrad in 1974, appears also in *Portrait*, pp. 119–21.

[3] Graham's long-widowed mother was the Hon. Mrs A[nne] E[lizabeth] Bontine (née Elphinstone Fleeming, 1828–1925). A descendant of Andalusians and Scottish Whigs, she still took a vigorous interest in politics and the arts. On behalf of the War Office, her son had gone to South America, searching for new supplies of beef.

[4] Gibbon's humorous and affectionate letter tells of his fortunes as a correspondent for the *Daily Chronicle* on the Italian Front, including a narrow escape from wounds at the Battle of Gorizia, an abundance of wine, and a dearth of butter. Showing that he thinks a lot of Jessie as well as Joseph, Gibbon asks 'When in God's name shall we all three be together again?' His relations with Maisie, his wife, were troubled: see *Letters*, 5, pp. 688–9.

[5] Dating this letter [1917], Jean-Aubry places it among those written in March. One good reason for concurring is that during February and March, Neville Chamberlain (1869–1940) made a series of announcements about inclusion of older civilians in the National Service scheme, announcements that provoked energetic debate. In March, moreover, Conrad was frail but no longer bedridden.

would ask you to tell me who John Freeman is.[1] I know he wrote two vols of verse and I judge he must belong to Mrs Meynell's circle.[2] Anyway I am grateful to him for what he found to say about my work. I would like to see him and perhaps to know him – but just now one has no heart much for anything.

Pray send me a ch. made out to M[r] C. Lonkhurst[3] for 8. 2. 6. There's no end to accts coming in.

I don't know what to do as to Nat. Service.[4] It was no good to send my name while I was in bed. Now I am out of it but can hardly move for lumbago. And what could I do? I could perhaps be employed about the docks or something of the sort; but men between 50 & 60 are doing it now, no doubt. With my uncertain health I feel that it's hardly worth while, for the infinitesimal use I may be, to throw away the chance of doing my own work – such as it is. And I also feel very wretched about it.

Yours ever

J Conrad.

To J. M. Dent
Text MS Berg; Unpublished

[letterhead: Capel House]
13 Mch 17

Dear Mr Dent.

I shall of course sign photographs and books for you with the greatest pleasure and I own I am flattered by your request.

Thanks for the advance copy. The get up pleases me very much. I don't like to distribute my books very much but I am afraid in this case I shall want six extra copies, which pray send me with the stipulated six which will only do for wife and a few intimate friends. France – A. Gide and a couple of friends of the N. R. Française[5] – will claim 3. Here I must send a copy

---

[1] A poet and critic, John Freeman (1880–1929) published *The Moderns* in 1916; it contains chapters on Shaw, Wells, Hardy, Maeterlinck, James, Patmore, Francis Thompson, Bridges, and Conrad (pp. 243–64).

[2] The circle of Roman Catholic poets gathered around Alice Meynell (1847–1922), among them Conrad's acquaintance Agnes Tobin (1864–1939).

[3] Charles B. Lonkhurst, a Ham Street farmer.

[4] Apart from those in reserved occupations, healthy civilians under 60 (the age Conrad would reach in December) were required to sign up for work of national importance.

[5] Besides Gide, friends and acquaintances associated with the *Nouvelle Revue Française* included Jacques Copeau, Jean Schlumberger, and Henri Ghéon.

to Northcliffe (a return-civility)[1] and to some seamen friends I made during my visit to the coast last year. But if I want any more I shall buy them in the open market. The copy you have been good enough to send me in advance is going to the Front by to-nights post.

Sidney Colvin will review for the *Observer*. I've sent him the revise sheets yesterday.[2] Are the other books on sale yet? I should like to see them. Believe me

Yours faithfully

Joseph Conrad

To B. Macdonald Hastings

Text MS Colgate; Unpublished

[letterhead: Capel House]
Wednesday. [14 March 1917][3]

My dear Hastings.

I would take it as a great kindness on your part if you would (if at all possible) come down here on Saturday after your interview with Irving.

We would have the talk I have wished for, this many a day. And if you must be back to duty on Monday early there is a good train from here about 3 o'clock on Sunday. Otherwise I hope you will stay another night.

It isn't prudent for me (they say) to take a run up. I don't look very bad but the gouty bronchitis hangs about me still.

Trains at 4.30 and 7.15 from Char + go to Hamstreet (change in Ashford). The train at 5.25 from Char + only to Ashford. If you wire in good time (say about 2 o'clock) we will meet you at either station.

Yours

J Conrad.

P. S. A good train from Ash to Lond 5.38 Arr. Lond 6.58 on Sunday if necessary

---

[1] Perhaps Lord Northcliffe had sent Conrad a copy of his *At the War*, published by the British Red Cross in 1916.

[2] A second or third set of proofs? The letter to Colvin of 21 February apparently refers to an earlier set.

[3] The letter to Sandeman of this date mentions the upcoming 'interview with Irving'.

To Christopher Sandeman
Text J-A, 2, 183[1]

Capel House.

14 Mch., '17.

My dear Sandeman,[2]

I am scandalized by your unpatriotic choice of disease,[3] but I hope you have repented and got rid of it by this time. You should model yourself on me and (if you must have something) employ the best brand of gout, as patronized from time immemorial by the Nobility and Gentry of this country and its most distinguished statesmen, beginning with the two Pitts, Palmerston, J. Chamberlain[4] and many others in between.

Of course you will say that it is my snobbishness. Anyway I have been indulging in gout for the last six weeks and am ready to pass it on (cheap) to anyone who wants something really distinguished. For I am weary of that luxury – oh! how weary! . . .

Your suggestion is most welcome and the object of it seems most interesting from your description.[5] A dash of Orientalism on white is very fascinating, at least for me; though I must say that the genuine Eastern had never the power to lead me away from the path of rectitude; to any serious extent – that is. I am afraid you will be shocked by the frivolity of these remarks.

I hope my adaptor (M. Hastings) will be able to come down this Saturday after the final interview with Irving, and I shall then put forward the name and back it up in the terms of your letter. I agree totally with your opinion of Irving. At first, you know, he had Jones in his eye. Then he veered around to Heyst (a mistake, I believe). The consequence was that poor H. had to alter the 1st and 2nd and rewrite completely the 3rd act. A horrid grind, but it improved the play beyond question. Of course it isn't the play as I would have tried to write it, but it's first rate stage-work – or I am much mistaken.

---

[1] As always in J-A, without the farewell and signature.

[2] Rather than follow the family tradition of making port and sherry, Christopher or 'Kit' Sandeman (1882–1951) became a journalist, lecturer, and author. Opera, politics, poetry, history, and botany all fascinated him. Between the wars he led several expeditions to Peru and Brazil, rafting on the headwaters of the Amazon and the Huallaga, and collecting orchids for British herbaria. From 1914 to 1918, he served in the Intelligence Corps.

[3] According to Jean-Aubry, German measles.

[4] William Pitt, Earl of Chatham (1708–78), William Pitt, his second son (1759–1806), Henry John Temple, Viscount Palmerston (1784–1865), Joseph Chamberlain (1836–1914), two Tories, a Whig, and a Liberal Unionist.

[5] A suggestion to cast Mona Limerick as Lena. In the letter to Hastings of the 19th, Conrad writes that her personality is 'Irish with something oriental added'.

The point of criticism you raise in *Victory* (the novel) is not so apparent in the play. Perhaps you are right. But I still think the psychology quite possible. My fault is that I haven't made Lena's reticence *credible* enough – since a mind like yours (after reflexion) remains unconvinced. I need not tell you that while I wrote, her silence seemed to me truth itself, a rigorous consequence of the character and the situation. It was not invented for the sake of "the story." *Enfin!* What's done is done. And I am unfeignedly glad that you like the book as a whole.

Did I tell you we had our boy here on leave after a year in France? He celebrated his 19th birthday here. He is the M[echanical] T[ransport] officer of a battery of 6-in. howitzers and from his last letter (received yesterday) I see between the lines that our heavy guns are being trundled forward after Fritz pretty steadily. I was very pleased with him and with what he had to tell me. My poor wife snatched 10 days of fearful joy and paid for them afterwards, but she is her own calm self again now. A great relief to me.

To Hugh R. Dent
Text MS Berg; J-A, 2, 186

[letterhead: Capel House]

19. 3. 17

Dear Mr Dent[1]

Thanks very much for your letter and the copies of the book. I have now eighteen of them of which two will go to the US to two Collectors – friends of mine who always get *All* the English editions – but to whom I always send the first signed by myself.

Can't say I am delighted at the Russian revolution. The fate of Russia is of no interest whatever to me; but from the only point of view I am concerned about – the efficiency of the Alliance – I don't think it will be of any advantage to us. Political trustworthiness is not born and matured in three days.[2] And

---

[1] Hugh Railton Dent (1874–1938) joined his father's firm in 1888 and became an editor of the Everyman's Library series in 1909; when J. M. Dent died in 1926, Hugh succeeded him as chairman of the board, a position he held until his own death.

[2] Conrad refers to the initial events of the March Revolution: the street protests in St Petersburg and the Duma's call for the Tsar to abdicate in favour of a parliamentary government. These events would of course have drastic military and political consequences for Britain, France, and other Russian allies in the war against the Central Powers.

as to striking power an upheaval of that sort is bound to affect it adversely for a time at least. However we shall see.

Yours

J. C.

To B. Macdonald Hastings
Text MS Colgate; Unpublished

[letterhead: Capel House]
19 Mch 17.

My dear Hastings.

Sorry you couldn't come here. Better luck next time. I have Your note of the 18th and am glad to hear of the satisfactory interview with H. B. I[rving] and H. Clark.[1]

The only thing "on my chest" now is the question of the actress. What would you think of Mona Limerick.[2] She has a strange uncommon personality (Irish with something oriental added) but the main point is that she "gets across the footlights". She is not good-looking, she has some mannerisms. I am told she rehearses rather badly – but she has a quality which gets home every time and if she may exasperate her audience I am certain she will never bore it or leave it indifferent.

She had excellent notices in J Echegarray's play (Cleansing Stain. – Pioneer Players).[3] There's a suggestion of trouble and sorrow about her which would just do for Lena – and I think she has force. At any rate she has Art.

Do you know her? Or could you manage to get to know her? Just to see. I think it would be worth the trouble.

Yours

J. Conrad

---

[1] The actor E. Holman Clark (1868–1925), famous for his Christmas-time performances as Captain Hook in J. M. Barrie's *Peter Pan*. Clark had a financial interest in the Savoy Theatre, where he was currently rehearsing the role of Polonius.

[2] Mona Limerick was born in South America; for almost a decade she acted with the first and most significant of provincial repertory companies, Miss Horniman's at the Midland Theatre and the Gaiety, Manchester. She appeared there in plays by Ibsen, Synge, and Shaw. Subsequently, she spent the winter of 1913–14 at the Fine Arts Theatre, Chicago. Her last London appearance was in 1929.

[3] Although in his native Spain José Echegaray (1832–1916) was considered a tedious reactionary, *The Cleansing Stain* was not cleansed enough for the theatrical censorship in Britain; hence the production was an unlicensed one, limited to a single performance at the Queen's Theatre on the afternoon of Sunday, 4 February. The *Observer* (11 February, p. 5) praised the 'intelligence and finish' Mona Limerick brought to the part of Enriqueta.

To J. B. Pinker
Text MS Berg; Unpublished

[Capel House]

19. 3. 17.

Dear Pinker

This is the birthday of the book you have commanded to *be*. And here it is, heralded by a trumpet-blast from W. L. Courtney – perhaps you have heard it? (in last Thursday's D[aily] T[elegraph]).¹

It's a great stroke of business; but apart from that I think that I am glad now you had that inspiration.

This morning too I've had a note from M. Hastings from which I see that the formal agreement with H. B. I[rving] will be the next *act*. I imagine that the great American scene will follow as prepared by you. Another of your "strokes". Of course its material size no man can foresee; but whatever it may be my dear Pinker I want you to participate in the theatrical gamble(?) to the extent of 20% (as for the high priced stories) for indeed all those possibilities came out of your hand every bit as much as out of mine – and even in a sense more from yours ——

Please send me a cheque to *Lewis & Hyland*² for £40 and will you pay as much to the L[ondon] & West[minst]ᵉʳ bank into my acc*ᵗ*?

Yours ever

J. C.

PS. Do you know anything about an actress called Mona Limerick? Christopher Sandeman wrote to me the other day suggesting her for the part of Lena, as the very thing required. I am awfully afraid of H. B. I. sticking that pretty creature Jessie Winter[s]³ into the play – which would be awful. If you have any influence with M[acdonald] H[astings] turn his mind towards Mona. She had magnificent notice[s] for her acting in J. Echegarray's play *Cleansing Stain* quite lately.

PPS I conclude You had good news from Eric. We had a short letter from B[orys] on Sat: extremely elated tho' of course telling us nothing.⁴

---

¹ Having given it an advance notice, W. L. Courtney (1850–1928) reviewed *The Shadow-Line* on the 21st ('The Cult of the Uncanny', p. 3), linking it to other recent books with a supernatural atmosphere. Courtney had been reviewing Conrad's work since 1897, when he wrote on *The Nigger* for the *Daily Telegraph*.
² A firm of drapers in Hythe.
³ Born in London, Jessie Winters made her début there in 1904 and had since been in many West End productions; her current role was in *Under Cover* at the Strand.
⁴ The Germans were dropping back under the threat of a renewed Allied offensive.

To John Quinn
Text MS NYPL; Unpublished

[Capel House]
19. 3. '17

My dear Quinn
This is the day of pub^{on} of the Shadow-Line my new (small vol) book.

I keep your own inscribed copy here till the submarine hurrah[1] subsides a little, or till happier days altogether: unless you wish me to send it along at once.

We are fairly well (I've got over my Febr^{y} gout) here. No use writing a lot since one doesn't know if this will reach you at all.

My wife joins me in the feelings of the greatest regard. I am my dear Quinn
Always yours faithfully
J Conrad.

To Christopher Sandeman
Text J-A, 2, 190[2]

Capel House.
[c. 19 March? 1917][3]

My dear Sandeman,
Merci mille fois. I have started a strong agitation for X.[4] My *adaptateur* did not come down but I have dispatched one letter to him and another to my agent. I am very much indebted to you also for the warning against the other woman.[5] I have a secret terror of all actors and (not so much) of actresses since they murdered for me a one-act play I wrote once (off my own bat) and had some illusions about.[6]

I am sending you a short piece of writing of mine – of no particular importance – but Dent insisted on publishing it now; and I had to let him for the sake of peace and quietness. Don't trouble to write, pray, on *that* account.

---

[1] The U-boat attacks on North Atlantic shipping.

[2] Only Jean-Aubry's text has survived: the ellipses and the suppression of names are his.

[3] Jean-Aubry dates this '[End of April]' but references to the appearance of *The Shadow-Line* and to recent correspondence about casting Mona Limerick as Lena suggest a date closer to 19 March, and in any case prior to 3 April, date of further comments about the other 'X' – the diplomat.

[4] Mona Limerick, Sandeman's suggestion.

[5] Jessie Winters? She is mentioned unfavourably in the letter to Pinker of the 19th. The letter to Pinker of the [29th], however, cites Sandeman as a witness against Lily Elsie.

[6] *One Day More* had a three-day London run in June 1905: Conrad's reactions at the time varied from 'My play is not a success tho' [a] good many kind things have been said' to 'Complete failure I would call it': *Letters*, 3, p. 275 (to Norman Douglas), p. 288 (to H. G. Wells).

We are getting good news in so far at least that it breaks up the subtle, deadening effect of stagnation. And I think it is good in itself too.

X . . . , I understand, is a *diplomate de carrière* – which is a great advantage.[1] Perhaps he will be the first *Ministre Polonais à la Cour de St. James.* What you say of the Poles is true enough. But you must remember that in great affairs they have had no experience for generations. In such circumstances natural aptitude will run into *un peu trop de finesse.* We can't expect certain virtues from people conscious of having been regarded for ages as a political nuisance – an insoluble and embarrassing problem.

Absolute sincerity, I begin to think, is not natural to man; it's acquired by a long training in self-confidence. And poor X . . . was not even certain of his backing while he had to speak out. *Enfin!* I hope you are quite well now.

To J. B. Pinker
Text MS Berg; Unpublished

[Capel House]
Wednesday [21 March 1917][2]

My dear Pinker.

Thanks for your good letter with enclosure. I was glad to hear you had heard from Eric. I had an idea he would be very busy just now.

The Irving news is satisfactory certainly. I had no hope that he would be so prompt. I thought of Doris too – but she is very busy still with her Romance.[3] Anyway I am pleased there is no question of J. Winter[s] for the part.

---

[1] A strong candidate for the identity of 'X' here and in the letter of 3 April is August Zaleski (1883–1972). From 1906 to 1911, Zaleski lived in London, where he took a degree at the London School of Economics. He returned in 1915 to work with the Polish Information Committee (PIC), whose elected President he became; he also taught Polish at King's College, London University, and advised the Foreign Office on Polish affairs. The PIC's pamphlets appeared in collected form as *Poland's Case for Independence* (1916) with contributions from both Poles and Britons. In November 1916, the PIC announced its intention of working for the creation of an independent Polish republic, a prospect that alarmed its more cautious supporters. For instance, the influential Slavicist R. W. Seton-Watson wrote: 'I regard it as a theoretical ideal, but quite unrealisable; the international situation and our relations with Russia make it impossible for any serious person in this country to give it their support' (quoted by Norman Davies, 'The Poles in Great Britain 1914–19', *Slavonic and East-European Review*, 50 (1972), p. 73). After the war, Zaleski represented Poland in Switzerland, Greece, and Italy; from 1926 to 1932, he was Polish Foreign Minister. In 1939, he returned to London, serving as Foreign Minister and later President of the Polish Government in Exile at 43 Eaton Place. In August 1915, Conrad wrote a guarded introduction on Zaleski's behalf to the *English Review* (*Letters*, 5, p. 502).
[2] Following up on the topics of the 19 March letter: Irving's response to the revisions, Pinker's share of US royalties on the play, and Eric's well-being.
[3] Doris Keane (1881–1945) had the lead in Edward Sheldon's *Romance*, which had been running since October 1915, first at the Duke of York's, then at the Lyric, and showed no sign of closing.

Indeed My dear Pinker this is the least I could do. It isn't even bare justice. I am very proud of your belief and of your interest in me.

Ever yours

J. Conrad

PS That donkey Lynd begins his review with the words Mr *Conrad will be sixty this year.*[1] It gave me quite a shock to see it in print. Having had gout for more than 24 years I never look on it as an *age-disablement* and I am not conscious of any other, because no doubt the gout covers them all up to my consciousness. But I am not calling him a donkey on that account. Imagine he reviews to* Shadow-Line from a <u>Ghost-Story</u> point of view!! Would you believe it? Is it stupidity or perversity, or what?

To Iris Wedgwood

Text MS Private collection; Unpublished

[letterhead: Capel House]
22^d Mch 17.

Dear Mrs Wedgwood.

Pray believe in our heartfelt sympathy with You and the General in this visitation bringing so cruelly home to you both the never-ending sorrow of this war.[2] How kind and dear of you to write me such a letter at such a moment. It shall be preserved with especial care and pride as proof of the friendship I have been fortunate to find under Your roof.[3]

Indeed dear Mrs Wedgwood my application to you meant nothing more than a natural anxiety to find out whether there was anything against the boy. His last letter consists of a very few lines of execrable handwriting in a tone of elation, whence I conclude that his battery is moving forward. I am certain he's too busy and generally delighted to think of the second pip just now.[4]

---

[1] This was not the first time a review by Robert Lynd (1879–1949) had offended: his piece on *A Set of Six* presented Conrad as a linguistically challenged cosmopolitan whose only home was the sea: see *Letters*, 4, p. 107, n. 6. In the present review, *Daily News*, 19 March, p. 2, Lynd again restricts Conrad to the status of a maritime novelist – this time a maritime novelist whose venture into the uncanny fails to offer enough 'grue'.

[2] Ralph Wedgwood's younger brother, Arthur Felix Wedgwood, a captain in the North Staffordshire Regiment, had been killed in action on the 17th.

[3] Conrad visited the Wedgwoods in July 1914, while they were living in Harrogate, Yorkshire. He thanked them for their 'charming hospitality' in the dedication to *Within the Tides* (1915).

[4] To think of promotion to lieutenant.

My wife who sends her dear love is touched by the interest You have been good enough to take in the matter. As to me I feel quite compunctious at having trespassed so much on your thought and your time.

Believe me dear Mrs Wedgwood with our love to the children and warm regards to the General

Always your faithful friend and servant

Joseph Conrad.

To Sir Sidney Colvin
Text MS Yale; Unpublished

[letterhead: Capel House]

23 Mch '17.

My dear Colvin.

I see the Obs^(er.) every Sunday and I am awaiting the next N° with great impatience.

I am aware that the D[aily] T[elegraph] and the T[imes] have had their notices out. But I haven't seen them. I don't think I will. The newspaper notice is so generally uninteresting that I imagine I won't miss much by my abstention.

My mistrust of the weather prevented us from pressing you for the visit now very much overdue. But the first shift of wind you must come.

B[orys]'s last letter consists of a very few lines (of most execrable handwriting) in an elated tone, from which I conclude that he's very busy trundling his "lovely" guns forward. As to this retreat[1] c'est une phase comme une autre, from which it is impossible to conclude anything. The Russian affair, from the only point of view which interests me (that is: the Alliance), can hardly be expected to increase the *driving* power. On the other hand I don't think it will diminish the *resisting* power of Russia to any great extent. For the rest political trustworthiness is not born and matured in 3 days. If the peasantry rises there will be an immense bloodletting. But it may not happen till after the peace.

Our love. In haste to catch post.

Yours

J. Conrad

[1] The German retreat from the Oise to the heavily fortified Hindenburg Line, completed by 5 April.

To Sir Sidney Colvin
Text MS Rosenbach; Unpublished

[Capel House]
25. 3. '17.

My dear Colvin

I am *delighted* with your article in the Obs^{er}.[1]

Thanks for your letter rec^d to-day. I shall certainly see the article in the Nation as I expect the cutting will be sent to me in the usual course.

At this moment wet snow is falling heavily – quite like a blizzard, but melting on the ground instantly. Very curious effect.

Our love

Yours

J. C.

To J. B. Pinker
Text MS Berg; Unpublished

[Capel House]
26. 3. '17

My dear Pinker.

The pub^{on} of Western Eyes at 1/- now or at some future time is a matter for you to decide.

If they were to re-issue the 2/- edition (or bring it to public notice) now it might perhaps sell on account of the subject.[2]

The notices of the S Line I have seen are in the main very respectful. Land & Water is very good. Colvin in the Obs^{er} is really better than I expected. The Scotsman's $^1/_2$ col: very satisfactory. I have heard that the Nation's review is worth reading being "real criticism".[3] I haven't had that cutting yet.

---

[1] 25 March, p. 4. Colvin praises Conrad for offering the pleasures of popular as well as literary fiction; as ever, the new book embodies 'the double, the two-handed power of thrilling narrative and penetrating, unflagging human interpretation'. Better still, 'Mr Conrad's English is nowhere more of a model by its rhythm, its flexibility, its economy, its faultless fitting of words to things'. Colvin adds, however, that the autobiographical element in *The Shadow-Line* leaves it 'somewhat lacking in organic structure'.

[2] Revolutionary tumult. The first edition sold for 6 shillings, and the 'third and cheaper' edition of August 1915 for 2; in November 1917, Methuen brought out an edition crammed into 320 pages which sold for one and three, i.e. threepence more than the customary shilling.

[3] *Land and Water* (where 'The Warrior's Soul' would shortly appear) gave *The Shadow-Line* only one paragraph, but in that space Lucian Oldershaw describes it as 'a wonderful little story, as intense as *Lord Jim*, as eerie as *Falk*' (22 March, p. 16). The unnamed reviewer for the *Scotsman* notes an affinity with Coleridge's 'Rime of the Ancient Mariner', admires Conrad's

Heard from M. Hastings who seems pleased generally. I guess from the tone that you must have established excellent relations with that man who has the name of being difficult to deal with.

Yours ever

J. Conrad.

PS. The Times' reviewer is out of his depth a little.[1] *Pray* 'phone Dent to send me six more copies and ask him to send *you* the acc[t] for the *whole lot*.

To E. L. Sanderson
Text MS Yale; Unpublished

[letterhead: Capel House]

26. 3. '17

Dearest Ted[2]

Thanks for your good letter – all friendship and charity. I have been seedy for weeks and weeks. Mind as sick as the body. Trials find one out.

It was the greatest comfort to read your good news. Your success in Elstree is a great achievement a wonderful assertion of a handicapped personality which makes me very proud of the friendship "Torrente inchoata".[3] I suppose I am not such a miserable rag as I feel if You still will touch me – without tongs.

Upon the whole I am glad the dear boy is appointed to *the* flagship.[4] I suppose he is too. As he grows older in the service he will no doubt (like others) grow shy of flagships. But for his début it is excellent. Give him my love and my warmest wishes for this the first real step on the road of his choice.

pictorial quality, but has reservations about 'the sentimentalising tendency that occasionally mars his work' and is 'prominent in his idealisation of the crew' (22 March, p. 2). The rich and substantial unsigned review in the *Nation* (24 March) may be found in *CH*, pp. 304–8.

[1] Both style and judgment might reasonably suggest incompetence: 'So Mr Conrad's wise men, his salted old sea captains of cogent hints and intimations, preach, by a livelong aggregation of example to the least possible dilution of precept, the way to salvation.' 'The serene assurance of the imagination which is the outcome of all the finest work of Mr Conrad's genius is here broken and uncertain. The moral overbalances the story' (*TLS*, 22 March, p. 138).

[2] Edward Lancelot ('Ted') Sanderson (1867–1939) took passage in the *Torrens* in 1893. On that voyage, Conrad read him a draft of *Almayer's Folly*. Sanderson taught at Elstree, his family's preparatory school in Hertfordshire. After service in the Boer War he and his wife, Helen, remained in Africa, first in Johannesburg then in Nairobi, where he served as Town Clerk; he returned in 1910 to be Headmaster of Elstree.

[3] The Latin play on words allows for several meanings, but the basic one is 'begun in the *Torrens*'. 'Handicapped personality' may be a reference to Sanderson's ill-health, which had occasioned the original voyage. Like Ransome in *The Shadow-Line*, he had a weak heart.

[4] Ted and Helen Sandersons' son Ian Campbell MacDougall Sanderson (1900–79) had been appointed to HMS *Malaya*.

We had a few lines (of execrable handwriting) from B[orys] last Friday. Nothing in them but a tone of elation, whence I conclude he has been trundling his "lovely" howitzers after Fritz.

Jessie's health gives me some anxiety tho she does not complain. But I see. Our dear love to You both and your daughters.

Yours ever

J Conrad.

To Richard Curle
Text MS Indiana; Curle 38

[letterhead: Capel House]

27. 3. '15 [1917][1]

Dear Richard[2]

This is only to tell you that your copy of The Shadow Line has been put aside here – till better days.

For the rest I am still like a man in a nightmare. And who can be articulate in a nightmare? Borys had a 10 days' leave from the front. He was impatient to get back to his guns. Enfin!

I simply *can't* write.

Yours toujours

J. Conrad.

Jessie had a note from Cordelia[3] the other day. Apparently all well. We are very lonely here. No one down for months and months.

To J. M. Dent
Text MS Berg; J-A, 2, 186

[letterhead: Capel House]

27. 3. '17.

Dear M[r] Dent:

It's very pleasant to hear that the first ed: of 5000 has been sold. The war-shortage of paper is of course regrettable. But one must put up with these

---

[1] In his edition, Curle corrected Conrad's slip; all the references point to 1917.

[2] Richard Henry Parnell Curle (1883–1968) was Scots by birth but English by residence and education. His passion for travel appears in such books as *Into the East: Notes on Burma and Malaya* (1923) and *Caravansary and Conversation* (1937), and his psychological curiosity in *Women: An Analytical Study* (1947). His first book, *Aspects of George Meredith* (1908), was followed by many other studies of writers, including Browning, Hudson, Hardy, and Dostoevsky. In his relations with Conrad, about whom he wrote three books and many articles and pamphlets, Curle became both protégé and protector – a combination of sympathetic critic, bibliographer, collector, acolyte, entrepreneur, and friend.

[3] His wife, née Fisher: they married in 1912. Curle omits this and the following sentence.

things without repining. We will do better with the next book. My writing days are not over. I am not an "old" author. I was 38 when my first book was published – and that was in the year in which I finished writing it.[1]

I return here M[r] St Clair's letter as requested.[2] Of course, like everybody else, I was a reader of the Singapore Free Press which was *the* paper of the East as between Rangoon and Shanghai.[3] But I didn't know the Editor's name, and indeed I knew very little of and about shore people. I was chief mate of the S. S. *Vidar* and very busy whenever in harbour. And anyway I would not have cared to form social connections even if I had had time and opportunity. Naturally I knew something of most of the people he mentions. I also knew some whom he was not likely to meet at the Club and of whom he could not have had other than merely journalistic knowledge – the most inexact thing in the world. I will drop him a line in a day or two – for the sake of old times. His recollection of Capt Ellis does not seem very exact. (He's a journalist – see?) Capt E was certainly big but not "a raw-boned Irishman".[4] It was a fine, dignified personality, an ex-Naval officer. But journalists can't speak the truth – nor even *see* it as other men do. It's a *professional* inability – and that's why I hold journalism for the most demoralising form of human activity, made up of catch phrases of mere daily opportunities, of shifting feelings.

I shall certainly call on you the very first time I come to town. But I am still very lame. Believe me

Yours faithfully

J. Conrad.

PS Yes Colvin was good. I don't think I'll see the other notices. I never look at them (unless by somebody I know) though my wife makes a collection I believe. I've heard that the *Nation*'s review was "real criticism". I'll look at it.

---

[1] Conrad finished revising *Almayer's Folly* in May 1894; Unwin published it in April 1895, when Conrad was 37.

[2] See Conrad's reply, 31 March.

[3] The *Singapore Free Press* was founded in 1835. St Clair became editor in March 1887.

[4] The Master-Attendant of Singapore Harbour, Captain Henry Ellis (1835–1908), was Irish, kindly, large, and famously irascible; in 1924, St Clair described him as a 'bigboned Ulsterman', but his large frame seems to have been well-padded rather than 'raw-boned': see *CEW*, pp. 195–205, 315; see also pp. 212–17. In January 1888, a month before he retired, Ellis appointed Conrad Master of the *Otago*. Their only meeting figures in *The Shadow-Line*, where Captain Ellis is the 'deputy-Neptune'. In 'The End of the Tether' and *Lord Jim*, he is scantily disguised as Captain Elliot.

To C. K. Shorter

Text MS BL Ashley 2923; Unpublished

[letterhead: Capel House]

27. 3. 17

Dear Mr Shorter.

Many thanks for the most noble-looking copies.[1] I am truly delighted with the appearance you have given to that trifle which now looks quite imposing.

Pinker is a severe watch-dog but I am sure he doesn't even think of growling in this connection. He identifies himself with my feelings and he knows how pleased I am.

Thanks once more for your friendliness and your generosity in allocating five copies to me.

Always yours cordially

Joseph Conrad

To J. B. Pinker

Text MS Berg; Unpublished

[Capel House]

Wednesday [28 March 1917][2]

My dear Pinker.

I had a letter from Dent telling me that upwards of 5,000 copies of the S-L have been sold (all the 1st Ed:) and that there is no paper to print more.

Would you ask *L & W* if they mean to send me proof of my story which they intend to publish shortly in a special number?[3] I should like to see it.

Jessie was immensely tickled by the portrait business. I suppose that when a paper publishes the photo of One's wife it is Real Fame.[4]

Effect of S-L – which you didn't foresee, I suppose. I've had yesterday a batch of long reviews sent me which I —— but that's not the point. Are *you* pleased?

My part in this business consisted mostly of funking it. All these cuttings should be wreathed round your head – not mine – in the manner of laurel-leaves.

---

[1] Of *One Day More* in an edition of 25.

[2] Dent announced the sales figures on the 26th (TS carbon Berg). The letter to Pinker of 31 March continues the discussion of Irving's *Hamlet*.

[3] 'The Warrior's Soul' appeared in the 29 March number of *Land and Water* with illustrations by Dudley Hardy.

[4] This portrait remains untraced.

We had the most ridiculous rumours flying about here last Sunday.[1] Thereupon John got very flighty indeed and neglected his Monday's lessons utterly.

Ever yours

J. Conrad.

PS I hear indirectly that H. B. I[rving] (so they say in town) intends to produce Hamlet after the *Professor*. Please tell me what you know of it.[2]

To Elizabeth Dummett

Text J-A, 2, 187

Capel House.

29. 3. '17.

Dear Mrs. Dummett,[3]

Thanks ever so much for your kind and delightful letter. The first time I come to town I shall repeat my thanks in person.

This morning we had the great and unexpected pleasure of receiving a letter from dear don Roberto dated 21st Feby. from Cartagena, and written obviously in good health and spirits. It fairly glows (like all he writes) with his inextinguishable youth and his love for the visible world, which he has enriched by his understanding and his creations with the art of a compassionate magician.

The few lines he gives to Cartagena brought to me for a moment the feeling of my vanished youth. I saw the place for the first and last time in 1875.[4] It seems not to have changed a bit.

Jessie sends her dear love.

I am, dear Mrs. Dummett,

always your most faithful friend and

servant.

---

[1] Unfounded rumours that the German retreat had become a rout?

[2] A revival of J. M. Barrie's *The Professor's Love Story* was playing at the Savoy; *Hamlet* opened there on 26 April.

[3] Elizabeth 'Toppie' Dummett (née Miéville, 1868–1940) was widowed in 1891. A fine horsewoman and a lively talker, she held court for gatherings of writers, painters, and musicians at her home in Brompton, West London. Her close friendship with Cunninghame Graham lasted until his death.

[4] Conrad made two voyages to Martinique in 1875 and one in 1876; precisely what he did while the *Mont Blanc* and the *Saint-Antoine* were in the roads off Saint-Pierre remains a mystery, but on the third voyage at least he may have been running guns to the Catholic and conservative faction in the Colombian civil war of 1876. Cartagena, at the mouth of the Sinú river, is a possible model for Sulaco in *Nostromo*.

To Gladys Langham [?]
Text MS Private collection; Unpublished

[Capel House]
29. 3. '17

Dear Miss Gladys¹
    I blushed immensely (with pleasure) on reading your letter. This is praise indeed; and the more pleasant because, I'll confess to you, I like the *Nigger* very much myself.
    Believe me

yours faithfully

Joseph Conrad.

To J. B. Pinker
Text MS Berg; Unpublished

[Capel House]
Thursday [29 March 1917]²

Dear Pinker
    Perhaps you will be interested in the enclosed disquisition on actresses by Christopher Sandeman – the only *really* rich man I know. But he is quite a good fellow and fairly intelligent. If you can put spokes into the Lily Elsie's wheel pray do so.³
    The D. Mail notice (quite sympathetic)⁴ is another leaf in your laurel wreath.
    The Copy of the play is for the Yanks when you are ready to give it to them.⁵

Yours ever

JC.

---

¹ Tentatively identified as Gladys Langham, one of Jessie Conrad's friends. The letter is dropped into a copy of *The Nigger*.
² Although letters to Sandeman of 14 and [19] March indicate that he had already expressed his opinion of various actresses, there are two reasons for placing this text at the end of the month: the review in the *Daily Mail* came out on the 27th, and this review added another leaf to the crown offered to Pinker on the [28th].
³ Lily Elsie (1886–1962), a Yorkshirewoman, had had a great success in *The Merry Widow* (1907). When she married, she quit the stage, but returned three years later, in 1915, to star in charity performances. On 5 May, Hastings told Conrad that he could 'appreciate your concern about the threatened engagement of Lily Elsie for Lena' (*Portrait*, p. 122).
⁴ Like several other reviewers, 'C. W.' of the *Daily Mail* sees a resemblance to the 'Rime of the Ancient Mariner'; this review notes, however, that the scenes of macabre lassitude are offset by the young skipper's exuberance. It is 'a book which all those should read who believe that the art of fiction is not a mere anodyne' (27 March, p. 4).
⁵ The script of *Victory*? Negotiations over a US production were under way.

To J. B. Pinker

Text MS Berg; Unpublished

[letterhead: Capel House]

31. 3. '17

My dear Pinker

Thanks for your letter.

In reference to the Irving agreement "perf^{ce} before October" means really that *Victory* would be put on in the autumn. Is that so?

Have *you* heard anything of Irving thinking of Hamlet? (suppose for May-June). I should like to know whether there is any talk of it, for a special reason – connected with a girl. This in your character of the General Manager of my existence will give you something to think about.

And in this connection: has there arrived a letter or parcel for me c/o of You "till called for". I don't suppose so but pray just drop a *yes* or *no* into Your next letter.

After this I hope you will feel as if you were driving a skittish horse.

Remember me to E[ric] when you write. B[orys] has been silent. I reckon these young men will have a little breathing-time if rains set in.

The "Russian Scene" is interesting to watch tho' the Liberal enthusiasms leave me cold.[1]

From the alliance point of view I doubt if there will be any advantage. But perhaps it wont be worse. This is the very beginning tho'. One feels anxious.

Yours ever

J Conrad.

To Catherine Willard

Text MS Berg; Unpublished

[letterhead: Capel House]

Saturday [31 March 1917][2]

Dear Cathleen*.[3]

I have had a letter from Pinker which is not definite, in so far that, as he writes me, he has just sent the agreement to H. B. I[rving] for signature. It has not been returned yet, and as it stipulates performance *before* Sept^{er} 1917,

---

[1] At first, Lloyd George, the Liberal Prime Minister, welcomed the March Revolution and agreed to introduce a parliamentary motion expressing solidarity. When the Russian war effort began to flag, his enthusiasm waned: see Trevor Wilson, ed., *The Political Diaries of C. P. Scott, 1911–28* (Collins, 1970), pp. 270–1, 294–302.

[2] The contents mesh with those of the letter to Pinker of this date.

[3] Catherine (or Catharine, but not Cathleen) Livingstone Willard (1895?–1954), an actress, was born in Dayton, Ohio; her mother was Grace Robinson Willard, an interior designer, journalist, and friend of the Conrads. Catherine Willard trained in Paris and in 1915 made her British début in *The Taming of the Shrew* with F. R. Benson's Company. From 1918 to 1920, she was a leading player at the Old Vic, where her parts included Olivia, Hermione, Lady

I don't like to write anything that would give H. B. I. the idea that I don't know what is being done in my name. It wouldn't be fair to Pinker who is a very able and devoted agent.

If H. B. I. accepts the condition then I imagine the Hamlet prod^{on} is not likely to take place – unless for a very short run. But in a day or two we shall know what he says; and if there's the slightest chance to forward your wishes you may be certain I'll write to him as warmly as is possible under the circumstances.[1]

What do you think – you who are du théâtre? Is it *likely* H. B. I. would put Hamlet on for, say, May-June, in any case? Have you heard anything more of this? For if you can tell me anything *positive* I'll write at once. It seems to me now that Victory can't very well come on before the Autumn. Yet – I don't know. I am utterly ignorant of affaires du théâtre. Only don't imagine Chère Enfant that I am hanging back. If you can tell me: – "oui, marchez" – je marche. Our love to you and Mama Grace.[2] Tell her that I am much concerned at the news. We do hope to see you both here before long.

Your[s] affectionately
Joseph Conrad.

To W. G. St Clair
Text Malay Mail; CEW 316 (in part)

Capel House,
Orlestone,
nr. Ashford.
March 31, 1917.

Dear Mr St Clair,[3]

Dent communicated to me your letter and enclosed your card, for which much thanks.[4]

Macbeth, and Beatrice – her favourite. In 1921 she returned to the US, where she took many roles in Boston and New York. She was married from 1925 to 1931 to William E. Barry and from 1931 to 1945 to Ralph Bellamy; both marriages ended in divorce. Her obituary in the *New York Times* gives 1900 as her date of birth; theatrical reference books give 1895. In November 1919, Conrad told Frank Vernon she was twenty.

[1] Clearly she was hoping for a part. A long run for *Hamlet* at the Savoy would of course delay the production of *Victory*.

[2] Grace Robinson Willard (née Cameron, 1877–1933), Catherine's mother, was for a time the London correspondent of *Vanity Fair*. During a long residence in England, she also applied her talents to interior design. The Conrads, who met her through Jo Davidson, the sculptor, took her advice on furnishing Oswalds.

[3] William Graeme St Clair (1849–1930), born and educated in Scotland, taught in Burma and then moved to Malaya in March 1887 to edit the *Singapore Free Press*. He was also conductor of the Singapore Philharmonic Society and a major in the Singapore Voluntary Artillery. When he retired in 1916, he moved to Colombo, but was visiting Britain in 1917.

[4] St Clair had come across the serial version of *The Shadow Line* at the Sports Club in Saint

Yes, I remember Bradbury. It was he who let me off port-dues when I put into Singapore in distress with *all* my crew unfit for duty (1888). It is a very difficult thing to shove everybody into a tale even as autobiographical as *The Shadow-Line* is. My Capt. Giles was a man called Patterson, a dear, thick, dreary creature with an enormous reputation for knowledge of the Sulu Sea. The "Home" Steward's name (in my time) I don't remember. He was a meagre wizened creature, always bemoaning his fate, and did try to do me an unfriendly turn for some reason or other.[1]

I "belonged" to Singapore for about a year, being chief mate of a steamer owned by Syed Mohsin bin Ali (Craig, master) and trading mostly to Borneo and Celebes somewhat out of the usual beats of local steamers owned by Chinamen.[2]

As you may guess we had no social shore connections. You know it isn't very practicable for a seaman. The only man I chummed with was Brooksbanks,* then chief officer of the s. s. *Celestial* and later, as I've heard, Manager of the Dock at Tan-Jong Pagar. I've heard of course a lot about the men you mention. Old Lingard was before my time but I knew slightly both his nephews, Jim and Jos, of whom the latter was then officer on board the King of Siam's yacht.[3]

In Bangkok when I took command, I hardly ever left the ship except to go to my charterers (Messrs Jucker, Sigg and Co.) and with the chief mate sick I was really too busy ever to *hear* much about shore people. Mr Gould, Consul-General and then Chargé d'Affaires in the absence of Sir E. S[w]atow, was very kind to me during the troubled times I had in port.[4]

James's Square and made inquiries first of the *English Review*, then of Dent, emphasising his former position with the *Singapore Free Press*.

[1] The port dues incident appears in *The Shadow-Line*, but without mentioning Bradbury, Captain Ellis's assistant. For Captain Patterson, see also the letter to Colvin of 27 February; the Sulu Sea separates Borneo from the Philippines. The inhospitable Superintendent of the Sailors' Home for Officers was C. Phillips, an ex-soldier, temperance proselytiser, and Inspector of Singapore brothels (*CEW*, p. 183).

[2] Over a period of four and a half months (August 1887–January 1888), Conrad made four voyages to Borneo and the Celebes in the *Vidar*, James Craig, Master, sailing under the Dutch flag. The Arab trader Syed Mohsin bin Salleh al Jooffree had his head office in Singapore and branches in Berau and Bulungan; he owned several steamers (*CEW*, pp. 29–31, 107–8). Syed Abdulla, the character in *Almayer's Folly*, was his eldest son (Captain Craig's written response to questions by Jean-Aubry, MS Yale).

[3] For Frederick Havelock Brooksbank and the *Celestial*, see *CEW*, pp. 27–9; he was the son-in-law of Captain William Lingard ('Old Lingard', 1829–88), a model for Tom Lingard in *Almayer's Folly*, *An Outcast*, and *The Rescue*. Sherry (*CEW*, pp. 135–8) notes the resemblances between Lord Jim's life in Patusan and the actual experiences of 'Tuan Jim' Lingard. When Conrad first came to Singapore, in 1883, Joshua Lingard was commanding the SS *Paknam* (*CEW*, pp. 116–17); according to St Clair, *Maha Chakkri*, the royal yacht, doubled as flagship of the Siamese navy.

[4] Jucker, Sigg were general merchants and teak exporters. Conrad spent about a fortnight in

Naturally, like everybody else, I was a diligent reader of the excellent and always interesting *Singapore Free Press* then under your direction. I keep my regard for that paper to this day. It was certainly the newspaper of the East between Rangoon and Hong-Kong. Last time Sir Hugh Clifford (a friend of many years)[1] was here we talked appreciatively of the *S. F. P.* I imagine you must have been generally friendly to him on public matters. I wonder what the attitude of the paper was at the time of the B[ritish] F[ederated] Borneo Governorship and resignation.[2] He did not mention it and I did not ask him. We passed on to other memories, for he will never cease to regard his Malayan days.

All my literary life (since 1893) I've been living in the country, coming to town but seldom – and now less than ever. I hope you are recovered by now; and perhaps later, if your health will permit, you will come down here for a day. And then indeed I may hear something really worth knowing about Singapore and the straits of which truly I know very little.

Believe me,

Yours Faithfully,

Joseph Conrad.

To Helen Sanderson

Text MS Yale; J-A, 2, 195

[letterhead: Capel House]
[late March–early April 1917][3]

My dear Helen.[4]

Jessie will be writing to you in a day or two, but meantime I want to tell you how much I appreciate the kind things you say about the S-Line. Strangely

---

Bangkok. E. M. Gould, the British Consul there, had initiated the search for a new master of the *Otago* by wiring Captain Ellis in Singapore. Sir Ernest Mason Swatow (1843–1929), famous for his pioneering consular work in Meiji period Japan, was the British Minister Resident in Bangkok from 1884 to 1887.

[1] Perhaps Conrad had forgotten that Hugh Clifford published the first general appreciation of his writing in the *Singapore Free Press* ('Mr Conrad at Home and Abroad', 1 September 1898, under the pseudonym 'The Book-Worm'). Their correspondence began in 1899 and continued until Conrad's death. Both had known Singapore in the late 1880s, Clifford as a member of the Governor's staff.

[2] In 1899, Clifford was appointed Governor of Labuan and North Borneo. As the nominee of the Colonial Office (which had plans for a federation of British territories in Borneo), Clifford was caught in a power struggle with the chartered British North Borneo Company, and resigned in 1901.

[3] Jean-Aubry dates this letter [1917], placing it between letters from May and September. The references to *The Shadow-Line* and to Ian's joining his ship suggest an earlier date.

[4] Helen Mary Sanderson (née Watson, 1875–1967) married Ted in 1898. She was a Scotswoman from Galloway, full of moral and intellectual vigour. As 'Janet Allardyce', she contributed sketches of East African life to *Scribner's Magazine*.

enough, you know, I never either meant or "felt" the supernatural aspect of the story while writing it.[1] It came out somehow and my readers pointed it out to me. I must tell you that it is a piece of as strict autobiography as the form allowed – I mean the need of slight dramatisation to make the thing actual. Very slight. For the rest not a fact or sensation is "invented". What did worry me in reality was not the "supernatural" character but the *fact* of Mr Burns' craziness. For only think: my first command, a sinister, slowly developing situation from which one couldn't see any issue that one could *try for*; and the only man on board (second in command) to whom I could open my mind, not quite sane – not to be depended on for any sort of moral support. It was very trying. I'll never forget those days.

I hope that dear Ian will be comfortable in his first ship. You are right. The Naval training has a peculiar quality, and forms a very fine type. For one thing it is strictly methodised to a very definite end which is noble in itself and of a very high idealistic nature, while on its technical side it deals with a body of systematised facts which can not be questioned as to their value, which can not be discussed apart from their reality – say on the ground of personal taste, for instance. That steadies the young intelligence and faces it with life not as it is written about but as it actually is. Last year I saw many Naval Officers from Admirals to Sub-lieutenants and I have noticed that the Navy thinks rightly on all questions. I don't say this in the sense of the Navy thinking as I do. But whatever conclusion a naval officer arrives at, even if distasteful to me, I can't help recognising that he arrives at it on sound grounds, making use of his intelligence and not by way of petty prejudices or ignorant assumptions. I was at sea for 10 days and coming on shore I went into a couple of drawing-rooms and one or two newspaper offices; and what I heard there made a painful contrast.[2] Borys is well and absolutely serene. Please tell dear Ted that he is very much what he was when Ted saw him [in] Rye[3] and approved of him. One of the greatest pleasures I had in my life.

Our dear love to you all.

Your affc^te friend and servant

Joseph Conrad.

[1] Conrad returned to this issue in his 1920 'Author's Note': 'I believe that if I attempted to put the strain of the Supernatural on it it would fail deplorably and exhibit an unlovely gap.'

[2] Soon after his perilous voyage in the *Ready*, Conrad failed to persuade Lord Northcliffe, the most powerful and most opinionated newspaper magnate in the country, that submarines could not attack each other: see *Letters*, 5, p. 679.

[3] The ancient former sea-port in East Sussex, about ten miles by train from Capel House.

To Sir Sidney Colvin
Text MS Yale; Unpublished

[Capel House]
2. 4. '17

My dear Colvin

Let it be then next Sat: week (the 14th) as Jessie will be away all day on Thursday.

Could you – would you – take the 11 AM from Ch^g + and (change in Ashford) come right down to Hamstreet? It will be easier to arrange for transport from that station. If more convenient to you there is a train something after 4 which does get connection in Ash^d and will bring you to H'street about 6. 30.

I am so glad you like my L & W story. It belongs to 1916[1] and was out 12 months ago in The Metropolitan Mag U. S. A.

I really think myself that for a pot-boiler c'est assez bien. But it isn't really *done*. I can *do* nothing now. I'll show you where I got the hint for it in Phillippe* de Ségur.[2] There's a hint for another in him but I fancy too macabre (and improper) for use. Our love to dear Lady Colvin and yourself.

Yours

J. C.

To B. Macdonald Hastings
Text MS Colgate; Unpublished

Capel House
2. 4. 17.

My dear Hastings.

I have just posted you a pamphlet and a letter. As to this here[?] – if it weren't for you being so worried I would simply think it comic. A good subject. *The Play. A comedy in 16 acts.* I absolutely don't understand what the man means. I simply wonder what will come next – and then next – and then at every second rehearsal . . .[3]

---

[1] Conrad finished revising 'The Warrior's Soul' (previously 'The Humane Tomassov') in May 1916: see *Letters*, 5, p. 584.

[2] Philippe-Paule, comte de Ségur (1780–1873), a veteran of the Grande Armée, wrote a memoir recalling his service with Napoleon: *Un aide de camp de Napoléon (de 1800 à 1812)*. Yves Hervouet points to the passage where Ségur rescues a Cossack from drowning in an icy Moravian lake; a year later, the Cossack returns the kindness by coming to Ségur's aid when he is taken captive in Poland: *French Face*, p. 315, n. 115.

[3] Perhaps a first response to E. Holman Clark's request for further rewriting. If so, the interminable comedy would have starred Clark as a champion fusspot. By the 4th, Conrad felt calmer about the situation.

This a matter for your competent decision. I can only re-affirm my confidence in you whatever You do.

Yours cordially

J Conrad

To J. B. Pinker

Text MS Berg; Unpublished

[Capel House]

Monday. [2 April? 1917][1]

My dear Pinker.

Would you order for me (you can do it by 'phone) the book mentioned in the enclosed cutting.

I am at work again. Slow. Dam' slow, for I am still gouty and – most abominably depressed.

We had a long letter from B[orys]. Very busy and somewhat worried because his recommendation for promotion sent up last Sept[er] has produced no effect yet. But obviously he hasn't much time to think of such personal matters. He says: "things are very interesting here".

Yours ever

J Conrad.

To Hugh R. Dent

Text J-A, 2, 187

[Capel House]

3. 4. '17.

Dear Mr. Dent,

I return Twentyman's letters. He was one of the score or so of boys that passed through my hands when I was chief officer of various ships.[2] It's pleasant to see that the pains I took to make good seamen of them are not forgotten by those grizzled men. When I last saw him he was 17 and I 27 in Samarang.[3]

---

[1] Borys did not get his promotion until late in the year: see the letter of [10 October]. The state of Conrad's health suggests March or April. The letter of [11? April] tells Pinker that he expects to finish an article within the week; although that was not the case, these are the first signs that Conrad had started writing again.

[2] Ernest William Gain Twentyman (1868–1946) served as an apprentice in the *Highland Forest* when Conrad was mate; he recalls the apprentices' high spirits in Section IX of *The Mirror of the Sea*, mentioning Twentyman by name. The latter was now in London, having resigned his position as Harbour Master of Suva, Fiji Islands, to volunteer for the Royal Naval Reserve. A surviving letter to Conrad of 26 October 1916 appears in *Portrait*, p. 116; for a quotation from Twentyman's initial approach to Dent, see J-A, 2, p. 187, n. 4.

[3] Conrad left the *Highland Forest* in Semarang, Java, in July 1887, when he was 29.

Christopher Sandeman
Text J-A, 2, 188

Capel House,
3. 4. '17.

My dear Sandeman,

I am grieved to hear of the neuritis. What a beastly thing to happen to one. I am much disturbed to think that you have inflicted on yourself the pain of writing your most welcome letter.

It's the sort of thing that'll make me shy of writing to you, to my great loss, because (you may have noticed it) I do turn to you to ease my mind on various matters in which I feel I'll be understood by you better than by anyone. *Vous êtes mon correspondant très spécial.*

I wonder what form X's activities will take now. The Russian proclamation is very fine but – ²⁄₃rds of the Polish territory (on the basis of the 1772 frontier) are in German hands.[1] And peace will have to come soon. From our point of view Russia, I am afraid, will be non-existent for some time, and that, of course, makes one think anxiously of the Western front.

Had another elated letter from the boy dated six days ago. I believe the whole army is elated.[2]

Tout à vous

To B. Macdonald Hastings
Text MS Colgate; Unpublished

[Capel House]
Wednesday [4? April 1917][3]

My dear Hastings

From Pinkers letter received today I see that Irving seems inclined to put the play into rehearsal immediately.

That's rather good – if there's no risk to spoil the American side of the business thereby. I suppose you and P know more about these things than I do – who knows nothing.

---

[1] In 1772, by the First Partition, Poland lost territories to Prussia, Austria, and Russia. Had Conrad gone by pre-1772 boundaries, even larger areas could now be said to be under German control. German armies had occupied Warsaw in August 1915 and Vilna (Vilnius) in September 1916; the Front now lay even farther east, in Latvia, Byelorussia (Belarus), and Ukraine. On 30 March 1917, despite the loss of ground and perhaps in the hope of stirring up resistance against the Austrians and Germans, the Provisional Government of Russia decreed Poland's independence, but left specifics to a future Constituent Assembly. For 'X' (August Zaleski?), see the letter of [c. 19 March?].

[2] Conrad's misgivings were justified: within two weeks elation was replaced by alarm, as it became clear that the Germans had retreated to strongly fortified positions. Germany, moreover, could now afford to concentrate on the Western Front.

[3] As the following letter to Catherine Willard shows, Conrad did not think he needed to participate in the latest round of revisions. He returns to the subject, however, in the

I want only to say here that if time is to be saved I am quite content to trust you entirely with the alterations (as suggested by H. Clark) and that you needn't send the copy down here – from that point of view. I had just as soon see the thing take life and shape on the boards since you have said that you are willing I should attend some of the rehearsals.

Yours

J. C.

To Catherine Willard

Text MS Berg; Unpublished

[Capel House]
Wednesday. [4 April 1917][1]

Dear Catherine.

I have written to the Great Man (I am still all of a shake) giving your name and address and asking for an interview for you —— daughter of a valued friend; two years with the Benson Co.[2] etc etc. And if there is a suggestion of "personal interest" well, chère enfant, it can not compromise you – whatever HBI[rving] may think of *me*. Seriously – I hope we won't be treated badly by the G. M. and that he will say something satisfactory.

He and Holman Clark want Victory revised slightly (for the third time) after which they prophesy success.

I don't believe it. But this strictly *entre-nous.*

Let me know if you hear from him and I shall do the same by you should he write to me. For I don't suppose he will drop the letter into the waste-paper basket? Croyez-vous?

Our dear love to Mama Grace and yourself.

Votre ami

J. Conrad

To Catherine Willard

Text J-A, 2, 188

Capel House.
Easter Monday [9 April], 1917.

Dear Catherine,

I only wish I could be an useful friend to you. H. B. Irving has dropped me a note, and I daresay you've heard from him already. I am afraid nothing can come of it now, but perhaps in the future – ?

---

letter of [11? April]. By the end of the month, the production date had been pushed back again.

[1] On [31 March] Conrad had not yet written to Irving; by [9 April] he had had a reply.

[2] F. R. Benson's was the resident company at the Stratford-upon-Avon Shakespeare Festival from 1886 to 1919; between seasons, the company toured Britain and Ireland.

I see from a paragraph in the *Observer* that you have a part in "Love for Love".[1] That Congreve is amazing and "L. for L." is certainly the best stage play, though I think that "The Way of the World" is a greater work. "Angelica" does not come up to "Mrs. Millemant*."[2] I am afraid Mama Grace will think it scarcely proper for me to talk to you about Congreve's plays. But you needn't read them yet. The rest is silence.

Our love to you (each in her own way) charming women.

Bien à vous

To J. B. Pinker
Text MS Berg; Unpublished

[Capel House]
Wednesday. [11? April 1917][3]

My dear Pinker

Please send to Jessie's credit at Lloyds Bank £20 besides her usual cheque.

Irving was most amiable about the girl – who is simply poor Catherine Willard. I am afraid there are some hard times ahead of her, as Mrs W (for some reason or other) lost her job with the American papers.

H. Clark's letter to Hast[gs] about the play was very appreciative and the final alterations he suggested very sound and simple to carry out. Mere cutting out of one scene, in effect.

I hope the business will go through notwithstanding the American warlike caper.[4] I don't know whether it was the shock of our great success[5] but I am going to have a gouty knee. I am going to bed presently.

Pray drop me a note about yourself Eric and such affairs as are going on. I shall have an Ad[miral][ty] article this week ready.*[6]

Yours ever

J Conrad

---

[1] At the Aldwych Theatre, 15 April, the Stage Society would give a Sunday matinée performance of the complete text; as a 'private' production it escaped the Lord Chamberlain's censorship, which was not friendly to Restoration drama.

[2] Mrs Millamant, the brilliant and resourceful heroine of *The Way of the World* and the rather less brilliant Angelica of *Love for Love*. Catherine in fact played Jenny.

[3] With news of Irving's amiability as expressed to Conrad in a note received by the 9th or as to Catherine Willard by the 19th? Allusions to current events favour the earlier date.

[4] The US Congress declared war on Germany on 6 April.

[5] The Nivelles Offensive, an Allied attack on the German Sixth Army launched on 9 April? Canadian troops captured Vimy Ridge on the first day.

[6] The one surviving 'Admiralty paper' is 'The Unlighted Coast', finished in January. Since 'Never Any More' describes the work of naval aviators, Conrad may originally have meant it to be one of the series commissioned by Sir Douglas Brownrigg. In any case, Conrad eventually contributed this account of his first and only flight to the June number of Hastings's magazine *The Fledgling*; as 'Flight', it is collected in *Notes on Life and Letters*.

PS. Please ask Halchards*[1] by phone to send me "Behind the Ger^{an} Veil" – J M Beaufort (Hutchinson. 6/-).[2]

To J. B. Pinker

Text MS Berg; Unpublished

[Capel House]

17. 4. 17.

My dear Pinker.

Please put cheque for £8. 2. 6. into the enclosed envelope (to J. Foot & Son Ltd[3]) and have it posted with your own letters in the usual way. I am giving Jessie a self propelling chair – a not very cheerful present for the 21st anniv^{ry} of our marriage,[4] but it's clear that walking is more difficult to her every day, and with the machine she may be able to get around the house at least without effort and pain.

Ever yours

J. C.

To J. B. Pinker

Text MS Berg; Unpublished

[Capel House]

Thursday [19 April 1917][5]

My dear Pinker.

Thanks for your letter and congratulations. I'd much sooner have given Jessie a trinket of some sort – but the chair is something for her to think about and to look forward to. Rather hard luck to be reduced to that at 43. She sends you her love.

Irving has been very nice to Catherine Willard. I am glad to hear you see the road clear ahead. That there would be turns and corners I never doubted, and it was a comfort to know you were holding the ribbons.

---

[1] Hatchards, the Piccadilly booksellers.

[2] Count J. Maurik de Beaufort, *Behind the German Veil: A Record of a Journalistic War Pilgrimage*, then just published. As a citizen of the Netherlands and thus a neutral, Beaufort was able to travel around Germany with credentials as a journalist and family connections to high-ranking soldiers and statesmen. He also spent fourteen days on the Polish Front, where he experienced 'Fascination, horror and cold' (p. 208). The book is strongly anti-German and pro-British.

[3] Invalid chair makers, 171 New Bond Street, London W1.

[4] Celebrated on 24 March.

[5] A sequel to the letter of the 17th about the anniversary present.

B[orys] wrote me to say he was pleased with the dedication. I've seen the 2^{d} Ed advertised last week – in the D[aily] C[hronicle][1] I think.

Yours ever

J Conrad

To Catherine Willard
Text MS Berg; J-A, 2, 189

Capel House

19. 4. '17

Dear Catherine.

Thanks for your note.

I am glad the G[reat] M[an] was gracious. I shall drop him a line so as not to lose touch for the future. I am sorry there is no woman's part beside Lena in *Victory*; I mean something that would be of use for you to attempt. There are two or three Orchestra Girls[2] but those are not "parts" in my sense.

I have taken a most desperate resolve to turn dramatist before long and then perhaps I'll write a part for you. It would have to be something très gentil et très malicieux en même temps. Somehow I fancy you could do that very well – sans avoir l'air d'y toucher,[3] you know.

Our aff^{te} regards to you both

Tout à Vous

J. Conrad

To W. T. H. Howe
Text MS Berg; Unpublished

Capel House

Orlestone. N^{r} Ashford

Kent

20. 4. '17

My dear Sir.

Many thanks for your interesting letter. I am sorry you have suffered persecution at the hands of the (frivolous, benighted and altogether-unworthy-to-live) persons who failed to discern at the first glance the Greatness of Conrad. However, I forgive them, and I hope you too will forgive (and forget) their

---

[1] 13 April, p. 2.   [2] Members of Signor Zangiacomo's Ladies' Orchestra.
[3] 'Without turning a hair'.

(untimely, scandalous and all-but-criminal) jests at the expence* of the True Believer.

We are then now, Allies! The enthusiasm here is not noisy but very deep. The service at St Pauls was very fine. However you would have seen our papers by the time you get this.[1]

Our boy's batt[er]y is now in position close to St Quentin. The army is full of confidence and rather pleased with itself.

If you have any of Conrad's characters to pose pray don't forget Alice Jacobus.[2] Freya (in the same vol) is not so picturesque. But indeed my women (with the exception of Nina and Aïssa) are not very picturesque. Linda Viola with her father (after the old man has fired his shot) would make a group. Also the couple in the Planter of Malata alone against the topmost rocky pinnacle of the island. But for that you'll want a young man with a Minerva profile (white drill suit, Panama hat) and a society belle who would have some character in her face (not all of them have, you know) and a rare lot of Titian-red hair. But all this would hardly repay the trouble (tho' the search for Titian-red hair may be amusing) and the fact must be recognised that neither my people nor the situations in my novels lend themselves to pictorial grouping. I only wish it were otherwise for your idea appeals to me very much. All success to you in your charitable enterprises.

I shall be delighted to have a token of my American friends kind appreciation of my work.

I shall try to get for you a first ed: of Almayer. Now and then one happens on the market. But if I succeed I shall keep it here for you till the submarine hurrah is over.

I close to catch the evening's mail in our village, but when this letter will actually leave our shores is hard to say – and whether it will ever reach your hands no one can be sure. Believe me

yours cordially.

J. Conrad

---

[1] On the morning of the 20th, a congregation of 3,000 filled Saint Paul's Cathedral for a dedicatory service to mark the entry of the United States into what one of the participating clergymen called 'this great war in defence of Liberty, Humanity, and Justice'. Among the congregants were the King and Queen, the US ambassador Walter Hines Page, and a contingent of Civil War veterans. The service included prayers, readings, a sermon by the Bishop of the Philippines, both national anthems, and the Battle Hymn of the Republic. By request of the Lord Mayor, buildings all over the City flew the Stars and Stripes.

[2] Of 'A Smile of Fortune'; the other women are from 'Freya of the Seven Isles', *Almayer's Folly*, *An Outcast*, and *Nostromo* respectively. In order to raise money for war charities, Howe was organising an evening of *tableaux vivants* representing scenes from Conrad's works.

To Sir Sidney Colvin
Text J-A, 2, 189

[Capel House]
Saturday, [21 April 1917][1]

My dear Colvin,

Many thanks for your letter and the cutting from the *Westminster Gazette*.[2] I am immensely pleased with it and very proud of that unreserved recognition – and also of having my name put down at the Athenæum with you as proposer.[3]

The only other member of the Athenæum (barring Hugh C[lifford]) that I know is Graves.[4] He has always been very friendly to my work and I remember him once going out of his way (I mean literally – in the street) to compliment me warmly on the *Secret Agent* when the novel was first published.

No, my dear Colvin, I meant that you should send *me* the revise sheets of the *S. Line* so that I could have them bound in a spare binding I've got by me; and I meant to reproduce the final corrections (as far as possible) before returning them to you. *That* was the understanding. Pray keep to it if it isn't too late.[5]

It's you, *cher ami*, who have been perfectly delightful during your visit here, leaving with us an impression of freshness and vitality, and that fidelity to early enthusiasms which keeps a man from ever becoming "aged" in the common sense of that word.[6] If I shocked you by flying out against Gambetta I am sorry. He *was* a great man, especially in regard of the other makers of the 3rd Republic. Freycinet, Léon Say, Challemel-Lacour were most distinguished personalities – but rather *hommes de cabinet*. Of the others (with perhaps the exception of the golden-tongued Jew, Jules Simon) the best

---

[1] Jean-Aubry's dating makes good sense and is confirmed by the description of lot 117 in the sale of Colvin's letters from Conrad (Anderson Galleries, New York, 7 May 1928). On the 2nd, Conrad invited Colvin for the 14th; this would be a reply to Colvin's thank-you letter after the visit.

[2] If this refers to the review of *The Shadow-Line* (24 March, p. 3), Conrad is being studiously tactful. The anonymous reviewer begins by classifying the work as a memoir – a continuation of *Some Reminiscences* – but goes on to discuss it as fiction, finding it unshaped and only barely credible.

[3] Conrad was elected to this august London club in 1918: see the letter to Colvin of 27 March 1918.

[4] Conrad knew Charles Larcom Graves (1856–1944), assistant editor of the *Spectator*, but mention of an enthusiasm for *The Secret Agent* suggests Alfred Percival Graves (1846–1931), the Irish editor and poet, father of Robert: see *Letters*, 3, p. 480.

[5] This bound set with MS corrections was Lot 42 in the sale of Colvin's library (Sotheby's, 21 November 1927).

[6] Colvin was born in 1845.

that can be said is that they were politicians.[1] They are now decently for-gotten. But the greatest figure of the times through which we have lived was The People itself, *la Nation*. For 150 years the French people has been always greater (and better) than its leaders, masters and teachers. And the same can be said of the English – indeed it's manifest in what we see to-day. The two great figures of the West![2] Only the French, perhaps, were more searchingly tried by the lesser stability of their political life. Yet I don't know. The evils which worked amongst us were more insidious in their methods.

Our heartfelt sympathy with dear Lady Colvin in her grief and anxiety[3] and our best love to you both.

P.S. I am an honest person, so seeing at a glance that the shirt wouldn't fit me, I decided with but little hesitation that it should be sent to the owner. I hope you've got it by now. Jessie thanks you for your inquiries. I saw her just now creep painfully across the room and could have cried.

---

[1] Both friends could claim to be arguing from experience. Conrad had lived in France during the early days of the Third Republic and associated with militants of the Left and Right (*Letters*, 1, p. 241, and *The Arrow of Gold*), while Colvin had met and corresponded with Gambetta (see the letter of 24 September 1919). The '*hommes de cabinet*' ('back-room men') were brilliant adminis-trators rather than great public speakers and all admirers or disciples of Léon-Michel Gambetta (1838–82). Charles-Louis de Saulces de Freycinet (1828–1923), by education a mining engineer, excelled at reorganising the French army and the railway system and was four times Président du Conseil (Prime Minister). As Finance Minister under seven administrations, the economist Léon Say (1826–96) ably faced the challenge of paying off war debts and indemnities. As Deputy (of the far Left) for the *département* of Bouches-du-Rhône, Paul-Armand Challemel-Lacour (1827–96) would have been a familiar name to Conrad during his Marseilles period; in 1876, Challemel-Lacour moved to the Senate, became ambassador to the United Kingdom in 1880 and (very briefly) Foreign Minister in 1883. Jules-François Simon (1814–96) taught at the Sorbonne and wrote *La Politique radicale* (1868), a major influence on the French Left; first elected to the Assemblée Nationale in 1848 (and evicted by Louis-Napoléon three years later), he was a member of the Government of National Defence during the war with Prussia, the Minister of Education under Thiers, and Président du Conseil in 1876–7. Gambetta himself made his name as a court-room advocate in political cases; his periods in office (President of the Cham-ber of Deputies, 1879–81; Président du Conseil, 1881–2) have less significance than his role as shaper and preserver of the Third Republic, not to mention his immense popularity with the public.

[2] An ironic reference to the Prime Ministers of France and the United Kingdom? Conrad certainly had a low opinion of David Lloyd George, whose pre-war politics were too populist and whose war-time politics too opportunist for Conrad's liking. Although the new Président du Conseil, Alexandre Ribot (1842–1923), was taking office for the fifth time, Conrad would have had stronger reason to focus his dislike on the more radical Aristide Briand (1862–1932), whose most recent of many ministries had collapsed in March, largely because of military failures in the Balkans.

[3] Over a relative missing in action?

To Warrington Dawson
Text MS Duke; Randall 191

[Capel House]
Sunday. [22 April 1917][1]
Cher Ami.[2]

"Mortonism" est une belle idée, as you make use of it; but the fact is (I mean a *fact* not a criticism) that your metaphysical connections with the subject-matter of the F[ourth] D[imension] are not graspable to *my* mind. If you remember, some years ago, when I read the work in type-script, I tried to convey this to you.[3] Vous n'êtes pas un homme ordinaire – moi je le suis (with a certain quality of tension, of vision, which make[s] me what I am). Therefore almost at every turn I run up against my limitations. What saves me is that I am aware of them. At the present time more than ever. That is why I have consistently refused for the last 2 years to write anything for the newspapers. In fact I can't do it. Even on matters not literary. Of the three papers I undertook for the Admiralty I wrote one. For the rest I am afraid I'll have to break my word. A l'impossible nul n'est tenu.[4] I can't come to terms with any sort of writing. The short book I've sent you was finished in 1914. I have done nothing since practically. 2 short stories – about 18000 in all in two years.[5] Voilà la verité.

I can assure you that in my shrinking there is no timidity as to saying what I think. And least of all any fear of compromising myself – against which your letter seems to be arguing. I should have thought you knew me well enough not to suspect me of *that* kind of wor[l]dliness.

---

[1] The envelope was postmarked on Monday the 23rd.

[2] Francis Warrington Dawson (1878–1962) came from Charleston, South Carolina. His father was a newspaper publisher, and his mother, who followed her son to Paris when he made it his headquarters, belonged to a family of faded plantation-owners. Throughout his life Dawson wrote prolifically: fiction, essays, newspaper stories. He covered strikes, wars, peace conferences, the French Senate and Chamber of Deputies. 'Furthermore', to quote Randall, 'he had a special taste and talent for conversing with the great and near-great' (p. 4). In 1909, while on safari in East Africa with Theodore Roosevelt, Dawson met Conrad's old friends the Sandersons. When he came to England in May 1910, intending to report the funeral of Edward VII, he carried an introduction to Conrad.

[3] Morton is a character in his novel *The True Dimension* (Secker, 1916), a semi-autobiographical sea-story with a psychic dimension. Conrad seems to have read a draft of an earlier version, 'The Purser's Shilling', in 1911 (*Letters*, 4, p. 504, and Randall, p. 143, n. 1). For Dawson on Conrad's attitude to 'Metaphysics', i.e. communication with spirits, see Randall, p. 100.

[4] 'You can't demand the impossible.'

[5] *Victory* was finished in 1914, but is hardly a 'short book'. The stories are 'The Tale' and 'The Warrior's Soul'. Conrad avoids any mention of *The Shadow-Line*: either he does not want to allude to his own uncanny maritime narrative, or he is fuzzing the date of completion (sixteen months prior to this letter) in order to dramatise his reluctance to write.

I suffer from it so little that if you ever cared to write yourself a critical exposé of your philosophy (as contained in your art) and send it to me I would be stimulated (peut être) to add thereto some par[agraph]s de ma façon and sign it and would see it published in every newspaper in the world not only without tremors but with sincere pleasure.[1] This is not a cynical joke. It would be curious. Years ago I thought I would like to do it for myself if the thing had been practicable. Explain my own work in all its "nuances" which no critic however able and sympathetic could be expected to detect. I mean Explain it – not puff it. But you wouldn't suspect me of that sort of thing.

My dear I never doubted of your recognition. It's coming – if it has not come yet quite. The story you sent me (I am glad to have it) I remembered of course very well. It isn't the sort of thing that is ever forgotten.[2]

Nous voilà donc Alliés! It is a great piece of luck for England and France. That's the sort of feeling one has: a piece of luck. And perhaps it isn't right to feel like that; but the way the thing came about, the contradictions of expressions, the mist of words the years of reserve so impartial (officially) as to be almost dreadful do leave that impression on one's heart if not on one's mind. Enfin! Le sort en est jété[3] – and old Europe will have to reckon with a quickened Americanism; that is if Americanism cares to assert itself continuously in the future. But in any case it is a tremendous event.

Yesterday (Sat) at 12. 15 AM Jessie and I sitting up late listened to the gunfire from Dover – a great burst of it which was over in 20 minutes; but we only heard to-day the news of two German destroyers sunk. Poor Jessie is not very well. The strain is telling on her. Last January she snatched the fearful joy of having the boy here for 8 days. He was impatient to get back to his guns and his men. Ever since he went to France in Jan 1916 he has been in command of the M[echanical] T[ransport] section of a 6 in howitzer battery. He celebrated his 19th birthday here. He said to me "I am a veteran". And it's true in a way. He was in the very first batch of the youngsters appointed

---

[1] In June 1913, Conrad commented critically and at length on Dawson's aesthetics as embodied in the manifesto of the Fresh Air Art Society (*Letters*, 5, pp. 236–9).

[2] According to Dawson, this double-edged compliment also refers to *The True Dimension* (Randall, p. 192, n. 7), but Conrad also read such stories as 'The Grand Elixir' and 'The Novel of George' (*Letters*, 5, pp. 228, 296).

[3] 'The die is cast': an echo of 'iacta alea est', Julius Caesar's words on crossing the Rubicon, thereby initiating the war against Pompey and his allies in the Roman senate. Decoud uses the French version in *Nostromo*, Part II, Chapter 4, p. 166. Initially, President Wilson had pursued a policy of strict neutrality, 'impartial in thought as well as action'; for his re-election campaign in 1916, the Democrats used the slogan 'he kept us out of war'. Continued U-boat attacks on neutral shipping, however, helped sway the President and Congress towards intervention, but another influence was the decoding of the Zimmerman note, in which the German Foreign Minister wrote of plans for an alliance with Mexico (to be rewarded by the re-acquisition of former Mexican territories in the US) if America should enter the conflict.

to be MT officers with heavy guns. It was quite a new thing then – so new that in his own words they: "had to learn their work under fire".

I don't know how you will receive this letter. With anger maybe. But perhaps it will not last and so pray remember that in this house there is warm affection and eager welcome for you, always.

There are periods in one's life – public and private – that don't stand being set down on paper even for a friend. I can't talk to you about myself just now; and when better days come then one will want to talk of other things. Still, some day – peut-être —— Meantime I am

yours as always

Joseph Conrad.

To Edward Garnett

Text MS Yale; J-A, 2, 192; G. 268

[Capel House]

[late April 1917]¹

Dearest Edward²

The trouble is that I too don't know Russian; I don't even know the alphabet. The truth of the matter is that it is *you* who have opened my eyes to the value and the quality of Turgeniev.³ As a boy I remember reading Smoke in a Polish translation (a feuilleton of some newspaper) and the Gentlefolks in French. I liked those things purely by instinct (a very sound ground but no starting point for criticism) with which the consciousness of literary perfection had absolutely nothing to do. You opened my mind first to the appreciation of the art. For the rest Turgeniew* for me is Constance Garnett and Constance

---

¹ Between 21 and 30 April. On [30 April], Conrad told Pinker he had answered Garnett's letter of 'last Sat.' (the 21st or 28th) with an invitation to Capel House. The date [2 May], which appears in the Nonesuch but not in the Bobbs-Merrill edition, should properly go with the subsequent 'Wednesday' letter about Garnett's impending visit. A mismatching of envelopes and texts probably caused the confusion.

² Edward William Garnett (1868–1937), a publisher's reader and critic, was the husband of Constance, the translator. Constance lived at the Cearne, a woodland house near Limpsfield, Surrey, which became a meeting-place for writers, artists, anarchists, socialists, and Russian refugees; Edward divided his time between the Cearne and London, where he presided over regular literary gatherings at the Mont Blanc restaurant. His encouragement of Conrad in the 1890s was typical of his generous and continuing attention to new writers, for example Edward Thomas, Robert Frost, D. H. Lawrence, and Dorothy Richardson. During the First World War, Garnett served in the Friends' Ambulance Unit; although Conrad disapproved of his pacifism and Russophilia, their friendship endured.

³ Garnett was preparing *Turgenev: A Study* (1917), made up in part of his prefaces to his wife's translations. A significant number of Conrad's fellow writers, among them Ford and James, regarded Turgenev as the supreme Russian prose-writer.

Garnett *is* Turgeniew.[1] She has done that marvellous thing of placing the man's work inside English Literature and it is there that I see it – or rather that I *feel* it. Upon the whole I don't see it. If I did see I could talk about it, perhaps to some purpose. As it is my dear I wouldn't know how to begin.

As far as I know You are the only man who had seen T not only in his relation to mankind but in his relation to Russia. And he is great in both. But to be so great and at the same time so fine is fatal to an artist – as to any other man for that matter. It isn't Dostojewski the grimacing terror haunted creature who is under a curse; it is Turgeniew. Every gift has been heaped on his craddle*. Absolute sanity and the deepest sensibility, the clearest vision and the most exquisite responsiveness, penetrating insight and unfailing generosity of judgment, and unerring instinct for the significant, for the essential in human life and in the visible world the clearest mind, the warmest heart, the largest sympathy – and all that in perfect measure! There's enough there to ruin any writer. For you know my dear Edward that if you and I were to catch Antinuous*[2] and exhibit him in a booth of the world's fair, swearing that his life was as perfect as his form, we wouldn't get one per cent of the crowd struggling next door to catch sight of the double-headed Nightingale or of some weak-kneed giant grinning through a horse-collar.

I am like you my dear fellow: broken up – or broken in two – disconnected. Impossible to start myself going impossible to concentrate to any good purpose. It is the war – perhaps? Or the end of Conrad simply? I suppose one must end some day, somehow. Mere decency requires it.

But it is very frightful – or frightening. I think the last, rather.

No my dear fellow. I don't think the short book "unworthy". It's dedicated to the boy. I got the notion into my head you were in Italy.[3] Your copy is here and I am sending it to you now. Of course it's nothing of importance. I wonder what is? I mean of what I have done.

I didn't see the Nation's review. I knew it was not written by you being under the impression that You did cut lo[o]se from literature (for a time) and were not in England.[4]

To be frank I don't want to appear as qualified to speak on things Russian. It wouldn't be true. I admire Turgenew but in truth Russia was for him

---

[1] As she would become for Chekhov and Dostoevsky. During her career, Constance Garnett (née Black, 1861–1946) published seventy volumes of translations from the Russian, seventeen of them works by Turgenev. Conrad spells Turgenev and Dostoevsky in a Polish manner.

[2] Antinoüs was the Emperor Hadrian's lover, accidentally drowned in the Nile and subsequently deified. His beauty and his sudden end made him a favourite subject for sculptors.

[3] He had served as a Red Cross orderly in the Dolomites; his eye-witness report of the Siege of Gorizia appeared in the *Manchester Guardian*, 10 January 1916, p. 6.

[4] In the past, Garnett had contributed regular unsigned reviews for the *Nation*; among the books discussed in this way were *The Secret Agent* and *Under Western Eyes*. At present, Garnett's principal contributions to the press were the satires collected in 1919 as *Papa's War*.

no more than the canvas for the painter. If his people had all lived in the moon he would have been just as great an artist. They are very much like Shakespeare's Italians. One doesn't think of it.

But my dear Edward if you say definitely I've to do it – well I'll try.[1] I don't promise to bring it off tho'! As I've told you I don't seem to be able to get hold of anything. The Shadow Line was finished in Jan. '15. Since then I just wrote two short stories. Say 12000 words.[2] I have destroyed a few pages. Very few.

This is the true state of affairs. And it's getting very serious for me too.

I've been gouty and almost continuously laid up since Febr^y. I've just got up after the last bout.

Perhaps if you would come down and talk a little you could wake me up. Who knows? For indeed my dear to refuse anything of the kind to you seems intolerable.

Give it a trial. Jessie back[s] this suggestion with all the force of her affection for you. I will say nothing of mine. You either believe in it – or You don't. I have sometimes wondered ——

Ever Yours

J. Conrad

To J. B. Pinker
Text MS Berg; Unpublished

[Capel House]
Monday. [30 April 1917][3]

My dear Pinker

I am sorry my note failed to get inside the envelope with the signed agreement (2 copies).[4] I've just discovered it under the blotting paper.

Thank you my dear fellow for all your work and care in the Irving matter. It strikes me as a most satisfactory document. I didn't expect anything like that in the whole of its stipulations and conditions. I hope H[astings] is satisfied too. Do you get on with him?

I am sorry to say I have been again in bed, with a bad hand (left) and some temperature. Of late all my attacks bring on temp^{re} – and that makes one feel so beastly ill and then so weak afterwards. I make desperate efforts to pull myself together but I don't ever seem to get the time for it. A change of abode would be a stimulus (it has often been so in the past) but its not to be thought of during the war.

---

[1] To write a preface to Garnett's *Turgenev*, as he did in short order.

[2] 'The Warrior's Soul' runs to about 7,800 words and 'The Tale' to about 6,700, for a total half way between the one given here and the one just offered to Dawson. Conrad finished the draft of *The Shadow-Line* in December 1915.

[3] Between the letters to Garnett of [late April] and [2 May].

[4] The signed contract for the stage production of *Victory*.

It's pretty bad upon the whole but you know me well my dear Pinker and you can trust to my *tenacity*. (I lay no claim to energy). It has pulled me through worse periods and out of deeper depressions. It isn't as if I had no ideas. I have. Even too many. But my grip fails me too often. Yet not altogether. Perhaps you would like to know that your idea of publishing the S-Line has in effect helped me through a very beastly time.

Another item in the record of your friendship; the sort of item whose value is to be appreciated fully only by myself – and perhaps by poor Marwood if he were alive now.[1]

Edward Garnett wrote to me last Sat. I asked him to come down and talk Turgueniev over, as soon as he likes. Warrington Dawson wrote to me too, a lamentable letter. We all have our troubles – but you seem to be the only man who doesn't talk about his own.

Ever Yours

J. Conrad

PS Would you order for me a book called Psychology of the Unconscious 21/-. It's published by the Broadway House. It's Routledge & Sons I think.[2]

To Catherine Willard

Text MS Berg; J-A, 2, 191

[letterhead: Capel House]

30. 4. '17.

Chère Catherine.

I am truly sorry H B I[rving] did not do anything. If my health permits I'll run up and go to the Savoy at your intention. Perhaps in a talk with HBI I'll be able to slip a word in. I do feel sorry to be so powerless.

The girls in *Victory* do have some lines to speak. One of them more than the others. Y pensez-Vous?[3]

And a propos: I've signed the agreement. It stipulates performance before the end of the year. That means probably October.

B[orys] is an impertinent young cub. But then on the other hand consider that he must have been meditating on the subject in the crashing of shells. That's a sort of compliment. Personally I like your short hair. Always did. But I can't attack him very well; for only think, if it came out that a father

---

[1] Conrad's close friend Arthur Pierson Marwood had died almost exactly a year earlier.

[2] C. G. Jung's *Psychology of the Unconscious*, translated by Beatrice M. Hinkle and published by Routledge-Broadway House in 1916.

[3] 'What do you think about it?'

and son are quarrelling about your hair – quel scandale! So I had better say nothing. You must squash him yourself. Women know how [to] do that thing almost from babyhood. I remember the squashings I got in my young days. But I must ask you not to be too hard on him. After all the graceless wretch *is* my son. Our love to You both.

Votre ami

J. Conrad.

To B. Macdonald Hastings
Text MS Colgate; Unpublished

[letterhead: Capel House]
[April? 1917][1]

My dear Hastings

Flowers would be a difficulty. There are no "ground" flowers in the tropics but I would let the artist invent them.

I would suggest the scene as to back-cloth a few rocks say left and then a very luminous blue sky away to the horizon line and a darker blue sea. And for the wings heavy tree-trunks (on left). No folliage*.

It's a forest without undergrowth. Only trunks with some orchids spikes hanging down and just boughs overhead.

Must try for effect of intense light; and if one could contrive a patch of shade on the stage for Lena to sit in (rock or tree) it may be effective.

Pardon scrawl. Am in bed and in great pain.

Yours

J C.

To J. B. Pinker
Text MS Berg; Unpublished

[letterhead: Capel House]
1 May '17[2]

My dear Pinker

Please pay for me the encl[d] batch of bills none of them for any big amount which I ought to have attended to before.

Yours ever

J. Conrad.

---

[1] The absence of a watermark from the Capel House stationery suggests a date in the first third of 1917. Gout kept Conrad in bed for long spells between February and April; in April, Hastings was working on revisions and thinking about sets.

[2] This is the first dated use of a new batch of Capel House stationery. The letterhead does not change, but the paper now carries a watermark: CRIPPLEGATE with a picture of a fortified gateway.

PS A. A. Farrar's cheque for John's tuition (£5. 5) is also due. Pray send it
to me.

To Edward Garnett
Text G. 271

Capel House
Orlestone
Nr Ashford
Wednesday [2 May 1917][1]

Dearest Edward,
    We are very glad to hear you are coming, to stay with us, on Monday. The
station is Hamstreet and the train arrives about 1. 15. You'll have to change
on* Ashford Junction.
    I expect to have something roughed out for you to see by that time. I think
to write it as if to *you personally* would be the easiest for me[2] – and perhaps
the most effective.
    I am looking up your marvellous prefaces to-day. They are great.
                                                    Yours ever
                                                    J. Conrad

Jessie's love

To J. B. Pinker
Text MS Berg; Unpublished

[letterhead: Capel House]
Wednesday. [2 May 1917][3]

My dear Pinker
    Thanks for your letter. Indeed by insisting on the S-Line being published
you have displayed the insight of a doctor who knows his patient thoroughly.
I may be an unsatisfactory patient – but I am not an ungrateful one.
    Edward announces his coming for Monday next. I shall rough out a preface
for him by then. I think of it in the form of a letter taking a wide sweep
around the subject. Literarily such a form is easy and safe enough. But what
do you think of it from a business point of view? Just tell me. I know you
will have trouble enough with that book, and I really want to be helpful. But
perhaps the form doesn't matter much. Anyway I mean to give him a good

[1] These are arrangements for the visit of 7–8 May.
[2] This is what Conrad did. The preface is collected in *Notes on Life and Letters*.
[3] Dated by Garnett's impending visit.

measure (more than the 3–4 pp he asks for) if I only can stick it out. And I think I can. You know E is a sort of tragic figure in letters. I say this seriously. Yes. Poor Dawson. Isn't it awful! And, you know, he isn't a fool exactly, but there's no doubt that he is hopeless in a sort of mysterious, exalted fashion. O! those Americans! They all seem to have something just a little wrong with their brains and it shows in a variety of ways – which are *not* amusing.

Ever Yours

J. Conrad.

PS I believe you keep my letters. Well please tear-up this one anyhow. I had a letter from Dent with proofs of Lord Jim.[1] But I don't intend to correct for this edition except in one place. Am writing to him.

To Catherine Willard

Text MS Indiana; *L. fr.* 137

[Capel House]

Jeudi. [3 May? 1917][2]

Chère Catherine

Vous croyez? Le role de la violiniste? Elle a a peine six repliques.

J'imagine que HBI[rving] ne pense pas encore a Victory. Mais si Vous voulez je veux bien lui écrire tout de suite; car je crains fort de ne pas être en état d'aller à Londres de sitôt. Reflechissez un peu et envoyez moi un petit mot. Moi, Vous comprenez ca me fera le plus grand plaisir de Vous voir dans la pièce. Ce qui me fera de la peine c'est de Vous y voir dans un rôle si insignificant.

En ce moment a ce qu'il parait HBI, H. Clark et M. Hastings sont en train de "chercher la femme". Pour Lena, vous comprenez.

Affectueusem^t

Votre vieil Ami

J. Conrad.

Translation

Dear Catherine

Do you think so? The role of the violinist? She scarcely has six lines.

I imagine that HBI is not thinking about Victory yet. But if you wish, I would be happy to write to him immediately, for I am rather afraid that I won't

---

[1] The second British edition, priced at six shillings.

[2] A sequel to the letter of 30 April, which suggests that Willard consider a role other than Lena.

be fit to go to London so soon. Think about it a little and drop me a line. For my part, you understand, seeing you in the play would give me the greatest pleasure; what would grieve me would be seeing you there in such an insignificant role.

At the moment, it seems HBI, H. Clark and M. Hastings are in the process of "chercher la femme". For Lena, you understand.

Affectionately

Your old Friend

J. Conrad.

To B. Macdonald Hastings

Text MS Colgate; Unpublished

[letterhead: Capel House]
6. 5. '17 [early May 1917][1]

My dear Hastings

I didn't suggest that particular form for Schomberg's hotel because its more like the bungalows on the island.[2] This is a private house I imagine. But if you and H. B. I[rving] like it that sort of thing will do very well.

I suppose you've signed the contract by this time. Are you satisfied with it? I think that looking at the whole of its terms and stipulations it's very fair indeed. The American agreement is the next act; but that I know you regard as satisfactory. Then comes the production!

And *then* . . . we shall see. I do hope my dear Hastings you'll not have to regret your time and Your labour expended on the work, which is very much Yours – and yours alone.[3]

I've been reading through your plays again. You are "très fait"[4] as the French say. Tell me, had E[den] P[hillpotts] much to do with the *Angel*?[5] It seems to me pure Hastings.

Kindest regards.

Yours cordially

Joseph Conrad

[1] The date on the letter reads '6. 5. '17', but the letter from Hastings to Conrad of 5 May (TS/MS Berg; *Portrait*, pp. 121–2) is indisputably a reply to this one. Although the mistaken date could be Hastings's, Conrad had a long history of such slips.

[2] In his reply, Hastings mentions sending a friend's snapshot of a hotel in Surabaya.

[3] 'You are kind enough to say that the work is very much mine, but I am sorry that you should say such a thing of such a ready made drama as your novel' (Hastings to Conrad, 5 May).

[4] 'Quite experienced'.

[5] *The Angel in the House* (1915), a comedy in three acts by Eden Phillpotts (1862–1960) and Hastings, which was available in an acting edition from Samuel French. Remembering Conrad's interest in methods of collaboration, Hastings insisted that 'it is quite as much Phillpotts's work as mine'.

PS What about Lena? This is the only thing that gives me some concern. The last name you mentioned in that connection fills me with dread.[1] But it isn't for me to say anything.

To B. Macdonald Hastings

Text MS Colgate; Unpublished

[letterhead: Capel House]

[c. 6 May 1917][2]

Dear Hastings

Thanks for your good letter. I'll drop a note to Irving as you advise, but I feel I ought not to interfere. I will try to express my general feeling without mentioning names since as a matter of fact I don't know the individuals. I know that M[ona] L[imerick] has done some very fine, very temperamental work, in certain plays in Manchester and more recently has some success in London in the Spanish play. She may not be very *safe*. One would have to make sure that she understands the part.[3]

I am sorry and disconcerted at the news of your departure for France. Couldn't we meet before you go? I am awfully crippled yet. Is it too much to hope you may find time to come for the night here?

Re French trans[on] I had a letter from André Gide about various matters and in writing to him I'll mention that there is a play and that I am thinking of translating it.[4] That *may* bring a proposal from some quarter. I would rather it came from the other side. This anyway is not a good time.

Yours sincerely

J Conrad.

PS Yes, my dear fellow. The house is first rate. I was only thinking of the other bungalow. I like it very much otherwise. Can I have a copy of the play for a few days. Or could I get P[inker] to have a copy made for me? He has one I suppose.

---

[1] 'I can appreciate your concern about the threatened engagement of Lily Elsie for Lena. I only regarded the engagement as a commercial proposition. As I think I have told you before, I regard the dramatization of your story as a purely commercial proposition. Otherwise this actress would never have occurred to me' (Hastings to Conrad, 5 May).

[2] Between the letter from Hastings of the 5th and the letter to Hastings of the [10th].

[3] On 19 March, Conrad had lobbied for Mona Limerick, citing good reports of her performance in *The Cleansing Stain* in letters to Hastings and to Pinker. In his letter of 5 May, Hastings told Conrad that Irving was ready to see her 'at the first opportunity'.

[4] Neither this letter nor Conrad's response has survived.

To John Quinn
Text MS NYPL; Unpublished

[letterhead: Capel House]
6 May '17.

My dear Quinn

Thanks for your letter. My wife holds a corrected typed copy of Victory for you till better times. As to the 1st Ed. copy of Sh-Line I'll hold it too for awhile. Nothing's safe for 5 minutes at sea just now. The first Ed: was small and it was followed by a *Reprint* (of the 1st Ed). But that's not what you want for an inscribed copy. The *Second* Ed is being advertised now.

I am sorry to say the corr^d typescripts of Sh-Line and of the short story (I am glad you like it) have not been preserved.[1]

The coming in of the US is no doubt an enormous piece of luck for the Western Powers. There is a certain unreality in the motives as set forth in the speeches. We here we don't fight for democracy or any other "cracy" or for humanitarian or pacifist ideals. We are fighting for life first, for freedom of thought and development in whatever form, next. For the old, old watchwords of country and liberty – in fact. The army has no doubt about it. It cares nothing for political formulas, and for academic distinctions between nations and governments which it looks upon as mere piffle.

I must be excused from joining in the extacies* about the Russian revolution.[2] Apparently a revolution can be made in 24 hours but a nation's nature can't be changed in that time. Russia was an untrustworthy ally before – and it remains so still. The immediate result is to eliminate it as an *active* factor from the war. It counted for little – and now it counts for just nothing. The Germans saw at once that they would be able to reduce their Eastern front by one-third of their effectives at least. I think they have done it already and that most of the reinforcements on the West front come from the East. Though of course some of the new reserves have been used too no doubt. Lwoff Miliukov & Co[3] so far from being able to repress anybody

---

[1] Two TSS of 'The Warrior's Soul' were in the Hodgson sale of Conrad's library, 13 March 1925.

[2] Quinn had written: 'The revolution in Russia is the greatest thing that has happened in political revolutions since the French revolution.' Even more provocatively he added: 'I feel now that something may be done in Ireland soon. The handwriting is on the wall' (Quinn to Conrad, 16/17 March, TS carbon, NYPL).

[3] When the Tsar abdicated, Georgy Yevgenyevich, Prince Lvov (1861–1925) formed a Provisional Government; his Foreign Minister was Pavel Nikolayevich Miliukov (1859–1943), a well-known liberal historian. Under pressure from Bolsheviks and Socialists, Miliukov resigned in May and Lvov in July.

run a good risk of being hanged themselves before very long. There's no government of any sort whatever there now. There are speeches from balconies. The experts in organisation[1] you intend (so the papers say) to send to Russia will have a startling and curious experience. Something like being thrown overboard in a storm to organise the waves of the sea. We shall see! Jessie sends her kindest regards. Had a letter from the boy yesterday. Too busy to write much. In position about 6000 yards from St Quentin I guess. And so it goes on. Strain, and more strain – and still more . . . Believe me

always yours

J. Conrad.

To J. B. Pinker
Text MS Berg; Unpublished

[Capel House]

[8? May 1917][2]

Dear Pinker

I am sending you this letter for information – Do you think taking the play and the present circumstances into consideration that it would be worth while for me to undertake the translation?[3]

In any case pray have a copy of the play made for me personally. I imagine you have copy from which it could be done.

Edward just left. Preface finished. I shall send it to him tomorrow typed and corrected. He seems pleased.

Yours ever

J. C.

PS Please send Edward copy of Secret Agent to 19. Pond Place Chelsea.

---

[1] Disciples of Frederick Winslow Taylor, the prophet of 'Scientific Management': see Patricia Carden, 'Utopia and Anti-Utopia: Aleksei Gastev and Evgeny Zamyatin', *Russian Review*, 46 (1987), 1–18.

[2] Written on the back of Hastings's letter to Conrad of 5 May. On Monday the 7th, Jessie Conrad mentioned Garnett's presence to Pinker (MS Berg); the reference to a forgotten shaving-brush (see the letter of [11 May]) shows that Garnett stayed at least until the morning of the 8th.

[3] In response to Hastings's speculation that the stage *Victory* might be 'done in Paris . . . the translation to be your own' (*Portrait* p. 122).

To B. Macdonald Hastings

Text MS Colgate; Unpublished

[letterhead: Capel House]

Thursday [10 May 1917][1]

Dear Hastings

On reflexion I think I had better wait to see how the play goes here before I tackle the French trans*on*. But I've asked P[inker] to have a copy typed for me at once. Don't think I am shirking it. Somebody from France is sure to come over – and then we may be approached from there. It will be better I think.

I still hope for a sight of you before you cross over.[2]

Kindest regards

Yours sincerely

J. Conrad

PS. I have told André Gide about the play as a bit of personal news and it's certain to get about in the literary world.

To J. B. Pinker

Text MS Berg; Unpublished

[Capel House]

Thursday. [10 May 1917][3]

My dear Pinker.

Thanks for your letter. You will receive the corr*ed* copy of the preface from Edward to whom I've sent it yesterday. Pray have 2 copies made – one for me. Perhaps you won't mind glancing at it yourself.

I am writing to H. B. I[rving] on the subject of Lena's part, and shall write to M. H[astings] in the sense of your advice as to the French translation. You are perfectly right in what you say.

A. Gide has sent me typed transl*on* of Typhoon.[4] It's wonderfully done – in parts. In others utterly wrong. And the worst is that with all my knowledge of the two languages I can't do much either in the way of suggestion. I was not fully aware how thoroughly *English* the Typhoon is. I am immensely proud

---

[1] Conrad asked Pinker for a fresh copy of *Victory* on [8? May].

[2] Hastings had been ordered to France with a labour battalion, but the order was later rescinded.

[3] The same day as the 'Thursday' letter to Hastings.

[4] As part of his plan to publish a complete translation of Conrad's work, Gide assigned 'Typhoon' to Marie-Thérèse Muller. Unhappy with the results, he took over the work himself. *Typhon* (the novella, rather than the whole collection of stories) appeared in two March 1918 issues of the *Revue de Paris*, and in book form later the same year. There were only 300 copies of the original Nouvelle Revue Française edition, but the Gallimard publication in 1923 was aimed at a

of this, of course. There are passages that simply cannot be rendered into French – they depend so much for their meaning upon the very genius of the language in which they are written. Don't think I am getting a "swelled head". It's a fact.

Yours ever

J. Conrad.

To J. B. Pinker
Text MS Berg; Unpublished

[Capel House]
Thursday [10 May? 1917][1]

Dear Pinker

Since I posted my letter, Jessie has struck me for a trip to town. As she has not been away since Jan[y] last I must let her have it. So please send me tomorrow £5 in notes to go up with on Monday.

I shall then see you on Monday about 12.30

Ever yours

J. C.

To Edward Garnett
Text MS Texas; G. 272

[Capel House]
Friday. [11 May 1917][2]

Dear Edward

Thanks for your letter. There is no note of irony in it and I don't believe you wanted to put it in   in this case.

I didn't want my scrawl back. I really thought you told me to send it on. Why didn't you light the domestic fire with it? P[inker] will have a clear copy made for me too from the corr[ted] type.

Awfully good of you to send me the portrait of M[ona] L[imerick].[3] I think she will be It if she only cares for the part. Am writing to Irving to-day.

---

larger readership. (Joseph de Smet published an earlier translation in the magazine *Progrès*, July 1911.) For assessments of Gide's achievement, see René Rapin, 'André Gide et sa traduction du *Typhon* de Joseph Conrad', *Revue des Lettres Modernes*, 374–9 (1973), 187–201; Sylvère Monod's Note in Volume 2 of the Pléiade edition (Gallimard, 1985), pp. 1329–32; and the essays in *Bulletin des Amis d'André Gide*, 21:100 (1993).

[1] Likely to be the second letter of the Thursday before the Conrads' three-day visit to London, which started on the 14th.

[2] Just after Garnett's visit and the drafting of Conrad's preface to *Turgenev*.

[3] The confusion in Garnett's footnote between stage versions of *Victory* and *The Secret Agent* does not invalidate his identification of the picture he sent.

Letter to W[alter] de la M[are][1] goes this post.

Seriously my dear fellow it was comforting and warming to have you here, all to myself and laugh, and ironise, and squabble with you as in the days when the wine was still red and women more than a mere memory of smouldering furies (of all sorts) and diabolic excentricities*. It's true that we always treated these subjects literarily. The loftiness of your sentiments and the austerity of your demeanour intimidated me. Even now during your visit I wanted once to be impertinent to you and simply couldn't do it. The Prestige! Your undying prestige! It's true that I managed to get furious with you for about 7½ seconds, but that, really, was a sort of inverted tribute. If you think there are many men for whose words I care enough to get furious with them you are mistaken. There is in fact only one – yourself. For contempt at a certain temperature may resemble fury. But you get the genuine article. The rest of mankind may flatter itself ——

The book and the shaving brush left last night. Jessie and John send their love.

Ever Yours

Joseph Conrad.

PS J[essie] cant lay her hands just now on the N° of L & W containing the story.[2] It will come along presently. But its nothing really. Pot-boiler.

To J. B. Pinker

Text MS Berg; Unpublished

[letterhead: The Norfolk Hotel,
Surrey Street, Strand,
London W. C. 2.]
Tuesday. [15 May 1917][3]

Dear Pinker.

We are going to Leigh[4] for the day so I shan't see you till to-morrow.

It did me good to get [in] touch with you. I've also seen Jack and Ada.[5] They were charming. Colvin called too. He was very much alarmed by H[ugh] W[alpole]'s letter which I showed him – I'll write W tonight.

---

[1] Walter de la Mare (1873–1956), poet, novelist, and anthologist, whose works include *Peacock Pie* (1913), *Memoirs of a Midget* (1921), and the children's anthology *Come Hither* (1923). This letter has not survived among his papers in the Bodleian Library.
[2] 'The Warrior's Soul' in the 29 March number of *Land and Water*.
[3] Conrad wrote the predicted letter to Walpole on Friday the 18th.
[4] Leigh-on-Sea, Essex, to visit G. F. W. Hope and family? The Pinkers lived in the village of Leigh, near Reigate, Surrey, but Pinker would hardly need information about a visit to his own house.
[5] Galsworthy.

I have a good mind (if we're back in time) to see Irving in Hamlet this evening.[1] Do you think I could send him my card and see him for a few minutes after the performance? Or would the sending of the card be incorrect?

Pray send over the watch-chain (if it is in your office) and five £1 notes. We saw Faust last night.[2] A very decent performance.

Yours ever

J. C.

To J. B. Pinker

Text MS postcard, Berg; Unpublished

[letterhead: Norfolk Hotel]
[c. 17 May? 1917][3]

J. B. Pinker Esqre

I am detained but will come for you with Jessie about One o'clock. We are leaving this afternoon. Please pay 25 to my acc^{t} as I'll have to draw a cheque here.

Your

JC.

To Sir Sidney Colvin

Text MS Duke; Unpublished

[Capel House]
Friday. [18 May 1917][4]

My dear Colvin.

It's very good of You to have taken so much trouble for John's sake.[5] He is very grateful and sends his love.

I am going to write to H[ugh] W[alpole] this afternoon a tête reposée[6] after all the current correspondence has been expedited.

I won't say more just now. Our dear love to Lady Colvin and yourself

Yours ever

J. Conrad

---

[1] In the production at the Savoy, Irving had the title role.
[2] Charles Gounod's opera, staged at the Garrick Theatre by the Royal Carl Rosa Company.
[3] Filed in the 1917 correspondence at the Berg: the Conrads ended a visit to London around 17 May, and that seems the most likely date for this postcard.
[4] The date of the letter to Walpole.   [5] John Conrad's sake.
[6] 'With a calm mind'.

To Hugh Walpole

Text MS Texas; J-A, 2, 194

[letterhead: Capel House]

18 May '17

Dear Mr Walpole[1]

It is gratifying to know that a few pages of mine – and of the sort too for which there seemed to be little justification – have helped to tide you over the difficult hours that precede the dawn. It appears then that they have not been written in vain.

I have heard of your accident. To fall between a ship and her quay is an abominable experience. I understand it was a very close call too and that you are en quelque sorte un "Revenant".[2]

Having come back from so far, I wonder whether you think it was worth while. I shouldn't like to say positively, chiefly for the reason that owing to my "age and infirmities" I am so completely out of it. A very hard fate this, I can assure you. But speaking generally I think that decidedly: – yes, it is always worth while. One gets a sort of moral satisfaction out of it. I suppose you'll smile – and to be quite candid with you I don't know myself very well what I mean by it. But – that is what I feel. And I am not an idealist either. Any hopes are of a strictly limited kind. — And yet ——

I have been (like a sort of dismal male witch) peering (mentally) into the caldron into which la force des choses[3] has plunged you bodily. What will come out of it? A very subtle poison or some very rough-tasted Elixir of Life? Or neither? Just mere Kvass[4] so to speak. It's very curious. I feel startled when I remember that my foster-brother is an Ukrainian peasant.[5] He is probably alive yet. What does he think? I am afraid that what he thinks bodes no good to the boys and girls with whom I used to play and to their

---

[1] Hugh Seymour Walpole (1884–1941; knighted 1937) was born in New Zealand, but his parents soon returned to England, where his father became Bishop of Durham. As a young man, he admired and was admired by Henry James. As a novelist, Walpole first met recognition with *Mr Perrin and Mr Traill* (1911) and *The Duchess of Wrexe* (1914). In *The Dark Forest* (1916), he drew on his experience of working for the Russian Red Cross. Among the most popular of his later novels were the Herries Chronicle series, set in the Lake District, and the Jeremy series, set in public and preparatory schools. Before meeting Conrad, who was to treat him as a protégé, Walpole had already published his critical appreciation *Joseph Conrad* (Nisbet, 1916; revised edition, 1924), but they were yet to meet.

[2] A ghost, like the deceased captain in *The Shadow-Line*. At Liverpool Docks in February, Walpole had fallen between ship and quayside when trying to embark for Arctic Russia. Since he was wearing a fur coat ready for the winter ahead, he proved particularly difficult to rescue from the freezing water (Hart-Davis, *Walpole*, p. 158).

[3] A play on Verdi's titles? 'La force des choses' translates *La Forza del Destino*, and that opera does have a Gypsy fortuneteller, Preziosilla; the true witch, however, complete with cauldron and noxious vapours, is Ulrica in *Un Ballo in Maschera*.

[4] The Russian beer made with rye or barley flour or bread.

[5] That is, the son of his wet-nurse. Conrad was ever fascinated by the Cain and Abel story.

children. Are those gracious shades of my memory to turn into blood-stained spectres? C'est possible, Vous savez! And those houses where under a soul-crushing oppression so much noble idealism, chivalrous traditions, the sanity and the amenities of western civilisation were so valiantly preserved – are they to vanish into smoke? Cela, aussi est très possible! And at any rate moral destruction is unavoidable. Meantime I have been asked to join in the public ecstasies of joy.[1] I begged to be excused. Le monde est bête. It's a positive fact. – Pardon this scrawl and believe me

very sincerely Yours

Joseph Conrad.

To J. H. Retinger
Text MS PAN; Najder (1983, 2); Original unpublished

[letterhead: Capel House]
19 May 17[2]

Mon cher Joseph[3]

Merci pour le Paris-Midi qui vient d'arriver.

Nous imaginions que Vous étiez en Suisse. De grace donnez-nous des nouvelles de Tola car Jessie ne fait que s'inquieter.[4]

---

[1] As director of the Anglo-Russian Bureau (also known as the British Propaganda Office), Walpole was based in Saint Petersburg (Petrograd, at the time). There he had witnessed the March Revolution, which initially he favoured. He wrote to his mother: 'Of course all one's sympathies were with the revolutionaries, and whatever troubles there are in store, what has happened is a tremendous thing for Russia' (Hart-Davis, *Walpole*, p. 161). Perhaps some of this sympathy informed the letter that 'very much alarmed' Colvin and provoked Conrad. In his reply, Conrad imagines the horrors of class-warfare, but the threat of ethnic hostilities was not far behind: the Bobrowskis and Korzeniowskis were after all Catholic and Polish, but their tenants were neither; one result of the March Revolution was the emergence of the Ukrainian Central Rada (Council); by November 1918, newly independent Poland was at war with the West Ukrainian Republic over possession of Eastern Galicia.

[2] Najder (1983, 2, 229) reads this as '19 March', but the contents support the reading '19 May'. The contract with Irving, for example, was not signed until late April.

[3] Józef Hieronim Retinger (1888–1960), a native of Cracow, wrote in French and English as well as Polish. He capped his law degree from Cracow with a doctorate from the Sorbonne; his dissertation appeared as *Le Conte fantastique dans le romantisme français* (Paris: Grasset, 1909). Political urgencies frustrated his hopes of taking yet another degree from the London School of Economics. During the war, he devoted his energies to polemical activities in the Polish cause, becoming as a consequence the victim of slanders and intrigues that led the French government to deport him to Spain; he advanced his ideas about the future of Poland in *La Pologne et l'équilibre européen* (1916). In the 1920s, a sympathiser with the revolution, he worked as an agent of the Mexican government. Later, he became a courtly advocate of European unity. He and his first wife, Otylia ('Tola', 1889–1984), came to know the Conrads well, and it was Otylia Retinger's mother who invited them to Poland in 1914. Retinger wrote his memoir of the friendship *Conrad and His Contemporaries* (1941; US edition 1943) with panache; the details, such as the claim of a first meeting in 1909, call for scepticism.

[4] Otylia Retinger was pregnant.

Je ne vous parle pas des affaires. Les événements recents m'ont deprimé. Ici il y a eu une joie tout-a-fait idiote – vu la situation.

Ma santé a été assez mauvaise depuis Votre départ. Jessie devient nerveuse a la longue. Les nouvelles de B[orys] sont bonnes. Il est quelque part en position contre St Quentin. Il semble content des* toutes choses et de tout le monde. Tant mieux.

Nous attendons un mot de Vous sur le Grand Evenement. Jessie and John send their dear love to you all.

Yours as ever

J. Conrad

PS Ni vu ni entendu personne depuis votre départ. Sand[eman] m'écrit une ou deux lettres – sur les actrices en disponibilité. Contrat pour Victory signé avec Irving. Comme travail – rien!!! Le spectre de la Ruine rôde autour de Capel House. Il faudra voir a lui fermer la porte au nez – mais je n'ai pas beaucoup de force.

Translation

My dear Joseph

Thank you for the *Paris-Midi* which has just arrived.

We thought you were in Switzerland. For pity's sake send us news of Tola because Jessie does nothing but worry.

I am not going to talk about current affairs with you. Recent events have made me depressed. There has been a gaiety here that is absolutely idiotic – given the situation.

My health has been rather poor since you left. Jessie grows anxious as time goes by. The news from B[orys] is good. He is somewhere in position near St Quentin. He seems happy with everything and everybody. So much the better.

We await a word from you about the Great Event. Jessie and John send dear love to you all.

Yours as ever

J. Conrad

PS Neither seen nor heard from anyone since you left. Sand[eman]: writes me one or two letters – about available actresses. Contract for Victory signed with Irving. As for work – nothing!!! The spectre of Ruin prowls round

Capel House. The door should be shut in its face – but I don't have much strength.

To J. B. Pinker

Text MS Berg; Unpublished

[Capel House]
[26? May 1917][1]

Dear Pinker

I got this after posting my letter to you. It may interest you. I transmitted the request to Irving – nothing more. Do you think she will do?[2]

I pointed out to HBI that what was wanted was a safe actress with a simple, quiet conception of the part. No great genius is needed there.

Ever yours

J. C.

To J. M. Dent

Text MS UNC; Moore

[Capel House]
Tuesday [29 May? 1917][3]

Dear Mr Dent

I'll try what I can do. But in any case it will be something quite short.

You'll hear from me on Friday at latest. I need not tell you that I too am anxious that the edition should be a success for both our sakes. Let me tell you that in our intercourse I feel on your part a friendliness, a desire to make the best of me to which I am very sensible. I am not likely to disregard wilfully any wish of yours.

Yours sincerely

J. Conrad.

---

[1] On the verso of a letter from Lillah McCarthy (see note 2) written on the 25th.

[2] McCarthy (1875–1960) was a partisan of contemporary drama. As manager of the Kingsway Theatre, she staged Schnitzler, Ibsen, and Shaw, encouraging a restrained style of acting appropriate for scripts by authors who despised Romantic excess. She herself had appeared in major productions of works by Shakespeare, Shaw, and Harley Granville-Barker (her first husband). Now McCarthy wanted to play Lena.

[3] Dent wanted an Author's Note for the new edition of *Lord Jim*. On 6 June, Conrad told him that the MS had gone to Pinker for typing. If the present letter was written on 5 June rather than 29 May, Conrad must have acted with extraordinary speed.

To the Paymaster General
Text MS PRO T1/12178/29480/18; Unpublished

[letterhead: Capel House]
2 June 17.

The Rt. Hon.
The Paymaster General

Sir[1]

I beg to inform you that I wish to give up my pension[2] at the end of the current year.

As to the income-tax form sent me with the last two pension-warrants I regret not to be able to fill it in just now as I have not received yet my accts from my agent. I expect to have them in the course of this month.

I am Sir

Your obedient servant
Joseph Conrad

To [?]
Text MS Yale; Unpublished

[letterhead: Capel House]
3 Jun '17.

Dear Sir.[3]

As a matter of fact I've nothing to do whatever with the production of the play; I know nothing of theatrical matters; I am not competent. But why should you not drop a line to M[r] H. B. Irving or to my excellent adaptor B. Macdonald Hastings?

His address is: Corp[al] M. H. N[o] 2 Off[er] Cadet Wing. R[oyal] F[lying] C[orps] Hursley Park, Winchester. I think that he will be on leave in town at the end of the month. My impression is, however, that all the parts are filled with the exception of Lena. But I really don't know.

Your letter interested me very much. But my experiences of that part of the world were over in 1888[4] – long before your time. As to Heyst himself

---

[1] The Paymaster General, responsible for disbursement of government funds, was the Right Hon. Arthur Henderson (1863–1935), a Labour member of the coalition Cabinet. The reply to Conrad's request came from Charles Llewelyn Davies (1860–1927), Assistant Paymaster General from 1910 to 1924 (6 June: *Portrait*, p. 123).

[2] Presumably as a contribution to the war effort, Conrad wanted to give up the Civil List pension of £100 a year granted in August 1910. The Civil List was a discretionary fund controlled by the Prime Minister's office.

[3] Unidentified: evidently an actor with some experience of East Asia.

[4] His first voyage in the *Otago* was his last in Asian waters.

he dates further back still. I had my visual impression of the man in 1876: a couple of hours in an hotel in St Thomas (West Indies).[1] There was some talk of him after he left our party; but all I heard of him might have been written down on a cigarette-paper. Except for these hints he's altogether "invented".

I am afraid I won't be able to meet you at the end of this month. There are all sorts of things in the way of my coming to town then. I am sending your letter to B. Macdonald Hastings rather than to H. B. I. whom I only saw once in my life. MH will certainly be interested and something may come of it. One never knows.

Yours faithfully

Joseph Conrad.

To J. M. Dent

Text MS Berg; Unpublished

[letterhead: Capel House]

Monday [4 June 1917][2]

Dear Mr Dent.

I was under the impression the pp have been sent back.[3] Anyway they are approved. I am awfully sorry for the delay.

My wife sent you some time ago a set of photographs. At least I sent them, but they are her property. She is dunning me for them now.

Yours sincerely

J. Conrad.

To B. Macdonald Hastings

Text MS Colgate; Unpublished

[Capel House]

Monday. [4? June 1917][4]

Mon caporal.

I am *ever* so glad you like my Mighty Effort. Pray accept an un-venerable old man's blessing for yourself and your Fledgeling*[5] – all your fledgelings.

I enclose here a letter from a man. He's funny. He thinks the world began with his coming on the scene. My experiences in the East were over in 1888

---

[1] In the Author's Note to *Victory*, the date given is 1875, and the man is the prototype of Mr Jones; Conrad visited St Thomas, one of the Virgin Islands then under Danish rule, in both years.

[2] Replying to a letter from Dent of this date (TS carbon, Berg).

[3] Proofs of the second British edition of *Lord Jim*. Conrad mentioned them to Pinker on [2 May].

[4] Close to 3 June, when Conrad wrote to the would-be actor.

[5] Conrad had contributed 'Never Any More' (the account of his one aerial experience reprinted in *Notes on Life and Letters* as 'Flight') to the first issue of Hastings's *The Fledgling*, 'Monthly Journal of the No. 2 Officer Cadet Wing, Royal Flying Corps' (June 1917).

when he ran about in short frocks most likely. I never heard of him in my life. Is he an actor? Would he be of some use? Have we a Ricardo? According to what he says he ought to have a good notion of the surroundings – the material "millieu*".

And in this connection – is Holman Clark likely to be Jones? His Polonius was quite a conception and well realized too. Very well. The other day I sneaked in to see Hamlet – but please keep that a *profound secret*, for a time at any rate. Till I relieve you of the oath you are supposed to have taken.

Lillah McCarthy wrote to me.[1] She hankers after Lena's part. I mentionned* this to H. B. I[rving] because she asked me to do so. I haven't seen her act since Galsworthy's *Strife*.[2] H. B. I. wrote me a non-comm[it]^{al} letter. What do you think?

Yours very sincerely

J. Conrad

To H. F. T. Cooper
Text MS Private collection; Unpublished

[letterhead: Capel House]
6 June 17.

Dear Sir[3]

Of course there is no excuse. None whatever. But you don't know what an elusive thing a slip of the pen is. One may look over the proofs ten times and yet miss it. I can only say I am shocked at myself and am sorry.

I send you an American copy of the Shadow Line so that you should have something that can't be bought in this country – at any rate.

Yours

J. Conrad.

To J. M. Dent
Text MS Berg; Unpublished

[letterhead: Capel House]
6 Jun 17.

Dear Mr Dent

I've posted the Author's Note to Mr Pinker asking him to have a typed copy made and to forward it to you.

---

[1] See *Portrait*, p. 123.   [2] In 1909.

[3] The remark that the American edition 'can't be bought in this country' suggests that Cooper was one of Conrad's British admirers. The copy of *The Shadow-Line* accompanying this letter is inscribed 'H. F. T. Cooper with compliments and thanks from Joseph Conrad June 1917'.

I think it is what you want, about a thousand words of by no means solemn character.

You'll get the Typescript on Friday I presume. Please send me a (duplicate) proof in due course. I may want to make some verbal alterations.

Yours sincerely

J. Conrad

PS I reserve to myself the faculty to use that note for the Lord Jim vol of the Ed^{on} de Luxe when that appears.

J. C.

To A. T. Saunders

Text MS South Australia; *CEW* 295

[letterhead: Capel House]

14.June 17.

Dear Mr Saunders.

You are a terror for tracking people out! It strikes me that if I had done something involving penal servitude I wouldn't have liked to have you after me. However, as I have done nothing of the sort and am not likely to, now, (too old) I can enjoy without misgivings the evidences of your skill, tenacity and acuteness. Many thanks for your letter with the enclosures giving the history of those lively ladies, the daughters of the late lamented Hayes.

Mostly all the inferences and surmises in your letter are correct. I did go to Minlacowie.[1] The farmers around were very nice to me, and I gave their wives (on a never-to-be-forgotten day) a tea-party on board the dear old "Otago" then lying alongside the God-forsaken jetty there. *The Smile of Fortune* story does belong to the "Otago Cycle" if I may call it so. The *Secret-Sharer* in the same vol: also does in a way – as far as the Gulf of Siam setting goes. The swimmer himself was suggested to me by a young fellow who was 2^d mate (in the '60[s]) of the *Cutty Sark* clipper and had the misfortune to kill a man on deck.[2] But his skipper had the decency to let him swim ashore on the Java coast as the ship was passing through Anjer Straits. The story was well remembered in the Merchant Service even in my time.

---

[1] From 22 February to 21 March 1889 (*CEW*, p. 35): Minlacowie (Aboriginal 'Sweet Water', present-day Minlaton, South Australia) lies at the centre of a wheat-growing district in the interior of Yorke Peninsula, across Gulf Saint Vincent from Adelaide. The *Otago* was berthed in Spencer Gulf, on the peninsula's west side; the very last grain clippers sailed from there in 1949.

[2] The killing really happened in September 1880. For a discussion of Conrad's sources, see *CEW*, pp. 253–7.

To a man of letters and a distinguished publicist so experienced as yourself I need not point out that I had to *make* material from my own life's incidents arranged, combined, coloured for artistic purposes. I don't think there's anything reprehensible in that. After all I *am* a writer of fiction; and it is not what actually happened, but the manner of presenting it that settles the literary and even the moral value of my work. My little vol: of autobiography of course is absolutely genuine. The rest is a more or less close approximation to facts and suggestions. What I claim as true are my mental and emotional reactions to life, to men, to their affairs and their passions as I have seen them. I have in that sense kept always true to myself.

I haven't the time to write more at present but pray believe that I appreciate very highly the kind way you are keeping me in mind. In a few days I'll dispatch to you a copy of the new ed^{on} of Lord Jim which is about to be published by Dent's.

> Believe me sincerely yours
>
> Joseph Conrad

To W. T. H. Howe

Text MS Berg; Unpublished

[letterhead: Capel House]

15 June 17

Dear Mr Howe

Your letter was very welcome and I am ashamed of the delay in answering it. I wanted an altogether free half hour but somehow of late a lot of vexing affairs have been turning up.

The effects here of the general's arrival, of his few words and just now of President Wilson's speech have been excellent.[1] The arrival of some of your ships has pleased the People very much and is highly appreciated by our navy and government. Altogether the feeling is that the co-operation has begun well and that you on your side have got hold of the thing with good will and understanding. It is a great piece of luck for Gt Britain this *understanding* (intelligent sympathy) with* seems to us here to grow with every day of the young Alliance, to judge from the reported words and actions across the Atlantic.

I can't tell how much complimented I feel by the friendly and earnest spirit with which you are tackling the "Evening with C's People" celebration.

---

[1] General Pershing and his staff docked at Liverpool on the 8th and travelled to London the next day. The London press of 15 June carried President Wilson's speech on German war aims delivered the previous day at the Washington Monument.

Do you realise that you are there engineering a very considerable event in my life? I assure you that I am deeply touched by this sign of friendliness and appreciation coming to me all the way from Cincinnati. It *is* a considerable event. Too considerable for me to make any suggestions. (You don't really want them) I can only send you a word of gratitude.

The charming photographs of your "residenz" arrived safely. I can't send you anything of the kind in return. Our "palazzo" has not been photographed inside. The other day a charming American girl[1] (her maternal grandparents live actually in Cincinnati) sitting outside with me laughed suddenly. I asked: "Why do you laugh?" and she said: "It's the house. It looks like a property house on the stage". And as a matter of fact it does. An ordinary limousine coming in front of it extinguishes it completely in a most absurd manner.

We heard today from the big boy. He's in this new push[2] apparently. But it's difficult to be certain as those young fellows will never say. All we know is that about six weeks ago he had 48 hours in Paris (on service) and that some "delightful Americans" he met at Hotel Meurice were most friendly to him. Since that time he has been "up to his eyes in hard work", and his letters have been very, very short. Well – I must close. Believe me always

Yours

Joseph Conrad.

To John Quinn
Text MS NYPL; Unpublished

[letterhead: Capel House]
17 June '17

My dear Quinn.

Thanks for the program-tickets of Follett's lecture.[3] I knew nothing of it. I need not tell you I feel immensely complimented by your taking the chair. I also appreciate the importance of you consenting to do so. You are great in the part of "A Friend".

You no doubt know the names of some of your men prominent in the steel industry, now in France on business. Well it's like this: a month ago the boy was in Paris (48h leave) where he got in tow with some "most charming"

---

[1] Catherine Willard?

[2] The attack on German positions along the Messines-Wytschaete Ridge which began on 7 June with a heavy artillery bombardment and the explosion of colossal mines under the German trenches.

[3] Delivered in Chickering Hall, New York, on 29 May by Wilson Follett (1887–1963) of Brown University, who would soon begin a new career as editor and publisher. Conrad had liked his *Joseph Conrad: A Short Study*, published in 1915 (*Letters*, 5, p. 575).

Americans (at Meurice's) who "were awfully good" to him. One of them
(the important steel man) said to him at parting. "I don't know if you are
a hard worker Mr Conrad but if you are and are thinking of engineering,
don't forget to call on me after the war. I can help you to enter any great
engineering firm you like".

His name is Batchett – or something like that. That boy's handwriting is
like the scratching of a paralysed hen, anyhow. Is there in the steel world a
man of mark with a name something as above?[1] The boy is impressed but a
saying like that may mean something or nothing, according to the personality.

I stop short here because I want this to catch the next mail-boat and for
that noon is the latest hour.

My wife sends her friendly regards

Yours

J. Conrad

To J. B. Pinker
Text MS Berg; Unpublished

[letterhead: Capel House]
Tuesday [19 June 1917][2]

My dear Pinker.

We had the confounded lot of machines right over our house about 20
minutes or so before they reached Folkestone.[3] Jessie counted them correctly.
I only managed to see one; but the roar in the air was most impressive. The
whole country-side was vibrating with it.

All Jessies brothers are gone now and as there is a lot of women to look
after we must do something. There are two lots – wives and sisters and so
please send me two cheques for £25 each, made out to me as I don't know
yet the names of the vicar and the solicitor who will be put in charge of
that arrangement, and I have promised to settle it this week. This is the
contribution for the next 12 months. *In addition* there is Mrs George (the
Mother) now just over 70 and in regard to her please send Jessie on every
first of *June-Sept-Dec* and *March* a special cheque for £6 made out to Mrs Jane
George. I will remind you at the dates but I am telling you now of the whole
arrangement, which pray carry out tho' I didn't consult you beforehand.

---

[1] In his reply of 18 July (TS carbon, NYPL), Quinn reported on the confidential inquiries he
had made. The man's name was Batsholts and neither the US Steel Products Company nor
the Royal Bank of Canada could find anything bad to say about him: 'Manifestly, he is not an
adventurer, but a man who does things and deals in large affairs.'

[2] In content, close to the letters of 15 and 17 June.

[3] German planes had attacked Folkestone, a seaport about fifteen miles from Capel House, on
27 May.

Had a letter from B[orys] telling us he was given 48 hours' leave to Paris – where he seems to have got amongst a lot of Americans of pretty good standing. Amongst them Mr Batchells (I don't know if I've spelt the name right) a personage of some importance in the steel syndicate who said to him: "I don't know Mr Conrad if you are a hard worker; but if you are and wish to serve an engineering firm I will be happy to use my influence either in US or in the "Old Country" for the son of Mr Joseph Conrad". There was also the representative of the "Peerless Lorries" who fell on his neck and made offers of service to him – because B has a high opinion of the P. L. which are being used with his batt[er]y's guns.

That cub went to Hotel Meurice(!) where he fell in with all that American lot including Jane[1] – "and many other charming ladies" (but Jane beats them all out of sight). I wrote to him cautioning his inexperience against the "hearty" American speeches; saying (what I do believe) that 5 words from an Englishman are worth 5000 from an American, any time. But perhaps it is just as well that the kid should have something cheerful to think about as to his future. As to Jane (who seems to have taken him in tow there) he's hit in the midriff, hard; but after all if he must meet a "Jane" it's better he should meet her at 19 than at twenty-four. Anyway it couldn't be helped, and besides he's back again and "up to his eyes in work". This last remark makes me think that something is preparing down Somme way.

W. T. Howe the agent of the Am Book C^o in Cincinnati writes me they are organising a performance of 21 living pictures from J Conrad's novels. It's going to be a great social affair for a war charity – $10 tickets. I've sent him some suggestions (as requested); for it's all good for business. And besides he tells me that the Conrad readers in that most enlightened town are sending me a token of regard in the shape of a Rookwood pottery vase specially designed.[2] The second firing of the same came off successfully, and it's going to be sent off shortly in defiance of the submarines. This is some success. I ought to give you half of it, but as that wouldnt work I think I shall leave it in my will to Eric – so that it should stand in the office when we both are no "longer there". I thought of you at first, but I intend us both to live a long time and You would have retired when I go off the hooks and Eric will be carrying the tradition on.

Yours ever

J Conrad.

---

[1] Jane Anderson (c. 1888–?), American war correspondent and fiction writer. Although its precise nature is debatable, the impression she made on the Conrad family was indisputably vivid. See *Letters*, 5, p. 627 and *passim*.

[2] Founded in 1880 by Maria Longworth Storer of Cincinnati. The pottery, inspired by Japanese models, is famous for the quality of its glazes.

To J. B. Pinker
Text MS Berg; Unpublished

[Capel House]
[c. 22 June 1917][1]

My dear Pinker.

Thanks for your letter. *Pray* send me word who is Miss Maud Robertson. I can't keep her off, any longer. She's coming next week. And though I know the name I can't for the life of me remember whether she is an Actress or a Poet or[2] . . . Can't find her in Whos Who, and I have no other reference books. But you have. And moreover you are supposed to know everything and to be able to help me out of *any* hole at 5 minutes notice.

Ever yours

J. C.

PS If *poet* perhaps you could get a vol of hers or so for me, to assuage my distress.

B[orys] in his last letter recognises the justness of your saying about Americans. The steel man was not of Jane's gang but at a lunch party given by Retinger at which there was a secretary of our Embassy and two govern[t] Frenchmen of importance. So probably a responsible sort of person.

Mrs. Ret[inger] delivered safely of a daughter in Switzerland – and immensely delighted. He himself still in Paris – extremely busy.

To J. H. Retinger
Text MS POSK; *Conrad News*; Najder (1983, 2)

[Capel House]
22 June '17

Très cher Ami.

This moment we receive a pc from dear Tola which has relieved our very great anxiety. Our warmest congratulations and most affectionate welcome to Miss Retinger.[3] May her shadow grow bigger and bigger for the proper number of years – and thereafter "never grow less".

You have been very dear and good to our big child in Paris. We had a long letter from him. We are very grateful to You.

---

[1] On or close to the day of Conrad's congratulatory note to Retinger.
[2] Maud Gordon Robertson (née Mosher), by origin an American and the author of *A Woman of Moods* (novel, 1903), *The Minx* (dramatisation of the above, 1906), and *Hints to Lady Golfers* (1909). See also the letter of [23 June].
[3] Malina Wanda Retinger, born in Lausanne.

Jessie is writing to your wife and sends her love to you. We both long to see you both. But when will that be?!

Ever Yours

J. C.

To W. G. St Clair
Text Malay Mail

Capel House
22nd June, 1917

Dear Mr. St. Clair,

I hardly dare to apologise for the delay in acknowledging your portrait.[1] It seems a very fine piece of work and worthy of the personality – not to speak of the locality where it perpetuates the memory of your services. Pardon this scrap of paper, the hurry of this short scrawl; but I am determined not to delay further with the thanks I owe to you for your kind letter. I hope with all my heart you will have a good time and return to town in good health.

Believe me, sincerely yours,

Joseph Conrad.

To J. B. Pinker
Text MS Berg; Unpublished

[Capel House]
[23 June 1917][2]

My dear Pinker

You are very good. Sorry I worried you. The mystery is solved. She's the wife of the Right Hon. J. M. Robertson author, critic and politician. J. M. R. was one of my earliest prophets in the old days – before Nostromo.[3]

She's bringing a man to make a drawing of my head.

I report progress.

Yours ever

J. Conrad

---

[1] When St Clair retired in March 1916, his Singapore friends commissioned a portrait of him. It is reproduced in Walter Makepeace, Gilbert E. Brooke, and Roland St J. Braddell, eds., *One Hundred Years of Singapore*, Vol. 2 (Murray, 1921), opposite p. 292. No doubt St Clair had sent Conrad a reproduction of this portrait.

[2] On [27 June], Conrad refers to the 'note posted on Sat:'.

[3] The Right Hon. John Mackinnon Robertson (1856–1933), author, lecturer, member of the Privy Council, and former cabinet minister, continued to express his admiration in 'The Novels of Joseph Conrad', *North American Review*, 208 (1918), 439–53. Conrad had corresponded with him in March 1915: see *Letters*, 5, pp. 448–9.

To J. B. Pinker
Text MS Berg; Unpublished

[Capel House]
Wednesday 11 AM. [27 June 1917][1]

My dear Pinker

This for your consideration and ultimate decision when the question arises – when we hear what M. T. thinks of the part.[2] My personal opinion is that M. T. is the right actress for the part – and that it is good policy to give the play every chance. We don't want less than 100 performances – do we? And the right woman may secure that for us.

M. T. has a position, has her public and at any rate is an actress – not a painted image. At least that's my impression. But you know these things ——

I'll just drop a line to M. Hastings saying that Madge is worth thinking over.[3] Nothing more. But I won't write till to-morrow (Thursday) ev^g so that you may stop me by wire if you want to.

Imagine my misfortune. I've broken short off two of my front teeth on a cherry stone. Horrible.

Jessie started typing the story. Progress continues. But the app^t with the dentist for tomorrow won't help me very much with to-days. The breach in my mouth feels big enough to drive a coach and four through.

I have received this morning the enclosed demand note.

Yours as ever (but much distressed)
J. Conrad

PS Sorry I worried you about M. Robertson. I suppose you had my note posted on Sat: last to say that the mystery was solved.

Ever Yours
Joseph Conrad

---

[1] Written on the verso of Hastings to Conrad, 25 June (*Portrait*, pp. 124–5), and a sequel to the correspondence about Maud Robertson.

[2] A member of a widely travelled theatrical family, Madge Titheradge (1887–1961) had played in everything from pantomime to Shakespeare. She was particularly famous for her Christmas performances in the title role of *Peter Pan* at the Duke of York's; her recent work included appearances at the Haymarket, Coliseum, Garrick, and His Majesty's.

[3] Agreeing with Hastings, who had suggested her in his letter: 'She is a handsome girl with much magnetism and above all the ability to rise to a big situation. There are very few such women on the English stage.'

To J. M. Dent

Text MS Berg; Unpublished

[letterhead: Capel House]

[3 July 1917]¹

Dear Mʳ Dent

I am sorry for the delay. Yes, pray send me the proof of Youth Vol: and I will try to concoct a little "Note" for it.²

Yours faithfully

J. Conrad.

To J. B. Pinker

Text MS Berg; Unpublished

[letterhead: Capel House]

[c. 3 July 1917]³

My dear Pinker

I delayed for a few days paying the rent thinking you might find it possible to run down here in the matter of the new house. But as I've had a reminder, please send a ch: for £45 to *Edmund W. Oliver Esqʳᵉ*,⁴ New Place, Lingfield. Surrey.

Pray have the 20 pp or so which I send you run through the machine (one copy) for me and returned. I want to see how they look and to start correcting, and Jessie's Blick[ensderfer] wants some small repairs.⁵

No particular care is necessary. Its only for correction.

Re. *Western Eyes*.

No. No need for proof. What is this cheap Edᵒⁿ? A 2/- one has appearᵈ already. Is it a 1/- horror?⁶

———

I am to look over the Youth vol for Dent and shall write about a thou: (or less) words by way of prefatory note.

Ever yours

J Conrad.

---

¹ Date-stamped in Dent's office on the 4th.
² The Author's Note that appears in the second British and later editions.
³ Mention of the 'prefatory note' gives the approximate date.
⁴ One year's rent to the owner of Capel House: see *Letters*, 5, p. 587.
⁵ Around 1910, she had obtained 'one of the earliest portables, a Blick[ensderfer] typewriter' (*MFJC*, p. 13).
⁶ See the letter to Pinker of 26 March.

To J. B. Pinker
Text MS Berg; Unpublished

[Capel House]
Monday [9 July 1917][1]

Dear long suffering Pinker
Pray have this typed 2 cop[ies]. It is the Note to Youth. And *do* please read it through before sending it to Dent. I want your judgement in case there should be anything inopportune, some false note perhaps?
I should like to know. Of course if you pass it you needn't write.

Ever Yours

J Conrad

To J. B. Pinker
Text MS Berg; Unpublished

[Capel House]
Saturday [14 July? 1917][2]

My dear Pinker.
I've received everything. It's very good of you to write in commendation. Yes. I have a notion that these notes will do for the Ed: de Luxe.
I wouldn't even expand them. Of course I can't rivalise with poor dear H[enry] J[ames][3] and I don't know that it would be wise even to try. Besides I don't feel the need somehow. And then I have formed for myself a conception of my public as the sort of people that would accept graciously a few intimate words but would not care for long disquisitions about art. And, lately, I have no "aims" to explain.
Thanks for attending to the spoiled Mrs Joseph Conrad. That vagabond woman seems to have told you that the ground belonging to the house was 4 acres. It isn't a matter of desperate importance but you may just as well know that it is 24 acres (twenty-four). 3 good fields at the back.

Your[s] ever

J. Conrad.

---

[1] Dent thanked Conrad for the Note on 16 July (TS carbon, Berg).
[2] Among the 1917 letters at the Berg, and soon after writing an Author's Note. Conrad completed three of these prefaces in 1917: *Lord Jim* in June, the *Youth* volume in July, and *Nostromo* in October. Since Jessie Conrad was then too ill to be 'vagabond', October does not fit; of the other two dates, July is more likely, given the quest for a new house mentioned on the 3rd. In that case, the 'commendation' was for the Author's Note to *Youth*, sent to Pinker on 9 July. The next dated communication to him is a telegram of 24 July asking if he would be in town the following day (Berg).
[3] With James's monumental Prefaces to the New York Edition of 1908.

To Lieutenant H. J. Osborne

Text NLA MS 8650/8605;[1] Osborne

[letterhead: Capel House]

20 July '17

My dear Osborne.[2]

Infinite thanks for your kind letter which gave me the greatest possible pleasure. After reading it I've given three cheers for the old ship, her Captain[3] and all on board of her. I am glad the luck came in your way – for, though You can't speak plainly, I imagine the job was done thoroughly since you've been 25 minutes at work.[4] I wish I could get alongside of you and hear the whole yarn with all the details. You and all your crowd ought to get some leave after that piece of business. But I suppose that under the present circumstances people of your sort cannot be spared from the "fishing". May the best of luck attend you always and may you all come through safely every time.

No. I didn't think I was forgotten. For myself I can assure you my dear Osborn[e] that I brought away from our short cruise the highest possible regard for you as a man, a sailor and an officer. I only hope that *our* Service will never lack men of your stamp and that you'll find a place in it worthy of your merits. For I suppose peace will come – some day. But the road seems long and the leading marks are not in sight yet.

Thanks for your kind reference to the wife and the boys. We had our big boy on leave here for a few days. His batt[er]y has been in the thick of it lately. The small boy has helped me in giving three cheers for the Freya's ship's company with right good will. I heard from S[utherland] not a long time ago and he sent me some photos of the old ship one of which has a very good, full length likeness of you.[5]

---

[1] The National Library of Australia has a photocopy of the original, which is in a private collection.

[2] Lieutenant Henry Joseph Osborne (born 1891), a temporary lieutenant in the Royal Naval Reserve since March 1915, was serving in HMS *Ready* when Conrad sailed in her in 1916. In 1917, Osborne won the Distinguished Service Cross, and in 1918, after engaging two German submarines and sinking one, the Croix de Guerre. During his later career, he was stranded in the Gulf of Corinth, 1921, and made voyages to Australia, North America, and South Africa.

[3] A decoy vessel, *Ready* was disguised as a Norwegian timber freighter (named *Freya* in honour of Conrad), and sailed with a merchant skipper, Mr W. Moodie, as well as a naval commander, Captain John Georgeson Sutherland. In his *At Sea with Joseph Conrad* (Grant Richards, 1922), the latter tells us that 'Moodie', a Shetlander and 'a shy, retiring, soft-spoken man, charmed' Conrad (p. 25). By the time he wrote to Conrad, Osborne had taken Sutherland's place.

[4] Laying depth-charges. Under Osborne's command, *Ready* had engaged two German submarines, destroying one.

[5] This likeness appears opposite p. 60 of Sutherland's book.

Pray thank Mr Moody* for his kind remembrance of me and give him my best regards.

Yours cordially

Joseph Conrad.

To J. M. Dent
Text MS Berg; Unpublished

[Capel House]
21 July. [1917]^1

Dear Mr Dent.

I am so sorry I can't do what you ask me to do.^2 It's ridiculous and vexing but I am totally unable to grapple with anything but the work I am at now. And even that is constantly slipping from my grasp.

Yours faithfully

J. Conrad.

To William Rothenstein
Text MS Harvard; Unpublished

[letterhead: Capel House]
2^d Aug 17.

My dear Will.^3

Thanks for your pamphlet,^4 to which I responded with every feeling and conviction that go to make up my "less perishable" being. And how beautifully all those deeply felt truths are said! Only a few days ago I was telling some people that you were a master of language too. There's no doubt that you are. Master of a very personal, very fine prose.

We had just a few lines from B[orys] this morning. His batt[er]^y is about Lens somewhere.

---

^1 The date of receipt in Dent's office confirms the year.

^2 On 16 July, Dent had asked for a contribution to a war annual put out by the Young Men's Christian Association (TS carbon, Berg).

^3 William Rothenstein (1872–1945; knighted 1931), a friend of Conrad's from 1903, was notable for his portrait graphics, paintings, and drawings. Max Beerbohm described him as a young phenomenon in 'Enoch Soames' (*Seven Men*): 'He wore spectacles that flashed more than any other pair ever seen. He was a wit. He was brimful of ideas . . . He knew everyone in Paris.'

^4 *A Plea for a Wider Use of Artists & Craftsmen* (Constable, 1916), the printed version of a lecture given at the Sheffield Technical School of Art, 8 November 1916.

I begin to be able to write a little, but my health is not good. Jessie too shows signs of the war-strain.

I close in haste to catch our only post. Our love to you all.

Yours ever

J. Conrad

To John Quinn
Text MS NYPL; Unpublished

[letterhead: Capel House]
8 Aug '17

My dear Quinn.

No end of thanks for your kindness in taking so much trouble for a thorough answer to my inquiry.[1] I am glad of this sign of your interest in the boy who would be a very lonely and unsupported being in life except for the good-will of men who have honoured me with their friendship for the sake of my work. Of men like you, I mean. You understand how anxious I am to see him in the way of making something out of existence before I "hand in my checks". We had a letter last week from which we learn he has managed to get another 3 day's* leave to Paris, (It will make him altogether 16 day's* leave in a year and a half at the front) which apparently he spent amongst charming women; entre autres Miss Root and also Miss Crocker.[2] It looks as if America were fated to get him. Not a bad fate for the boy.

Pray, when you see Follett, give him a warm greeting from me. His little book is one of these things one does not forget. I saw some time ago a study of Galsworthy by him (and a lady who must be either his wife or his sister) which within the limits of a magazine article was simply admirable for insight and expression.[3]

Fancy you going to preside at that lecture with a big stick and laying about you with such vigour on the most respectable heads![4] I suppose the admirers of these men will be waiting for me with guns under the hedges. Nevertheless I enjoy the mental picture of John Quinn on the war-path on my

---

[1] About the American steelmen Borys had met in Paris. See the letter to Pinker of 15 August.

[2] One was a niece of Elihu Root (1845–1937), US senator and 1912 winner of the Nobel Peace Prize; of the other, Quinn wrote: 'There are Crockers and Crockers, but *the* Crockers are from California and wealthy . . . But not all crockery even is first class china' (to Conrad, 25 August, TS carbon, NYPL).

[3] This essay on Galsworthy is reprinted in *Some Modern Novelists: Appreciations and Estimates* (New York: Henry Holt, 1917) by Helen Thomas Follett and her husband Wilson.

[4] Taking the chair at Wilson Follett's lecture on Conrad, 29 May, Quinn had made fun of several contemporary English writers, especially H. G. Wells (Quinn to Conrad, 18 July, TS carbon, NYPL).

account. It surpasses my wildest dreams. I begin to think myself a person of consequence.

Thanks for the E. Pound book.[1] I haven't opened it yet as one must be in the right mood for that sort of reading. And nowadays it's difficult to get any sort of mood to last – except the war-nightmare mood which makes one a little sick of life. That's so. No use concealing it. – Page made a jolly good speech in Plymouth.[2] As ambassador he is a success.

Believe me

always Yours

Joseph Conrad.

To Sir Sidney Colvin
Text MS Haverford; Lucas 305

[letterhead: Capel House]

9 Aug[t]. 17.

My dear Colvin.

I see that it is to your friendship and to your authority I owe the (lavish? – magnificent? – gorgeous?) tribute from over the sea.[3] You may be sure it is very welcome. Authors, as you cannot but know, can stand a lot of jam on their bread. And apart from that I prize particularly every word said in favour of my reminiscences.

I think I'll drop this enthusiastic young man a line. But not yet as I am in bed with some sort of internal disturbance – and writing in bed even on an invalid table worries and exasperates me beyond reason. I am a ridiculous person.

We are truly glad to have a good report of your holiday. But I am afraid the weather will be changeable all this month.

We had a few lines from B[orys], this morning; quietly cheerful as usual but, also as usual, saying very little. Last month he had 3 days in Paris. That, including his home visit, totals up to 16 days' leave in 18 months' service at the front. Not enough to make of him an officier de salon. We had news of that Paris visit otherwise too. Il me semble que ce garçon aura de la chance avec les femmes.[4]

---

[1] *Lustra, with Earlier Poems.* Quinn had been seeking a US publisher for this collection inspired in part by Li Po (Reid, *Man from New York*, pp. 254–5). Conrad's copy, inscribed by Quinn, was lot 69 in the Hodgson sale of Conrad's library, 13 March 1925.

[2] Walter Hines Page (1855–1918), formerly editor of the *Atlantic Monthly* and Doubleday's partner, was now US ambassador to the United Kingdom. Addressing a rally on Plymouth Hoe on 5 August, he alluded to the site's associations with the defeat of the Spanish Armada and the voyage of the *Mayflower*. His general themes were 'the union of two great peoples' in the war effort and 'the heroic times in which we live' (*The Times*, 6 August, p. 8).

[3] Lucas could not find the source of this eulogy (p. 305).

[4] Although Borys is not an 'officier du salon' (a drawing-room warrior), 'It seems to me that boy will have good luck with women.'

I set this down in the face of all the shells flying over his head. Allah 'hu Akbar! What is written is written.[1] Meantime I prefer to think of him in tow of girls like Miss Root and Edith* Cleveland[2] (they seem to have given him a "good time") than battant le pavé idly in Paris. Retinger gave him a lunch with some young diplomats – American. It strikes me I'll have to be mighty civil to a good many Americans after the war. Our love to Lady Colvin and yourself.

Yours ever

Joseph Conrad

To J. B. Pinker
Text MS Berg; Unpublished

[Capel House]
[9 August 1917][3]

My dear Pinker

Will you deal with this request as you think fit?[4] I've just finished corr^g proof of *The Tale* for the *Strand*.[5]

John is going to school at last – Ashford Grammar School. Very elated at the prospect. We shall have him for weekends here so as to ease Jessie down gently. Afterwards Bedford (modern side) will be the right thing for him, I think.[6]

Heard from B[orys] today. A longish letter about Ret[inger] and a few other people. I hope you had news lately and that you are keeping well. We had a succession of people lately here. I haven't the strength of mind to keep them off. I'll be writing you in a day or two. I continue working to some effect.

Yours ever

J Conrad.

---

[1] 'Allah 'hu akbar': 'Allah is great.' 'What I have written I have written': the words of Pontius Pilate in St John's Gospel, 19.22.

[2] As identified below, Esther Cleveland (1893–1980), daughter of Grover Cleveland (1837–1908), US President 1885–9 and 1893–7. Her marriage to W. S. B. Bosanquet, another English officer, took place in Westminster Abbey the following year.

[3] On the verso of J. A. Hammerton to Conrad, 8 August; the letter to Colvin of the 9th gives the day when Borys's letter arrived.

[4] John Alexander Hammerton (1871–1949; knighted 1932), editor of Library Publications, wanted permission to include 'An Outpost of Progress' in an international anthology of modern fiction.

[5] For its October number.

[6] John Conrad could attend the school in Ashford as a day-boy; when he went on to Bedford he would have to board. A sixteenth-century foundation, Bedford School became the first in its county and one of the first in the country to offer classes in engineering.

To J. B. Pinker
Text MS Berg; Unpublished

[letterhead: Capel House]
Thursday noon. [9 August 1917]¹

My dear Pinker

Did you get Jessie's letter containing the mis[s]igned cheque? I ask because another letter from us did not reach its destination apparently. But perhaps I'll have something from you by the afternoon's post.

Pray send me ch to A. A. Farrar Esqre £5. 5 John's tuition and another £*14 10* to Messrs G. H. Hunter Ltd.²

B[orys] was in Paris 10 days ago for 2 days and was entertained by Root's niece, Crocker's daughter (you know "The Boss") and Esther Cleveland. America has got him – but it's a fact that it is a funny team – for you may remember that Senator Root was Crocker's great enemy at the time.³ What is clear is that I'll have to be civil to a lot of Am^{cans} after the war. Retinger expects to be over in a few days. We had also a letter from B (6 days on the way) from the front but I don't think he's actually in the Flanders push.

I am at work quite steady – tho' afflicted by a mysterious tummy-ache which may be caused by the wet.

I hope you are well.

Yours ever

J. C.

To J. B. Pinker
Text MS Berg; Unpublished

[Capel House]
Monday [13 August 1917]⁴

My dear Pinker

Thanks for the ch[eque]s received on Friday.

I am feeling better.

I've heard from Cincinnati. The living pictures from Conrad's work was a very fashionable affair and highly successful. To be repeated, on a larger scale, soon.

---

¹ The second letter of the day, as suggested by 'noon'; here Conrad expands upon the news from Paris.
² George Harrison Hunter, High Street, Ashford, clothier, tailor, and hatter.
³ If Miss Crocker was related to the mighty, she could have been a granddaughter of the formidable banker and chief of the Southern Pacific Railroad, Charles Crocker (1822–88), but he was neither notorious as 'The Boss' nor young enough to be an antagonist of Elihu Root.
⁴ This letter acknowledges the cheques requested on the [9th], and is close in date to the reply to Howe of the 16th.

W. Follett is at work at an extended study of J Conrad to be pub[lished] by Doubleday.[1] I hear that from Quinn.

Ever Yours

J Conrad.

To J. B. Pinker
Text MS Berg; Unpublished

[letterhead: Capel House]

15th Aug '17

My dear Pinker.

Nothing could have given me greater pleasure than the reception of Ld *Jim* reprint. Almost like a new book. There was over a column in the *Times* – perhaps you've seen? Squire (in L & W) gave me a page, almost,[2] and has been extensively quoted in a popular weekly paper. Generally the press has "taken notice" remarkably. At the same time The *S. Line* has come out on top (with Beresford's book) in a popular competition in Sat: West: Gazette as the subject of a prize essay (by a prisoner of war) on 1917 fiction.[3] And thus your wisdom continues to be justified – and my (much shaken) belief in my own existence receives a welcome support.

The new story – I fear – will be no shorter than the S. Line.[4] Such is the truth.

John goes to school on 21^t Sepr. It will cost about £50 a year and he will get good value for the money, for that school is very successful in getting

---

[1] This expanded version of the short study did not appear.

[2] Dent had just brought out the second British edition. After summarising the new preface, the anonymous *TLS* reviewer (Virginia Woolf) went on to welcome the re-appearance of the book in which Conrad 'seems to have found once [and] for all the subject that brings out his rare and wonderful qualities at their best'. Among these qualities are Conrad's 'moments of vision' and his 'gift of seeing in flashes' (26 July, p. 355). J[ohn] C[ollings] Squire (1884–1958) was literary editor of both *Land and Water* and the *New Statesman*. His review in the former is titled 'Mr Conrad's Masterpiece' (26 July, p. 15): pairing Conrad with James, Squire praises the moral seriousness of *Lord Jim* and wonders why it was not more widely admired on its first appearance.

[3] The Saturday supplement of the *Westminster Gazette*, a London evening paper, had sponsored a competition for the best essay on 'The Tendency of English Fiction in 1917'. The results appeared in the issue of 4 August. 'Karshish', the POW who shared the first prize of 10 guineas, cited *The Shadow-Line*, J[ohn] D[avys] Beresford's *House-Mates*, and Clemence Dane's *Regiment of Women*. About Conrad's novel, 'Karshish' wrote: 'Always he gives the impression of one who tells a tale while subjected to drawn-out mental or physical pain. The tale, it seems, would not be told were not the need to tell it imperative, and the pain is a spur hastening the action.'

[4] He had resumed work on *The Arrow of Gold*, now in the process of growing from a story to a novel much longer than *The Shadow-Line*.

scholarships and so on. We went over there yesterday and settled the thing. It's all one cadet-corps and John is going into uniform with W. Kent yeomanry[1] badge.[†]

Will you pay £20 to Jessie's acc[t] in Ashford and 15 into mine in London.

Quinn sent me information about the American Batchells who made offers to B[orys] for after the war. He is the partner of a million-dollar man called Cromwell(!) in some steel works in Cincinnati (or somewhere thereabouts) and they are both men of the highest standing.[2] Quinn obtained information about them from two directors of the Steel Trust and also from a couple of banks, which he has sent to me neatly typed. I forwarded it to B. Is it possible that this Cromwell is your Cromwell?[3] A steel-man (but I rather think he's "general-business" man) with leaning towards stage-ventures? It would be funny.

　　　　　　　　　　　　　　　　Ever yours

　　　　　　　　　　　　　　　　　　J. Conrad.

[†] The school detachment as a whole – m[achine] guns, inf[antr][y] and signallers won the shield for "general efficiency" from all the public schools in Eng[d] at Marlborough camp a week ago. The schoolmaster is simply treading on air!

To W. T. H. Howe
Text MS Berg; Unpublished

　　　　　　　　　　　　　　　[letterhead: Capel House]
　　　　　　　　　　　　　　　　　　16 Aug[t] '17
Dear Sir

　　Thanks for your friendly and cheering letter.

　　Yesterday the American troops on the march had a great reception in London.[4] I hope they understood that the London crowd doesn't get into

---

[1] Cadet forces had become a feature of public-school life well before the war. School contingents were attached to army regiments, such as the West Kent Yeomanry.

[2] See the annotation to the letter of 17 June.

[3] John Cromwell the American producer: see the letter to him of 7 June 1918. Hastings and Pinker were negotiating with him for an American run of *Victory*, which war-time conditions were to make impossible.

[4] In two long columns headed '"Old Glory" in London', *The Times* (16 August, p. 7) reported on the grand parade 'behind the flag of the great Republic' from Waterloo Station to Wellington Barracks. Although the plans for the march had been announced only two days previously, there was a large turnout of spectators. At Buckingham Palace, just before the contingent

such a state more than once in a century perhaps. I was immensely impressed. Your men looked extremely fine and wonderfully fit. A great day in London history and the people really *felt* that it was great.

Thanks ever so much for the promised tile. I shall frame it for my study (when I get one). For goodness' sake keep the vase back! Keep it back till the first day of the preliminary armistice – no longer. For I confess that I am extremely impatient to behold it.

I don't, really, feel competent to suggest a picture. It's the static quality of a grouping that disconcerts my imagination. When writing I visualise the successive scenes as always in motion – a flow of closely linked effects;[1] so that when I attempt to arrest them in my mind at any given moment the first thought is always: that's no good! And I get discouraged. I would like however to know that Alice Jacobus[2] may get a chance. Either the introduction scene ("This is Alice") or the last (either "I love nothing" or the kiss on the forehead). But if so pray see to it that the young captain wears the white suit (tunic) of the tropics and nothing with brass buttons on it.

But – that's no good.

The boy (three lines this morning) is well. A month ago he had 3 days' leave in Paris where he was introduced to some American ladies, amongst others to Miss Root. Americans are awfully nice to him. Last night Red Cross trains were passing Ashford every half hour with wounded from Flanders. And so it goes on. Believe me

cordially and gratefully yours

Joseph Conrad.

reached the barracks, 'One band played "The Long, Long Trail", and the crowd took up the refrain in great voice, helping the strains of the brass with a fine volume of sound. When the Stars and Stripes came past, the King and all the military officers . . . paid the proper compliments.' There had been an even warmer welcome in Paris on 4 July. Because of submarine attacks, ferrying US troops across the Atlantic proved very difficult; at the time of the London parade, only about 14,000 US troops had reached Europe. Nevertheless, their presence gave promise of multitudes to come. Despite earlier plans to hold these soldiers in reserve until the summer of 1918, they went into action for the first time on 2 November (Martin Gilbert, *The First World War* (New York: Henry Holt, 1994), pp. 341–2, 360, 372–3).

[1] Cf. Ford's remarks on collaborating with Conrad: 'In writing a novel we agreed that every word set on paper . . . must carry the story forward and, that as the story progressed, the story must be carried forward faster and faster and with more and more intensity. That is called *progression d'effet*, words for which there is no English equivalent' (*Joseph Conrad: A Personal Remembrance* (Duckworth, 1924), p. 210).

[2] From 'A Smile of Fortune': cf. the letter of 20 April where Conrad asks Howe to be sure to include her.

To John Rothenstein
Text MS Rothenstein; *Summer's Lease* 43

[letterhead: Capel House]
28 Augst '17

My dear John.[1]

Thanks for your charming idea to write me about Victory. I am very pleased to hear that you like the book. I have a little weakness for it myself. Still nicer, if possible, are your friendly references to Borys. I hope the time will come soon when you'll be able to renew your acquaintance and lay the foundation of a friendship which will carry on in the future the warm affection and the great regard I have for your Father. We had news from B. lately. He is on the Ypres section of the front and very busy. We have heard he is going to be promoted lieutenant in a few days, which, no doubt, please[s] him, after 2 years of active service. Pray give our love to your Mother and Father.

Yours affectio^ly

J. Conrad

To E. L. Grant Watson
Text MS Wright; Unpublished

Capel House
Nr Ashford
Kent
29 Aug. '17

Dear Mr Grant Watson.[2]

Pardon the long delay. I only secured lately not so much the leisure as the proper freedom of mind, to read through and get on terms with your novel.[3] Not that the getting on terms was a difficult matter. The book is captivating enough, in all conscience, as a piece of writing and of course as a story too. I thank you heartily both for the pleasure it has given me and for the kind thought of sending me a copy.

---

[1] John Knewstub Maurice Rothenstein (1901–92), the son of Alice and Will, was one of Borys Conrad's boyhood friends. Rothenstein became an authority on modern British painting and was director of the Tate Gallery from 1938 to 1964. His publications include the three-volume *Modern English Painters* (1952–73) and an autobiography in three parts: *Summer's Lease* (1965), *Brave Day, Hideous Night* (1966), and *Time's Thievish Progress* (1970).

[2] Elliot Lovegood Grant Watson (1885–1970) took a first in natural sciences at Cambridge. In 1910–11, he joined a scientific expedition to north-western Australia. Thereafter he devoted himself to writing essays, fiction, and studies of natural history.

[3] *The Mainland* (Duckworth, 1917), a *Bildungsroman* whose hero experiences life in the Australian bush as a farmer, miner, and pearl-fisher.

Progress – or I should say development – is very visible in these pages. The theme has been treated fairly often lately; but I won't quarrel with you for that since you have given it its own particular colouring in a masterly manner. As to the depth I won't say anything about it just now because it is a ticklish subject at the best of times and especially so at the present time.[1] And the theory that the less deep you go the nearer you remain to "reality" may have some truth in it (amongst other obvious advantages). However the pages have been felt – that's obvious – before they were written, and that is enough to secure for them my respect and sympathy. My best wishes for health and good work and all the happiness that may flow from these things.

Yours

Joseph Conrad

To J. B. Pinker
Text MS Berg; Unpublished

[letterhead: Capel House]

Thursday [30 August 1917][2]

My dear Pinker

I am sending you this type so as not to have both MS and type in the same house for fear of accidents – as with End of the Tether years ago.[3] The set is not corr*ed* at all and generally not fit to be seen.

I am working. Don't be vexed with me for the slowness. I am thankful to do even that much. At any rate what I do write remains. It is good enough in every sense.

I have authorised Doubleday to print the new prefaces in his Am. editions of Youth and Jim. He asked me.

Strangely enough a letter from B[orys] tells us of a possible leave in a fortnight. I hope it will come off as he expects; but considering that he is on the Ypres sector I must say I am surprised.[4]

I'll be writing you early next week again.

Yours ever

J. C.

---

[1] In war-time, when aesthetic arguments might be thought superfluous? At a time of literary debate over the value and nature of realism? Conrad had just been reading the essay by a pseudonymous prisoner of war on 'The Tendency of English Fiction in 1917'.
[2] Dated by Borys's impending leave and the 'sp[ecial] cheque', due in September.
[3] On 23 June 1902, when the serial of 'The End of the Tether' was already under way in *Blackwood's*, an overturned oil lamp flared up, destroying a batch of MS and TS.
[4] The Third Battle of Ypres had begun on 31 July.

PS Please pay the encl^d small bill for B's tobacco.¹ I remind you also of a sp. cheque to Jessie £6 – (quarter) for her Mother, as arranged before.

To John Galsworthy
Text MS Forbes; J-A, 2, 196

[letterhead: Capel House]
3^d Sept '17

Dearest Jack²

This is a gripping piece of writing.³ I got as far as p. 47 before it dawned on me that these were marvellous opening pages. The others are not less so. My dearest Jack they are sheer delight to read from line to line in their ampleness and in their detail, and in the quiet sense of maîtrise (mastery?) that pervades them and is profoundly satisfying to the mind – which never for a moment is left in doubt. And thus there is nothing in the slightest degree to check the feeling which from first to last and all the time is with you – the artist – and therefore with your creation and all its scenes, great and small.

I wonder what the reception will be. This is almost the only one – at any rate the one *big* thing of yours which has no public life. All that is de la vie intime – it may even be called: secret life. And even the only way the outside world acts on her is by the few words overheard at the ball – forcing on as it were the enlightening conversation with the Major. But that already is of the "intime" order. It's very curious. It is a profound study of a personality but I imagine that 99% of the critics won't see its wide connections. The girl will dominate them. Strange that one should think of her always as a girl that one has known in the early days and then hears her story with the utmost sympathy, some sadness and a profound conviction that it had to be.⁴

I could write pages about facts and persons that are all without exception worthy of you and most searchingly lighted up by your particular Galsworthy

---

¹ Among the 1917 files at the Berg is a note to Pinker dated 'Saturday': 'My dear Pinker Many thanks. Herewith the tobacco bill. Your J. C.' Perhaps Conrad forgot to enclose it with this letter.

² John Galsworthy (1867–1933) met Conrad in the *Torrens* in 1893. His early work was tentative, but in 1932 he won a Nobel Prize (an honour denied his friend) for his fiction and his plays. Like the Forsytes, his family was well supplied with money, and he helped Conrad over many years with gifts and loans as well as constant encouragement.

³ Galsworthy's *Beyond*, a newly published novel of almost 500 pages, dedicated to Thomas Hardy.

⁴ The novel concerns the intense attachment of Major Charles Winton to his motherless daughter 'Gyp', and the challenge to that attachment when Gyp finds an 'unsuitable' lover.

rays. Aren't they good! The Major is absolutely wonderful. However You must trust my word that I haven't missed anything. Très fort tout ça. I haven't been so delighted for I don't know how long. Our dear love to you both

Ever Yours

J. Conrad.

PS I've seen your most charming article on the French in the Fortnightly.[1]

To Sir Sidney Colvin
Text Private collection; Unpublished

[letterhead: Capel House]

8 Sepr 17

My dear Colvin.

We shall be delighted to have you on the 17th. Jessie suffers now from a slight bronchitis, but she is improving already and shall be quite her own self by then.

I suppose I shall have an autographed Keats.[2] The moment approaches and I am looking forward with impatience to a copy "fresh from the oven".

Our love to Lady Colvin and yourself

Tout à Vous

J. C.

PS Expecting B[orys] on leave before many days

To J. B. Pinker
Text MS Berg; Unpublished

[letterhead: Capel House]

[13 September 1917][3]

My dear Pinker.

The news of Eric's decoration[4] must have warmed your hearts your wife and yours. And your friends are delighted that an opportunity did come to a young man who (no one who knew him had any doubt) knew how to seize it

---

[1] 'France, 1916–1917: An Impression' in the September number of the *Fortnightly Review*, reprinted in *Another Sheaf* (1919).
[2] Colvin's *John Keats: His Life and Poetry, His Friends, Critics and After-fame* (Macmillan, 1917).
[3] The first of a sequence from the time of Borys's home leave, 13–24 September. Undated or partially dated letters within the sequence establish the order; references to the AUP interview and the *TLS* review of *Youth* in explicitly dated correspondence confirm the period.
[4] Eric Pinker had won the Military Cross, a high honour for junior officers who carried out 'distinguished and meritorious services in battle'. Since the press did not announce the award until the 27th, the Pinkers must have been informed in advance.

with honour. All luck to him – and may his head grow peacefully grey above that bit of ribbon and that bit of metal that are so little and mean so much. Please send him a hearty hand-clasp from me.

Ever affct^{ly} yours

Joseph Conrad.

PS I only asked about Irving because of the other play's suggestion.[1] I am not surprised. Neither do I worry. It's all safe in your hands.

I had to give an interview to an Am. United Press man. I enclose it and hope I haven't committed an indiscretion in your sight.

This moment wire from B[orys] arriving Ashford 4. 30.

To J. B. Pinker

Text MS Berg; Unpublished

[letterhead: Capel House]

Thursday. [13 September 1917][2]

My dear Pinker.

Please let my boy telephone from your office to his colonel (that was); and give him five pounds in my name.

I am a bit worried about Jessie's bronchitis which seems to have taken hold.

Ever Yours

J. Conrad.

To John Galsworthy

Text MS Forbes; Unpublished

[letterhead: Capel House]

Friday [14 September 1917][3]

My dearest Jack.

Thanks for your good letter. I am looking forward to the Five Tales proofs[4] with the greatest possible curiosity.

Yes my dear fellow. Do let us see each other soon. Jessie is still kept indoors with her bronchitis – which was very nasty indeed. B[orys]'s arrival yesterday

---

[1] A suggestion of mounting another play at the Savoy before *Victory*? Or the suggestion of another collaboration with Hastings?

[2] The second letter of this date, preparing for Borys's visit to town on the 14th. On reaching England, he would have travelled directly from Dover or Folkestone to Ashford rather than going via London.

[3] The second day of Borys's visit.   [4] Heinemann published *Five Tales* in 1918.

on 10 days' leave bucked her up no end. But I shudder when I think of his departure. He's gone up today to dine with his C. O. Col: Lithgow,[1] an invitation which he could not refuse and indeed did not want to, as there seems to be a great affection between those two. They had many close shaves together. But from to-morrow we shall have him to ourselves in this rural solitude.

I am sending this to your town address.[2] I understand my dear Jack the longing for the scenes of your youth.

With our dear love to you both

Yours ever

J. Conrad.

To J. B. Pinker
Text MS Berg; Unpublished

[letterhead: Capel House]
15 Sept. '17.[3]

My dear Pinker.

I thought that was their idea; and as I told you at the time I don't want to do anything of the kind.[4] Moreover your judgment in the matter is absolutely right. Whatever price you would get for it would not make up for the interruption. It's altogether my feeling. I ought to stick to the desk and keep hold of my thoughts for dear life.

I return the Otis Wood letter, as requested.

There was no time to communicate with you about the interview – so I accorded it as a matter of policy. A quite inoffensive young fellow came, and in due course sent me his stuff. I wrote to him most politely praising him up, but pointing out that in this matter shades of expression were very important and hoping he would not be offended if [I] sent him a draft-interview based on his suggestions. So what you have read is J. C. interviewed by J. C. every word of it. The dear child thanked me effusively and confessed artlessly – "it's much better than anything I could have done".

[1] James Lithgow (1888–1952; baronet, 1925) came from one of the great Clydeside shipping families. During his military service in France, he was mentioned in despatches. Invalided out in 1916, he was appointed Director of Merchant Shipbuilding, Admiralty, a position he held until 1919. Returning to Scotland, he became Chairman of the Board, Lithgows, Ltd, and later served as the President of the Federation of British Industries.
[2] The Galsworthys divided their time between London and Devon.
[3] Changed by Conrad from 'August'.
[4] On 24 July, the Otis Wood Newspaper Syndicate had asked Conrad his price for four 2,000-word articles on the US Navy (TS Berg).

So everybody is pleased – and I consider myself now an interviewer of genius.

Yours ever

J Conrad.

PS. Jessie seems to be getting over the beastly bronch: at last.

To Christopher Sandeman

Text J-A, 2, 196

Capel House

15 Sept., 1917.

My dear Sandeman,

I don't know what you think of me by now. The fact, however, is, for what it is worth, that for weeks on end I could not use my right hand; and my mentality has grown so feeble that the simple idea of asking my wife to drop you a line has never occurred to me. Perhaps you thought I was dead? I am forwarding you this proof to the contrary with mixed feelings. This is as near as I dare to give you a hint of them.

Je me demande what on earth one can write to a friend in these times? A speechless stare would about meet the situation, but one can't send that in a letter. And words somehow die on one's lips. Well, at any rate, I can tell you that I rejoice to know that your health is improving, or at least tending that way. I am no longer elastic; so, though I can use my hand, I remain flattened out as before. I can't even produce a bitter smile at the Russian antics;[1] and as to the phraseology of the Press, that has ceased to amuse me a long time ago. My store of cynicism is exhausted. The democratic bawlings of our statesmen at Mme Germania[2] would be dull enough, if history were a comic libretto. But one somehow can't look at it in that way – tho' I believe, in the Victorian Age, a literary man of liberal conditions wrote a comic History of England.[3] That was in the days of the Manchester School;[4] but the days through which we live would make Stupidity itself pause.

Do send me a line of forgiveness with news of your health.

---

[1] The most recent development was the arrest of the Commander-in-Chief of Russian forces, General Lavr Georgiyevich Kornilov (1870–1918), on charges of attempting a coup in Petrograd. The charges originated with his by now bitter opponent Aleksandr Feodorovitch Kerensky (1881–1970), head of the Provisional Government.

[2] The allegorical figure ubiquitous on postage stamps and medals of the period.

[3] *The Comic History of England* by the lawyer and humorist Gilbert Abbot à Beckett (1811–56) with illustrations by John Leech (1817–64), published by *Punch* in 1847.

[4] An appropriately loose grouping of *laissez-faire* economists and politicians associated with that booming industrial and commercial city: the most notable among them were Richard Cobden

To J. B. Pinker

Text MS Berg; Unpublished

[letterhead: Capel House]

20 Sept '17

My dear Pinker

John is off to school today. Will you please send ch. for £16-16-0 to A. S. Lamprey Esqre.

Ashford Grammar School[1]

Ashford Kent

I can hardly yet use my hand.

Ever Yours

J. Conrad

To J. B. Pinker

Text MS Berg; Unpublished

[letterhead: Capel House]

Friday. [21 or 28 September? 1917][2]

My dear Pinker

Thanks for letter and all the cheques. Give my hearty greetings to Eric – and all good luck to him. I shall certainly want to hear when I see you all about his adventures and his views.

No more to-day.

Ever Yours

J. Conrad.

To J. B. Pinker

Text MS Berg; Unpublished

[letterhead: Capel House]

Saturday [22 September 1917][3]

Dear Pinker

B[orys] having undertaken to get a lot of things for the A[rtillery] Park's theatrical troupe finds himself short of cash and has asked me to lend him

---

(1804–65) and John Bright (1811–89). One of their major achievements was the repeal of the Corn Laws in 1846.

[1] Arthur Sydney Lamprey was Headmaster.

[2] Evidently Pinker's son had been granted home leave: by [7 October] he had gone back to the Front.

[3] In the last few days of Borys's leave.

£15. Please do that for him. He will be passing through town on Monday on the way to front and will call at about 12.30.

Yours ever

J. Conrad.

Youth's reception also good. Times a column.[1] Other papers taking notice too. It's a tonic. Hand better.

To J. B. Pinker
Text MS Berg; Unpublished

[letterhead: Capel House]
27 Sept 17.

My dear Pinker.

I've just had a set of Nostromo proofs. Personally I've been glad to see them. I suppose you've had your say as to the advisability of publishing so soon after Youth.

I am attending to the proofs, and I rather like it. Jolly good stuff. But I had a bad time writing it. And it was your first big contract for me. I shall never forget how pleased you looked getting out of the hansom on your return from seeing Harvey.[2] It was like laying the first stone. —

Am sorry to say Jessie has to stop in bed and have ice treatment for her knee for a few days. I am much better, as you can see from the handwriting, and am working.

You will let me know if anything is done with Irving. Mere curiosity. I am not worrying about *that*. It isn't my own pidgin.[3]

Yours ever

J Conrad.

---

[1] Virginia Woolf's unsigned review is generally eulogistic, celebrating Conrad and Hardy as the period's major figures. *Youth* shows 'Mr Conrad at his best . . . It has an extraordinary freshness and romance. It is not so subtle or so psychological as the later mood' (*TLS*, 20 September, p. 451).

[2] George Brinton McClellan Harvey (1864–1928), President of Harper & Brothers from 1901 to 1915, published *Nostromo* on both sides of the Atlantic. The meeting would have been in May 1903.

[3] 'It's none of my business': the *OED* defines 'pidgin' as 'A Chinese corruption of Eng. *business*, used widely for any action, occupation, or affair'.

To Roman Dmowski
Text Giertych

[letterhead: Capel House]
1st October, 1917

My dear Sir.[1]

Thank you very much for sending me your contribution towards the solution of the great problem. I would have written before only all the last fortnight I was deprived of the use of my right hand.

Your arguments and your conclusions seem to me absolutely incontrovertible.[2] I trust your words won't fall into deaf ears. The scrupulous fairness of your Polish Scheme and the force of your reasoning should secure assent in any sphere competent to appreciate a statesmanlike proposition.

Believe me

very faithfully yours
Joseph Conrad

Problems of Central and Eastern Europe

Dr. Roman Dmowski

---

[1] Roman Dmowski (1864–1939), a prominent Polish nationalist writer and politician, had just contributed a chapter to *Russian Realities and Problems*, ed. J. D. Duff (Cambridge University Press, 1917). His brief, privately printed statement on *Problems of Central and Eastern Europe* also appeared in 1917. His first book, published in 1903, was *Myśli nowoczesnego Polaka* (*Thoughts of a Modern Pole*). According to Dmowksi, the modern Pole, while embracing Polish tradition, should be suspicious of inherited privilege – and of such Polish 'outsiders' as Jews and Orthodox or Uniate Ukrainians. Before the war, Dmowski led the National Democratic Party in the Russian Duma, where he argued for Polish independence within a Pan-Slavic context; in Warsaw, he organised boycotts of Jewish businesses. Converting to the cause of full independence during the war, he founded the Polish National Committee, which moved from Lausanne to Paris in 1917. Along with Paderweski, Dmowski represented Poland at the Paris Peace Conference and thus was a signatory to the Treaty of Versailles. He was briefly Foreign Minister in 1923.

[2] In *Problems of Central and Eastern Europe*, Dmowski argues that the chief problem is German imperialism. Once Germany is defeated (with the aid of Polish volunteers), a new Poland can emerge: 'A fundamental reconstruction of Europe, which would reduce German power to the natural limits of the German race . . . is indispensable to the re-establishment of European equilibrium' (p. 14). By no means all Poles agreed; followers of his bitter enemy Marshal Józef Piłsudski (1867–1935), for example, considered Russia at least as great a threat.

To Edith Wharton
Text MS Yale; Karl

[letterhead: Capel House]
1 Oct 17.

Dear Mrs Wharton.[1]

I couldn't write before because I was disabled in my right hand. An accident that occurs often, alas!

Many thanks for thinking of me. You can not guess how your gracieuseté has been comforting to me in these hard times. On the very morning the book arrived[2] our eldest boy went away after the usual 10 days' leave from the front. C'est un très brave garçon who tho' he's only nineteen understands his father in a heart-ensnaring way. Somehow the parting was even harder than the time before. Then on returning from the Rway station I saw the summer-blue book on my table.

The first 60 pages might well have been written with one of these quill-feathers one finds lying on some quiet field on a hot brooding summer day. The others too – du reste. But I am not thinking of anything so gross as a goose-quill. It is Chamfort[3] (I think) who says that Racine wrote "avec une plume de tourterelle". I suppose that is the quill-feather *you* found before beginning to write *Summer*. C'est un oiseau qui a la voix douce et une ame passion[n]ée.[4]

You may imagine with what interest I followed step by step your Charity with her bewildered wilfulness and her innate generosity. You know I once attempted too to deal with an untutored soul[5] and in comparison with your maîtrise it seems to me the clumsiest thing in the world – even allowing for the difference of characters. As to old Royall il est immense.[6]

---

[1] Among the novels already published by Edith Newbold Wharton (née Jones, 1862–1937) were *The House of Mirth* (1905), *Ethan Frome* (1911), and *The Custom of the Country* (1913). Among the work to come would be *The Age of Innocence* (1920) and her autobiography, *A Backward Glance* (1934). In 1910, she had gone to live in France for good. During the war, she worked on behalf of refugees, and included Conrad's 'Poland Revisited' in her fund-raising anthology *The Book of the Homeless* (1915).

[2] Wharton's *Summer* (1917), published in Britain by Macmillan.

[3] The playwright and aphorist Nicolas-Sébastien-Roch Chamfort (1741–94).

[4] Racine was said to have written 'with the quill of a turtle-dove'; the turtle-dove is 'A bird with a soft voice and a passionate soul'.

[5] Lena? Flora de Barral? Amy Foster? Charity, the heroine of *Summer*, leaves her backwoods family to live with relations in a genteel country town.

[6] 'Superb'.

But a piece of writing like Summer is not to be talked about in that way. That book, no matter where one opens it presents itself en beauté – toujours en beauté. And everything is in that; every "name" one wants to look for in it – is in that.

Pardon me for inflicting on you so much of this unlovely scrawl. But before I end I must tell You that I've always loved your rhythms so very fine, distinct and subtle. On opening the book I let myself be carried away by them and I must tell you in all sincerity that it wasn't difficult even under the circumstances. Truly it was a great delight.

Believe me, dear Mrs Wharton,

always your very faithful admirer and
servant

Joseph Conrad.

To J. B. Pinker
Text MS Berg; Unpublished

[Capel House]
2ᵈ Oct 17.

My dear Pinker

Please pay in something (say £15) to my accᵗ.

Yesterday Dr. Campbell came in from Salisbury[1] and I had to pay 6 for the petrol he picked up in Ash[ford]. Of course he will pay me back but meantime the che: must be met.

I am much exercised by the *Note* to Nostromo. I assume you wish this book to have one? I myself feel it wouldn't be fair to let it go out without. And yet it's awfully difficult to decide what to say about a work (as N is) of pure imaginative invention.

I am getting worried about Jessie. Everything points to the disease of the bone having set in. I don't know how long she will have to remain in bed. In herself she's well. Without John the house is desolate and he himself doesn't seem to be very happy. We've got to live all that down.

Ever affˡʸ yours
J Conrad.

---

[1] Probably Kenneth Campbell, a friend who sometimes gave Conrad professional advice; he was an eye specialist currently serving with the Royal Army Medical Corps in camp near Salisbury. See the letter to him of 21 June 1919.

To J. B. Pinker

Text MS Berg; Unpublished

[Capel House]

Thursday [4 October 1917][1]

My dear Pinker.

To-morrow (Friday) I'll send you preface to Nostromo – the best that's in me in that way – by the morning train. Please give instructions for it being typed (about 1200 words) and returned to me for correction at once (one copy).

I'll send that back on Monday for clean copies (two) one for Dent and one for Am: if D[oubleday] & P[age] want it.

I enclose here a letter from Doubleday. What does he mean by moaning about Dent? What has he to do with it? Has he been thinking of getting out still another cheap edition? There are two now permanently. The buckram cover and the "Deep Sea" in leather. I think D[oubleday] wants watching, so that we should get *all* the share that is our due.[2]

Ever Yours

J. Conrad.

To J. B. Pinker

Text MS Berg; Unpublished

[letterhead: Capel House]

Sunday Night [7 October 1917][3]

My dear Pinker.

Jessie typed the thing in bed – I wrought on it with the pen – and so you may have *two* clean copies made of it straight away. (about 2000 w.)

When done please glance at the thing. I think that I give nothing away in it, and that it will not hurt the interest as a *note*. But *at need* it could be printed as a post-script.[4] Your impression ought to settle the point.

When I think that I owe to you this revival, this second chance for my Poor Nostromo I feel more than ever that what you've done for me cannot be reckoned up fairly either in figures – or in adequate words.

---

[1] Written on the verso of Doubleday to Conrad, 17 September, and continuing the agenda of 2 October.

[2] After congratulating Conrad on the quality of the Author's Note to *Youth*, Doubleday wrote: 'I deeply regret that we cannot get out the complete edition. I see Mr. Dent's imprint on this proof – I had hoped that we might do it with him, printing his copies in this country. We have already got a format which I understand is satisfactory to you. But I will cease from bothering you on this subject.' In the margin of this paragraph, Conrad wrote: 'Does he muddle it with the *de Luxe*? Do write to the blighter for me. J.C.'

[3] Continuing the sequence of letters about the new edition of *Nostromo*.

[4] The Author's Note appears among the preliminaries, dated October 1917.

What I said of Doubleday was in regard to his trying to play sudden tricks with new editions without warning. You can't suppose surely that I doubted your vigilance over the whole lot of them.

I felt for you, seeing Eric off. It's rather awful. One lives in hope but with set teeth all the time. Did I tell you that B[orys] got his lieutenancy a week ago?

I should like to see you.

Yours ever aff[ty]

J. Conrad

To Hugh R. Dent
Text MS Berg; Unpublished

[letterhead: Capel House]
Monday. [8 October 1917][1]

Dear M[r] Dent.

Herewith the pages: 353–432.

The beginning of Chap. VIII got into the 1st Ed[on] without being corr[d] and pruned by me at the time.[2] The 1st Ed[on] was most unsatisfactory. You'll find several passages deleted bodily. Pray have all that carried out even if it costs some trouble. For they are really superfluous and this edition of Nostromo (the Cinderella of all my books) may even be reviewed as a new book.

The *Note* will be over 2000 words long. P[inker] has the MS and will send you a typed copy without loss of time. Send me proof of it early to be thought over a little.

Yours sincerely

Joseph Conrad.

Hugh Dent Esq[re].

To J. B. Pinker
Text MS Berg; Unpublished

[Capel House]
Tuesday. [9 October 1917][3]

My dear Pinker.

I have today finished with the proofs of *N* which are going to Dent by this post.

Will you please pay a little into Jessie's acc[t] – say 15, and settle this bill for me?

---

[1] Another letter in the *Nostromo* sequence.   [2] Conrad was unwell.
[3] The proofs arrived on that day: Dent to Conrad, 9 October (TS carbon, Berg).

As to Jessie it is absolutely necessary that she should be seen by somebody. For the knee to get into that state while she was actually in bed with bronchitis is a sign of some serious mischief. As I can not shove her easily to town I have accepted the suggestion of our doctor who is a friend of Wilfrid* Trotter – the surgeon[1] – and who proposes to ask him to come and see Jessie the very next time he comes to stay with him in Ashford, which he does fairly often. Perhaps next week.

I am anxious. She just can stand and no more and it doesn't seem to improve in the least. It has never been like this since the operation.[2] After the ice treatment the pain has subsided but that's all. Otherwise her health and spirits are good.

John has settled down after two weeks at school and no doubt will be as much of a monkey there as he was at home. I am working. *N* interrupted me a little of course. The first edition was full of misprints (Dent set up from it) the others came on top of that – so it took some "reading". Besides I went over the text (cutting out here and there and altering passages) because I hope it will be "noticed" almost as a new work – who knows? I have been cheered up and stimulated greatly. Quite a mental change.

Ever Yours

Joseph Conrad.

To J. B. Pinker
Text MS Berg; Unpublished

[letterhead: Capel House]
Wednesday. [10 October 1917][3]

My dear Pinker.

Herewith copy for D[oubleday] P[age] and I hope they will make good (business) use of it. I am glad you approve of it as a preface. I feared I had given away too much of the inside, though Jessie thought not.

My dear fellow I'll be most happy to come – perhaps on a Friday so as to get back home in good time for the Sunday. John coming on Fri: evening would relieve me with Jessie. It's awfully dull for her in that low darkish room; and there's nobody here but Lady Millais[4] likely to call on her, as most

[1] Wilfred Trotter, surgeon and Lecturer in Principles and Practice of Surgery at University College Hospital, London.

[2] In November 1904. She had been suffering from a displaced cartilage in her knee for fourteen years. The operation brought some relief, but the knee continued to afflict her for the rest of her life.

[3] Dated by allusions to Dent's letter of the 9th, the Author's Note to *Nostromo*, and the forthcoming visit to Pinker's country house, 25–6 October.

[4] Jessie Conrad's friend and neighbour Lady Millais, daughter-in-law of the painter Sir John Everett Millais. See the letter to her of 28 January 1918.

people we know are gone. Then there is still the surgeon business. I should like to know on what date he may be down in our neighbourhood, before I suggest a day for you to see whether it would be convenient for Mrs Pinker. By that time I'll have also, I hope, my hand out of cotton-wool. I am using it in bandages yet and I don't like to exhibit myself in that state. 'Tisn't pretty.

I am sending you also a letter I had from the Ven[erable] Dent. Do you know anything of the book whose advent stirs his heavy bosom with fear?[1]

Can't the Esthetic Israelite[2] be induced to do a republication of the Nigger (with the suppr^{ed} preface) and of Typhoon with an Author's note? But perhaps it would not be worthwhile —

B. Macdonald Hastings (who is in Hastings) has applied for leave to lunch here on Saturday. I'll throw into his dead-level brain the grain of a play which I have had in my mind for some time. That is if I observe him in a receptive mood. I suppose it will be safe? He seems "indifferent honest" as Shakespeare says.[3]

Thanks for your good words to us, and for your message to the boy which I'll send on to him at once. He's been promoted under the "Winston Scheme". A whole batch of them, bosom friends from Salisbury Plain days,[4] got their second pip together after 2 years' service.

Ever afftely yours
Joseph Conrad.

To J. B. Pinker
Text MS Berg; Unpublished

[letterhead: Capel House]
Friday. [12 or 19 October? 1917][5]

My dear Pinker.

Thanks for letter with the startling news of your intention to play another joke on Dent. I will do my best to help.

---

[1] Because Murray was going to publish an American novel with a similar background, Dent wanted to hasten publication of the new edition of *Nostromo* (Dent to Conrad, 9 October, TS carbon, Berg).

[2] Conrad laboured under the curious delusion that all publishers were Jewish. The specific reference here is to William Heinemann, who had published *The Nigger* and *Typhoon and Other Stories*.

[3] *Hamlet* 3.1.125.

[4] Long a training ground for soldiers. Having just returned from commanding a battalion at the Front to become Minister of Munitions, Winston Churchill (1874–1965) was alert to the frustrations of serving officers.

[5] Written on a full sheet of watermarked stationery and from the 1917 files at the Berg. Several references suggest a tentative dating to the middle of October: the possible collaboration with Hastings, the posting of copy to the United States, and John's elation, perhaps on account of a success at his new school. The American edition of *The Shadow-Line* had appeared at the end of April.

Johns head, just now, is too big for *any* hat.

G Barker's opinion as to my playwriting chance is interesting.[1] I do think of it. However I don't know – if it were a question of assistance I would just as soon let in Hastings who's more of an average man and a good stage hand. He would "mec[h]anise" a play for me with neatness and dispatch and probably would be easier to manage

If *Victory* goes at all it will give me a great impulse.

Ever aff[ly] yours

J. Conrad.

P. S. Yes. Aren't the misprints in Am. editions exasperating! I didn't like to worry you with it before but since you feel like this will you my dear fellow arrange (if at all possible) that the proofs that go to US (for setting up) are the "revise" English proofs; and that D. Page & C[o] send me a set of proofs to look over. The S. Line has some horrible misprints and was obviously set up from first proof.

To J. B. Pinker

Text MS Berg; Unpublished

[letterhead: Capel House]

Sunday. [14 October 1917][2]

My dear Pinker.

I am giving you no peace but you must forgive me. The present request is whether you would be good enough to telephone from your office for a pair of crutches for Jessie. I ask you instead of writing direct because in this war-time one firm may not be able to take the order and another may. It'll save time.

The first people to try would be Arnold and Sons.[3] But I put all the particulars on a separate piece of paper which you can give to Miss Allen for the actual inquiries.

M. H[astings] spent a whole afternoon here. I hinted casually at the play-subject and he became so keenly interested that we talked of nothing else for $3\frac{1}{2}$ hours on end. We became lost to the world and (pray don't faint) after agreeing on the march of the action and on the character of the personages (10 in all) we settled the first act, which H promised to send me roughly written, together with the complete scenario of the whole, in about a fortnight.

---

[1] Harley Granville-Barker (1877–1946), playwright, actor, director, and critic, certainly a more formidable presence than Hastings.

[2] Hastings came to lunch on Saturday the 13th.   [3] In the City, at 5 & 6 Giltspur Street.

He said: I want to go to work at once under a fresh impression. It can't do us any harm to have a play ready. – So far he is right. The idea is that he will write on folded sheets so that I have half the space for modifying the dialogue which must be Conradesque.

He didn't seem to think me impracticable – quite the contrary. My ideas appeared to him new but struck him as good – I mean in details. The whole idea of the play is wholly mine and that he has wholly accepted from the first. So that point is beyond question. Subject: Faked old Master. Scene Italy. People *all* English (including one Jew). Four women. Six men. Stage setting: the big drawing-room and the terrace outside it in an old Italian Palazzo in the hills, near Sienna*.

I don't think there's any risk with M. H. really. And anyway it wouldn't be great. It isn't any new discovery in the way of a plot and has no value in itself.

H told me (but perhaps you know it?) that C[romwell] means to try V[ictory] in Atlantic City first, then maybe in a few other places before bringing it to N. Y. H regrets that neither of us can go over to assist with the actual production. He really tried to sound me on the subject, I believe.

Ever Yours

J. Conrad.

To B. Macdonald Hastings
Text MS Colgate; Unpublished

[letterhead: Capel House]
[mid October 1917][1]

My dear Hastings.

It was a great pleasure to have you here and I am glad to hear that you have been lastingly interested in our conversation.

I too have been thinking about it and it strikes me that there will *have to be* a scene (I don't see it) some scene, *the scene* which everybody will want to go and see. We will have to invent it, contrive it, discover it – anyway get it in somehow, extract it from the subject, which in itself has a fine level of romantic, dramatic, tender and even comic possibilities – but it is a level. And we may even make it a pretty high level by our united efforts (personally that sort of excellence would please me most) but the question is: will it be enough for the public?

You would know best.

I want also to ask you before you take the plunge into collaboration to read once more with special attention that one act play of mine.[2] And this for the

---

[1] Soon after Hastings's visit on the 13th.   [2] *One Day More.*

reason that it will give you the fullest information both as to my temperament and my principle of technique (as apart from stage-craft). And after all you may just as well know. We are going to work together. The play will have to be a blend of our distinct mentalities. I shall have no doubt in the course of our colla^{on} to stand up for myself. And that little one act will show You (if you care to know) the inner "nature of the beast" with whom (or which) you'll have to deal.

I beg to point out for instance that it contains nothing like the proportion of *mere chatter* that, say, *Ghosts* [does]. Of course the subject is bigger than most that Papa Ibsen[1] ever tried. Then the exposition goes together with the action from the very first. The psychological note of the relation between father and daughter is struck in a dozen "replicas" so that only a mentally deaf person could fail to hear it. The whole secret (fact and psychology) of the girl's friendship with the crazy man next door is absolutely disclosed in one short scene, and the dramatic situation established, clearly enough for the meanest understanding, in readiness for the "denouement" between the girl and the sailor, so that every word that passes between them is full of dramatic significance – for the spectators. And all the characteristics of the work (not the play as play) are the outcome of my mental attitude as prompted by my temperament. I'll be always trying for the same things (I couldn't help myself) in a dramatic rendering of any given subject.

As you are the "tied" man of us two, I shall be always ready to run over for a talk when you feel that it would help you. Kindest regards from us both

Yours

J. Conrad

To J. B. Pinker
Text MS Berg; Unpublished

[letterhead: Capel House]
Wed. [17 October 1917][2]

Dear Pinker

I am so sorry to keep on worrying. Allen & Hanbury[3] sent crutches only 38 in long instead of <u>forty</u>-eight – which I am sending back of course.

---

[1] The 'sacrosanct Ibsen, of whom like Mrs Verloc of Ossipon, I prefer to say nothing' (*Letters*, 3, p. 503).
[2] Conrad ordered the crutches the next day; by Wednesday the 24th, his wife was using them.
[3] The chemists: their surgical-appliance branch was at 48 Wigmore Street, London W1.

Since Arnold & Son seem to have a stock would you ask them to send any pair at once, *providing* they are of such make that they can be shortened here to the exact length.

Yours ever

J. Conrad.

To J. B. Pinker
Text MS Berg; Unpublished

[Capel House]
Thursday [18 October 1917][1]

Dearest Pinker

I have ordered the stock crutches from Arnold.

Pray pay in £5 to my bank to make sure in meeting Arnold's cheque.

Yours ever

J. C.

To John Galsworthy
Text MS Forbes; Marrot 479

[letterhead: Capel House]
21st Oct '17.

Dearest Jack.

The only thing that can be said of the stories[2] without the slightest qualification is that they are. I mean they are from the first line to the last. Tho' I've read them more than once I should like to keep the vol. till we meet either here or in town. Anyway in work like that there is no choice to make. The first is in studio language très fort. The second is apart from the wonderful characterisation of all these people a most entertaining tale in its, what would be called in a play, intrigue. But perhaps the one of the whole lot which appeals to me most is the story of poor M' J. Forsythe's* last coup-de-coeur. There are things in it that for delicacy and insight and tenderness of treatment can't be matched anywhere – out of your own pages.[3]

I am still half paralysed mentally; but what's worst poor Jessie is laid up with something that's happening in that wretched knee. I fear another operation will be necessary. She's more crippled than ever before and a month's rest has done absolutely nothing. – Do drop me a line as to your movements. Our love to you both

Ever Yours

J Conrad.

[1] Again, the crutches.   [2] The proofs of *Five Tales*.
[3] Conrad refers to 'Indian Summer of a Forsyte'.

To J. B. Pinker
Text MS Berg; Unpublished

[Capel House][1]
Wednesday. [24 October 1917][1]

My dear Pinker.

Brownrigg[2] having asked me to lunch with him I suggested to-morrow (Thursday) and shall be in your office between 12 and one. B-gg will 'phone in the course of the morning.

It strikes me that Jessie having her crutches now, and her sister coming tomorrow for the day, and the weather being good that perhaps you would have me for the night tomorrow? We could go down together[3] and go up on Friday morning (still quarrelling violently).

Anyway I'll bring a bag and leave it at Ch^g + on the chance that you'll find it convenient. But pray don't let me be a nuisance to Mrs Pinker who may not like sudden invasions. It's just a suggestion.

Yours ever

J Conrad.

To Edward Garnett
Text MS Indiana; G. 273

[letterhead: Capel House]
27 Oct '17.

My dearest Edward.

I asked Jessie to drop you a line on receipt of the book[4] which was delayed somehow.

I got back home last night. Dead lame, as usual after an excursion. While away I saw the Outlook article[5] which in its prosy way seemed to me good.

Your opening pages are excellent, excellent! I was much delighted with your masterly thrusts at all that thick-headed crowd.[6] As to the rest of the book you know that I *do* know it well. I re-read your prefaces often. You have fused them together with great skill and judgment and I suppose you had to do that; but for my part I regret every word left out – no doubt wisely, but still —

---

[1] Conrad thanked Mrs Pinker for her hospitality on the 28th.   [2] Chief Censor, Royal Navy.
[3] The Pinkers lived about forty minutes by train from London.   [4] *Turgenev: A Study*.
[5] The admiring notice of Garnett's book in the 20 October issue (pp. 382–3) which cites from the preface Conrad's praise of Turgenev's characters: 'human beings, not strange beasts in a menagerie or damned souls knocking themselves about in the darkness of mystical contradictions'. Like Conrad, the reviewer firmly believes in Turgenev's superiority over Dostoevsky.
[6] In his opening chapter, 'Turgenev's Critics and His Detractors', Garnett argues against critics such as Maurice Baring (1874–1945), who complained that Turgenev's vision was too limited and his work not as 'true' as Dostoevsky's.

Do remember us affectionately to your wife. I suppose D[avid][1] doesn't remember those two figures from the immemorial past when he was five or thereabouts and sailed in an (iron?) tub with me. Those were good times! These Ghosts send a warm greeting to him.

Ever yours

J. Conrad

Jessie's love. She's laid up with the knee.

PS B[orys] was here for 10 days about a month ago. He's just got his second star after 18 months at the front. He was recommended for promo[ti]^{on} after the Somme push but these things are slow in coming. He inquired affectionately after you – and so did Hope[2] when he was here last July.

To Mary Pinker
Text MS Morgan; Unpublished

[letterhead: Capel House]
28 Oct 17.

Dear Mrs Pinker.[3]

I hope that the visit to the dentist was not too painful. Hanging about all the morning in the dusty corridors and the grimy dens of the Admiralty I gave you a sympathetic thought more than once.

Lunching with your husband I recovered my spirits, which had sunk very low in that cavern – I mean the Admiralty. He's kindness itself, but next time I shall hire a man to follow me or adopt the practice of the late Dr Hueffer (the father of Ford Madox)[4] who used to go visiting in the country with a tooth-brush and a pair of socks in the pocket of his frock-coat for all luggage. I can't have J. B. P. carrying my bag. And it was no use protesting. He is a masterful personality and indeed when I have to argue with him I prefer to do it by letter, always.

I hope you will get this before the end of the month. I missed the post last night – not by my fault though. My wife thanks you for your kind message and sends her love. She will be radiographed on Monday and the

---

[1] Constance and Edward's son, David (1892–1981), the future novelist.
[2] The 'Director of Companies' and former merchant seaman G. F. W. Hope (1854–1930): Conrad's friendship with him went back to the early 1880s.
[3] Mary Elizabeth Pinker (née Seabrooke, 1862–1945) married J. B. while he was working in Turkey.
[4] Francis Hueffer (1843–89), music critic of *The Times*, and regular contributor to the *Fortnightly Review*. His doctorate was in philology. Conrad knew him only through the stories Ford loved to tell.

Great Man is coming to see her in the course of next week, and give his verdict.

It was delightful to see you and not the oldest but the most helpful in *every* way, and indeed I may say the most devoted of my friends in your home surroundings. With my warm thanks for the charming friendliness of your reception I am, dear Mrs Pinker

always your very faithful and obedient servant

Joseph Conrad.

To J. B. Pinker
Text MS Berg; Unpublished

[letterhead: Capel House]
31 Oct 17.

My dear Pinker.

The surgeon is coming down here on Sat next. (Wilfrid* Trotter). His fee may be merely nominal and in any case will not be very heavy but please send into my acc^t £20, so that I may write him a cheque.

I think there can be no doubt of there being an operation in Dec^{er}. Jessie's idea is to shut up the house completely, to sell the piano (she even is offering it for the price we paid) so that we can get a better instrument next spring; for herself she prefers to go to an hospital (Lond. Univ. Hosp) as paying patient than to go to a nurs^g home. As to me I think I had better take a small flat (2½ gns per week. I see several advertised) where Nellie Lyons can do the housekeeping for me and look after me too in case of gout. There I could work too – which I couldn't do in a hotel.

It will be a matter of fully six weeks before we can return down here. But it neednt be six weeks lost to me. On the contrary I'll feel more at ease when something has been done.

Coming to see you has done me good. I've done some good work since my return. I didn't look yet at the Naval reports.[1] I may do so next Sunday.

I wonder where Eric will be sent *now*! B[orys] is still at the old front.

Ever Yours

J. Conrad.

PS Pray send £25 *to C. Hayward & Son. New Rents* Ashford. Kent.[2] There will be no more of such extravagance in the future.

---

[1] With a view to an article?   [2] Garage proprietors.

To G. Jean-Aubry

Text MS Yale; *L. fr.* 138

[letterhead: Capel House]
3 Nov. '17.

Cher Monsieur.[1]

Je regrette bien vivement de ne pas pouvoir vous prier de venir ici sans plus tarder. Le fait est que ma femme est bien souffrante en ce moment-ci. Il est question d'une operation et nous attendons demain un medecin de Londres qui prononcera.

Peut-être a Votre retour d'Ecosse nous pourrons arranger une entrevue ici ou a Londres. Ce sera un grand plaisir pour moi.

Croyez moi

bien a Vous

Joseph Conrad.

Translation

Dear Sir.

I greatly regret being unable to ask you to come here without further delay. The fact is that my wife is very unwell at present. There may be an operation, and we are expecting a doctor from London tomorrow who will deliver a verdict.

Perhaps on your return from Scotland we could arrange a meeting here or in London. That would give me great pleasure.

Believe me

sincerely yours

Joseph Conrad.

---

[1] Jean-Frédéric-Émile Aubry (1882–1949) wrote as G., Georges, or Gérard Jean-Aubry. Born in Le Havre, he became a friend of many composers, including Debussy and Ravel; both de Falla and Roussel wrote settings of his poems. From 1908 to 1915, he travelled in Europe and Latin America, promoting the cause of contemporary French music. From 1919 to 1930, he edited *The Chesterian*, a music magazine published by a firm of instrument makers. His books on music include *La Musique française d'aujourd'hui* (1916, translated 1919) and *La Musique et les nations* (1922). Conradians know him for *Joseph Conrad in the Congo* (1926), *Joseph Conrad: Life & Letters* (1927), *Lettres françaises* (1929), *The Sea Dreamer: A Definitive Biography* (1957), and numerous French translations of Conrad's works.

To J. B. Pinker
Text MS Berg; Unpublished

[Capel House]
Sunday. 1. pm. [4 November 1917][1]

My dear Pinker.

The great man has been and gone.

Verdict: very serious; but he wishes to have another exam^{on} under Chloroform – (will have to come to town for that) before deciding whether operation is to be done at once or after 3 months' preliminary treatment to reduce the nervous hyper-aest[h]esia[2] of the nerves involved.

All this means amputation. But, as he said to me: no surgeon will take a limb off without making certain beyond all doubt that it *must* be done.

Many thanks for Your letter. I'll write again soon.

Yours ever

J Conrad.

To J. B. Pinker
Text MS Berg; Unpublished

[Capel House]
Wednesday. [7 November 1917][3]

My dear Pinker.

Thanks for your lines. Trotter must get in touch with Dr Tebb who has seen the operation in 1904 and will be able to tell him what B. Clark[e] has done or left undone.[4] Tebb is inspecting certain factories for the Gov^t and it may take some time to catch him; so I don't expect to hear from Trotter till next week.

---

[1] Conrad had told Pinker about the surgeon's impending visit on the 31st.
[2] Over-sensitivity, especially of the skin.   [3] A sequel to Mr Trotter's weekend visit.
[4] Albert Tebb (1863–1943) was a London physician who attended the Conrads, the Hueffers, and the Rothensteins among other literary and artistic families; Bruce Clarke of St Bartholomew's Hospital operated on Jessie Conrad in 1904. The Ministry of Munitions was employing Tebb to investigate the medical hazards of work in ammunition factories; his research was published as 'An Inquiry into the Prevalence and Aetiology of Tuberculosis among Industrial Workers with Special Reference to Female Munition Workers' (1918): see Martin Bock, 'What Has Happened to Poor Tebb?: A Biographical Sketch of Conrad's Physician', *The Conradian*, 23 (1998), 1–18.

His fee here was ten g[uinea]s and for the next exam^{on} in London it won't be so much probably. It will be on another footing I guess since he's going to take up the case either for treatment or for operation. That being so I've written to an agent for letting flats as the treatment will have to be in London. Say 3 months.

Bad as it all is (for Jessie really is having an awful time) I know I wanted a change; and now I shall get it (there is no option) and it'll have its effect for all the attendant worry. The mere knowledge that something is to be done for Jessie has enabled me to get hold of my thoughts and concentrate on the story. It is *really* going on.

B[orys] saw R[etinger] off to Switzerland from Paris – very ill. The Italian business has apparently finished him off. And there is that poor girl with a 6 months' baby in Lausanne. Tragic affair, for as you may imagine peace or no peace the Germans and Austrians won't forgive him in a hurry.[1] A lot of his books (some fine editions) and a piece of furniture or two are stored in London. His old housekeeper has written to us. I shall write once more to him to ask whether he wants us to take them out of warehouse for him or not. I shouldn't like them to be sold for charges without making an effort to save the things.

Jane's leaving Paris (for the xth time) on Friday for London. Friday is a bad day. But if she really manages to get away it will [be] good for Jessie to whom she is very devoted.[2] It will be a fine opportunity to show the devotion for the next 2–3 months won't be a cheerful time, whatever happens. —— I hate to be always asking *you* for money but there is *Miss N. Lyons* Ch: (£5), due now. —— I passed revise of Nostr^{o} preface last Thursday. Are they really going to publish this year?

Ever Yours

J. Conrad.

---

[1] For the views expressed in his *La Pologne et l'équilibre européen* (1916). Retinger would have been demoralised by the massive defeat of the Italian army at Caporetto, north of Trieste, on 24 October. In his letter to Colvin of 12 November, Conrad gave his own opinion of this disaster.

[2] Concerning Jane Anderson, Conrad once wrote to his wife: 'I never cared to see you kissing other women as you know. But this one is different' (*Letters*, 5, p. 663).

To H. L. Mencken
Text Blodgett

Capel House
Orlestone
Nr. Ashford
11 Nov. 17

Dear Mr. Mencken:[1]

Thanks for your friendly note. The book too has arrived[2] – and I need not tell you that the appreciation of a mind so alert, so penetrating and so unprejudiced is a matter of the greatest possible gratification and interest to me, I can't help feeling that you make perhaps too much of what there is in me. But as on one hand I have the greatest respect for your critical faculty (*respect* as apart from admiration which is there too) and on the other I am conscious of absolute sincerity (as I look back on my work) well then, I suppose it must be so. It remains for me to thank you warmly for the generous terms in which you express your judgment, for the tone of friendliness toward the man – and his effort.

There are a few little matters of fact: as for instance the impression (expressed by dear Clifford)[3] that I ever hesitated between French and English. I could not have done so. If I hadn't had the English to write I would never have written at all. You may take my word for it. I certainly was not writing or even working at Alm: Folly for five years. I carted it about with me for that length of time, simply because I have the habit of sticking to things but I had even no opportunities to think about it (still less to toil over it). The MS (which J[ohn] Q[uinn] has got right enough) is the freest from erasures of all my MSS. What did I care – what did I know then? To address my fellowmen at large on any subject or even with a

---

[1] Henry Louis Mencken (1880–1956) worked for an array of newspapers in his native Baltimore. With George Jean Nathan he founded the *American Mercury* in 1924, remaining as editor until 1933. Often considered the most brilliant and the most cantankerous polemicist of his lengthy day, Mencken revivified the American language. A shrewd literary as well as social critic, he published many books, some compiled from his fugitive pieces and some written from scratch; among his works are *George Bernard Shaw – His Plays* (1905), *In Defense of Women* (1917), *The American Language* (1918), and the six series of aptly named *Prejudices* (1919–27). In the Fifth Series (New York: Knopf, 1926), pp. 34–41, Mencken describes the stories in *Youth* as the century's finest. True to form, the Conrad he admires is a sardonic absurdist whose God is not 'a loving papa in carpet slippers, but a comedian'.

[2] *A Book of Prefaces* (1917), which has a chapter on Conrad, pp. 11–64.

[3] Hugh Clifford had expressed this opinion in an article for the *North American Review* in 1904; Conrad refuted it publicly in the Author's Note to *A Personal Record*: 'English was for me neither a matter of choice or adoption ... if I had not written in English I would not have written at all.'

yarn, did not seem to me a serious occupation. I have learned since, by arduous experience that it is – or that it can be. But the experience (very bitter at times) was purely personal, belonging to "ma vie interieure" as the French say. No MS of mine – not a single one – was hawked about.[1] Unwin accepted *Al Folly* and asked for the next. Henley accepted the *Nigger* on the strength of 3 chapters for the "New Review," and Heinemann did the same for book form of that work. The contract for *Typhoon* stories was signed 3 years before the book appeared. I sent Karain to Mr. Blackwood (and marked my own price on it) who accepted it. Everything else that appeared in Maga was asked for and Heart of Darkness was written by special request for the M number of that venerable periodical.[2] My contracts here with Methuen and now with Dent were business transactions for works unseen – unwritten.

The difficulty was the writing: ill health, blank weeks, nay months, that won't (in the words of Winnie Verloc) bear thinking about. And for the rest I can only say: Nous avons vecu.[3] One boy of 19 at the front since 1915 – another of 11 at school, and the solitude and silence (conditions of life) so loyally shared without a shadow of repining by my wife go on – as before. Two, three more books may yet come of it. Quien sabe.

I was especially pleased by your references to *Nostromo*.[4] A new edition is coming out with a short preface. I shall send you a copy. I enclose here a photograph taken in Poland in 1914. Something that hasn't been knocking about in illustrated papers.

Yours cordially,

Joseph Conrad

[1] Mencken, who has much to say about Conrad's struggle for financial survival, alludes to Quinn's expenditures on manuscripts, and repeats a story about Pinker's trying to sell the US rights to 'Poland Revisited' for an unrealistically steep price (p. 57).

[2] *Maga* was a familiar name for *Blackwood's Edinburgh Magazine*. When the request for a contribution to *Blackwood's* thousandth number arrived, he was already at work on 'Heart of Darkness' (*Letters*, 2, p. 139), and negotiations over 'Karain' were more protracted than implied here (*Letters*, 1, p. 356, n. 7, p. 364), but this account of Conrad's successes is substantially true.

[3] The plural version of one of Conrad's favourite quotations: 'J'ai vécu' ('I am still alive' or 'I have gone on living'), the words of the Abbé Emmanuel-Joseph Sieyès (1748–1836) on surviving the Jacobin Terror.

[4] Mencken praises Conrad's ability to handle a sensational tale inhabited by 'the whole stock company of Richard Harding Davis and O. Henry' with psychological depth and veracity. 'One leaves "Nostromo" with a memory as intense and lucid as that of a real experience. The thing is not mere photography. It is interpretative painting at its highest' (*A Book of Prefaces*, pp. 48, 46–7).

To Sir Sidney Colvin
Text MS Hofstra; J-A, 2, 197

[letterhead: Capel House]
12 Nov. Monday 1917.

My dear Colvin

This morning on opening my eyes I saw the noble vol[1] delicately deposited by my side, while I slept, by Jessie's instructions (I live en vieux garçon, in the spare-room now); and now after reading the preface and looking at the illustrations I sit down en robe-de-chambre and pantoufles[2] to thank You for the copy, for the inscription, and for your invariable friendship in letters and in life, and, in association with dear Lady Colvin, extended to my nearest and dearest on earth.

You have been very much in my thoughts of late, for I can feel with you (and for you) in the present posture of Italian affairs. This morning Gibbon's corr[espoden]*ᶜᵉ* in the D. C. is very reserved.[3] For me there seems nothing possible but the Brenta-Astico line, the first river-position which is not liable to be outflanked from the north. It's true that Venice would be then on the right of the front but the allied squadrons could cover it efficiently, and in any case the brunt of the enemy's attack could not be delivered along the sea-shore where our heavy naval guns would come into play. I don't know anything about the state of water in both these rivers. It is no doubt torrential and variable; but the mere river-bed is an advantage in front of a solidly occupied position. The Adige line would give up too much all at once it seems to me; and then (one hates to write it) in case of further reverse on the Brenta there would be *that* to fall back on. – I have been fearing this for the last 3 months. I told Borys when he was here in Sept. It seems to me that a blind man could have seen that those people were hanging on by their eyebrows in the north: As to treachery I simply don't believe in it. Poor Cadorna spoke in the bitterness of his heart – unreasonably. It was a purely military defeat.[4] And that can be retrieved. It is moral rottenness that is irretrievable. But I can't believe that an army, who had gone through a most arduous campaign

[1] Colvin's new book on Keats: Conrad had hinted his desire for a signed copy on 8 September.
[2] Living like a bachelor, sitting in dressing-gown and slippers.
[3] Gibbon's signed article appeared on the front page of the *Daily Chronicle*. Routed at the Battle of Caporetto (24 October–4 November), the 300,000 remaining Italian soldiers had regrouped on the River Piave, near Venice. Gibbon's vivid article took an optimistic line, arguing that now the Italians were fighting on home ground they would put up a much more spirited resistance.
[4] At Caporetto, a lengthy stand-off between Austrian and Italian troops was broken by the arrival of German troops. The surprise attack devastated the Italians: 500,000 were killed or injured, 250,000 captured, and 350,000 deserted. As a consequence of this débâcle, General Luigi Cadorna (1850–1928) lost his post as Chief of Staff. On 27 October, Cadorna had sent a cable from the Front blaming the army's collapse on domestic rather than foreign enemies ('L'esercito non cade vinto de nemico esterno, ma da quello interno'). Versions of this allegation were widely quoted in the European press.

with credit and had just won a notable success, could go suddenly rotten in patches – like this. An army is not a parliament. Italians are not Russians who (nobody would believe me in 1914) are born rotten. Of course it is a great blow, and I don't think the arrival of the great and mysterious Col. House[1] makes up for it – quite. We shall telephone to you our arrival in town, which may be this week. Our dear love to your house.

Ever Yours

J. Conrad.

To J. B. Pinker
Text MS Berg; Unpublished

[letterhead: The Norfolk Hotel,
Surrey Street, Strand,
London, W. C. 2.]
[17? November 1917][2]

My dear Pinker

We arrived (by road) yesterday afternoon. I am off flat-hunting, so as to get out of this hotel as soon as possible, and shall turn up at your Office about 12–30.

Ever Your

J. C.

To Alice Rothenstein
Text MS postcard Harvard[3]; Unpublished

[Norfolk Hotel]
November 25th. [1917]

Our address after today will be as follows. —

4 Hyde Park Mansions
Flat C.
Marylebone Road N. W.

Shall be glad to see you[4] anytime. Will let you know when I leave.

Yours.

J. Conrad

---

[1] Edward Mandell House (1858–1938), an honorary colonel in the Texas Rangers, was President Wilson's close adviser on military and diplomatic affairs. In 1915 and 1916, he sought ways of negotiating a peace. After the United States entered the war, he assumed the task of co-ordinating Allied efforts, not least upon the Italian Front.

[2] According to the letter of [27 November], the Conrads stayed at the Norfolk for nine and a half days, leaving on the 26th.

[3] In Jessie Conrad's hand.

[4] Alice Rothenstein (née Knewstub, 1867–1957), an actress whose stage name was Alice Kingsley, married Will in 1899. Her family had ties with the Pre-Raphaelites.

To J. B. Pinker
Text MS Berg; Unpublished

[letterhead: Norfolk Hotel]
26th. Nov 1917.
Dearest Pinker

I have signed agreement for flat up to 26 Febr [19]18 on Sat and given them a cheque for the whole term which with the cost of agreement and fee for taking the inventory amounts to £57–4–6.

The agreement for paying in advance seemed to be in the usual form, and any discussion as to that would have prevented us coming in this morning. And I *do* want to get in and sit down to work.

Jessie will be leaving here about 2 o'clock in a Rolls Royce car(!) lent by a friendly doctor. I'll be off presently to the flat with most of the luggage.

I'll have to draw a cheque for the hotel acct today. The surgeon has not fixed yet the date for exam^{on}. Can hardly be before Friday on account of Sir R. Jones' arrangements.[1] I'll run in and see you about 12. 30 if I can.

Yours ever

J. C.

To J. B. Pinker
Text MS Berg; Unpublished

[letterhead: Talbot House,
Arundel Street,
Strand,
London WC2.][2]
Tuesday. [27 November 1917][3]
My dear Pinker.

Sorry I missed you. What do you think of our taking Miss Hallowes on[4] (half time) to take from dictation and also to type from MS? Somebody will

---

[1] Sir Robert Jones (1858–1933; knighted 1917), the distinguished orthopaedic surgeon, who from 1917 onward figured prominently in attempts to ease Jessie Conrad's plight. See the letter to him of [12 December 1919].
[2] Pinker's office letterhead.   [3] The day after leaving the Norfolk.
[4] Lilian Mary Hallowes (1870–1950) first worked for Conrad in 1904. With substantial interruptions, she remained his secretary for the rest of his life; he depended on her especially in his later years, when he was dictating both correspondence and work in progress. She also did much to organise his dealings with agents and publishers. According to Jessie Conrad, Miss Hallowes 'used to declare that proofs would be found imprinted on her heart when she died' (*Joseph Conrad and His Circle* (Jarrolds, 1935), p. 228).

have to do that last anyhow, and I believe the girl will be useful to me in many ways.

Have you a wine merchant in London? And would you mind ordering him to send me a case of Beaune (red) and ½ doz Chablis (white)? I detest buying wine in grocers' shops. You don't mind?

The Hotel bill was £33 odd for 9½ days. 4 people so I havent much left in the bank. We are settled down. I worked last night and this morning.

Yours

J. C.

To B. Macdonald Hastings
Text MS Colgate; Unpublished

4.C Hyde Park Mansions
Marylebone Rd NW.
28 Nov '17

My dear Hastings.

I've just had your letter and I agree with your views completely. I can't say I would feel *very* unhappy if Irving were to drop the play, for to be frank I believe in the play much more than in the actor.

I quite understand that you are too busy with the actualities of your present life to give much (or any) thought to the projected play. The time will come sooner or later, for this (or some other) subject to be taken up by us again. We are at the above address for the next three months. Pray remember should you by some chance be in town during that period that the Edgeware* Road (Met) Station is within a minute's walk from 4 Hyde Pk Mans^ons (Flat C) and the Edg. Road (tube) Sta. only 5 minutes walk.[1] I don't send you the tel No. because I am not on the telephone in this place.

It would be a very great pleasure to see you at any time. My wife will be probably in a nursing home for some six weeks. But as a matter of fact the surgeons have not pronounced yet as to what is to be done with that unlucky knee.

United kind regards

I am always your

J. Conrad

---

[1] One Edgware Road underground station was on the Metropolitan and Circle Lines, the other on the deeper Bakerloo Line.

To J. B. Pinker
Text MS Berg; Unpublished

[4C Hyde Park Mansions]
Wednesday. [28 November 1917][1]

Dear Pinker

I send over Nellie as I want to go on working till six today when I am under promise to go to Brixton to see Catherine Willard in *Ghosts*.[2]

Please give N. five notes for me; and pray when you send Jessie her money let her have it in notes, as cheques are not any use here, in this strange land inhabited by suspicious natives. So sorry to give you all these various kinds of trouble. But it won't be so all the time.

I shall see Miss Hallowes to-morrow and arrange with her for giving me part of every day. I am sure she will be very useful.

I dined yesterday with Jack – Sir James (most amiable and quite lively) and Massingham.[3] You are quite right as to him. A man of worth; but he was somewhat dismal. We walked down the Strand together at 11 pm and he was very friendly.

John's going back to school on Thursday.

I am to meet W. L. George next Sunday week at lunch. Is he one of your men? Anyway can you tell me which is considered the best of his novels. I want to read something of his. I have heard people enthusing over *The Bed of Roses*.[4] If you happen to have that book please lend it to me. Jessie's love.

Yours ever

J. Conrad

Do you feel at all disposed to look us up? Taste the house-lunch or something of the sort. We will send out for the beer. Edgware Road (met) is nearly opposite our door.

---

[1] The dinner was on the 27th (Marrot, p. 433).

[2] She was playing Regina in a touring production of Ibsen's play which had opened at the Kingsway Theatre on 28 April. Since the script was unlicensed it could only be performed once at each venue.

[3] John Galsworthy ('Jack'); Sir James Matthew Barrie (1860–1937), the Scottish playwright and novelist; the Liberal journalist H[enry] W[illiam] Massingham (1860–1924), from 1907 to 1923 editor of the *Nation*, where many of Galsworthy's essays and stories appeared. Conrad dined with them again on the 6th.

[4] For the novelist W. L. George, see the letter to him of 24 August 1919. Appearing in 1911, *A Bed of Roses* went through nine impressions in a year. 'Friendless, penniless, and unskilled', Victoria Fulton turns to prostitution, successfully enough to buy a comfortable country house where, at the end of the novel, she is being wooed by the local squire. Responding to libraries' refusal to buy the book, the shilling edition of 1913 included a combative Preface 'Which the Author Would Like You to Read'. There, George argues that had he been a cynic, he would have written a sentimental romance in the manner of Nat Gould or Marie Corelli and ended with his heroine degraded or dead.

To Sir Sidney Colvin
Text MS Duke; Unpublished

4.C. Hyde Pk Mansions
Marylebone Rd
30 Nov. 17.

Dearest Colvin.

You may be sure I would have called this afternoon with a report, only unfortunately I got a touch of gout during the night and only just managed to give Jessie a look-in in her "home" about 9. 30 this morning. I have been nursing the wretched foot ever since, and it's much better.

Sir Robert Jones and Mr Trotter examined Jessie yesterday at six pm. The verdict generally is against the amputation. The details I hope to give viva voce to Lady Colvin and Yourself on Sunday afternoon. I am only 2 stations from Nott[in]^g Hill Gate (on the Met:) and that will be my route to your Castle henceforth.

Jessie took the anaestethics* very well. As Sir Robert said: she went off smiling and came-to smiling. The night was not very good – but then she's used to bad nights. I found her at 9. 30 sitting up very good knitting a sock. She chased me back to the flat promptly to put my foot up but not so promptly as to forget to send her dear love to Lady Colvin and Yourself.

– in which I humbly join. A bientôt donc.

Ever yours
J. Conrad.

PS J. will be in the home till Monday, at least

3. York Place
Baker S^t.

She wanted me to tell you she was very comfortable there and surrounded by kindly attentions.

To J. B. Pinker
Text MS Berg; Unpublished

[4C Hyde Park Mansions]
Friday. [30 November 1917][1]

Dear Pinker.

Jessie will remain a couple of days in the nursing home 3 York Place. Baker St.

Sir Robert Jones took a nominal fee only 5 g[uinea]s. and Wilfrid* Trotter declared to me that he was not going to take any more of my money. He

---

[1] The contents parallel those of the preceding letter to Colvin.

will look after Jessie till she can be made to walk either by treatment or otherwise. There will be some splints of a special kind to get and Sir Robert Jones intends to fix it himself when he is again in London in 10 days' time. Apparently also without a fee!

I've been quite upset in a way by those men's kindness. The whole business yesterday has not cost more than seven gui[nea]ˢ (including the anaestethist's* fee). I have given cheques for that amount and there may not be quite enough in the bank to meet them. Jessie has the cheapest room – 1 g[uine]a a day.

The worst is that I've got a bad foot and can't come myself to tell you all about everything. Dʳ Mackintosh¹ had John for 3 days now, and is coming today to see me. Another generous soul.

Ever Yours

J. C.

To Richard Curle

Text MS Indiana; Curle 39

4.C. Hyde Park Mansions.
Marylebone Rᵈ
N. W.
2ᵈ Dec. '17.

My dear Richard

We are at this address for 3 months so that Jessie should be treated for her unlucky knee joint. Of late she was fairly in the way of becoming a cripple for the rest of her days. Something has to be done.

We had news of the success of the operation; and we send you here our affectionate congratulations on your final escape from the disease which has hung on to you so long.

I had a lot of worry and anxiety of late, about Jessie of course, and also other things. Such days have to be lived through. As to news – Well! All one's interior and private life is knocked into a cocked hat every morning by the public news of which you know as much as I do.

As 13 years ago, when Jessie was going to be operated, Nostromo is coming out. History repeats itself. Only I hope that this time N won't be the black frost² he was at his first appearance. I wrote a short preface, "très intime".

---

¹ Robert Duncan Mackintosh, an old friend, practised medicine in Barnes, South-West London; see the letter to him of 17 July 1918.

² A translation of the French '*four noir*': ostensibly, a cold oven, but used colloquially to mean a deadly frost; an expression Conrad often used to describe the commercial failure of *Nostromo*.

But all these things seem to have no importance now. One can't imagine a single human being likely to be the least bit interested in such matters. Unless perhaps You!

And so I have preserved most carefully *for you* the corrected (first) proof of the new Edition where you will be able to see at a glance all the corrections and the few changes I have felt myself compelled to make. Some of them do bear on the very passages you quote in your book on me.

This you must pardon me. I thought a great deal about you before making them. Of course the changes are merely verbal and affect no more than a dozen words.[1] Moreover I think you'll approve – in the end.

It's late. I am tired and nervous and chilly. So – "au revoir", for the present. Jessie sends her love.

Yours ever

J. Conrad.

To J. B. Pinker
Text MS Berg; Unpublished

[4C Hyde Park Mansions]
Tuesday. [4 December 1917][2]

Dear Pinker

The enclosed speaks for itself. I am awfully sorry. What may be said is that of the amount she would have expected the £20 of the relinquished pension.[3] So it isn't *quite* as bad as it looks.

If I can go on only as I've begun (under adverse circumstances) there will be soon something complete in your hands.

My face is going down under treatment and I may be able to dine with Jack and E. V. Lucas[4] on Thursday as I've been asked to do.

Ever yours

J. Conrad.

PS I've answered the man saying the matter would be put right in a few days.

---

[1] 'There were considerably more than a dozen' (Curle's note).
[2] Conrad was able to dine at the Automobile Club on the 6th.
[3] The Civil List pension relinquished in June.
[4] Edward Verrall Lucas (1868–1938), critic, journalist, surreal humorist, and one of Methuen's employees. The other diners were Gilbert Murray (1866–1957), his daughter Agnes (1894–1922), Barrie, Massingham, and Ada Galsworthy (Marrot, p. 434).

To Arthur Symons
Text MS Virginia; Hunter (1985, 3)

[4C Hyde Park Mansions]
Sat: evg. [8 December 1917][1]

My dear Symons[2]

I can't fix a day as Sir R. Jones may turn up from L'pool any day (after Tuesday) to put on the splint himself and that visitation is sure to happen some time in the middle of the day. And I should like to be present, of course.

I would have named Monday but for that day I've an old engagement which it is impossible to throw over, as it's *my* invitation. So sorry!

I'll drop you a line immediately after Jones has been and done it.[3]

I think that short piece[4] very fine indeed. Gets home all right both in idea and in the whole detail of expression.

Our love to you both[5]

Ever Yours

Joseph Conrad.

To B. Macdonald Hastings
Text MS Colgate; Unpublished

[4C Hyde Park Mansions?][6]
Wednesday. [12 December 1917?][7]

My dear Hastings

I have meditated a little on all the interesting points of your letter to C[romwell] and have come to the conclusion that those are not the things for my intelligence. But it does not matter. My confidence in you is absolute – and after all – or before all – this is *your* adaptation. Don't imagine I am not interested. I am immensely, and I very much appreciate Your friendly

---

[1] On [30 November], Conrad expected Sir Robert's visit in ten days' time. Hunter assigns this text to [July 1920] but the reference to splinting matches the earlier date.
[2] Yeats's friend Arthur William Symons (1865–1945) wrote poetry, essays, and fiction. As a critic, he showed broad tastes in literature, music, and painting, and spoke up for such then-neglected or misread figures as Baudelaire and Blake. In 1896, Symons took 'The Idiots', the first short story Conrad ever sold, for the *Savoy*. Symons underwent a severe mental breakdown in 1908 and could not return to his Kentish home until 1910. In 1925, he published *Notes on Joseph Conrad*.
[3] An echo of 'You've been and gone and done it', a catchphrase from the music halls.
[4] Symons's 'Joseph Conrad', *Land and Water*, 1 November 1917, pp. 14–15.
[5] Rhoda Symons (née Bowser, 1874–1936), Arthur's wife, was an actress and musician.
[6] Letterhead: Capel House, watermarked, but if the dating suggested below is right, Conrad must have taken some stationery to London.
[7] This and the next two letters are hard to date. Conrad refers to Madge Titheradge as a prospective actress on both 27 June 1917 and 7 September 1918. Negotiations with the American producer John Cromwell began in March 1917 and continued even during the US try-out of *Victory* in May 1918 (Cromwell to Pinker, TSS Berg). Relations between Cromwell and Hastings, however, reached an especially prickly stage at the end of 1917. On 14 January 1918, Cromwell wrote

proceeding of sending me [a] copy of your letter to C. of which I admire the diplomacy and the firmness and the workmanlike, sound sense. How does the Madge T[itheradge] suggestion prosper?

Yours sincerely

J. Conrad

To J. B. Pinker
Text MS Berg; Unpublished

[4C Hyde Park Mansions?]
Wednesday eve^g [12 December 1917?][1]

Dear Pinker.

I send you this correspondence. But perhaps You know all about it already.

I think M. H[astings] makes a pretty convincing reply, and I presume that C[romwell] will either accept it as decisive or cry off his contract.

For myself I am with MH entirely. But I have no call to interfere.

Should C back out those people from whom we heard this morning might perhaps be approached. Whether it would be good policy is for you to say.

Anyhow the Victory stunt seems to have gone shaky all over. But I am not upset and hardly even sorry.

Yours ever

J. C

To B. Macdonald Hastings
Text MS Colgate; Unpublished

[4C Hyde Park Mansions?]
Saturday ev^g [15 December 1917?][2]

My dear Hastings

All I can do is to assure you of my sympathy with you in the vexation of that Correspondence.

You know by this that Pinker endorses every word of your reply. He tells me that he "doesn't care a rap if C[romwell] gives up the play". And as he

a conciliatory reply (TS carbon, Berg) to a 'frank' letter from Hastings, which may be the diplomatic but firm one Conrad discusses here. Neither Cromwell's 'brainless' threat to break the contract nor Hastings's response survives, but Cromwell's letter of 14 January makes it clear that he had threatened to drop the play but was now willing to carry on. If Conrad's letter belongs to this period of transatlantic brinkmanship, other correspondence suggests a more exact placing: since they share an agenda, the 'Wednesday eve[nin]g' text must belong to the same date as this one; the evening letter mentions Pinker's having just received a proposal to stage *Under Western Eyes* from an American producer who might be induced to take over *Victory*; two letters of the [17th] refer to this producer (H. Neagle) as someone of current interest.
[1] The second letter concerning the reply to Cromwell.
[2] If a copy of Hastings's letter went to Pinker on the [12th], the next Saturday was the 15th.

knows my great and abiding interest in our common venture this means that
he sees other ways to bring it out.

C. strikes me as a stupid sort of person. And indeed after that anxious
and brainless letter of his I'd just as soon he *did* give up. I can't have any
confidence in him any longer.

Still you and P must decide on the steps that are to be taken in all possible
eventualities. You'll find P loyal to you for your own sake (apart from his old
friendship with me). Kind regards from us both

Yours

J. Conrad

To J. B. Pinker

Text MS Berg; Unpublished

[4C Hyde Park Mansions]
Monday. [17 December 1917][1]

My dear Pinker

On Friday I got an attack of gout which came on with great severity while
I was dining out.

However, it didn't stop the working, tho' it laid me up. I shan't be able to
go out for another 3–4 days yet – if even then.

I am writing to M. H[astings] today, both as to Miss L McCarthy[2] and the
American proposal relative to the Western Eyes dramatisation. Should he
be willing to take that up (with me) the arrangement of the best terms with
H. Neagle[3] would not take you very long, I suppose. This after all is not an
affair which need be pushed on with any haste.

At best we couldn't deliver the play before six months from the signature
of contract.

Ever Yours

J. Conrad.

To B. Macdonald Hastings

Text MS Colgate; Unpublished

[4C Hyde Park Mansions]
[17 December 1917][4]

My dear Hastings

This letter speaks for itself. If you don't see any harm in letting her see the
play, let me have it here. I'll call on her in any case.

---

[1] Hastings answered the letter anticipated here on the 18th.
[2] Lillah McCarthy was still interested in playing Lena and, in a letter of 11 December (TS Berg),
had asked to see the script of *Victory*.
[3] A New York impresario.   [4] The letter Conrad told Pinker he was going to write that day.

H. Neagle (dramatic organisation in New York of which You know no doubt) wrote me asking for a dramatisation of Western Eyes by myself if possible. Pinker wrote a diplomatic letter. The Question would be whether you have any inclination that way – the way of collaboration. I should like to know what you think of the material and mental possibilities of the thing coming off in reasonable time – supposing they make it worth while for us to undertake the job. Will you please open your mind to me on this without reserve.

Yours sincerely

J Conrad

To B. Macdonald Hastings
Text TS Colgate; Unpublished

[4C Hyde Park Mansions]

19 Dec 1917.

My dear Hastings

These are my sentiments entirely, both as to "Western Eyes" and the diplomatic conduct you recommend me to follow with Lillah.[1]

G[ladys] C[ooper] certainly is much more promising[2] and I wish you all luck in the negociations*. In regard to "Western Eyes" I have already presented the "gold bag" view to Pinker with all the force of which I was capable.[3] I think we may trust him to do the best from that point of view. I share your opinion as to the play to be got out of W[estern] E[yes]. But those people are asking for it themselves and I think we could work at it together in goodwill and harmony.

Yours very sincerely

Joseph Conrad

PS I am forwarding Your letter to P who will know how to proceed.

---

[1] For the full text of Hastings's letter of the 18th (TS Berg), see *Portrait*, pp. 127–8. Because of his negotiations with Gladys Cooper, Hastings proposed temporising with McCarthy: 'Put her off delicately for the present . . . Promise her the script of course.'

[2] Gladys Cooper (1888–1971: DBE, 1967), the well-known West End actress; she had recently become joint-manager of The Playhouse.

[3] Hastings had written: 'there is a very great and noble play to be made of the story, but as I've told you before I don't believe there's a brass sixpence to be made by any manager who produces it'. Nevertheless, he added: 'But I think Pinker should agitate for a mighty bag of gold representing if possible that I am almost as terrible a person as you are.'

To J. B. Pinker

Text MS Berg; Unpublished

[4C Hyde Park Mansions]
Wednesday. [19 December 1917][1]

My dear Pinker.

I send you the enclosed for your information. As to what there is to do you know it best. I mean as to the Neagle(?) proposal.

I have been doing well since I began to dictate.[2] No day less than 500 words the first week and an average of 700w per day the second week.

Edward saw a lot of pages and seems to think the stuff good.[3] Miss H[allowes] leaves town for a week, on Friday. I shall see then how I get on with pen and ink. Pray send me £5 in notes (when you send Jessie's money) for my Ch^mas expenses.

My best wishes to you and all yours.

Will you be at all in the office during the Xmas week? I should like to know.

I am not fit to get out yet. If you do come to the office next week then the day you do so should be the day for lunching here with us.

Ever Yours

J Conrad

To Sir Sidney Colvin

Text MS Duke; Unpublished

[4C Hyde Park Mansions]
30 Dec. '17

My dear Colvin.

I just got out for one half-hour the other day to raid Your library and carried off one Maine, two Carlyles (of Froude) and two Goncourts.[4]

---

[1] Conrad enclosed Hastings's letter of the 18th; allusions to Christmas confirm the date.

[2] Conrad dictated a substantial portion of his memoir *A Personal Record*, as well as some passages of *Nostromo*, but *The Arrow of Gold* was the first novel to be written almost entirely by dictation.

[3] A return to the working methods of the nineties, when Garnett read and commented on most of Conrad's drafts.

[4] Sir Henry James Sumner Maine (1822–88), who took a comparative approach to the evolution of customs, laws, and institutions in such works as *Ancient Law* (1861) and *Village Communities in the East and West* (1871); James Anthony Froude (1818–94), historian of eighteenth-century Ireland and Tudor Britain, edited the letters of Jane Welch and Thomas Carlyle and wrote a two-volume biography of the latter (1882–4); Edmond and Jules de Goncourt (1822–96, 1830–70): Conrad might have borrowed some of their novels, such as *Soeur Philomène* (1861) and *Germinie Lacerteux* (1865), or part of their nine-volume *Journal*.

I left the other lot of books but made no attempt to replace them on the shelves.

I was grieved to hear of your cold. I hope it is over and that you will begin the year 18th free of all ailments.

I have no such hope for myself. This thing sticks to me but still I've been able to work all through it, and I hope that by Wed*ay* I will be able to move freely out of doors.

A Naval Officer just gone out. Great regret afloat and ashore at the change of First Sea Lord. Jellicoe accepted the peerage[1] I suppose on account of his wife (a Miss Cayzer – of Cayzer Irvine & C°. Shipowners) who is rich. And they haven't given up yet the hope of a boy.

Our dear love and best wishes to you both.

Ever yours

Joseph Conrad.

To Edward Garnett

Text MS Free: G. 274

[4C Hyde Park Mansions]

Sunday [30 December 1917][2]

Dearest Edward.

Will you come early and spend the first evening of 1918 with us (Tuesday)? No need to answer this unless you can't come.

My heart failed me at the last moment when on the point of sending you my MS. But don't flatter yourself. It was the Post Office (in the holiday rush) that I was afraid to trust. If that copy had gone astray it would have been a disaster as there is no other yet.

It's here provisionally corrected waiting for you.

Do try to come. All our loves

Yours ever

J. Conrad.

If we dont hear by Tuesday midday we shall expect you for supper according to precedent.

---

[1] Lloyd George had just forced the resignation of Admiral Sir John Jellicoe (1859–1935) as First Sea Lord (the senior political position at the Admiralty) after only a year in office. He was now relegated to the purely naval post of Chief of Naval Staff and took a seat in the House of Lords as Viscount Jellicoe.

[2] Garnett's date is [3 December], but the invitation for New Year's Day pairs this letter with an envelope postmarked on Monday the 31st.

To André Gide
Text MS Doucet; *L. fr.* 138

4.c. Hyde Park Mansions
Marylebone Road
London N. W.
Dec 30. '17

Très cher Gide.[1]
Rien que quelques lignes pour Vous envoyer nos souhaits du jour de l'an.
Merci de Votre lettre. I[l] y a eu dans le "Times" une etude sur vous.[2] L'avez vous vue? C'est intelligent jusqu'à un certain point et c'est respectueux. Mais ça manque de profondeur et puis c'est trop court. On ne peut pas dire grand chose sur A. Gide dans deux collonnes* du Supp^ment Littéraire du Times. Du reste il y a la une admiration contenue qui perce sous les phrases assez ternes et qui rend l'article sympathetique en son ensemble.
Je ne travaille pas. J'ai presque cessé de penser au travail. Je pense a mes amis en vérité mais je n'ai rien a leur dire. Une fois la plume a la main c'est un recul comme de peur. Enfin.

a vous de coeur

Joseph Conrad

PS Nous sommes ici pour six semaines pour que ma femme puisse suivre un traitement pour son genou malade qui la tourmente fort.
Ma femme, Jean, vous envoient leur amitiés bien affectueuses. Le grand garçon est quelque part près de Cambrai.[3] Ses lettres sont courtes et rageuses. Quelle bête d'affaire!

---

[1] Of all the literary friends of Conrad's later years, André-Paul-Guillaume Gide (1869–1951) was the most distinguished, the most artistically remarkable. He received the Nobel Prize for literature in 1947. A born-again pagan and a recidivist puritan, his strengths lay both in intimate autobiography and in ironic fictions. Among his works are *Les Nourritures terrestres* (1897), *L'Immoraliste* (1902), *La Porte étroite* (1909), *Les Caves du Vatican* (1912), and *Les Faux-monnayeurs* (1926). His writings, his creation of the *Nouvelle Revue Française*, and his vast network of friends and correspondents placed him at the centre of French literary life. He first met Conrad in July 1911 and dedicated *Voyage au Congo* (1927) to his memory.

[2] The article, a review of his achievements to date, observes that Gide's mind 'is rare and complex, subtle and evasive, and, though it has less of power than of attraction, is an influence to be valued and reckoned with, in the last resort chiefly because M. Gide has followed his own precept, pursued and tried his own individuality, and so made of himself, within his province, *le plus irremplaçable des êtres*' (*TLS*, 27 December, p. 647).

[3] In France, near the Belgian border: the Battle of Cambrai, November–December, involved the largest deployment of tanks yet seen.

Translation

My very dear Gide.

Just a few lines to send you our good wishes for the new year.

Thank you for your letter. There was a study of you in the "Times". Have you seen it? It is intelligent up to a certain point and respectful. But it lacks depth and is too short. One can't say much about A. Gide in two columns of the Times Literary Supplement. Otherwise, an evident admiration shines through the commonplace phrases and renders the article agreeable as a whole.

I am not working. I've almost stopped thinking about work. True I think of my friends, but I have nothing to tell them. Once the pen is in my hand, there is a recoil as of fear. So.

Yours affectionately

Joseph Conrad

PS We are here for six weeks, so that my wife can undergo treatment for her injured knee which gives her great pain.

My wife and John send you their affectionate regards. The big boy is somewhere near Cambrai. His letters are short and ill-tempered. What a brute of a business!

To T. Fisher Unwin
Text MS Colgate; Unpublished

4.c. Hyde Pk Mansions

Marylebone R^d

NW.

30 Dec '17

Dear Sir[1]

Thanks very much for the extremely interesting book on the Adelphi.[2] I ought to have thanked You before for the 4 vols of Service's verses.[3] The fact is the books reached me only the day before yesterday as they have been delayed in the country, till the people got our instructions to send everything up.

---

[1] Thomas Fisher Unwin (1848–1935) published Conrad's earliest works. Neither his business practices nor his adherence to the Liberal party endeared him to Conrad.

[2] Perhaps John Swarbrick's *Robert Adam and His Brothers* (Batsford, 1916). The Adam brothers designed the great series of terraces between the Strand and the river known as The Adelphi (1768–72), where Unwin had his office.

[3] Robert Service (1874?–1958), the popular Scots-Canadian poet of frontier life. In the first years of the war, he served as a stretcher-bearer. Unwin published his *Songs of a Sourdough* (1907), *Rhymes of a Rolling Stone* (1913), and *Rhymes of a Red-Cross Man* (1916).

We are here for a month to get surgeons advice on my wife's knee. I can't say I enjoy being in town. It's simply awful.

Pray accept for Mrs Unwin and yourself our best wishes for the coming year.

Believe me

very faithfully yours

Joseph Conrad.

To Elizabeth Dummett

Text J-A, 2, 199

4c Hyde Park Mansions,
Marylebone Road, N. W.
31 Dec., 1917.

Dear Mrs. Dummett,

Our best wishes for the New Year, – as far as one dares to formulate wishes in those years of never-ending deceptions.

As I have no doubt that don Roberto will appear *chez vous* tomorrow with his felicitations, will you please give him from us his share of these timid but sincere good wishes and the assurance of our great affection?

My *Nostromo* is to re-appear in Jan[uar]y; don't be surprised if you have to wait a little for your copy. I am having it specially bound for you and I apprehend there will be the usual "war-time" delay in that as in other things.

I must thank you for the special pleasure you gave me that day I lunched at your house. I didn't say anything then, being intimidated by W. L. George and W. L. George's wife.[1] But I was delighted to hear that you liked my last story in the *Between the Tides* vol:- I mean the story about Anne.[2] I have been much abused for it, – privately and publicly – and your words were like dew in the desert: for I too have a weakness for that story.

Since, I had no opportunity to speak to you. When you called the other day, I was much grieved at not being presentable. Don Roberto talking of Colombia[3] and other things was perfectly delightful. I hope he got rid of the cough which was tormenting him.

Directly I am fit again to appear amongst my fellowmen I shall come *vous saluer chez vous*, and perhaps may bring the book with me. Till then I remain as always your most faithful and obedient friend and servant.

---

[1] At the lunch on the 9th foreshadowed in the letter of [28 November]. George's second wife was Helen Agnes Travers, née Madden, who died in 1920.

[2] 'Because of the Dollars', collected in *Within the Tides* (1915).

[3] Cunninghame Graham had been travelling there in search of beef for British troops. His experiences gave rise to *Cartagena and the Banks of the Sinú* (1920).

To Ada and John Galsworthy

Text MS Forbes; Unpublished

[4C Hyde Park Mansions]
31 Dec. '17.

Dearest Ada¹ and Jack.

All good to you in this new year. I am glad to hear you are beginning it "nearly well" in health. In these times that's pretty good. I envy dear Jack his hot fit of work. I am chilly, chilly. Still I do something every day but it all seems without relief and colour and strangely remote – directly I lay it aside. Every morning is a new, painful start and a calling for help to the gods who are deaf – every morning.

I am really no worse than in other years, but in town one feels it more. At Capel I could crawl to the door in my dressing gown (and on two sticks) for a little air and sun. If only for 5 minutes. Here it's like being in jail. John stands London wonderfully well. Never bored. That kid has more than a spoonful of brains in his head. What it will come to of course no one can say.

Mons. B[orys] expects his ticket of leave any day, and in the end may not get it till God knows when. Meantime Jessie expects to see him walk in any moment. She begins to feel the confinement and the suspense; and there is a good deal of pain too.

Our dear love to you both.

Ever Yours – not very exhilarated
but faithful

J. Conrad

To E. L. and Helen Sanderson

Text MS Yale; J-A, 2, 198

[4C Hyde Park Mansions]
31 Dec 17.

My dear Helen and Ted.

Our warmest New Year wishes to you to dear Ted and to your children near and far.

Ever since that evening when I was so unfortunately out when you called I've been more or less laid up with gout decorated with bronchial

---

¹ Ada Nemesis Galsworthy (née Pearson, 1864–1956), was adopted by Ernest Cooper, a Norwich doctor. As a teenager she studied the piano in Dresden, and later she composed songs. Conrad wrote a preface to her translations from Maupassant, *Yvette and Other Stories* (1904). Although long involved with John, she had been officially and unhappily married to his cousin Arthur until 1904, when the death of John, Senior, eased the threat of family sanctions.

symptoms – a very artistic specimen indeed. And I am thoroughly sick of it. I darent put my nose outside the door; and my fine projects of haunting the Elstree School doorstep seem but mad dreams to my sobered fancy.

And all through it, with groans and imprecations, I have been working every morning. You can imagine what sort of stuff that is. No colour, no relief, no tonality; the thinnest possible squeaky babble. And when I've finished with it I shall go out and sell it in the market place for 20 times the money I had for the Nigger – 30 times the money I had for the Mirror of the Sea ——

It is a horrible prospect. And because I have not enough Satanism in my nature I can't enjoy it. I am really a much more decent person than you would think. It's a great disadvantage.

I don't know why I've told you all this; but I feel better for it. Our dear love to you all. Remember me specially to Ian.

A young naval officer[1] has just been to see me with a fine story [of] a fight with a submarine. They bagged the beast after a 20 minutes' action.

Our dear love to you all.

Ever yours in heart and mind
Joseph Conrad.

To J. B. Pinker
Text MS Berg; Unpublished

[letterhead: Capel House]
Saturday [May–November 1917][2]

My dear Pinker

Ever so sorry to bother you but the Inc: Tax man begs me to fill in the form.

Could you just send a note of inc[ome]: no detailed statement is necessary as the man knows me – and as a matter of fact fills in my form himself. We do it together in his office.

Ever Your

J. C.

[1] Lieutenant Osborne of HMS *Ready*?
[2] The acquaintance with the tax inspector suggests that this was someone Conrad knew in Kent rather than in town. Since Conrad's dealings with the Inland Revenue were not confined to the end of either the calendar or financial years, this fiscal idyll could date from any time in 1917 between his purchase of watermarked stationery and the beginning of his extended stay in London.

To J. B. Pinker

Text MS Berg; Unpublished

Sat: [May–December 1917][1]

My dear Pinker

Thanks for my cheque and for the 2 books which reached me to-day.
You are very good to let me worry You thus.

Ever yours

J. C.

---

[1] Like the previous letter, located in the 1917 files at the Berg; this one written on the bottom half of a sheet watermarked CRIPPLEGATE. Conrad may have had some Capel House stationery with him in London: see the letter to Hastings of [12 December?]. Another note from 1917, written on scrap paper, reads: 'Dear P Yes. Please pay this Your J. C.'

1918

To John Galsworthy
Text MS Forbes; Unpublished

[4C Hyde Park Mansions]
1st Jan. '18. even^g

Dearest Jack

Our congratulations on seeing letters and good service honoured in your person.[1]

I've just seen the paper, having worked all the morning, and then read and dozed through the usual p. m gloom. This indeed is like life in death. I haven't been out yet but may make a timid excursion as far as Arundel St tomorrow – on business.[2]

No sign of life from the Surgeons and this suspense and confinement begin to tell on Jessie. She ought to look better. I wish B[orys] would come and "tonic" her up a bit.

Our love

Yours ever

J. Conrad

To J. B. Pinker
Text TS/MS Berg; Unpublished

4C Hyde Park Mansions,
N. W. 2[1]
January 1st. 1918

My dear Pinker

With the exception of three days in the Christmas week I worked every day and that story without a name[3] is progressing well. It's now more than a fortnight since I have been outside the door of the flat, but I think I will venture out to-morrow – Wednesday – and I propose to call on you between 12 and 1 if you are disengaged. I will have to worry you about my affairs and John's affairs[4] and affairs at large. With those things off my

---

[1] Immediately before Christmas, the Government offered Galsworthy a knighthood. He declined the honour on the grounds that 'the work of Literature is its own justification', but because his telegram did not reach the Prime Minister's office in time, news of an impending award went out to the press. Before Galsworthy could countermand the story, his friends and admirers had sent him 175 letters and 20 telegrams (Marrot, pp. 435–8).
[2] At Pinker's office.   [3] It would become *The Arrow of Gold*.
[4] Homesick and lonely, John was about to change prep schools: see the letter of 10 January and John Conrad, *Joseph Conrad: Times Remembered*, pp. 110–11.

mind I shall sit down and finish this MS before we leave town at the end of February.

The thing'll sound like a mockery but still – happy New Year to you.

Ever Yours

J. Conrad

To J. B. Pinker
Text TS/MS Berg; Unpublished

4C Hyde Park Mansions,
Marylebone Road,
N. W. 2[1]
Jan. 3rd, 1918

My dear Pinker.

Including the 800 words done this morning the MS so far contains 26,000 words on the lowest estimate. As I told you yesterday I will want that much more to finish the story, also on the lowest estimate. You will see then that the size of the story will approach almost a full length novel and will be a handy one for serialising.

I don't send you the pages because I haven't been doing much correcting as yet, but next week I intend to correct all I have and then I will send it to you for clean typing in the usual way. As a matter of fact I will be glad to know that there is more than one copy in existence.

In reference to the bills I spoke to you about. Please send me ch: £45. Made to Mes[s]rs: Lewis & Hylands; and I enclose here the "inhabited house" tax paper.[1]

The other 3 or 4 bills won't be anything like the above. I'll write to you about them next week. I feel most compunctious.

Yours ever

J. Conrad.

PS Please send me also a ch: for £1. 10 for Miss L. Hallowes.

---

[1] The Inland Revenue levied duty on occupied houses; the occupant of Capel House would be liable at a rate of ninepence per pound of annual rent. The total would come to £1 13s 9d (one pound thirteen shillings and ninepence).

To Edward Garnett
Text G. 279

[4C Hyde Park Mansions]
6 Jan 1918

Dearest Edward,

Will you come on Friday or any day before Fri. dropping me a line to that effect?

I've an ad^ce copy of the *Nostromo* re-issue for you here. Shall I keep it till you come?

I am still a prisoner, lame, not a little sick of it. I've been working however at the rate of four of my pages per day – but without pleasure and only feeling now and then in touch with my subject.

I forgot to give you the pages last time.[1] I shall have another copy made and then I'll be able to trust the post. Now I am "afeared".

Jessie's love.

Yours ever

J. Conrad

Have *you* been doing anything?

To J. B. Pinker
Text TS/MS Berg; Unpublished

4C Hyde Park Mansions,
Marylebone Road,
N. W.
Jan. 10th. 1918

My dear Pinker.

Are you aware that an old story of mine "IL CONDE" (Cassel[l]s' Magazine 1908, Set of Six, Vol.) has appeared in the January number of the "Storyteller Magazine"? I am calling your attention to it because I don't know if it has been done with your knowledge or whether those people have a right to use it as many times as they like. The Storyteller is, I believe, a Cassel[l]'s publication. I can't say it is very pleasant to see one's stuff in that lot of rubbish and one's name amongst all those magazine hacks.[2]

---

[1] Garnett was reading *The Arrow of Gold* as successive batches of the draft became available.
[2] The *Story-Teller*, a Cassell publication, went in for lively popular fiction. As well as 'Il Conde', the January number featured stories by H. A. Vachell and Baroness Orczy.

The surgeons are coming to-day at six to fit the splint. Trotter of course will have no fee. But Aitken[1] will have a cheque and there will be the account for the special splint. I only hope the thing will do some good and enable Jessie to move without pain with the aid of a stick.

Yours ever

J. Conrad.

PS Work is going on steadily and on the whole I am satisfied with what I do.
PPS Pray send me Miss L H[allowes]'s ch. 1. 10. and 2 notes for myself. I don't send MS for clean copy this week as there was such a lot to correct that I am not quite through with it yet. I'll be done on Monday.

To J. B. Pinker
Text MS Berg; Unpublished

[4C Hyde Park Mansions]
[10 or 11 January 1918][2]

My dear Pinker.

In the matter of the bills which I mentionned* to you: Please send me a cheque for £8. 13. 0 and another for £17. 5. 8.

There will be one more Ashford acc^t to settle but I don't know the amount yet.

For the school business I must ask you to post a ch: for £16. 1. 2. to A. S. Lamprey Esqre The Grammar School. Ashford. Kent. and to send one for £33. 19. 6 to R. M. Pearce. Esqre Ripley Court. Ripley Surrey (term fee for John Conrad) so that he receives it on Friday (the 18th) next as John joins on that day.

Poor Oliver[3] having departed from this troubled earth a month ago I received the enclosed letter asking for ¹/₂ years rent.

The surgical appliance didn't fit. An awful disappointement* for Jessie. A week's delay. We conclude that we will return to Capel end of Febr^y. The splint will have to be worn 4 months at least. So no use staying and paying

---

[1] Wilfred Trotter of University College Hospital and David McCrae Aitken of the Military Orthopaedic Hospital, Shepherd's Bush; Aitken and Sir Robert Jones were joint authors of several papers on leg surgery.
[2] Immediately after the visit from the surgeons.
[3] Edmund Ward Oliver, proprietor of Capel House.

two rents. Better go back and take with us Miss Hallowes on a 3 months' arrangement. For even if the Story of Rita is finished *here*, I could tackle the Rescue in the same way or have a try (by dictation) at a play. – Am progressing regularly at 600 words p. day. Part III begun but if it turns out too long I will split it in two. Anyway it's the last. Shall try to bring you MS for clean copy myself on Thurs: about one o'clock.

Ever Yours

J. C.

To J. B. Pinker
Text MS Berg; Unpublished

[4C Hyde Park Mansions]
Sunday ev^g [13 January 1918]¹

My dear Pinker

If I had been able to run about myself I would have made (or at any rate attempted to) a better arrangement. But the time is getting short and John has got to be fixed and there is really nothing at all today as there has been a procession of visitors ever since 11 o'clock.

I suppose I made it clear enough to you that besides the new school there will have to [be] 15 g[uinea]s to pay the Ashford school in lieu of notice.

Ever Yours

J. Conrad

To B. Macdonald Hastings
Text TS Colgate; Unpublished

4C Hyde Park Mansions,
Marylebone Road,
N.W.
Jan. 14th. 1918.

My dear Hastings.

I believe I didn't acknowledge receipt of the play. I am sorry. I got the MS. in the morning and early that afternoon it was in L[illah] M[cCarthy]'s hands. I haven't heard from her yet. Perhaps she will write to you direct. I can't say I am much concerned at her eventual decision. I don't see her as Lena somehow.

Sincerely Yours,

Joseph Conrad

---

¹ The first Sunday after the request for two lots of school fees.

To J. B. Pinker
Text MS Berg; Unpublished

[4C Hyde Park Mansions]
Sunday [20 January 1918][1]

Dearest Pinker

I am, definitely, to lunch with Walpole (and Percy Anderson the artist[2]) on Wed: next. Pray get the publisher of the *Dark Forest*[3] to send me a copy. I really must see it before I meet the man.

Sorry to be incessantly worrying you with requests of all sorts – but I am really much crippled in my movements as you know.

Ever Your

J. Conrad

To Lady Millais
Text MS Private collection; Unpublished

4.C. Hyde Pk Mansions
Marylebone R[d]
N. W.
28 Jan 1918

Dear Lady Millais.[4]

I went at once about obtaining for You the copies of the Inter[nation][al] Mag. with Mrs Langtry's memoirs.[5] My agent thought he could at least borrow them in a certain quarter here. But apparently they are not to be had in this country at all. At least not yet. So the order for them is gone to

---

[1] Walpole's diary shows that he first met Conrad over lunch on Wednesday 23 January (Hart-Davis, *Walpole*, p. 168).

[2] Percy Anderson became Walpole's 'ideal friend' in 1910 and was the dedicatee of *Mr Perrin and Mr Traill* (1911). An artist and theatrical designer, Anderson (1851–1928) created the costumes for Beerbohm Tree's lavish Shakespearean productions, Henry James's disastrous *Guy Domville*, and most of the Gilbert and Sullivan operettas (Hart-Davis, *Walpole*, pp. 78, 87–9).

[3] A novel based on Walpole's experiences in war-time Eastern Europe (Eyre & Spottiswoode, 1916).

[4] Lady Mary St Lawrence Millais (née Hope-Vere, 1861–1948), a Scotswoman, was Jessie Conrad's close friend and neighbour; she lived at Leacon Hall, Warehorne. Widowed in 1897, she was the daughter-in-law of the painter Sir John Everett Millais. In later years, she served as a Justice of the Peace.

[5] Née Emilie Charlotte Le Breton, married as Lady de Bathe, Lily Langtry (1853–1929), the 'Jersey Lily', was one of the first society women to take up a theatrical career, which she did with gusto, playing everything from music hall to Shakespeare. Her liaison with Edward, Prince of Wales, became an open secret.

America in his weekly cablegram to N. York; but I regret to say it may be weeks before we get the copies here.

We are very anxious to hear your news; but we know that you must be very tired and hardly dare ask you for a line. We hope that the state of that pluckiest of sufferers[1] is gradually improving, by now. Our warmest sympathies go to you both.

We expect to leave here of* the 26 Feb[y]. for home. Two days ago the surgeons put Jessie's limb into the apparatus; and as far as the pain goes it is a success. But the weight of it is appalling and she wont be able to move about much while she wears it.

With our united love to Sir John and Yourself believe me, dear Lady Millais,

always your faithful and ob[t] servant

J. Conrad

To J. B. Pinker
Text MS Berg; Unpublished

[4C Hyde Park Mansions]
Monday. [28 January 1918][2]

Dear Pinker

Pray send me cheque to *Messrs. Bentalls*[3] for £11. 4. 0.

The surgeons put the limb into the apparatus on Sat. ev[g] and as far as relief from pain goes it's a success. But the inconvenience and the weight of it are appalling. She won't be able to move about much while she's wearing it.

Percy Anderson starts his portrait of me[4] on Thursday morning. On Friday I am going to see (by invitation) the main Orthopaedic hospital at Shepherds Bush. But I have arranged with Miss Hallowes to give me the afternoon on these two days as I don't want to interrupt the work. John seems to have settled down happily in the new school. We are still expecting Borys – any day.

Ever Yours

J. Conrad

---

[1] Lady Millais' son, Sir John Millais, Bart (1888–1920), a naval officer, was suffering from tuberculosis.
[2] Two days after the surgeons fitted the apparatus.
[3] The department store in Kingston-upon-Thames.
[4] A water-colour, now in the National Portrait Gallery, London. See Plate 11.

PS. I've drawn a cheque for £4. 4. o for machine and there will be one to Dr Aitkin* soon to the same amount probably.

To Helen Sanderson

Text MS Yale; Unpublished

[4C Hyde Park Mansions]
28 Jan 1918.

Very dear Helen.

It was like my cheek to invade you and have to be specially catered for – but you and all those people under your wing have been so kind that I hardly feel like a great sinner. We shall expect Ted on Thursday about 3. 30 in the hat devised and designed by himself on the model patronized by his remote ancestors.

As you observe I dont even attempt to thank you for your reception yesterday; but I've been warmed, moved, and made to feel welcome under that hard-won and yet paternal roof of the Sandersons,[1] as in no other place on earth. And I am indeed grateful to you all.

Our dear love to you both and all the children.

Ever your

J. Conrad.

To J. B. Pinker

Text MS Berg; Unpublished

[4C Hyde Park Mansions]
Tuesday. [29 January? 1918][2]

My dear Pinker.

I am obliged to send the tax man's inquiry to you. The other is Dr Aitken's small acc^t which please settle for me.

Ever Yours

J. C.

---

[1] Elstree School, Hertfordshire, just north of London.
[2] On the 28th, Conrad was expecting a bill from Mr Aitken.

To Arthur Symons

Text MS Yale; Unpublished

[4C Hyde Park Mansions]
Tuesday [29 January 1918][1]

Dear Symons

I am truly sorry I can't come on Thursday. A very old friend whom I have few opportunities to meet has selected that day to come for a long afternoon's talk. I can't possibly put him off.

Désolé mon cher[2]

Yours ever

J Conrad.

To Edward Garnett

Text G. (B-M) 255[3]

[4C Hyde Park Mansions]
Wednesday [30 January 1918][4]

Dearest Edward.

This is to warn you that H[ugh] W[alpole] will turn up to supper on Friday. If you prefer to have your old J. C. all to yourself come tomorrow, Thursday. If we don't see you by a quarter past seven we will conclude that you have decided to put up with the presence of H. W. at the weekly symposium.

Yours ever

J. Conrad.

PS It was impossible to keep him out on the Friday. Am sorry.

---

[1] The envelope was postmarked on the 31st, a Thursday. The 'very old friend' was Garnett, who was bidden for that day.

[2] Perhaps in recompense for not answering a letter or not seeing him in Kent or London, Conrad gave Symons a copy of *Victory* inscribed 'in a spirit of compunction and with a still lame right hand . . . 1918' (Private collection). The most likely date is August; on the 15th or 16th, Conrad told Walpole that his hand was 'still very lame'.

[3] The text survives only in the US edition of the letters to Garnett.

[4] Dated [9 January] in the Bobbs-Merrill edition, but the first meeting with Walpole was on the 23rd, and he was invited for supper on the 30th.

To E. L. Sanderson
Text MS Yale; Unpublished

4 Hyde Pk Mansions (Flat C.)
Marylebone R^d
NW.
Wednesday. [30 January? 1918][1]

Carissimo Eduardo.

Thanks for the pocket-book. I couldn't imagine where I had left it. The only thing I was absolutely certain of was that it wasn't in Elstree. Therefore Jessie decided to telephone there at once. She knows me well. But to this moment I can't get rid of the absurd impression that you must have picked my pocket. —

Your and your dear wife's reception warmed my heart as nothing else in the world could have done. Kitty is a delightful personality.[2] Her manner with you as you stood together for a moment under the light charmed and moved me. Blessings on all your heads.

Yours ever

J Conrad

PS The surgeons are still keeping us in suspense. Jessie sends her dear love

To Hugh Walpole
Text MS Texas; J-A, 2, 200

4.c. Hyde Pk Mansions.
30 Jan. 1918

Dear Mr Walpole.

Nostromo left for Bury St this afternoon 3 hours before your letter arrived. This is decisive.

Yes. Do come. As late as you like and stay to supper – un repas quelconque – if you can. As Flesh and Fowl are uncertain nowadays[3] it will be probably Red Herring. The plates'll be chipped in true camp style.

Pray drop us a line an* account of the "Missus" who will naturally want to disguise that Herring for the occasion.

Sincerely Yours

Joseph Conrad.

---

[1] Conrad visited Elstree on the 27th, but the pocket-book may have been retrieved on some other visit.

[2] The Sandersons' daughter Katherine, now in her late teens.

[3] Because of war-time shortages.

To Edward Garnett

Text MS Colgate; G. 279

[4C Hyde Park Mansions]

Thursday. [31 January 1918][1]

Dearest Edward.

It's perfectly ridiculous, but as you insisted on it, you are hereby assured that M^r & Mrs J. Conrad are expecting you tomorrow evening at the usual time.

Do come my dear fellow. The days are running out and I am anxious to learn of *all* the ways and means of "offending your taste" so as to make my last[2] novel as perfect in perversity as possible.

Our love

Yours ever

J. C.

To Elizabeth Dummett

Text MS Syracuse; Barringer

[4C Hyde Park Mansions]

2^d Feby. 1918

Dear Mrs Dummett.

Please give room in your house to this copy of the revived *Nostromo*. It isn't in the least necessary that you should read this long and rather too political book. But some of my (literarily) best women are in it, and I would like you to be friendly to them to the extent of letting them dwell under the same roof with yourself.

Pray forgive me for not bringing the vol: myself. I am again detained indoors with a bad foot; and I won't even be able to go tomorrow with Jessie to see our small boy at his school.

With our united love I am, dear Mrs Dummett,

Always most faithfully yours

Joseph Conrad

---

[1] Another stage in the negotiations about supper; the envelope was postmarked on the 31st.
[2] Most recent.

To John Quinn
Text TS/MS NYPL; Unpublished

4C Hyde Park Mansions,
N. W. 1
Feb. 6th. 1918

My dear Quinn.

I have just read your letter to Jessie, who is immensely flattered and pleased at her friendly correspondence with J. Q. Speaking of that same lady I will tell you that the surgeons entertain good hopes of mending her thoroughly in the course of 6 to 8 months. And meantime a cleverly devised apparatus which she has to wear on her damaged limb has relieved her from the pain from which she has suffered for the last 14 years. She can look forward to the future now with renewed confidence.

My outlook too has been altered for the better in consequence. This thing has been like a nightmare oppressing our life for a long stretch of years.

Thank you very much for the books. Monahan I like.[1] E[zra] P[ound] is certainly a poet but I am afraid I am too old and too wooden-headed to appreciate him as perhaps he deserves. The critics here consider him harmless; but as he has, I believe, a very good opinion of himself I don't suppose he worries his head about the critics very much. Besides he has many women at his feet; which must be immensely comforting. But I am very grateful to you for sending me that bibliographically valuable copy.[2]

Whatever happens Russia is out of the war now.[3] The great thing is to keep the Russian infection, its decomposing power, from the social organism of the rest of the world. In this Poland will have to play its part on whatever lines her future may have to be laid. And at the same time she will have to resist the immense power of germanism which would be death too, but in another shape. Whether that nation over-run, ruined and shaken to the very foundations of its soul will rise to this awful task I really don't know. What assistance she will be able to get from the Western world nobody can tell. Never was there such a darkness over a people's future, and that, don't forget, coming after more than a century of soul grinding oppression in which apart from a few choice spirits the Western world took no interest. Fine words

---

[1] The poet and essayist Michael Monahan (1865–1933), whose work Quinn admired (Reid, *Man from New York*, p. 292). Monahan's latest books were *At the Sign of the Van* (1914) and *New Adventures* (1917).

[2] *Pavannes and Divisions* (1918): a copy inscribed by Quinn was in the Hodgson sale of Conrad's books, 13 March 1925.

[3] A consequence of the October Revolution.

have been given to it before. And the finer the words the greater was always the deception. One evening in August in 1914[1] in a dimly lit, big room I spoke to a small group of Poles belonging to the University and the political life of the town of Cracow. One of the things I said was: "Rest assured that whoever makes peace in six months (that was all the talk then – that the war couldn't last) England will go on for ten years if necessary". But I had also the courage to tell them: "Have no illusions. If anybody has got to be sacrificed in this war it will be you. If there is any salvation to be found it is only in your own breasts, it is only by the force of your inner life that you will be able to resist the rottenness of Russia and the soullessness of Germany. And this will be your fate for ever and ever. For nothing in the world can alter the force of facts".

And if I had to speak to them to-morrow I would repeat these very words. I don't remember now what Mr Wilson said in his latest utterance. There is an awful air of unreality in all the words that are being flung about in the fact of such appalling realities. For the closer they are looked into the more appalling they are. And the tragedy of the situation for all the hearts, that are not the Devils' or the Angels' but those of Men truly worthy of the name, is this: that they can't contemplate either Peace or War otherwise than with an equal dread.

That is the tragedy – the inner anguish – the bitterness of lost lives, of unsettled consciences and of spiritual perplexities. Courage, endurance, enthusiasm, the hardest idealism itself, have their limits. And beyond those limits what is there? The eternal ignorance of mankind, the fateful darkness in which only vague forms can be seen which themselves may be no more than illusions.

In this enormous upheaval of Forces and Consciences all Hopes and all Fears are on an equality. Either can lead mankind equally astray. And there is nothing in the world to hold on to but the work that has to be done on each succeeding day. Outside that there is nothing to lay hold of but what each man can find in himself.

My wife sends her kindest regards. The news from Borys is good. John has gone to school for good and the "Old Folks" are feeling very lonely.

Believe me dear Quinn

Yours most sincerely

Joseph Conrad

---

[1] The Conrads reached Cracow on 28 July of that year and left for the relative safety of Zakopane on 2 August.

To W. T. H. Howe
Text TS Berg; Unpublished

4C Hyde Park Mansions,
Marylebone Road,
N. W. 1
Feb. 12th. 1918

Dear Mr Howe.

My warm thanks for the Christmas card and the Hurl[e]y book¹ and for the general friendliness of your feelings towards me of which you give me so many proofs.

Your letter of Jan. 15th makes very pleasant reading indeed. Somehow I didn't expect the S[hadow] L[ine] to have a very wide appeal but many people of all sorts and conditions seem to like it. Your critical appreciation of that handful of pages is of course specially gratifying. May I be always able (as long as the breath lasts) to please you and my other good friends in Cincinnati and elsewhere. Pray accept for the group of which you form part my friendly greetings and my best wishes for their individual prosperity and for the triumphant success of U. S. arms in alliance with the Western Powers. My wife joins me in all good wishes and kindest regards.

Believe me yours faithfully
Joseph Conrad.

To J. B. Pinker
Text MS Berg; Unpublished

[4C Hyde Park Mansions]
12. II. 18

My dear Pinker.

Pray settle those 2 bills for me. The one to Larden² is for the unavoidable repairs to the house.

Ever Yours
J. Conrad

---

¹ Since Howe lived in Cincinnati, the book could have been *The Town of the Beautiful River* (1915), illustrated with etchings by the local artist Edward Timothy Hurley, or *Cincinnati: Prints from the Etchings of E. T. Hurley* (1916).
² J. and L. Larden, local plumbers and glaziers.

To J. M. Dent
Text TS Berg; Unpublished

4C Hyde Park Mansions,
Marylebone Road,
N. W. 1
Feb. 15th. 1918

Dear Mr Dent.

I don't call on you with congratulations on recovery because I imagine you are very busy after a long absence.

Mr Hugh has no doubt explained to you the matter of the M. S.[1] so I will only say that I am gratified by the interest you take in the progress of my book.

Yours very faithfully
Joseph Conrad

To Cecil Roberts
Text TS Churchill; Unpublished

4C Hyde Park Mansions,
Marylebone Road,
N.W. 1.
Feb. 15th. 1918.

Dear Mr Roberts.[2]

I think it fair to warn you that we will have on Sunday two dear ladies, great friends of ours, but who will certainly be in the way of the good talk I promised myself to have with you. My wife has just told me of these invitations. However, if you have the necessary courage, we will be delighted to see you at seven o'clock on Sunday next.

Yours faithfully
Joseph Conrad.

---

[1] Perhaps Conrad had talked to Hugh Dent about the progress of the new novel.

[2] Edric Cecil Mornington Roberts (1892–1976) was to become a best-selling novelist, acclaimed playwright, and cosmopolitan *bon vivant*. Among his books were *Pilgrim Cottage* (1933) and *Victoria Four Thirty* (1937). During the First World War, he was a correspondent with the Dover Patrol, the RAF, and the Allied armies in France while doubling as literary editor of the *Liverpool Post*. Between 1920 and 1925, he edited the *Nottingham Journal*. For an account of his first meeting with Conrad, which was arranged by Grace Willard, see 'Joseph Conrad: A Reminiscence', *Bookman* (London), 49 (1925), 95–9.

To Hugh Walpole
Text TS Texas; Unpublished

4C Hyde Park Mansions,
Marylebone Road,
N. W. 1
Feb. 15th. 1918.

My dear Mr Walpole.

Sorry I did not answer your friendly note before. My character is anything but capricious, and I honestly think that you may trust the stability of my feelings. I am sincerely glad of your friendliness towards myself, which I may or may not deserve – all future things are uncertain – but which I am never likely to take otherwise than seriously. We must certainly meet again before I go back to Kent. I will drop you a line soon.

Yours

J. Conrad.

Pardon type. Painful wrist.

To Samuel A. Everitt
Text TS carbon Yale; J-A, 2, 200[1]

Capel House
Orlestone
Nr. Ashford
Kent
Feb. 18th, 1918.

N. B. It is understood that the contents of this letter are not for publicity in the daily or weekly press, but only for the use of Messrs. D. P. & Co. travellers.

Dear Mr. Everitt[2]

Many thanks for your friendly letter received to-day, which I answer at once.

---

[1] Text for the body of the letter comes from the Yale carbon copy, which Conrad signed. Jean-Aubry's version includes what must have been holograph additions, given here as a headnote and a PS. On the 18th, Conrad was still in London but used his Capel House address because any reply from the USA would arrive after his return on the 26th.

[2] Samuel Alexander Everitt (1871–1953): after graduating from Yale in 1895, he began a career in publishing. He became treasurer and executive vice-president of Doubleday, Page, and retired in 1930.

No. Mr. Doubleday never talked to me of your business and publicity arrangements, but I quite understand. I am very willing indeed to accede to your request except as to the specimen pages. No one sees my manuscript till it is ready for the printer. A specimen page is nothing. A piece of literature is not a bag of wheat and I should think that in the case of a writer of my standing as an artist even the very booksellers ought to feel a certain amount of confidence as to the character of the wares they are going to receive.

The title of the book is another point on which I can give you no information, for the reason that, so far, I don't know it myself. It was like this with "Victory." I didn't hit upon that title till the very end; and the word itself was the very last written of all the MS. I had thought of many titles before, but I am very glad I waited for what, you cannot deny, was a true inspiration. And thus it is in this case. Lots of titles pass through my head (in my idle moments – which are few) but not one of them gives me the exact feeling of rightness. If it had been a book in French I believe I would have called it "L'Amie du Roi" but as in English the gender is not indicated by the termination (The Friend of the King) I can't very well do that. People would think perhaps of a friend with a great beard and that would be a great mistake. The title of "The Goatherd," which would have been possible too, is open to the same objection. They would be both a little misleading because the connection of the story both with goats and kings is very slender. "Two Sisters" would be a title much more closely related to the facts but I don't like it.[1] It's too precise and also too commonplace. On the other hand, "Mme. de Lastaola" is foreign in appearance, besides looking pretentious. "The Heiress," which is closest to the facts, would be the most misleading of all; and it is also very unimaginative and stupid. We must wait for the title to come by itself.

As you see, the above are all connected with a woman. And indeed the novel may be best described as the Study of a woman who might have been a very brilliant phenomenon but has remained obscure, playing her little part in the Carlist war of '75–6,[2] and then going as completely out of the very special world which knew her as though she had returned in despair to the goats of her childhood in some lonely valley on the south slopes of the Pyrenees. The book, however, is but slightly concerned with her public

---

[1] In 1896, Conrad had abandoned work on 'The Sisters', leaving only a fragment to appear posthumously in 1928; one strand in the plot follows two sisters from the Basque country.

[2] Like its predecessors, the Third Carlist War was fought mainly in the Basque country, heartland of the Carlists – upholders of tradition, the unchallengeable authority of the Catholic church, and the illegitimacy of female succession to the throne of Spain. The Carlist claimant at the time was Don Carlos (1848–1909), Duque de Madrid, whose supporters regarded him as King Carlos VII.

(so to speak) activity, which was really of a secret nature.[1] What it deals with is her private life: her sense of her own position, her sentiments and her fears. It is really an episode, related dramatically and in the detailed manner of a study, in that particular life. That it is also an episode in the general experience of the young narrator (the book is written in the first person) serves only to round it up and give it completeness as a novel. The narrative is divided in[to] four parts, each part containing three or four long chapters. There will be something of Paris in it, and something of the sea, but the actual milieu of the story is the town of Marseilles. The colouring is Southern. However, all the interest is in the personages. Of these, two women and four men play an active part, the others being only mentioned in the narrative, which I want to tell you, is dealing with facts and not at all with self-analysis and psychology.

Of the artistic purpose of the writing I won't say anything: it is a matter between myself, my conscience and my critics. But I am confident that an experienced and intelligent American bookseller, allowed to see what I have written to you here, would be able to form a pretty clear notion of what he would have to deal with in handling the book. In length it will be shorter than "Victory." What we might call a mediumsized novel.

Believe me, dear Mr. Everitt,

Very faithfully yours,

Joseph Conrad.

P. S. Yes. I've seen "Contact's" work.[2] It is very good. But he's not the only one.

To B. Macdonald Hastings

Text TS Colgate; Unpublished

4C Hyde Park Mansions,
Marylebone Road N. W.
Feb. 19th. 1918

My dear Hastings,

Pray pardon the delay in returning you the enclosed letter. C[romwell] has obviously backed down before your masterly vindication of your point of view. As to his proposals and suggestions the decision must be taken by you in conjunction with P[inker].[3]

---

[1] In terms of sexual intrigue, political intrigue, or both?

[2] 'Contact' was the author of *An Airman's Outings* (Blackwood, 1917).

[3] Cromwell had replied to a strong letter from Hastings on 14 January (TS carbon, Berg). If he could get a cast together and if the National Controller of Fuel did not close all theatres, Cromwell was now willing to arrange a try-out of *Victory*. Nevertheless, he felt Act One needed heavy pruning: 'For after all doesn't the dramatic action of the play and by that I mean

We are leaving here in a few days and will be home at Capel on the 26th of this month.

Kindest regards from us both.

Yours sincerely,

Joseph Conrad

To J. B. Pinker

Text TS/MS Berg; Unpublished

4C Hyde Park Mansions,
Marylebone Road,
N. W.
Feb. 19th. 1918.

Dearest Pinker.

I am sending you here a letter I received from Doubleday's partner and my four pages in answer.

I wanted to accede to his request and this is the only way I found possible to do it in. The blessed letter is a morning's work, but The Trade must be treated with consideration. And my time is surely a great consideration just now. If you think it will do, perhaps you will be kind enough to have it forwarded to S. A. Everitt, Esq. in his poetical Garden City.

The work has been hung up for a day or two. I had a great number of people to see. But it is not brought to a standstill, you understand, it's only interrupted. I have got a lot of stuff in my head which I want to get on to the paper as soon as possible. Yesterday I met Francis Howard of the Grosvenor Gallery. Of use to my projected play about the faked picture, in which he was much interested. Says that the fact on which I build my plan of the play has actually happened. Apparently a small (very rare) book has been written about it which he promised to send me.[1] It may help. At any rate adds to interest. But Rita must be got out of the way first.[2] Interest in that too. Edward very delighted with it and I almost blushed at his enthusiasm.

---

the culminative action, begin at the arrival of the three men on the island?' Nevertheless, what remained after the cuts should feature Mrs Zangiacomo more prominently than at present.

[1] While not enjoying quite the éclat it had had in the late nineteenth century, the Grosvenor was still one of the major London galleries. Its honorary Managing Director was Francis Howard (1874–1954), artist, collector, critic, founder of the International Society of Sculptors, Painters, and Gravers and the National Portrait Society. He may have had in mind one of the numerous anecdotes of artistic chicanery in Alessandro Foresi's booklet *Tour de Babel, ou Objets d'art faux pris pour vrais et vice versa* (Paris and Florence, 1868). Nothing came of the play.

[2] By attending to the roughed-out short story that became *The Arrow of Gold*.

Shall try to call on you to-morrow, Wed. about three. Will be leaving the flat on Monday evening and Town on Tuesday.

Ever Yours

J Conrad

PS I'd like to give Lieut B. Conrad £10 towards his leave expenses. Would you send him a cheque here. He's leaving us on Thursday 7 am – Means to call on you to-day or to-morrow.

To Cecil Roberts

Text TS Churchill; Unpublished

4C Hyde Park Mansions,
Marylebone Road,
N.W.
Feb. 19th. 1918.

Dear Mr Roberts.

Next Friday is our last in Town and it is Edward Garnett's evening. E. G. has done a lot for literature in the '90s and anyway is an interesting and worthy personality. If you would like to meet him come in about seven and we will have a three-cornered talk. E. G. is a moody and somewhat freakish personage, and he belongs of course to a past, the glory of which has passed away,[1] but I don't suppose you will mind that.

Wife joins in kind regards

Yours Faithfully

J. Conrad.

To John Galsworthy

Text MS Forbes; J-A, 2, 220

[4C Hyde Park Mansions]
Monday. [25 February 1918][2]

Dearest Jack.

I am of course with you entirely both as to the matter and the expression of the Agricultural pamphlet.[3] Thanks very much for sending me the copy.

---

[1] With his support for writers as original as Dorothy Richardson and D. H. Lawrence, Garnett was as influential as ever.

[2] Jean-Aubry dated this [1919]; Najder established an accurate date in consultation with John Conrad (*Chronicle*, p. 591, n. 165). From paragraph two, the Jean-Aubry text omits 'of (I suppose) . . . who will understand'.

[3] *The Land: A Plea* (Allen & Unwin, 1918), in which Galsworthy argues that the establishment of more smallholdings would lessen a perilous dependence on imported food and improve the

It shall be duly treasured both on account of its body and its soul – which is the soul of a great truth.

We went yesterday (by car!) to see John. He looked happy enough. But for me it was sad to behold the dear little pagan in the Eton jacket and horrible round collar of (I suppose) the most Christian civilization in the world. I say this without the slightest bitterness, of course. And I say it only to you and Ada who will understand.

Those people are really full of kindness and tact (I can see it plainly) but they have not the slightest conception of what he is. They will understand him presently when he has become like one of themselves. But I shall always remember the original – the only genuine John – as long as I live. Borys too had a particular impression of "The Kid" which he could not define any better than I can mine. And he too will be sorry. As to Jessie they were too close together, she really loved him too much to see him clearly. She'll be always delighted with him. We took Nellie with us. On the way back she said: "Doesn't John look well!" (He was most gracious to her). Then after a long while she said as if to herself: "Poor John".

After this there's no more to be said. Our love to you both

Ever Yours

J Conrad.

To John Drinkwater
Text MS Yale: Unpublished

[letterhead: Capel House]
28 Febr. 1918

Dear Mr Drinkwater.[1]

Your letter reached me only this afternoon.[2]

I am immensely flattered that you consider the play good enough. I regret I havent the text to send you. Neither can I find the license*,[3] but perhaps it will not be necessary.

Believe me very sincerely yours
Joseph Conrad.

---

national diet. He advocates better education in nutrition and agricultural methods, support for the allotment movement, and the breaking up of great estates.

[1] John Drinkwater (1882–1937) was a prolific dramatist, essayist, and poet. His plays included *Abraham Lincoln* (1918), *Oliver Cromwell* (1921), and the comedy *Bird-in-Hand* (1928). For many years he worked with the Birmingham Repertory Theatre, originally The Pilgrim Players.

[2] Writing on the 22nd, Drinkwater had asked permission to stage *One Day More* for a one-week run at Birmingham Rep, starting 16 March; he offered Conrad 2.5% of the gross takings. The text appears in *Portrait*, p. 128.

[3] The Lord Chamberlain's licence, necessary for any public performance.

To J. B. Pinker
Text MS Berg; Unpublished

[Capel House]
[c. 28 February 1918][1]

My dear Pinker
I consented. You'll see to the fees.

J. C

To Lewis Rose Macleod
Text TS Lubbock; Unpublished

[letterhead: Capel House]
March 4th. 1918.

Dear Sir.[2]
May I ask you not to cut this contribution[3] into bits with leaded headings?
I notice that some of your contributors are spared this sort of collaboration
for which I do not care. I am sure you will be merciful to my weakness in
this respect. I tried to keep strictly within the limits named by you, but if by
chance the exigencies of space demand the elimination of a few lines I beg I
may be given the job myself. I will know best where to strike. I don't mean
to say that I would like to do it. But I am a reasonable person who believes
in the limitations of time and space.

Believe me very faithfully Yours
Joseph Conrad

To J. B. Pinker
Text TS/MS Berg; Unpublished

[letterhead: Capel House]
March 4th. 1918

Dearest Pinker.
This is the article. Will you kindly have it done in two copies with the
greatest possible care and if I am not to see it before it goes to the D[aily]
M[ail] will you have it compared word for word with my copy by some
skilled person. For I can't expect to get a proof. Pray also preserve my own
copy. Please my dear fellow pay the net proceeds into my account whence I

---

[1] About the same date as the reply to Drinkwater, written on the verso of his letter of the 22nd.
[2] Born in New Zealand to Scottish parents, Lewis Rose Macleod (1875–1941) began his journalistic career in New South Wales; in 1905 he moved to South Africa, where he became editor
of the *Johannesburg Sunday Times*. From 1916 to 1924 he was literary editor of the London *Daily
Mail*, where several of Conrad's essays first appeared. Macleod returned to Johannesburg in
1924 to edit the *Rand Daily Mail*.
[3] 'Tradition', published in the *Daily Mail*, 8 March, and collected in *Notes on Life and Letters*.

will distribute it amongst deserving objects. I have done it as it were in my own time. And in this connection let me congratulate you on your skill in extracting teeth from editors. I shall turn my energies to the "Story without a Name"[1] and when Miss Hallowes arrives in about twenty days time it shall run like greased lightening* off the machine. Meantime think indulgently of

Ever Yours

J. Conrad.

Please look at enclosed letter to lit^{ry} ed: of DM before sending in with clean type properly addressed. I dont remember his name.

To J. B. Pinker
Text Telegram Berg; Unpublished

[South Ashford, Kent
5 March 1918
12. 00]

Bookishly L[on]d[o]n

Pray give mail following corrections[2] page three line six from bottom delete comma after eye page five line seven from top delete the before sea page six line four from top delete comma and the word and after extreme page six line four from bottom print look outs instead outlooks page seven line ten from top delete after under page eight line six from bottom print were instead was

Conrad

To J. B. Pinker
Text MS Berg; Unpublished

[Capel House]
[6 March 1918][3]

Dearest Pinker

Here's N'cliffe's wire. Am I to accept the sum – that *is* the question.[4]

If you think *not* please take action in my name advising me by wire in the morning.

Yours ever

J. C.

---

[1] *The Arrow.* [2] These corrections are to 'Tradition'.
[3] Northcliffe wired Conrad on the 6th (Berg); as requested, Pinker wired on the morning of the 7th.
[4] He was offering the remarkable price of 250 guineas for 'Tradition', a rate of half-a-crown a word, £1 for eight words.

PS The way this draft is crossed I don't know whether you'll be able to pass it through your acc*ᵗ*. So I enclose here my cheque to you for £26. 5. o which I believe is right.

J. C.

To Lord Northcliffe
Text MS Harmsworth; Unpublished

[letterhead: Capel House]
7 Mar. 1918

Dear Lord Northcliffe[1]

It is a fact that I acceded to the Dly Mail's request because it was conveyed to me in terms implying your personal desire that I should write on the subject which, of course, could not be indifferent to me.

Everything else I left to my agent; and I did not really know what he had arranged till I received your wire late yesterday. I am certain there is no other man in the U. K., or even in the Empire, that would put such a value on any contribution of mine.[2] But it is not for me to argue against your testimony. I can only thank you for it, and assure you that I accept it "de bon coeur" (as the French say) – as, I am sure, it was offered to me.

Believe me, dear Lord Northcliffe,

always very faithfully Yours
Joseph Conrad.

---

[1] The original Press Lord, Alfred Charles William Harmsworth (1865–1922) became Baron in 1905 and in 1917 Viscount Northcliffe. Prepared by life as a teenage reporter and copy-boy, he started the popular magazine *Answers to Correspondents* in 1888. With his younger brother Harold (later Lord Rothermere), Harmsworth went on to buy the London *Evening News* in 1894, give the world the first halfpenny morning paper, the *Daily Mail*, in 1896, and found the *Daily Mirror* in 1903. Like Hearst in the United States, the Harmsworth brothers used the latest publishing techniques to cater to a rapidly expanding readership eager for simple, vivid writing and aggressively presented opinions. In 1908, the Harmsworths acquired a controlling interest in *The Times*. There and in his more popular newspapers, Northcliffe promoted his often alarmist political ideas. During the war, his strident criticisms of Kitchener and of Asquith's Liberal and Coalition governments were heard variously as patriotic or self-seeking, malicious or urgently necessary.

[2] Northcliffe's wire reads in part: 'There is obviously some mistake dear master in the suggestion that you should be paid only 50 guineas for anything you may care to write' (Berg).

To J. B. Pinker
Text TS/MS Berg; Unpublished

[Capel House]
Thursday. [7 March 1918][1]

Dearest Pinker.

Your wire came this moment. I have written to Lord N[orthcliffe] saying that I accept his "testimony to the value of my contribution in the same spirit in which I am sure it is offered to me".

This is a windfall which will enlarge the sphere of "deserving objects" and also will get rid of some bills with which I did not want to worry you till the novel was finished (the repairs to the inside of the house for instance – and other small matters), but which I'll be glad to get off my mind. Jessie pleads too that she is a "deserving object". I suppose she'll have to be recognised a[s] such.

I am going on in tolerable health and in good spirits with the novel – "writing-up" the dictated stuff. Miss H[allowes] is due here on the 23, and will find me quite ready to go on.

J's love.

Ever Yours

J. Conrad.

To J. B. Pinker
Text MS Berg; Unpublished

[Capel House]
14. 3. 18.

Dearest Pinker

I've just been notified of my election to the Athenæum under Rule II (as an "eminently distinguished" person) by the Committee.[2] I send you here the part of Colvin's letter bearing on the matter.

It is rather appalling at first sight to have to pay £40 for the honour. Luckily Lord N[orthcliffe] was there! To be frank I didn't think the thing would come off so well. I must admit that I am pleased. And at this junction I turn to you as a man whose part in this (or any other) success has been a preponderant one, with affectionate gratitude.

Pray send me two £5 notes for which I enclose cheque.

---

[1] The same day as the dated response to Northcliffe.
[2] Rule II of this august London club stipulates that every year its committee should offer membership to 'a certain number of persons of distinguished eminence in science, literature, or the arts, or for public services' (*Rules and List of Members*, 1891).

I have been in bed for 3 days with a bad wrist and feverish symptoms. This place no longer suits my health – I verily believe. Chill clay. But God only knows. However the attack in London was nothing as severe as this one. I didn't feel so ill. I could work to some purpose. Whereas this time I was really bad. A real illness.

But I am picking up and shall follow a course of treatment for a month to check this wearisome recurrence – if we can.

Ever Your
J Conrad.

To Allan Wade

Text MS Wellington; J-A, 2, 202; Knowles

[letterhead: Capel House]
15. 3. 18.

My dear Mr Wade.[1]

I wonder whether this reminder will catch You? For all I know You may be at the gate this moment – for I suppose You've not forgotten us, though no doubt we have grown shadowy as real people will do. It's only stage personages that keep their outline unblurred. Apparently art is mightier than life.

And you too are a shadow! But don't vanish – Dont! It would be unkind, to say the least of it.

I feel extremely shadowy to myself – I mean the C[onrad] of the London days. There is a great silence around me here – in which I am listening for the rustle of your shadowy footsteps. Send us a line of ghostly handwriting soon.

Yours cordially
J. Conrad.

To J. B. Pinker

Text MS Berg; Unpublished

[Capel House]
Tuesday. 20. 3. 18

Dearest Pinker.

Thanks for your letter and for the £10 received last Sat:

Will you please pay a quarter's rent (£11. 5. 0) to the firm of solicitors to whom you paid rent for me last December. I can't remember the style and

---

[1] Allan Wade (1881–1955), a theatrical manager and producer, began his career with Frank Benson's Shakespeare company. Wade was frequently associated with companies that fell foul of, or had to circumvent the Censor of Plays: from 1906 to 1915, he was Harley Granville-Barker's assistant and script-reader; from 1912 to 1916 he was secretary of the Incorporated Stage Society; in 1919, after a stint in Paris, he helped found the Phoenix Society and produced nearly all their plays. When Conrad wrote to him in 1918, he was business manager at the Royalty Theatre; the history of their earlier meetings is not known.

address of the firm, or I wouldn't give you the trouble. You however must have their receipt which gives the information.

I never doubted your sentiments as to my career. I like to think I am doing honour to your bringing up – which has given you trouble and anxiety enough. Seriously my dear fellow, I feel there's no-one in the world but you to take a close interest in what happens to me.

Ever aff^{ly} yours

J. Conrad

PS Apples magnificent. Almost reconciled me to see[ing] them baked on the table – they look so pretty in that state.

PPS In writing to them would you also give a 12 months notice to terminate tenancy.

To J. B. Pinker
Text MS Berg; Unpublished

[Capel House]
20. 3. 18

My dear Pinker.

The parcel of papers reaches me by this post.

Yes. Certainly let the Dep^t of Information have all the translation rights they like to have for the D. Mail article.

Yours ever

J. Conrad.

To Hugh Walpole
Text MS Texas; Unpublished

[Capel House]
20. 3. 18

My dear Walpole

I was just on the point of dropping you a reminder of your promise to come and see us. Your room is ready for you. Bring your MS along and see what you can do [with] it in this silence and solitude.

The Green Mirror[1] reached me all right. I asked the Missus to acknowledge it at once. She forgot to do so. A very rare thing with her.

I didn't write to You about it as I expected almost every day to have you here for a talk about that and other things.

In haste catch postman (at cross-roads)

Always yours

J. Conrad

---

[1] *The Green Mirror*, published by Macmillan in 1917.

To Lewis Browne
Text TS Indiana; Unpublished

[letterhead: Capel House]
March 27th. 1918.

Dear Sir.[1]

You must excuse me answering your categorical enquiries as to my religious beliefs. I don't feel inclined to, so to speak, bare my innermost heart to the world. I don't think the world would be very much interested in it and I don't think that such a performance can ever be altogether sincere. I ask myself whether it can be even possible in the sense in which you mean it, unless to a theologian who takes his standpoint in a dogmatic system. I am no theologian and I am too modern even to pretend that I am. I have not seen any of H. G. Wells's books on his religion[2] but I have not the slightest doubt that his religion is very good for him.

Believe me,

very faithfully yours

Joseph Conrad

To Sir Sidney Colvin
Text TS Colgate; Unpublished

[letterhead: Capel House]
March 27th. 1918.

My dear Colvin.

Thank you very much for your good, dear and sympathetic letter. For the last few days I haven't been able to concentrate either on thinking or reading or, in fact, on anything.[3] One needs to summon all one's fortitude only to watch with composure the cruel hours that fall like lead into one's heart. Don't think this is the expression of a purely personal feeling. I feel and think nationally; and though I must confess that I had no illusions for the last two years it doesn't make the reality any easier to bear. For I had hopes, to which I clung, and to which I cling yet, for they are not all dead even now, at this supreme moment.

---

[1] London-born, Lewis Browne (1897–1949) emigrated to the USA when he was fourteen. At the time he wrote to Conrad, he was studying for the rabbinate at Hebrew Union College and a bachelor's degree at the University of Cincinnati. When his vigorously socialist views cost him his first appointment as a rabbi, he became a professional writer and lecturer on religion. Among his popular successes were *Stranger Than Fiction: A Short History of the Jews* (1925), *Since Calvary: An Interpretation of Christian History* (1931), and *How Odd of God* (1934).

[2] Probably H. G. Wells's *God the Invisible King* (1917), an uncharacteristic justification of the war on religious grounds.

[3] On 21 March, the Germans had launched a huge offensive, forcing the British Fifth Army to retreat westward into Picardy.

B[orys] is right in the thick of things. At the beginning of things he was in the neighbourhood of Holnon Wood in independent command of an advanced ammunition depot of a group of three batteries, I think; his own being the 111th. That was about 12 miles from St. Quentin.[1] Even while he was on leave he was very anxious about that part of the position which was then being very heavily shelled. Those youngsters seem to know a lot. He was absolutely convinced that the main German effort would bear on that part of the front. He told me his reasons for it and assured me that before the month was out there would be, in his own words: "a pretty considerable slaughter" over there. After he rejoined there was of course nothing material in his letters which were written in a cheerful tone, the last letter being dated the 17th. This morning we had a field p. c. dated the 24th so we know that up to then he has been neither killed, nor wounded nor mopped up by the Germans. I conclude also that his battery has been saved, since I feel sure that in the contrary case one of the above three things would certainly have happened to him.

I am very sorry not to hear any better report of your health. Mine is very indifferent too as you may guess from this letter being dictated. I was in hopes of being able to come up to London before the 5th of April but that is very improbable now. It's ever so good of you to put yourself at my disposition in that way and I hope you won't think me insensible or ungrateful if I don't make a special effort to take advantage of your kindness. The fact is that there is no special effort left in me. I don't mean morally altogether. It is also physically that I am not up to it. The fine weather we had (and I assure you I am quite old enough to appreciate every moment of it) doesn't seem to have made much difference to the gouty symptoms who cling to most of my joints as if they loved me. I repay them with hatred too deep for words.

I paid my entrance fee and subscription within 24 hours of the notification of my election. On receiving a further letter from the secretary saying that he will report my acknowledgement of the notification at the next meeting I wrote begging him to convey to the Chairman and the Committee my sense of the honour done to me under Rule 2. I don't know whether it is done or not usually but I went by the light of nature by which this sort of thing seemed to me convenable.[2]

Our dear love to you both.

Yours ever

Joseph Conrad.

---

[1] British forces had taken Holnon Wood in April 1917; it was lost during the current attack.
[2] A gallicism for 'correctly done'.

To Edward Garnett

Text TS Private collection; G. 280

[letterhead: Capel House]

March 27th. 1918.

Dearest Edward.

Our warmest thanks for your brotherly sympathy with our natural anxiety about the boy. He is right in the thick of things, for at the beginning of this attack he was only about 12 miles from St. Quentin.[1] This morning we had a field p. c. dated the 24th.

Yes. Jack's testimonial, if he would give you one, would be trustfully accepted by the more or less intelligent mass.[2] As to some Big Pot, you know my dear fellow that I have no more notion of them than of Big Tango Dancers of the day;[3] so I can't suggest anyone who might serve. I would love to see the whole set of Nineteen, but not to make any suggestions. For the pleasure. For the aesthetic appeal, and to see its whole effect.

To throw a rope round the whole thing is rather a good idea, but even as to this I can't make a suggestion. I can't think consecutively and the few distressed thoughts that are knocking about in my head I am totally unable to put into words. Its a most distressing and depressing state to be in. One marches staggering along the very edge of despair hour after hour, day after day, feeling that one will never get anywhere.

Ever affectionately yours

J. Conrad.

PS Jessie's love. She will be writing to you presently.

To J. B. Pinker

Text MS Berg; Unpublished

[letterhead: Capel House]

4 Ap. '18

My dear Pinker.

This is only to tell you that the work proceeds (since last Monday) at about the same rate as in London. We have news of B[orys] up to the 30th. Please

---

[1] The focus of the German army's surprise attack.

[2] Garnett wanted Galsworthy to endorse the set of nineteen sketches that appeared in 1919 as *Papa's War and Other Satires.*

[3] Hard on the heels of ragtime, the tango reached Britain in 1913. In the *Daily Graphic* of 12 May, 'A Peeress' described it as 'a most graceful and beautiful dance' (*OED*). Since it was also a hard dance to learn, demonstrations by Argentine stars became the rage in salons, cafés, and fashionable hotels.

send Jessie £12 instead of 10 as she says she can't quite manage on the ten
per week.

The gout has left me for the time. The faithful Nellie is coming up to
London to take delivery of John at W'loo Station, for his Easter holidays. It
will be a comfort to have him here for 3 weeks.

Ever yours

J. Conrad.

To J. B. Pinker
Text TS/MS Berg; Unpublished

Capel House,
Orlestone,
Nr Ashford.
April 8th. 1918.

Dearest Pinker

That unspeakable Patron of Letters[1] has sent me the enclosed complaint
and also copies of his correspondence with you. I have answered him with
more civility than he deserves and I send you the copy herewith.

It relates strictly only to *A. F.* and it keeps closely to your suggestion of
royalties. But should he want to re-publish the other two books and wish
to get prefaces for them too he ought to pay for these in cash, unless your
diplomacy can extort from him a new agreement increasing the royalties,
which, as you know, are very low; only 12 percent, I believe.

The two books I mean are the *O. of the I.* and *T. of U.*[2]

The work progresses here. I wont say I can already see the end but I can
smell it distinctly. When I do actually see it, it isn't likely I will write to you
about it. I will be too busy running after it. John is very much home indeed.
I am not free from small pains and aches altogether but there is nothing to
stop the work.

Ever affec^ly yours

J. Conrad.

I suppose you've had news from the front. This is a horrible time.

---

[1] Conrad's (and Garnett's) long-running nickname for T. Fisher Unwin.
[2] No doubt his first publisher had noticed the recent editions of Conrad novels. As the following
letter to him shows, Unwin wanted to bring out a fresh edition of *Almayer's Folly* with a preface
by the author; he also held rights for *An Outcast of the Islands* and *Tales of Unrest*. His TS letter
to Conrad of 6 April is in the Pinker files at the Berg, as is his letter of the 9th, on whose verso
Conrad has written 'Here's the snake's reply'.

To T. Fisher Unwin
Text TS copy Berg; Unpublished

[Capel House]
April 8th. 1918.

Dear Mr Unwin.

I am in receipt of your communication of April 6th, together with two enclosures consisting of Mr Pinker's letter and of your letter to Mr Pinker, which, as a matter of fact does not reply to Mr Pinker's proposal of the terms on which I would be prepared to write a preface for a new edition of "Almayer's Folly".

The communication itself reproaches me for not answering your letter personally. I assure you that no discourtesy was meant. Your letter contained a business proposal and Mr Pinker deals with all business matters. He knows my mind on all these questions. I sent him your letter without loss of time and as he is on the spot the whole thing might have been settled in five minutes at a personal interview if you had wished it. As it is, though I am answering your communication, I really don't know what to say since in the enclosed correspondence you make no reference to the suggestion Mr Pinker has put before you in my name. It is very simple. I will re-state it here: I would be willing to furnish a preface for A. F. providing you give me an interest in the book. This could have been accepted in principle by a simple Yes. There would have been no difficulty as to the details of the arrangement, which is not prompted by any sort of rapacious instinct on my part. I think it's only natural that after something like 22 years I should like to acquire some slight interest from a business point of view in my first work.

To J. B. Pinker
Text MS Berg; Unpublished

[letterhead: Capel House]
16th Ap '18

My dear Pinker

Thanks for your letter which I ought to have acknowledged in my last to you. I had yesterday a letter from F[isher] U[nwin] which I enclose. I don't think it is worth answering – but you know best.

I have entered the period of tension with the story. After all the end *is* near. It will in the long run reach 75000 words and therefore come, I suppose, under the agreement with Dent, the first of the three.[1] It will be something

---

[1] Conrad had signed a three-book contract with Dent in 1913.

either good or bad but at any rate it won't be mediocre. The critics will have an opportunity to pile on to me if they are in that humour.

I should like to see you but I suppose I am always a sort of interruption when I come. I am concerned as to the way this last act[1] will affect you, and this concern my dear fellow is not utterly selfish, whatever a cynic might think. I am trying to keep myself steady but it is hard. Our last news is from the 11th. When did you hear from Eric?

That we should have to go through this after all these years is awful. It isn't a plaint – it's a groan I could not keep in.

> Ever Yours
>
> J. Conrad.

PS Please pay something to my ac.[*] (12 will do) as I am 6 overdrawn and may want a pound or two to run up with.

To Helen Sanderson

Text TS/MS Yale; J-A, 2, 202

[letterhead: Capel House]
April 20th. 1918.

Dearest Helen.

Your report of what poor Ted has got to go through is appalling. Those cures are atrocious things but what you describe is more like a procedure of the middle ages, when medical men treated their patients with ruthless ferocity strangely in accord with the spirit of the time. Whether the spirit of our time is less ferocious one may well doubt. It's a despairing reflection. We hope with all our hearts that dear Ted's tortures will benefit him in the end.

The last f[ield] p.c. we had from Borys is dated on the 14th. During the first days of the German attack I lived in an agony of apprehension for I knew that his battery was in the very thickest of things, its position being near Holnon Wood. At last a few lines arrived dated the 30th and we knew that he was neither killed nor wounded nor mopped up by the Germans in the first rush.[2] The battery too had been pulled safely out of that mortal scrimmage and the boy was very much pleased with his work and very enthusiastic about his own particular men, who, he tells us, "performed miracles". It was rather

---

[1] Latest military action: i.e. the British retreat after the Battle of Saint-Quentin.

[2] The Fifth Army was hard pressed during the Battle of Saint-Quentin, and the subsequent retreat provoked unmerited scorn in the domestic press. Looking back on the battle, General Gough wrote: 'Of the survivors, an average of little more than 1000 could still stand to arms in the divisions whose strength on paper should have stood at 10,000 infantry. Some battalions were reduced to 50 men' (*The Fifth Army* (Hodder & Stoughton, 1931), p. 329).

bad luck for him to have been transferred from the 3rd to the 5th Army only last September. When on his last leave he was very uneasy about what was coming and was obviously anxious about the position of the battery to which he is attached. I don't think that anything that has happened, unless perhaps his own escape unscathed, was a matter of surprise to him. But its no use dwelling upon these things.

Jessie who sends her dear love to you both is suffering a great deal of pain but she remains hopeful and on the whole well enough in health. I've a gouty thumb, but am working. I really dont understand how I manage it, but I do. It's probably rubbish. Oh yes. You shall see me in May and I hope you won't call the police to remove me till after a decent interval.

My dear Helen my heart is like lead. I don't think I had many illusions from the first; but this is so different even from a mere half of what one was led to expect!

Love to you both and pray give my love too to Ted's charming secretary and my thanks for her private line in Ted's letter, and my love to the other two dears when you write.

Ever your affc^{te} friend and serv^t
J. Conrad.

To Sir Sidney Colvin

Text MS Duke; *MFJC* 128

[Capel House]
22^d. 4. 18

My dear Colvin.

Pardon this scrap of paper. I have been at it all day and I haven't the energy at this hour (11. 30 pm) to go downstairs and get a whole sheet.

And truly I wouldn't have enough news to cover it. We had letters from B[orys] dated up to the 20th inst. His batt^{ry} has been sent back for a rest (the first time this happens to him since he went to France) and he writes the letter of the 20th from some town (either Rouen or Havre I guess) seventy miles still further back, where he and some other officers had run for a day or two to get clothes and some provisions. I reckon those boys must have lost all their kit in that infernal "bagarre".[1] But the batt[er]y is safe and the kid is unhurt so far. He's a good child. He remembered hearing me say once that

---

[1] 'Brawl'.

I liked a special kind of olives, saw some in a shop and is sending me a jar of them – out of the very jaws of death as it were. I feel horribly unworthy.

The work progresses – such as it is. I hope you are getting better in earnest. I may have to run up to town for a few hours on Thursday. Great nuisance. Pray give my love to Lady Colvin and forgive me this empty chatter.

Ever affect^ly yours

J Conrad.

To Alice Rothenstein
Text MS Harvard; Unpublished

[letterhead: Capel House]

22^d Apr. 1918

Dearest Alice

Ever so many thanks for card and invitation.[1] Yes, I'll come since You will have me. Please drop me a line to say where I am to meet You and our dear great man. Or if you prefer, 'phone Pinker's office *Gerrard 1809* after 10 am on Thursday giving time and place. I'll be there about 11 o'clock.

Our warmest sympathy goes to Will and You in this bereavement.[2]

Always dear Alice

your affct^te friend and servant

Joseph Conrad

To J. B. Pinker
Text MS Berg; Unpublished

Capel.

Tuesday [23 April 1918][3]

My dear Pinker

Will Rothenstein has asked me to lunch and to the opening ceremony of his exhibition on Thursday. I shall leave here early and look in at your office soon after eleven, just for a moment.

I've done so well with the MS all the last week that I may give myself a day off.

Ever Yours

J. Conrad

---

[1] To a preview of Will Rothenstein's war-pictures at the Goupil Gallery, London, on the 25th.
[2] The loss of her brother, George Knewstub.
[3] This comes between the dated letters of the 22nd and 27th, one written before, the other after Rothenstein's opening.

To Borys Conrad

Text MS Boston; *Listy* 369; Original unpublished

[letterhead: Capel House]

27. 4. '18

Dearest Boy.[1]

Thanks for your letter, which is not the first you wrote me since your leave. We communicated before, with each other direct, on matters which need not be alluded to at present.

Between the 20th March and the 30th when your first f[ield] p.c. reached us I had the most anxious time of my life. I dreaded lest you and the battery should get mopped up by the Germans in the first rush. The relief from that first apprehension was immense. Then we had a note from Will Rothenstein, who (as he was being chased away from the front) made inquiries as to the battery and heard vaguely that it was in the neighbourhood of Lassigny – of all places in the world.[2] Will's intention was to see you again and make a pencil drawing of you for your Mother.

Last Thursday I went to see his show of war-pictures at the Goupil Gallery. Very fine. Your friend H. A. L Fisher (Minister of Education)[3] made an opening speech. Not bad. We lunched together before the function. Lunch very bad. Mother's portable bag of sugar[4] (which I produced) a great success with the Minister. Will was evidently very pleased with You and with his reception at your mess. He and Alice send their love.

I was very much touched my dear boy by you remembering my taste in olives. That's "real friendly". But I hope you don't imagine I attach too much importance (or any) to that sort of thing. It's you[r] action that pleases me – even if the olives never turn up.

The only par: I rem'ber in *Truth* is a rebuke to the foolish talk about the 5th Army. I was glad too to read in all the papers a very high testimony from a

---

[1] Alfred Borys Conrad (1898–1978), the Conrads' elder son, was educated at private schools and in HMS *Worcester*. He showed an early interest in cars and engineering which helped to earn him a commission in the 'Mechanical Transport' section of the Royal Army Service Corps at the age of 17½. He never entirely recovered from his war experiences which included being gassed on one occasion and temporarily blinded on another. After the war, his occasionally erratic behaviour strained relations with his father (but not his mother).

[2] Rothenstein had gone to France as an official war artist. Lassigny, a small place between Roye and Noyon, was the scene of heavy fighting in June and again in August 1918. Perhaps Rothenstein had worked there, but he makes no mention of the town in his memoir *Men and Memories: 1900–1920* (Faber, 1932).

[3] Herbert Albert Laurens Fisher (1865–1940), historian and statesman: as Vice-Chancellor, he had encouraged Borys's application to read engineering at Sheffield University.

[4] Containing part of the family's allocation: sugar was strictly rationed and hoarding forbidden.

French General.[1] London is the silliest place in the world. It's* chatter sounds both absurd and heartless very often. The press with its "Enemy defeats" is exasperating too. The people of this country are not *all* infants. And on top of that comes the "back to the wall" proclamation.[2] I could hardly believe my eyes. I think it is a most improper expression to use in connection with His Majesty's Forces, under *any* circumstances – and certainly in the present circumstances. I think that the general in the Peninsular* War who rode up to his part of the line just before the French attack "en masse" and said simply: "Die hard, men" was better inspired.[3] No more for the present my dear boy. Our thoughts are with you and our hearts are anxious – but not heavy. The tone of your letter has comforted me immensely. All our loves to you.

Ever your affec^te Father

J. Conrad.

To Hugh Walpole

Text MS Texas; Unpublished

[letterhead: Capel House]
Sat. 27 Ap. '18

My dear Walpole.

I saw you too but the only effect on me was to make a mental note to tell you that you had a double perambulating the town. I was talking to a very decent fellow (on the press) called Tomlinson.[4] Afterward I proceeded to the

---

[1] On 10 April, *Truth* had urged critics of General Gough and his Fifth Army to 'stay their tongues until they are in possession of all the facts' (p. 462). The 19 April issue carried an interview with an unnamed French general (in fact General G. L. Humbert), who praised the conduct of British troops at Saint-Quentin, giving particular credit to the artillery. Meanwhile Lloyd George had denounced Gough in Parliament and relieved him of his command. Borys, however, could have drawn his father's attention to an earlier item: a complaint about a shortage of officers in Borys's own unit (3 April, p. 432).

[2] The commander of the British Expeditionary Force, Field Marshal Douglas Haig (1861–1928), issued a general order to his troops on 11 April in which he stated: 'There is no other course open to us but to fight it out. Every position must be held to the last man; there must be no retirement. With our backs to the wall, and believing in the justice of our cause, each one of us must fight on to the end. The safety of our homes and the freedom of mankind alike depend on the conduct of each one of us at this critical moment.'

[3] 'Die hard, 57th! Die hard!' were the words of Lieutenant-Colonel Inglis when wounded at the Battle of Albuhera, 16 May 1811.

[4] H. M. Tomlinson was on leave from France, where he was accredited as a war correspondent. He much admired Conrad, who had a marked influence on his fiction. See the letter to Tomlinson of 20 March 1919. Their correspondence began in 1912.

Goupil Gall^y to look at Will Rothenstein war-pictures – which was really my object for coming to town.

Could you? – would you? come down on the 4th (Sat) of May. On the 14th we hope to be in the Metropolis with comp[let]^{ed} MS of a sort of novel, and stay for a week. Of course coming now needn't stop you coming on 1st June which we will make a firm date in any case. But do try to turn up on the 4th. I've been grinding ever since you saw me last (I don't mean in the Strand),[1] and your company till Mond^{ay} 6th (perhaps run to town together) would brace me up for the final pull.

Jessie's friendly greetings.

Yours always

J Conrad.

To Sir Sidney Colvin
Text MS Duke; Unpublished

[letterhead: Capel House]
28. 4. '18

My dear Colvin.

Your letter has saddened me, but I can very well understand the mood of a slow difficult recovery from such a depressing illness as a severe influenza. I wish I could run over and see you. I am however now in bed myself – the usual thing. I hope however to meet you in London on the sixth or seventh of May, and to be initiated into the Mysteries of the Temple (of Athena) under your friendly guidance. I hope you will be improved sufficiently to carry out your intention of coming to town. As to me, I shall certainly come if I can put foot to the ground.

The tone of your reference to the days (not so very distant) when I used to raid your library touched me by its kindness. Your friendship is a very considerable thing in my life – you can not doubt it – and Lady Colvin's genius for sympathy, understanding and kindness has made it a thing of the greatest price for Jessie and myself. Our thoughts are with you daily in anxious but hopeful affection.

B[orys] is well. He writes cheerily (letter dated 23^d). I fancy the boy is pleased with the way he played his part at that time when he didn't "take off his boots for a fortnight". It was awful he says and goes on to add "and yet I enjoyed it in way". What could a Napoleon's officer say

---

[1] A play on 'grinding', which could mean working hard or having sexual intercourse; the Strand itself and its side-streets were notoriously the resort of prostitutes. Such jokes are rare in Conrad's letters.

more – or less? There is a military vein imbedded* somewhere in that child's temperament.

No more at present but with our best love to You both I am
Ever affct^ly yours
Joseph Conrad.

To André Gide
Text MS Doucet; *L. fr.* 139

[letterhead: Capel House]
28. 4. 18

Très cher ami.

Merci mille fois pour votre bonne lettre. Vos paroles m'apportent le plus grand réconfort (je suis au lit en ce moment) et l'espoir de vous voir chez nous, ici, nous a remplis de joie.

Je ne puis vraiment vous exprimer ma reconaissance pour l'intérêt fraternel que vous prenez dans mon oeuvre. J'en suis fier – cela va sans dire – mais surtout j'en suis profondément touché. C'est un grand bonheur qui m'arrive vers la fin de la vie – car me voilà sexagénaire – un homme inutile!

Borys est indemne jusqu'a present (lettre du 23 courant). Il servait depuis plusiers mois a l'extrême droite en contact avec l'artillerie française pour laquelle il a la plus grande admiration du Monde – comme du reste pour toute votre armée. Qui ne l'aurait pas?

Votre idée d'une petite edition du Typhon me fait un grand très grand plaisir Vous pensez bien.[1] En verité vous me gatez. C'est très agréable d'être gaté par un ami tel que Vous. Je me demande seulement ce que j'ai pu faire pour gagner cette affectueuse amitié qui est certainement le 'Grand Prix' de ma vie litteraire. Mais a quoi bon? C'est un cadeau des dieux.

Je pense que la revolution russe a fait vieillir plus que de raison mon Western Eyes; mais j'attends avec le plus grand interet les premieres pages de la traduction que Vous me promettez.[2]

Je suis en train de finir une espèce de roman dont l'action se passe, ou plutôt est située, en France – si Marseille est bien en France et non en Phénicie.[3] Du reste, ça importe peu. La localité est indiquée seulement. On a honte de pincer la lyre pendant que Rome brûle. Enfin.

A vous de coeur.

Joseph Conrad.

---

[1] *Typhon*, Gide's translation, published later that year.
[2] Dr Philippe Neel (1882–1941) had undertaken the translation, published in 1920. See Walter Putnam, 'A Translator's Correspondence: Philippe Neel to Joseph Conrad', *The Conradian*, 24 (1999), 59–91.
[3] Having recently begun as a Phoenician settlement.

Translation

Very dear friend.

Many thanks for your kind letter. Your words give me the greatest consolation (I am in bed at the moment) and the hope of seeing you at our home, here, has filled us with joy.

I can't truly express to you my gratitude for the fraternal interest you take in my work. I am proud of it – that goes without saying – but above all I am deeply touched by it. It is a great blessing to befall me towards the end of my life – for now I am a sexagenarian – a useless man!

Borys is unharmed so far (letter of the 23rd inst.). He served for several months at the extreme right in contact with the French artillery, for which he has the greatest admiration in the world – as for your army as a whole. Who wouldn't have?

Your idea of a small edition of Typhoon gives me great, very great pleasure, as you can imagine. In truth, you spoil me. It is extremely pleasant to be spoiled by a friend like you. I only keep asking myself what I have done to earn this affectionate friendship, which is surely the 'great prize' of my literary life. But what's the point? It is a gift of the gods.

I think that the Russian revolution has made my Western Eyes look terribly outdated; but I await with the greatest interest the first pages of the translation that you promise me.

I am currently finishing a kind of novel in which the action occurs, or rather is set, in France – if Marseilles is indeed in France and not Phoenicia. However, this matters little. The locality is only mentioned. One feels ashamed of plucking the lyre while Rome burns. Enough.

Yours affectionately.

Joseph Conrad.

To Edmund Gosse
Text MS Berg; J-A, 2, 203

[letterhead: Capel House]

1 May '18

Dear Mr. Gosse.[1]

My warmest thanks for the inscribed copy which arrived yesterday. The first time I read the book was in 1908,[2] the last was in '12 or early in '13

---

[1] Edmund Gosse (1849–1928; knighted 1925), poet, literary historian, biographer, and reviewer, exercised a powerful influence on the later Victorian and Edwardian literary world. His critical enthusiasms ranged from Ibsen to Donne.

[2] The year after Heinemann published Gosse's autobiographical *Father and Son*.

when the copy disappeared – as books will vanish from the best regulated households: especially books that are often on duty because they can be always depended upon, at any hour and almost in every mood of the reader.

Directly the little, friendly-looking, vol: was put in my hands yesterday afternoon I read – toute affaire cessante – the intro: and the first 15 pp where there are passages for which I have a special affection: such as the opening paragraph striking the first clear and touching note of the work, and the one where the walls of the little house containing these exalted lives are seen open above to the "uttermost heavens".[1]

On my return from town I had to go to bed for 48 hours. I am always being laid up by the heels in that wearisome manner. It was only on Monday[2] that I could write to my agent to find me a copy of my Reminiscences (ce titre là est bête) in a *good* condition. This may take a little time. There was only one edition of, I believe, a thousand only. I need not tell you how pleased and indeed touched I was by your asking for that particular book. I've always had and shall keep to my last day a very vivid sense of Your invariable generous appreciation of my work.[3] Believe me, with the greatest regard

Yours

Joseph Conrad

To J. B. Pinker
Text MS Berg; Unpublished

[Capel House]
Friday. [3 May 1918][4]

My dear Pinker

Will you procure me a copy of my *Rems*: for Ed: Gosse who sent me his *Father & Son* with a most civil request for the other and an infinity of comp[lts].

The work is going going – not gone out of my hands yet. The beastly thing is like an india-rubber band. Stretches.

---

[1] Of his fervently devout parents, Gosse wrote: 'They lived in an intellectual cell bounded at its sides by the walls of their own house, but open above to the very heart of the uttermost heavens' (1907 edition, p. 17).

[2] The 29th – the day before receiving Gosse's gift, if we take this narrative literally. Either Conrad knew of the book's arrival but was not well enough to handle it, or a combination of courtesy and influenza has scrambled the chronology.

[3] In 1894, Gosse read the MS of *Almayer's Folly*, and in 1902 he helped to procure Conrad's grant from the Royal Literary Fund.

[4] The only Friday between the letter to Gosse and the second inquiry to Pinker about *Some Reminiscences*, 9 May.

Miss H[allowes] takes John half-way to school while I shall correct, scrape score, polish and twist many pieces of M.S., today. Then on Sat: the last part will get started. And won't I be glad when it's done and the "murder is out" at last.

Pray give Miss H £3 for expenses as I had to borrow the amount from Jessie. Her love. When will you run down?

Ever yours

J Conrad

To Barrett H. Clark

Text TS Yale; J-A, 2, 204

[letterhead: Capel House]
May 4th. 1918.

Dear MʳClark.[1]

No. I am not continually besieged by the sort of correspondence you have in mind. I will admit that what there is of it is for the most part fatuous and not at all like your communication, which, by its matter and still more by its friendly tone, has given me great pleasure. You must not mind me answering it on a typewriter,[2] as on account of the state of my wrist the handling of the pen just now is a matter of difficulty.

You are right in thinking that I would be gratified by the appreciation of a mind younger than my own. But in truth I don't consider myself an Ancient. My writing life extends but only over twenty-three years, and I need not point out to an intelligence as alert as yours that all that time has been a time of evolution, in which some critics have detected three marked periods – and that the process is still going on. Some critics have found fault with me for not being constantly myself. But they are wrong. I am always myself. I am a man of formed character. Certain conclusions remain immovably fixed in my mind, but I am no slave to prejudices and formulas, and I shall never be. My attitudes to subjects and expressions, the angles of vision, my methods of composition will, within limits, be always changing – not because I am unstable or unprincipled but because I am free. Or perhaps it may be more exact to say, because I am always trying for freedom – within my limits.

Coming now to the subject of your inquiry I wish at first to put before you a general proposition: that a work of art is very seldom limited to one

---

[1] A publisher, editor, and author, Barrett H. Clark (1890–1953) devoted his life to the theatre. He was literary editor for Samuel French, New York, from 1918 to 1936; in the latter year he became executive director of Dramatists' Play Service; his own books included *British and American Drama of Today* (1915), *Contemporary French Dramatists* (1915), and *Eugene O'Neill* (1926); his labours as an anthologist included the 58-volume series World's Best Plays (1915–26).

[2] With Miss Hallowes at the keyboard.

exclusive meaning and not necessarily tending to a definite conclusion. And this for the reason that the nearer it approaches art the more it acquires a symbolic character. This statement may surprise you who may imagine that I am alluding to the Symbolist School of poets and prose writers. Theirs however is only a literary proceeding against which I have nothing to say. I am concerned here with something much larger[1] . . . But no doubt you have meditated on this and kindred questions yourself. So I will only call your attention to the fact that the symbolic conception of a work of art has this advantage that it makes a triple appeal covering the whole field of life. All the great creations of literature have been symbolic, and in that way have gained in complexity, in power, in depth and in beauty.

I don't think you will quarrel with me on the ground of lack of precision; for as to precision of images and analysis my artistic conscience is at rest. I have given there all the truth that is in me; and all that the critics may say can make my honesty neither more nor less. But as to "final effect" my conscience has nothing to do with that. It is the critic's affair to bring to its contemplation his own honesty, his sensibility and intelligence. The matter for his conscience is just his judgment. If his conscience is busy with petty scruples and trammelled by superficial formulas then his judgment will be superficial and petty. But an artist has no right to quarrel with the inspirations, either lofty or base, of another soul.

Of course, your interpretation of "Victory's" final aim, of its artistic secret as it were, is correct; and indeed I must say that I did not wrap it up in very mysterious processes of art. I made my appeal to feelings in as clear a language as I can command; and I don't think there is a critic in England or France who was in any doubt about it. In one or two instances the book was attacked on grounds which I simply cannot understand. Other criticisms struck me by their acuteness in the analysis of method and language. Some readers frankly did not like the book; but not on the grounds of irony. And yet irony is not altogether absent from those pages, which, I am glad to think, have not failed to move your feelings and imagination. Pray accept this long screed as warm acknowledgment of your sympathy with my work. With my best wishes for your success in the life of your choice, believe me

very cordially Yours

Joseph Conrad.

---

[1] Although Conrad suspected that all literary formulas were narrow, the rejection of Symbolism may also have to do with its cult of the spiritual, well summed up by Arthur Symons's definition of Symbolist writing as 'a literature in which the visible world is no longer a reality, and the unseen world no longer a dream' (*The Symbolist Movement in Literature* (2nd edn, rev., Constable, 1908), p. 4). Against this validation of the 'unseen world', one might remember Conrad's words in the Preface to *The Nigger*: 'art itself may be defined as a single-minded attempt to render the highest kind of justice to the visible universe' (p. vii).

To W. H. Chesson
Text TS/MS Rosenbach; *Listy* 372; Original unpublished

Capel House,
Orlestone,
Nr Ashford
Kent.
May 6th. 1918.

Dear M[r] Chesson.[1]

Thank you very much for your letter. Some time ago Adelphi Terrace[2] wished me to write a preface for a reprint of Almayer's Folly, offering payment for the same. I suggested that instead of cash I should be given a small interest in the book which some twenty-three years ago was sold outright for £20; but A. T. for reasons no doubt of high policy did not see Its way to accept that modest arrangement. For my own part I will confess I was not very anxious to write the preface, and so the matter dropped. But if A. T. must have a preface I am really very much obliged to It for pitching upon you for that thankless job.[3] I am sure that you will bring to it all your literary acumen, a sympathetic mind and every possible grace of expression. I consider myself lucky in being confided to your pen. I haven't forgotten the days when we used to see a little of each other and when you used to speak kindly to me and no doubt of me also. Those are very old times; and to tell you the truth I don't value them highly except for a few personalities for whom I have never ceased to care, such as yourself, Edward Garnett and perhaps one or two others.

There is nothing interesting in the way I came in contact with T. F[isher] U[nwin]. I knew nothing about publishers and one name was very much like another to me. But at that period of his existence T. F. U. had published some paper-bound books by various authors and I had bought one or two of them: Mademoiselle Ixe and The Pope's Daughters, I believe. My ignorance was so great and my judgment so poor that I imagined that Almayer's Folly would be just suitable for that series.[4] As a matter of fact it was much too long, as you know, but this was my motive in the choice of publisher. I sent

---

[1] As one of T. Fisher Unwin's readers, Wilfrid Hugh Chesson (1870–1952) was among the first to see the MS of *Almayer's Folly* and was swift to appreciate its promise. As a reviewer for the newspapers, Chesson later contributed several perceptive appraisals of Conrad's fiction.

[2] T. Fisher Unwin's headquarters.

[3] The job was never done. In any case, an unpublished Author's Note to *Almayer* already existed, which Conrad retrieved from Quinn in April 1919 for the collected edition.

[4] The Pseudonym Library: Unwin's publicity for the series hinted that many of the authors were literary celebrities in disguise. *Mademoiselle Ixe* by 'Lanoe Falconer' (Mary Hawker) was one of the most successful volumes, appearing in 1891 and being reprinted as late as 1924; *The Pope's Daughters* should be *The General's Daughter* (1892) 'by the author of *A Russian Priest*' (I. N. Potapenko). Conrad was prepared to adopt a Malay nom de plume, 'Kamudi'.

the MS. by messenger boy, instructing him to get a receipt, which the boy brought to me all right, and I have an invincible notion that it was signed by you; but I didn't preserve that document of the literary history of our time. The acceptance came some three months later in the first type-written letter I ever received in my life. The rest you know. It isn't a very exciting story. You won't be able to make very much of it and indeed the whole book is a small affair – the shortest I believe of all my long novels.

Believe me my dear Mr Chesson, with great regard,

Cordially yours

Joseph Conrad.

P.S. I venture to differ from you in what you say of the Rem^ces vol. I think it does throw some light on my first book. Indeed the *Rems* were written with that purpose in view:- my first book and my first contact with the sea. Vide preface.

To J. B. Pinker
Text TS Berg; Unpublished

Capel House
Orlestone,
Nr Ashford,
Kent.
May 9th. 1918.

My dear Pinker.

I had the receipted account from Mrs Pearce[1] for which thanks.

As to the matters touched upon in my letter: can you tell me whether a copy of Rems. out of Nash's stock can be obtained from J. M. Dent, or from some bookseller? Please send to Jessie the three pounds for which I asked.

I have this moment finished Chap. One of Part Five, which is the last part. Two more Chaps. will finish it. I don't suppose it can be done by the 14th, which is Tuesday, but I intend anyway to come up to town with Jessie, as we have two Stage Society tickets for a Congreve Comedy.[2] I must give myself that treat. We intend to get back the same day by the 7.15 train; and you may reckon that on the Saturday after, the story will be finished with the exception, perhaps, of the foreword and the after word which I will write while the clean copy is being typed – perhaps 4000 words altogether – very probably less. Will you lunch with us on Tuesday at one in the Waldorf Grill-room?

Ever Yours

J. Conrad

[1] Proprietor and Headmistress of Ripley Court, John's private school in Ripley, Surrey.
[2] *The Way of the World* at the King's Hall, Covent Garden; the cast included Catherine Willard.

To Hugh Walpole
Text MS Texas; Unpublished

[letterhead: Capel House]
9th May [1918][1]

My dear Walpole.

I think our arrival in London will be delayed till the 18th or thereabouts. Jessie thanks you for the invitation which she's delighted to accept.

We will return here on the 25th with the typed copy of the story for me to correct – which will be done by the time your visit here falls due.

I've been seedy for the last fortnight, again.

Yours

J. Conrad

To Caroline Marwood
Text MS Yale; Unpublished

[letterhead: Capel House]
11. May '18

My dear Caroline.[2]

I am certain it is most wise of you to have resolved not to face the difficulties of existence (which I must say I have foreseen) bereft of all support and companionship which your new alliance will give you. Pray accept for yourself and your future husband our sincere wishes for your united happiness. You who have so well proved your capacity for most steadfast devotion need not fear of any one suspecting you of forgetfulness. We who know how much you were appreciated are pleased to think that life may yet give you your reward at the hands of the man of your choice.

Believe me, my dear Caroline,

always affectionately yours
Joseph Conrad

To W. H. Chesson
Text MS Rosenbach; Unpublished

[letterhead: Capel House]
12 May '18

Dear Mr Chesson

Thanks for your letter in answer for mine. I don't think that the works you name as "not read" by you would be of the slightest help to writing a preface for A's Folly.

---

[1] References to literary plans and travel supply the year.

[2] Caroline Marwood (née Cranswick, 1868–1952) married Conrad's close friend Arthur Marwood in 1903; Conrad often visited their Kentish farmhouse about ten miles from Capel House. Arthur died in 1916; her husband-to-be was called Walter Pilcher.

That book must be judged on its demerits alone. Your indulgence will find a way to pal[l]iate them persuasively. I only ventured to mention My Rems*ces* in a postscript of my last letter because the genesis of that "first work" is expounded there at length – amongst other matters.

Cordially Yours

J. Conrad

To Lewis Browne
Text TS/MS Indiana; *New Republic*

[letterhead: Capel House]
May 15th. 1918.

A copy of this will follow by the next mailboat. J. C.

Dear Proffessor* Brown[e],[1]

Thank you very much for accepting my answer to your first letter in that friendly spirit. I somehow had an idea that you would understand.

Thank you very much also for advising me of what F[rank] H[arris] had thought fit to publish about my origins.[2] Not that I have any racial prejudices but being from long descent an "Old Christian" – a *Cristiano viejo* as the Spaniards say[3] – I feel absurdly scrupulous about a falsehood of that kind. I only saw F. H. once in my life, as far as I can remember. He was brought to my house by Austin Harrison (1913) who did not consult my wishes in the matter, and I received him politely but without enthusiasm. They stayed three hours. On that occasion F. H. laid a claim to having "made my reputation" on the strength of an article of a laudatory kind by H. G. Wells published in the Saturday Review which was then (1897)[4] the property of F. H. H. G. W. on the other hand had told me some years before that he had the greatest

---

[1] An undergraduate at the time, Browne had probably written to Conrad from a university address.

[2] James Thomas 'Frank' Harris (1856–1931) grew up in Ireland, emigrated to the US, later moved to London where he became editor first of the *Fortnightly* then of the *Saturday Review*. Later, he edited *Pearson's Magazine* in the US, in which according to a subsequent letter from Browne to Conrad, Harris published his comments: 'When F. H. called you a Jew he did so, as you righ[t]ly imagined, to insult you. He said that the trashiest hack can become popular and recognized if only he advertize himself as one of the oppressed race' (*Portrait*, p. 132).

[3] The phrase which, in the days of the Inquisition, signalled an ancestry in the faith rather than recent conversion from Islam or Judaism.

[4] The visit was in 1910 (*Letters*, 4, p. 381). In *My Life and Loves* (W. H. Allen, 1964, Vol. 4, Ch. 2), his autobiography, Harris again took the credit for Wells's spontaneously enthusiastic notice in the *Saturday Review*, 15 June 1895 (rather than 1897), p. 797.

difficulty in making F. H. print the aforesaid article – and as between the two it is of course Wells that I would believe.

In 1915 I had a letter or two from F. H. (from U. S) of, to put it mildly, a pro-German character. I didn't answer them. That very year, or perhaps the next, he sent me a copy of his book on Oscar Wilde[1] which I didn't care to have, both on account of the author and of the utterly uninteresting subject; and I took the earliest opportunity of returning the gift with a message explanatory (as above) through a friend of F. H. who wrote to me on some matter I don't remember now.

This is the history of my dealings with F. H. Of his origins I know nothing. His character is well known.[2] As to my origins anybody who has read my "Personal Record" with a certain intelligence of things European, can have no doubt of what they are. I imagine that F. H. called me a Jew in his publication as a manner of insult and in the hope of causing me extreme annoyance.

But I don't feel annoyed in the least. Had I been an Israelite I would never have denied being a member of a race occupying such a unique place in the religious history of mankind. I send you this disclaimer simply in the interest of truth.

I imagine there is no scruple which would prevent F. H. from calling me Mahommedan or a worshipper of Baal, for some reason of his own, or from the mere love of lying. Neither is there anything in him to prevent him calling me a forger, a burglar, a pickpocket or a card-sharper. He however for some reason prefers to call me a Jew. This is a statement of fact which can be disproved as follows:

I am in possession of the following documents:[3]

1st A passport in the name of Alexander II Emperor of all the Russias, and signed by Prince Galitzin, Governor of the Province, granted in 1868 to my father "the Nobleman Apollinary N. Korzeniowski and his son Conrad aged ten years, to travel abroad for the benefit of his health for three years etc. etc."

2d Copy of my parents' marriage certificate from the registers of the Roman Catholic Consistorium of the Govt. of Vol[h]ynia.

3d My baptismal certificate delivered in the usual way by the officiating priest and registered in the parish Church.

4th The Act of Decease of my father (28 May[4] 1869 Cracow) delivered by the parish priest of that quarter of the town, Minor Canon of the Cathedral,

---

[1] *Oscar Wilde: His Life and Confessions* (1916). [2] As a lecher and a braggart.
[3] From here on, every leaf of the typescript bears Conrad's penned initials as if it were a legal document.
[4] He died on the 23rd.

stating distinctly that the deceased died in the Roman Catholic religion and duly shriven according to the rites of the Church.

5th An official advice from the Burgomaster certifying that I had been elected Burgess of the City of Cracow with the remission of the usual fees, "to honour the memory of his father as a Patriot and Man of Letters", and addressed to the Highborn Lady Teofila Bobrowska as the (maternal) grandmother and the natural guardian of the minor (1869) Conrad Korzeniowski.[1]

(This last document establishes my descent on my mother's side).

In sending me these and other documents in 1894 when I became a British subject my maternal uncle advised me that if I wanted to know something more about my descent I would find it in the archives of the Province of Podolia relating mainly to the 18th century, but (he wrote to me at the same time) that he had had researches made already, which showed that during that century my paternal ancestors were men of substance and what may be called "prominent citizens" frequently elected to provincial offices of trust, and forming alliances in their own modest sphere after the usual several years service in the armies of the Republic.[2] My paternal grandfather served in the Polish army from 1807 to 1820 when he sold his land in Podolia and came to live on his wife's estate in Vol[h]ynia. Their fortune which descended to my father, his brother and his sister, was confiscated by the Russian Govt. in consequence of the rebellion of 1863.[3] Those are the origins and this is my history before my arrival in England. After that it is carried on documentarily by a series of my discharges (V. G. as to "character" and V. G. as to abilities) as seaman and officer in the British Merchant Service up to the year '94. From that time to the present day it is carried on by my written and published pages, 18 volumes in all, which have obtained a certain amount of recognition. The police of the County of Kent have nothing against me[4] – in fact, if anything, I am rather honourably known to them; even to the extent that one day when our car broke down on the road the son of our local superintendent of police came out to the rescue (5 miles) in his own car, and was perfectly charming. But that may have been on account of my wife who is a very popular person and (I may also add) *not* a Jewess.

---

[1] Teofila Bobrowska was made his guardian in 1870; she died in 1875.
[2] Conrad became a British subject in 1886. The relevant letter from his uncle Tadeusz Bobrowski has not survived. The fullest account of Conrad's ancestry in his own correspondence is in a letter to Garnett of 1900 (*Letters*, 2, pp. 244–7).
[3] The year in which Teodor Korzeniowski, the paternal grandfather, died.
[4] This avowal of respectability had a particular resonance in war-time, when suspicion of those who looked or sounded foreign could be easily aroused. Conrad himself had been questioned by the East Riding Constabulary in 1916, when he landed from his expedition in the *Ready* (*Letters*, 5, p. 689).

So if it pleases F. H. to declare me an anarchist, a forger of bank notes or anything like that I trust you will be good enough to affirm to everybody that it can be disproved on documentary evidence.

Seriously my dear sir, I would be under an obligation to you if you would kindly make public in the right quarter such part of this communication as you may judge necessary. Pardon all this long story and believe me with the greatest regard and the friendliest sentiments

Yours

Joseph Conrad.

The documents are in my drawer but I don't take the trouble to have them photographed. I think You will take my bare word on all these matters.
PC* I may add that a lot of my Father's MS are deposited in the Library of the University of Cracow. They consist of verse and prose deeply imbued with religious feeling (but free from all Ultramontanism[1]). I saw them in 1914.[2]

To Edward Garnett
Text G. 281

Capel House,
Orlestone,
Nr Ashford,
Kent.
May 16th. 1918

Dear Edward,

You are quite right in thinking that I know nothing of those people of whom you speak.[3] I don't even know their names. The one or two I have

---

[1] The variety of Catholicism that locates all secular as well as spiritual authority in Rome, on the far side of the Alps.

[2] Conrad visited the library of the Jagiellonian University at the end of July 1914.

[3] Conrad is replying to a letter of 13 May (*Portrait*, pp. 128–9). Garnett, who had been serving as a medical orderly in Italy, now faced the prospect of being conscripted for war work that went against his conscience: 'As you know I have no earthly objection to killing the responsible people who engineered the war or who are prolonging it, but I refuse absolutely to do military service for objects I do not believe in—such as the conscription of Ireland, the break-up of Austria, the recovery of Alsace-Lorraine, or other such objects (open or secret) of our ruling caste!' Rejecting the alternative of conscientious objection, 'which apparently will relegate me to the land, to Dartmoor [Prison] or any other job fixed upon as sufficiently unpleasant by officials', Garnett asked for Conrad's help in finding 'some Gov[t] job of a civil nature. If you can think of any amiable official person known to you who might help me to that end I wish you would send me a letter of Introduction.'

come in contact with must have carried away the very worst impression of my irreverent attitude and my sceptical state of mind. Like the rest of us poor mortals they resent the slightest independence of opinion and dislike those who do not swallow them whole. As to any magnanimity of conduct that is a thing almost inconceivable to their minds and truly abhorrent to their prudence.

Since leaving town I haven't been able to get hold of the young man Roberts,[1] whom I suppose you mean. He didn't answer our letters inviting him here, addressed to the Automobile Club. He may be either ill or gone away or in some other manner out of reach; but we shall make it our business to discover his private address from Mrs Willard who has introduced him to us. She too may be out of town, and in any case she is not very quick in answering letters, but Jessie will write to her to-day.

I return to you the type and the proof which you have sent me. The *English Review* thing is wonderfully done and, of course, from a certain point of view it is absolutely unfair, as you know well yourself.[2] Truth has not only been heard, it has even been chewed over and over again, and its true flavour has sunk into the very soul of the people. It is a bitter flavour but bitterness is the very condition of human existence, and mankind generally is neither guilty nor innocent. It simply *is*. That is misfortune enough. Men die and suffer for their convictions and how those convictions are arrived at doesn't matter a bit. That's why, my dear fellow, satire seems to me a vain use of intelligence, and intelligence itself a thing of no great account except for us to torment ourselves with. For directly you begin to use it the questions of right and wrong arise and these are things of the air with no connection whatever with the fundamental realities of life. Whereas in the region of feeling there is nothing of the kind. Feelings *are*, and in submitting to them we can avoid neither death nor suffering which are our common lot, but we can bear them in peace. The Edward Grey in Paris article[3] is very cleverly done. It is mordant, it is witty. But the greater the evidence of your extraordinary gifts in that way I will confess to you, my dearest fellow, the sadder I feel, not in antagonism but in real sympathy with you; with the deepest feeling for the inner tragedy of your existence – because it is nothing less than that

[1] Cecil.
[2] 'Truth's Welcome Home', to be published in the June number of the *English Review*: this and the other squibs mentioned in Conrad's letter were collected in *Papa's War and Other Satires* (1919).
[3] 'A Week in Paris'; Sir Edward Grey, later Viscount Grey of Fallodon (1862–1933), was Foreign Secretary between 1905 and 1916.

for you and for anybody who understands your temperament (inclined to remorseless analysis) and the exquisite sensitiveness of your mind.[1] Send me the *All-Highest* article as soon as you can. I shall not presume to advise any alterations because I am convinced that in such a matter nobody has any right to interfere with your mental and still less with your verbal inspiration which is simply admirable. And any way don't please be angry with me for writing as I do.

Ever yours

J. Conrad

Jessie's love. Borys all well on the 11th. Pardon type. Bad wrist.

To Sir Sidney Colvin
Text TS/MS Yale; Unpublished

Capel House,
Orlestone,
Nr. Ashford,
Kent.
May 17th. 1918.

My very dear Colvin.

Thanks for your dear long letter. I grieve that your report about yourself is not more definitely favourable, but I find some comfort in the opinion of the doctor who has your complete confidence. It is really very good of you to take the trouble and make the effort of writing a long letter. I am not, just now, answering it as I ought; but the fact is I am engaged on the last chapter of my novel and find it very difficult to concentrate on anything else. This letter is being dictated in the interval between two pages of MS. If I were to wait until the end of the day's work I wouldn't be able to produce two consecutive thoughts out of my emptied head.

Of course I have been very distinctly aware of the second edition of your Keats. Macmillan's timidity is a very well-known thing, but in this case it has worked for good by giving you an opportunity to correct, expand and, as it were, make perfection more perfect. I am ordering a copy of the second edition and when you come down here – which may the gods permit to [be] soon! – you will point out to me the additional work you have put into the book.

[1] In effect, Conrad turns Garnett into a character from the novels, a Razumov, Decoud, or Heyst.

You can't be expected to remember but I have given you some two years ago a summary view of the subject of the novel I am working at.[1] It is the story of a woman presented without action (in the theatrical sense) but elucidated by a progressive sequence of situations having a dramatic, "intime" quality of their own. The critics will have a chance to say that J. C. has turned over still another leaf. The proprieties however won't be outraged, at least no more than is inherent in the subject. The whole thing is full of conversations and is divided into five parts: as it were – Acts.

Je baise les mains de Milady and with our united love to you both am

Ever Yours

J. Conrad.

PS 1ˢᵗ or 2ᵈ June seem very possible days. We shall have Walpole here on the 1ˢᵗ and I may come up with him.

To G. Jean-Aubry

Text TS Yale; Unpublished

[letterhead: Capel House]
May 17th. 1918.

My dear Sir.

We will be delighted to see you and we suggest Monday next because on Sunday we will have visitors who will stay all day and would prevent us from all intimate talk. Even on Monday there may be people to lunch but they will go away afterwards and perhaps you could stay over night, or, if you can't do that perhaps you wouldn't mind going home by the last train which wouldn't get you to London till about ten o'clock. If so we would dine at seven o'clock which would give you time to catch the train of which I speak.

In any case you will come to lunch by the 11 o'clock train from Charing Cross, which will bring you to Hamstreet Station (the first station after Ashford, where you change) at *1.15.* Some sort of conveyance will meet you there even if I can't manage to come myself.

I will confess to you that I don't know on which translation you have been engaged.[2] André Gide has never written to me about that. Of course I am immensely interested to meet any of my translators on whom I look as my particular friends; with an added feeling of gratitude due to them

---

[1] In conversation, perhaps? In the extant correspondence, the first allusion to what became *The Arrow of Gold* occurs in a letter to Pinker from February 1915 (*Letters*, 5, p. 441).

[2] The translation of *Within the Tides*, published in 1921.

for undertaking a task in its nature so thankless and calling upon so much patience and labour on their part.

My wife joins me in kind regards

Believe me very faithfully Yours

Joseph Conrad.

To J. B. Pinker

Text MS Berg; Unpublished

[Capel House]
Monday 27 May. [1918][1]

My dear Pinker.

Herewith agreement only signed. Jessie's coming up by car to see surgeons on Wed: and shall be by your door about 12. 30. Let her have £5 for which she will send up her maid. She will bring with her parts: II & IV of Arrow of Gold to be clean-typed. Pts III & V will follow as soon as possible. I've III to revise and v to finish – last 10–15 pp. Devil of a pull. Whats done of p^t v is almost all revised already.

Pray send to Jessie's acc^t Lloyds Bank (Ashford) £20 (in lieu of relinquished pension).

Of course if I can I'll come up with her to hear what Trotter and R Jones will have to say. She'll return here at once unless the surgeons detain her.

Ever Your

J. C

To Hugh Walpole

Text TS Texas; Unpublished

[letterhead: Capel House]
May 28th. 1918.

My dear Walpole

I hope you will leave your scruples in the cloak-room before you come along here. They wouldn't harmonise with my state of mind which is expectant, looking forward and acutely aware that generally speaking the sands are running out. The work will be done by the time you arrive and even if it isn't you may be confident that you will do me good. Try to catch the 4. 28 from Char. X. and take your ticket to Hamstreet, which is the next station after Ashford, where you change. Some sort of conveyance will be waiting for you there, and if there is more than one proclaim your destination in a

---

[1] The imminent conclusion of *The Arrow* confirms the year.

bold, loud voice because the police know nothing against me (so far) and your reputation will be safe. Kindest regards

Yours

J. Conrad.

To J. B. Pinker

Text MS Berg; Unpublished

[Capel House]
Tuesday. 4. June. [1918][1]

Dear friend.

Finished this moment. But I won't come up till Thursday as I must have a day with the last pages. If you are engaged on that day (at one) pray drop me a note and I will come at three.

Ever yours

J C.

4.30 pm.

To J. B. Pinker

Text MS Berg; Unpublished

[Capel House]
Wednesday. [5 June 1918][2]

My dear Pinker

Just glance at this - it's answer to Cromwell. I don't understand all these things; and, frankly, I haven't tried much – as I am writing well now, have my own problems to worry about, and don't want to unsettle my mind which is a thousand miles from Victory and all stage tricks connected with it. But my general impression is that H[astings] is a loyal workman and that C seems to be in earnest about the undertaking. And so everything's for the best – whatever they decide – from a business point of view. Don't you think so?

Pray send me a ch for £10. 17. 0 to pay an acct. with.

Jessie has reported to me her conversation with you. Your warnings and advice would always have decisive weight with me; and the more so if, as in this case, they are in accord with my feeling about things in general.

---

[1] A combination of Tuesday's being the 4th and news of a book's completion establishes the year.
[2] The only known letter from Conrad to Cromwell is dated 7 June, a Friday. In a letter to Pinker of 27 May, Conrad mentions Jessie Conrad's imminent visit to town, a visit that offered the chance for the conversation between agent and wife. A 'Friday' letter to Pinker, assigned here to [7 June 1918?] asks him to send or withhold a communication to 'C'. If 'C' was Cromwell, and if the letter to him was the one that survived, Pinker could have suggested redrafting an earlier version sent for his inspection on the 5th.

You know me well so I won't say much more except that I don't by any means feel hopeless about myself. Things will get done, all right. This is not the end. It may be even a beginning of a new phase. Nevertheless I know that every word you said to J is perfectly sound. As to my restlessness and (perhaps) fancies they may be genuine enough (I don't get them up on purpose) but they will have to be suppressed; and to that too I am equal.

Ever yours with great aff^{on}

J Conrad.

To John Cromwell
Text TS copy Berg; Unpublished

[Capel House]
June 7th 1918.

PRIVATE

Dear Mr. Cromwell,[1]

My friend and agent, Mr. Pinker, communicated to me a copy of the letter you addressed to Mr. Hastings after the trial performance of "Victory" in Syracuse.[2]

I read it with the greatest interest and feel moved to write to you direct, first of all to express to you the pleasure your friendly and appreciative references to my work have given me, and then to express my general concurrence with the spirit in which you deal with the whole question of adaptation of a novel for the stage.

I write to you confidentially because the adaptation of "Victory" is altogether Hastings' work. He toiled very hard at it. I like the man and wouldn't hurt his feelings for anything. It is also clear that I have no standing for intervening in this particular case; but I may say that I have been struck

[1] John Cromwell (1887–1979), born in Toledo, Ohio, as Elwood Dager Cromwell, made his professional début as an actor in 1907; as a stage actor, director, and producer, he had considerable success on Broadway. In 1928, he moved to Hollywood, where he directed such films as *Of Human Bondage* (1934), *Little Lord Fauntleroy* (1936), *The Prisoner of Zenda* (1937), and *Anna and the King of Siam* (1946). A few months after the try-out in Syracuse, Cromwell was conscripted and had to abandon his plans for the stage version of *Victory*, but in 1940 he directed a cinema version for Paramount Studios.

[2] On hearing that Cromwell intended to stage *Victory* in Syracuse, NY, on 6 May, Hastings wrote to Pinker: 'Syracuse is not a very good hopping off place. The entire population are batty. But we will hope for the best' (3 May, TS Berg). The best did not occur: with only brief pauses, the production ran for $3\frac{1}{4}$ hours, delighting neither the critics nor the public. Cromwell wrote to Pinker on the 14th saying that the play would have to be rewritten entirely and enclosing a dismal statement of receipts. On the same day, he sent Hastings a $3\frac{1}{4}$-page, single-spaced critique, which is the letter cited here (TSS Berg).

by your masterly exposition of the theory of adaptation.[1] All the adapter should convey is *Primo* the spirit – the sentiment – of the book, and *Secundo* the development of the tale, since as a matter of fact the two are inextricably connected like the soul with the body. For that purpose personages may be eliminated or added, (for the sake of the tale) providing they act in accord with the spirit in which the author views the events. To attempt to convey the author's actual prose on to the stage seems to me a frantic undertaking from a theatrical point of view. I did hint something of this to H. and even sent to him bits of dialogue in given situations, as I felt it ought to go. Not a word of them was in the book; and yet, in a sense, they could not have been spoken by anybody but Mr. Jones (for instance) and rendered his psychology as accurately as any words he utters in the book. However, Hastings' point of view was different; and as it was understood between us that he was going to do all the work and have all the responsibility I refrained from further suggestions and offered no remarks upon the finished adaptation. Now, of course, it would be out of the question for me to interfere, the more so that I am not prepared to collaborate actively in a fresh adaptation. I shrink from the effort of carrying my successive points against a man whose general feeling of the task does not accord with mine and who moreover is professedly a dramatist. To do it myself would perhaps be easier but there I shrink from the task of erecting the scaffolding, as it were, because in my inexperience I mistrust my power for the scenic management of a tale. I did attempt it once in my life, and the little play is certainly not altogether inept from a stage point of view, but to do it on a larger scale would be, I am afraid, too anxious a labour.

It remains for me to thank you for the earnest thought and sympathy you have given to the production of the dramatised "Victory". I can only hope that it will not be all lost, and that you will be able to inspire Hastings with your point of view and with the necessary courage to undertake the task once more.

Believe me, dear Mr. Cromwell,

Very faithfully yours,

Joseph Conrad.

[1] 'I had too great a reverence for Mr Conrad and a love for this book, to remember that the only one and successful way to make a play from a written story, is to roughly digest it, and then *put it aside*. It has cost me no small sum to have that proven to me again. I can well understand your temptation to use Mr Conrad's dialogue, but I have proven to my satisfaction that it is not active, actable dialogue. The audience did not understand Heyst, they did not understand the conflict between him and Lena, they did not even accept the mystery of Mr Jones' . . . 'The play without Conrad would be the most utter rot, but Conrad without a play will not succeed in the theatre. And believe me, he should be there.'

To J. B. Pinker
Text MS Berg; Unpublished

[Capel House]
Friday [7 June 1918?][1]

My dear fellow.
   Herewith my letter to C. I leave the sending or the withholding of it to you.
   It is really of no importance

Your J. C.

To J. B. Pinker
Text TS/MS Berg; Unpublished

Capel House,
Orlestone,
Nr Ashford.
Kent.
June 7th. 1918.

Dear Pinker
   I have just received clean copy as follows –

Part Two. Sections ı, ıı and part of ııı. ⎱ double set
Part Five. Sections ı, and part of ıı.   ⎰

   Also corresponding *original corrected type* of both.
   Let me point out that it's imprudent to enclose *all* the copies together because if that parcel had gone astray in some way we would have been deprived completely of that part of the book. Pray for the future keep the *original corrected type* in your office, till I have returned to you the double sets of clean type, passed for the printer. And please send me the completed lot as soon as possible. Till then I will keep what I have just received here, because I don't want to have bits of the book flying about to and fro by post.
   I am now looking over Part One. I have come to the conclusion that Part One also will have to be clean typed – though it has been already done once. I'll send it to you by Sat. evening's post.

Yours always
J. Conrad.

---

[1] See the note to the letter of [5 June]: the linking of this note to the long letter to Cromwell must be tentative.

To Hugh Walpole

Text TS Texas; J-A, 2, 206

Capel House,
Orlestone,
Nr. Ashford.
June 7th. 1918

My dear Walpole.

I want to thank you at once for the little book[1] and to tell you that I am profoundly touched by many things which you have found it possible in your heart and conscience to say about my work. The only thing that grieves me and makes me dance with rage is the cropping up of the absurd legend set afloat by Hugh Clifford (who ought to have his K. C. M. G. taken away from him for that) about my hesitation between English and French as a writing language.[2] For it is absurd. When I wrote the first words of *A. F.* I had been already for years and years *thinking* in English. I began to think in English long before I mastered, I won't say the style, (I haven't done that yet) but the mere uttered speech. Is it thinkable that anybody possessed of some effective inspiration should contemplate for a moment such a frantic thing as translating it into another tongue? And there are also other considerations: such as the sheer appeal of the language, my quickly awakened love for its prose cadences, a subtle and unforeseen accord of my emotional nature with its genius. To that last, my dear Walpole, you bear witness yourself in your critical sketch – or I have misunderstood you completely![3] You may take it from me that if I had not known English I wouldn't have written a line for print in my life. C. and I were discussing the nature of the two languages and what I said was: that if I had been offered the alternative I would have been afraid to grapple with French which is crystallised in the form of its sentences and therefore more exacting and less

---

[1] Walpole's *Joseph Conrad* (Nisbet) came out in June 1916. At the time, Conrad was too preoccupied with the war to get a copy (*Letters*, 5, pp. 610, 626).

[2] Sir Hugh Clifford, Knight Commander of the Order of St Michael and St George, wrote several influential articles about his acquaintance including 'The Genius of Mr Joseph Conrad', where the story of a linguistic dilemma surfaces (*North American Review*, 178 (1904), 842–52).

[3] Walpole called the third chapter of his study 'The Poet'. He devotes ten pages of that chapter to tracing the evolution of Conrad's style (pp. 72–82), distinguishing three phases. In the first, Conrad writes as if thinking in a foreign language, and his prose can be too lyrical for its own good. In the second, the 'lyrical impulse can be seen at its perfection' (p. 79): 'Youth', 'Typhoon', and 'Heart of Darkness' are as poetic as Whitman's 'When Lilacs First in the Door-yard Bloomed' and Keats's 'Ode to a Nightingale' (pp. 80–1). In the third phase, the 'cool and clear-headed . . . slightly ironic artist' has taken over, and in works like *The Secret Agent* and *Under Western Eyes*, the former lyricism has disappeared.

appealing . . . But there was never any alternative offered or even dreamed of. Somehow C. transformed a general remark into a personal statement. There must have been on that day a particularly dense fog under that imposing bald pate of his.

Another matter of fact.

You say that I have been under the formative influence of Madame Bovary. In fact, I have read it only after finishing *A. F.* as I did all the other works of Flaubert; and, anyhow, my Flaubert is the Flaubert of *St. Antoine* and *Ed[ucation] Sent[imentale]*[1] and that only from the point of view of the rendering of concrete things and visual impressions. I thought him marvellous in that respect. I don't think I learned anything from him. What he did for me was to open my eyes and arouse my emulation. One can learn something from Balzac, but what could one learn from Flaubert? He compels admiration – about the greatest service one artist can render to another.

The tale of the "Arrow" is finished. There are only the preliminary and the final Notes to write; for it is going to be specifically and by declaration on the title page "A Story between two Notes".

It is quite on the cards that we will come to London next week. Something will have to be done with Jessie's knee at once. The thing is becoming impossible. I am considerably worried about the immediate future in this and other respects.

Thank you for your enquiry after the boy. Yesterday we had a letter dated the 3rd. He is doing Captain's duty with his battery, that officer being now on leave in England. The boy seems to like it but he confesses that the strain of waiting is becoming almost unbearable. Still he is with men, superiors and inferiors, whom he positively loves and trusts; and so, if it must come to that, it will be easier to die in their company.

Affect[ly] yours

Joseph Conrad.

---

[1] In style, milieu, and concept, the realist *L'Éducation sentimentale* (1869) and the experimental *La Tentation de saint Antoine* (1874) are as disparate as any two works by Flaubert could be. Elsewhere, Conrad's allusions to the Carthaginian extravaganza *Salammbô* (e.g. *Letters*, 2, p. 100) suggest that this, too, was a favourite work. In 1892, well before finishing *Almayer's Folly*, Conrad wrote of rereading *Madame Bovary* 'avec une admiration plaine* de respect' (*Letters*, 1, p. 109). For an incisive survey of Conrad's enthusiasm for Flaubert, see Hervouet, *French Face*, pp. 10–13. The remarks about Flaubert are on pp. 77–8 of Walpole's book. The marginalia in Conrad's own copy show him as much more willing to acknowledge the extent of Flaubert's influence than he is in this letter (Hervouet, *French Face*, p. 13).

To Edmund Gosse
Text TS/MS Syracuse; Barringer

[letterhead: Capel House]
June 11th. 1918.

My dear Mʳ Gosse.

It is very delightful to me that this old book for which I care very much should have drawn such a letter from you. I have put into it, honestly, all that there was in me of love for the language and of sympathy for mankind.

I cannot help trying to justify Nostromo before you, who, like all the early friends of my work, are part of that extremely limited audience for which one writes with a desire to please and to convince. Nostromo is a man suffering intensely all the time from an exaggerated *amour propre*. I present him at first as complaining that, after he had brought the old Englishman, (rich enough to pay for a whole railway) from the mountains, he had not enough money in his pocket to buy himself a cigar, because his wages were not due till next week. He is a man with instincts for magnificence. His prestige with the great populace is the very breath of his nostrils. The episode when he cuts (or rather lets the girl cut) the silver buttons off his coat in the view of the assembled people gives the note of his psychology. Afterwards he may be supposed to reflect as men of the people often do: Yes, I am a great man but what do I get for it? This state of mind is, so to speak, kept up by the constant railing at his unrewarded devotion by Signora Teresa: the only woman he may be said to respect and love with a filial sentiment. And, generally, all the time he suffers from non-recognition. It seems to him that people take his greatness (of which he is aware too much) as a matter of course. All those traits mark in him a man of the People. He begins to believe that, as old Viola says, the rich keep the people to fight for them like dogs.

He gives his best to those Ricos. The great affair of saving the silver appears immense to his understanding. It is, as he says to the dying Teresa, the "most desperate enterprise of his life". He half believes that to it he has sacrificed the salvation of a woman's soul. He refuses her request to fetch a priest to her bedside. Great as is his scorn for the priests he reflects that, after all, it is impossible to know that what they advance is not true. He refuses Teresa's request for the sake of the "most desperate enterprise of his life".

When it fails, in the way I describe, all the vanity of his past and the misery of his present position overwhelm him in a way. The conversation in the Custom-House with Dr Monygham, whom he dislikes and distrusts, tips the scale on the side of secrecy. Monygham (quite innocently from his own point of view) makes light of the silver-saving business and even advances the opinion that the silver would have been of much greater use ashore. In the first moment indignation seals Nostromo's lips. Afterwards, you will observe, he is not obliged to lie. Everybody he meets takes the loss of the silver for granted. He has only to hold his tongue.

You will note that Gould is not Nostromo's employer in any sense. His employer is dear old Captain Mitchell for whom he has a certain affection but no respect whatever. He won't go to him. He goes to old Viola; and if he undertakes his legendary ride to Cayta it is only really in deference to the last appeal of the dead woman: "to save the children" – and, incidentally, all the Blancos of whom he thinks with the bitterness, resentment and scorn of an unappreciated man.

Afterwards in the confusion of the first days, after the saving of Sulaco, he wanders about the wharves disregarded and idle. Why should he give the silver back to those people who seem already to have forgotten all about it?

Moreover days and days have passed. Nobody inquires after the silver. That repugnance to speak of it, compounded of many motives and feelings, has grown upon him. His interview with Charles Gould is a very formal affair. Charles Gould his mind full of the greatest possible interests, the future development of the mine, the founding of the new state, is hardly aware of the part Nostromo has played – as it often happens to the humble instruments of fate. Charles Gould has dismissed the lost silver from his mind . . . I have indicated all this in narrative form. Perhaps I ought to have presented the very scene. But Nostromo's fate was hurrying me on and I really did think that his conduct was sufficiently *motivée* by the man's character and by the force of circumstances.

The death of Decoud and the disappearance of four ingots is a fact of minor importance, yet decisive. Nostromo doesn't understand it. It is impossible for him to understand Decoud. In the bitterness of his spirit he says to himself: Why! Those Ricos, they are perfectly capable of thinking I have killed him or sacrificed him in some way – what do I know? And in truth he would be utterly unable to explain the shortage of four ingots. N. himself probably believes that Decoud has committed suicide; and he may advance this as his personal opinion, with proofs which he can offer. But supposing, even, that everybody believed him, still that wouldn't explain the disappearance of four ingots. People would say: Well, yes. It looks as if D. had committed suicide. But he has shot himself, hasn't he? A man does not require four ingots to help him shoot himself with a revolver. In his bitterness Nostromo is perfectly capable of thinking that those people who never understood his greatness would always suspect him of a mean theft.

But Nostromo is not a thief. He is a strong man succumbing to a temptation of which mere greed is the smallest possible ingredient. And even while succumbing to the temptation he still remains a strong man. He is not going to succumb to remorse. He will let nothing tear this treasure from his grasp; and at last the treasure gets hold of him and becomes the direct cause of his tragic end. In the very hour of death he is reluctant to disclose his secret to Mrs Gould. Perhaps it is only then that Nostromo secures that recognition of his character for which he had been thirsting all his life, when Mrs Gould, the perfectly sympathetic woman, is obscurely moved to refuse the confession (which she sees it costs him so much to make) with the words: "No, Capataz. Let it be lost for ever."

Now as to the question of geography. Of course you have seen yourself that Sulaco is a synthetic product. The geographical basis is, as you have seen, mainly Venezuela; but there are bits of Mexico in it, and the aspect presented by the mountains appertains in character more to the Chilian seaboard than to any other.[1] The curtain of clouds hangs always over Iquique. The rest of the meteorology belongs to the Gulf of Panama and, generally, to the Western Coast of Mexico as far as Mazatlan. The historical part is an achievement in mosaic too, though, personally, it seems to me much more true than any history I ever learned. In the last instance I may say that Sulaco is intended for *all* South America in the seventh decade of the nineteenth century.[2]

Pardon this long defence. Your opinion matters too much to me to let it go by without trying to make a case for my point of view. Many thanks for the book. I read the sketch of De la R. psychology with great delight. Vauv*es* I've read before in the pamphlet of the R.S.L. and was touched by your warmhearted sympathy of presentation.[3] It *is* good of you to have written at length about my poor Nostromo.

Believe me with very sincere regard

Yours

Joseph Conrad.

[1] 'Costaguana is no particular S. Am: State but a compound of many, mostly of Mexico, Argentina and Paraguay, with a dash of Banda Oriental and traces of Venezuela' (Conrad to Michael Holland [1913?], *Letters*, 5, p. 325). 'Chilian' was a customary spelling in the nineteenth century.

[2] Cunninghame Graham, Conrad's chief informant, worked and travelled there in the following decade, the 1870s.

[3] In *Three French Moralists and the Gallantry of France* (Heinemann, 1918), a study of François, duc de La Rochefoucauld, Jean de La Bruyère, and Luc de Clapiers, marquis de Vauvenargues. 'R.S.L.' stands for the Royal Society of Literature, but Gosse's book is an enlargement of three lectures given at the Royal Institution.

To J. B. Pinker
Text MS Berg; Unpublished

[Capel House]
[11 June 1918]

Dearest Pinker.

We may get at any time orders to proceed to town. Have you paid anything into my acc^t at the bank? I may want to draw a cheque any time.

"First Note" to *A. of G* finished and typed *clean* in two copies to be joined to the clean sets when comp$^{te.}$ "Final Note" will be ready to-morrow.

No further clean copies have reached me up to now: *Tues^y. 11th June. 4. 30 pm.*

Ever Yours

J. Conrad

To J. B. Pinker
Text MS Berg; Unpublished

[Capel House]
Wednes^d 12th 4. pm. [June 1918][1]

My dear Pinker

I am being rather dunned for an account. Will you send me £20 ch:?

The final Note of the A of G finished to-day and will be clean-typed to-morrow. All we want now is the clean-type of MS. I received yesterday double copy of further 28 pp of Part II clean copy.

The book is now complete.

Ever Yours

J. Conrad

To J. B. Pinker
Text MS Berg; Unpublished

[letterhead: Capel House]
Thursday. [13 June 1918][2]

My dear Pinker

MS (type) just received. Part v. But it is not the balance of the same. It is some few pp *short*. No doubt they will turn up in due course.

Thanks for the 20 paid in.

Miss Hallowes has in hand the clean-typing of the 2^d note (end of book). I shall join it (as well as the 1st Note) to the complete sets when I have them all here and then send the sets to you.

---

[1] The month of finishing *The Arrow.*   [2] A nearly immediate sequel to the previous letter.

I propose to keep here the batches I have received till the two sets are complete. Does this meet with your approval?

Ever your

J. Conrad

We haven't heard yet from Sir R^t Jones, but I guess next week will see us in town.

To Edmund Gosse

Text MS BL Charnwood 70949; Cox 77

[letterhead: Capel House]
15th June '18^1

Dear Mr Gosse

While the hunt for a decent copy of Rem^s proceeds (several scouts are out) I've had a copy of Nostromo bound and beg You to give it the hospitality of Your shelves.^{2} I have a great weakness for that work as my biggest creative effort. There are also other grounds for that special affection. This reprint (after 14 years) has got a bit of a preface of the autobiographical kind, on which perhaps You will cast an eye which I know to be friendly now as much as in the early days.

Believe me

very sincerely Yours

Joseph Conrad.

To G. Jean-Aubry

Text TS Yale; Unpublished

4 Hyde Park Mansions, Flat C.
Marylebone Road,
N. W. 1.
21st June 1918

Dear Mr Aubry

I return you the MS. of The Planter^3 and I am very sorry I made you wait for it so long. I have been so busy finishing my novel that I had no time

---

^{1} '15th' is a hard reading, but marginally preferable to '18th'.
^{2} It carries the inscription 'Edmund Gosse with grateful regards from Joseph Conrad' (Sotheby's sale catalogue, 30 July 1928, lot 22).
^{3} Jean-Aubry's translation of 'The Planter of Malata'.

to read with attention the other three stories. But from my rather hurried perusal I can see that they are admirably done.

We are come* to London for two months. The surgeons decided that an operation is necessary. My wife is going to a nursing home on Tuesday and the operation itself will take place on Thursday. I hope you will give me the pleasure of seeing you frequently during my stay here. If you are not going out of town for the week-end perhaps you will find time to call on us on Sunday afternoon about five. My wife asks me to tell you that it will be a great pleasure to her to see you before she retires from the world for six weeks or more. The Edgware Road stations, both Metro and Bakerloo, are quite close to the Mansions. The number of the Mansion is 4, and the flat has got the letter C on the door. It is on the ground floor on the left of the entrance, the only door. I am sorry to say we have no telephone.

Venez si vous pouvez

Bien à Vous

J. Conrad.

To J. B. Pinker
Text MS Berg; Unpublished

4.c. Hyde Pk Mans:
Marylebone R^d
NW. 1.
24 June 1918

My dear Pinker

Of the £45 you paid in to my credit I paid £37 for the flat (till 16th Augst) and something like £7 at the hotel. Since then I had to draw cheques (today) for 8 and 5 pounds. I must be a good bit overdrawn at my bank. I must ask you to pay in a fifty as there will be a few bills (this is the month of June) and of course I must have something in reserve. The operation will cost nothing but the 2 guineas of the anaesthetist.

Miss Hallowes was at your office to complete and put in order the *original* corr^{ed} type of the A of G which I believe you wish to deliver to Dent. But pray my dear fellow *don't* let him set up from that copy. The two clean sets will be in your hands in a couple of days. I am at work on them – though I have a gouty finger on my right hand.

I will ring You up at 11 am so that you may be saved answering this by post.

André Gide is here with a lot of translated stuff for me to look over and approve. Very interesting. Jack's article was done on Sat.[1] We have John here looking very seedy.

Ever Yours

J Conrad

To Sir Sidney Colvin
Text TS/MS Indiana; Unpublished.

4C Hyde Park Mansions,
Marylebone Road,
N.W. 1.
June 25th. 1918.

Dearest Colvin.

Pray send the enclosed to P. A.[2] as I can't make out the address he gives at the head of his letter.

Jessie and I will be counting the days till Lady Colvin's and your return, if only for a short time. Jessie sends her dear love to you both. I am going to take her to the nursing home this afternoon. Her last visitor before her seclusion will be Andre Gide, who is in England for a few days and has promised to call at four o'clock.

It's the greatest relief to my mind to know that I shall see your dear wife and yourself before long. I kiss her hands.

Ever your

J. Conrad.

To B. Macdonald Hastings
Text TS Colgate; Unpublished

4C Hyde Park Mansions
Marylebone Road,
N.W.1.
June 26th. 1918.

My dear Hastings.

You must forgive me the delay in answering your letter and confirming my wire. The finishing of my novel and the preparations for taking my wife to London are responsible for it. The surgeons have decided to operate

---

[1] Galsworthy had been writing a series of articles for the *Daily Chronicle* on 'The Resettlement of the Land', a longer version of his pamphlet on the subject.
[2] The artist Percy Anderson?

upon her to-morrow morning. I shall be at this address for the next two months.

It goes without saying that I am ready to give you complete freedom, without any reservation or stipulation whatever, to dramatise "Victory" on the lines of Cromwell's suggestion, if you think it worth while to undertake the task. I will even consent not to see it at all if you prefer not to show it me. I know your work. And I am certain that you will make a very good play of the story.

Believe me very sincerely Yours

J. Conrad.

To Sir Sidney Colvin
Text MS Duke; Unpublished

4.c. Hyde Pk: Mans:

27. 6. '18. 9.30 pm.

My dear Colvin.

Many thanks to you both for the wire which I will show to Jessie tomorrow. The report from the Home is that she is going on most satisfactorily. (9. p. m)

The knee was septic. How it got infected Sir Robert could not say. Very likely during the Polish journey. However Sir R. took away the knee-cap, excised all the cartilages*, but without touching the bones, and made a new socket. There is every reason to believe that the junction will take place easily and that Jessie will have a very useful stiff joint completely free from all pain.

When I saw her at 3 o'clock she was recovering and told me that (apart from the pain left by the operation itself) she felt greatly relieved. She asked me in a faint voice to send her love to Your wife and Yourself.

It was good of you to write me a long letter. Obviously the only thing is to keep away from London. I shall take the utmost liberties with library.

Borys arrived on sp[eci]*al* leave on Tuesday evening. This made Jessie quite happy. We shall have him with us for another 10 days and by that time Jessie'll have made considerable progress.

No more at present. I am going to bed with my mind more at ease that* it has been for years – in that particular respect. My dear love.

Yours

J. Conrad

To J. M. Dent
Text TS/MS Berg; Unpublished

4C Hyde Park Mansions,
Marylebone Road,
N.W. 1.
[28 June 1918]¹

Dear Mʳ Dent

Thanks very much for your friendly letter acknowledging the receipt of the MS. of the *A. of G.* I trust that when sending it to you Pinker made it perfectly clear that you must not set up from it as the clean copies now in my possession have been much corrected, mainly in the way of eliminating superfluous words and phrases and generally pulling together the style. It would be positive hardship for me to have to insert on the proofs the further corrections I have made and am making now on the clean copy.

I assure you that yours are the only eyes (barring Edward Garnett's) that have seen the story as a whole so far.

You mustn't take it ill if I don't accept your invitation for Wednesday next. My wife has been operated on yesterday and for the next week or so I am spending every moment of my time with her. One can do no less for a friend of so many years standing.

I am delighted with your good opinion of *Western Eyes*. That book had an enormous success in Russia I've been told. Yes! I too wish You had it in your hands.² Pray give my regards to Mʳ Hugh.

Yours faithfully
Joseph Conrad

To J. B. Pinker
Text MS Berg; Unpublished

[4C Hyde Park Mansions]
Wednesday. [3 July 1918]³

My dear Pinker

This is the Nursing home bill which please settle for me. I am in for flu', I fear

Yours ever

J. C

---

¹ Written the day after the operation and date-stamped in Dent's office on 1 July.
² Methuen owned the rights.
³ Around the period of his wife's operation on Thursday, 27 June, Conrad was still in fair health. By [5 July] he was ill and in the care of Dr Mackintosh.

To Jessie Conrad
Text MS Yale; *JCLW* 33

[4C Hyde Park Mansions]
Friday. 7. pm. [5 July 1918][1]

Dearest Girl[2]

Mac[3] has been and prescribed for B[orys] and also for me. B has some temp*re* but it is going down. It is certainly a pretty sharp attack of 'flu. I am getting on all right and have no reason to apprehend any new develop*ts*. Mac is coming to-morrow.

I've just got your note and also a message that you want N[ellie] to come in the evening. I am sorry to say that she won't come. She has been attending on B and may carry infection. I won't let you run that risk. And any way if I am not allowed to see you I don't see why anybody else out of the flat should see you. I had no 'flu and no temp*re* myself.

Directly B's temperature falls to normal he won't be infectious and you shall have visits from everybody. Write to me by post. Mac gave me an excellent report of you. All will be well presently.

Your Most loving

Boy.

To J. B. Pinker
Text TS/MS Berg; Unpublished

4C Hyde Park Mansions,
Marylebone Road,
N. W. 1
July 5th. [1918][4]

My dear Pinker

Thank you very much for the cheque and the letter for Borys which he received this morning. Yes. Pray send on to Jessie's account as requested by her. That money keeps the household expenses here going and wages

---

[1] For the sequence of letters about the family's health, progress reports in the dated letters of the 6th and 13th establish the period, and holograph days of the week clarify the order.

[2] Jessie Emmeline Conrad (née George, 1873–1936) probably met her future husband in 1894. One of nine children, she was working as a typist and living with her widowed mother in Peckham, South London. The Conrads married in March 1896. Both biographers and those who knew her disagree about her personality: some disparage her stolidity or patronise her want of formal education, others admire her fortitude and her shrewd management of a somewhat cantankerous family. An accident to her knees in 1904 exacerbated a previous injury, leaving her lame and in pain for the rest of her life. She wrote two books about her husband, *Joseph Conrad as I Knew Him* (1926) and *Joseph Conrad and His Circle* (1935); her *Handbook of Cookery for a Small House*, accepted by a publisher in 1906, did not appear until 1923.

[3] The Conrads' medical friend, Robert Duncan Mackintosh.

[4] The year of resuming work on *The Rescue*, finished in May 1919.

both here and at Capel. The Nursing Home fees will amount to about £72 for the six weeks; but with your diplomatic handling a couple of articles would earn that and more, here and in America.[1]

That is why I suggested doing them if opportunity offered. My view is that those articles, (if any are written) won't interfere appreciably with my work on the "Rescue" and it would be satisfactory to cover the extra expenses as they occur. I am really anxious to do that as at any moment we may be called to pay the first half of the income tax which, as far as I remember, will be £220. At the same time I shouldn't like to undertake a series unless you think it necessary for me to do so. A series of articles would occupy my mind too exclusively. I wish to avoid that in view of the necessary concentration to proceed with the "Rescue" which, I understand, you wish me to do.

With any sort of luck the "Rescue" will be finished this year. I am reading it over now for the 20th time at least. I must try to catch on to the old style as much as possible. But if I can't it will have to be done anyhow.

There may be some small household bills to pay which I can't manage [and] I'll have to send to you.

In haste

Ever Yours

J Conrad

To Jessie Conrad
Text MS Yale; *JCLW* 41

[4C Hyde Park Mansions]
Saturday. [6 July 1918][2]

Dearest Girl.

Thanks for your letter. You are a great treasure.

Boy has still a temp: but no headache this morning. Mac[kintosh] has promised to see him today and give him a certificate for the War Office.

John is gone with Miss Hallowes to the Bank. I had a letter from Mrs Pearce arranging to meet his train on Mond: afternoon. The best thing for John is to go back to school.

I am still a bit shaky.

Edward was here last night and left his love to you. Aubry came about 9 o'clock and sat up with me till nearly one. I was very glad of the company.

Boy got easier about 3 am and I fell asleep like a stone till 8 this morning. Bones[3] got up at six – she says – to have a look at B. and then got all our

---

[1] By the 16th, Conrad was planning the first of three articles for the *Daily Chronicle* about the war-time achievements of the Merchant Navy.

[2] Borys's high temperature persisted, but he had recovered by Saturday the 13th.

[3] The family nickname for Nellie Lyons, who was very thin.

breakfasts ready by 8. 30. I am keeping very quiet for indeed I am not very fit for much flying about.

This letter is to be taken to you by Doris.[1] Nellie has made up a parcel as instructed incl 2 bott sham.[2]

Our love to you

Ever your Boy.

To Jessie Conrad
Text MS Yale; *JCLW* 43

[4C Hyde Park Mansions]
5.30 pm. [6 July 1918][3]

Dear Treasure.

Mac[kintosh] would have told you about B[orys] and myself. I went to the W[ar] O[ffice] this afternoon in a taxi John attending me very nicely.

B still very hot but head easy. He had some lunch – a help of spagh^{tti} cooked in milk and some peaches (cooked).

Everything is infinitely horrible to go through, without you to boss the show and cheer one's heart with your dear eyes. I worry a bit about you being in so much pain. Still to think of You making such splendid recovery does cheer one.

I don't think I'll phone to-night. I shall keep dead-quiet for I am still a bit shaky.

Ever tenderly Yours

J. C. Boy.

To André Gide
Text MS Doucet; *L. fr.* 141

4c Hyde Park Mansions.
Marylebone R^d
N.W. 1.
6 Juillet. 18.

Mon cher Gide.

Juste un petit mot pour Vous dire que ma femme va aussi bien que possible. L'opération a été un grand succès.

---

[1] Unidentified: perhaps another maid, but not one of the Vinten sisters, who worked for the Conrads in the post-war period.

[2] Champagne.

[3] Since John went back to school on the Monday, he and his father must have gone to the War Office on the day Mackintosh produced the medical certificate.

M. Ruyters[1] est venu me faire visite. Je me sens beaucoup de sympathie pour lui. Du coup après l'avoir vu, j'ai compris *le Mauvais Riche*[2] d'une façon plus complète.

J'ai eu une legère grippe. Mon grand garçon l'a eu severement. Il est encore au lit et son congé en sera prolongé d'une semaine au moins.

Mes felicitations les plus chaudes au sujet de Votre filleul et neveu.[3] Du reste j'ai toujours senti qu'il y avait un fond héroïque dans la nature française. A présent le monde entier le sait – mais mois je suis un 'vieux croyant',[4] et mon cœur se dilate de voir ma croyance établie comme une grande vérité aux yeux des hommes.

Je suis profondement touché de savoir que deux jeunes Français ont trouvé le temps (et le désir) de parler de ma prose là bas – la bas![5]

A bientôt, j'espère.

Tout a vous

J. Conrad.

Translation

My dear Gide.

Just a line to tell you that my wife is doing as well as possible. The operation was a great success.

M. Ruyters paid me a visit. I liked him a good deal. Once I'd seen him, I understood *Le Mauvais Riche* more fully.

I had a slight cold. My older boy came down with it badly. He is still in bed and his leave will be extended for at least a week.

My warmest congratulations regarding your godchild and nephew. Moreover, I have always felt that there was an heroic depth to the French character. Now the whole world knows it – but I myself am an 'old believer', and my heart swells to see my belief established as a great truth in the eyes of men.

---

[1] The Belgian novelist and poet (originally Ruijters, 1876–1952).

[2] A collection of pieces in several genres published in 1907. The title-story alludes to the young man in the gospels who 'had great possessions' and 'went away sorrowful' when Christ told him to give them to the poor (Matthew 19.16–22).

[3] On his very first day in combat, Dominique Drouin, Gide's nephew and godson, had won both the Croix de guerre (with palms) and the Médaille militaire for leading a raid behind enemy lines.

[4] Perhaps an allusion to the *Raskolniki* or Old Believers, the spiritual heirs of those who broke with the Russian Orthodox Church in the seventeenth century over the issue of liturgical reform. Robert (*Dictionnaire alphabétique et analogique de la langue française*) gives 'vieux croyant' in this sense, citing Jules Verne's *Michel Strogoff* (1876).

[5] In the trenches?

I am deeply touched to hear that two young Frenchmen have found the time (and the desire) to speak of my prose down there – down there!

Hope to see you soon.

Yours truly

J. Conrad.

To Jessie Conrad
Text MS Yale; *JCLW* 39

[4C Hyde Park Mansions]

Sunday. 2 pm [7 July 1918][1]

Dearest Chica

Mac having not turned up till now I am sending John and Bones to take you the flowers left by Aubry this morning and the few letters which arrived by last night's post.

All here is going tolerably well. B[orys]'s temperature is but a degree or so above normal. He has some appetite. I fancy it is safe now for John to see you for a few minutes. However let the Matron decide that. Would Miss Clapperton[2] lend you a couple of books for Borys to read? If so I should ask also for Sir Frank Swettenham['s] book.[3] It is on the *topmost* of the bookshelves in the dining room. I am not certain of the title. That however is of no great importance.

I am still a little shaky but am getting on steadily. Bones is doing her best but she is slightly distracted all the time. Still the machine works after a fashion. Since yesterday I am using your Foot's chair.[4] It's a great comfort; and it also seems to bring something of your personality into the flat. Its good to think that when you've your place in it it will be no longer to suffer agonies but just to enjoy its friendly comfort. My tenderest love to you best of women.

Ever Your Boy.

B sends his love. He looks very big in our bed where I put him from the first. John and I occupy the small room. John must go to school tomorrow.

---

[1] The day before John's return to school.
[2] The Colvins' obliging cook? See the letter to Sir Sidney of 4 August.
[3] Sir Frank Swettenham (1850–1946) began his administrative career in the Malay Archipelago in 1871 and was particularly active in negotiations with Malay rulers; in his last years of service there, he was High Commissioner for the Malay States and Governor of the Straits Settlements. Among the books Borys might have picked up were *Malay Sketches* (1895), *British Malaya* (1907), or *Also and Perhaps* (1912).
[4] The wheelchair purchased as an anniversary present in April 1917.

To William Archer
Text TS BL Ashley 45291;[1] Facsimile, Fletcher 108

4C Hyde Park Mansions,
N. W. 1.
July 10th, 1918

Private

My dear Archer[2]

I have your letter dated from Wellington House.[3] I don't know what is the Department occupying that address, an ignorance which I share with 95 per cent of the subjects of the Crown.[4] You make it also a point of explaining to me that I wouldn't be eating your dinner but a dinner offered by a Department. As a matter of fact I would much sooner dine with you than with the best of Departments, but I can't accept an invitation from a Department Unknown to dine with one or two(!) Americans whose name (or names) are with[h]eld from me.

You really cannot expect me to come out to a dinner of that sort like an imbecile without even knowing whom I am going to meet. No personal distinction, even as great as yours, no exalted official position, and not even a close intimacy of many years gives a man a right to send out such an invitation. I wonder whether you would have asked in such terms a barrister of any standing, or a doctor, or a clergyman. I very much doubt it. "One or two Americans!" I am sixty, – I have 25 years of honest literary work behind me and it is highly improper for a Department to address me in this manner as if I were a youngster who ought to be glad of any sort of notice being taken of him.

[1] Yale owns a TS draft corrected in pen. The corrections are incorporated in the text sent to Archer, which does not restore the deleted phrase 'There is their Ambassador whom I know personally, for instance—'.

[2] William Archer (1856–1924), a Scot, began his career as a drama critic in 1879, with the *London Figaro*. Later, he wrote for the *World, Nation, Tribune, Morning Leader*, and *Manchester Guardian*. An editor and translator of Ibsen, he fought to make the British stage more serious.

[3] The offending invitation reads 'A small dinner is being arranged by this department in hono[u]r of 2 or 3 distinguished Americans, notably Professor Canby of Yale who is anxious to meet you. It is to be at the Reform Club on Monday the 15*th* at 7.30 for 7.45. I hope you will be able to come. You will not be my guest, of course, but the guest of the department.' Archer did not specify the department ([9? July], MS pencil draft, BL; *Portrait*, p. 130).

[4] In 1914, Ford's friend C. F. G. Masterman (1873–1927) set up the War Propaganda Bureau, recruiting novelists, playwrights, essayists, and historians sympathetic to the Allied cause. Their mission was to influence world and especially neutral opinion. Headquarters were in Wellington House, a converted block of flats in Buckingham Gate formerly the offices of the National Insurance Commission and still bearing that name as a cover. The bureau became the Literature Department of the new Ministry of Information in 1917, and its chief was now the Scottish author and former imperial administrator John Buchan. Archer headed the department's Scandinavian section.

On the other hand it is very easy to leave Joseph Conrad alone. He doesn't thirst for that sort of recognition. As to the distinguished Americans whose name[s] you don't think worth while to communicate to me, if they really want to meet Joseph Conrad they must find some other way. It wouldn't be very difficult.

Believe me

Very faithfully Yours

Joseph Conrad.

To William Archer

Text MS BL Ashley 45291; Unpublished

4C Hyde Park Mansions,

N. W. 1

July 12th. 1918.

My dear Archer.

I am compunctious, yet, really, how was I to know?[1] If You had said – my Dep^t proposes to ask you to meet some Americans – will you accept? I would have understood. However the slowness of my wits is punished sufficiently by a wretched cough which has descended on me yesterday. As I've had a touch of 'flu' already I am going to 'phone to my doctor who may, for all I know, intern me in this beastly flat for a week. It occurs to me also that I may not have time to get down in time my dress-suit which somehow has got left behind in the country. Upon the whole I think it is safer for me to express my regret and to plead inability.

Believe me

Always faithfully yours

Joseph Conrad.

To Helen Sanderson

Text TS/MS Yale; Unpublished

4C Hyde Park Mansions,

N. W. 1.

July 13th. 1918.

Dearest Helen.

My dismay at your tidings would have been much greater if I didn't know the stoutness of your heart. The bright spot of course is the good report of

---

[1] Archer had replied to Conrad with a contrite letter identifying the department and the guests, both American and British (11 July, TS carbon, BL; *Portrait*, p. 130). For details of these guests, see *ibid.*, p. 130, n. 1.

Ted's health, and I can imagine what comfort and help dear Kit must be to you both in this horrible gale of wind.

In an hour or so I will be taking your letter to Jessie at the Nursing Home. She has been thinking and talking very much of Elstree lately and was very much disappointed when B[orys] and I had to give up the hope of coming to Elstree if only on a couple of hours visit. Both our 'flus are better and if it had not been for your letter received last night we would have asked permission to come to lunch on Sunday. But as it is I won't have the happiness of presenting the kid to your friendly eyes before his departure for the front.

He is very anxious to get back to his column and his guns in view of the expected push. His brigade of heavy guns has been transferred to Flanders and he wants to become familiar with the country and all its roads before the business begins. His stories of the great retreat in March have been extremely interesting and both appalling and inspiring in their details. His battery retired fighting all the time and came out of it with its proper number of guns. Not all the same guns, but still the proper number. You must understand that in those days six-inch howitzers could be had for the trouble of picking them up in the fields.

Poor Jessie is having a rather bad time just at present. She is facing the pain cheerfully; what frightens her a little is the prospect of a long imprisonment in the nursing home. She will write to you today or to-morrow. I want to see you all before You leave Hill House at the end of the term, but I won't come over till you tell me I may do so. B. will start for France on Tuesday next, and then my loneliness will be awful. Without Jessie I am like a lost soul. Give my love to Ian when you write. Love to all the house.

Ever Yours

J. Conrad.

To G. Jean-Aubry
Text TS copy Yale; *L. fr.* 142

[4C Hyde Park Mansions]
lundi 16 juillet [15 July] 1918[1]

Cher Monsieur,

Comme mon fils ne part pour le front que jeudi matin, il nous faudra remettre la soirée de lecture (que nous avons fixée pour mercredi) à plus tard dans la semaine.

---

[1] Monday was the 15th. The confusion of dates could be Conrad's own or Jean-Aubry's. At the bottom of the Yale text is the annotation: 'copie d'une lettre adressée à G. Jean-Aubry et donnée par lui à Mlle Irène Rakowska (Mme. L. Luniewska) cousine de Joseph Conrad'.

Je me trouve engagé pour jeudi soir. Le vendredi j'aurai Garnett, de sorte que je ne vois guère que le samedi. Ca vous conviendra-t-il? Ou peut-être dimanche dans l'après-midi.

Envoyez-moi un petit mot.

Amitiés

J. Conrad.

Translation

Dear Sir,

As my son does not leave for the front until Thursday morning, we must put off the reading evening (which we fixed for Wednesday) until later in the week.

I am engaged on Thursday evening. On Friday, I will have Garnett here, so the only possibility is Saturday. Would that be convenient? Or perhaps Sunday afternoon.

Drop me a line.

Regards

J. Conrad.

To J. B. Pinker
Text TS/MS Berg; Unpublished

4 C Hyde Park Mansions,
N. W. 1.
July 16th. [1918][1]

Dearest Pinker.

I send you here two sweet documents, one of which is unavoidable and the other I couldn't avoid. Please put the bank right giving me also a credit of £20.

I know you will be glad to hear that Jessie is going on so well that she may be out of the nursing home by the end of this month. All the unfavourable symptoms have subsided, the reabsorbtion* of fluids is proceeding quickly and the surgeon tells me that in a fortnight or so it will be possible to put the joint into plaster of Paris. This will have to remain for some six months and then we will have to come up to town again to have it taken off and for a three week's* course of massage for the upper muscles. And that will be the end of the job.

---

[1] Borys's 'flu' and Jessie Conrad's stay in the nursing home identify the year.

It is pretty certain now that we will not need to prolong our tenancy of this flat beyond the two months which have been paid for already. They expire on the 16th Aug. but I think we will be home in the country before that.

Personally I am not very well. My touch of 'flu' left behind a most abominable cough which exhausts me and makes me feel seedy. In addition I have a gouty right hand and a fit of shivers every evening. You won't be surprised to hear that I don't feel particularly cheerful just now.

B[orys] had most violent 'flu'. He is leaving for the front on Thursday, and next week John will be coming back from school. More bills! I shall tackle the Chronicle article[1] in a day or two and you may be sure, my dear fellow, that if I can make it a series of three I will do it. I haven't been out anywhere for days except for my visit to Jessie with whom I spend the afternoon every day.

I feel I want to see you to renew my confidence and vitality. I shall make the attempt before long.

Ever yours

J. Conrad

To R. D. Mackintosh
Text MS Alberta; Jellard

[4C Hyde Park Mansions]
17. July 18.

My dear Mackintosh.[2]

I sit down to send you the good news. Aitkin* has told Jessie that she may hope to be out of the home by the end of the month. The re-absorption of fluids takes place quickly and Aitkin* thinks he may be able to put the joint into plaster in a fortnight from today.

Jessie no doubt will be writing to you herself but meantime she desires me to give you her love. She looks better than she did last week but she has not got her appetite back yet.

I have been racked by a most horrible cough (perhaps of gouty origin) but it is better today. Borys is leaving tomorrow morning – and that's our greatest trouble just now.

Your friend John went back to school ten days ago and is now working at his exams with some success – I hear. B rushed over today to see him for an hour.

---

[1] This became the tripartite 'Well Done!', *Daily Chronicle*, 22–4 August.
[2] Robert Duncan Mackintosh (1865–1934) practised medicine in Barnes, South West London. From 1909 to 1921, when they had a falling out, Conrad valued the company and the advice of this Scottish doctor, an amateur playwright and inventor described by his great-niece as 'an unpractical enthusiast and dreamer'.

I expect we will be able to leave for the country about the 15 Augst.
Goodbye for the present

Always Yours

Joseph Conrad.

To Mr Batty

Text TS Yale;[1] Unpublished

4 C Hyde Park Mansions,
N. W. 1.
July 19th. 1918.

Dear Mr Batty.[2]

Your letter has given me great pleasure as evidence of recognition on the part of British seamen amongst whom I have spent the best years of my life. I call them the best because those were the earliest years of my independent existence.

They are very far away now, but looking at this distant past impartially I feel moved to express my deliberate opinion that the sea-going generation of forty years ago, those with whom I worked, who taught me my business and by their precept and example formed my character, were in every respect as good men as those of to-day to whom the nation accords, as a body, the reward of its gratitude, praise and affection.

The root of the matter was in those men, the friends and fellow-workers of my youth. They lived their hard lives obscurely. The opportunity was not for them, the opportunity to show the great worth of the sea training and the sea tradition.

The opportunity was reserved for the men of to-day. They have answered its demands most nobly. The nation has discovered the high qualities of its civilian seamen. It seems to me that it has discovered them with some surprise. One remembers with a little amusement and not a little indignation the prophecies of several distinguished men (who ought to have known better) that the first half dozen sinkings by U-boats would clear the sea of all merchant ships. To an old seaman like myself it seemed a very strange pronouncement: for in the twenty years and more of my sea life I had never perceived that chicken-hearts were a part of the equipment of any ship or fishing-boat that ever went to sea.

---

[1] Incidental corrections to the TS are in Miss Hallowes's hand, but the greeting and signature are in Conrad's.

[2] Mr Batty must have been a sailor and perhaps a journalist as well. Conrad's letter seems designed for circulation among sailors, perhaps in a seafaring magazine. Its tone and content are close to those of 'Well Done!', published in the *Daily Chronicle*, 22–4 August.

Therefore as an old seaman I am very proud of but not a bit surprised at the fidelity and courage of the men of to-day – coasting-men, fishermen, deep water sailors – all the men who, from their early youth had found their work cut out for them at sea. And I am glad to have this occasion to express to them through you my warmest admiration and my brotherly regard.

Very faithfully yours

Joseph Conrad.

To Jessie Conrad
Text MS Yale; Unpublished

[4C Hyde Park Mansions]

Sunday. [July or August 1918][1]

My dearest Chica

I have just had your message. No dear, I'll not come out today. You think it will be more prudent not to do so. Anyway I have taken some fizzy medicine this morning and am expecting the usual consequences.

Young Chatteris [?][2] called yesterday and proposed to visit me this afternoon. He has got his hen with him – but the old Birds are away for the week end. It's funny.

Can't say I feel very bright yet. Still I have no particular pain anywhere today and I didn't have a bad night. I am horribly bored with the situation and I am unhappy at being separated from my kitty. Bless you my dearest darling.

Ever your own

JC

To Sir Sidney Colvin
Text TS/MS Berg; Lucas 309

4C Hyde Park Mansions,

N. W. 1

Aug. 4th. [1918][3]

My dear Colvin.

Yesterday I was well enough to go out in a taxi and raid your book-cases. I looted four volumes of different works which shall be put back religiously in the places where they came from. Your cook was most amiable and received me like a long-lost friend and generally made me feel at home; but to enter into the house made me feel vividly how much I missed Lady Colvin and you.

---

[1] The circumstance of Conrad's being unable to visit his wife points to the summer of 1918. He had influenza in early July and lumbago in early August; the absence of dated letters from late July suggests he was also ill then.

[2] Unidentified.   [3] The Conrads' health and Gibbon's activities identify the year.

I really wouldn't dare to come down to you for a night. I can't shake the gout off definitely, my left hand is still crippled; and in addition I have had a severe attack of lumbago which made me crawl about bent double like an ancient gaffer and, generally, makes me unfit for civilised society.

Jessie is getting on well, generally, with slight ups and downs which is to be expected. She can't possibly leave the nursing home till the end of the week – if then. There is no use in coming to the flat unless she can help herself more than she is able to do as yet. The confinement tells on her a little bit, but upon the whole her general health is holding out wonderfully. I ought to be immensely bucked up but as a matter of fact in consequence of my gouty state I feel horribly depressed.

I doubt whether we will be able to get away by the 15th. I am sure it will be best for all of us to be in the country. John is looking well and passed his twelfth birthday in a cheerful frame of mind, mainly induced by the large tip he received from his adopted uncle Perceval Gibbon.

P. G. has seen me several times and asked me to send to Lady Colvin and yourself his affectionate regards. The poor man is not happy. He yearns for his girls whom he had* not seen for three years.[1] He is now in the service of the Admiralty and has the rank of a Major of Marines. I think he is doing very good work. He is off to-morrow on a mission of 30 days to the French and Italian Navy. He has learned Italian and acquired an immense love for Italy, and he sleeps with the Div[ine] Com[edy] under his pillow. B[orys] wrote the other day. He's well and cheery but rather overworked. He's now in Flanders.

With my dear love to you both

Ever yours

J. Conrad.

To Jessie Conrad
Text MS Yale; *JCLW* 35

[4C Hyde Park Mansions]
5 pm. [4 August 1918][2]

Dearest own Kit

Thanks for your letter. I love to see your handwriting when I can't see you yourself.

I am just finishing 2^d article for Dy: Chron:[3] Had mustard plaster for 1 $^1/_2$ hours on my back this afternoon. Back still smarts but lumbago easier.

---

[1] Because their parents were estranged.
[2] The day before Jessie Conrad's letter to Pinker of the 5th (MS Berg), which reports progress on the articles and gives news of Conrad's health.
[3] 'Well Done!' appeared in three instalments.

Cheque gone. Writing painful so finish here with a great long hug and many kisses on my poor Kitty.

Ever

your Boy.

To Jessie Conrad

Text MS Yale; *JCLW* 37

[4C Hyde Park Mansions]
[c. 8 August 1918][1]

Dearest Girl

Don't be angry with me but I think I will stay in all day and see what a course of steady heat and rest will do to improve my back-ache. At the same time I shall be correcting steadily my artc*les* for the DC. I finished the last this morning. Ask Mac to call on me if he turns up in your place first.

My appetite is not bad – only that back worries me still a little. I want to be as fit as possible for the journey.

You are a very dear good, charming plucky, sweet, pretty kitty-faced girl and I love you very much.

Ever

your Boy.

Poor Sidie.[2] I am sorry!

To J. B. Pinker

Text MS Berg; Unpublished

[4C Hyde Park Mansions]
10. AM. [c. 8 August 1918][3]

Dearest Pinker

Articles will be with you *clean* typed on Monday as I can't finish my correcting and typing till Sat:

Pray advance me on the 100 agreed to be paid into my acc*t* from proceeds of D. C. articles two cheques. *£11. 18. 0.* and *£9. 3. 6.* (made to me). I am

---

[1] The same day as, or at most a day or two before, the '10. AM.' letter to Pinker promising revisions: that letter was probably written before the 9th; Conrad spent the 8th in bed and on the 9th managed to visit Jessie.

[2] A nickname of Sir Sidney Colvin. Cf. the reference to an undelivered message in the letter to Lady Colvin of the 9th.

[3] The family indeed left London on Tuesday the 13th, so Conrad meant to finish revising the articles on the 10th. Use of the phrase 'till Sat:' rather than 'tomorrow' hints at a date before Friday the 9th.

being rather dunned and I want those people (in the country) to have them this week.

I take it you will pay bal^ce of the £100 to my acc^t on Monday. I shall bring the articles to your office before one o'clock.

Give a word of verbal answer to the bearer and please let her have £4 in cash for me (four.)

Ever Your

J. Conrad.

We'll be leaving town on Tuesday for certain.

To Lady Colvin

Text MS Nielson; Unpublished

[4C Hyde Park Mansions]
Friday ev^g [9 August 1918][1]

Dear Lady Colvin[2]

I was horrified to hear from Jessie that no message was sent to you yesterday morning. I was in bed very seedy and unable to put foot to the ground all day. I can't tell you how sorry I was not to be able to see you.

Today I managed to creep down to a taxi and go to see Jessie. But I am not certain I'll be able to repeat the feat to-morrow. I shall try to get down to lunch at the club at one and perhaps you'll allow me, on my way to Jessie to run in for a moment. Vous baisez la main. Our time here is getting short.

Always dear Lady Colvin

your most faithful friend and servant
Joseph Conrad.

To Hugh Walpole

Text TS Texas: Unpublished

4C Hyde Park Mansions,
N. W. 1.
Aug. 12th. 1918.

My dear Walpole

I have been beastly seedy all the time. I have done nothing. I have seen no one; and, as you see, I am not yet able to use the pen.

---

[1] Close to the departure from London: the letter to Sir Sidney of the 4th shows that the Colvins were still out of town at that time, so a dating of the [2nd] would not be feasible.

[2] Frances, Lady Colvin (née Fetherstonhaugh, 1839–1924): after separation from her first husband, the Revd A. H. Sitwell, she made a living as an essayist; when she married Sidney Colvin in 1903, she had known him for more than thirty years. Their friend Robert Louis Stevenson venerated her as his 'madonna'.

This is only to tell you that we are leaving for home to-morrow morning. We hope you will let us know when you return to London and that you will be able to come down and see us in the course of September.

Ever yours

J. Conrad.

To J. B. Pinker
Text MS Berg; Unpublished

[Capel House]
Augst 14th Wedn^{ay} [1918][1]

Dearest Pinker

This is the D'day's letter I mentioned to you on Tuesday. The figure of the royalties interested me naturally. It would have been comforting if relating to 'old' works. But it occurred to me that Sh. Line was published that year and that a considerable part of that amount included perhaps the "advance on publication" of the S. Line? Is that so? And if so tell me roughly how much that was. One would like to know what the "old" books have brought in in 1917. A pardonable curiosity.

We arrived safely at 4 yesterday. Local doctor has seen Jessie last night. She sends her love. I feel the more cheep[?][2] of the two.

Ever yours

J. Conrad.

To Hugh Walpole
Text MS Texas; Unpublished

[letterhead: Capel House]
Thursday. 16[15?] Aug [1918][3]

My dear Walpole

Let it be the earliest date – the 24th. We shall be delighted to see you, hear your news of yourself and the novel and be generally cheered up (I am speaking for my depressed self) by this evidence of your friendship. I am infinitely flat. Jessie of course preserves her serenity and has resisted 7 weeks' close confinement wonderfully.

Pardon scrawl. Hand still very lame.

Always Yours

J. Conrad.

---

[1] Accompanying a letter from L. McNaughton of Doubleday, Page, dated 18 July 1918 (TS Berg).
[2] Meaning, perhaps, 'cheap'? To judge by the next letter to Walpole, certainly not 'chirpy'.
[3] The 16th was a Friday; Jessie's condition gives the year.

To J. B. Pinker
Text MS Berg; Unpublished

[letterhead: Capel House]
Sat. [17 August 1918][1]

Dearest Pinker

Thanks for your letter. It is indeed most gratifying to see the "old books" show so much life. That I should have held out long enough to see this I owe to your assistance since 1902 when you took my tangled affairs in hand.[2] It is a story that in my mind and heart will never grow old.

– Can you let Dent have a clean copy and get back the one he holds now, for me?

The question of the title is bothering me – I can't think of any other. I shouldn't like to make a change *after* serialisation.

– Please send that £20 to Jessie's acc* so that she may make a fair start with her housekeeping.

– I am doing nothing and in fact am not fit for anything. To-day I feel better. Next week Walpole is coming down; and about 2ᵈ Sept Miss H[allowes] will appear to help push Rescue to its delayed end.

Jessie sends her love.

Ever yours

J Conrad

To G. Jean-Aubry
Text MS Yale; *L. fr.* 142

[letterhead: Capel House]
Dimanche [18? August 1918][3]

Cher Monsieur

Mille fois merci pour Votre bonne lettre. Tout a bien marché pendant le voyage. Ma femme souffre un peu du genou. Pour ça il n'y a que la patience.

Moi je ne suis pas bien. Le lumbago me tient encore. Le poignet aussi fait mal et généralement je suis déprimé. Je ne peux pas réagir contre cette oppression. Mais – patienza!, comme disait Dominique[4] quand nos affaires ne marchaient pas.

---

[1] A week before Walpole's proposed visit on the 24th. Also from this period comes a note on the back of an envelope from the Gas Light and Coke Company, Westminster, postmarked on the 16th: 'Dear P. Please settle this for me. Yours C.' (MS Berg).

[2] Pinker began working with Conrad in 1900 (*Letters*, 2, p. 294).

[3] Jean-Aubry's date is [August 1918]: soon after the return from London on the 13th.

[4] Dominique-André Cervoni (1834–90), born in Luri, Corsica. Originally encountered as first mate of the *Saint-Antoine*, he was Conrad's nautical mentor in Marseilles. The 'Tremolino' section of *The Mirror of the Sea* gives a lively description of him. Evidently Conrad had been telling Jean-Aubry tales of his youthful adventures.

Je me demande quand je pourrai me remettre au travail. En ce moment il me semble que jamais.

Pensez a venir nous voir au retour de vos vacances. J'arrête ce gribouillage tout court car le poignet n'en veut plus.

Croyez moi toujours bien à Vous

J Conrad.

My wife's kind regards.

Translation

Dear Sir

Many thanks for your kind letter. Everything went well during the trip. My wife suffers a little with her knee. For that there is only patience.

I am not well myself. Lumbago still grips me. My wrist is also painful and generally I am depressed. I can't fight off this oppression. But – patienza! as Dominique used to say when our affairs weren't going well.

I wonder when I can go back to work. Never, it seems to me just now.

Consider coming to see us on the way back from your holiday. I am cutting this scribble short because my wrist won't stand for more.

Believe me always sincerely yours

J Conrad.

My wife's kind regards.

To J. B. Pinker

Text MS Berg; Unpublished

[Capel House]

20 Aug '18

My dear Pinker.

I find it necessary to get a bath-chair for Jessie. She can't remain indoors for months.[1] Please enclose £5 in the letter addressed to J. Foote* & Son ordering the same.

Jessie wishes to try to do without a nurse so the one now with us will leave next Monday and that expense will be stopped. The doctor of course has to see Jessie twice a week at least for the next two months.

Yours ever

J. Conrad

---

[1] She already had a self-propelled chair purchased from J. Foot and Son, but a Bath chair was better suited for outings, because it afforded more leg-room and could be pushed by another person while its occupant steered.

To J. B. Pinker
Text MS Berg; Unpublished

[Capel House]

Thursday 22^d Aug. [1918][1]

My dear Pinker.

Thanks for your letter received this morning. Thanks also for the promise of obtaining the correc^d copy from Dent.

I have an invincible dislike for calling the novel *Doña Rita*. I fancy it would be unlucky. You must allow me to be unreasonable in this instance.

Do you know of a* still another edition of the *Mirror of the Sea* issued by Meth: at 3/6 in red suede leather, in a neat cardboard case? Perfectly charming. But the type and paper seem identical with the 5/- edition.[2]

They ought to have given me a chance to correct a few misprints. I saw it in the hands of a French friend.[3] I should like to have a couple of copies.

I find it difficult to forgive Meth:, for not following the typographical arrangement of the first 6/- ed: either in the 5/- ed or in this last 3/6 one. It is treating one with contempt.

Ever Yours

Joseph Conrad

To J. B. Pinker
Text MS Berg; Unpublished

[letterhead: Capel House]

Sat. [24 August? 1918][4]

Dearest Pinker

Your letter arrived this moment. I bless your insomnia – and also your wide awake brain. Another man might have lain awake for a year and nobody the better for it to the amount of one penny. This is really a great stroke of genius.

---

[1] A sequel to the letter of the [17th] with its request for a clean copy and its uncertainty about a title.

[2] Methuen issued a five-shilling edition in April 1918 and a shilling edition in November; Harrap then brought out a three-shilling 'new edition' in time for Christmas.

[3] Gide?

[4] Written on watermarked stationery and filed among the 1918 correspondence, this letter must be about serialising *The Arrow of Gold*. Although he mentions the wrong magazine, Conrad knew by the morning of the 31st that the serial had been taken for a high figure. In the letter assigned to [6 September], Conrad deals with an embarrassment caused by Walpole's loose talk about a 'remarkable stroke of business'. Walpole was expected at Capel House on the 24th and thus would have been there for first-hand news of the handsome offer if it arrived on that day.

You understand my dear fellow that you take 20% on this – and even so it's just the double for me of what I expected to get in this country. In fact I hoped for 350 – with luck.

Jessie thanks you for your reference to her. She begs me to express to you her admiration of your brain-wave.

Amazing affair!

I close now – post time. I will write to you on Monday.

Ever Yours

J. Conrad

PS Jessie had *not* her cheque to-day and has struck me for a loan. I will never see it back – of course.

To J. B. Pinker

Text MS Berg; Unpublished

[Capel House]
Sat. morning [31 August 1918][1]

Dearest Pinker

I have to appeal to your friendship in a matter which may not commend itself to your wisdom but in which I believe you will understand my feeling. It is the matter of saving poor Joseph Retinger from a miserable and lonely end in Spain where he is now (why – I don't know) ill and penniless and without a soul to turn to.[2] He has appealed to us (in two distressing letters) to get the English Government's permission to come here. Walpole promised to act for me as I can't travel to town. Bennett no doubt will help too in that.[3]

I have received yesterday a further appeal for material assistance which it is impossible to disregard and I turn to you in all confidence in your sympathy to ask you to find for me a hundred pounds *for that object* of which we would send him fifty (telegraphically as he asks) as early in the week as possible and hold back the other fifty ready for what may turn up – his passage here when that is arranged – or any further help.

I have no doubt you will assist me in this matter of feeling. After all it is this man's friends who were infinitely kind to me and all mine in Poland, lent me

---

[1] This is the first of three letters about Retinger's plight all written on the same Saturday. The third, the more public of the two to Walpole, establishes the date.

[2] He had been hounded out of France, perhaps at the instigation of Polish émigrés anxious to distract official attention from their own activities (Najder, *Chronicle*, p. 434, footnote).

[3] The novelist Arnold Bennett (1867–1931), also a Pinker client. Bennett and Walpole could be helpful because both were doing war-work at the Ministry of Information, Walpole in the Russian Section and Bennett as director of British propaganda in France.

money and took infinite pains to enable us to get to Vienna at the beginning
of the war. I needn't say more except that we all have a great affection for him.
    Pray answer this by a word.

Ever yours

J. Conrad.

Address: J. Retinger. Hotel de France. Fuentarabia. Spain.[1] If there are difficulties for transmission of money, Walpole assured me he can arrange. I am
writing to him by this post too. If you 'phone to him he will know all about
the matter already.

Please Note: Of course that amount is for that *particular* purpose. There are
my own requirements – which will be John's school term about 35. end Sept.
Then I will have to ask you for £24. an old debt which I would like to settle,
first week in Sept. and early in Oct £25 house rent.

    I need not tell you that I am ready to write a piece (as soon as you say the
word) for a paper to help all this out. Miss H[allowes] arrives on Wednesday,
here and I shall start on Rescue at once. Nurse goes to-day.

    What do you say to *The Lost Arrow* for title? If no objection please notify
the Lond: Mag: people before they start advertising a serial by J. C.[2]

To Hugh Walpole

Text MS Texas; Unpublished

[letterhead: Capel House]

Sat even^g [31 August 1918][3]

Dear Walpole.

    Did Jessie drop you a line of thanks for the little vol?[4] My hand still hurts.
I started reading my inscribed copy right away. How well (and freshly) all
this is done! The dinner party – the tea-party – the opening of the umbrella
tragedy! Perrin's psychology is no small potatoes – let me tell you. You make a
lot of points as you go along that make one look with increased consideration
at your early years.

    As I expected I had an appeal from poor Retinger for material assistance.
I have written Pinker to provide and send the £50 *telegraphically* as asked for.

---

[1] Very near the border with France. The modern spelling is Fuenterrabia.

[2] *The Arrow of Gold* was serialised in *Lloyd's Magazine*. The *London Magazine* had published 'The
   Black Mate' (1908), 'A Smile of Fortune' (1911), and 'Freya of the Seven Isles' (1912). From
   extant correspondence it is not possible to tell whether Conrad mixed up the names or Pinker
   engineered a last-minute switch.

[3] Although meant for 'next post', the other letter to Walpole identifies the Saturday.

[4] A recent reprint of Walpole's *Mr Perrin and Mr Traill*, first published in 1911. Drawing upon
   its author's unhappy experiences of schoolmastering, the novel depicts the petty tyrannies
   suffered alike by pupils and staff of a minor public school.

(I suppose the poor fellow held off as long as he could). Pray give Pinker your advice and help if there are any difficulties – or special steps to take – for transmission. I shall send you the statement of my relations with R by next post – to your rooms. This I address to the Ministry.[1]

Ever yours

J. C.

Jessie's kindest regards

To Hugh Walpole

Text MS Texas; Pomian 42

[letterhead: Capel House]
Kent.
31st Aug. 1918

My dear Walpole.

My acquaintance with Joseph Retinger dates back to 1912. He came to our house with an introduction from A. Bennett who had met him in France. R. told me then that he had a general mission from the National Committee (Galician) to raise the Polish question in the press of France and England.[2] An impossible task then, in view of the state of European alliances. He confessed to me that he could get no one to touch the subject – out of regard for Russian susceptibilities – but his intention was to remain in the West and persevere in his efforts.

He was very often here for week-ends and talked to me openly of his hopes. Both himself and his wife gained very soon our regard and affection. Our journey to Poland was undertaken on Mrs Retinger's mother's invitation to spend the month of August (1914) at her country place near Cracow – but just over the Russian frontier. We never reached there. The declaration of war caught us in Cracow and [I] must say that it was R's friends, political and others, who treated us with the greatest possible kindness, lent me money (which, of course, I owe them yet) and took infinite trouble to get the consent of the local authorities for our departure for Vienna where the efforts of M[r] Penfield Am: Ambassador procured our release.[3] I owe them indeed a large debt of gratitude.

---

[1] Perhaps the other way round: the personal letter to Walpole's flat, the testimonial to Walpole's office? In any case, Walpole wrote to the DMI (Director, Ministry of Information) on 4 September, asking the Ministry to help Retinger (TS carbon Texas).

[2] The Committee represented nationalists in the parts of Poland and Ukraine occupied by Austria.

[3] Frederic Courtland Penfield, US ambassador to the Austro-Hungarian Empire from 1913 to 1917.

I saw a good deal of R in the years '15 and '16. He was very open with me as to his thoughts, his hopes and his feelings. All these were perfectly sound; and it is incredible that a man should seek out a recluse only in order to lie to him by the hour. His activities during that period are known to the English and French Govts. He was personally known to Mr Asquith, to Mr Balfour, Lord N'cliffe; at our Foreign Office, at the French Embassy. In Paris he was known to M. Berthelot and to Count Andrew Zamoyski[1] – a personality above suspicion.

In '17 R. remained in Paris and his health broke down. I had rather alarming reports from friends and also from Borys who spent his 3-days' leave there in nursing R during one of his heart attacks. In 1918 I heard from him from Madrid. How and why R went to Spain I do not know. The question for me is to save this, in many respects, loveable human being broken in health and fortune from perishing miserably as if abandonned* by God and men. For that is how the situation looks to me. If we could get him over here we would look after him. I hope you will do what you can to help me for I am absolutely unable to come to town yet and time presses.

Yours ever affect^ly

Joseph Conrad.

To J. B. Pinker
Text MS Berg; Unpublished

[letterhead: Capel House]
Sunday [1 September? 1918][2]

My dear Pinker

Very good of you to think of getting me double set of proof. I hardly expected any.

Today I am worse again. I can neither sit, lie or stand in comfort with that sort of lumbago that has got hold of me. Nevertheless you may see me in the course of the week. A tragic affair of that poor Retinger for whom I must attempt something in London.

Ever Yours

J. Conrad.

---

[1] Herbert Henry Asquith (1852–1928), Prime Minister, 1908–16; Arthur James Balfour (1848–1930), Prime Minister, 1902–5, Foreign Secretary, 1916–19; Philippe Berthelot (1866–1934), diplomat, a prominent official at the French Ministry of Foreign Affairs from 1904 to 1919. Rather than Andrzej Zamoyski (1800–74), the 'White' nationalist leader who was expelled to France in 1862, Conrad may have meant Maurycy Zamoyski (1871–1939), Vice President of the Polish National Committee in Paris.

[2] Or 25 August? Retinger's woes suggest the period.

To C. K. Shorter

Text MS BL Ashley 2924; Unpublished

[letterhead: Capel House]
1ˢᵗ Sepᵗ 1918

Dear Mʳ Shorter

Pardon the delay in thanking you for your letter and returning the proof.[1] I can hardly hold the pen yet on account of a gouty wrist which has been worrying me for the last six weeks.

The very next time I am in town I shall give myself the pleasure of calling on you. But I must say that half my life now is devoted to cultivating the charms of gout. That can be done only indoors – and mainly in bed. This naturally makes me somewhat of a recluse.

Pray accept the assurance of my warm regards.

Yours

Joseph Conrad.

PS Certainly. The *Well Done* is at your disposal.[2]

To J. B. Pinker

Text MS Berg; Unpublished

[Capel House]
Tuesday 5 pm. [3 September 1918][3]

Dearest P.

No end of thanks for your promptness. Pray decide between the two titles: *Lost A* or *A of G*.

Affectˡʸ yours

J. C

Yes like to see Hastings last version

The Lost Arrow not The Last Arrow as in your letter.

---

[1] Of *The First News, an Essay*, one of Shorter's limited-edition pamphlets; this essay was previously published in *Reveille*, August 1918.
[2] Shorter brought it out as a pamphlet later in the year.
[3] Here Conrad thanks Pinker for his prompt response to questions in the letter of [31 August].

To J. B. Pinker
Text MS Berg; Unpublished

[letterhead: Capel House]
4 Sept '18

My dear Pinker.

I would rather the D[aily] C[hronicle] gave me some hint of a subject or two.[1]

Thanks for your letter of this morning. W[alpole] wrote me too to say he was doing his utmost.

Miss H[allowes] arrived. We have been putting a lot of papers in order this morning. This week is given up to visitors, American and others. It will have to be stopped; it's too expensive. Please send me a ch. for £15.

I will write the article (or articles) for the D. C. before starting on *R[escue]* I think.

I am concerned at the news of your health. What is it my dear fellow? I need not tell you how happy we will be to see you here – especially if that is going to be the sign of your perfect recovery.

What news of Eric? They are beginning to move forward on his part of the front. We haven't heard from B[orys] for nearly a week.

I suppose the ser[ialisati]^{on} in the Lloyds Mag: will take about six months.[2] You may take it that if life last[s] the *R* will be in your hands in Jan^y *at the latest*. That will give you plenty of time for negotiations – won't it? – since the *Arrow* can't possibly come out as book till spring. I imagine I can dispose as I like of the rights of translation (French) of *Well Done*. I've been asked.

Jessie sends her love.

Ever yours

J Conrad.

---

[1] The *Daily Chronicle* suggested an article on the Bolshevik revolution, but Conrad was too ill to write it. See the notes to the letter to Pinker of 17 September.

[2] It ran from December 1918 to February 1920 for a total of fifteen episodes. In terms of Conrad's changing readership, Pinker's choice of publication is significant: *Lloyd's* was the successor to *Baby: The Mother's Magazine*; in the 1918 edition of *Newspaper Press Directory* its contents are described as 'What women want to know'. The first instalment of *The Arrow* appeared in the Christmas Double Number alongside stories by Ethel M. Dell, E. Phillips Oppenheim, Compton Mackenzie, and Mrs Belloc Lowndes; this number also presented a symposium on 'The Potential Wife–Mother'.

OSWALDS,

BISHOPSBOURNE,

KENT.

22 . 11 . 19.

Dearest Don Roberto

I am just fresh from the
second reading of your
vol. My dear friend the
track of your unshod horses
may be faint but it is
imperishable.

There is a tone, a deep
vibration in these latest
pages of yours which

1 To R. B. Cunninghame Graham, 22 November 1919

THE SHADOW LINE

THE SHADOW LINE

The "shadow line" is that dim boundary that divides youth from maturity. How a young first mate, who unexpectedly finds himself in command of a sailing vessel, leaves his carefree youth behind forever in the agonizing responsibility of a twenty-one day voyage from Bankok to Singapore. His ship is becalmed, the whole crew stricken with fever and no quinine in the medicine chest! A tale which shows Mr. Conrad's gifts at their highest level.

"The Shadow Line" ranks with "Typhoon," "Youth," "The Nigger of the 'Narcissus,'" and Mr. Conrad's other classics of the sea.

By
Joseph Conrad

THE SHADOW LINE

WHY DID THE CAPTAIN AND THE SILENT CREW OF THE SHIP IN THIS STORY OF THE FAR EAST HAVE SUCH GREAT AND MYSTERIOUS DIFFICULTY IN PASSING LATITUDE 8° 20′?

JOSEPH CONRAD

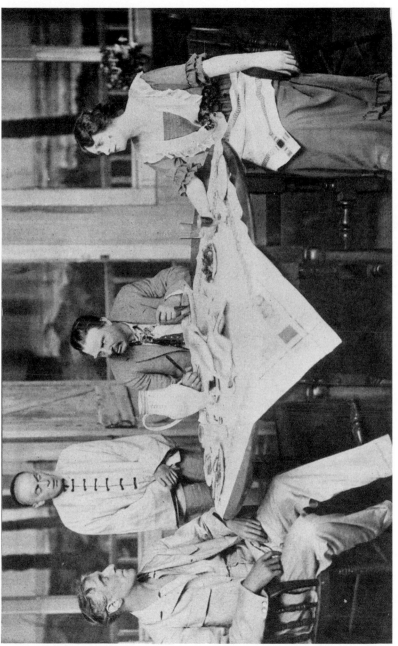

3 *Victory* at the Globe Theatre: Murray Carrington (Heyst), George Elton (Wang), Sam Livesey (Ricardo), Marie Löhr (Lena)

above:
4 Sir Hugh and Lady Clifford
('Mrs Henry de la Pasture')

right:
5 Sir Robert Jones

"Force," repeated Lingard. "I think not—if it can be
helped . . . and it rests with you. I tell you plainly
I cannot let you speak any vessel in these straits."

Drawn by Dudley Hardy

6 *The Rescue*, illustration by Dudley Hardy, *Land and Water*, 30 January 1919

"You propose to go out on deck like this?" muttered Mr. Travers, with downcast eyes

DRAWN BY MAURICE GREIFFENHAGEN, A.R.A.

7　*The Rescue*, illustration by Maurice Greiffenhagen, *Land and Water*, 22 May 1919

8 Perceval Gibbon

9 Conrad in 1918, by Percy Anderson

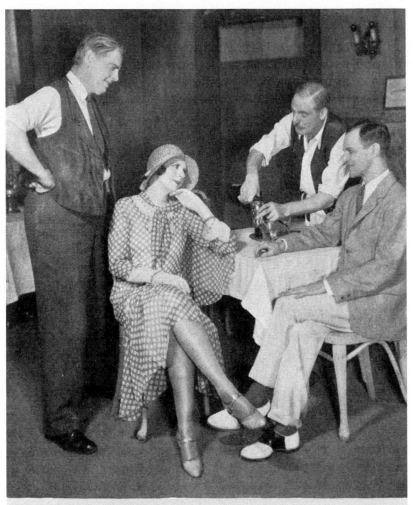

Thurston Hall, Catherine Willard, Edward Donnelly, and Benjamin Hoagland in Don Marquis's pleasant little comedy at the Assembly, "Everything's Jake!"

10 Catherine Willard on Broadway

To J. B. Pinker
Text MS Berg; Unpublished

Friday evening [6 September 1918][1]

Dear Pinker

I am no end sorry for W[alpole]'s indiscretion re A of Gold.

He saw me depressed, and to his remark on that I said I had really no reason to be. Things were going on well I said; and I added that I had just heard from you that the novel was excellently well placed as serial in Eng^d. He asked in what periodical, and I named the London. Nothing more was said.

My dear fellow I could see no reason for keeping secret your remarkable stroke of business. I mentioned no figures. The mere fact came out in the course of conversation – naturally. I can't tell you how sorry I am if it is to cause you the slightest annoyance. I shall be careful in the future what I say to W. Our friend Curle, who had business experience, would have held his tongue. I used to be very open with him and as far as I know he never chattered.

Ever affct^ly yours

J. Conrad.

Hand still hurts when I write. Give my best regards to Mrs Pinker. Jessie gets on. She sends her love. I hope and trust you are feeling better. Paddock Wood is on the main line – on your way.[2] You could look at the horses between two trains.

---

[1] If Walpole's indiscretion originated in a conversation with Conrad on 24 August, the 30th would be the earliest date for this letter, but correspondence in the Pinker archives makes 6 September more likely and would also coincide with Conrad's state of health, Pinker's notion of a visit, and, above all, the use of the definitive title. A letter to Pinker from S. Nevile Foster, 3 September (TS Berg), rebuts an allegation by Walpole that *Land and Water* would not offer a decent price for serial rights and continues: 'I am naturally disappointed that I was not even given the opportunity of seeing the story, and the least I can do is to make sure that Mr Conrad thoroughly appreciates our position in the matter.' Thus this letter would be a reaction to Foster's complaints.

[2] On his way to see the Conrads? Paddock Wood lies on the main line from Tonbridge to Ashford.

To J. B. Pinker
Text TS Berg; Unpublished

[letterhead: Capel House]
Saturday Sept. 7th. 1918.

Enc: M. H[astings]'s play.[1]

My dear Pinker

Having read the other two versions I have just only looked at this one and have also taken the opinion of three very different minds which, together, would no doubt reflect truly enough the effect which would be produced upon an audience of play-goers. The general impression (which I share from what I have seen) is that this version has much more go than the other two; and all the readers agree that no part drags. My criticism is that, admitting Hastings' arrangement without any question at all, he doesn't perhaps make enough of the opportunities of the mere dialogue. But after all I may be wrong. Those speeches backed by the personality of the actor may sound effective enough on the stage. Of course my assent to any version that M. H. would produce was secured beforehand, so that I have really nothing to say in the matter.

My attention has been called to the company now playing at the Garrick in the "Pigeon Post". That play will probably run to the end of the year, or perhaps even a little longer, but I am told that Madge T., A. Wontner and A. E. George,[2] and one or two others, would be very suitable for the parts in "Victory". Perhaps you will throw out this suggestion to M. H.

Thanks very much for your letter and the enclosed cheque received yesterday. I hope you have found it possible to send the money to R[etinger] this week. I am very glad to hear that your indisposition is but slight and I hope to see you here before many days pass over our heads.

I am sorry to say that Jessie is receiving another set-back with inflam[m]atory symptoms in the wound. I am beginning to think that there may be something serious behind. The doctor himself can't say yet but I see that he too is somewhat concerned. She sends her love.

Ever Your

J. Conrad

---

[1] The latest version of *Victory*, now supposedly less encumbered with dialogue from the novel.
[2] A. Page's *By Pigeon Post* had been playing at the Garrick since March; its cast included Madge

To Sir Sidney Colvin
Text TS Hofstra; Unpublished

[letterhead: Capel House]
September 9th. 1918.

My dear Colvin.

From the appearance of this letter you will gather that my wrist is still worrying me. Somehow or other I can't shake off my general gouty state, and though I am not actually laid up I can't trust myself away from home or else I would have run over to see you long before this. I may safely say that my thoughts are all the time with you both in all possible affection and tenderness. But it is my fate to be a useless individual, unable to show my care and concern for my best friends. I trust you are now getting really better. It's nearly a week now since we heard from dear Lady Colvin, to whom please give my duty and my love.

We have heard from H[ugh] W[alpole] since his visit to you. He is a charming person and is proving to me that he can be a very good friend in need. He and Jessie are excellent friends and his friendly disposition towards my two boys gratifies me exceedingly.

Jessie has had a slight set-back with her wound which is annoying though not serious. Her habitual serenity is but little disturbed by it and her general health is good. We had cheery letters from Borys lately and if we only could get definitely a good report of you there would be no reason for our minds to be otherwise than at ease about things in general. We had here to lunch two American officers, Bostonians. They informed me that They had come to finish the war; which is very cheering, though I don't suppose that the French and ourselves and the Italians are to sit down and fold our arms. At any rate I am glad that we have done something towards the beginning of the end off our own bat, as it were. For that is how it looks; though, of course, it will be a very long time yet before President Wilson will take the head of the table at the Peace Conference – as they evidently expect him to do. After which Europe generally will have to take a back seat. No more at present. Dictating is poor fun.

Our dear love to you both.

Ever Yours

J. Conrad.

Titheradge and Arthur Wontner, who had won some celebrity by replacing Holman Clark as Captain Hook in the annual production of *Peter Pan*. A. E. George does not figure in any of the theatrical directories.

To Major Gordon Gardiner
Text TS Harvard; Unpublished

[letterhead: Capel House]
Sept. 9th. 1918.

Dear Major Gardener*[1]

It was a great pleasure to hear from you. I have kept a very vivid memory of our fore-gathering in Edinburgh,[2] and I look forward with immense pleasure to seeing you here; that is if you don't mind visiting a house which has got a slight flavour of hospital about it. My wife is recovering after a heavy operation on her knee, from which she has suffered for something about fourteen years, but she is visible, though she doesn't leave her chair yet. I have at present a swollen ankle and a gouty right wrist (that is why this letter is dictated) but I am not laid up. If this state of affairs is not too repellent to you we suggest Wednesday for your visit. There is a train from Rye which arrives at Hamstreet about 1. 12 p. m, and if you will kindly wire (*Conrad. Hamstreet.*) we will arrange for a conveyance of some sort to meet you. If that day is not convenient to you perhaps you will suggest another this week or the next, in which case a word on a postcard will be sufficient. It looks as if the weather were going to keep fine for a few days.

    With our united kind regards

Sincerely yours

J. Conrad.

To B. Macdonald Hastings
Text MS Colgate; Unpublished

[letterhead: Capel House]
[between 9 and 14 September 1918][3]

My dear Hastings

I sent the play to P last Sat. I'll make no remarks except the general one that I even prefer this version to the 2[d] one. As to matters of detail with my lack of scenic experience I prefer to say nothing now. But if You don't mind

---

[1] An Aberdonian, Gordon Gardiner (1874–1937) was a major in the Border Regiment seconded to Scottish Command as an intelligence officer; his duties included spy-hunting and the surveillance of enemy aliens. Before the war, although often troubled by ill health, he had been a civil servant in South Africa (where he went through the siege of Kimberley), a tea-planter in Ceylon, and a student at Harvard. After the war, he worked as an arbitrator of industrial disputes and as secretary of the National Club, London. The posthumous *Notes of a Prison Visitor* (1938) record some of his experiences in befriending convicts. His novels include *The Reconnaissance* (1914), *At the House of Dree* (1928), and *The Man with a Weak Heart* (1932); at his death, he was working on a study of Napoleon.
[2] During Conrad's visits to Edinburgh in 1916, when their friendship began.
[3] Conrad sent the new version to Pinker on the 7th; since that was 'last Sat.', the date must fall between then and the 14th, and the 8th seems too close to the 7th to use 'last'.

me imparting my impressions to you during rehearsals I will do so. I hope to goodness You will be there to see the thing through.

Pray accept this copy of my only dramatic effort. There are only 25 of them so it will be a bibliographical curiosity for your shelves. At the same time I would be glad to know whether you think it shows a hopeless incomprehension of the stage. I saw it performed by the S[tage] S[ociety] with Const[an]ce Collier and J. L'Estrange in the principal parts, and it was a painful experience — I assure you.[1]

Don't forget your promise to run down here when possible.

Yours

J Conrad.

To C. K. Shorter

Text TS Berg; Unpublished

[letterhead: Capel House]

Sept. 14th, 1918.

Dear Mr Shorter

I return you the proof on account of three punctuation corrections of no importance, but we may just as well have the text as correct as it can be.

I am still laid up and as far as ever from coming to town. But when I do I shall not fail to present myself before you after an interval of something like 21 years.

Meantime I send you my thanks for the copies of "First News" which reached me the other day.

Believe me,

Yours very sincerely,

Joseph Conrad

To G. Jean-Aubry

Text TS Yale; Unpublished

[letterhead: Capel House]

Sept. 17th. 1918.

Dear M. Aubry.

Thanks for your letter. Apart from your letters being always a pleasure I am glad to know that you are back in London and as it were nearer to us. I have had a very beastly time of it as far as my health is concerned and I

---

[1] The Stage Society gave three performances of *One Day More* in June 1905. Conrad wrote at the time: 'At any rate the reception of the play was not such as to encourage me to sacrifice 6 months to the stage' (*Letters*, 3, p. 272). The leads were Constance Collier (1878–1955) and Julian L'Estrange (also known as Jules, 1878–1918).

can't really say that I am certain of having taken a turn for the better yet. I have done no work and didn't enjoy my leisure, and all this makes me very savage and misanthropical. Neither is my wife's recovery as advanced as we expected it to be by this time.

I shall be dropping you a line in a day or two suggesting a week-end. At this moment we are expecting some people and this house is so small!

Tout à Vous

J. Conrad.

To J. B. Pinker
Text TS Berg; Unpublished

[letterhead: Capel House]
Sept. 17th. 1918.

My dear Pinker.

John will be going to school next Friday but I don't think I will be in London myself that day. I have been extremely seedy for the last three weeks but I am getting better, or at least I hope so. I have had of late so many returns of gout that I hardly dare hope for a continuous week of complete freedom.[1]

Something about moving to another house will have to be decided soon, but I don't worry you with a long letter about it because we still hope to see you here before long, when I will expound you my views and ask you for your advice.

H. Dent was down in Ashford on some business and so we had him here for lunch yesterday. It's 20 years since I had a publisher at my table. S. S. Pawling was the first in '97 just before they published the "Nigger";[2] and now Dent, who is quite a decent fellow to talk to.

I needn't tell you that I haven't done a line of work since our return here. I was absolutely unable. I am both worried and exasperated by this state of affairs.

Pray send me five one-pound notes for John's travelling expenses.

Jessie sends her love.

Ever yours

Joseph Conrad

---

[1] Two letters from Miss Hallowes to Pinker concern Conrad's health at this period: on the 12th she wrote to say that he was not well enough to do an article on the Bolsheviks for the *Daily Chronicle*; on the 14th, she reported that he still could not walk (MSS Berg).

[2] Sydney Southgate Pawling (1862–1922), William Heinemann's partner, was one of Conrad's first admirers.

To Hugh Walpole
Text TS Texas; Unpublished

[letterhead: Capel House]
Sept. 17th. 1918.

My dear Walpole

I have had another beastly relapse but I believe that now I shall really get better for a month or two.

If you see ahead a week-end that you can spare pray let us know of it. I have given up all idea of coming up to town for a month or more. I simply dare not risk it.

Jessie's recovery has had another set back. Her general health however is good and this is but another call on her inexhaustible fund of patience. We had a letter from Borys this week in which he says he has written to you. The books seem very much to his taste.

I hope that the Rettinger* affair got through successfully. It is very dear of you to have taken it on your shoulders. Pray give my affectionate regards to Arnold Bennett who for so many years has kept me in his mind.[1] A man who like me has lived so completely out of men's sight can't but feel touched and gratified by such fidelity.

Jessie's love.

Ever Yours

J. Conrad.

Major Gordon Gardiner
Text MS Harvard; Unpublished

[letterhead: Capel House]
18 Sept. '18

My dear Major.

We are grieved at the news of your ill-health. You must not run the slightest risk and I am comforted to think that you are being cared for – and restrained for your own good.

I wrote to town for a copy of Victory in anticipation of your visit. I am glad to say I've obtained a 1st ed:. As I am not able to bring it to you myself I am sending it with this letter.

Pray drop us a line as to your health.

My wife's sympathy and kind regards. Believe me always

most faithfully Yours

Joseph Conrad.

[1] Bennett had often expressed his admiration for the work of Conrad, whom he had known since 1902: see, especially, *Letters*, 5, pp. 139–40.

To J. B. Pinker
Text MS Berg; Unpublished

[Capel House]
Sat 21 Sep^t [1918]^1

My dear Pinker.
Please pay Mrs Pearce's acc^t for me.
I am somewhat better.
Thanks for your letter with notes.

Yours ever

J. Conrad.

To G. Jean-Aubry
Text MS Yale; Unpublished

[letterhead: Capel House]
Merc: 25 Sep^r '18

Cher Monsieur.
Voulez-Vous venir nous voir ce Samedi? Si vous prenez le train de 4.30 pm
a Charing Cross pour *Hamstreet* Vous arriverez ici a 6.21. Envoyez-nous un
petit mot pour que la voiture puisse venir vous chercher a la gare.^{2}

Tout à vous

J. Conrad.

Translation

Dear Sir.
Would you like to come to see us this Saturday? If you take the 4.30 p.m.
train at Charing Cross for *Hamstreet* you will arrive here at 6.21. Drop us a
line so that the car might come to meet you at the station.

Sincerely yours

J. Conrad.

---

^{1} Mention of John's Headmistress, Mrs Pearce, locates the year.
^{2} On Friday the 27th, Conrad sent Jean-Aubry a telegram: 'We are coming to town thursday
for a week Conrad' (Yale); it is not clear whether this message meant that the visit to Capel
House was cancelled.

To J. B. Pinker

Text TS/MS Berg; J-A, 2, 207[1]

[letterhead: Capel House]
Sept. 25th. 1918.

My dear Pinker.

Thank you very much for your two letters. I had Mrs Pearce's receipt this morning.

I am glad to hear that Eric is well and in good spirits. All good luck to him. The stoppage of leave looks as though we intended to push on our advantage without respite. That indeed is the right spirit for this job. It looks indeed as if out there we were out of the wood at last. It is at home that I can't help feeling that we are still in the dark about the truth of the situation. Those strikes are really inexcusable[2] and seem to me either the result of moral blindness or of a very sinister recklessness of purpose, strangely un-English – at least as I have understood the character of Englishmen in the past. It may be simply a lack of imagination, a kind of stupidity, but it's hard to believe that it is nothing else but that. And anyhow, stupidity or wickedness, the consequences will be equally deplorable unless good sense or repentance come to the rescue.

I am sorry to say that things are not at all well with Jessie. The state of the joint has taken a decided turn for the worse, I mean apart from the condition of the wound itself, which in one place still refuses to heal for no reason that our doctor here can discover. But it is the internal state of the joint that gives cause for anxiety. There is a return of pain and mysterious swellings which must be caused by some source of mischief inside. It is the bitterest sort of disappointment.

I have been talking with our doctor this moment. He says that it is no use waiting any longer as three months have now elapsed since the operation and the state of the joint is apparently worse now than it was when she first arrived here. She must be taken up to London to be seen by both surgeons who operated: Aitken and Sir Robert Jones. Sir R. is expected from Italy on Monday as Mrs Watson, his daughter,[3] writes us. Aitken of course is in London. I am writing to the Nursing Home today to retain a room for Jessie as from Thursday Oct. 3rd. which is the earliest date they can give me. Under

---

[1] Minus the PS.

[2] At one time or another during the previous month, striking workers had included women bus and tram employees in London, London police, and Yorkshire miners; now the South Wales railwaymen had come out, and a wider railway strike seemed imminent.

[3] Hilda, the elder daughter, married to the writer and editor Frederick Watson (who had once proposed a collaboration with Conrad: *Letters*, 5, pp. 69–70). The Watsons lived in North Wales, where they were joint masters of the Tanat Valley hunt.

the best conditions this means a week in town. I propose that Miss Hallowes and myself should stay at the Norfolk which is both near your office and the Temple station from which I can get round easily to Baker St. which is very near the Home; so that even if I am lame I can manage to go and see Jessie with very little actual walking.

As to the work which I must and want to do – a small hotel-room at the Norfolk is not a very good place for it, but I thought that for a few days you would perhaps let me have Eric's room from about ten till one if you are not making any special use of it; but I beg you to be quite frank with me if you don't like the idea of what after all would be an intrusion on your business premises. I won't say anything more just now as I am really very upset by this unlucky development with its attendant anxiety and expense.

Your suggestion for developing the Polish episode[1] is helpful and I would accept it at once if it weren't for the thought that I could hardly avoid in that case touching the political side of the present situation, which I am very shy of doing, both in regard to its effect in this country and also in Poland, where everything I write does make its way. It may be absurd shrinking but there it is. However if nothing else offers I could do even that, as I want to help the situation with some additional cash, as you know. I don't offer writing a short story for two reasons which you will understand very well. First because it would be comparatively a long job, and next because it will take me too much out of the mood for the "Rescue" which I have been cultivating most earnestly for the last six weeks and have in a measure attained now. Three newspaper contributions of three or four thousand words in all are not open to those objections. You know me too well not to see at once the point of this argument. Meantime till we leave here next week I intend to stick to the "Rescue" exclusively. After all every page of that is money too – only not immediate. Pray drop me a line to say you are not utterly sick of me and my disasters which always come to roost on your shoulders.

Yours ever

J. Conrad

P. S. The doctor saw me again before leaving the house. There's no use blinking the fact that (in his opinion) the bones failed to grow on the inner side of the joint. This means laying the articulation open again and wiring them

---

[1] 'First News', published in the August issue of *Reveille*, describes Conrad's experience of hearing that war had broken out just as the family arrived in Poland. For further references to a projected article on Poland, see the letters of 12 and 15 November. Between 12 and 27 December (date on TS, Yale) Conrad wrote 'The Crime of Partition', which, as its title suggests, is more political than anything Conrad envisaged in September.

together. The mere thought of this cut upon cut makes me shudder. It may leave surface trouble for years. Or a metal outside plate may meet the case, to be worn for years. But that only if there is no tendency in the joint to become septic. Anyway this is a matter for Sir R. J. alone to decide upon. Jessie keeps wonderfully calm and outwardly cheerful but it must be [a] terrible blow for her. I know she dreads the mere thought of another operation. Luckily I am better tho' still lame a little. The doctor has offered to lend us his car for the journey to London. It will save anything from 12 to 16 pounds for I would have had to get something from town. He's a good fellow.

J. C.

Major Gordon Gardiner
Text TS Harvard; Unpublished

[letterhead: Capel House]
Sept. 27th. 1918.

My dear Major Gardiner.

You are a penetrating critic I must say. Whether you are right in regard to your own work or not I would not like to say. With the greatest possible capacity for detachment it is very difficult to be fair to oneself. Perhaps it is even impossible. At any rate you are very interesting in the analysis of your own novel;[1] but making all possible allowances for your insight, which I may well call remorseless, I have a suspicion that you are a little too clear-eyed in your examination. It seems to me that there are things in your work which have escaped your appreciation.

I will confess at once that I have read the book only once, and that, of course, is not enough; just as one audition is not enough to judge a piece of music; the more so because you are obviously a man whose pen does not run easily into emphasis. Whether an artistic presentation of life can be made effective without the help of artifice I can't say. But whether or no, I imagine that all artifice is utterly uncongenial to your temperament, I ought perhaps to have said your character. But we are now talking of writing, which of course is a temperamental thing. What I can feel in your writing is what your analysis would miss naturally; the indefinable quality of charm. There is also the quality of interest – I don't mean the subject itself; I mean in the writing. The subject in itself is certainly a very difficult one because of

---

[1] His first, *The Reconnaissance* (Chapman & Hall, 1914).

its deep nature and its necessarily superficial aspects.[1] As to its treatment it is of the most transparent sincerity. One can't mentally object to a single phrase or a single attitude of those people. The picturesque opening pages are wonderfully done.

This is all I am going to write to you to-day. I hope and trust we shall meet before very long and by then I would know the book better. Pray send us a word on a postcard about the state of your health. We are both very anxious to hear from you on that matter and of your future movements. My wife sends her kindest regards.

> Believe [me] always Yours
> Joseph Conrad.

Pardon the type. My wrist hurts too much to write more than a few lines.

To J. B. Pinker
Text TS/MS Berg; Unpublished

> [letterhead: Capel House]
> Sept. 30th. 1918.

My dear Pinker.

As I have not heard from you I conclude that you were not in your office towards the end of last week. I do hope that your absence is connected with agriculture and not with your health.

Now I have to add to my former news that yesterday (Sunday) I have been told to lose no time in getting Jessie to town. The state of affairs is such that apparently even one day would make a difference. The danger now is of her getting a suppurating joint, which of course would be a fatal development. The only remedy for it would be amputation and I have been warned by Mackintosh who came out here yesterday from town on purpose to see her that that would be a serious matter in the given conditions. I have therefore made arrangements for a car (the one offered by the doctor not being available till later in the week) to take us up to town to-morrow morning straight away to the nursing home, where Aitken and Mac[k]intosh will see her that very afternoon.

As I will want to be there I doubt whether I will be able to look you up on Tuesday. Pray pay in £20 to my account as I will have to draw a cheque or two on my arrival in London. I have wired for rooms in the Norfolk and I will come over to see you on Wednesday about 12 o'clock unless you let

---

[1] The subject is distinctly Conradian: a gentlemanly trooper who has won the Victoria Cross in South Africa becomes afflicted by debilitating self-doubt.

me know that it is inconvenient to you. It would be very good of you if you would tell Walpole on the 'phone that we are coming up and that I will be at the Norfolk after five o'clock on Tuesday. Will you also get Methuen to send me over to the hotel a copy of Lucas's latest book.[1]

This is a lot of requests. It is your unfortunate position to be the only friend on whom I can rely but I'll try not to be a great nuisance to you.

I am very lame and can only crawl slowly. I am dreading the journey tomorrow as Jessie is in considerable pain.

Ever yours

J. Conrad.

To T. J. Wise
Text TS BL Ashley 2953; J-A, 2, 209

Norfolk Hotel,
Surrey Street
Strand, W. C. 2[2]
2. 10. 1918

Dear M[r] Wise.[3]

Thank you very much for your friendly letter enclosing the cheque. It is very delightful for me to think that the possession of the MS. is a matter giving you so much satisfaction.[4] As Mr Aubry may have told you, Mr John Quinn of New York possesses all the series of my manuscripts of the books which have been already published. Some of those MSS. being mere fragments, others complete and in a good state. You however are now in possession of the MS. of a novel that certainly will not be published till 1920.

---

[1] The third edition of *A Boswell of Baghdad* (1918)? It was published by Methuen, E. V. Lucas's employer.

[2] Conrad wrote this and the letters of the 6th and 7th on Capel House stationery, cancelling the letterhead and subsituting the hotel's address.

[3] Thomas James Wise (1859–1937) was a collector – and creator – of bibliographical rarities, particularly those of the Jacobean, Romantic, and Victorian periods. Having prospered as a dealer in lavender and other essential oils, he built up a considerable collection of books and manuscripts, many of which are now in the British Library's Ashley Collection, and enjoyed a solid reputation as a scholar and enthusiast. Meanwhile he was forging, and selling at high prices, spurious early editions of such authors as Wordsworth, Tennyson, Swinburne, Shelley, George Eliot, Charlotte Brontë, and the Brownings. His fakery was first exposed by John Carter and Graham Pollard in 1934. Since then, David Foxon has shown that Wise enriched his own holdings by stealing leaves from books in the British Museum. Wise came to replace John Quinn as the preferred purchaser of Conrad's MSS, TSS, and corrected proofs; he was also of service by reprinting individual Conrad essays in small and therefore costly limited editions.

[4] The MS of *The Rescue* in the state described below. Since this was not the MS of a completed work, selling it did not go against the letter of the agreement with Quinn but did go against the spirit.

This MS. also holds a special position in so far that it is the only one which has a history extending over twenty years. Begun in 1898[1] as my third planned long novel it was laid aside finally at the end of '99 so that a whole pile of pages belongs wholly to the twentieth century. The preservation of those pages I owe entirely to my wife who insisted on keeping them in one of her drawers long after I lost all interest in the MS. *as MS.*, for several typed copies have been taken of it each introducing changes and alterations till this last (I believe the 4th) typed copy on which I am working now and intend to finish the tale by dictation. Thus you will understand that there will be no further pen and ink pages. The first complete state of the novel will be a typed copy bearing pen and ink corrections and alterations.

Though I suppose John Quinn would like to have it and indeed may be said to have a moral claim on it, I will, if you at all care for it, reserve it for you, so that you should have the very last as well as the very first of the conception and execution of "The Rescue". The two texts side by side may form a literary curiosity showing the modifications of my judgment, of my taste, and also of my style during the 20 years covering almost the whole writing period of my life.

As soon as my wrist becomes less painful I will write for you an extended note on the history of the MS. accounting shortly for the reason of its having been laid aside for so long.

Believe me very faithfully yours
Joseph Conrad.

To John Quinn
Text TS NYPL; Unpublished

Norfolk Hotel,
Surrey Street,
Strand, W. C. 2.
Oct. 6th. 1918.

My dear Quinn.

It is a very long time since I have given you any of our news. I don't know whether my wife has written to you lately. She is a much better correspondent than I am. I ought to be very much ashamed of myself but instead of offering explanations I prefer to throw myself on your indulgence.

We are now in town for about a fortnight. Last June the operation on my wife's knee was successfully performed and we returned to Capel to

---

[1] Conrad wrote the earliest passages of 'The Rescuer' in 1896.

await in peace and confidence the complete healing of the actual cut (it was enormous) and the gradual growing together of the bones which were to give her a stiff but perfectly dependable limb, with, of course, absolute freedom from the pain and discomfort she had suffered from for nearly fifteen years. Sir Robert Jones operated – a surgeon of European reputation for dealing with big joints. All the prognostics were good. Unfortunately things did not proceed quite normally; and instead of being able to walk about by now she has not at this date put her foot to the ground yet. Some small complications set up not only in the wound itself but also, we fear, in the joint, delaying her normal progress and causing me a lot of anxiety. It is indeed a very severe disappointment. She bears it with her usual serenity which has been of such great help to me in the various difficulties of our life.

The upshot of it all is that I brought her here for further advice and action. Sir Robert Jones' assistant and right-hand man (a very able surgeon himself) assures me that there is no reason for anxiety. He is positive that ultimately everything will come right – according to plan. Patience and care are the proper remedies. Jones himself (he is a General in the R[oyal] A[rmy] M[edical] C[orps]) is on a visit to the Italian front now. He will be back in London on the 10th and will then decide what has to be done. Perhaps a small incision will be necessary; but we all hope that it will not be. My wife herself is not particularly anxious to be carved any more. I am glad to say that her general health is excellent and I may say that, at this moment of writing, she looks better than she has done for the last five years. She sits up in bed in the Nursing Home holding receptions with the utmost cheerfulness; and as the room is small the husband when he turns up has to sit on the doorstep as it were. The great improvement in the general situation and the numerous if scrappy letters from our big boy are an immense help to her spirits under this fresh ordeal.

The big boy is with the 2nd Army in Flanders under Plumer.[1] Good army, good commander, good spirits and good hopes are his lot now. An inspiring change from March last when he was involved in the 5th Army breakup retreating his battery of 6-inch howitzers from position to position as if they had been field guns and coming out without the loss of a piece, though with severe losses amongst the men. It was a wondrous tale which he told me last June as he had special leave then to attend his mother's operation. At the end of the affair the Artillery and the Mechanical Transport Corps were officially congratulated on their behaviour, his battery being specially commended and

---

[1] General Sir Herbert Plumer (1857–1932), famous especially for co-ordinating the Allied attack on Messines.

given a fortnight's rest. The Batt[er]y returned then to the line in support of the Canadian troops which had stopped the German advance, and remained there till things improved and the whole artillery brigade was ordered to Flanders where the boy is now sharing in the successes gained over the very ground on which he began his active-service life in January 1916, when little more than a child.

He had not much opportunity to see American troops but of the little he has seen he spoke to me with the warmest admiration. But as to that all the British army feel the same. Now of course he is a long way off from the American troops in line, the 2nd Corps being, as you perhaps know, associated with the Belgians and a few French divisions.

My wife has preserved carefully the first and original typed copy of my latest finished novel – The Arrow of Gold – corrected, scored and interlined in ink. And this is the only draft that exists, with the exception of the opening of the tale, about 36 pages, actually written with the pen. The rest of the story for various reasons I was compelled to dictate. I don't know whether you will care to have this typescript, but at any rate you know now that it is in existence – the only authentic first draft (with added corrections) of the story.

When the novel will be published I can't really tell you. I will send you of course a copy of the first English edition as soon as it comes out. But that cannot be very soon. The serialisation in this country will not begin till January, and as to serialisation in U. S. I doubt whether it is even arranged for, as yet.

This year my health has been simply deplorable. Half the time I have been a cripple and at least half of that again I have spent in bed. But I won't enlarge on this state of affairs, of which I am getting profoundly weary.

The small boy John has grown considerably. He is bright and intelligent enough but not particularly industrious. He has been at school now for about a year, but we will miss him from home very much. For 21 years there has always been a child in the house and now with John's departure the house feels somehow empty.

My wife has recommended to me very earnestly not to forget to give you her kindest regards. She hopes that one of the first pleasures after the war will be to actually behold you in your proper person under our roof. May it be soon!

Believe me my dear Quinn

always Yours

Joseph Conrad.

To Hugh Walpole
Text MS Texas; Unpublished

[Norfolk Hotel]
Sunday. [6? October 1918][1]

My dear Walpole.

I have Your note. It's very obvious that till that report is done You'll have no time for frivolities. I had half a mind that evening to say something to that effect but felt shy. By the same post Sobanski[2] writes me that he's called suddenly to Paris and Italy. So the lunch on Wed[nesd]^ay with him is off too. He professes to be sorry and points out that we are doubly fellow-countrymen as Poles and as Podolians. All Podolia's sons are very fond of their romantic province. But I have never seen it[3] – and am not likely to, now.

Affect^ly Yours

J. Conrad

To Lewis Browne
Text TS Indiana; Unpublished.

[Norfolk Hotel]
Oct. 7th. 1918

Private

My dear Prof Brown[e]

Two copies of the New Republic[4] and your friendly letter arrived at the same time. It was very good of you to take the matter in hand so earnestly. Personally I did not attach a very serious importance to what F[rank] H[arris] said and I don't suppose that anybody in the U. S. would attach any importance to his activities, whatever they are or might have been. A couple

---

[1] The rather formal greeting suggests a date early in the correspondence. At the beginning of October, Walpole found himself having to prepare a report for the War Cabinet, summarising the work of the Ministry of Information: 'A particularly hair-raising job and one for which I feel quite unfitted' (Hart-Davis, *Walpole*, p. 176).

[2] Władysław Sobański.

[3] Conrad's paternal grandfather, Teodor Korzeniowski, came from Podolia, as did Prince Roman Sanguszko (1800–81), the original of 'Prince Roman' (1911); the province lies in Western Ukraine, between the Bug and Dniester rivers, south-east of Volhynia.

[4] The 24 August issue with a long extract from Conrad's letter to Browne of 15 May under the heading 'Mr Conrad is not a Jew' (16, 109). For Browne's undated reply to the present letter, see *Portrait*, p. 132: a reference there to muted victory celebrations requires a date after 11 November.

of years ago I understand, they were pro-German.[1] He was, I imagine, always a worthless personality and I should think is discredited completely by now.

My appreciation of his character in my letter to you was meant for your ear only; and as to the statement of my origin I imagined you would communicate it to certain individuals in a private manner. But since you have judged it necessary to give it a wide publicity I must thank you for taking all this trouble in the cause of truth which, even in such a small matter, has its own ethical claim.

I must say that I am rather glad the New Republic has with[h]eld the full name.[2] My unfavourable view of the man's character is based on general impressions depending on old facts nearly forgotten by the world, and which I myself remember but vaguely now; and on the general consensus of opinion amongst men of standing and rectitude with whom I happened to talk about the individual in question. As I have said, I meant my appreciation for your ear only, though I omitted to state this explicitly in my letter to you.

About an hour ago we have read of the Austro-German Peace overture to President Wilson.[3] Frankly I don't know what it means, but I do know what it will do. It will unchain and unmuzzle all the pacifist activity in the new and the old world and bring more trouble to the hearts and consciences of honest men of various feelings and opinions. And from that point of view it is undoubtedly a very clever move. The question of sincerity and good faith does not arise at all. Germany has forfeited the confidence of mankind; but it is obvious that all her declarations must be accepted on their face value if anything in the way of negociation* is to be done at all. Well – we shall see.

Believe me

                                          very faithfully Yours

                                                          Joseph Conrad.

---

[1] Early in the war, Harris published a series of articles in the *New York Sun*, which he expanded into *England or Germany* (1915); he took the line that the British were too tainted by colonial misdeeds to claim any moral superiority over Germans.

[2] Harris's name does appear in the article. There is no mention, however, of Conrad's asking Browne in the letter of 15 May to 'make public in the right quarter' the novelist's Christian genealogy. The article in the *New Republic* begins 'A friend of Mr Conrad's has kindly communicated to us the following letter.'

[3] In January 1918, Woodrow Wilson (1856–1924) had presented his Fourteen Points, the set of principles he believed necessary for the establishment of peace, justice, and good order in Europe and its hinterlands. On 4 October, Prince Maximilian of Baden (1867–1929), the German Chancellor, sent a note to the Allies offering an immediate armistice and expressing willingness to negotiate a peace along the lines of Wilson's principles.

To Richard Curle

Text TS Indiana; Curle 40[1]

[Norfolk Hotel]
Oct. 9th. 1918.

My dear Richard

My last letter to you, I have every reason to think, has been submarined and I was just preparing to try my luck again when yours of 14/8/18 arrived. I am very glad of the generally good news you send me both as to your health and your activities. The image of you as editor of an African rag is startling. I should like to see some of your leaders, but that, I suppose, will never be. Don't forget to send me the promised pamphlet of the Anonymous Englishman's letters.[2]

I am dictating this because I have a crippled right wrist. Gout has been clinging to my various limbs ever since the beginning of this year, practically. I am going now to repeat to you in an abridged form the news contained in the drowned letter.

Early this year we spent some time in London on account of Jessie's knee. The surgeons put the limb in splints of a particular kind and assigned a three months period to observe the result of that truly infernal-looking implement. It brought instant relief; and though the beastly affair weighed nearly six pounds she managed to go about a good deal with Borys who was on leave just then. Those two racketted together for a fortnight, dined in a club with Mrs Wedgwood, who was charming to them both, visited theatres undeterred by the numerous air-raids and generally had a good time. I had gout. Then B. returned to France to be involved in the 3rd Army's mess[3] and we went back to Capel to await developments. It was a horribly trying time.

The developments not being favourable (except in so far that I managed to finish a novel – *The Arrow of Gold* – on the 14th of June) we proceeded to town at once for further advice; the upshot of which was that a very big, if not exactly dangerous, operation on the knee was performed by Sir Robert Jones with apparent success. Borys fresh from the disastrous retreat, through which he had pulled out his battery entire after a lot of rear-guard fighting, obtained a special leave for the operation, and was a source of great comfort to me, not to speak of his mother. She having her two boys with her preserved a wonderful cheerfulness through it all. At the end of six weeks in a nursing home I took her back to Capel; but unluckily various small complications set in and now we are again in town for a fortnight,

---

[1] Leaving out the last three sentences of the first paragraph.
[2] Untraced: Curle had been working in South Africa.   [3] The unfortunate Fifth Army.

the prey of the surgeons. However I am assured on all hands that the ultimate success is certain. The bones have grown together, I am told; and considering that the joint has been in a horrible condition for upwards of fourteen years the slight set-back after the operation is not to be wondered at. Yesterday she has actually put her foot to the ground and walked a few steps in her room in the nursing home, for the first time in more than three months.

The present disposition of the family forces is as follows: Mr and Mrs J. Conrad are going to retreat to Capel House next week, according to plan. Lt. B. Conrad is advancing in Flanders with the 2nd Army and is much bucked up. Master John Conrad is interned in a preparatory school in Surrey for his third term and is now reconciled to his horrible situation. I can't tell you very much about further operations beyond the fact that they include a frontal attack upon the "Rescue", which was indeed begun some time ago but, I am sorry to say, has been pushed feebly and has died out for a time. However, in the present more favourable circumstances it shall be taken up with vigour and is expected to achieve a success by January next at the latest.

These are all the news up to date from my front.

Rest assured, my dear Richard, that I return with the greatest warmth your regard and affection. You too are often in our thoughts. During the anxious passages of the last ten months I have more than once missed your unfailing and friendly support. We both look forward impatiently to seeing you again but we both understand perfectly your feeling of reluctance. But don't tarry too long on the way. I am getting on – I mean in years. After sixty, one begins to count the days; and gout, however faithful, is not a cheerful companion. I am getting awfully crippled and it's about time Jessie ceased to be so. And if that happens I don't really mind very much if I have to end my days in a wheeled chair like Macaulay's Lord Holland. He kept his wits to the end and I have the advantage over him that my wife is not a Lady Holland.[1] But one wants to have all one's friends within reach.

---

[1] Elizabeth Vassall, Lady Holland (1770–1845), was a woman of pronounced opinions, a hostess legendary for her dinner parties at which artists, politicians, savants, and aristocrats talked under her firm supervision. Her second husband, Henry Richard Vassall Fox, the third Lord Holland (1773–1840), continued the traditions of his Whig dynasty as an orator and statesman. The essay on Lord Holland by Thomas Babington, Lord Macaulay (1800–59), makes no mention of the wheelchair but commends his serenity and fortitude in ill health. Those who knew him, Macaulay wrote in 1841, 'will remember that temper which years of pain, of sickness, of lameness, of confinement, seemed only to make sweeter and sweeter' (Lady Trevelyan, ed., *The Works of Lord Macaulay* (1875), Vol. 6, p. 542). Curle's note refers to Lord Holland as 'a character of whom Conrad was very fond of talking'.

I am delighted to hear of the travel book.¹ Perhaps you remember that I was always rather enthusiastic over that work. I wonder whether you changed in any way its plan and its tone. We shall see. I am warned² that there is very little space left so I will end here abruptly with love from Jessie and myself.

Ever yours

Joseph Conrad.

To J. B. Pinker
Text TS Berg; Unpublished

Norfolk Hotel,

Surrey St.

Strand.

Friday. [11 October 1918]³

Dear Pinker

It struck me after you left yesterday that the MS. of R. was actually here with me and I propose to look it over on Saturday and Sunday morning and deliver it to you on Monday before leaving for home. Like this the L. and W.⁴ people will have it a week sooner for the information of their artist.

Do you remember whether the little book on "Joseph Conrad" published by Doubleday for distribution was written by William Follet or some name like that.⁵ I need the information for a bibliography which is being made by J. Aubry for a collector. Perhaps you have a copy in your office which you could spare or at least let me see. I am going to get up to-day and shall certainly call on you on Monday with the Rescue typed copy.

Yours ever

J. Conrad

P.S. In the matter of the little book or anything else that you wish to say, Miss Hallowes will be downstairs so that you may call up on the telephone (without troubling to write) on receipt of this. I return Candler's book⁶ with many thanks.

---

¹ *Wanderings: A Book of Travel and Reminiscence*, published by Kegan Paul in London and Dutton in New York (1920), dedicated to Conrad.
² By Miss Hallowes.   ³ Just before the Conrads returned to Capel House.
⁴ *Land and Water*, the predecessor of *The Field*, had agreed to serialise *The Rescue*.
⁵ In 1916, Doubleday gave away free copies of Wilson Follett's *Joseph Conrad: A Short Study* (1915).
⁶ *Siri Ram* (1914): see the letter to Candler of 12 November.

To John Quinn
Text TS/MS NYPL; Unpublished

[letterhead: Capel House]
Oct. 16th. 1918.

My dear Quinn

I have written to you not a very long time ago. You may be sure that our sympathy was with you during all your heavy trials. You will have, my dear friend, to moderate your altruistic activities for whatever may be the call of humane ideals a man in sound morals must be also just to himself.[1] We shall wait with impatience the further news of the improvement in your health resulting from the operation.

My wife, I am sorry to say, is not getting on after her operation as well as we all expected but the improvement we hope will come in time. I have been almost continually ill since the beginning of this year but that is a pretty old story by now.

I will tell you frankly that we don't think much about Irishmen now.[2] As long as they didn't actually and materially add to the deadly dangers of our situation we were satisfied. I am speaking now of the bulk of the people, not of our politicians. We had asked the Irish to come to some arrangements among themselves. They couldn't or wouldn't; and then the active, living interest in the problem died out. Even what America thinks of all this has ceased to occupy our thoughts. I, who have seen England ever since the early eighties putting on the penitent's shirt in her desire for conciliation, and throwing millions of her money with both hands to Ireland in her remorse for all the old wrongs, and getting nothing in exchange but undying hostility, don't

---

[1] In his letter to Conrad of 15 September (TS carbon, NYPL), Quinn had written of a serious illness and consequent operation: 'My illness has made me horribly sensitive and tender of suffering in others. Before when I did kind or considerate things, they were perhaps mostly intellectually kind – kind without tenderness – except of course to my sisters and my parents and my brother when he lived. But tenderness must be felt. It cannot be described. It does not mean sentimentality. I never before realized what a power for good money could be if there was tenderness and love, as well as intellect in its use.' Of the time just before the operation, he wrote: 'I felt that there was so much I wanted to do that I could only do a few things to make things easier for others. If ever I lived selfless days, those five days were selfless.'

[2] 'Don't think much' in the sense of 'don't have a high opinion of' rather than 'don't think often'? Conrad's 'sally' responds to passages in Quinn's letter about the controversy over imposing conscription in Ireland: 'There is no denying the fact that Ireland has suffered in this country because of her attitude on conscription. But the English are deceiving themselves if they think that opinion in this country does not sympathize with Ireland's claims to self-government. I am sure that conscription by coercion will be a stupendous blunder for England . . . She cannot urge that she is fighting for the freedom of Belgium if she has got conscription press-gangs in Ireland.' Quinn wrote as an Irish-American of moderate views and an influential Democrat alert to public opinion.

wonder at her weariness. The Irishmen would not be conciliated.[1] That's a fact. And I don't presume to judge whether they were right or not. I only know that they took the money and went on cursing the 'oppressor' with renewed zest. Their able men scrupled not to make their careers in England and exploit all the advantages that arose from a connection with a great and prosperous empire. I have seen those things, I, who also spring from an oppressed race where oppression was not a matter of history but a crushing fact in the daily life of all individuals, made still more bitter by declared hatred and contempt. A very different thing from an historical sense of wrong and a blundering administration: which last I will admit if you like. But what administration could be free from, so-called, blunders when dealing with a people that being begged on bended knees to come to some understanding amongst themselves is incapable or unwilling to agree on the form of its free institutions. I can't help asking myself, if Gladstone's Home Rule Bill had passed[2] what our position would be now, with an independent power (for it would have come to that by this) with an army and a navy just across St. George's Channel, still nursing the sense of historical wrong as their dearest possession and chumming-up with Germany in sheer lightness of heart and for the sake of a jolly good fight. However they will get their independence, I haven't the slightest doubt, in some way or another; but I suppose it won't matter very much then, because by that time President Wilson's Millen[n]ium will reign on earth and even the carrying of walking sticks will be strictly prohibited amongst the members of the League of Nations.[3] And Ireland will still remain discontented! For what's the use of independence without the power to break England's head. However the genius of a people will out; and I have an idea that the Angels on the Central Committee running the League of Nations will have their hands full with the pacification of

---

[1] The Liberal policy of conciliating Irish, particularly Nationalist, public opinion originated in the early 1880s as an alternative to maintaining the often bloodily contested status quo. Land ownership, tenants' rights, and rural development were among the urgent issues. Over the following decades, legislation provided for tenants who wished to buy their holdings from the great estates, labourers who needed decent housing, and country people in general who might benefit from railways and better roads. Funding came from the public purse, and thus from the British – and Irish – taxpayer. In the 1920s and '30s, the UK and Irish Free State governments would argue bitterly about defraying the cost of these reforms.

[2] William Ewart Gladstone (1809–98) introduced two bills for granting Home Rule to Ireland, one in 1886 during his third premiership, and one in 1893, during his fourth; both were voted down. Parliament finally passed a bill in September 1914, but its enactment was postponed for the duration of the war.

[3] The last of President Wilson's Fourteen Points advocated 'A general association of nations...for the purpose of affording mutual guarantees of political independence and territorial integrity to great and small states alike.'

Ireland. It will be the only state that will be not weary of fighting, on the whole round earth.

Of the war and its more or less approaching end I won't speak in this letter. We had news of the boy yesterday. He writes cheerfully as he has always written for the last three years. I am in good hopes, for I have always said that it is a trait of German character to go to pieces suddenly under a strain. My wife sends you her warm greetings and all the sympathy of a fellow sufferer. She knows what you had to go through. Don't be angry with me for my sally at the Irish. I wish them all possible happiness.

Yours cordially

J. Conrad.

To Messrs Hachette et Cie
Text TS Private Collection; Unpublished

[letterhead: Capel House]

Oct. 17th 1918.

Messrs Hatchette* et Cie.,
Chandos St,
Charing Cross,
London.

Dear Sirs,[1]
    Will you kindly send me the following books, enclosing the account, to the above address: –

> Adolphe: par Benjamin Constant.
> Raphael: par Lamartine
> Dominique: par Eugene Fromentin[2]

Yours faithfully,

Joseph Conrad.

---

[1] The French booksellers and publishers had a London bookshop.
[2] *Adolphe* (1816) by Benjamin Constant (1767–1830) and *Dominique* (1863) by Eugène Fromentin (1820–76) are autobiographical novels; *Raphaël* (1849) by Alphonse de Lamartine (1790–1869) is a memoir with fictional elements. All these works present a doomed love affair between a young man and an older or inaccessible woman. Whatever blend of experience and fantasy went into its making, *The Arrow of Gold* treats of similar obsessions. On the presence of Constant's life and works in *Victory*, see Hervouet, *French Face*, pp. 122–35.

To J. B. Pinker
Text MS Berg; Unpublished

[letterhead: Capel House]
Thursday. [17 October 1918][1]

My dear Pinker.

I was going to write you when this agreement[†] arrived.[2] So I return it by rail as I wish this letter to reach you today.

Please send to Jessie's credit in Ash[ford]: (Kent) Lloyd's Bank £20 – and ten to mine in Lond.

The object for which I was going to worry you today in any case is this: will you come down? not to comfort a sick friend but to give advice to the aforesaid in the matter of a house, which has offered rather unexpectedly – and *seems* a possible (though not a simple) proposition. *We* think it suitable – or as near thereto as we are likely to get. But I want to know your opinion not only as a matter of business, but also as to your feeling as to that move in regard to myself – whom you know.

It just strikes me: as you do not come to town on Sats – would you run down on Friday by some early *PM* train and we could proceed to *The Grange* straight from Ashford station. Just have a look at it. And then you could leave us on Sat: morning in time probably to get to your own home to lunch. My idea is to keep you away from your wigwam as little as possible during the weekend.

Please, if you find you can come out on the war-path with us this week to fire a wire into* us as arrangements with caretaker and motor-bandit will have to be made at the earliest possible moment.

Yours ever

J Conrad.

PS On reflection: let off a wire in any case please

[†] Emi[nen][*tly*] Satis[facto][*ry*]

To Cecil Roberts
Text TS Churchill; Roberts (in part)

[letterhead: Capel House]
Oct. 17th 1918.

Dear M[r] Roberts.

We have only just returned home and found your letter. Strangely enough almost by the same post my wife had returned to her through the Dead

Letter office the one she addressed to you at the Automobile Club as far back as the month of March. We wondered what had become of you, and now we are very glad to know it was nothing absolutely fatal. Joking apart we are heartily glad to hear that your health is re-established and that you have been so busy with congenial work.

It came at last to my wife having to undergo a serious operation on her knee. I have got her back down here but she is not getting on so well as we all hoped she would. This is the only reason why we don't ask you at once to come and see us here. Her slow convalescence has complicated matters very much in this small house which is very full at present. But before long I hope we will be able to ask you to visit us. We shall pick up the threads of our old talks in these rural surroundings.

Your R.A.F. paper is very good[1] – but I don't think the age is so very wondrous unless perhaps in spots, like the curate's egg. Otherwise humanity is at its old game, the same old game from the beginning of ages and I really believe that the invention of the bow and arrows was a much more wonderful feat than the invention of flying machines – when you dispassionately think of it. But the young men are all right.

A gouty wrist prevents me writing more than a line or two at a time. Hence this type for which I apologise.

Very sincerely yours

Joseph Conrad

To Christopher Sandeman
Text J-A, 2, 210

Capel House.
Oct. 17, 1918.

My dear Sandeman,

I was delighted to receive your letter from Seville. It was eleven days on the way. This helps me to realize that feeling of moral remoteness from the world and its war which you describe to me.

I am not surprised to hear of our improved standing in the view of the Spanish people. Nothing succeeds like success. Mankind is made that way. Neither am I surprised to hear that our sympathizers, as distinguished from partisans, have not increased. But I must say that the general attitude towards Spain here is by no means resentful.[2] The economic difficulties are well

---

[1] Roberts's articles on the Royal Air Force were collected as *Training the Airmen: How They Fly* (Murray, 1919).
[2] Spain remained neutral all through the war.

understood and the pro-Teutonic character of the Spanish press is simply ascribed to German money. Not very complimentary for the press: but the nation as a whole is not associated with it.

Somehow an air of mystery hangs upon the clearest utterances, like a cloud over an open landscape. The force behind these plain words is immense. Immense in every sense. The fact is that the mind uttering these momentous declarations is a non-European mind; and we, old Europeans, with a long and bitter experience behind us of realities and illusions, can't help wondering as to the exact value of words expressing these great intentions.[1]

I will say no more of this. Time will show. And it is very possible that if this letter were to turn up in fifty years' time, it would appear very foolish to its discoverer. It is very possible also that he would not understand it at all. But I am sure you understand what I mean – and so enough of this.

I have been distressingly gouty all this year, but I managed to finish a novel. The news from our boy is good. He is now with Plumer in Flanders and I suppose, in a sense, enjoying himself. This letter is typed because my gouty wrist hurts so much when I write that a few lines is all that I can do. All luck to your play in its Spanish dress.[2] We must, my dear Sandeman, see each other when you return. You have been much in my thoughts – tho' as to letter-writing I behave abominably to my friends – not excepting you.

À vous affectueusement.

To J. B. Pinker
Text TS/MS Berg; Unpublished

[letterhead: Capel House]
Oct. 18th. 1918.

My dear Pinker.

As I expected it to happen Jessie's knee has been put into plaster again by the surgeon here and we must settle down again to wait for the result.

The agent who has got the letting of the "Grange" is very anxious to proceed to business. I have told him that a move will be made in the course of next week. I am not writing this in order to make myself a nuisance to you, but I must say that I should like very much to be able to make up my mind on that matter; which somehow I can't do till I have heard your dispassionate opinion. Great issues of peace (my private) and work, hang upon the solution

---

[1] These comments, strikingly reminiscent of Marlow's opinions of Kurtz, probably concern the 'non-European mind' of Woodrow Wilson, especially in the context of his Fourteen Points.
[2] A staging of *Widow's Night* in Spain? In Britain, this had been the only one of Sandeman's scripts to be cleared for public performance (Lord Chamberlain's inventories of licensed plays, Nov. 1916, BL).

of the house problem. It may sound ridiculous but it's quite true; and you, knowing us both pretty well, and looking at the thing from outside may save us from a false step.

On Tuesday morning I called on Foster with the type of the Third Part,[1] not to show him the text, of course, but to let him see certain typographical arrangements of paragraphs and conversations which I want them to carry out in print. They both agreed at once, and at the same time promised me to set up without the slightest delay and send me the proofs as soon even as the end of this month, providing they get the copy next week. This will be very convenient to me as I don't want to be bothered with proofs in December, when I am in the swing of composition of the last part of the book. I refused to listen to any stories about the *Arrow* business,[2] saying that in this matter as in any other Mr Pinker and I were one and moreover I said: "What's the good of talking about what's done, since you have now a story much more appropriate to the character of your paper and lending itself so well to a display of illustrations". – All this passed in a most friendly tone anyway. I was glad to hear that they contemplate a run of six months. The last instalment would then come out in May. I tell you all this because perhaps a date could be arranged for book publication in May too. Would that be too late for the Spring season? – that is if American arrangements can be carried out for that month too. But all that is none of my worry. It all depends on your judgment and rests in your hands.

The artist they have in view is Brangwyn.[3] This seems to me all right, but I would be glad to hear what you think. They also spoke of Dudley Hardy, the idea being to have two illustrators perhaps. Of D. H. I know absolutely nothing[4] except some humorous London types in low life.

This my dear fellow is all I've to say at present: except to ask you to see that my "original" type is carefully preserved, and when the copies are made returned to me here. I want to have it back as soon as possible.

Pardon this long letter

Ever Yours

J. Conrad

[1] On S. Nevile Foster, editor and Managing Director of *Land and Water*, with the latest section of *The Rescue*. The 'they' later in Conrad's letter suggests the presence of an assistant.
[2] See the notes to the letter to Pinker of 'Friday evening' [6 September].
[3] Born in Belgium to Welsh parents, Frank Brangwyn (1867–1956) was first apprenticed to William Morris, and later went to sea. During the war, he served as an official war artist, known in particular for his sombre etchings of ruined towns and villages; after the war, he worked on large-scale murals such as those in the Guildhall, Swansea.
[4] In fact, *Land and Water* had commissioned Dudley Hardy (1867–1922) to illustrate 'The Warrior's Soul' in 1917. Widely known for his posters for the Gaiety and Savoy Theatres, Hardy was also in demand for work on books and magazines. For Conrad's reactions to the illustrations for *The Rescue*, see the letter of 12 December.

To Sir Sidney Colvin
Text MS Virginia; Unpublished

[Capel House]
21 Oct. 1918

My dear Colvin.

Pardon this scrap of paper. I happen to have a copy of "Youth" here and I shall dispatch it to-morrow to the address in Hampstead. There's no kindness there. I am in fact highly flattered by appreciation in that quarter. As to the Hist: of the British Army[1] it is "tout bonnement admirable!" No other phrase can do justice to it.

We have heard this morning that Borys is in hospital in his own words: "shaken up and slightly gassed". This is dated the 17th. As the day before we had a cheery letter dated the 15 it must have happened sometime on the 16th. The boy writes that he went to the hospital on his own two feet and submitted to being put to bed "under protest". He expects and hopes to be back with the battery in a week. He confesses however that being "out of it" he feels "very tired". No doubt he must have had a most strenuous time of it ever since last July.

I own I am a bit anxious. Jessie is firm as a rock, what with her pride in the boy, her love for me and her profound unquestioning patriotism. She had now all but 3 years of anguish and is not at the end of her fortitude yet. But I do hope there will be a word from him tomorrow.

Our dear love to you both.

Ever yours

J. Conrad.

To Borys Conrad
Text MS Boston; Unpublished

[letterhead: Capel House]
21 Oct 1918
10 pm.

My dearest Boy.

Your letter of the sixteenth (from the hospital) arrived today. I hasten to tell you that mother took it very well, though of course one can't expect her not to feel anxious. I won't say anything of myself. I hope a few lines of your ever-desired handwriting will turn up tomorrow morning to help her in her fortitude which has been so severely tried for nearly 3 years now.

---

[1] Perhaps J. W. Fortescue's *History of the British Army: Extracts from British Campaigns in Flanders (1690–1794)*, which had appeared in April.

You can't know dearest how much you are to her. No one can know. I can but dimly feel something of the terrible strain under her serene cheerfulness. Her pride in you helps her to keep it up. She's not the sort of woman that "breaks down". But she had a very hard time of it which all my love for her could not make easier to bear.

You may take it from me that her general health is good – even very good. As to the result of the operation Fox[1] assured me very earnestly that success is not doubtful at all to his mind. It was a relief to me to see the leg in plaster again. After a month or so I shall write to Sir R. Jones about that worrying pain-spot. It may be improved by that time considerably. But in any case it isn't anything that cannot be remedied – and Sir R. Jones has solemnly promised her to see her walk.

I am better since our return here; and if I can only stick to my work the situation looks very well. So far I am sticking to it. The negociation* about the Grange will be resumed this week I hope. It isn't exactly the house we want. The surroundings and the grounds are not good enough in fact. Too suburban. But if nothing else that is "just right" offers I shall conclude, providing the people show themselves reasonable. We had this evening a letter from John who seems cheerful enough. A boy broke his collar bone. That school appears to me unlucky in a way. Still he has taken to it by now. Accept my paternal hug.

Your ever affec^{te} father

J. Conrad.

To J. B. Pinker

Text MS Berg; Unpublished

[Capel House]

Wednesday. [23 October 1918][2]

My dear Pinker.

Thanks for your letter. We are glad to know Mrs Pinker and You had a cheering sight of your First-born. It's the day they leave one that is the devil.

B[orys] had a shell shock and was slightly gassed about a week ago, with his batt[er]y major. He expected to be out of the hosp: in a week. But we heard

---

[1] Campbell Tilbury Fox (1870–1949), MRCS, LRCP, medical officer at the Ashford Cottage Hospital. His name gives a clue to the period of a note headed only 'Thursday': 'Dear Pinker Will you please settle this bill for me[?] Your J Conrad'. On this note, Pinker has scribbled 'Ask Fox'. Another note, this one headed 'Tuesday ev^g', reads: 'My dear Pinker I forward you the Nurs: Home acc^t which I found on my return home. Ever Yours J. Conrad' (MSS Berg). This note is undatable, simply one of many attesting to the costs, financial as well as psychological, of Jessie Conrad's sufferings.

[2] The news that Borys had been gassed arrived on the 21st.

to-day that he has been sent to a base hospital (N°8 R. Cross) I imagine in Boulogne. He describes himself as much bruised with stones and very shaky when he gets up. Otherwise all right. Jessie's wound is closed at last. She sends her love.

Yours ever

J. Conrad

To André Ruyters

Text MS Yale; Unpublished

[letterhead: Capel House]
Kent
23 Oct 1918

Mon cher Monsieur.[1]

Voulez [-vous] venir Samedi prochain et passer le Dimanche avec nous? Si cette date Vous convient envoyez un petit mot et prenez le train de 4. 25 (je crois) a Char + pour Hamstreet (on change a Ashford Junc^on^) ou vous arriverez a six heures vingt minutes. Une voiture vous attendra là – mais je ne peu[x] pas promettre d'être present moi-même. J'y tâcherai cependant.

Je suppose que vous avez reçu le livre avec le MS? J'etais bien fâche de ne pas Vous voir la veille de notre depart. Force majeure.

Bien à Vous

J. Conrad.

Translation

My dear Sir.

Would you like to come next Saturday and spend Sunday with us? If this date suits you drop us a line and take the 4. 25 train (I believe) at Charing Cross for Hamstreet (change at Ashford Junction) where you will arrive at 6. 20. A car will be waiting for you there – but I cannot promise to be there myself. I will try, however.

I suppose you received the book with the MS. I was very annoyed not to have seen you on the eve of our departure. Force majeure.

Yours truly

J. Conrad.

---

[1] André Ruyters (originally Ruijters, 1876–1952), the Belgian novelist and poet, was a friend of Gide and one of the founders of the *Nouvelle Revue Française*. His translation of 'Heart of Darkness' was serialised in the *NRF* (1924–5).

To Sir Sidney Colvin
Text MS Duke; *MFJC* 130

[letterhead: Capel House]
[c. 23 October 1918][1]

My dear Colvin.

B[orys] has been sent after all to a base hospital (n 8 R+) which I guess is in Boulogne. He was with his batt[er]ʸ Major at the time and they were both much bruised with lumps of earth and flying stones. He describes himself as perfectly right while in bed but feeling shaky when he gets up. He regrets being away from his column at this exciting time, but has no idea how long they are going to keep him in the hospital. He talks of his enormous appetite and is obviously pleased to have plenty to eat. Methinks our Flanders army has been advancing on a light diet.

Our dear love to Lady Colvin and yourself.

Yours ever

J. Conrad.

To William Rothenstein
Text MS Harvard; Unpublished

Capel House
Nr Ashford
Kent
24 Oct 1918.

My dear Will.

We are here again after a fortnight in London. Jessie had to give up all walking attempts for a month. The wound is completely healed at last but there is pain in the joint which shows that all is not well there. I am afraid something further will have to be done there. Time will show.

Borys is in Nº 8 Red Cross base hospital after being knocked down by a H.Z.[2] and also gassed. When this happened he was with his battʸ Major. They were both much bruised and shaken. I got a shock from the War office wire. A most horrid fright. However as they report him officially as a slight case all is well – till next time. The Boy himself wrote cheerily only regretting to be away from his "work" at this exciting time.[3]

I just manage to crawl about and by keeping myself warm (while I can) find existence possible. Last July I finished one novel and now I've to hurry up and finish another (already sold for serial in Land & Water), an old thing laid aside

---

[1] Carrying the same information as the letter to Pinker of 'Wednesday' [the 23rd].
[2] Howitzer.   [3] All along the Western Front, German forces were retreating.

many years ago, its very mood forgotten – dead. I am trying to rescucitate*
it: a miracle, I suspect, not worth performing, even if I do manage it. This
writing is an odious business.

I am certain your move to London will be a very good thing for You all.[1]
We here haven't even any imbeciles (to whom I don't object personally) or if
there are any they leave us alone.

I trust you will soon get away to France since it is your heart's desire and
we all will gain much by it. You omit to say anything about John and Billy[2] –
the unknown to me. I just remember him a very little chap. Give all your
House our dear love.

Ever Yours

J. Conrad

To J. B. Pinker

Text MS Berg; Unpublished

[letterhead: Capel House]
Monday. [28 October 1918][3]

My dear Pinker

Thanks for Parts i & ii which reached me safely. Please send me the p^t iii
as soon as it is done with, without waiting for pt iv, as there's something in
it I want to look up.

I am going on steadily with the R. without forcing the pace however as yet.
I have solved one of the difficulties that rather bothered me (in the action)
and I think that I have glimpsed last night a good solution of the other. This
is encouraging. My greatest desire and ambition is to deliver the balance *in
clean copy* to the L & W before the 15 Jan. '19. I believe I can do it too.

You'll have had Jessie's letter proposing you should arrive on Monday for
lunch. It's a good notion in so far that it will not waste more than one day
of your time. We could see the place in the afternoon and have an evening
together and on Tuesday you could be in your office by noon or soon after.
Its very good of you to give us your time and trouble in this affair.

Give my affect^{te} regards congratulations and wishes of the very best luck
to Eric, and remember us warmly to Mrs Pinker. I suppose she will come up
to town for the investiture.[4]

---

[1] The Rothensteins had been living in a bucolic Cotswold village.   [2] The Rothensteins' sons.
[3] A sequel to the letter of the [17th] with its request for Pinker to inspect The Grange.
The present Monday would be the one immediately after the 26th, when the doctors were to
examine Borys.
[4] The formal award of Eric Pinker's Military Cross?

Pray drop us a line as to Jessie's proposal so that I can arrange for the viewing order and the conveyance in good time.

Ever Yours

J. Conrad

B[orys] writes he's still very shaky and sleepless, but can eat and smoke with relish, while the effects of gas have almost passed away by now. He was to be examined again on the 26th. I hope they will give him time to recover completely.

To J. B. Pinker

Text MS Berg; Unpublished

[Capel House]

30. 10. '18

My dear Pinker

Please settle this for me. The acc^t is exactly £24 as I have noted on the letter.[1]

Many thanks for the MS Rescue pts III & IV received safely.

Yours ever

J Conrad

To Katherine Sanderson

Text MS Taylor; Unpublished

[letterhead: Capel House] Kent

1st Nov. '18

My dear Kitty[2]

The delay in answering your letter arises from the state of my wrist, which sometimes pains me too much to write – and really I couldn't dictate a letter to you on the type-writer. You would have justly looked on it as an outrage.

We were very much concerned at the news of your Grandmother's illness.[3] It would be very dear of you to let us know by a word on a card whether the improvement is maintained.

As to the specific question you put about my work (in a tone bordering on severity) I beg humbly to explain that one novel is finished and that I am

---

[1] This letter has not survived.

[2] Katherine Sanderson (born 1899, married name Mrs C. E. Taylor), the Sandersons' eldest child, a long-time resident of Kenya and latterly of Devon.

[3] Ted's mother, Katherine Susan Sanderson (née Oldfield, c. 1843–1921), a great admirer of Conrad's work and his confidante on visits to Elstree in the 1890s; Conrad dedicated *The Mirror of the Sea* to her in 1906.

grinding hard at another. But nothing will appear in book-form before May next – and that only if fates are propitious. Why it should be thus it would take too long to explain. But you may be sure that the first advance copy will find its way to Elstree without delay.

Our eldest boy has been shell-shocked and gassed severely enough to be sent to a base hospital just about 3 weeks ago. He expects to be allowed to get up in a day or two. What they will do with him further we don't know. Of course he's horribly vexed to be out of the advance. He was with Plumer – 2^d army. I understand his frame of mind; but I very much doubt whether he will be fit for another month or more.

One can't say positively how things will be by then. There may be still a kick left in Fritz. But I doubt it. In any case however a general fleet-action is out of question altogether by now.[1] When you write to Ian pray remember me to him with all possible affection. And the same to you my very dear Kitty, together with thanks for your good, friendly letter to this ancient person who appreciates your charm and graciousness infinitely. Give my best love to your parents.

Your friend Joseph Conrad.

PS From middle of June till about 3 weeks ago I haven't had two days together of decent health. This is the only thing which kept me from running over to see you all.

To Meredith Janvier

Text TS Private collection; Unpublished

[letterhead: Capel House]
Nov. 6th. 1918.

Dear Sir.[2]

I am quite willing to sign for you the little pamphlet of the Suppressed Preface[3] belonging to Mr Bonestell of Fresno. I have a particular regard for Californians both from personal acquaintance and from correspondence with some of them.[4]

---

[1] Since the German fleet was bottled up by the naval blockade, her sailor brother was probably out of danger. In any case, the war was close to an end.

[2] Lawyer, photographer, book dealer, amateur strong man, Meredith Janvier (1872–1936) lived in Baltimore. A contributor to the *Baltimore Evening Sun*, he collected some of his essays in *Baltimore in the Eighties and Nineties* (1933) and *Baltimore Yesterdays* (1937), the latter with a preface by H. L. Mencken. Mencken once observed that 'Janvier reveled in buying books as a cat revels in catnip.'

[3] To *The Nigger*.

[4] Among these, Agnes Tobin (1864–1939), James Marie Hopper (1876–1956), and Mary Austin (1868–1934).

I have not the smallest doubt that you are "all right". I have lately written
to Richard Curle in answer to his letter telling me, amongst other things, that
his book of travels has been finished and dispatched to Knopf for publication.
I trust it will meet with reasonable success, for what I have seen of it some
three years ago seemed to me very promising both as to matter and manner.
I imagine it will be more of a piece of literature than a book of travels is
generally.

When you send me the Suppressed Preface pamphlet pray let me have in
a friendly way (that is if you can spare a copy) Wilson Follett's Short Study
(No. 171. unpriced). D[oubleday] P[age] and Co. did send me three or four
copies some years ago but they have all disappeared from the house and I
want one to keep for myself.

Your instructions as to returning the signed preface will be followed carefully. However I imagine that there will be no other but "Act of God" risks on
sea passages now. If you happen to have another unsigned Preface which you
would like to have signed before disposing of it I will be very glad to sign it
for you. I mean you personally, since this one, I understand, is Mr Bonestell's
property already.

Yours faithfully

Joseph Conrad

To G. Jean-Aubry

Text MS Yale; *L. fr.* 143

[Capel House]

Mercredi 7. 30 pm [6 November 1918][1]

Cher Monsieur

J'ai été obligé de m'absenter de la maison cette semaine, de sorte que nous
n'avons pas pu vous demander de venir entre les Dimanches. Mais si [vous]
pouvez le faire venez Lundi prochain pour lunch et pour passer la nuit. Le
week-end lui même est pris par H. Walpole qui aura a me causer des ces
affaires à lui. Et puis comme vous savez nous n'avons qu'une chambre d'ami
puisque l'Infante Hallowes[2] occupe celle de Borys.

---

[1] Jean-Aubry's dating, which there is no reason to question. This letter fits between a telegram
of 1 November asking Jean-Aubry: 'Can you come tomorrow till Monday arriving Hamstreet
1.12 if possible' (Yale) and a telegram of the 15th reading: 'Expecting you Ham St. Saturday
for lunch 1.12 will meet you Conrad' (Yale).

[2] A musical pun on *L'Infant Harold*, the French name for Byron's hero Childe Harold and thus the
inspiration of Hector Berlioz's symphonic poem for viola and orchestra *Harold en Italie*. 'Childe'
denotes a chivalrous adventurer rather than a child in the modern sense. Miss Hallowes was
born in 1870.

Si vous pouvez trouver un jour libre plutôt dans le courant de la semaine (après Lundi je veux dire) Vous n'avez qu'a nous envoyer un petit mot. Si tout cela est impossible alors il faudra fixer le week end après celui de Walpole.

Tout à Vous

J. Conrad

Translation

Dear Sir

I had to be away from home this week, so that we could not ask you to come between the Sundays. But if you can, come next Monday for lunch and spend the night. The weekend itself is taken by H. Walpole who has private matters to discuss with me. And then as you know we have only one guest bedroom since Childe Hallowes has Borys's.

If instead you can find a free day during the week (after Monday, that is) you need only send word. If all this is impossible, then it will be necessary to set the weekend after Walpole's.

Yours truly

J. Conrad

To J. B. Pinker
Text TS/MS Berg; Unpublished

[letterhead: Capel House]
Nov. 8th. 1918.

My dear Pinker

I have seen Hartley Manor[1] and I must say that it seems the very thing, both as to the house itself and the grounds, which are so arranged that one gardener and another man (who would also do to wash the Ford car which I hope to get after the Peace) will be able to keep it in order.

The place is modest but has great character and indeed is the very thing for Joseph Conrad. It is excellently fitted out, and apparently in running order, because the man Harris, who resides in Grosvenor Square,[2] has been using it up to last month as his weekend house. The furniture is delightful certainly, and I understand that he wants to sell it as he has no room in his town house for it. However that is not a condition, and I have no doubt that he would let me have part of it as selected, either by rooms or by pieces.

---

[1] In Longfield, near Hawkhurst, Kent.
[2] The Rt Hon. Frederick Leverton Harris, 70 Grosvenor Street, Mayfair.

I myself would like to have the drawing-room, the hall and two bedrooms. The rest we could temporarily manage. However Jessie must see the place first, as I dare not take it for her, and I propose, if at all possible, to arrange to take her there on Wednesday. We would bring with us her light bath-chair which could be used inside and in the grounds too; so that she has a thorough examination of the house and its surroundings; after which at about two o'clock on Wednesday I will wire you the decision from Longfield, so that you can get at once in touch with Hampton,[1] as you so kindly offered to do. I can't tell you how grateful I am to you for your offer. I only wish you could see the place yourself. But meantime perhaps you would drop a line to Hampton saying: that Mr Conrad hesitates very much because of the smallness of the rooms; and it requires some consideration whether the advantages of the place would make up for that.

We might get an abatement of about £15 on the rent on that account, because the rooms *are* small. As to the premium they ask we could no doubt get an abatement on it because I think it is really too high (£500). Perhaps you would ask them also to mention how much they would want for the whole of the furniture; just to give us an idea of the value they put on those things, which, I must say look thoroughly fine and appropriate.

Ever yours affect[ly]

J. Conrad.

PS I've had a good batch of proofs from L & W.
PPS I understand that you will arrange for the architect to go over the place if we decide to proceed.

To Sir Sidney Colvin

Text J-A, 2, 211

Capel House
11. Nov., 1918, 11. 30. A. M.[2]

My dear Colvin,

Just a word on this historic date to ask how you are and to tell you all is fairly well with us. The patrol airship has just gone home from his beat – not needed any more! His usual hour was seven in the evening. The bells in

---

[1] Hampton & Son, estate agents, 3 Cockspur Street, five minutes' walk from Pinker's office.
[2] Half an hour after the signing of the armistice.

the village are ringing; and we two sit here soberly thankful for the end, giving our thoughts to those homes where no losses can be made up, and our gratitude to those who will never return. It is indeed a solemn day. The great sacrifice is accomplished, bringing with it a thrill[1] of wonder and awe at the inscrutable ways of mankind on this earth.

We have had a letter from B[orys] this morning. He is in Havre still, awaiting his Medical Board. I imagine they will give him sick leave now. Of course, there is a lot yet for the Army to do, but no doubt the numbers will be rapidly reduced.

My love to Lady Colvin

To J. B. Pinker
Text MS Berg; Unpublished

[Capel House]
11 Nov. '18

Dear Pinker.

Our warmest congratulations on Eric coming safely through the fiery furnace[2] which, we may take it, is finally put out now. It has been an awful time. I measure the stress by the feeling of limpness that has come over me today.

It did not prevent me from doing some of the Rescue today. I've sent also to the L & W. the whole of the Part I corrected. Good riddance – but not rubbish, or not so much as I feared it was.

Please pay into Lieut A. Borys Conrad's acc^t at Sir C. R McGrigor & Co 39 Panton St Haymarket S.W.1 [3] twenty pounds.

The aforesaid Lieut is detained in Havre awaiting further exam: by the Med: Board and is short of cash. I don't think he is very well in health either. I do hope they will send him home on sick leave preliminary to discharging which may follow soon now.

Ever Yours

J. Conrad.

---

[1] Quoting this passage, the sale catalogue of Colvin's letters from Conrad reads 'sense' rather than 'thrill' (Anderson Galleries, New York, 7 May 1928, lot 141).
[2] Like the three Jews who had refused to worship the statue of Nebuchadnezzar, King of Babylon (Daniel 3).
[3] Private bankers who specialised in military accounts.

To E. L. and Helen Sanderson
Text MS Yale; Unpublished

[letterhead: Capel House]
11 Nov. '18

Dearest Ted and Helen.

We are thankful to know that your boy as well as ours is safe out of the fiery furnace. On this day of sober joy one's thoughts turn to the homes where no losses can be made up and one's gratitude [to] the multitude of those who will never return.

Our warmest love to you all

Yours ever

J. Conrad.

To Hugh Walpole
Text MS Texas; J-A, 2, 211 [1]

[letterhead: Capel House]
11 Nov '18

Dear Walpole.

A word on this great day to take part in the sober joy you must feel. The great sacrifice is consummated – and what will come of it to the nations of the earth the future will show.

I can not confess to an easy mind. Great and very blind forces are set free catastrophically all over the world. This only I know that if we are called upon to restore order in Europe (as it may well be) then we shall be safe at home too. To me the call is already manifest – but it may be declined on idealistic or political grounds. It is a question of courage in the leaders who are never as good as the people.

We are thankful to know you are better. I shall try to see you in the course of this week. I imagine you'll be still interned in your flat on Thursday.

Affect^ly Yours

J. Conrad.

PS I did not write to thank you for your kindness and trouble in the Ret[inger]: affair, but pray believe in my sincerest gratitude.

---

[1] Without the PS.

To Edmund Candler

Text TS Morgan; Candler xxxvii

[letterhead: Capel House]
Nov 12th. 1918.

My dear Candler.[1]

I ought to have thanked you before for the book[2] which I read directly it reached my hands. This book adds to the great consideration I always had for your work and for yourself. Because the work is the man, generally; and in your case particularly so. Indeed it is a very fine book. You have rendered marvellously the aspects of nature, more profoundly perhaps than in any of your other work; and as to the humanity of it, I have been immensely struck by the lofty impartiality of your insight and the sincere sympathy of your treatment.[3] I have read those pages with sustained interest, and I have left them with a distinct sense of enlightenment in the intricate matter of racial psychology and with a firmer conviction of the difficulty of the problem which politicians at home are so ready to handle on mere party lines. Let me congratulate you with all my heart on the success, the artistic success, which you have attained in dealing with a most difficult subject.

My warmest thanks to Mrs Candler and yourself for your truly friendly invitation to come and stay in your house when I am in London. Nothing would give me greater pleasure since you are so willing to take the risk. But as a matter of sober truth I am in such a position that I must grudge every day spent away from my work. This situation will last till the middle of January next, and till then, I shan't appear in town unless absolutely forced to do so by some matter of business that will brook no delay.

[1] Edmund Candler (1874–1926) read classics at Cambridge. From 1896 to 1903, he taught in Indian schools and colleges, and from 1906 to 1914 he was Principal of Mohindra College in Patiala. He wrote about his extensive travels in Asia for the *Outlook*, *Blackwood's*, and the *Allahabad Pioneer*; in 1904, he was gravely wounded while covering the Younghusband Mission to Tibet for the London *Daily Mail*. He served as an official correspondent with the Indian Expeditionary Force in Mesopotamia, 1917–18, and as a roving reporter for *The Times* in the Transcaucasian Republics, 1918–19. After a spell as Director of Publicity for the Punjab, 1919–21, he retired to Southern France. In addition to his accounts of war and wandering, he published novels, short stories, and *Youth and the East: An Unconventional Autobiography* (1924).

[2] *Siri Ram, Revolutionist: A Transcript from Life, 1907–10* (1914).

[3] Openly rooted in his experiences as a teacher in India, Candler's novel tells the story of Siri Ram, who is jailed for publishing an inflammatory newspaper; when released, he assassinates a British judge and takes poison while under sentence of death. In a note to the second edition, Candler clarifies his own position: 'Siri Ram was a nationalist – I have given him that credit – and a revolutionist – a nationalist because his true instincts were patriotic, a revolutionist because these instincts had been perverted to violence and race-hatred' (p. 308).

Yesterday brought us a feeling of deep and almost mournful thankfulness. One looks back with awe at the greatness of the sacrifice. Whether the future will be worthy of it time alone will show.

My wife joins me in kindest regards to Mrs Candler and yourself. Believe me with the greatest regard

Yours

Joseph Conrad.

To J. B. Pinker
Text TS Berg; Unpublished

[letterhead: Capel House]
Nov. 12th. 1918.

Dear old friend.

I return to you the agreement of *A. of G.* duly signed and initialled. I am glad to see the five year clause and thank you very much for having had it accepted. I consider it a most important thing to have our hands free at the end of a fixed period. I also note the raising by £100 of payment in advance of royalties. I think "Victory" was only £400. Those are good terms. 20 per cent was also in the Victory agreement, I think, for the cloth edition ($1. 30). I thought I had the same amount: that is about one fifth of the published price, for the Blue Leather; but as the Blue Leather is sold at $1. 50, twenty five *cents* is equal only to *one-sixth* of the published price; roughly speaking 1/- per copy. I don't know why I should get less royalty for the edition which I have an idea has a greater sale than the cloth one. I never liked that edition. If you remember D[oubleday] sprang it on us in 1912 without communicating with you in any way and altogether off his own bat. Without in any way wishing to influence your judgment I suggest that at some fitting moment you could perhaps point out to D. that C[onrad] thinks he ought to have a uniform rate of 20 per cent on all the copies of his works in D.'s. hands. From something young Page told me a couple of years ago when he was here,[1] I have an idea that it is the Blue Leather edition that they are mostly pushing on to the public.

It strikes me that if Lloyd's Mag. are going to begin *A. of G.* in their Jan[uar]y issue your time for serialising in U. S. is getting short. I wish you every success in that matter. I know it would please you as much as it would please me. You have done so well with that novel (we never had so much

---

[1] Frank Page, youngest son of the American diplomat and publisher Walter Hines Page, visited the Conrads in November 1916 (*Letters*, 5, p. 679).

for serial rights in England) that I think that whatever sum you can obtain for serial rights of it in U. S., if its only a few greenbacks, you ought to have 20 per cent. I put down this plainly here so that there should be no mistake as to my intention and also as to my *sole* initiative in this matter. I intend to drop [in] on you about noon on Thursday next. I am coming up for lunch with Sobanksi to talk about that article with photographs for L. & W.[1]

Always your affect[te] and grateful

Joseph Conrad.

To J. B. Pinker

Text TS Berg; Unpublished

[letterhead: Capel House]

Nov. 15th. 1918

Dearest Pinker

This is a letter of two requests. The first one is that if you have a spare American copy of "Victory" (either edition) you will send it to me for presentation to an old lady to whom I want to be very civil. The print of the English edition is very tiring to the eyes. But if you have not a U. S. copy that you can spare pray order Methuens to send one to me at once.

The other request is for the statement of income about which the tax-gatherer in Ashford is worrying me persistently. That will be for the year 1917. Make it as summary as you like, but I don't want them to assess me off their own bat as there would be no end of bother in claiming a reduction since they are sure to assess me too high.[2]

I had a very good time yesterday. I suppose there is no doubt that L. & W. would print the Polish article.[3]

Yours ever

J. Conrad

PS Miss Hallowes dispatched the corr[d] proof to you of R. this morning by rail.

---

[1] The 'Polish article' mentioned in the next letter. *Land and Water* carried no illustrated article about Poland and nothing under Sobański's signature in the following months. Conrad's name and face often appeared, but only in connection with the serial of *The Rescue* (e.g. 26 December, Supplement, p. 6; 16 January, p. 21).

[2] In the margin, another hand has pencilled in the figure '£2160.10.3.'

[3] Although the answer must have been 'no', this projected article could have been the origin of 'The Crime of Partition', published in the *Fortnightly Review*, May 1919.

To G. Jean-Aubry

Text TS/MS Yale; Unpublished

[letterhead: Capel House]
Nov. 19th. 1918.

My dear Aubry.

I forgot to put this matter before you when you were here. It is this: Lieut.
Commander *R. R. Rosoman*, of the Royal Navy, was the officer responsible
for the preparing and fitting out of the ship "Vindictive" for the Ostend
expedition and also was 1st Lieut. of her during that operation.[1] The
British Government rewarded him by promotion and Admiral Keyes, (the
Commander in Chief) tried to get him a British decoration, with the result
which the enclosed letter from my old friend Commander Walter Saunders,
D. S. O. shows.[2] Of course promotion is of more advantage to an officer
without fortune of his own; but Rosoman is very anxious to have a French
decoration, particularly in view of the fact that there is a general impression in the Dover command that the French Government thinks the people
concerned with the preparation of that enterprise worthy of recognition.

I don't know why Saunders thinks that I have any influence in the French
official world in London. I have none, as you know very well; but perhaps
you could mention the case in some influential quarter. The man certainly
has done good work and is very anxious to get some mark of recognition
from France.

I believe that other officers connected with the enterprise have been or
are about to be decorated by your Government.

As a seaman myself I know of what importance a thorough and conscientious preparation is for securing success in an operation of that kind. Pardon
me for troubling you with this affair. Du reste mon cher ne vous donnez pas

---

[1] A system of canals connected the German submarine base in Bruges with open water.
The raids on Zeebrugge and Ostend were intended to block the mouths of these canals. On
the night of 22/23 April 1918, the cruiser *Vindictive* under the command of R. R. Rosoman
landed a party of naval and marine volunteers on the fortified breakwater at Zeebrugge and
then stood by under heavy fire while the landing party blew up gun emplacements and a railway viaduct. The U-boats were penned up for three weeks, and eight of the raiders won the
Victoria Cross: Sir Henry Newbolt, *History of the Great War*, Vol. 5: *Naval Operations* (Longmans,
Green, 1931), pp. 241–77.

[2] For his role as deviser and leader of the raids, Rear-Admiral Roger Keyes (1872–1945) received
a knighthood as well as honours from the French, American, and Belgian governments;
R. R. Rosoman, who had been shot in both legs during the raid, received a promotion but no
decoration. Commander Saunders was in charge of armed drifters – fishing vessels adapted
to naval service; the acquaintance went back at least to Conrad's tours of naval defences in
1916; besides raising the case of Commander Rosoman, Saunders asked if Conrad was writing
his book on the drifters (10 November: MS Yale).

trop de mal a ce sujet. Comme Vous voyez beaucoup de monde j'ai pensé que Vous pourriez trouver une occasion de placer un mot en faveur de Rosoman qui est un fort brave homme.[1]

J'ai dicté cette lettre car j'ai mal au poignet un peu.[2]

Tout à Vous

J. Conrad

PS Je viens de recevoir Votre lettre relative au Wise reprint.[3] C'est parfait. Merci.

To J. B. Pinker

Text MS Berg; Unpublished

[letterhead: Capel House]
Wednesday. [20 November 1918][4]

My dear Pinker.

I had the book from Meth: Thanks.

Pray pay 20 additional into Jessie's acc^t this week. In regard to the pension of which she was deprived she has a right to this.

I will be sending you the last chap: (IV) of Part *four* of Rescue – for clean typing and handing over to L & W. With that chap: they will have in hand *four complete* parts of R.

Chaps. I. & II. of Part *Five* are finished. The III is nearly so, but as I have done no correcting so far I hold them back till next week.

The work proceeds steadily.

Ever Yours

J. Conrad.

PS Did I tell you that B[orys] has been passed fit for duty? What happened was that he was pinned under a collapsed wall for an hour, breathing all the time chlorine gas.

---

[1] 'Anyway, my dear, don't give yourself too much trouble on this matter. As you see a lot of people, I thought you could find an occasion to say a word on behalf of Rosoman, who is a very gallant man.'

[2] 'I've dictated this letter because my wrist hurts.'

[3] In Wise's dealings with Conrad, Jean-Aubry played the go-between: see in particular the letter of 27 November; letters from Jean-Aubry to Conrad of 21 and [26] November show that Jean-Aubry knew much more than Wise about the location of contributions to periodicals.

[4] A sequel to the letter of the 15th: here Conrad thanks Pinker for ordering a copy of *Victory* from Methuen.

To J. B. Pinker
Text MS Berg; Unpublished

[letterhead: Capel House]
Nov. 21st. 1918.

My dear Pinker,

I send you here the *last* chap: of Part *Four* of the Rescue. I don't know how many copies you will have typed, but I should think two will do: one for L & W and one (I presume) for Dent's copy. I do not know if you have a set of Rescue in America which would require to be completed for the purpose of negociating* a serial. As to Doubleday he will have the corre*d* proof to set up from.

I must have been more overdrawn than I thought at my bank as I've had another reminder this morning. Pray send them another £20 – (apart from Jessie's extra for which I asked you in my letter of last Tuesday). I have two complete chapts of Part Five but I won't send them to you till later. There would be no object in that just now, unless you should wish it.

Yours ever

J. Conrad.

To J. B. Pinker
Text TS Berg; Unpublished

[letterhead: Capel House]
Nov. 22nd 1918.

My dear Pinker

Thank you for your letters received to-day. I had also a letter from Hamptons advising me that they had communicated with Mr Hulkes at once.[1] I haven't the slightest wish to commit myself to anything with those people, and, directly I hear further from Hamptons, I will send you their letter. As to the rent, I must tell you that the house has been let for several years to a Mr Manuelle (obviously a business man in the City)[2] at £145, who has, I must say, left it in very good order, both as to buildings and the grounds, of $3\frac{1}{2}$ acres. I offered £120 providing I get the house as it stands, with all Manuelle's improvements and the whole collection of lamps, without paying any sort of premium. Perhaps I did offer too much, but it is not at all certain that Hulkes will entertain the proposal. Most proposals laid before me contain the premium stipulation.

---

[1] Cecil James Gladdish Hulkes, JP, of Tonbridge, owned Pettyns Court, Ash, near Wrotham, Kent.

[2] George Schenck Manuelle.

The shooting is not worth much being mostly grass land and so near London; but the right of ranging at liberty over 200 acres of hill and wood is very fascinating to me. The place is within an hour's rail from London (Victoria or Holborn) on two lines. The distance from each station is about the same – 4 miles. The house is very good but in no way distinguished. It will take some furnishing because the rooms are very much larger than here and there are four more of them.

I should like very much your architect to go and have a look at the place. I should like also to ask him to give his opinion as to the possibility of setting up an electric light installation and the size of the plant required. Electric light is a very great convenience and in the way of expense I believe it pays for itself in three or four years.

I heard from Candler. He is going to the near East for the Times and I have sent him my best wishes for his success for he is a very good fellow. His Indian novel is a very remarkable piece of work in more than one respect.

Jessie sends her love.

Ever Yours

Joseph Conrad.

To J. B. Pinker

Text MS Berg; Unpublished

[Capel House]

[22? November 1918][1]

Dear Pinker.

I send you copy of my letter to Hampton. I wrote direct to save you the trouble of the preliminaries but I hope, if it comes to anything you will conclude the business for me.

The place has good points. I want to get in without paying anything in the way of premium. If the man accepts my condition I think it will be fair value for £120. This is to include the 170 acres of shooting that go with the house. Very poor I believe being all grass land and so near London; but what I would like is the right of entry on to these acres and it would be nice for the boys to get a rabbit now and then.

Yours ever

J. C.

---

[1] Furthering the agenda of the first letter about Pettyns Court.

To J. B. Pinker
Text MS Berg; Unpublished

[Capel House]
Sat: [23 November 1918][1]

Dear Pinker.

Thanks for your letter. You have mine of yesterday. Don't imagine I want to act rashly in any matter – house or other. I don't care particularly for that house and as to electricity talking about it costs nothing. What I really want is change. It is a real need; but even if I had not you to advise and guide me I wouldn't rush into it headlong. My feeling about it is exactly yours. It requires consideration at every step and I rely entirely on You to tell me what can or can not be done. My only scruple is as to taking up your time and so much of your thought; but I feel that you will not grudge me that.

I'll forward you Ha[m]ptons letter as soon as I hear from them. Many thanks.

Ever Your

J. Conrad

PS Can you order for me from Hatch[ar]^{ds} all the pub^d poems of Sassoon. He wants to come to see me next week.[2]

To John Galsworthy
Text MS Forbes; Unpublished

[letterhead: Capel House]
25 Nov '18

My dearest Jack.

I don't ask Sassoon this week because I have ordered everything he has published to be sent to me. I know his verse only in extracts and I want to see it all before I meet the man.

I am slaving at a novel and not feeling very bright. Jessie is trying to walk bravely. But there's no use concealing from ourselves that all the trouble is

---

[1] Pinker has evidently responded cautiously to either or both of the preceding letters.

[2] Poet, soldier, sportsman, and critic of military policy, Siegfried Sassoon (1886–1967) had been put on long-term sick leave in July when a bullet grazed his scalp. Sassoon greatly admired Conrad's work. He took *Nostromo* and *A Set of Six* with him to France in February 1917, and quoted a passage from 'The Informer' about the effect of 'terror and violence' on men of good will while in hospital later that month. In 1918, he read *Chance* and reread *Lord Jim* (Rupert Hart-Davis, ed., *Siegfried Sassoon: Diaries, 1915–1918* (Faber, 1983), pp. 131, 134, 217, 244). This was the year of his most widely acclaimed collection of poems about and against the war, *Counter-Attack*. In November, Sassoon visited Thomas Hardy, Robert Bridges, and John Masefield. Around the end of the month, he went to stay in Rye, a few minutes by train from Capel House (John Stuart Roberts, *Siegfried Sassoon* (Richard Cohen, 1999), pp. 128, 131–2, 135).

not over yet. The pain-spot persists and even grows larger I fear. It's rather depressing; but she wants to give it every chance to subside (if it means to do so) before appealing to Sir R. Jones.

Borys is still in Rouen busy with such duties as come in his way, in the hope of being ordered back to his battery in the end. He feels rather sick at having missed the triumphal advance and the opportunity (as an M[echanical] T[ransport] officer can) of doing some service to the liberated populations.

Our dear love to you both

Ever Yours

J. Conrad.

To Graham Tils
Text TS Berg; Unpublished

[letterhead: Capel House]
Nov. 25th. 1918.

My dear Mr Tils.[1]

I do not think really that I am to blame. I have worked for twenty years in obscurity and withdrawn from the world. How on earth could I get any notion of the feelings and desires which sway the souls of collectors for whom I have the most profound respect? It's only very lately that I got a very small insight into that world and discovered that my works are an object of interest to it.

Twenty-one years ago, when I was a perfectly unknown man with only two published books to my credit, Clement Shorter, then chief editor of the Illustrated London News, volunteered to publish a novel for me on the mere view of a few introductory pages which he obtained at the house of a friend. It was not only money but the wide publicity and a very striking appearance with splendid illustrations that he offered to a beginner without literary friends, influence or connections. At that time I did not even know of his existence. He wrote to me and I went to see him. From that time to this we have never met again. If his proposal came to nothing it was entirely my fault. It went so far as my receiving the proofs of the first part of the novel, and then, for reasons into which I need not enter, I decided to lay that particular work aside. Though my failure must have occasioned him great inconvenience C. S. entered into my reasons with complete sympathy.[2] In the years that elapsed we used to send each other messages through our common friends. At the beginning of this year he wrote me a letter asking me for permission to

---

[1] A collector of whom we know little beyond his irritation with Conrad, Shorter, and Wise. In a letter to Wise of 24 May 1919, J. A. Spoor describes Tils as 'a man in Chicago . . . a collector . . . a customer of Hill' (TS BL).

[2] 'I saw Shorter who didn't eat me', Conrad told Garnett in February 1899, after backing out of the arrangement with the *Illustrated London News* (*Letters*, 2, p. 169).

print 25 copies of "First News" and "Well Done"; and of course I assented at once. I could not have refused him that small satisfaction; and I will tell you frankly that if all the world were angry with Mr Clement Shorter it would not alter my satisfaction at having done something he had asked me to do.

The point of view you expose in your letter could not possibly have occurred to me.

Since then and while I was still in a state of ignorance a friend of mine, Mr Thos. J. Wise, of London, bibliophile, collector of MSS., and author of some remarkable bibliographies,[1] has asked me for the same sort of permission relating to three or four short pieces of mine contributed to the daily press; and I saw no reason to refuse him. Mr Wise had behaved in a very friendly manner towards me on one or two occasions, and it was a pleasure for me to give him the required permission. But whether he will take advantage of it and to what extent I cannot tell you.

It is my intention to communicate to him the contents of your letter;[2] and as he and Shorter know each other very well I believe that, no doubt, the latter will also learn your views on the subject. Whether those will have any effect I really cannot say; but this is the utmost I can do in recognition of your special grievance. I also wish to say that I regret very much that you and other collectors should deem themselves treated unfairly. I acted in ignorance for which I can hardly be blamed as I am not a collector myself. That particular range of emotions is a closed book to me. I never collected anything in my life, not even postage stamps, as so many boys do. This is no doubt regrettable, but I am afraid I am an imperfect human being, mentally and morally, in other ways too. Pray forgive my imperfections.

Believe me dear Sir

very faithfully Yours

Joseph Conrad.

To G. Jean-Aubry

Text TS/MS Yale; Unpublished

[letterhead: Capel House]

Nov. 25th. 1918.

My dear Aubry.

Thank you very much for your letter and the kind interest you take in my "naval officer." Ceci est d'un vrai ami. Whatever happens my gratitude is acquired* to you.

---

[1] Wise had already compiled bibliographies of Coleridge, the Brontës, Tennyson, Borrow, Wordsworth, Ruskin, and both Brownings.

[2] Referring to Tils in a letter of 18 February 1919, Conrad wrote 'I regret now I sent his letter to Mr Wise. It was very funny.'

I enclose here a letter from America which will speak for itself.[1] The hidden passions of the world of collectors are simply frightful. I shouldn't be surprised if a collector came over to shoot me. Pray show my letter to Mr Wise. I want him to know that I run risks for his sake. I would be also glad if Shorter had a view of it.

I answered the man that even if the whole world were angry it wouldn't affect my satisfaction at being able to do something which Mr Shorter and Mr Wise have asked me to do.

Heaven is my witness that I didn't know anything of your intention of sending a note on the "Rescue" to L. & W.[2] Or is it that I have so completely forgotten? Maybe. My mind is so completely taken up with that novel that I have lost my grip upon everything else. Do you want me to write to them?

J'arrête ma lettre ici pour retourner a ma tâche. C'est imperatif. Rappelez moi au bon souvenir de M. & Mme Halpert et de Mme Harding.[3]

Tout à Vous

J. Conrad.

To G. Jean-Aubry
Text TS/MS Yale; Unpublished

[letterhead: Capel House]
Nov. 27th. 1918.

Mon cher ami.

I return to you the cheque duly endorsed, and I am very glad you have been able to do a deal with Wise in the corrected type of "Nostromo". I only wish it had been more; but considering the fragmentary state of those things I think the price not so bad. I wish you every possible success in the negotiation about the Bibliography. The remarks you make on it are very just; there is no reason to treat collectors with special consideration. Such wares have a fanciful value, altogether independent of the author's intrinsic worth. But as to your Bibliography that is a thing that has its own value and is the result of a very conscientious and wearisome labour.

---

[1] The letter from Graham Tils.

[2] There is no note on *The Rescue* in *Land and Water* that might be attributed to Jean-Aubry; the substantial piece in the issue of 16 January, the week before publication, is signed by Robert Lynd.

[3] 'I finish my letter here to return to work. It's imperative. Remember me to Mr and Mrs Halpert and Mrs Harding.' For Louise Alvar Harding the singer and hostess: see the letter of 3 November 1919. Alexandre (born c. 1856) and Beatrix de Halpert (née Corbet, c. 1860) married in Stockholm in 1878; although Swedish-born, Mme Halpert had English parents and her husband was French.

Therefore I can't but highly approve of all your dealings in this matter with Mr Wise.

With L. & W. the position is somewhat different. You have engaged my personal responsibility in a matter of which I know nothing. Not that I have the smallest doubt as to the value and character of the Note you have written on "Rescue"! My point is that it lays me open to the charge that "Conrad looks after his own advertisements". And it isn't either as if the proprietors of L. & W. were personal friends of mine.[1] They are strangers to me and might misinterpret my interference. It looks as if I had tried to intrude on what is purely their own business; and Englishmen are, as a general rule, very tender on that point. Also, as it happens, it accords badly with my general attitude to the publishing world and to those two men in particular. In my only interview with them I took up the position that I didn't care a bit whether they took up the "Rescue" or not, before it was finished. It was their own affair and as far as I was concerned I took no further interest in it but the revision of proofs. Thus the situation is made a little awkward for me. I haven't heard from them on the subject so far. However if they write to me I will back you up to the extent of saying that I approve of the Note and that you are a very good friend of mine.

As to the two pamphlets: my impression was that I had given them to you to hand over to Mr Wise. On reflection, however, I imagine that if Wise knows Shorter personally he will get them from him by way of exchange for his own pamphlets when he publishes them. Therefore I think that you had better keep them for yourself. But pray if you dispose of them to the Chicago man, which I think would be a very good thing, let it be for yourself and *not* for me. Pray don't let it appear as if *I* were selling those pamphlets. I have given the permission to re-print out of friendship to Shorter from no interested motives and it would annoy me very much if the contrary impression got about, either in England or America.

I have here 94 pp. of pen and ink MS. of "Arrow of Gold". Those are probably the very last pages of my work that will ever be written by my own hand. I was thinking of sending them to America but if, as it seems to me (from first par. in the copy of your letter to Wise) Mr Wise would care even for fragments of MS. from my pen and if he thinks the above specimen, which very probably will be my last, worth to him rather more than ten shillings a page, I would be disposed to part with it for £50. If you care to mention it to him at all it must be understood that the transaction has to be concluded before Wednesday next as I have a special use for that money. In order to

[1] One was S. Nevile Foster, editor and managing director; the other is unknown.

save time I am sending you those pages now, and you can send them back to me or bring them with you next time you come to see us if Mr W. declines or you don't like to move in the matter. Je Vous en prie ne vous genez pas pour me le dire.

Ma femme et deux de nos bonnes ont en la (ou *le* – je ne sais pas) 'flu'. Pas très serieusement, mais au plus fort de la chose. Borys est arrivé en permission de 15 jours qu'il va tâcher de convertir en congé d'un mois; de sorte que nous avons l'espoir de l'avoir ici pendant les fêtes de Noel. Le garçon a assez bonne mine. Ma femme naturellement est au lit pour une semaine encore je pense. Elle vous envoie les 'kindest regards'.[1]

Tout à Vous

J. Conrad.

To J. B. Pinker

Text MS Berg; Unpublished

[Capel House]

Wednesday [27 November? 1918][2]

Dearest Pinker

I answered this letter appropriately at once.

Has the Lloyd News* begun A of G already? I saw a small par: in a daily which is not quite clear to me.

Won't those people send me any proofs? Pray tell them to behave decently and send me early copies of the Magazine too. Editors used to have manners – once!

I think Hulkes (of Peltyn's* Court) will take no notice of my offer – so far he's taken no notice.

Ever Yours

J. C.

---

[1] 'My wife and two of our maids have had the "flu" (I don't know if the word's masculine or feminine). Not very seriously, but right in the thick of things. Borys has arrived on a fortnight's leave which he will try to convert into a month's break, so we hope to have him here over the Christmas holidays. The boy looks quite well. My wife, naturally, will be in bed for another week I think. She sends you "kindest regards."'

[2] Written on the back of a letter from H. E. Maule of Doubleday, Page, dated 6 November. Unless the mails were unusually slow, Conrad would have received this letter well before the 27th, but the theme of Mr Hulkes's indifference belongs to the end of the month. One might speculate that Conrad sent Pinker the communication from Doubleday some time after he had answered it. On 3 December, Conrad asked for proofs from *Lloyd's Magazine* in a tone of annoyed reiteration. On 4 December, he wrote what amounts to a point-by-point reply to Maule's letter as though Pinker had seen it already and expressed his opinions.

To J. B. Pinker

Text TS Berg; Unpublished

[Capel House]
28 Nov. 1918

My dear Pinker

As you see this man wants to negotiate personally.[1] I haven't heard from him yet but I expect I shall very soon, and unless one gives up the notion there is no reason to refuse to meet him. I can't expect you to leave your business and run about the country for me; but my general idea would be to get into a habitable house without having to pay any premium. The rent I offered covers also a four-roomed cottage. The house itself is very well built and very dry, which is a consideration for me. There would remain then only the question of the furniture. As to the light it would be for the future. At any rate there is no necessity for me to conclude on the spot. I will have a thorough look at the place (which I haven't had yet) and will be able to send an architect before we definitely agree.

I am not particularly anxious for that house, you must understand. I only say that it will do. I am only writing to you like this in order that you should send me any suggestions that may occur to you.

Jessie is laid up with 'flu' but is getting better. One of the maids is very ill. I am fairly well myself but could work better if I had not all these worries. The day before yesterday B[orys] arrived on a 15 days' leave which we hope he will manage to get extended over Xmas. He looks fairly well but he is not quite himself yet and hasn't yet quite lost his gas cough. I will be writing to you at the end of this week on the general situation.

Yours ever

J. Conrad

To T. J. Wise

Text MS BL Ashley 2953; Unpublished

[letterhead: Capel House]
Kent.
2^{d} Dec 1918

Dear Mr Wise.

I was about to pack the *Arrow of Gold* (typed corr^{d} copy and the MS pp) for America when it occurred to me that you might like to have the MS pages as a curiosity, as all the chances are there will never be any more pen and

---

[1] Conrad wrote on the back of a letter from Hampton's of 27 November which passed on an invitation to meet Mr Hulkes.

ink pages of my work in the future. My right wrist seems permanently out of order and the use of the pen starts it aching after a page or two. The typed corr^d first copy I meant to dispatch to N. York. Aubry however writes me that you wish to have it together with the MS pages.

That copy is the original of the story as dictated. It consists of about 520 pp. I am having them numbered consecutively in *blue* pencil – all other numbers to be disregarded. The corrections are mostly in black pencil, but a good many are in ink. I don't think there are in the whole lot ten pp without corrections. On two or three the corrections (in ink) are not in my handwriting. I dictated them on a day when my wrist was too bad to be used at all. The text is divided into: First Note – Five Parts – and Second Note. It is absolutely complete, the clean copies for the printers having been typed from it. These, as they come back to me (in England at any rate) with the proofs, will be destroyed. America will set up from revised proofs (duplicate) which I am sending over for that purpose.

The thing being for about 460 pp (out of 520) the *only* original text in existence I can't very well throw it in as a make-weight to go [with] MS. p. p. It is either interesting or not interesting from a literary point of view. But if it *is* interesting then there is nothing more interesting in existence – from that point of view. On that ground I have no doubt I could get a hundred in U. S., for the whole lot after some little delay. But if you will give me £70 I will be very pleased to forward it to you at once. It is my first work (novel or story) which may be said to be wholly dictated.

Your typescript copy of *Rescue* is being carefully preserved, as far as it goes, while I am completing the novel. I have been able to work fairly well lately and I expect to finish it by, say, the 15 of Jan^y, 1919. I hope you will have the whole in your hands before the end of that month. Meantime if you like to have what is ready delivered at once (parts I. II. III. IV) into your possession I'll send it on with pleasure.

Believe me, dear Mr Wise,

very faithfully yours
Joseph Conrad.

To G. Jean-Aubry
Text MS Yale; Unpublished

[letterhead: Capel House]
2^d Dec '18

Cher Aubry.

Je viens d'écrire a Mr Wise que ceci etant le seul premier texte qui existe je ne peux pas le lui donner pour rien. Le tout aux E. Unis produirait bien

£100, mais s'il veut me payer 20 livres extra (£70 en tout) je prefère conclure l'affaire avec lui.

Merci de tous le mal que V[ou]s vous êtes donné. Je suppose que vous avez chez Vous les pp manuscrites. Vous les donnerez a Mr Wise s'il Vous les demande – n'est-ce pas?

Ma femme a eu une mauvaise 'flu'. Voilà 9 jours qu'ellest* au lit. Ça va mieux depuis hier. Borys est arrivé en congé. Moi, je travaille est* même j'avance. Quand ma femme sera debout nous vous prierons de nous faire une petite visite.

Tout à Vous

J. Conrad.

Translation

Dear Aubry.

I have just written to Mr Wise that this being the only original text in existence, I cannot give it to him for nothing. The whole lot would bring £100 in the United States, but if he wants to pay me 20 pounds extra (£70 in all) I prefer to settle the matter with him.

Thank you for all the trouble you've gone to. I suppose you have the manuscript pp at home. You will give them to Mr Wise if he asks you for them – isn't that so?

My wife has had a bad bout of flu. She's been in bed for 9 days. Things have improved since yesterday. Borys has arrived on leave. As for myself, I am working and even making progress. When my wife is up and about, we will ask you for a brief visit.

Yours truly

J. Conrad.

To J. B. Pinker

Text MS Berg; Unpublished

[Capel House]

3 Dec. 18

My dear Pinker

Please insist with Lloyds Mag. to send me proof with corresponding type of each instalment. It's only proper. I want to be treated decently.

Will you also remind L & W that they promised early proofs of all the parts in their possession. I had p^t One nearly a month ago and nothing more since. I don't want to be bothered with proofs end Dec^{er} and in the first days of Jany when I'll be engaged with the last pages of *R*.

I am going on steadily tho' not so fast as I would like.
The man Hulkes gives no sign about the house.

Ever Yours

J. Conrad

To J. B. Pinker
Text TS/MS Berg; Unpublished

[letterhead: Capel House]
Dec. 4th. 1918.

My dear Pinker.

1. I have no confidence in D[oubleday] P[age's] judgment. Their request strikes me as pretty cool, too. Unless you think the chances of serialising Arrow so poor as to be not worth holding to, D&P. proposal must be met by a negative on the ground of needless sacrifice, merely.

2. Besides: January next won't be a good time for publication. The mind of the public will be busy with peace negotiations and political controversy then and for two months more at least.

3. Also: the time between this and, say, January 30th will be too short to make proper publicity arrangements for a Conrad book.

4. Lastly: The impression would be bad if the U. S. serialisation of Conrad failed in two or even in one instance. Those things get talked about. I get letters from U. S. frequently. I am thinking of my own prestige of course. No other would be engaged. The question of money is secondary. On the other hand hawking about would not be a good thing. There was talk of it in regard to the Polish Journey. (In print by Mencken).[1] You'll weigh these matters with better judgment than I can.

5. But if you feel inclined to give serialization in US up (and you wouldn't do that except for very good reasons, I know!) you must tell me so plainly and you will find me perfectly amenable to your advice – even against my own inclination.

6. Only: We've almost agreed that Rescue is to precede Arrow. There are three good reasons for that course. One of them is that R. will be ready first for book form. Second: a matter of dedication to ex-ambassador Penfield.[2] Third: that the Rescue is really an earlier book than the Arrow.[3] My own preference for that course is a secondary matter.

7. Finally: I beg you most earnestly to settle finally the mode of publication of these two books so that by chopping about they should not get

[1] One of Mencken's essays includes an anecdote about Pinker's vain attempt to get $2,500 for the US rights of 'Poland Revisited' (*A Book of Prefaces* (New York, 1917), p. 57).
[2] Who rescued the family in 1914 by securing Austrian exit permits despite the Conrads' status as enemy aliens.
[3] Earlier by far in its inception.

into each other's way. If you prefer to talk to me rather than write I will come up on Friday. I've numbered the pars of this for your convenience in answering.

Ever affectionately Yours
Joseph Conrad.

To J. M. Dent
Text TS/MS Berg; Unpublished

[letterhead: Capel House]
Dec. 6th. 1918.

My dear Dent.

My warmest greetings on your safe return from the States, I presume in good health and, as I see, with no abatement of your spirit of enterprise.

The pamphlet idea is very new to me.[1] Personally I don't attach any importance to those articles and the prospect of writing another one is not exactly fascinating, especially at the present time, as I am up to my ears in the last part of "Rescue". It isn't the sort of job one can get through while one whistles. I really cannot promise you any copy before January next, when I hope to have the third novel of our contract finished and off my mind. Meantime you may fix up the business side with Pinker, for indeed I am not averse from* the idea.

Believe me sincerely yours
Joseph Conrad

PS My greetings to Mr Hugh. It was a pleasure to have him here for a few hours. His very sympathetic* and his kindness in sending books to my wife while she was in the nursing home was much appreciated by both of us.

To J. B. Pinker
Text TS/MS Berg; Unpublished

[letterhead: Capel House]
Dec. 6th. 1918.

My dear Pinker

Thank you for your full letter.

First: On the point of time between the publication of the two books, I see that you have planned no less than an eight months interval and possibly ten. This is exactly the view I take.

---

[1] Dent wanted Conrad to write a shilling pamphlet on the Royal Navy along the same lines as Kipling's *The Irish Guards in the Great War*, 'because I want it to lie on the stalls, and to popularise your name, as well as to do the people good' (5 and 9 December; TSS carbon, Berg).

Second: As to the order of publication. Taking into consideration also Dent's natural impatience to publish Arrow here as soon as possible perhaps the best way would be to deal with the book as you suggest. That is: If A. remains unsold till say the end of January (and no negotiation[s] are proceeding at that date) then give Doubleday his head and let him publish Am book no earlier than the end of March. But here arises the question whether Dent will be free to publish at the same time? I am afraid that Lloyds will spread this thing over six months or more, which would put off English book form till end June. Bad time. It will make thus the Arrow a 'spring book' in America and an 'autumn book' in England. Would that be safe from the material point of view?

Third: On the other hand L & W being a weekly, may finish Rescue in March, in which case simultaneous book form could come out in April in U. S. and U. K, the Arrow in that case being held back.

Fourth: My preference lies that way; but you understand that I would not on that ground alone forego any chance of the serialisation of Rescue. And in this connection I must tell you that Doubleday, years ago, volunteered to me assurances of help in serialising the Rescue, for which they do not pay any advance on publication. I mention this to you for what it is worth; not attaching any value to it as it stands, but with a view of asking him privately for his good offices as a sort of set off for my consent to publish Arrow in the spring. After all, those people are on the spot. They must have influence. They are my publishers for the whole of my work; and perhaps I could venture to write personally in that strain with some effect and without compromising either you or me.

5th: The whole problem is very intricate. Each course presents certain complications and difficulties; but it would be unwise on our part to lose sleep and appetite over it. I still think that "Rescue first" is a good principle; unless indeed serialisation offers before say middle of March, in which case we could release Arrow in America at once for book form.[1]

You have here my full view of the situation. The decision will rest with you; and I will be perfectly satisfied as long as there is an assurance of a proper interval being preserved between the two book forms both in England in America.

Ever afft^{ly} yours

J. Conrad

PS Writing to D'Day is the merest suggestion of a possibility and I wouldn't dream of doing it without your *fullest* assent. And indeed I am anything

---

[1] *The Rescue* was serialised in the United States (*Romance*, November 1919 May 1920); *The Arrow* was not.

but anxious to do that thing, I assure you! You have all the weight of my affairs on your shoulders. A little more money would make things easier for us both. The Napoleonic novel[1] may take 18 months in writing. I would like too to have a look at Elba and Corsica before I get too deep into the tale – say next winter. But I am sure you will not misunderstand me.

To G. Jean-Aubry
Text TS Yale; Unpublished

[letterhead: Capel House]
Dec. 9th. 1918.

Mon cher ami.

I think I told you last week that I wrote to Mr Wise. As I haven't heard from him yet perhaps you will be good enough to send me back those MS. pages of Arrow of Gold which you have; as I think I will send the whole lot to America without waiting much longer. My wife sends her kindest regards. She is much better now. Borys has got a prolongation of leave and is staying with us. Do you think you could find time to come down for a day, before Christmas? I don't think we could arrange to put you up for the night just now, but we should like to see you very much. For myself I doubt whether I will be in London this year, though it is possible. My health is now fairly tolerable and I am going on with the book but not getting on as fast as I would like to.

I hope you will drop us a line soon.

Tout à Vous

Joseph Conrad.

To Arthur Symons
Text MS Virginia; Hunter (1985, 3)

[Capel House]
Monday 9 Dec. [1918][2]

My dear Symons.

We were very sorry to hear of the horrid bad time you and your wife have had lately. Jessie is still laid up – after a severe flu and bronchitis; but I expect her to get up to-morrow. One of our maids was very dangerously ill and altogether it was not a cheerful house these last days.

---

[1] The long-projected historical novel that finally took shape as *Suspense*.
[2] The report on Borys locates the year.

I saw the Times article – a nasty and stupid thing which a man like you may disregard.[1] That vol: is full of charm and contains many pages of rare distinction and luminous like pearls, which – as we know on the highest authority – are not appreciated by swine.[2] Let them grunt!

I look forward to the book your letter promises me.[3] Your prose delights me even more than your verse tho' that too has its marvellous side.

We are glad to hear of the doctor's verdict. I hope your cough is nearly gone by this time and no longer prevents you whispering sweet nothings in the ears of the Russian Ballet.[4] We admire your capacity for 'whirlwind' life. You are eternally young.

Our eldest boy is home on convalescent leave after being wounded and gassed during the victorious advance of the 2^d Army. Hard times after doing 3 years of work to miss all the shouting at last. He looks however fairly well by now.

I am hard at work on another novel which is approaching completion. Pray give us a line of news about you both. Jessie's kind regards.

Ever yours

Joseph Conrad

To J. B. Pinker

Text MS Berg; Unpublished

[letterhead: Capel House]

10 Dec '18

My dear Pinker.

Herewith 2^d part Rescue corr[ect]ed proof – American set. The *L & W* set has been sent to them by this morning's post.

I had proof from Lloyds of 2^d inst of Arrow. I forgot to count the words but it is now much longer than the first which was a bare 5000. But if it had been double, 10. 000, it would take 10 months to run the story through. *Arrow* is just over 100. 000.

Heard from Hulkes. We are to meet at the house this week – it seems. Am doubtful of it coming to anything. If it does I depend on you to see to

---

[1] An unfriendly review of Symons's *Colour Studies in Paris* (1918) (*TLS*, 5 December, p. 596). Writing to John Quinn on the 10th, Symons quoted Conrad's words of reassurance (Karl Beckson and John M. Munro, eds., *Arthur Symons: Selected Letters, 1880–1935* (Macmillan, 1989), p. 243).

[2] 'Neither cast ye your pearls before swine, lest they trample them under their feet' (Matthew 7.6, quoting Jesus).

[3] *Cities and Sea-Coasts and Islands* (Collins, 1919), a collection of essays and reviews.

[4] Symons had a tendresse for the Polish ballerina Lydia Lopokova (later Keynes), and through her knew Diaghilev (Karl Beckson, *Arthur Symons: A Life* (Oxford, Clarendon Press, 1987), pp. 292–3).

324

the agreement. I hope to see you next Monday when I come up to meet John.

Ever Your

J Conrad.

PS Borys staying on extended leave to attend another Med. Board. Jessie much better. Sends her love.

Send me the *name* of the principal owner of L & W. I forgot it.

To T. J. Wise
Text MS BL Ashley 2953; Unpublished

[letterhead: Capel House]
10 Dec 1918

Dear Mr Wise.

I am so sorry to hear you have been tormented by our common enemy.[1]

Thanks for the cheque.[2] The typed copy goes out by the same post with this. I have personally seen that it is in order. Of course it does look not very fresh. *All* the work of the book has been done on it. I signed p 1. and p. 519. after inking over myself the text on that page which was written in pencil and looked dangerously faint and smudgy. The other corr^{ons} (in pencil) I did not ink over. I have also joined to the copy a "note" (one page) giving a few facts as to the origin of the story, which I signed also.[3]

My wife thinks that there is somewhere in the house a complete short story in MS. I doubt it. However she intends to hunt it up when she gets better after her bad attack of flu. Don't think pray that I am planning to unload it on you. It cannot be anything very good as MS. As it is I am afraid Quinn will want to take my scalp when he hears of our transactions.

Believe me

very faithfully Yours

Joseph Conrad

---

[1] Gout.   [2] For the TS of *The Arrow of Gold* offered to Wise on 2 December.

[3] This must be the note reproduced in Wise's *A Bibliography of the Writings of Joseph Conrad* (Richard Clay, 1921), p. 81. 'The subject belongs to my early life. I was conscious of it through all the years of my writing life, but I was reluctant to take it up, not seeing my way, and not feeling the mood, though I thought of it more than once. It was only in 1917 that I brought myself to consider it seriously.'

A second note is an MS fragment at Yale. 'Note for Mr Thomas J. Wise[.] The pgs bound in this vol are the *only* MS pp of the first draft of The Arrow of Gold. The rest of the first draft was dictated straight to the machine and afterwards corrected in pen and ink. That corrected typed set embodies of course the 94 pen and ink pp of this Ms as modified late by me. Joseph Conrad.'

To Messrs Chatto & Windus

Text TS Private collection; Knowles & Stape

[letterhead: Capel House]
Dec. 11th. 1918.

Dear Sirs.

I have read your letter most carefully,[1] but I can't, as you ask me to do, give my serious consideration to a proposal from which all mention of time is excluded. No doubt many writers can shake 50,000 words out of their sleeve in their spare time but I have not that facility. The work I am doing now I cannot possibly lay aside for another six weeks.[2]

Yours faithfully

Joseph Conrad.

Messrs. Chatto & Windus.

To J. B. Pinker

Text TS/MS Berg; Unpublished

[letterhead: Capel House]
Dec. 11th. 1918.

My dear Pinker

I am very sorry to cause more trouble about the year '17 accounts, but it isn't altogether my fault. Looking at the two enclosures you will realise what has happened. I was asked to call by the Surveyor,[3] who called my attention to the fact that both your communications related to the year 1917 and wanted to know which of them was right.

What happened was this, as he explained: He is a new Surveyor and he asked me for a statement not knowing that his predecessor had already done so early in the year. I am ashamed to say that I had forgotten completely myself that I did ask you for a '17 statement just before leaving London in March, had received it from you in April and had forwarded it to the man who has now left, and obviously had not warned his successor.

---

[1] Chatto & Windus, the long-established London publishers, wrote to Conrad on 10 December to ask if he would supply 40–50,000 words of text for a book reproducing the paintings and graphics of naval activities currently displayed in the Sea Power Exhibition at the Grosvenor Gallery, London (TS carbon, University of Reading; *Portrait*, p. 5).

[2] A reply to this letter dated 13 December assured Conrad that 'there is no reason why you should not delay beginning the work for the matter of six weeks or so . . . but as a preliminary to any negociations we should naturally be glad to know how long you would be likely to take over the work when once you had started on it' (*Portrait*, p. 135).

[3] Of taxes.

The new man while waiting for a reply to his enquiry discovered the statement rendered in April. I imagine that the first statement is correct and that when making the second statement some payments made in 1918 have crept in, being entered by mistake as being made out of the 1917 income. There is also a discrepancy in the amount of premiums on life policies which was pointed out to me and I couldn't explain. I regret bothering you with all this but this matter must be somehow cleared up. Pray have the statement posted to me before five o'clock on Monday because I am going on Tuesday to Ashford to see the man and fill in and sign my return.

Thank you for your letter of the tenth. I will just drop a note to Doubleday as it can do no harm, as you say. Of course they must send proofs. I hope they won't begin till February as otherwise I shall be overwhelmed with proofs from L. & W., from Ll. Mag., and from Doubleday; and these last will require some looking into as they will be for a book-form set up from a type-written copy. I have had a letter from Chatto & Windus which I am sending you here. It seems to me very obvious that Henry Newbolt is the right person.[1] I must say that this letter does not impress me very favourably. They talk about arranging for America and all this sort of thing, which is obvious; and about translation into foreign languages, which means very little; and also about the 'assured publicity' which seems to be a sort of bait. But while they ask me to give serious consideration to this vague proposal they don't say anything about the time. It doesn't seem very serious to me. In such books pictures are the thing for which people buy them, and if I wrote 40, 000 or 50, 000 words I would much prefer publishing them by themselves.

Ever Yours

Joseph Conrad.

PS Thanks for your letter. I've written to N. Foster about the drawings. Please pay in £20 to my acc*. I fear I won't be able to see you on Monday as I expect to see M*r* Hulkes on Monday in Ashford. I'll run up later in the week and be able to tell you something re house.

JC.

---

[1] Sir Henry Newbolt (1862–1938), patriotic poet and writer on naval affairs. When Conrad received a grant from the Royal Bounty in 1905, Newbolt acted as one of two trustees in charge of the funds.

To S. Nevile Foster
Text MS copy Yale; Unpublished

Capel House
Dec: 12th 1918.

Dear Sir,[1]

I have had today from Mr Pinker two full page illustrations of the "Rescue". I hesitated whether I would write to you. For all I know the number may be ready by this time; but I must put on record the protest of a man whose work has been illustrated in many publications for upwards of 15 years and who, as an artist himself in another medium, has always been treated by his illustrators with a certain amount of consideration; and, before all, with that loyalty which is due from a conscientious artist to the conceptions of another. For some of them, like Mr. Maurice Greiffenhagen who illustrated my "Typhoon" in 1902, I have preserved to this day a sentiment of real gratitude for the sympathy of workmanship, for the honest effort to render in another medium – if not all the details or even the hard facts, then the spirit of my conception.[2] I feel in the same way towards the illustrator, whose name I don't recall, who did the drawings for my "Mirror of the Sea"[3] – towards many others too, in Harpers, in the Metropolitan,[4] who, with various degrees of success, made me feel that they had read at any rate my text and had responded to it according to their temperament, but always with skill & knowledge.

---

[1] S. Nevile Foster was editor and managing director of *Land and Water*, the forerunner of *Country Life*. For the duration of the war he abandoned the magazine's usual fascination with the pursuit of fish and game in favour of covering the war's strategic and political aspects. He continued to publish fiction, however, and considered taking *The Shadow-Line*, but decided that it lacked incident.

[2] Maurice William Greiffenhagen (1862–1931), head of graphic design at the Glasgow School of Art, illustrated the serial of 'Typhoon' for the *Pall Mall Magazine* and the book form for Putnam's (both 1902). He also did the illustrations for 'The Inn of the Two Witches: A Find' in the *Pall Mall Magazine*, March 1913. His best-known illustrations were those for Rider Haggard's romances. Reacting to Conrad's protest, Foster commissioned Greiffenhagen to work on later instalments of *The Rescue* (for a sample of what he did, see Plate 7, taken from the issue of 22 May, p. 33). In the interim between Hardy's departure and Greiffenhagen's arrival, H. L. Bacon illustrated the episode of 20 March, and Christopher Dudley the episode of 3 April.

[3] The graphics for *The Mirror of the Sea* were those done by David B. Waters for the serial publication of some sections in the *Pall Mall Magazine*.

[4] See *Letters*, 4, Plate 7, for an example from *Harper's Magazine*: a moment from 'The Secret Sharer' drawn by W. J. Aylward. Other *Harper's* illustrators of Conrad's work were Anton Otto Fischer, Wolcott Hitchcock, and Thornton Oakley. The *Metropolitan Magazine* commissioned Clifford Ashley, Frederic Dorr Steele, and H. J. Mowat.

Has M$^{r.}$ Hardy[1] ever seen a yacht's gig,[2] the most elegant thing afloat? Has he ever seen in a boat of that description a man fool enough to stand in the attitude of that ugly blob, which is, properly speaking, monstrous? Will he show me anywhere a boat of any description that will look like what is meant for a boat in that illustration? Has he ever seen a square-rigged vessel under any circumstances of light or trim look like a collection of unsightly bags without character, outline, or anything else? Has he looked with an artist's eye ever in his life at the leech of a sail, either full or aback, the most definite & expressive line in the world?[3] The whole thing is false enough to set one's teeth on edge; and of unpardonable ugliness. I won't speak of the heavy tonality, of the opaque quality of that tropical sky, which at the moment he selected is clear, as I distinctly state. For Carter sees the star-rocket soar up from behind the land and take up its position like a new star in a constellation, before he sees it burst. And don't imagine for a moment that I wanted M$^{r.}$ Hardy to draw the stars for me. There are ways of rendering the luminous quality of a tropical night & there was no reason to cram ugliness into the very sky.

I write strongly because I feel strongly. I don't suppose M$^{r.}$ Greiffenhagen for instance had ever seen the appearances of a typhoon, but he had imagination enough to understand the words I had written. He tackled his problem like a man. The types[4] in that story have been inspired by a sympathetic reading of my text. In the rendering of the details, such as the inside of the wheelhouse or the glimpse of the overwhelmed foredeck, he displayed a fidelity to my vision by which I was deeply touched.[5] McWhirr, Jukes, the engineer, the very Chinamen, were treated in a way to bring their individualities out in accord with my vision & with a scrupulous care. But really in the scene with the two figures drawn by M$^{r.}$ Hardy the limits of the widest license* are overstepped. It almost amounts to gross contempt and I tell you this plainly because I feel it strongly. What does he mean by sticking a fur cap on the head of Lingard? What is it – a joke? Or is it to display a fine independence in a story whose action takes place in the tropics? And what is that face? (Lingard is a man with a beard – I say so.) – that face which

---

[1] Dudley Hardy, whom Foster had chosen to illustrate the serial: see the letter of 18 October.

[2] A gig is a light ship's boat propelled by oars, sails, or both, which may be stored on board, towed, or sailed independently. The offending illustration appeared as p. 22 of the 6 February episode.

[3] Leech: 'Either vertical edge of a square sail; the aft edge of a fore-and-aft sail' (*OED*). A sail is full when the wind blows it away from the mast and aback when the wind pushes it against the mast.

[4] Stereotyped plates.

[5] This acknowledgment of fidelity to a vision recalls the Preface to *The Nigger*.

says nothing, which suggests no type, might belong to a hotel waiter or a stock broker, and with that whole figure which might be that of a burglar, meeting an about 35-year-old railway guard in some nondescript place that might be a cellar! I asked a visitor staying in the house "where do you think those two men are?" & I got for answer "Well, it might be a cellar". I defy anybody to guess that this is supposed to be a ship's cabin. I have described that cabin. It was panelled white with gold mouldings. The steward had lit the cabin lamp (does Mr Hardy know the difference between a lamp and a lanthorn?¹) and the place in which the first vision of possible disaster comes to Lingard in the midst of his success is characteristically gay and martial with its light decorations & the glint of musket barrels – brilliant, full of light, blazing! Not a nondescript black hole without air wh[ich] I see on the plate before me. Lingard himself is described as in his flannel shirt, with a sash & bare-headed. Carter is defined in four lines as a young man, looking still more youthful, with smooth cheeks & a tiny moustache. Pray look at that railway guard conception. Is that a youngster just come on board, after four days in a boat, an officer of clippers, without enough manners to take off his cap when he comes into another man's cuddy.² I wonder also why M^r· Hardy didn't dress up Lingard in a Pierrot costume, instead of the fur cap. It would have been at least funny, and, in so far better than the dully forcible treatment of that scene; and every bit as truthful. May I ask you whether in your mind those types are settled and are going to be continued right through the story? Whatever happens pray take note of this protest, which is the first and the last I will make. It is perfectly justified on the ground not only of mere truth to facts but of the artistic conception. As it stands it is sheer disloyalty. However, you may be sure that mine is strong enough towards the publication wh: has opened to me its pages to keep my lips closed as to my real feelings before the rest of the world. I have written to you so strongly just because I mean this to remain between ourselves, though, of course, I am not afraid of M^r· Hardy knowing what I think. Perhaps you could convey it to him in a form wh: may do some good in the future? But I am afraid he can't possibly care for the story. It may be uncongenial to his temperament, you know.

   Believe me

                              Y[ours] e[ver]

                                                      J. C.

---

¹ A lanthorn or lantern is the glass-and-metal casing; a lamp is the source of light itself.
² Cuddy: a captain's private cabin or the cabin where officers take their meals: here, the former. For this scene, see Plate 6, reproduced from the issue of 30 January p. 20. Before publication, Hardy managed to remove Carter's and Lingard's headgear.

To G. Jean-Aubry

Text TS Yale; Unpublished

[letterhead: Capel House]
Dec. 14th. 1918.

Cher ami.

My wife has discovered a place to put you up in. It will be a very small room but I suppose you won't mind that. Therefore we hope that you will come to see us on Saturday by the 4. 30 train and stay on till Monday morning. Please drop us a line that you will.

Kindest regards from everybody in the house.

Tout à Vous

J Conrad

To J. B. Pinker

Text TS/MS Berg; Unpublished

[letterhead: Capel House]
Dec. 14th. 1918.

My dear Pinker.

I will be very glad if you would dispose of Chatto and Windus' proposal in the sense of your letter. Thank you very much for your reply to mine with the subjoined statement for the Surveyor of Taxes, as to the correct income for the year 1917. They have meantime assessed me at £2400 but I am going to protest and I have no doubt that it will be amended down to the amount stated in your letter.

I have arranged to meet Hulkes re house on Tuesday. I shall hear what he has got to say and make a note of it without committing myself in any way. On Wednesday I intend to run up and see you about 12 o'clock and perhaps we may lunch together, as I want to talk to you in detail about certain ideas and needs of mine.

Poor Jessie's limb is not getting on and I am beginning to be worried. Another appeal to Jones will have to be made and what the consequences of it will be God only knows.

I had a letter from Land & Water and it is arranged that Hardy will come to see me, to talk over the illustrations, one* some day between Xmas and the New Year. Without going into the spirit of those illustrations I am not at all pleased at their technique which wants to be forcible and is only dull. And what the devil does the man mean by putting a fur cap on Lingard's head and in a story whose action is in the tropics? That's beyond a joke. I must say that

I have been accustomed so far to be taken seriously by my illustrators; and whatever I may have felt about illustrations I have been always very grateful to them for their loyalty, beginning with M. Greiffenhagen, who was my first illustrator when you first took my fortunes into your hands by serialising "Typhoon" in the Pall Mall.

Ever Yours

J. Conrad

PS Heard also that L & W won't begin *Rescue* till 2^d week Jany. It's rather convenient for me. I've begun a Polish Article with Harpers in view,[1] planning for about 4000 words.

To John Galsworthy

Text MS Forbes; Unpublished

[letterhead: Capel House]

16 Dec. '18

Dearest Jack.

B[orys] being in town tried to see you but heard that you were away. He's gone to Canterbury for the Med^{al} Board today. I hope they will extend his leave or else mark him for home duty. He looks well enough and the gas-cough is nearly gone now. But he is undoubtedly shaken and not quite himself yet.

I couldn't ask Capt Sassoon to come here because of Jessie's flu. It was pretty severe. Poor Nellie Lyons was ill too and I much fear the faithful creature's existence is near its close. We had her moved to the Cott^{ge} hospital and our Doctor told Jessie that her chance was very slight. It seems to be a general break up. Her hold on life was always very frail tho' she never complained of anything.[2] We had been uneasy about her for some time. Jessie and I are trying to make arrangements to render her last days on earth as easy as possible amongst her own people. For she may last a month or even longer we are told.

Jessie after her flu has developed a swollen throat. She has struck a vein of bad luck. As to her knee I am afraid we will have to appeal again to Sir R. Jones' skill and kindness. It's evident there is something wrong still there.

---

[1] 'The Crime of Partition', which first appeared in the *Fortnightly Review* on 1 May 1919 as 'Poland: The Crime of Partition'.

[2] To the point of keeping silent about her debilitating stomach ulcers in 1909 lest the household be disturbed and work on *Under Western Eyes* interrupted (*Letters*, 4, p. 285).

It's a rather difficult position. We are naturally most reluctant. But it is now six months since the operation and she has made up her mind to write herself. It cant be left as it is. Our dear love to you both.

Ever Yours
J. Conrad

To F. N. Doubleday
Text TS/MS Princeton; J-A, 2, 213

[letterhead: Capel House]
Dec. 21st. 1918.

Dear Mr Doubleday,

I was just thinking of writing to Garden City when I heard of your arrival in this country. I am very glad that your presence here may give us an opportunity to meet each other after the holidays. I would have come up of course to see you, as I fear that with your many important engagements it will be impossible for you to give us the pleasure of receiving you under our roof here this time; but in any case I will be under the necessity of bringing my wife to London in the course of next month, probably for another operation; the one performed on her knee in June last not having entirely answered our expectations. All the year 1918 has been passed in endeavours to relieve her from her crippled state and I have had rather an anxious time in consequence.

It didn't, however, prevent me, as you know, from finishing a novel, about which I had lately a very appreciative letter from a member of your staff. It was extremely pleasant. But all the communications I receive from Garden City are extremely pleasant, though they are generally signed each by a different name. Mr Saxton's signature is the only one I saw more than once; but I believe he is no longer with you.[1]

The Arrow of Gold is a subject which I had in my mind for some eighteen years, but which I hesitated to take up till now. This state of mind may to an American appear very dilatory and ineffectual; and I won't attempt to apologise for my opinion that work is not to be rushed at simply because it can be done or because one suffers from mere impatience to do it. A piece of work of any sort is only fully justified when it is done at the right time; just as the potentiality and the energy of a fire-brigade is only justified when a house is on fire. To rush out and deluge the citizens' houses with streams of water simply because the pumps are new, the organization perfect and a laudable energy must have an outlet, would be an absurd proceeding and, very likely,

---

[1] Eugene Francis Saxton (1884–1943) worked for Doubleday from 1910 to 1917; he and his wife, Martha Plaisted Saxton, greatly admired Conrad's work.

give serious offence to the reasonable part of the public. Some feeling like this, just as strong but of a different order, has restrained me. But having found the mood I didn't tarry much on my way, having finished that novel in about ten months. This for a piece of creation depending so much for its truth on actual brush-strokes, one may say, is rather a short time; especially as it was also an essay, I won't say in a new technique (there is nothing new under the sun) but in a method of presentation which was a new departure in J. C.'s art – if such a thing as J. C.'s personal art exists. I wouldn't like to have to demonstrate this in set terms; but some people say that it does exist.

You have too much knowledge of human nature not to understand after what I have said, that I feel a particular interest in that book, which is so much of a portraiture of vanished years, of feelings that had once their actuating power and of people who probably are all at rest by now. I am sufficiently* of a democrat to detest the idea of being a writer of any 'coterie' of some small self-appointed aristocracy in the vast domain of art or letters. As a matter of feeling – not as a matter of business – I want to be read by many eyes and by all kinds of them, at that. I pride myself that there is no sentence of my writing, either thought or image, that is not accessible, I won't say to the meanest intelligence (meanness is a matter of temperament rather) but to the simplest intelligence that is aware at all of the world in which we live. Therefore I will confess without shame that the failure in serialising the "Arrow of Gold" has affected me to a certain extent. The question of what is or is not fit for serial publication reduces itself, when all is said and done, to the single point of 'suspended interest'. That I judge is the 'master-quality' of a serial; and it is not always to be obtained by the mere multiplicity of episodes. One single episode out of a life, one single feeling combined with a certain form of action (you'll notice I say *action* not analysis) may give the quality of 'suspended interest' to the tale of one single adventure in which the deepest sensations (and not only the bodies) of the actors are involved.

I put this point of view with some diffidence before a man eminently successful in one of those forms of human activity that deal with mankind in the mass. I may be wrong. I think however that I was right in the objections I raised against the proposal to publish A. of G. in book form in January. First of all, it seemed to me that, at the date the proposal reached me, there was not enough time left to make the business and publicity arrangements for a novel by J. C. whose merit is not of that kind that could secure a response without all the help that the standing, influence and organisation of Doubleday, Page & Co. can give him. I also doubted the advisability of publishing a book at a time when, for the next three months or more, the public mind is bound to be absorbed by the problems of peace and the settling of political questions all over the world. Besides, I felt that in justice to myself, and also to your efforts on my behalf, I must see the proof sheets; not for material alteration, but for the exact setting of the text. I felt this the more because your printers would be setting-up from a type-written copy which I myself had not seen, but which, I am sure, contains the usual amount of errors and mistakes of a kind that cannot be easily discovered by the most conscientious of proof readers. I am perfectly aware that I had no book proofs from you for the previous books, but this was only because then the setting-up at Garden City was done from printed texts which were already carefully revised by me.

The "Rescue" is approaching completion and I believe that the last words will be written before the end of January. The serialisation of that story will be another problem in which if opportunity offers, I feel I can count upon your assistance.

I hear that it is your intention to come to some agreement with Mr. Wm. Heinemann as to the publication in England of a certain proportion of the 'limited edition' which has been held in suspense during the war. Nothing would give me greater pleasure than to see the English issue in Mr Heinemann's hands. I have preserved a very vivid sense of that firm's friendly attitude towards my earlier work. They did everything that was possible to give a chance to the "Nigger of the "Narcissus" – a pretty hopeless book at that time; and later, when I failed in my engagement to them, they treated me with a delicate consideration which I am not likely ever to forget.[1]

My wife sends her most friendly regards. She charges me to say that she is glad you have found support in that friendship and devotion which give to the life of a man of action its greatest value.[2] I need not say that I associate myself warmly with her sympathy and felicitations. My eldest boy begs to be remembered to you kindly.

Believe me

Very faithfully yours
Joseph Conrad.

PS Our best Christmas wishes for all your family circle. I trust you will have good weather for your time of ease.

---

[1] Largely thanks to S[ydney] S[outhgate] Pawling (1862–1922), Heinemann's were notably forbearing about Conrad's failure to deliver *The Rescue*, on which they had paid him a substantial advance.
[2] Doubleday, whose first wife had died in February, married Florence Van Wyck (1866–1946) on 27 November.

You'll pardon this long letter. I don't often overwhelm you with long missives. But you are my publisher. The care of my reputation and my fortunes in the New World are in your hands, and being very sure of Your friendly sentiments I have written to you all that was in my mind.

To Edward Garnett

Text MS Indiana; G. 283

[letterhead: Capel House]
22 Dec '18

My dear Edward.

I was just going to drop you a line when your precious little note arrived. I missed you immensely my dear old friend during all these days.[1] The resumption of our intercourse has been very precious to me. It was a great and comforting experience to have your ever trusted and uncompromising soul come forward again from the unforgotten past and look closely at my work with the old old wonderful insight, with unimpaired wisdom and in unalterable friendship.

I was sorely tempted to ask you to come down for a few days; but 'flu' was raging all over our country-side, the weather was atrocious, Jessie herself was struck heavily (with consequent bronchitis too) and one of our maids nearly died in the house. Capel was not a healthy place to ask a friend to; while from a moral point of view it was a detestable atmosphere thick with gloom which even your "powerful intellect" could not have resisted, I believe. How I survived I don't know. At any rate here I am still very feeble in every respect except in respect of my affection for you.

I am afraid I'll have to bring poor Jessie again to London and deliver her once more to the surgeons. I am convinced that another carving is necessary before she ceases to be a cripple. The prospect of getting again in touch with you is a positive comfort – and the only one at this juncture. Borys who is here on convalescent leave (after being gassed and wounded) asks to be remembered to you. John who is too much of a pagan to regard the amenities of a Christian festival merely exclaimed at the mention of your name "I like him" and rushed off somewhere. We will leave it at that. But Jessie and I send you our deepest regard and love with all the best wishes proper to this season which, somehow, doesn't *feel* so festive as one expected it to be. A cloud of unreality hangs about men, events, discourses, purposes. The very

---

[1] As a non-combatant but at considerable risk, Garnett had served with an ambulance unit in Italy. Since his understanding of Allied military aims and methods was, to put it mildly, more sceptical than Conrad's, the difference of views had sometimes come between them; nevertheless, their intimacy went back for nearly a quarter of a century.

relief from longdrawn anguish is touched with mistrust as if it were if not a delusion then at least a snare.[1]

Ever Yours

J Conrad

To J. B. Pinker

Text TS Berg; Unpublished

[letterhead: Capel House]

Dec. 22nd. 1918.

My dear Pinker

Thank you very much for having written to the Surveyor.

I went to see last Friday the house for sale near Canterbury. I am certain that it could be got cheap; but it's not a transaction upon which I would venture.

The urgency of this letter lies in the fact that Jessie did not receive her week's money due last Friday. Pray send it on to her on Monday, and perhaps, at the same time, you would remit also the money for the Xmas week, as I don't suppose you will be in the office after Wednesday.

Borys thanks you very much for having thought of him in connection with employment by the firm of Vickers.[2] He would consider himself very lucky if the thing could be managed, the more so that he presumes that an employment of the sort would secure his release from the army easier than in any other way. He is extremely anxious to go back to civil work. He wonders whether you would give him an interview for half an hour or so after the holidays. I told him that you would certainly see him and listen to what he has to say. I hope, my dear Pinker, you will drop us a line giving your day and hour when you have leisure, because his sick leave will run out very soon and once he is sent off to some camp it might be difficult for him to come up to town.

I had a friendly letter from Doubleday, who wants me to come up and see him after Xmas. I made a suitable answer. I am very much afraid that we will all have to come up after Xmas on account of Jessie's knee. I think a supplementary operation is unavoidable but I also think that all the chances are that it will put her right definitely and close this worrying chapter in our life.

Ever Yours

Joseph Conrad.

---

[1] 'A snare and a delusion' is the familiar version of Thomas, Baron Denman's warning that trial by jury would, if tampered with, become 'a delusion, a mockery, and a snare' (*Regina* vs *O'Connell*, House of Lords, 4 September 1844).

[2] The great Midlands engineering firm.

To Ada and John Galsworthy
Text J-A, 2, 215

Capel House.
24 Dec., '18.

Dearest Ada and Jack,

You have been both very much in my mind but it's clear that I cannot hope to see you this year. So I send these few lines to carry to you the united affection (both boys are at home) of us all and all possible good wishes for unbroken felicity in your new home and many years of peace.

At the same time I'll confess that neither felicity nor peace inspire[s] me with much confidence. There is an air of the "packed valise" about these two divine but unfashionable figures. I suppose the North Pole would be the only place for them, where there is neither thought nor heat, where the very water is stable and the democratic bawlings of the virtuous leaders of mankind die out into a frozen, unsympathetic silence.

I haven't had any gout for a long time. I am sure I don't know why, and I am afraid to rejoice over much. I have been working, – or is it playing? – at a novel. But I am not unduly elated. The gloom of the last two weeks (I mean atmosphere) was enough to cure the worst case of laughing sickness.

Ever affectionately yours.

To F. N. Doubleday
Text MS Princeton; Unpublished

[letterhead: Capel House]
[late December 1918?][1]

This list contains the approximate number of words (assuming every line to be full) in Conrad's books:-

1)	Romance	190,000
2)	Nostromo	180,000
3)	Lord Jim	150,000
4)	Chance	150,000
5)	Victory	133,000
6)	Under Western Eyes	130,000
7)	An Outcast of the Islands	130,000
8)	Youth	130,000

---

[1] In the bound volume of Conrad's letters to Doubleday at Princeton, this list is placed between letters of 21 and 31 December, and was perhaps posted with one or the other. The estimates of length must be for the Collected Edition.

9)	The Secret Agent	109,000
10)	Typhoon	100,000
11)	A Set of Six	90,000
12)	'Twixt Land & Sea	87,000
13)	Almayer's Folly	80,000
14)	Tales of Unrest	73,000
15)	Within the Tides	70,000
16)	The Mirror of the Sea	69,000
17)	The Nigger of the *Narcissus*	60,000
18)	Some Reminiscences	55,000

I have not been able to examine a copy of The Inheritors – but it is amongst the shorter books.[1]

To F. N. Doubleday
Text TS/MS Princeton; Unpublished

[letterhead: Capel House]
Dec. 31st. 1918.

My dear M[r] Doubleday.

I shall be with you at one o'clock on Thursday unless indeed something very unforeseen and fatal happens before then. It will be a great pleasure for me, first to see you as a friend, and next to talk over with you those matters relating to my work and prospects in which I am so glad to feel you interested.

I have this moment heard that the Cosmopolitan is nibbling at the "Rescue".[2] There is a cable from your house asking for a synopsis (or else a rush of copy) for the Cosmopolitan people. P[inker] has also seen the Cosmopolitan representative here. I have sent P. an extended answer to the request and only hope that it may be satisfactory. It seems rather absurd to me that with three fourths of the story in hand there should be a request for a synopsis from a writer like Conrad. Don't imagine pray that I am hinting at being too great a person for that sort of thing; but with eighteen volumes of imaginative and creative work before the public and with a recognised very personal characteristic note in my art, I should have thought that no magazine editor need have worried himself about the last, say 120 pages. But

---

[1] This list adds up to 1,986,000 words; by Hans van Marle's calculations, the proper figure would be approximately 1,700,000. In the right-hand margin, a pencilled note in another hand gives more word counts: 'The Inheritors 80 th[ousand] The Shadow-Line 42'. More accurate counts for these volumes would be 63,600 and 39,700.

[2] A nibble but never a bite.

perhaps the editor of the Cosmopolitan had never read a line of my writing before. I should of course be sorry if the thing failed therefore I made the best answer it was in my power to give. But I will tell you about it when we meet.

Believe me
very faithfully Yours
Joseph Conrad.

PS I do indeed hope that I will have the honour of being made known to Mrs Doubleday at some future occasion.

To J. B. Pinker

Text TS/MS Berg; J-A, 2, 212

[letterhead: Capel House]
Dec. 31st. 1918

My dear Pinker.

I quite understand that people can not be expected to buy a pig in a poke but I submit that buying a Conrad work is not exactly that; and that the style, character and trend of the tale can be sufficiently seen from the M.S. in the state it is in now.

I may also point that the New York Herald, seven or eight years ago, was not afraid to begin before "Chance" was finished.[1] I mention this fact because the N. Y. H. is certainly a very American paper, with a large public, and I have no reason to think that they regretted it.

Much as I would be pleased to appear in the Cosmopolitan I am afraid I can do nothing in the way of a rush; and as to any sort of synopsis of events, apart from the difficulty I would have to give an abbreviated account, I am afraid it would be of no help, because the interest of that romance is all in the shades of the psychology of the people engaged – as is obvious from the four parts already completed. It is sustained by the presentation alone. You may however assure the representative of the Cosmopolitan Magazine that the story will end as romantically as it began, and that no one of any particular consequences will have to die. Hassim and Immada will be sacrificed, as in any case they were bound to be, but their fate is not the subject of the tale. All those yacht people will go on their way leaving Lingard alone with the

---

[1] The *New York Herald* began serialisation on 21 January 1912, and Conrad finished the serial version, considerably longer than the book form, on 25 March. *Chance* was not the first Conrad novel to be finished while the serial was running; the same had happened with *Lord Jim, Nostromo,* and *The Secret Agent.*

wreck of the greatest adventure of his life. For indeed what else could have happened? Any tragedy there is in this 'denouement' will be all in the man's feelings; and whatever value there may be in that must depend on the success of the romantic presentation. This statement, I have the right to hope, will be enough for the mature mind which directs the editorial department of the Cosmopolitan Magazine. There are many kinds of romance and this one is not fit for juvenile readers, not because it raises any sort of problem but on account of the depth and complexity of the feelings involved in the action, which in itself does not aim at any great originality and can be pretty well foreseen from the beginning.

Always yours

Joseph Conrad.

PS The above is written with the idea that you may like to show it to the Cosm^{an} man here after tearing off this strip. You might even leave it with him.

I ought to have thanked you before for your readiness to see McLeary[1] on Thurs: at 3. He will be punctual. On the same day I am driving up to lunch with D[oubleday]. I hope you will give *me* an interview in the morning. I want to get your guidance as to what I may or may not with discretion say to D. Also I'll bring the Polish article.

Ever affectly yours

J. C

[?]

Text MS Private collection; Unpublished

[letterhead: Capel House]

Saturday [October 1918–March 1919?][2]

My dear Sir[3]

Thanks very much for your sympathetic book. It is vividly interesting (I am on p 70) and am flattered to think that its writer, who *knows* so much of human

---

[1] McLeary's identity is not known.

[2] 2 October 1918, the date the Allies entered Damascus, and 25 March 1919, the date the Conrads left Capel House, define the period.

[3] This unindentified correspondent travelled in the Middle East and wrote about his adventures there. Among those who match this description are the Revd Joseph Thomas Parfit (1870–1953), author of *Among the Druzes* (1917) and *Twenty Years in Baghdad and Syria* (1916), an Anglican missionary and educator; Mohammed Marmaduke William Pickthall (1875–1936), translator of the Qu'ran, novelist, and author of memoirs such as *With the Turk in War-time* (1914)

affairs thinks so well of my work. I trust we may meet if only for a moment on your return from Damascus next year.

Yours cordially,

J. Conrad

and *Oriental Encounters* (1919); and the Hon. Aubrey Herbert, soldier, MP, master of disguise fluent in many languages, a model for John Buchan's stories of hazard and intrigue whose military reminiscences *Mons, Anzac, and Kut* (1919) describe campaigning on three fronts. By 1919, T. E. Lawrence (1888–1935) had only published *The Wilderness of Zin* (1914), a collaborative account written with C. Leonard Woolley of their archaeological expedition to the Negev (which served as a cover for military mapmaking), but as one of Conrad's later acquaintances, he is another possible recipient.

1919

To T. J. Wise
Text MS BL Ashley 1986; Unpublished

[letterhead: Capel House]
2ᵈ Jan '19
Dear Mʳ Wise

I ought to have thanked you before, for the very curious pamphlet containing Swinburne's sweet little joke.[1] I enjoyed both the verse and the prose (especially the prose) immensely.

With best wishes for this new year and all the many years to come. I am my dear Sir

Very faithfully yours
Joseph Conrad.

To J. B. Pinker
Text TS Berg; Unpublished

[letterhead: Capel House]
Jan. 7th. 1919.
My dear Pinker

Thank you for your letter disposing of F[isher] U[nwin]. You would laugh but that animal upset me so much by his impudence[2] that I got an attack of gout and am now in bed with a swollen knee, since the day before yesterday.

Miss Hallowes and I have been hard at work on the galley slips for the book form of the "Arrow". The work will be done to-morrow and I shall send you then the corrected galleys for transmission to U.S.

The car has been delivered to me to-day in perfect order and a good bargain. As we arranged please send C. Hayward & Son, New Street, Ashford, cheque for £186 of which £180 is for the car and £6 for the duty for the year 1919.

---

[1] After Algernon Swinburne died in 1909, Wise talked his way into The Pines, the house in Putney where the poet had been living under the care of Theodore Watts-Dunton, and acquired every literary relic he could find (Nicholas Barker and John Collins, *A Sequel to an Enquiry into the Nature of Certain Nineteenth Century Pamphlets by John Carter and Graham Pollard* (Scolar Press, 1983), p. 56). In all, Wise published seventy items trawled from the sea of unpublished letters and MSS, usually with an editorial introduction by Edmund Gosse. Easily the most entertaining of these would be *A Letter to Ralph Waldo Emerson* (1918), Swinburne's reply to rumours in the American press that Emerson had denounced him as 'a perfect leper and a mere sodomite'.

[2] The 'impudence' may concern either Conrad's remaining obligations to Unwin or Unwin's reluctance to permit a British collected edition. See Conrad to Pinker [c. 12 March] and 15 March.

I have been in too much pain to-day to work but I did a few pages yesterday and I hope I shall work to-morrow.

Ever Yours

J Conrad.

To J. B. Pinker

Text TS Berg; Unpublished

[letterhead: Capel House]

Jan. 14th. 1919.³

Dearest Pinker

Allison and Hardy¹ failed to turn up yesterday on account of the fog. I was hardly fit anyhow to see them, for it is a very bad bout of gout from which I am just beginning to recover.

Would you please 'phone to L & W to tell them that I am sorry. I see they have not fixed the actual date for beginning R. and if they could put it off to the first week in February it would be very convenient because I am badly shaken up and every day gained would relieve my anxiety to a certain extent.² Perhaps you could arrange.

Borys will attain his majority to-morrow. John goes to school in a week's time. We will have to come up to London in the first week of February for Robert Jones, but I suppose Jessie has written to you about it. I feel very weak and depressed just now.

Ever Yours

Joseph Conrad.

To Jessie Conrad

Text MS Yale; *JCLW* 45

[Capel House]

[15 January 1919]³

Dear Heart.

My soul is weary for the sight of you. I hope you will have a passible* night. What a comfort it is to have the two kids with us in these trying times – and especially the big kid who twines himself round my heart even more than when he was a small child.

---

¹ Murray Allison of *Land and Water* and the artist Dudley Hardy, who, to Conrad's displeasure, had been illustrating *The Rescue*. The visit was postponed to 12 February.

² The serial began in the 30 January number.

³ Jessie Conrad's own note reads: 'This letter was written in February, 1919, when Conrad was upstairs confined to bed by his old enemy, gout, Mrs. Conrad being downstairs unable to move after an operation.' Borys reached his majority, however, on 15 January.

I worry about you all, and I fret at being laid up on his twenty first birthday. What must be will be – and after all I have all possible confidence in the future. Good night dearest and give me a friendly thought before you go to sleep.

Your Boy.

To J. B. Pinker

Text TS Berg; Unpublished

[letterhead: Capel House]
Jan. 18th. 1919.

My dear Pinker.

I am getting better but I don't pretend to say I am fit to work yet. I may be in three or four days able to make a start.

The failure of Jessie's operation, for it was that, there is no disguising the fact, the prospect of another and the incertitude of the result with all the trouble and disturbance of coming up to London are really a crushing worry to my mind. Perhaps if I were well myself I could stand it better. I have had several most horrid sleepless nights of late. However I feel that directly I can lay hold of my work again I will be able to go on with it. That in itself is no worry except that I am a little bit anxious about the time going on. Your friendship, goodwill and guidance are really the only comfort I have in these trying hours. Jessie and I are touched at your remembering Borys's birthday.

Have you seen Robert Lynd's page on me in L. & W.?[1] Very nice indeed. There are four or five men like this who have been writing about me in a most friendly and appreciative manner for a good many years whom I don't know personally.[2] I hope to be able to see them before I go off the scene, for after all they have helped too and one really does feel grateful in one's heart to them though it is difficult to write formal letters of thanks.

Pray pay £25 to my account in the bank which I am advised is overdrawn.

B[orys] ran over to see the Sevenoaks house yesterday. It is not to be thought of. It would have had to be something really ideal to be worth the money asked. And it is far from being that. Moreover your remark to B. that I wouldn't like the inhabitants of the district was perfectly just. Even if the

---

[1] 'Mr Joseph Conrad', 16 January, p. 21, with a full-page photograph of Conrad on the facing page. Lynd observes that since Hardy has abandoned fiction, Conrad is 'the only novelist now writing in English with the grand tragic sense . . . He lifts the curtain upon a world in which the noble and the beautiful go down before an almost meaningless malice.'

[2] Robert Lynd (1879–1949) had often annoyed Conrad by dwelling on his supposed unfamiliarity with the English language. In 1908, Conrad had wondered: 'Couldn't someone speak to him quietly and suggest he should go behind a counter and weigh out margarine by the sixpennyworth?' (*Letters*, 4, p. 108).

house itself had been cheap it is a neighbourhood of rich men which would not have been appropriate to us.

In his wanderings about the country B. discovered a house belonging to Warner the cricketer. He himself has been killed, as you know,[1] but Mrs Warner wants to let it. I understand she asks £100 rent for it. The house itself is very interesting and would do well enough to live in. Very light and high rooms and just enough of them. But there is very little ground with it and no means of housing the car unless one were to enlarge a tiny coach house which they have there. It is three miles from Maidstone station and on the borders of Leeds Castle park, in a very pretty bit of country. It has got a very perfect system of central heating. However there are disadvantages too which require consideration. I wish to goodness we could find something possible, for this unsettled feeling is really not good for me and I am really impatient to make a start with my next novel.

Yours ever

J Conrad.

To J. B. Pinker

Text MS Berg; Unpublished

[Capel House]
21 Jan '19

My dear Pinker.

Our faithful Nellie died yesterday.[2] I wrote to her mother that Ill be responsible for the burial expenses, and unless B[orys] is ordered to duty before he will go over to represent the family with a wreath.

John is gone to school to-day. I presume you had my letter (re bank) of last Friday. I had to draw a small cheque today.

I am recovering from everything but some natural anxiety. But don't anticipate any catastrophe. It's evident that the damn[d] thing is not going to kill me this time, and I can reasonably hope for a three months' interval of tolerable health.

I rather dread the London journey – and the London stay – not to speak of a rather sinking feeling when I think of the ultimate result as to Jessie. She sends her love.

Ever Your

J Conrad.

---

[1] Not Pelham ('Plum') Warner, who died in 1963, but his much less famous brother R. S. Aucher Warner, who in 1900 captained the first West Indies side to tour England.

[2] Nellie Lyons, the Conrads' maid for many years, was 36. Her family lived in Sturry, near Canterbury.

To Sir Hugh Clifford

Text TS Clifford; J-A, 2, 216;[1] Hunter (1985, 2)

[letterhead: Capel House]
Jan. 25th, 1919.

My dear old friend.[2]

I cannot delay any longer answering your letter[3] and I would rather dictate it than put it off until I am able to sit up and write. I have been a prey to gout for many days and the state of public affairs does not help recovery in any great degree. True, the war is over, but in the success of our arms I had never a doubt. The future, however, is obscure enough and I cannot defend myself from discontent and anxiety. It may be more instinctive than rational, but yet it cannot be denied that there is something ill-omened in the atmosphere in which the peace and reconstruction problems are being tackled. The intervention of the United States was a great piece of luck for the Western Powers, but luck too has got to be paid for. The assistance came late but the full price will have to be paid for it nevertheless. American influence in European affairs cannot possibly be good on account of those people's crudeness and ignorance backed by great material strength and an awakened sense of their power. Luckily there is a sort of futility about them which will probably make them less dangerous than they might be.

Of course my concern is for England, which engages all my affection and all my thoughts. I look at all the problems and incertitudes of the day from that point of view and no other. As to Poland, I have never had any illusions and I must render the Poles the justice to say that they too had very few. The Polish question has been buried so long that its very political importance is not seen yet. In this war it had not even an episodic importance. If the Alliances had been differently combined the Western Powers would have delivered Poland to the German learned pig[4] with as little compunction as

---

[1] As was his custom with remarks hostile to the United States, Jean-Aubry cut from 'American influence' to the end of the first paragraph.

[2] Sir Hugh Charles Clifford (1866–1941; knighted 1909), a colonial administrator, was serving as British Resident in Pahang, Malaya, when he wrote one of the earliest general appreciations of Conrad's work. Later, he was appointed to the governorships of Labuan and North Borneo, the Gold Coast, Nigeria, Ceylon, and the Straits Settlements. He published many volumes of stories and sketches, collaborated on a Malay dictionary, and produced a Malay translation of the colonial penal code.

[3] Sent from Accra on 18 November 1918, it is included in *Portrait*, pp. 133–4.

[4] Like the 'Russian mangy dog' a symbolic beast, embodying what war-time public opinion believed to be typically German: a combination of overloaded scholarship, pretentious culture, and thoroughgoing swinishness. 'Learned pig' became an English catchphrase in 1785, when a literate animal headed the bill at Sadler's Wells; Wordsworth, Coleridge, Wollstonecraft, and Blake all mention this gifted performer: see Ricky Jay, *Learned Pigs & Fireproof Women* (New York: Villard, 1986), pp. 8–27.

they were ready to give it up to the Russian mangy dog. It is a great relief to my feelings to think that no single life has been lost on any of the fronts for the sake of Poland. The load of obligation would have been too great; and certainly, it is better to die than to live under a charge of moral bankruptcy, which would have been unfailingly made before many years. The only justification for the reestablishment of Poland is political necessity, but that has never been very clearly seen except by a superior mind here and there, both in France and England. Nothing serious or effective will be done. Poland will have to pay the price of some pretty ugly compromises, as you will see. The mangy Russian dog having gone mad is now being invited to sit at the Conference table, on British initiative! The thing is inconceivable, but there it is. One asks oneself whether this is idealism, stupidity or hypocrisy? I do not know who are the individuals immediately responsible, but I hope they will get bitten.[1] The whole paltry transaction of conciliating mere crime for fear of obscure political consequences, makes one sick. In a class contest there is no room for conciliation. The attacked class cannot save itself by throwing honesty, dignity and convictions overboard. The issue is simply life and death, and if anything can save the situation it is only ruthless courage. And even then I am not certain. One may just as well defy an earthquake.

You and yours have been continually in our thoughts. I did not write to you before, dear friend, because what could one have written? The old order had got to die – and they died nobly – and at any rate the dead are at rest.[2] It is those who are left who may have yet to bargain for their souls with the most materialistic and unscrupulous of forces that have ever moved mankind. A humiliating fate.

Borys has been gassed and shell-shocked in October on the Menin-Cambrai road during the Second Army's advance. After several weeks in hospital in France he is now with us on a month's convalescent leave. Poor Jessie has got the prospect of another operation. I am going to take her up to London in the first week of February and I do not know how long we shall

---

[1] No foreign government had recognised the Bolshevik regime. Meanwhile, heavy fighting between Reds and Whites continued across swathes of Russia, and Allied troops had intervened on the side of the Whites. Supported by Woodrow Wilson, Lloyd George had proposed urging the belligerents to conclude a truce in order to send representatives to the Peace Conference. Clemenceau and Orlando (of Italy) strongly opposed inviting any Bolsheviks to Paris. The compromise was to ask all parties to a meeting on Prinkipo Island, in the Sea of Marmara. The London press reported these developments on the 23rd. The Prinkipo meeting never took place.

[2] Clifford had lost his son Max, who was reported 'wounded and missing' on the Somme, 1 July 1916. Seven days after the Armistice, Clifford had written: 'at least today I have the consolation of knowing that he did not give his splendid, vigorous young life in vain' (*Portrait*, p. 133).

have to stay there. What will be the end of it nobody can tell and frankly I am trying not to think of it. John is in a preparatory school. They are both of them very good children to us, but I look at them and ask myself how they will end! There is an awful sense of unreality in all this babble of League of Nations and Reconstruction and production of Commodities and Industrial arrangements, while Fisher prattles solemnly about education and Conciliation Boards are being set up to bring about a union of hearts while the bare conciliation of interests is obviously impossible.[1] It is like people laying out a tennis court on a ground that is already moving under their feet. I ask myself who on earth is being deceived by all these ceremonies? It is really comic, but you know that in human affairs the comic and the tragic jostle each other at every step.

You must forgive me this typed letter. I can write only with great difficulty. Thanks for your green book,[2] which I have read with the greatest interest. I feel for you in your disappointment in harbour making. I should think that is the most hopeless coast in the world for an undertaking of that kind.

I do hope I shall see you this leave. We are leaving this house in March but we haven't yet found a place to go into.

Pray give my duty to Lady Clifford. My congratulations on the success of the War-Workers. It is a talent full of charm and promise. I haven't seen the recent book yet.[3] I have read nothing of late; neither have I done in the last three years anything I care for.

Jessie begs to be remembered to you both affectionately.

Believe in my gratitude for your indulgent and unfailing friendship.

Yours always

Joseph Conrad.

---

[1] Conrad was usually more sympathetic to H. A. L. Fisher, the historian and innovative President of the Board of Education, but here he is writing to a correspondent whose contempt for the Liberal party and its present coalition with the Labour party was even more intransigent than his own. Intended to mediate between employers and employees, the Conciliation Boards were the successors to the war-time Joint Industrial and Whitley Councils. The end of the war had set off a flood of dammed-up claims for better pay and easier, safer working conditions.

[2] The annual *Gold Coast Blue Book*, the colony's official report to Parliament, and thus the record of Clifford's activities as Governor. Conrad's slip is a rare piece of evidence about his eyesight.

[3] Three members of the family had published a 'recent book'. Clifford's wife, Elizabeth Lydia Rosabelle (née Bonham, 1866–1945), wrote novels as Mrs Henry de la Pasture, her name by her previous marriage. Her latest work, however, was a memoir, *Our Days on the Gold Coast* (Murray, 1919). Lady Clifford's daughter Edmée Elizabeth Monica de la Pasture (1890–1943) was to become popular as the novelist E. M. Delafield. She drew on her war-time experiences as a nurse to write *The War-Workers* (Heinemann, 1918). Clifford's most recent publication was *German Colonies – A Plea for the Native Races* (Murray, 1918).

To André Ruyters

MS Private collection; Unpublished

[letterhead: Capel House]
28 Jan 1919

Dear Mr Ruyters.

It is unfortunate that we should have failed to meet once more before your departure from England. My wife asks me to express to you her profound regret.

I am going to bring her to London next week for a further operation. I am extremely worried as to the ultimate result. I am writing this to you from my bed being laid up with a severe attack of gout. Fortunately my eldest son is home on convalescent leave. It is a great comfort for both of us.

Sans adieu – for surely we shall meet I hope more than once yet. Pray believe in my sincere friendship and great regard.

Yours

Joseph Conrad.

To J. B. Pinker

Text TS Berg; J-A, 2, 218

Capel House,
Orlestone,
Nr. Ashford, Kent.
Jan. 30th. 1919

Dearest Pinker.

I have heard from Robert Jones, I will show you his note when I see you; it is hopeful. The consequence is that I am bringing Jessie to London, on Wednesday next. I will have to get a closed car from London. A remnant of bronchitis still hangs about her and there is no other way. That's expense. And there will be more expense. I will give you a statement of what I foresee when we meet, so that you can finance me through it. I write to you like this because I don't know how I stand with you. Though of course I am not frightened, I am naturally rather anxious. Truly, twelve months ago I hoped for better things.

I just manage to hobble along. My mind has got its grip again and just to test it I finished yesterday a Preface for the Outcast of the Islands; about 16 hundred words. The labour is not thrown away because I have promised prefaces to Doubleday for every volume of the limited edition. I wanted to test myself with something I could finish in one go as it were. I have done it, and it isn't at all bad.

Tomorrow Miss Hallowes proceeds to London to find some place for us to hang out in, and make every arrangement for our stay. We will be three to arrange for, Miss H., B[orys], and J. C. himself. B.'s extension of convalescent leave is the only piece of luck in these not very bright days.

During Miss H's absence in London I shall revise and correct the latest pages of Rescue. I suppose you understand that there is quite a batch of them – a good part of Part v, all done before this beastly gout knocked me over. The production of further copy shall begin on Thursday morning next, I say – and there is no doubt whatever about it. I hope one of those two books will make a hit – I mean a money hit. I fancy it is the Rescue which is picturesque and at the same time more conventional that will prove the best spec[ulation] of the two.

Don't grow impatient with me, my dear fellow. I shouldn't like to think I am nothing but vanity and vexation of the spirit.[1] Perhaps at last we shall win to comparatively placid years, where there will be no other problems but quiet writing for me and leisurely, astute and successful negotiating for you. Shall I ever get into real smooth water and you have no longer to stand by ready with ropes and life-buoys watching my flounderings anxiously? Well, I don't mean to give up that hope as long as life lasts.

Jessie's love

Ever yours

Joseph Conrad.

To Hugh Walpole
Text MS Texas; Unpublished

[Capel House]
Thursday. [30 January 1919?][2]

Dearest Walpole.

I have asked Miss Hallowes to leave with you at the Ministry a small box of cartridges (I've bought for Borys' automatic) for transportation here. So don't be surprised if she turns up on Friday. Many apologies.

Ever yours

J. Conrad

Expecting you at 6. 21 on Sat.

---

[1] 'All is vanity and vexation of spirit': Ecclesiastes 1.14.
[2] This letter must have been written before 25 February 1919, when Walpole left the Ministry of Information for good (Hart-Davis, *Walpole*, p. 181). He visited Capel House in June and August 1918, but the affectionate tone of the greeting suggests a later date. Walpole also went to see Conrad soon after *The Secret City* appeared in January 1919 (Hart-Davis, p. 179). Between the 17th, which was publication day, and the end of the month, Conrad was too ill to welcome a visitor, but Miss Hallowes ran errands in London on Friday the 31st, and Borys, who enjoyed rough shooting, was home on leave.

To J. B. Pinker
Text MS Berg; Unpublished

[Capel House]
1st Febry. 1919.

Dearest Pinker.

I was glad to get your letter of Friday last. My congratulations to Mrs Pinker and yourself and my best wishes to Eric on the resumption of his civil life where we all, your new men and your old men, will be glad to see him take his place by your side.[1]

The nursing Home can not take Jessie in till Thursday. We will arrive about 3 o'clock and I imagine that Sir R Jones will see her at 4. 30 as arranged. So I shall not see you till Friday when I hope I'll be able to tell you something definite.

The house here will be shut up and B[orys] of course is coming with us to town. The extension of his leave terminates on the 22 inst: which supposing Jessie is operated on the 10th will be still a very critical time, when I, with the Rescue to keep going, would need him to attend his Mother while I could devote myself to the work with an easier mind. He has been to the War office the other day. They told him that they can not release him on merely compassionate grounds (his parents needing him) but that if he could also produce an offer of employment of any sort he could be demobilized. (He joined the army in 1915 – so falls into the category)

It struck me that perhaps you could ask your friend (of whom you told me) to give B some temporary employment – if only for 3 months or so – either on the business or the technical side of engineering – of course without salary. I don't mean it to be a fraudulent transaction at all. It would be a trial of a genuine kind, to my and B's mind. He is really anxious to get hold of something to do – apart from his distaste for the idea of being shunted off to some depot or other for months, with the chance, maybe, of being suddenly sent abroad again. That last would be most unfortunate. He will have to begin life afresh when he leaves the army and every day that can be saved is of the greatest importance.

That is why my dear fellow I venture to worry you with this affair. I know you wish well to the boy and that you will understand the real grounds of my anxiety to get him released.

Thanks for the Yale letter. I never saw a copy of that Magazine but I've heard of it. It was pleasant to read the man's appreciation of the *Arrow*.[2] Many thanks for all you *have* done and have tried to do for that book.

---

[1] At Pinker's agency.
[2] The letter to Hodgson of 18 February points to George T. Keating (1892–1976) as the man from Yale, the university to which he left his magnificent collection of books and documents by

Jessie sends her love and her thanks for your sympathy.

Ever Yours

Joseph Conrad

To T. J. Wise
Text MS BL Ashley 2953; Unpublished

[Capel House]
1st Feb 1919

Dear Mr Wise.

Just a line to thank you for the pamphlets which are very nice. It was funny to read this stuff after 15 years.[1]

I am recovering very slowly after my gout. I hope you are well after your visit to Bath.

Believe me allways*

very faithfully yours

Joseph Conrad.

To J. B. Pinker
Text MS Colgate; Unpublished

[Capel House]
Wednesday. [5 February 1919][2]

Dear Pinker.

Snow began to fall at eleven today. I hope it won't block the roads. R. Jones wrote saying he will see Jessie on *Friday* afternoon.

I hope we will get through all right tomorrow with the car. I will bring with me the Polish Article[3] ready for print and 4 chaps of R. ready for clean typing.

---

and about Conrad. Keating must have been following the English serial of *The Arrow*, which had started on 1 December 1918.

[1] Wise had reprinted two essays first published in 1905, 'Autocracy and War' and 'Henry James', as limited-edition pamphlets. In the same manner he brought out 'Tradition', a newspaper article from 1918. All three would reappear in *Notes on Life and Letters*.

[2] If he kept to the plan laid out in his letter to Pinker of 31 December, Conrad drove to London with a typed copy of 'The Crime of Partition' on 2 January. On that and the previous day, however, the weather was benign, and Conrad's letter of New Year's Eve makes no mention of a consultation with Jessie Conrad's surgeon or a long stay in town. Thus the present letter does not easily fit a date of Wednesday, 1 January, but its contents do match the circumstances of Wednesday, 5 February. On that day, heavy snow blocked roads in Kent and the London suburbs. The appointments with Pinker and Sir Robert Jones are therefore minor postponements of those specified in letters of 30 January and 1 February, the four chapters of *The Rescue* are the ones Conrad revised while Miss Hallowes was in London finding accommodation, and the £80 would cover a lengthy visit.

[3] 'The Crime of Partition'. According to a note on the surviving TS (Yale), Conrad wrote it

As you may be prevented from coming to town on Friday I am asking you here to pay into my acct £80 (I reckon the product of the Polish article) – for my London expenses. I'll have to draw some cheques tomorrow.

I'll see you on Friday anyhow if you are in town – but this snowfall looks as if it meant to make trouble for all hands.

Ever yours
J. Conrad

To Edward Garnett
Text TS Yale; G. 285

Durrant's* Hotel
George St.,
Manchester Square.
W. 1.
Feb. 8th. 1919.

My dearest Edward.

We arrived here yesterday ready for a long stay. But the surgeons are sending Jessie home for another two months when they hope the state of the knee will improve sufficiently to render another operation unnecessary. We shall be returning home probably on Thursday.[1] I am still very lame after a very severe gout attack. Will you, my dear Edward, come and dine with me on Monday at the above address? Will you phone a message for me to the hotel; but if you cannot manage Monday then there are still Tuesday and Wednesday for your choice, for I will make no engagement of any sort in the evening. I want very much to see you. I didn't thank you for the book by letter because I knew I was coming to town at once. You know my opinion of all the pieces composing it.[2] I did admire them not only for the depth and feeling of the satire itself; but for the really marvellous visualising of actors

---

between 12 and 27 December. Pinker had had two clean copies made by 8 January, when Miss Hallowes acknowledged their arrival at Capel House (TS Berg). *Harper's* rejected the essay (F. W. Slater to Pinker, 30 January; TS Berg), as did *The Times* (J. Webb to Pinker, 4 February; TS Berg); eventually the *Fortnightly Review* took it for its May number. Whether he knew about the second rejection or not, Conrad was evidently bringing to London a new fair copy, perhaps embodying further corrections or revisions.

[1] The 13th.

[2] See the letter of 16 May 1918 for comments on individual pieces from *Papa's War and Other Satires*. When Garnett sent Conrad the new book on 3 February, he wrote: 'later on you will tell me whether you think they "come together" as a whole. In fact I value your opinion more than anybody's: because you have taken the Satires *artistically*, & not as a party man' (MS Lubbock; *Portrait*, p. 137).

and scenes which really makes me think that you have cheated the world of a great novelist. Our dear love to You.

Ever Yours

J. C.

To R. B. Cunninghame Graham [?][1]
Text MS Texas; Unpublished

[letterhead: Durrants Hotel]

Tuesday [11 February 1919][2]

Très cher ami.

The surgeons have put Jessie off for another 2 months. I will tell you more when we meet.

There's nothing for it but to take her home as fast as possible. We are leaving here on Thursday.

I refrained from getting in touch with you before, reckoning on six weeks in town. I myself am so lame that I cannot get about. Will you dine with me (very badly) here tomorrow (Wed:) at 7 o'clock? – and hear my report and explanations.

Only pray don't cancel any engagement you may have, on my account. I am in a detestable frame of mind; both anxious and discontented; and, after all, we shall see each other before long (I hope) at Capel.

Ever affect[ly] yours

Joseph Conrad.

To J. B. Pinker
Text MS Berg; Unpublished

[letterhead: Durrants Hotel]

12[th.] Febr. Wed[y] 1919.

My dear Pinker.

I am going this morning on B[orys]'s business to a factory in Mortlake[3] where he is offered a berth. In the afternoon I'll see M[urray] Allison and D[udley] Hardy here. So I must write you what I could not say yesterday and I am sending this by Miss H[allowes].

Please send Jessie her week's money here. She has perhaps written to you? I'll send you the Nursing-home acc[t] tonight – for one week. I don't want

---

[1] Although grouped at Texas with the Walpole collection, this letter begins and ends in a way more typical of the Graham correspondence (cf. 3 January 1917).
[2] According to the letter of the 8th, the Conrads planned to go home on Thursday the 13th.
[3] South-west London.

to pay it out of my money. I have been buying various necessary things – such as a couple of trunks as ours have given out. I gave Dr Mac[kintosh] a subscription of £10.10 for his Boys home in Putney. He has been looking after me all last year (when in London) without fee and also attended Jessie. I couldn't do less. Then there is the Hotel bill here for B and me and the car for the journey out and home alone will amount to £14 (7 each way). So there won't be much left anyhow.

B. will remain till Sat to put in his papers through the demobilisation office. It *may* come off. It is an auxiliary aeroplane engines factory and the berth is in the workshop.

Please phone message to hotel that you have received this as I won't see Miss H[allowes] again today.

Ever Yours

J Conrad.

To R. D. Mackintosh
Text MS Alberta; Jellard

[letterhead: Durrants Hotel]
Thursday. [13 February 1919][1]

Dearest Mac.

B[orys] saw John yesterday. The kid coughs and doesn't look well. Jessie is worried but she must go straight home.

You said that you would give the kid a look in if necessary. Do you think you could manage to get a sight of him within the next few days. It would ease the mother's mind.

Our love to you

Yours

J. Conrad.

To J. B. Pinker
Text MS Berg; Unpublished

[letterhead: Durrants Hotel]
Thursday. [13 February 1919][2]

My dear Pinker.

We are leaving in an hour or so. As we will be passing your office about 2. 30 we shan't pull up as you will be out. Jessie regrets not getting a sight of you this time. She has probably written to you to-day.

---

[1] The letterhead, the presence of both sons, and the imminent departure for home suggest February 1919 as the period and the 13th as the date.
[2] Again, the day of leaving Durrants Hotel.

You will get or perhaps you have received already a letter from Reggie.[1] He consulted me. You will see yourself my dear old friend that I could not very well tell him not to do it. Those things are for you to judge of. All I can tell you is that the statements therein are true. I saw a lot of him this time. He has knocked off his liquor to the extent of 90% which is better than altogether. B[orys] who sees him in town has told me that the change is genuine. On Tuesday I sent him off to begin a story and last night he brought me a good 1, 800 words of *The Carpet* (or *The Con[n]oisseur?*).[2] He can work and I believe he means to. The commission you have secured for him will I believe save him from drifting, but this difficulty he puts before you is I think quite real. – I trust you will not think I am meddling. I never suggested anything to Reg. My own affairs give me occupation enough.

Ever Yours
J. Conrad

The other page has Oliver's address
My landlord's address.

> Edmund G. Oliver, Esq*re*
> Messrs: Sutton Ohnuanny & Oliver
> 3 & 4 Great Winchester St.
> E C 2.

Years rent £50.

Next week – with the letter as requested – extension *for 3 months Within* a fortnight I must ask you for a che: for £48. and another for £26. 10.

If you think it needed I may give you an *article* while going on with *Rescue*. A story would be out of the question. But an article on a sugg*d* subject I could manage. I don't mean to say I would like to do it. But I can – and what between Eng and US it would cover the above amount. Anyway we have escaped six weeks of Nursing Home bills for J[essie] and as much of hotels for me.

Marquess of Connynghame* offers me dirt cheap a most charming house, and offers to put electric light in etc etc (near Canterbury).[3] But its too big. A fine farmhouse is vacant near Ashford. Too near but possible. Shall see it.

---

[1] Gibbon.
[2] This story appears as 'The Connoisseur' in Gibbon's collection *Those Who Smiled* (Cassell, 1920), pp. 259–83.
[3] Frederick William Burton (1890–1974), sixth Marquess of Conyngham, was the major landowner in the parishes of Bridge and Bishopsbourne.

To Sir Sidney Colvin

Text MS Lubbock; Unpublished

[Capel House]

Friday. 9.30 am. [14 or 21? February 1919][1]

Dear Colvin.

Excuse this scrap of paper.

Infinite thanks for all your kind deeds and words in the Borys affair.

We have been most concerned at your news. What a horrible visitation! Thank God the worst is over and that you are safely back in your home.

I have had a sight this morning of Lady Colvin's p. c. – reassuring upon the whole. Give her my dear love. I hope to see you both before very long. But *Resc*: keeps me at my desk – composing, correction re-correction. And the end is not yet!

Own up that I *did* ask you to leave the serial form alone. Why didn't you? And now my artist's vanity is very much hurt.

Seriously – some retrospect was inevitable. From now on however the story will proceed straight on to its last romantic scene. —— Whatever it may be.

Hardy is awful! Awful! I believe you've given me the word of the riddle. I couldn't understand. I thought that he was just simply an unspeakable idiot. Well, he certainly does *not* find truth in wine.[2] I am greatly afflicted. We have no house yet. The world is dark.

Ever yours

J. C.

To J. M. Dent

Text TS/MS Berg; Unpublished

[letterhead: Capel House]

Feb. 15th. 1919.

My dear Mr Dent.

Is it possible that, as my wife frightened me with this moment, I have failed to answer your letter on the subject of photographs! If so, pray accept my remorseful apology.

I cannot find the letter. But if you want those photographs for purposes of publication, Mr Will Cadby, of Platt Cottage, Boro' Green, Nr. Wrotham, Kent, has got the copyright of several he took of me not a very long time ago.[3]

---

[1] Soon after the visit from Murray Allison and Dudley Hardy on the 12th. References to house-hunting and work on the serial of *The Rescue* confirm the period.

[2] Insobriety could be added to a charge sheet already well-filled with artistic crimes: for Conrad's opinion of Hardy's illustrations, see the letter to Foster of 12 December 1918.

[3] In February 1915: see *Letters*, 5, p. 444.

I hope you and yours are all well. Pardon this short note. I am in the ultimate throes of Rescue.

Yours

J. Conrad

To Messrs Hodgson & Co

Text TS/MS Bodley Eng. c.4802; Unpublished

[letterhead: Capel House]

Feb. 15th. 1919.

Private

Dear Sirs.[1]

From a letter of yours sent to one of your clients in U. S. I see that some autographed *presentation* copies of my various books are from time to time sold in London. I do not blame the presentees but I do not see why they should be alone in that thing. It is not however of my published books that I am thinking. As you probably are well aware, both Mr Shorter and Mr Wise have printed certain articles of mine for private circulation only. In each case only 25 copies. Of that number I had five copies of each sent to me.

To my great surprise I heard last December from America that one or two copies (of those published by Mr Shorter) are already in the United States, and on the market, and autographed! I daresay you know more about the price which has been asked for them than I do but my information is that £30 was asked for each. Whether it was paid I don't know. But the mere fact of these rarities being offered for sale, removes my last scruples, and as I have five of those booklets which I do not need I want to know whether you would care to buy them from me.

The booklets are:

> One Day More: A Play in One Act (Printed by C. Shorter,
> February 1917). 1 Copy.
> Tradition. (Wise. 1919) Two copies.
> Henry James. (Wise. 1919) Two copies.

Would you kindly tell me whether you would give me £50 for the lot, which if you desire it I will sign; though it does go a little against the grain to sign copies destined for sale.

Yours faithfully

Joseph Conrad.

---

[1] Auctioneers: for the head of the house, see the letter of 18 February.

PS It would be the signature only; but the misprints (those I have spotted) will be corrected by my own hand.

To J. B. Pinker

Text TS/MS Berg; Unpublished

[letterhead: Capel House]

Feb. 15th. 1919

My dear Pinker

I have heard from Jessie through Lady Colvin that there is an agitation (the centre of which is the Ath[enaeum] Club) to put my name forward for O. M.[1] Kipling's is the other name.[2]

Of course I was not approached. It is the sort of thing one could not refuse. But I feel strongly that K. is the right person, and that the O. M. would not perhaps be an appropriate honour for me who, whatever my deepest feelings may be, can't claim English literature as my inheritance. My mouth however is closed. In such a matter not even a confidential hint could be safely given to a friend; because it could be misinterpreted (in more than one way) to my great disadvantage. My scruple I assure you is very real. I don't know what you will think of it.

There is however another distinction which has been mooted (by the R. S. L.[3]) and that is the Nobel Prize. That was in the air last year; and as it is an international thing and less in the nature of an honour than of mere reward, we needn't have any scruples about acceptance, if it ever comes in our way.[4] And as it is not at all an impossible development I must tell you of the thought which had occurred to me as to the policy to follow.

I think sincerely that "Rescue" has a particular quality. Novels of adventure will, I suppose, be always written; but it may well be that "Rescue" in its concentrated colouring and tone will remain the swan song of Romance as a form of literary art. The serial is being extremely well received. I myself have had many pleasant letters and one or two even remarkable. And my suggestion is this:

Would it not be politic (the award of Nobel Prize being made in July, I think) to let Dent publish *R.* here on termination of serial, disregarding

---

[1] The Order of Merit was established in 1902, its membership always restricted to twenty-four eminent men and women. In addition to soldiers, academics, and politicians, its current membership included Thomas Hardy and Sir Edward Elgar.

[2] Kipling was offered the Order of Merit several times but always turned it down (*Dictionary of National Biography, 1931–1940*, p. 514).

[3] The Royal Society of Literature, founded in 1820.　　　[4] It never did.

altogether the order of publication in U. S. and sacrificing whatever small chance there yet may exist of *Rescue* serialising there. Of course we don't want to spoil the market for book-sale in U. S. by anything we do. My idea is simply to let them take their own line. D[oubleday] insisted on having *A. of G.* published at once. We consented. Therefore *R.* must be the spring book of 1920 for *them*. Here, accepting my present suggestion, the order will be exactly reversed. *R.* would be the spring book of this year and the *A. of G.* the book of the early spring next year. For, it seems to me, we are agreed that to have two novels in the same year would be unadvisable, especially in England.

I hate putting in question again what has been settled already, but the considerations expressed above must be my excuse to you on this occasion. The organic condition of the Nobel Prize is that a book must be published in the year of the award. However, I believe that in the case of Kipling it was disregarded.[1] Still if there is any more in that direction it will be helped by the publication of the *Rescue* as early as possible. I am afraid you must be sick of the very names of *Rescue* and *Arrow*; but, my dear fellow, the war was a severe check to your success in working up my career; and now I have a feeling of renewed opportunity of this being the crucial time of both our efforts. I trust you will not think I am worrying you unduly.

Yours ever affect^{ly}

J. Conrad.

PS I am sending you two more pamphlets pub: by Wise privately. I want you to have your Conrad set as complete as possible.

PPS The rent due to Oliver is £45 – not 50 as I wrote you in error.

To Cecil Roberts
Text TS/MS Churchill; Roberts

[letterhead: Capel House]

Feb. 15th. 1919.

My dear Mr Roberts.

Your generously appreciative letter compells me to confess that those pages of which you speak have been written a long time ago. A very long time ago. This book was begun really before I knew my business. But I knew enough to feel this and to lay it aside. It was taken up from time to time till I felt that the time had come to finish it. What had been written has been severely revised and pruned; but I think that the storm-description is still too long;

---

[1] Kipling had won the Nobel in 1907, a year in which he published nothing new.

and it appears unfortunately still longer, because, as it happens, it fills the whole instalment. However, you like it; and it is not for me to argue against an opinion that gives me so much pleasure.

I must confess that I am surprised you should imagine that the "English Channel in peace time" phrase is in any way an allusion to the present war. The English Channel has known war for centuries, and has seen less of this war than of any other in English history. Great fleet actions have been fought in the Channel, off Sluis, off Beachy Head, off La Ho[u]gue in the Soundings.[1] In Napoleonic times the Channel was stuck full of line of battle ships; whereas in this war if there had been three of them seen there altogether that would be about the most. The phrase is natural in the mouth of Shaw, a man whose father was master's mate at the battle of Navarino.[2] The time of "The Rescue" is fixed precisely by Lingard's allusion to the war in China, when the "French helped" 1859–60.[3] Further on you may find passages that I beg you to believe have nothing to do with the present time. My dear Sir, the sentiments, the opinions, the phrases, the emotions, and the very catch-words of our time are as old as the hills. The voices of to-day are but the echoes of dead voices that were moved by the same thoughts, the same doubts, the same anguish and the same passions from which we suffer to-day. You may just as well reproach me for dragging in the Trojan war. It's there, you know. That ass Shaw gives his view of it rather fully.[4]

Yes. I am not myself without some anxiety as to keeping up at the same pitch. I have thrown into that tale, as into a desperate fight, all that I am, all that I have, in the way of romantic vision, expression, and feeling. *That* is the artistic aim of the story. I am telling you this but you need not communicate it to the world at large. Treat it as what it is – a confidence. Years hence when I am no longer amongst you, young men who think of me so kindly, and the subject happens to turn up in a reminiscent conversation

---

[1] Off Sluys, in the Low Countries, the English fleet defeated the French in 1340; off Beachy Head, on the coast of East Sussex, the French defeated the combined Dutch and English fleets in 1690; in 1692, in the linked battles of Barfleur and La Hougue, fought off the Cotentin Peninsula in Normandy, the English defeated the French.

[2] At the Battle of Navarino, 20 October 1827, the turning-point in the War of Greek Independence, the British, French, and Russians defeated the Turks. This was the last naval battle fought entirely with wooden ships.

[3] In 1859, France became involved in the Second Opium War (1856–60); the following year, a Franco-British flotilla travelled up the Pei-ho river and landed troops for the final assault on Beijing.

[4] Shaw's allusions to the war in China, Navarino, and the Trojan War ('this affair about a woman was long before that time') come from *The Rescue*, Part 1, Chapter 2, as does Lingard's comparison between the Borneo coast and 'the English Channel . . . in peace time' which, despite all the period detail, Roberts took for a reference to the present.

(everything is possible) you will be able to speak with authority: "Yes, Conrad wrote to me about it before the story was actually finished." For it is not quite finished yet. And this is also a confidence. Only a few friends know and by this confidence you are enlisted into their ranks.

My wife is still very crippled but things begin to look up, with her. She sends her regards. I give up this written supplement.[1] My wrist aches and aches. I hope we will meet in April when we shall come up to town.

Sincerely Yours

Joseph Conrad.

To T. J. Wise
Text MS BL Ashley 492; Unpublished
[letterhead: Capel House]
16 Feb '19

Dear Mr Wise

Many thanks for the pamphlets which are charming.[2] Very kind of you to remember me so unfailingly.

I am glad your health has been so much improved. I convalesce very slowly after my last attack. Any mental or emotional strain always works against recovery; and I have been very anxious about my wife lately – till about a week ago when Sir R. Jones saw her and declared himself satisfied with her progress. On the mental side the stress of finishing the Rescue will last for another 5–6 weeks yet, I fear. I don't get on very fast with my work while the instalments keep on coming out with dreadful regularity. I am very glad to hear that Part I pleased you in print. The reception was very good; but it's difficult to tell how much of it was genuine and how much mere publisher's fuss. I myself, without being elated, think fairly well of the story. The romantic feeling is certainly there; but whether I can manage to keep the interest of the tale going – that's another question.

Believe me, with kind regards,

very faithfully Yours

Joseph Conrad

---

[1] As was now his custom, Conrad would have dictated the typed portion of this letter to Miss Hallowes, then added more personal references in his own hand.

[2] Conrad acknowledged the reprints of his own work on 1 February, so these must be other pamphlets, perhaps from an earlier year. Wise's output in 1919 included a group of three letters from Robert Browning to his son; among his private publications in 1918 were five Swinburne items: *The Character and Opinions of Dr Johnson*, *Lay of Lilies and Other Poems*, *The Italian Mother and Other Poems*, *The Ride from Milan and Other Poems*, and *A Letter to Ralph Waldo Emerson*: for the last of these, see the letter of 2 January. The standard print-run was thirty copies.

To J. E. Hodgson
Text MS Bodley Eng. c. 4802; Unpublished

[letterhead: Capel House]
18 Febr. '19

Dear Mr Hodgson.[1]

Many thanks for your interesting and friendly letter; but to pit *Lord Jim* against an air-raid was not fair either to your Mother or to me – or, at any rate, to the book.[2] Pray believe that I prize greatly your appreciative attitude to my work. It made its way in the world slowly through the assistance of unknown friends (like yourself); but now a generation has grown up which really seems to know Joseph; for I get many letters from young men nowadays, of the kind that was well worth waiting for. It is a great reward.

Your question as to my correspondent will be answered by your own letter enclosed here. My correspondent was Mr Keating.[3] I can't find his letter. It was rather long but its main object was to ask me to sign a couple of copies (*Jim* & *Nigger*) which he was forwarding to me. The books arrived later and I signed them for him the other day.

The story of the booklets is as follows:-

Some time in 1918 Mr C. Shorter asked me for permission to print for priv: circ: an edition limited to 25 copies of the one-act play *One Day More*. I saw no reason to object. The text used was that in the *English Review*. There is one misprint. Afterwards a paper entitled *First News* pub^d in the first N^o of *Reveille* under the Editorship of John Galsworthy was printed on the same conditions.

Then Mr T. J. Wise took up the fad. He asked for permission to print (on the same conditions) *Autocracy and War* (Fortnightly 1905) *Tradition* (Dly Mail, middle 1918) and *Henry James* (*N. Am^{can} Rev.* years ago and republished in the *N. A. R.* soon after H. James' death[4]).

Of each of the above I had given me five copies.

The first I heard of these booklets being offered in U. S. was by a letter from an indignant collector.[5] He was furious with Shorter and Wise for printing,

---

[1] John Edmund Hodgson (1875–1952), director of the long-established London firm of auctioneers, dealer in fine books and manuscripts, and scholar, was a past president of the Johnsonian Society and would become the historian of British aviation in its pioneering years. Hodgson's widow Norma (née Lewis, later Lady Dalrymple-Champneys), an authority on eighteenth-century English poetry, became Librarian of Somerville College, Oxford.

[2] Hodgson and his mother had been reading *Lord Jim* during an air-raid (information from his widow).

[3] See notes to the letter to Pinker of 1 February.

[4] James died in February 1916.

[5] Graham Tils: see the letter to him of 25 November 1918.

and all but cursed me for giving my assent. His grievance was that his Conrad collection would never now be complete because he could never afford to pay $150 for a booklet (*First News*, I think). I regret now I sent his letter to Mr Wise. It was very funny. No doubt these things will be great rarities.

I am sending you here the five copies I mentioned, not to force your hand but because it's only just that you should see what for the present purpose is merchandise – before you buy. I did not sign them because I don't know where, eventually, you may wish me to sign them:— on cover, fly-leaf, title page or at end of text. I am sending them by messenger. Pray return by regis^{ed} post.

Believe me

very sincerely yours

Joseph Conrad.

To J. B. Pinker
Text MS Berg; Unpublished

[letterhead: Capel House]
Kent.
Wed: 19. Febr. 1919.

My dear Pinker

Your letter is decisive as the word of a pilot should be. You've piloted me up to this point and there is nothing more foolish than arguing with a pilot in whom one believes. And in fact your reply is quite convincing. Taking the average of the three instalments already out I see (by correcting the pages of typed text) that *L & W* has enough Old Copy for some 9 weeks more. The new copy will certainly require another 5 weeks. This will bring the last instalment into the very end of May which *is* too late for book-form. In truth I prefer in my heart that the *Arrow* should come out first and leave a clear road for the *Rescue*, the bigger thing of the two. On Monday I reached p 500 of type completing 102, 000 words. Yesterday I did 1900 words more. A record. But I don't sleep well. I also worry about many things. All this isn't very wise; but I don't think wisdom generally is my strong point. I have somehow outrun the constable in London. I did not quite realise the amount of cheques I left behind me in the country. So I gave some money to my tailor and bought some books and other things, which I need not have done, – tho' most of the books I got are connected with the subject of the Napoleonic novel, which is very much in my mind all the time. The consequence is that the bank tells me I am £23 overdrawn (just about what I've given to the tailor) and that I can't settle the bill for the car which was sent in the other day. Pray do it for me and if you pay 30 to the bank it will just give me a credit of £7 which will keep the account going. I am trying to sell 5 booklets of the Shorter & Wise's printing and I wouldn't have bothered you if I could have managed it by this. But these transactions take time and moreover I won't let them go for nothing. A copy of *First News* (Shorter booklet) was sold in Dcc^er last in Am: for £30, unsigned, and presentation copies of Victory and Chance for about 60$ each. There seems to be a Conrad boom amongst collectors. I had all this in a letter from Janvier the fine-book dealer in N. Y.[1] and also from a collector (of small means) who is indignant at the prices (as if it were my fault) and curses me for letting Shorter and Wise print these booklets. "Now" he says, "my collection of you can't be complete. I'll never be able to pay 150$ for a booklet." I sent the letter on to Wise to let him see what I have to suffer for my good nature.

Garnett has been sorting my letters to him (1895–1904)[2] and has asked me to look them over. It's very fair of him. I think that in my letters to you there may be 3 or 4 that had better be destroyed. Not that I could doubt for a moment your's* or Eric's tact and care in that matter – but letters do get into strange hands. What I have in mind are letters about other people. As between you and me I want all the world to know what you have done for me. But there is one period that might be pruned.[3] I do not suggest destruction but a separate packet. If the world were honest and fair-minded, it could be trusted with the whole truth. But it isn't. It will put the worst construction on any given episode and besmirch the real truth established by so many years of your determined belief in me and of my gratitude to you which, believe me my dear friend, has never been obscured for a moment in my heart, no matter what words might have been written on the spur of the moment.

Ever Yours

J. Conrad.

PS The Ev. News is ready to take an article from me when I am "well enough" to write one.[4]

---

[1] Meredith Janvier was a Baltimore dealer; see the letter to him of 6 November 1918.
[2] The first stage of the collection published in 1928.
[3] The period of his collapse in 1910, initiated by a tense meeting with Pinker and followed by a period of estrangement. Despite having to work through intermediaries such as Galsworthy and Robert Garnett, and despite the large amount of money owed him, Pinker continued to show faith in Conrad and represent his literary interests.
[4] Conrad wrote nothing for the *Evening News* until 1923.

To B. Macdonald Hastings

Text MS Colgate; Unpublished

[letterhead: Capel House]
20 Feb '19

My dear Hastings

I am heartily glad that Your perseverance and work are not to be lost.[1] I send you the agreement as requested by Pinker.

Our kind regards

Yours

J. Conrad

To F. N. Doubleday

Text TS Princeton; Unpublished

[letterhead: Capel House]
Feb. 24th. 1919.

Dear Mr Doubleday.

I was glad to hear from you. As it happens I shall have to be in town to-morrow (Tuesday) in connection with house-hunting. My health is not precisely brilliant and I am rather over-strained with my work on "The Rescue". The whole thing has got to be kept up on the top note to the very end; and after each morning's work I feel completely limp. There are about fifty pages (of print) still to do; the most difficult perhaps of the four hundred of which the book will consist. There will be an enormous sigh of relief when it's over. I mean to make the critics sit up with it – whether to bark or to bless I don't know – but sit up, anyway.

I am so possessed, penetrated and enwrapped by the spirit of Romance that I don't think I will be able to talk to you any sense at all. But all the same I should like to see you before you leave Europe. I wonder whether you will be at home at three o'clock? Would you telephone to Pinker in the course of the morning if that hour suits you. I shall be free then and my train does not leave till 4. 30.[2]

There will be a mighty hunt in this house for the old Preface to "Almayer's Folly" written at the time but never printed anywhere and, indeed, seen by very few eyes.[3] Should we not be able to find a typed copy here we would have to have recourse to Mr Quin[n], who has the actual MS in his collection.

---

[1] Now that a London production of *Victory* was a certainty.

[2] In the left-hand margin, Doubleday noted in pencil: 'Had a nice talk with him. He is very pleased with us.'

[3] Written in 1894–5, it remained unpublished until the 'Sun-Dial' edition of 1921. The MS of this preface had been sold to Quinn.

The "Nigger" of course has got its Preface and also the Author's Note for American readers, which I suppose you will want to reproduce. About a month ago I had the lucky inspiration to write an extended Author's Note for "The Outcast of the Islands"[1] – and those will be the first three books in the order of their original publication. I shall look at it again and leave it with Pinker for typing.

I can't tell you what a pleasure it is to me to hear that the final arrangements are made for the limited Edition.

Perhaps when my Napoleonic novel is finished – say towards the end of the year '20 – I may be well enough in mind and body to come over and see you in your kingdom of the Garden City.[2] More unexpected things have happened in this world which is so full of surprises of all kinds. I assume of course that my visit would be only a moderately disagreeable surprise to you.

With most friendly regards

Yours

Joseph Conrad.

To J. B. Pinker
Text TS Berg; Unpublished

[letterhead: Capel House]
Feb. 24th. 1919.

My dear Pinker

I am coming to see you about one o'clock (Tuesday)[3] and poison your lunch for you with a distressing tale. O Friend of my (literary) Youth! the position has grown desperate and you had better get ready your diving apparatus to fish me out from the depths of despondency. I don't think you will find it a heavy job (moreover you are used to it) but it will have to be done, or else I fear the bottom will come out of everything under heaven and the sixth and last part of "Rescue" will consist of the words "I can't go on with this nonsense any longer", which will be rather too short for the balance of the book and may impress unfavourably the readers of Land & Water.

However I hope to get through with my tale by the time we have finished the cheese. I shall also bring with me Part Five of "The Rescue" which is a little longer.

---

[1] Doubleday notes: 'Expect to bring this all home with me'. Conrad finished the Author's Note on 29 January.
[2] The Long Island home of the Country Life Press, built to resemble a college or palace of the late Middle Ages.
[3] Conrad is following up on a telegram sent at 2:04 p.m. on the 24th, a Monday: 'Can you see me tomorrow about one Conrad' (Berg).

I had a letter from F. N. D[oubleday]. My congratulation to you on fixing up at last that wobbly piece of business. If I have time I intend to see F. N. D. before catching the train home. I like to see him deeply moved. Hastings must have sent you the agreement for "Victory". I am very pleased and excited about it and intend, directly "Rescue" is finished, to gain an entry into the theatrical world and become the slave of Marie Lohr.[1]

Ever Yours

J. Conrad

To Henry Dana
Text TS copy Berg; Unpublished

[Capel House]
Feb. 26th. 1919.

Henry Dana. Esqre

Globe Theatre.

Dear Sir.[2]

My first impulse was to put myself unreservedly at the disposal of Miss Marie Lohr, but I think that before doing so I ought to explain that the adaptation of "Victory" is entirely the work of Mr. M. Hastings in conception, structure and every detail of stage-craft. While he was busy with it I was engaged on my proper work, which is novel writing, and though of course I read the adaptation and am taking the greatest interest in its presentation, the actual details of scenic effect are not now present to my memory with sufficient vividness. I have no copy by me at the moment. If under those circumstances Miss Marie Lohr still thinks it worth while to hear my view of "Victory" as the subject of a play (which can be merely the expression of my feeling) or bear any suggestions that may occur to me, I do put myself at her disposal with the greatest pleasure and appreciation of the implied compliment. For indeed I ask myself what suggestions of value could I offer to that accomplished artist? I may have my ideas on drama but I really know nothing of the stage.

---

[1] Born in New South Wales to a theatrical family, Marie Löhr (1890–1975) made her London début aged eleven. After many years as a West End actress, she acquired the licence of the Globe Theatre in 1918. In the actor-manager tradition, she did not give up performing; her most recent roles had been in *L'Aiglon* and *Love in a Cottage*; in *Victory*, she would both direct and play Lena.

[2] After a career as an actor, Henry Dana (1855–1921) became business manager of His Majesty's Theatre, then general manager of the Globe Theatre, St Martin's Lane; as such, he worked with the producer Marie Löhr on the staging of *Victory*.

Nevertheless, I am perfectly ready to carry out any arrangement you may make with Mr Pinker as to my coming up to town, say next week, on any day Miss Marie Lohr may name as convenient to herself.

Yours truly,

J. C.

To J. B. Pinker
Text MS Berg; Unpublished

[Capel House]
Wed: 26. Febr. '19

Dearest P.

Enclosed here also particulars of the house from which you'll see what we are to get for our money.[1] Strange to say the statements are perfectly true which in a document of the sort is not always the case.

As you once said to me that you would like to know our real feeling when opening negociations* I'll tell you that Jessie is very pleased indeed and I am really anxious to get that house in which she could recover her power of walking and I my composure (after Rescue); and concentrate my thoughts on the *Nap[oleonic]* novel in really beautiful surroundings.

As, for a permanency, we have our view fixed on another house, it would be better perhaps to fix this up till Michaelmas – say full 7 months. As to the difference of rent for shorter or longer period I reckon it will come to the same thing as in the first case Mrs: Ke[a]ys-Young[2] will pay the gardeners, and we really prefer they should be responsible to her. The cottage is an absolute condition. Whether its rent is to be included or not is not so very material as it will be part of the wages we pay to those people – in any case.

Faculty to extend tenancy (on say, three months notice) might be mentionned* as "Oswald's"* Bishopsbourne negociation* may fail and nothing else so suitable present itself for some considerable time.

I think this is all.

I've had a letter from Dana to which I shall reply and send you copy by to-night's post. Jessie's love.

Yours ever

J. C.

---

[1] Conrad wrote on the verso of a letter from Messrs Curtis & Henson, 17 February, giving particulars of a house situated between Staplehurst and Headcorn, Kent.
[2] Of Eylesden, Chart Sutton, Sutton Valence, Kent.

The main *fact* is:- that there is no other house at all possible for us to take refuge in, in view. Not the shadow of one —— The date of entry must not be later than 10th of April.

To J. B. Pinker
Text TS/MS Berg; Unpublished

[letterhead: Capel House]
Feb. 26th. 1919

Dearest Pinker

Herewith Dana's letter with copy of my reply.[1] As you see he says nothing as to the interview taking place in the company of Hastings. I myself don't care very much for having Hastings there, for we would be either cutting across each other, or I would have to back him up, or it may end in me holding my tongue and playing the part of a dummy. On the other hand I wouldn't upset Hastings for anything. You will observe that with my usual prudence I leave all this to your diplomacy which has never failed in my experience, yet.

I forgot to explain in delivering the whole Part Five to you that in the envelope marked for "Land and Water" there is a double set of Chapters I, II, and III (clean copy). One of them of course is for the U. S., but probably you have discovered all this for yourself.

I was with Doubleday for about an hour. From what I can see that man has electrotype plates of all my works on the brain and is possessed of a frantic desire to ram them down English publishers' throats. He apparently doesn't care a damn what I have written or what I am going to write or whether I ever write a line again in my life. He gave me the impression of a man who is the victim of a particular mania. It was dreadful. But by the very absurdity of it it was at times amusing in a ghastly sort of way.

Incidentally I learned that F[isher] U[nwin] told him that he had signed contract with me for a novel, which was a very horrible thing to hear. And also that he would never consider any proposal of parting with my copyrights for a mere sum of money. Doubleday seemed to say that he had made an actual offer of hard cash and was peremptorily choked off. But devil only knows! This whole business of listening to D. has left the impression of a dreary and unintelligible nightmare.

Of course we missed Reggie[2] after hanging about for him like two outcasts in the hall of an hotel and at the door of a house which might have been some Ministry or other. I was too weary to take any particular notice. Whether

---

[1] Dana's TS letter of the 24th is in the Berg Collection.   [2] Gibbon.

he has pushed through the offer of employment for Borys to a satisfactory conclusion I don't know. He seemed to say so on the telephone – but devil only knows! My whole time after I left you seems but a dismal dream.

Ever affect^{ly} yours

J. Conrad.

PS Found at home letter from Shorter asking permission to print for priv^{te} circ^{on} the 2 Titanic papers and my story *The Tale* (25 copies of each with 5 or even 10 for me). Do you see any objection as to the last which has not yet come out in book form.[1] If you haven't would you mind phoning him to go ahead and that I shall write to him in a day or two?

To B. Macdonald Hastings
Text TS/MS Colgate; Unpublished

[letterhead: Capel House]
Feb. 27th. 1919.

My dear Hastings.

I had the same sort of communication from that quarter. I answered saying that this was no collaboration and making it clear that the whole thing from general Conception to the smallest detail was wholly and completely your own work with which I had nothing to do; but that of course I took the greatest possible interest in your adaptation and its artistic fortune. I also added that I had not seen the text for some time now and that in consequence all the detail of scenic effects was not so vividly present to my mind as I would have liked it to be if I were to talk about the play with its chief interpreter. I finally asked myself (I mean in the letter) what in my ignorance of the stage were the suggestions I could offer to such an accomplished artist.

But, my dear Hastings, as the last thing I should want to be suspected of is indifference to your work and its adequate rendering I ended by putting myself at the disposal of Miss Marie Lohr any day her agent should arrange with Pinker next week. I think I could not have said less without giving a false impression of my attitudes. You may rest assured however that I will do no harm, as I intend to say very little and confine myself to generalities, making it also clear that in that matter your views, your wishes and your ideas are the only ones that count.

I hope that you will find her intelligent and amenable to advice. I know nothing about the psychology of actresses and I don't think I have ever met

---

[1] The 'Titanic papers' appeared under Wise's imprint, *The Tale* under Shorter's, all three in 1919.

three of them in my life, though I have a vague recollection of having been fed with chocolates by Mme. Modjeska somewhere back in the Middle Ages.[1] I trust you have an adequate Heyst in your eye and also a couple of men that won't play the clown with the parts of Jones and Ricardo.[2] For the rest I wish you all good luck in the strenuous time you will have for the next month or two. If you have no objection I should like to see one of the later rehearsals — not to pass remarks but from simple curiosity.

Sorry to hear of your cold. Don't play about with it even if Marie has got to wait. My wife wishes to be kindly remembered to you.

Yours very sincerely

Joseph Conrad

To J. E. Hodgson
Text MS Bodley Eng. c. 4802; Unpublished

[letterhead: Capel House]
28 Febr 1919

Dear M[r] Hodgson.

I didn't want to trouble you with a letter sooner, but I trust you did not doubt my sympathy with you in your loss.[3]

It had been a long life of endeavour, of merit, of success; but I am sure that the larger part of its happiness was in your long companionship and in your filial devotion. This thought will comfort you under that sense of emptiness and unavailing regret those whom we love leave behind them. You who have shared his hours of trial and difficulty may be able now he is no more to pronounce him a "happy man". Your letter gives me that impression. It will be for you an abiding consolation.

Believe me

Yours faithfully

J. Conrad

---

[1] In Warsaw or Lwów? Helena Modjeska was the American stage name of Helena Modrzejewska (née Opid; Chłapowska in her second marriage, 1840–1909). Born in Cracow, she became much loved for her performances of Polish drama. In 1868 she joined the company of the Imperial Theatre, Warsaw. A nationalist outspoken in her opinion of the Russian occupation, she left Warsaw in 1876 to try life in the United States. There she learned English and decided to settle, returning to Europe only for occasional tours of her homeland and one season in London. Her most admired roles in English were in Schiller, Dumas, Ibsen, and above all Shakespeare.

[2] The eventual cast included Murray Carrington as Heyst, W. Gayer MacKay as Jones, and Sam Livesey as Ricardo.

[3] Of his father, Henry H. Hodgson, formerly Master of the Stationers' Company, the City of London livery company (guild) of booksellers and stationers.

To J. B. Pinker
Text TS Berg; Unpublished

[letterhead: Capel House]
March 1st. 1919.

My dear Pinker.

I have accepted M[arie] L[öhr]'s invitation for Monday. I should like to see you for a few minutes before I go and if you are free in the afternoon I will drop in to tell you what was said. I hope Hastings won't be there, and from a note he sent me the other day I don't think he cares very much for a joint call.

I have begun Part Six, of *R.* It would be very kind of you to push the clean typing of Part Five (IV, V, VI) and send me my rough copy back, as at any moment I may want to refer to something in those three chapters.

There is a par. in the Daily News on Doubleday's authority that the publication of *A. of G.* is put off till "some time in the spring". Did you know anything about this?

I am sending you the two Shorter booklets which will make up your set. I have put your initials and mine on the fly-leaf. Did you communicate with Shorter? I had a communication from him whence it appears Wise has put him off from doing the three booklets he wanted to do. I should rather like to have the two "Titanic" articles done in that way, either W. or S.

I hope something definite will be known about the house by Monday. As you wished me to do I refrained from asking Mrs. Keays-Young by wire either yesterday or to-day. One is rather anxious, as there is nothing else whatever to take refuge in.

B[orys] has been ordered to Denmark Hill Hospital to be treated for neurasthenia.[1] He is awaiting now his order to report there. He is really much better; has recovered his confidence in his mentality, and is seriously thinking of the Faculty of Applied Science at the Lond. Univ. His old Headmaster (of the *Worcester*) and the Captain too,[2] have been preaching to him about that three weeks ago, but the only effect they produced was a sort of distress. I kept quiet, except for any remarks I could throw in, in general conversation, and the other day he opened the subject himself, and grew

---

[1] The Maudsley Hospital on Denmark Hill, South London, specialised in psychiatric disorders: from 1916 (when it first opened) to 1920, it was a military hospital where a great many victims of shell-shock came for treatment.

[2] T. R. Beatty, Headmaster of the Nautical Training College HMS *Worcester*, and David Wilson Barker (1858–1941), Captain-Superintendent.

more and more hopeful as he talked. Of course that would be the best thing that could happen. I didn't say much beyond assuring him that he might be sure of all the assistance it was in my power to give him in any reasonable wish for his future. I thought it better not to press him. Though he looked well and even fat on coming from France he has not been at all himself.

Jessie seems really to be getting on. She sends her love.

Ever Yours

J. Conrad.

To C. K. Shorter

Text TS Berg; Unpublished

[letterhead: Capel House]

March 1st. 1919.

My dear Mr Shorter.

Pardon this dictated letter. In the matter of "The Tale" I admit I was reluctant when Mr Wise asked me, but as to you my feelings are different and I only wanted to ascertain from Pinker whether from a publishing point of view it was a proper thing to do, as that story has not yet appeared in book form. I thought you might have heard already from Pinker on the 'phone. However it seems to be settled now through your interview with Mr Wise. I admit that I should like the two "Titanic" articles printed privately as a booklet. Those articles won't appear again but in a volume of Miscellanea when the tale of my work is ended.[1] The booklets you published are perfectly delightful in every detail of their get-up, but if you leave the "Titanic" things to Mr Wise I will be content with your decision.

I shall be delighted to dine with you and indeed I propose calling on you the first time I am in town. I haven't been very well lately but I am rather better now, but the end of "The Rescue" on which I am engaged at present keeps me tied up to my desk. I think it will be a matter of three weeks more and then there will be an end to that old song. How old, you know well![2]

Believe me my dear Mr Shorter

Yours with great regard

Joseph Conrad.

---

[1] They became two of the *Notes on Life and Letters* (1921).
[2] When Conrad abandoned *The Rescue* in early 1899, Shorter had been the disappointed editor.

To J. E. Hodgson
Text MS Bodley Eng. c. 4802; Unpublished

[letterhead: Capel House]
[4 or 5 March 1919][1]

Dear Sir.

I have your letter of yesterday and am sending you the booklets now by rail (which I trust more than the post-office).

Your discreet groan over the price has touched me deeply. In order to alleviate the pain somewhat I am sending you in the batch 2 extra booklets ("Titanic" papers ex Eng. Review 1914[2]) which reached me this morning "fresh from the oven" sent by M[r] Wise. It will make the whole lot a little less costly – to you.

With regards

Yours

J. C.

To J. B. Pinker
Text MS Berg; Unpublished

[letterhead: Capel House]
Tuesday. [4 March 1919][3]

Dearest Pinker

I didn't get away from the theatre till 5. 15 last night and just caught my train. I saw all the actors, I talked of scenery, dresses, psychology, and the art of acting, till my head buzzed. MH[astings] read the first act. It was very interesting and I learned more about actors in these 4 hours than my philosophy ever dreamed of. It's a long story which I will tell you when we meet. I have carried away an intense impression of general hopefulness and belief in the play, very pleasant indeed – but it may have been "put on" – who knows! Still I am glad I went. Everybody was there – scene painter, costume designer – and even the, I presume, senior carpenter of the stage.

No word having come this morning from You as to the "Valence" house I shall get in touch with Geering[4] about the 5gns a week place (for 6 months

---

[1] Conrad was in London on the 3rd; Hodgson's reply to this note arrived on the 6th. On the 7th, Conrad thanked Wise for the pamphlets.

[2] May and July 1912.

[3] The day after the visit to the Globe. Mention of the house offered by Mrs Keays-Young of Sutton Valence reinforces the dating.

[4] An estate agent with offices in Rye and Tenterden.

or £150 p. y.). If a cottage can be got near it the business will be done; but for that one will have to go and find out on the spot. If anything definite can be found out about that matter I'll try to phone you before 4 o'c today.

Meantime hold off (without breaking off) the other people till tomorrow. It goes awfully against the grain to pay £250 for a year's rent.

Ever Yours

J Conrad

To J. E. Hodgson

Text TS Bodley Eng c. 4802; Unpublished

[letterhead: Capel House]

March 7th. 1919.

Dear Mr Hodgson.

Thanks very much for the cheque received yesterday and your nice comment upon the two additional booklets. I think that of the whole of Wise's productions these have the best appearance. I promise myself some day to look you up in your Temple of Books.

Yours faithfully

Joseph Conrad.

To T. J. Wise

Text TS/MS BL Ashley 2953; Unpublished

[letterhead: Capel House]

March 7th. 1919.

Dear Mr Wise.

Many thanks for your kind gift of the deep-blue booklets. The get up is perfectly charming; and the text, in book form, won't be procurable till after I have left the scene, in the last volume of any collected edition of my works.

I trust you are keeping our common enemy[1] at arm's length. I never can really. He's like the wolf – always at the door.

Yours sincerely

Joseph Conrad.

---

[1] A variation on the line from Thomas Hood (1799–1845), ' that old enemy the gout' ('Lieutenant Luff').

To J. B. Pinker
Text MS Berg; Unpublished

[letterhead: Capel House]
Sunday. [9 March 1919][1]
My dear Pinker.

Herewith sec[ti]^{ons} IV. V. VI of Part Five Rescue with final corr^{ons} the copy marked U. S. being for the States.

I am quite willing to let Shorter print the F. O. paper[2] since you seem to think that it may be done. He sent me proof of *The Tale* booklet yesterday.

I enclose here 2 booklets (Titanic) just printed by Wise, for your collection.

I am negociating* for Capt Halsey's R. N. house near Wye[3] – fur[ni]sh^d – 6 months. It's a devil of a fight. Expect decision on Tuesday. If that fails there is nothing else whatever. But I will go all possible lengths rather than have to shift into a hotel – anywhere. In any case it will never be equal to what we were disposed to sacrifice for the wretched Keay[s]-Young woman's house.

The Hon: Mary (Mrs Bell) of the other (permanent) house[4] would want us to get in at Mich^{mas} no later. I'll have to go to see her next week and squabble over terms.

Had a nice letter from Marie Löhr. Sam Livesey for Ricardo *is* impossible, really.[5] M. H[astings] is quite right to have a great din about that. We all want the play to have every chance.

I'll write you on Tuesday either to report progress or to say that "All is lost!"

Meantime Rescue creeps on; but I hope to mend the pace directly the other worries are off my poor brain.

Ever Yours
J. Conrad.

---

[1] Captain Halsey's answer came on Monday the 10th.
[2] Conrad's memorandum to the Foreign Office, 'A Note on the Polish Problem': Shorter published it as *The Polish Question. A Note on the Joint Protectorate of the Western Powers and Russia*, and it was collected in *Notes on Life and Letters*.
[3] Spring Grove, Wye, between Ashford and Canterbury: for Captain Halsey, see the letter of 5 May.
[4] Oswalds, which would be Conrad's last home: the Bells lived at Bourne Park, Canterbury; the Hon. Mary Bell (née Dyke) had been a maid of honour to Queen Alexandra, and her husband was a retired army officer.
[5] Sam Livesey (1873–1936), a Scot, had recently acted in *Cheating Cheaters* at the Strand, *The Knife* at the Comedy, and *The Female Hun* at the Lyceum. Despite Conrad's misgivings, perhaps prompted by Livesey's lengthy history of starring in melodramas, he did play Ricardo.

PS Please phone C[lement] S[horter] to hold the booklet till he gets back the proof. (The Tale).[1]

To C. K. Shorter
Text MS Rosenbach; Unpublished

[Capel House]
[early March 1919][2]

My dear Mr Shorter
Could you spare me six copies. I've a friend a simple fellow who would like to have the story by itself for the sake of the subject. The other five all have their destination.

Yours sincerely

J. C.

To J. B. Pinker
Text MS Berg; Unpublished

[letterhead: Capel House]
Monday. 8 am. 11 [10]^th Mch. 19.[3]

Dear Pinker
I send you this word to say that against all probability I have had a letter from Capt Halsey's agents accepting my last offer for his house, Spring Grove, just outside Wye and under 4 miles from Ashford Station. I have been negociating* for the last fortnight. That house used to let at £10. 10 p. w. with June, July, Aug at 12. 12. I have got it for £7. 7 per week Halsey paying the two gardeners (of whom one runs the electric light), from Mch 25th to Michaelmas.

Those men's wages cannot be less than £3 per week (more likely 3. 10) therefore I get the house, very charming (a little too big) and in pretty surroundings, (stream, lawns and so on) for 4. 4 actual rent. When you see it, as we hope you will on the first day convenient to you, you will admit that it is good value. As to the rest all I can say to you is that directly I've finished

---

[1] Miss Hallowes wrote a second PS: 'Mr Conrad asks me to add that he has heard a rumour that Brady is after the Cinema rights of the novels and he would be glad to hear if there is any truth in this rumour!' Will (William A.) Brady began as a fight promoter, moved on to theatrical management, and then film production. In 1918 he left his $100,000 a year job as director-general of World Film to set up as an independent; little more than a year later, he was bought out and became an actor.

[2] The proofs of *The Tale* were almost ready to go back to Shorter on [9 March]; Conrad wrote this note on the title-page.

[3] Monday was the 10th.

Resc: (I am in ch: II of last Part [VI]) I will write a short (really short) story for the Met[ropolit]^{an} contract,[1] which (at £300) will pay for it amply, the other expences* being no bigger than here. When I say I'll write a story it means not merely the intention but that I have a definite subject and see the way of treating it. The change will do us both good and the extra cost must be treated as holiday expences*.

I have instructed Burrows & C^{o2} to prepare the usual agreement and also act for me in taking the inventory. All incidental disboursements* the story will cover easily. It will probably take me 3 weeks to write, the actual date depending on the termination of *R*. I'll say no more at present. If you have any preference as to the modest payment (say monthly in adv^{ce} – or in 3 pay^{ts} during the period) please send me word by *early* afternoon post today.

Ever Yours

J. Conrad

PS What induced Hals. to close must be the magic of my name. He's a peculiar individual and looked upon it as a favour on his part at 10 gns. Only yesterday the agent was telling me that the thing was more than doubtful. —— When you come to see us we will go over Ralph's future school – if he persists in the agricultural idea.[3]

To Edward Garnett

Text MS Dartmouth; G. 286

[letterhead: Capel House]
12 Mch '19

Dearest Edward.

I ought to have written you days ago to thank you for your letters about the Resc:.[4] I am deeply touched, my dear old friend, by the fidelity of your memory recalling not only the year but the very episode on which the story was interrupted. It has given me a strange impression of having lived always under your eye; of your thought never having abandonned* me during all these years of Your lonely wanderings in the jungle of "literary matter" where

---

[1] Conrad wrote nothing more for the *Metropolitan Magazine*.

[2] Alfred John Burrows & Co., land agents, had an office in Ashford.

[3] Ralph Pinker was considering the South-Eastern Agricultural College (now Wye College), a constituent of London University.

[4] One of these letters, dated 5 March (MS Texas), can be found in *Portrait*, p. 137. While praising the work 'up to "no one knows" – the Fourth instalment', Garnett suggests that the 'conversations are a bit *too verbatim*, not quite in harmony. They want working over, filing down a bit – sharpening perhaps.' For later Garnett letters on *The Rescue* (4 June, 8 July, 25 [?] September, 13 October 1919), see *Portrait*, pp. 138–42.

you alone pursued the spirit with a magnificent disregard of the parasites that fed on your substance.

Pray *do* by all means jot your remarks and criticism on the margin of the L & W text. It will make these numbers precious to me. You know dear Edward that my first impulse (and also the last) was always to agree with your pronouncements. In this instance you give a voice to the vague uneasiness I always felt from the first while writing the Rescue. And what You say is "la sainte vérité".[1] But I could offer thereon some explanations, which may be worthless but are at least sincere. Only not on paper! Not just yet!

We are going for six months into a furnished house (end Mch). You must come and be friendly, good and wise to me for several days. It's a bigger place. You could get your moments of solitude. It would change you a little from your type of country. Jessie's looking forward immensely to your coming for to her you are my Good Genius and she will show you her affection in her artless manner by concocting various dishes and in everything else showing great discretion. She is beginning to walk. She sends her love.

Ever yours

J. Conrad

To J. B. Pinker
Text MS Berg; Unpublished

[letterhead: Capel House]
[c. 12 March 1919][2]

Dear Pinker.

I have your note and copy of a letter addressed by F[isher] U[nwin] to you. You might point out to the Gentleman that no power on earth can make me sign an agreement with him – not even you. You could only refuse to have anything more to do with me and vindicate your position in that way. But nobody knows better than I that you are a man of your word and my regard for you and identity of feeling with you on these personal matters is such that I feel myself morally bound to execute what you have promised. I proved that in a small way in the Tauchnitz affair when only a month after telling T. in contemptuous terms that I would have nothing to do with him I signed without cavil the agreement you had entered into with T – in ignorance of my action of course.[3] Your word is my bond.

---

[1] 'The holy truth'.
[2] Close to the 15th, when Conrad had received two answers from Pinker and a letter from T. Fisher Unwin concerning Conrad's desire to escape any more obligations to Unwin.
[3] Usually paying very little, the Leipzig publisher Baron von Tauchnitz bought the continental European rights to English-language fiction which he marketed in paperback editions for travellers. The relevant letter to Tauchnitz has not survived, but in October 1907, Conrad

I have a superstitious feeling that any connection with F. U. will be unlucky. On the other hand our luck (apart from merit) has turned with Dent. But you *do* know me well and it is a fact that the idea of the Napoleonic novel going to F. U. *was* a sort of shock. I think that if I had known at the time of F. U. attitude with the 3 books I would have asked you to give up the idea of the English de Luxe edition (the Amer: one he could not have stopped) and wait for better times and some other opportunity to deal with F. U. I was somehow under the impression that the transaction was releasing the 3 copyrights entirely; and that was worth almost any sacrifice.

The transfer of the Arrow is a matter for you to decide upon. I have only to thank you for having thought of my personal feelings. On the whole I would be glad to be done with F. U. I will sign whatever you put before me, but in view of the F. U. letter (which I enclose) pray my dear fellow give me the assurance that this will be the last of F. U. and that there is no promise direct or indirect even by a most distant implication of another book for him. We must not upset Dent either. I owe a letter to H[ugh] Dent and I may if you like back up your negociation* by a personal request on the ground for instance of clearing our future relation of all complications. I need not tell you that I will write or do nothing till I hear from you – I mean in this matter.

Ever affcat^{ly} Yours

J Conrad.

To J. M. Dent
Text TS Berg; Unpublished

[letterhead: Capel House]
March 14th. 1919.

Dear Mr Dent.

I have been so beastly seedy all this time that I have not been able to attend to anything except my work on "The Rescue" – and even that was interrupted several times. Pray give my thanks to Mr Hugh for his last letter. I feel very compunctious at not having answered it at once, for indeed the news about "Nostromo" was very welcome. Thus is his wisdom vindicated as against my doubts; and I assure you I have never been so pleased as at finding myself wrong in this case.

Directly "The Rescue" is finished I will be ready to discuss with you any project you may have in regard to my occasional writings.[1] But I am not

---

wrote to Pinker denouncing Tauchnitz and refusing to do business with him again; nevertheless, Tauchnitz continued to publish Conrad titles, a fact that suggests the scenario described here: *Letters*, 3, pp. 497–8. For other dealings, see *Letters*, 1, p. 298, and 5, pp. 127, 428–9.

[1] Dent had returned to his proposal of 5 December for a shilling pamphlet about sailors at war; he now wanted it to consist of a new essay and two existing ones – presumably 'Well Done!'

really fit now to discuss anything, for all things seem to me very difficult, horribly fatiguing to look at, and infinitely remote.

Pinker has already or will immediately approach you with a certain proposal. Pray give it your best and most friendly consideration. My great object is, on the practical side, to get rid of that entanglement which complicates the even course of my relations with the House of Dent.[1] The engagement had to be entered upon to make a collected edition possible, and the other party would hear of nothing less than this. My greatest desire is to be done with that thing for ever. It rankles.

On the sentimental side there is the desire, very genuine on my part, that you should look after the fortunes of my Napoleonic novel which would be next in succession to the "Rescue". Yet if you cannot see your way to accept Pinker's suggestion it will have to go to that quarter, for a promise is a promise, and we had the consideration.[2]

The effect from the publishing point of view will be that the fulfilment of my present agreement with you will be put off for another twelve months after the publication of "The Rescue", which last of course will remain in your hands in any case.

Pray don't imagine that I want to press you unduly. You must consider your own interests; but in this connection I may remark that from the very nature of the subject the Napoleonic novel is bound to be a bigger thing and also have a wider popular appeal.

With friendly regards

Yours

Joseph Conrad

To J. B. Pinker
Text MS Berg; Unpublished

[letterhead: Capel House]
15 Mch '19. Saturday

My dear Pinker.

Thanks for your two letters the written and the dictated which I received this morning. Indeed I did not want to take up your time to that extent; but I am very glad to be informed of the whole situation. You know very well

---

and 'Tradition' (17 February; TS carbon Berg). Thus the scope of the pamphlet would now cover the Merchant as well as the Royal Navy.
[1] Presumably, Unwin would not yield the copyrights of Conrad's early fiction needed for the collected edition unless he were given *The Arrow of Gold*.
[2] An advance from Fisher Unwin.

that I have absolute confidence not only in your intentions but also in, what we may call, your policy.

To be explicit as to the matter now in hand: Yes. I'll be glad if the transfer of the *A of G* can be arranged. – I take note that there is no further engagement with F[isher] U[nwin]. I agree with you that Dent should not be upset. The man who sold 2000 copies of *Nostromo*(!) in 18 months deserves some consideration. – *I* would *not* be upset if the transfer failed.[1]

– I understand clearly the bearing of your view of the *Rescue* (as "old book") on the F. U. engagement. It would save the Napo[leon]*ic* Novel from his clutches but it would be at the cost of prolonged unpleasantness with that man who would make a great fuss. It would be better to satisfy him as soon as possible I think. But the point is worth consideration, later, if necessary.

———

Your energy with F. U. *has* done him some good. I had a letter (enclosed) from him, whose tone is, by comparison, almost decent. But it is character-istic – very. I don't know what power he had to prevent the collec*ed* Edition in the States; but if he had the power the fact of his boasting of not having behaved like an unspeakable pig gives away his moral blindness more than anything else in my experience of him. I am afraid that if you published that F. U. booklet with all our testimony people wouldn't quite believe it. They would think it sensational. But it would make good reading. I am ready to collaborate.

B[orys] is going to be invalided out by his next Med: Board on Wednesday. So at least he has been told by the O[fficer] C[ommanding] of the Maudesley* Hospital where he now is.[2] The Senior Tutor of Trinity Coll: wants to see him as soon as possible. Should he apply to you please let him have some money for his journey to Cambridge, as I want him to go there before he comes home for good – that is till Oct next. He will have to work pretty hard during the next six months and I want him to do it under my own eye rather than at a crammers – who are frauds mostly. But perhaps for the Vac: months I could get some young man to come to stay with us and help him through. There are plenty of decent young fellows who would be glad no doubt. It would also be company for B. But of all this I would want to talk with you later.

Ever affct*ly* Yours

J. Conrad.

———

[1] Unwin acquired *The Arrow*, opening the way for Dent to take *The Rescue*. Subsequently, Unwin brought out *The Rover* (1923) and *Tales of Hearsay* (1925).
[2] Being treated for neurasthenia or shell-shock.

To J. M. Dent
Text TS Berg; Unpublished

[letterhead: Capel House]
March 16th. 1919.

My dear Dent.

I answer your letter at once just to say once more that the proposal which you think will be so arbitrary and oppressive will be nothing of the kind.[1] You must not regard Pinker altogether as the Devil. We have both given very serious consideration to it in our reluctance to disturb the existing arrangement; and also recognising your right to meet us with a negative.

Far from being intended to loosen the relations between us the proposal would arise from the desire to clear up the situation. There can be nothing unfriendly in spirit in a suggestion to which, I repeat once more, you may say 'no' without disturbing the feeling of mutual goodwill and appreciation which exists between us at this moment. Pray remember that this complication has not been brought in after we entered into our present relations. Its origin lies in negotiations begun some time before you published the first Vol. of my short stories; and the obligation must be discharged some time or another. If Pinker approaches you at all, it will be to save me from the mental disturbance and irritation of which I admit it is the cause. It isn't good for my work and even (ridiculous as it may appear) it isn't good for my health either; and though I tried to keep it all to myself, P. who knows me well, has discovered this without telling. Here you have, without mentioning facts and names, the whole moral situation.

I hope to begin the so-called Napoleonic book next July, as I must have a couple of months off after finishing "The Rescue".

I fear I won't be well enough to come to town for two or three weeks yet. My work has been interrupted for several days but I feel fit enough to resume it now.

Yours sincerely

Joseph Conrad.

To G. Jean-Aubry
Text MS Yale; Unpublished

Capel House.
18. 3. 19

Cher Ami

Rien qu'un mot pour Vous féliciter du grand succès. Nous nous en réjouissons de tous nos coeurs si on peut s'exprimer ainsi.

---

[1] The previous day, Dent had written: 'I have not the slightest idea of the proposals Mr Pinker has to make to me, I am afraid it is sure to be very arbitrary, but if it is in my power to compass

Votre carte datée du six courant m'est parvenue hier seulement![1]

Nous quittons cette maison le 25 pour une autre a dix k'mètres d'ici que nous avons louée pour six mois. L'addresse sera

> Spring Grove
> Wye
> Kent

et la station du Ch[emin] de fer toujours Ashford.

Les amitiés de tout le monde

Tout a Vous

J. C.

Translation

Dear Friend

Just a word to congratulate you on the great success. We rejoice with all our hearts, if one can express oneself thus.

Your card dated the 6th inst. reached me only yesterday!

We are leaving this house on the 25th for another ten kilometres from here which we have rented for six months. The address will be

> Spring Grove
> Wye
> Kent

and the railway station remains Ashford.

Best wishes from everybody

Yours truly

J. C.

To J. B. Pinker
Text TS/MS Berg; Unpublished

[letterhead: Capel House]
March 19th. 1919.

My dear Pinker

The account of expenses connected with Nellie's illness, funeral etc. has come in yesterday – £19. 15. 8. Please send me a cheque made out to me so that I can settle with those people.

---

my love for your work and my regard for yourself it will tempt me to do anything possible' (TS carbon Berg). Dent may have intended 'arbitrary' to describe his own course of action rather than Pinker's 'proposals'.

[1] The postcard dated 6 March has vanished; probably it gave news of Jean-Aubry's successful lecture tour of the Netherlands.

B[orys] won't be able to go to Cambridge, I fear, till the end of April, unless he manages his demobilisation with extraordinary smartness. I have already sent all his papers, certificates and testimonials, to the tutor in charge of his application, and it really looks as if it were going to be "approved". It will be a great relief for me [to] see this matter settled in the right way and see the boy grappling with his studies on a definite plan. A general chorus of approval greets this development. That does not affect me very much, but I think, really, that from a certain point of view Cambridge would be safer for him than London. It would also be more formative; and I imagine that at the Engineering School, where everybody *must be* an earnest worker, he will get the spirit of the place without the nonsense.

Yesterday I had a wire from M. Lohr asking me to attend a rehearsal at eleven o'clock to-morrow (Thursday). It will be rather a scramble to catch the early train, but I think I will go – not because of real interest but from mere unworthy curiosity. However at the last moment my heart may fail me. So I won't promise to pay you a visit. I don't know how long that horror will last, how I will feel after it, or indeed whether I will survive it at all. It may be over by 1. 30, though I doubt it. In that case I could try to ring you up and ask what time you will be back at the office. My hope is to catch the 4. 30 down, because I do not feel particularly bright and don't want to knock about the country-side till a late hour. Meantime, with many groans and curses at the in-terruptions that constantly arise the "Rescue" goes on, very much 'according to plan'. The greatest pleasure I had this week was your telegram approving my letter to F[isher] U[nwin] which was accordingly dispatched by the very next post, with cries of savage joy.[1] But he won't squirm, you may believe me! Nothing but an explosive bullet can really subdue a rhinoceros. Dent wrote in a sentimental tone. I gave him (cautiously) to understand that whatever he may say or do we both really love him. That will buck him up for a time.

We are entering on our tenancy on the 26th on account of the wretched plumbers who won't be done before the 25th. The agreement which is in the usual form stipulates three months' rent in advance, i.e. 26 weeks at 7gs p. w. The estimate for removal will come in to-morrow when I will write you a short note of the monies to be provided for the shifting of our camp. Jessie progresses. She sends her love. Wonderful rumours reach me from the U. S. It seems N. Y. City is talking already of my Coll^d Edition and even quotes the price in pounds as 36! I am also the "most read" novelist. This you must understand is the talk of newly arrived Americans in London (of various kinds and degrees) and is transmitted to me by no less person than

---

[1] The savage joy may account for its subsequent disappearance.

Mrs Dummett.[1] Walp[ole] wrote to me that you behaved to him (lately) like an angel. As W. does not enlarge I won't ask what it was about.

Ever Yours

J Conrad.

To J. M. Dent

Text TS Berg; Unpublished

[letterhead: Capel House]

March 20th. 1919.

My dear Dent.

I was very pleased to get your letter[2] this morning. Thank you for your assent to the proposed arrangement. I assure you it is not what I wanted to do either, but you are by now so fully informed as to the whole transaction that I need not refer to this hard necessity any more.

I am very pleased to hear that you arranged with Pinker to re-publish the "Reminiscences". And in this connection I should like you to consider the matter of the title. My suggestion to Nash[3] was "A Personal Record", but Nash looked so frightened at such an eccentricity that I hastened to assure him that he could call it anything he jolly well liked. My title was used for the American edition which is very well known over there and is often alluded to in literary articles in the press. What is your feeling as to restoring it to the re-issue in England? My fear is that some buyers might be deceived and then feel angry at having bought a book they had already, under another title. Neither you nor I want to make that worthy class of people – the book buyers – angry. Could we guard against that danger by putting the English title as a sort of sub-title to the other. Thus:-

Joseph Conrad

———— ————

A PERSONAL RECORD

(*SOME REMINISCENCES*)

The collection of Occasional writings will want some little talking over, but we may leave that till we meet, which I hope will not be very long now.

---

[1] Cunninghame Graham's close friend.

[2] Of 19 March (TS carbon Berg), reporting on a meeting with Pinker. Dent agreed to let Unwin have *The Arrow*, telling Conrad: 'It is not what I wanted to do, I wanted very much to have every scrap you were to write from this time forward, but I understand the difficulty'; at least Dent could bring out *The Rescue*, prepare a new edition of *Some Reminiscences*, and 'wait eagerly for the great Napoleonic book which God speed you in writing'.

[3] Eveleigh Nash, who published the first British edition in 1912.

I am going on with "The Rescue" steadily but without haste; for, at the high pitch at which that romance was started, extreme caution is necessary not to let the reader down at the last. I have good hopes of success with that book, owing to the simplicity of the subject and the directness of the nar[r]ative. But the actual writing is, for those very reasons, a matter of considerable anxiety. Thanks for your good wishes. With kind regards

Yours sincerely

Joseph Conrad.

To J. B. Pinker

Text MS Berg; Unpublished

[Capel House]
20. 3. 19.

Dearest Pinker.

Herewith note by the house agent of payment to make on entry. The estimate for removal is not in – but it will be about £26 for moving part of things to Ashford Warehouse and part to Spring Grove.

I think that if you send ch. to agents and pay in £50 to my acc^t I will settle the removal and some other exp^{ns} such as inventory the cleaning of Capel House and so on.

Or if you pay in 150 I will write all the cheques connected with this earthquake. Pray let me know on Mond:

I did not go to rehearsal. Without the standing and authority to suggest and criticise I would have had [to] try to play the polite to Marie Lohr and all these. A silly position to be in. Abstention means £3 in my pocket and over 1000w of *Rescue* (and Good Words too) done this morning between 10 & One.

I had a nice letter from Dent, which I enclose. I am glad he agreed with you as to the *Pers:* Record. That Vol: of occasional writings must be talked over between you and me, as I have some views about that sort of thing.

Giving up the *A of G* to F[isher] U[nwin] makes one feel rather worse than leaving one's small boy at his first school. But I must thank you, first for thinking of this move, and then for carrying it through without making Dent scream with pain. And there's no denying the fact that there is a distinct feeling of relief. The story of the *A of G* is made of the unexpected – first the Ll[oyd's] Mag serial – then into F. U's clutches. Who would have dreamt of it! And it may yet make a hit – since that is the last thing I expect from it.

We are moving in on the 26th and Jessie expects to see you soon there.

Ever Your

J Conrad

To H. M. Tomlinson

Text MS Private collection; Unpublished

[letterhead: Capel House]

20: 3. '19.

Dear Tomlinson[1]

I write to thank you for the book in both our names. My wife, though still unable to move to any extent is busy ordering men and handling (by the force of her will) things in view of our removal from this house to another very near Ashford also.

I have already seen most of the papers composing your new vol:[2] and I have appreciated their graphic power, personal point of view and felicity of expression. I glanced in here and there with renewed pleasure. That book is a good Companion.

I am up to my ears in work – arrears of 3$^{1}/_{2}$ years my dear friend! We hope that you and all yours are well. Our eldest boy was invalided out of the Army yesterday. My wife is getting on slowly. I am not brilliant in any sense but am still holding my end up.

With our united kind regards

Yours sincerely

J. Conrad

To B. Macdonald Hastings

Text TS Colgate; Unpublished

[letterhead: Capel House]

March 21st. 1919.

My dear Hastings.

Thanks for your note received to-day. When writing to M[arie] L[öhr] some time ago I backed up your protest against that absurd creature[3] by

---

[1] Born in Poplar, Henry Major Tomlinson (1873–1958) grew up in London's dockland. In 1904, he left a miserably paid job in a shipping-office to write for the *Morning Leader* (later merged with the *Daily News*). He first made a name for his articles about trawlermen; a voyage to the Amazon as a ship's purser gave him the material for his first book, *The Sea and the Jungle* (1912). During the war he worked as a correspondent, first for the *Daily News*, then for GHQ France. Later, he published many volumes of essays, such as *Old Junk* (1918) and *London River* (1921), and novels such as *Gallions Reach* (1927) and *All Our Yesterdays* (1930). His fiction often has a Conradian tang.

[2] *Old Junk.*   [3] Sam Livesey as Ricardo?

recording my own unfavourable impression of the physique and personality. It was all I could do considering that I have no standing to interfere, the authorship being exclusively your own.

I was not well enough to go to the rehearsal to which I was invited and I don't think I will be well enough on the 26th[1] to risk a journey to and a night in London. I wrote to M. L. thanking her for the offer of a box and begging her not to reserve it for me as I doubted my ability to attend.

Your general good opinion of the company is comforting but I share your disgust at the chances of the play being jeopardised by these people's obstinacy.

My wife joins in kindest regards

Yours

J Conrad

To J. B. Pinker

Text TS/MS Berg; Unpublished

[letterhead: Capel House]

21. 3. '19

My dear Pinker

Thanks for your good letter and enclosed cheque.

You have seen by this Dent's letter written to me after the operation. I return here the agreement for Rems. duly signed. I am very glad to have the book revived. I remember perfectly why you were keeping it back. That it has escaped F[isher] U[nwin]'s imprint only adds to my feeling of relief at the settlement of that nightmarish business which you have effected with so much skill. – I think that your answer to McM[illan]'s representative[2] was in the highest degree right and proper. I think with you that D[oubleday] wouldn't wish to let the books go, if I can judge from his statements and protestations to me. He had declared them definitely to me as being profitable from the business point of view, and as otherwise being cherished in the innermost sanctuary of his heart. He gave me the impression that he would as soon part with his entrails. And I don't know that I would want him to do that – I mean part with the books. Bad as he is there is some sort of a human relation established now with those people of the Garden City;

---

[1] The opening night of *Victory*.

[2] Macmillan, New York, evidently planned to capture the collected edition from Doubleday.

and if he is going to do the de Luxe edition and work up the publicity racket about me in that connection we may just as well keep it with him. I understand that what you take up, in both our names, is a completely neutral attitude, and if you think it proper I am completely satisfied with it. I think that perhaps it would be just as well if Doubleday was to be made to understand that *we* didn't set McM's at him. From something he said I fancied he was afraid, or rather doubtful, of what we might suddenly do. I should like him to go about the Ed. de Luxe with a composed mind as to our future relations.

The house is upside down. An earthquake is nothing to it. It does not last so long. The R. is going on nevertheless – a little every day, but quite enough to make me feel safe with L & W. On the other hand I *do* long to be done with it – and see at last myself what it's going to look like! If April sees the end of it and also of the short story which is to follow I shall feel extremely virtuous.

I didn't connect Walpole's view of you (as an angel) conveyed in a letter to Jessie with his talk that Sat. evening. It was mostly about his visit to America.[1] As to the business part of his confidences I remember now telling him that the strictly business view was not at all unjust; but that in any case you did not look at the position you have attained as a "commercial" one. I did not encourage him to enlarge and he soon went off to something else. Hugh is volatile, but he certainly appreciates you warmly and seems to stand somewhat in awe of Your person. I've declined the offer of a box from Miss Lohr. I am still feeling gouty and don't want to provoke the devil needlessly. *R* is my exclusive preoccupation.

Ever Yours

J. Conrad.

PS No. I don't want to revise the Rems in any sense but of course Dent must send me proofs, so that his edition may establish the correct text. — Jessie claims the pension which would have been due this quarter and she is really entitled to it (£20) and stipulated for it when I gave it up. Pray satisfy her. I see the L & W have changed the illustrator apparently to great advantage. Hardy was becoming impossible.[2]

---

[1] The publisher George Doran had suggested a lecture tour of the United States; Walpole sailed in September 1919 and stayed six months (Hart-Davis, *Walpole*, pp. 178, 188–93).

[2] Cf. the letter to Foster of 12 December 1918. For an example of Greiffenhagen's work, see Plate 7.

To J. B. Pinker
Text TS/MS Berg; Unpublished

Spring Grove,
Wye,
Kent.
March 26th. 1919

My dear Pinker.

Thanks for the revised sheets of the A. of G. sent by D[oubleday] I will look one of the sets over and if there are any serious corrections we will send them a note by mail. It was understood that those sheets were for me to keep. The other set I am forwarding here and you may give it to F[isher] U[nwin] if you think you can trust him.[1] I believe he is quite capable of publishing the book suddenly with an utter disregard of Lloyd's Mag. rights. He is capable of anything that wouldn't actually get him into trouble with the police. That is the whole of his morality.

We went into residence yesterday and to-day I am laid up with a bad ankle. Nevertheless I have worked at "The Rescue" this morning, about 600 words, which for a man in a state of gouty irritation is not so bad. I handed over to the agents of Capt. Halsey yesterday afternoon a cheque for £96. 12. 0. three months' rent and 1½ gs for half cost of the agreement which is in the usual form.

Will you be good enough to send me a packet of type-writing paper, as you did last year. I can't get anything decent in the country here. This sheet is a sample.

I have actually forgotten till now that this is the day for "Victory". Frankly I have no feeling whatever in the matter. I avoided going to rehearsals and I begged Marie Lohr not to keep a box for me, as she offered to do. However B[orys] went in there to buy a stall and they discovered who he was and gave him the box. As to you, my dear fellow, you won't get a box from me till I write a play – that play with which I propose to surprise you before we both get too old to care a hang what happens, on or off the stage.

Jessie is displaying an amazing amount of activity, flying back and forth in the Studebaker between the two houses and actually climbing stairs. All the things we take with us won't be here till late on Friday. I have none of my

---

[1] The next day at 10:21 a.m., Conrad sent this telegram from Wye: 'Please send back arrow sheets defective must inspect them before delivery to Unwin Conrad' (Berg).

books with me and only one pair of breeks[1] – the rest of my luggage being composed of a dirty collar and a tooth-brush.

Ever yours

J Conrad

*P. C.** I don't know whether Eric wants me to say how glad I am to know him to be back in the office unchipped and with an M[ilitary] C[ross] to his credit – but I do say it with all my heart.[2]

To J. M. Dent
Text TS Berg; J-A, 2, 219

[Spring Grove]
March 29th. 1919.

Dear Dent.

The Reminiscences are not a collection of loose papers.[3] The book is an elaborately planned whole in a method of my own, and in the Preface to it is pointed out distinctly as being specially concerned with my first book and my first contact with the sea.

This, apart from the revelation of personality, is the subject; and I have nothing more to say about it. That is the complete raison d'être for the book as a piece of writing. It is the product of a special mood and of a day that will never come again to me. It is no more 'material' than my very heart is 'material'. That sort of thing is not done twice any more than a book like the Mirror of the Sea.

Nash made from it a very presentable six shilling volume in 1911.[4] Things have changed since, I know, but I am certain that the House of Dent will do its best under the difficult circumstances for that bit of prose which is closer to me than my own skin and can be neither stretched out nor

---

[1] A Scots word for 'breeches', i.e. trousers.
[2] Another telegram to Pinker went out at 9:13 a.m. on the 28th: 'Please send five pounds to lieut A. B. Conrad Maudesley* hospital denmark Hill Mac[kintosh] wired me joyfull* thank you for this chance too Yours Conrad' (Berg).
[3] Conrad writes in response to Dent's letter of the 21st (TS carbon Berg). Dent wanted Conrad to add new material and proposed that the title should read *Some Reminiscences / A Personal Record*. On the 31st, he apologised for requesting an expanded text: 'I ought to have known of its complete unity and not troubled you.'
[4] 1912.

have pieces let into it without losing its fundamental unity and its artistic character.

Yours

J. C

To B. Macdonald Hastings
Text TS/MS Colgate; Unpublished

[Spring Grove]
March 29th. 1919.

My dear Hastings.

It was very good of you to send me that cheerful wire. I accept your prophesy* in a spirit of childlike trust and shall at once order a Rolls-Royce and buy a house in Surrey commanding an extensive view. I will even go so far as to pay my tailor's bill. To do more would not be exactly prudent till we hear further about the bookings.

Seriously, my dear Hastings, nothing can give me more pleasure than the thought that your labour, patience and, I may say, devotion to that thankless task are not to go for nothing. From the letters I had they all seem to have done their best and my boy thinks that Jones and the Chinaman were really remarkable.[1] Hugh Walpole says that Marie rose much beyond his expectations in the great scene. In fact it seems to have been a personal success for each and all of them and for this opportunity they ought to be grateful to you. The personal success which neither you nor I expected and couldn't have foreseen was that of Sidney Colvin in the part of Joseph Conrad. He was in the box Marie L[öhr] had reserved for me and my boy writes me that in the corridors he was pointed out as J. C. which amused him very much. Pinker's impression was excellent. I mean of the play as a play. I haven't seen any newspaper notices, except the D[aily] T[elegraph] one.[2] I was laid up on the day and it will be some time, I fear, before I can come up and see your work. But I think I am safe in sending you my congratulations at once.

Cordially yours

Joseph Conrad

---

[1] W. Gayer MacKay played Jones; George Elton, Wang.
[2] The review in the *Daily Telegraph* described an enthusiastic audience responding to a lurid and melodramatic play which simplified Conrad's psychology and muted his pessimism (27 March, p. 10).

PS My wife, who from the first had the greatest confidence in the third version desires me to give you her kind regards and warm felicitations.

To J. B. Pinker
Text TS Berg; Unpublished

[letterhead: Spring Grove][1]
Kent
March 29th. 1919.

Dearest Pinker

I was very glad to get your personal impression. I have seen since a batch of newspaper notices of which perhaps three displayed some signs of intelligence. My instinct kept me off rehearsals and I am glad you approved of it. You know me well, my dear Pinker! No one knows me better, and your conviction that no one but myself could convey Conrad characteristics on to the stage has given me particular pleasure and real encouragement. Of course there may be no attempt after all, but, if it is ever made, that saying of yours will certainly stiffen my back.

The only significant thing I have received since Wednesday is the Hastings' wire which reads as follows – "Bookings landed. Think we will make much money." I don't quite understand it, but however it may be, those proceeds fall into the category of our special understanding in the matter of serial rights. I am perfectly certain that if this affair had been in other hands than yours it would have come to nothing. Don't imagine, pray, that I am excited by M. H.'s wire. I remain in a state of Philosophic Doubt; though, of course, I will be glad not to be even remotely associated with a conspicuous failure.

I am sending you in a parcel by the same post (1) Sheets of *Arrow*, complete and duly corrected for F[isher] U[nwin]. (2) An envelope containing directions for the same corrections which you will please send to Doubleday, Page, to be applied to the American text as a final revise. I have also changed the dedication, because Curle intends to inscribe his travel book to me[2] and I don't want the thing to look like an exchange of compliments. (3) One copy Shorter's booklet of "*The Tale*" and a copy of Beaumont's edition of "*One Day More*"[3] for your collection.

I would like immensely to get a sight of you and have a talk. It does me a lot of good always morally to unload on you things that I cannot say very

---

[1] The Spring Grove letterhead was made with an uninked, embossed die. Throughout the period of the Conrads' residence, the letterhead was often stamped on Capel House stationery. Sometimes the old letterhead has been crossed out, as on both letters of 10 April, sometimes, as on 3 April, it has not.

[2] *Wanderings*, which appeared in 1920.

[3] The newly published Beaumont Press edition of 274 copies, 24 of them printed on Japanese vellum and signed.

well to anybody else. I think that the weather will improve very soon and I hope that when you feel disposed you will let us know of a day that will be convenient to you. In another two or three days we will get settled down here fairly comfortably. I am better, and intend to go out on Wednesday to see Colonel Bell's agent¹ about a permanent house I have in view: Oswalds, Bishopsbourne, about 4 miles from Canterbury. It will be a great relief to me to have the future settled in that respect; and certainly the house is wonderfully convenient.

Ever affect^ly Yours

Joseph Conrad.

To B. Macdonald Hastings

Text MS Colgate; Unpublished

Spring Grove
Wye. Kent.
Sunday. [30 March 1919]²

Dear Hastings

Thanks for your note with the cuttings which I return. We had a few more this morning all good from the box off^ce point of view.

Sorry to have disappointed you as to the elevation of my mind. It *is* a low thing. That however is a secret which I confide to you here and which you must not divulge.

I've checked your calculations and your arithmetic is undeniable. May it also be prophetic!!

Our kind regards

yours cordially

J Conrad.

To G. Jean-Aubry

Text MS Yale; *L.fr.* 144

[Spring Grove]
Kent.
Dim^che [30 March 1919]³

Très cher

Je vous ai ecrit deux fois a la Haye quelques mots seulement pour V[ou]s dire la part que nous prenons a votre succès en Hollande.

---

¹ Colonel Matthew Gerald Edward Bell (1871–1926) served from 1898 to 1909 in the Second Rifle Brigade and the Somaliland Field Force; he owned much of the land in the parishes of Bourne and Bishopsbourne.
² The first Sunday after the opening?   ³ A postmarked envelope accompanies the letter.

Vive la Hollande!
Mort a Voltaire![1]
Je vais Vous écrire une note pour vous demander a venir nous voir ici
aussitot que n[ou]s serons installés un peu.
Amitiés de la part de tout le monde.

À vous

J. C.

Translation

Dear friend
  I wrote to you in The Hague twice, a few words just to let you know the
interest we take in your success in Holland.
Long live Holland!
Death to Voltaire!
  I will write you a note to ask you to come to see us here as soon as we have
settled in a bit.
Regards from everybody.

Yours

J. C.

To J. B. Pinker
Text MS Berg; Facsimile, Curreli (1999)

[Spring Grove]
[c. 1 April 1919][2]

My dear Pinker.
  I answered this by proposing to give him *The Tale* and referring him to you
for the text – if he cares to have it for *La Ronda*.[3] I like to be recognised by the
young. As to the proposed translation of a long novel I said that if he wants
to take it up at any time he must address himself to you for the terms.

---

[1] A reference to Voltaire's *Candide* (1759)? In the third chapter, the ingenuous hero believes that
 he will never go hungry in Holland because everyone there is Christian and rich.

[2] Cecchi wrote to Conrad on 26 March requesting something for his new magazine (MS Berg;
 Curreli (1999)). On 3 April Conrad thanked Pinker for enabling a gift to Dr Tebb.

[3] A Florentine living in Rome, Emilio Martino Gaetano Cecchi (1884–1966) was literary critic
 of the daily *La Tribuna* and had just helped to found *La Ronda*, a literary magazine. He moved
 to Milan in 1923 to become resident critic of the *Corriere della Sera*. He had already published
 books on Kipling (1910) and the English Romantics (1915) and translated Shelley's *Defence of
 Poetry*. Later he wrote many essays, narratives of travel, and studies in art history. His obituary
 of Conrad was reprinted in *Scrittori Inglesi e Americani* (1935). Mario Curreli describes him
 as 'Italy's foremost non-academic critic of the first half of the twentieth century' ('Conrad's
 Reception in Italy', *Con-texts*, forthcoming).

I hope you don't mind me giving away a trans[lati]^{on} right now and then. This is a special case and may lead to other proposals.

———————

There is a matter I have much at heart. Poor Dr Tebb who 18 years ago looked after Jessie and advised me too, without fee is now (I hear it indirectly) ill himself and in a rather tight corner (temporarily I hope).[1] He has been a very good friend. I should like to send him £50 – as a loan or something – or belated fee. Can I do it? (It would be a great relief to my feelings). If so pray pay in that am^t to bank and I will draw a cheque after I hear from you.

Ever Yours

J. C.

To J. B. Pinker
Text TS Berg; Unpublished

[letterhead: Spring Grove]
Kent.
April 3rd. 1919.

Dearest Pinker

Many thanks for your letter advising me that poor Tebb's matter may go through now.

The Preface to the Outcast of the Islands will reach you on Monday, as I want to correct and expand it a little. The existence of the Preface to Almayer's Folly dates back to the publication of the book. It's a fierce production which ought to be preserved and so we will print it in the Coll. Ed. Volume. Unfortunately I haven't got a copy here and the person who has the MS is John Quinn, of New York, to whom I will instantly write, asking him to send a typed copy to Doubleday for publication. That will be as quick as if I mailed it from here.

"The Rescue" is really drawing to a close. I have that peculiar feeling of hopefulness and damnable strain which is a sure sign.

The Italian gent. I imagine will be writing to you before long.

Jessie sends her love and suggests you should name a day next week for your visit.

Ever Yours

J. Conrad

---

[1] Dr Albert Tebb had attended the Conrads, the Hueffers, and the Rothensteins. For his misfortunes, see Martin Bock, 'What Has Happened to Poor Tebb?: A Biographical Sketch of Conrad's Physician', *The Conradian*, 23 (1998), 1–18.

To Hugh Walpole
Text MS Texas; Unpublished

[letterhead: Spring Grove]
3 Ap: '19.

Dear Walpole

Don't forget your promise to look us up before you depart for your beloved Cornwall.

This place is as cold as the last circle of the Inferno according to Dante.[1] Drop us a line as to day and hour. Come to Wye Station first after Ash[ford] on Canter^{ry} line.

Love from all.

Yours

J. C.

To G. Jean-Aubry
Text MS Yale; Unpublished

[letterhead: Spring Grove]
N^r Ashford. Kent.
[5 April 1919][2]

Cher Ami.

Voulez Vous venir le Samedi pour le "lunch" si ça V[ou]s convient ou par le train 4. 30 pm. Prenez votre billet pour *Wye* car en ce moment notre auto est chez le carossier et ce sera difficile de Vous prendre a la gare d'Ashford. Envoyez-nous un petit mot toute de suite – ou peut être une depêche.

Ma femme vous le [re]mercis pour le Souvenir de Hollande. Il n'existe plus – car il était bien bon.[3]

Tout a Vous

J. C.

Translation

Dear Friend.

Would you like to come for lunch on Saturday, if that suits you, or by the 4. 30 pm train? Get your ticket for *Wye* because at the moment our motor-car

---

[1] Dante places Satan in the lowest circle of Hell, frozen in perpetuity.
[2] Jean-Aubry's dating, noted on the MS.
[3] Jean-Aubry's letter of 27 March promised 'un souvenir comestible' of his Dutch tour.

is at the coachbuilder's and it will be difficult to pick you up from Ashford station. Send us a line at once – or perhaps a wire.

My wife thanks you for the gift from Holland. It no longer exists – because it was so good.

Yours truly

J. C.

To Lewis Rose Macleod
Text TS Lubbock; Rude

[letterhead: Spring Grove]
Kent.
April 5th. 1919.

My dear Sir.[1]

I am just now engaged on a work which gives me some anxiety, as the endings of novels generally do; and I am no good at going from one thing to another and back again. My brain is not built in watertight compartments (neither were the ships in which I used to sail[2]); the principle was not practically developed in my young days. I regret the defect very much, but there it is. The "forward view" of which you speak intimidates me also. The Liberty of Prophesying[3] is a fine thing but I have no practice in it. Besides, I feel more than usually stupid just now. One's imaginative view is confounded not only by the variety and multiplicity of facts but by the strange immobility of the situation. Events, ideas, action, and even principles themselves, seem to hang in the air, suspended from an invisible hook.[4] No doubt this impression does not prevail at Carmelite House[5] and may appear highly fantastic there, but it affects me all the same. On the other hand you can not doubt that I would like very much to show my readiness to accede to any wish of Lord Northcliffe; and so, since you are good enough to offer a helping hand, perhaps you will

---

[1] Born in New Zealand to Scottish parents, Lewis Rose Macleod (1875–1941) began his journalistic career in New South Wales; in 1905 he moved to South Africa, where he became editor of the *Johannesburg Sunday Times*. From 1916 to 1924 he was literary editor of the London *Daily Mail*, where several of Conrad's essays first appeared. Macleod returned to Johannesburg in 1924 to edit the *Rand Daily Mail*.

[2] Building watertight compartments for greater buoyancy and safety became possible with the switch from composite (wood and iron) to all-metal construction. The liner *Mauretania*, built in 1904, had 175 such compartments. Such precautions, however, did not save the *Titanic* in 1912.

[3] The *Discourse on the Liberty of Prophesying* (1647) is a plea for religious toleration by the great Anglican preacher and divine Jeremy Taylor (1613–67).

[4] A reaction to the Peace Conference under way in Paris?

[5] Headquarters of the Northcliffe Press.

suggest a subject and I will see what I can do.[1] But you mustn't be annoyed if it ends in my saying to you that I can do nothing.

Believe me

very faithfully Yours

Joseph Conrad.

Lewis Rose Macleod Esqre.

To J. B. Pinker

Text MS Colgate; Unpublished

[letterhead: Spring Grove]

Sunday [6 April 1919][2]

My dear Pinker

B[orys] will call on you about noon on Monday. Please let him have £20 for some expenses he has incurred for me and to pay for John's travelling home. J. is coming home on Wed 7.[3]

D. Mail has asked for an article for their Vic[ry]. N[o]. This does not appeal to me at all. Still I told Macleod to send a sugg[on] and I would see what I could do. My hands are very full of *R* and my head still more.

Ever Yours

J. Conrad

To Eric Pinker

Text MS Lubbock; Unpublished

[Spring Grove]

Wed. 9. Ap. 1919.

Dear M[r] Eric.[4]

I hope it isn't 'flu' that has laid your Father up.[5] Pray tell him how sorry we are. It would be very kind of you to let us know what is the matter.

---

[1] Northcliffe wanted an essay for the 'Golden Peace' edition of the *Daily Mail*; it appeared on 30 June and included Conrad's 'Confidence'.

[2] The day after the letter to Macleod.

[3] Wednesday would be the 9th.

[4] Upon leaving school, Eric Seabrooke Pinker (1891–1973) went to work for his father. During the war, he won the Military Cross for bravery under fire. When J. B. Pinker died in 1922, 'Mr Eric' became the firm's senior partner and thus Conrad's principal agent. Later, he moved to New York and in 1939 was sent to Sing Sing prison for appropriating $139,000 of his clients' funds.

[5] A telegram to Pinker's office sent on 9 April reads 'We are very sorry hope nothing serious pray give us news tomorrow regards Conrad' (Berg).

In the matter of rooms for Ralph, I don't offer to look for them myself because just now I am too crippled to go to the village, and anyway we haven't given up the hope of seeing Your Father here in the course of this month. Is your brother entered to begin next term? The school is very full I am told and a great many students are accom[m]odated in the village which is not very big. Will you ask your Father whether he wishes me to attempt anything? I hope to be able to hobble about quite briskly in a day or two.

The D. Mail [are] pressing me for an article for their Peace N° – I think I'll have to do it for them. I don't want to appear ungracious and I am well on with the end of *R*. So I can afford the time – but I grudge them the effort. If you should think of coming down here yourself we will be very glad to have you for the night either with or without your brother.

Kindest regards

Yours

J. Conrad

To Eric Pinker

Text TS Berg; Unpublished

[letterhead: Spring Grove]
10/4/19.

My dear Mr Eric.

Thanks for your letter. I am glad to know that it is nothing worse than neuralgia, though I am sorry for the bad time it must have given him. Pray tell him we will be delighted to see him on Monday with R[alph]. I shall meet the train at 6 o'clock in Ashford.

I return herewith Shorter's letter. To tell you the truth I don't like very much to give him the permission, because that paper (one of the first your Father placed for me) belongs to the very body of "The Mirror of the Sea" – a published book.[1] Of that C. S. doesn't seem to be aware. Do you think Methuens would object? I shouldn't like to hurt C. S.'s feelings. Perhaps you would tactfully talk to him on the wire in that sense.

I note you received the corrected copy of "Preface" for Doubleday. Would you please send me back the uncorrected one which was sent to you first and

---

[1] The *World's Work* accepted the 'The Faithful River' in May 1904 and published it in December; it forms Sections 30–2 of *The Mirror of the Sea*. Shorter's reprint is titled *London's River* (1919).

which I asked you to detain.[1] I like to keep a copy by me and it may be of use when the English collected edition is being got out.

Yours sincerely

J. Conrad.

PS Please settle enc^d account for me.

JC

To John Quinn
Text TS NYPL; Unpublished

[letterhead: Spring Grove]
Kent.
10/4/19

My dear Quinn.

I feel very compunctious at not having written to you before, and I hope you will not be angry with me when you discover that this letter is connected with business. I want to ask you to do me the favour to let Doubleday Page have the copy from the MS in your possession of the Preface to "Almayer's Folly", which was not published at the time and which I want now to use for the Collected Edition. You will find it in your collection of MSS, an item of, I believe, $2\frac{1}{2}$ pages. You will add immensely to the obligation by letting Doubleday have that text at your earliest convenience, as he wishes to start that Collected Edition about the middle of the year, I think. I was just going to write to you formally to declare my intention of dedicating my next book "To John Quinn" in just so many words. That book is "The Arrow of Gold" and the substance of it is so closely related to me personally that it can in fitness be inscribed only to a friend.[2] I hope that after more than eight years' intercourse (though we have not seen each other yet) your kindness has given me that status towards you. The corrected proofs with dedication as above have been already mailed to Garden City so that if you don't want to be compromised by any public association with that unspeakable Conrad you had better telegraph direct to Doubleday and threaten him with legal proceedings in case he disobeys your injunction.

Hastings' adaptation of my "Victory" has blazed up extremely on the London world. You will have probably heard of it by this time. It's possible

---

[1] The 'Preface' was to *An Outcast*. In a telegram to Pinker's office of 8 April (Berg), Conrad wrote: 'Please hold authors note wrong copy sent posting right copy tonight'.

[2] For the obstacle to this declaration, see the telegram of [30 April] and the letter of 3 May.

that it may turn out to be a mere fire of straw but at any rate there cannot be about it the suggestion of 'black frost'. Though this play is none of my business I shouldn't have liked to be associated just at present with even the suspicion of a failure. Marie Lohr has made a personal success of it which I, as a matter of fact, prophesied to her on the day of the very first rehearsal. And on that account, too, I am extremely pleased with the good reception the play had from the first.

Our boy has been invalided out of the army the day before yesterday. Your namesake John, (the second boy) has just arrived from school to this new address; and so we are all four together and for the first time in many years without a sense of terror hanging over our heads.

My poor wife who is not getting on very well after the operation sends You her kindest regards

Believe me always yours

Joseph Conrad.

To J. B. Pinker
Text MS Berg; Unpublished

[letterhead: Spring Grove]
Friday 11th. Ap. 1919.

My dear Pinker.

I was ever so sorry to hear of your neuralgia. I'll meet your train at 6 in Ashford unless my foot prevents me; in which case pray speak to any shabby driver you may see in the Station yard. Our own car is being cleaned out and painted.

I've just received proof of article from the Fortnightly, which I see is the same with the one for Harpers.[1] I wasn't particularly keen for *that* one to appear in Eng^d. However since it is coming out please credit my acc^t with whatever amount the Fort^{ly} has agreed to pay (less the com[missi]^{on}) in advance. I am being rather worried by Ret[inger] who is apparently in pawn in Barcelona Palace Hotel. As the article is partly based on a little pamphlet of his which was pub^{ed} in '15 or '16[2] – I think I may let him have the £30 he asks for – and then no more.

I've begun today the contr[ibuti]^{on} to D. Mail *Peace Number* for which they asked me on N'cliffe's instr^{ons}.

[1] 'The Crime of Partition' came out in the 1 May number of the *Fortnightly Review* and the 14 June issue of *Collier's Weekly* (rather than *Harpers*).

[2] *La Pologne et l'équilibre européen* (1916). For an earlier occasion when Conrad came to Retinger's aid, see the letters of 31 August 1918.

Begun also penultimate chapt[er] of *Rescue*. The last will be very short. I am by no means sick of the *R* but Oh! What a relief it will be!

Ever Affct^{ly} Yours

J. Conrad

PS Or would you send for me the tel[egra]ph[i]^c order to R^{er}? But don't let me be a worry to you if you are overwhelmingly busy . . .

To Sir Hugh Clifford
Text MS Clifford; Hunter (1985, 2)

Spring Grove,
Wye,
Kent.
14 Ap. 1919.

My dear Clifford.

Thanks for your letter. We are now in a new house which I have taken fur[nish]^{ed} for six months till we can settle permanently after Michaelmas.

Jessie is still very crippled after the operation. I shall have to bring her up to town in the first or second week of May for Sir R. Jones to pronounce whether anything more ought or can be done.

With our affectionate regards

Ever Yours

J. Conrad

P.S. We shall await a word from you.

To Lewis Rose Macleod
Text TS Lubbock; Unpublished

[letterhead: Spring Grove]
Kent.
April 16th. 1919

Dear Mr Macleod

Here is my contribution and I hope you will not be too much disappointed. I haven't given it a title but you might call it "Confidence". You have had "Tradition" before,[1] and "Confidence" will make a pair. The word in itself is not a bad word for a Peace Number.

As to my own confidence in the future I don't mind telling you privately that it isn't the confidence that dwells in one and runs like soothing balsam in

---

[1] *Daily Mail*, 8 March 1918.

one's veins. It is the sort of confidence one holds on to with teeth and claws for dear life. However I don't say that in my article.

Yours faithfully

Joseph Conrad.

To F. N. Doubleday

Text TS/MS Princeton; J-A, 2, 220[1]

Spring Grove
Wye.
Kent.
17 Ap. 1919.

My dear Mr Doubleday

I was very glad to hear of your safe arrival in the Land of the Pilgrim Fathers, which contains, if not exactly the Garden of Eden, then the charming grounds of the Garden City. This, the latest message from it, is as pleasant to read as all the others I have been privileged to receive. It is also eminently distinguished by proceeding directly from you, and is furthermore notable as the longest letter I have received signed by F. N. D.[2] This you may take as an exact fact established by careful comparison with other documents of the kind preserved in the family archives.

Seriously, my dear Mr Doubleday, I am very much gratified by the words of hope and encouragement you have been good enough to send me so soon after your return. I am also touched by the sympathetic response extended by yourself, and of your trusted associates in your work, to my letter of the 21 December. I wrote frankly, in the hope of being understood, and now I have the comforting certitude of it being so.

Let me thank you for all the trouble and also for the success of your efforts in serialising "The Rescue". I feel that your remarks on the advantages of appearing in the columns of a newly started magazine are eminently just.[3] Pinker will be sending you the complete text before very long. I am glad to say that the proprietors of "Land and Water" profess themselves very pleased by the reception given to the serial here, and by the good effect on the circulation of the paper.

My thanks are due to you also for securing a review from Mr Hergesheimer.[4] Will you please thank him from me, not so much for what

---

[1] Without the first three sentences of the last paragraph.

[2] Dated 1 April, a carbon copy is preserved at Princeton.

[3] *Romance*, a New York magazine, was going to publish the American serial of *The Rescue*, starting November 1919.

[4] The American novelist Joseph Hergesheimer (1880–1954), now remembered for *The Three Black Pennys* (1917) and *Java Head* (1919), reviewed *The Arrow* for the 'Books and the Book World' section of the New York *Sun*, 13 April, p. 1.

he found it in his heart to say as for the warm, human (*not* critical) friendliness of his insight and for the very terms in which he expresses his, to me immensely welcome, appreciation. You have given me great pleasure by sending me that article in advance.

I do hope the friendly prophecies of your young men as to *A. of G.* will be fulfilled. The news as to the progress of your plans for the collected Edition is also very cheering. The texts of *A.'s Folly, Outcast* and *Nigger* are now corrected and ready. The Author's Note for *Outcast* will have reached you before you receive this. The Preface for the *Folly*, written at the time and never published before, is to be found in a MS now in possession of Mr Quinn, to whom I have already written begging him to send you a correct typed copy. The *Nigger* is sufficiently provided, both with a preface and an Author's Note. I will send you in good time an Author's Note for the volume of "*Tales of Unrest*", which will of course be Number 4 in the order of publication. I haven't yet revised the text of that vol. but you may count safely on it being ready early in June. Can you give me an idea how many volumes you intend to send forth in 1919 and also in 1920? I want to do my little part worthily in that enterprise.

A fortnight ago I sent you seven pages of small corrections for *A. of G.* The dedication is to be: *To John Quinn.* I repeat this here because the name of Richard Curle has been sent in error with the typed copy. My wife is progressing but slowly. The boy has been invalided out of the army last week. Both are sending their kindest regards. Pray remember me to Mrs Doubleday and believe me

always very sincerely yours
Joseph Conrad.

To J. B. Pinker

Text MS Berg; Unpublished

[Spring Grove]
Wedsy [23 April 1919][1]

Dear Pinker

Borys is bringing you the Authors Note for the Tales of Unrest (Coll^d Ed^{on}) of which please have two copies made and return the original to me. Please give B £8 to pay for some things for me.

Just had a letter from Ralph announcing his arrival for Monday. His room shall be ready and either I or B will meet his train in Ash[ford] or Wye.

Ever Yours
J. C.

[1] By Wednesday the 30th, Ralph Pinker had arrived.

To J. B. Pinker

Text TS Berg; Unpublished

[letterhead: Spring Grove]

30. 4. 19.

My dear Pinker.

Please do for Jessie what she is writing to ask you to do for her. I am feeling so much better this afternoon that I can even dictate a letter to you. I was in too much pain to ask Ralph to come in and see me but I shall do so to-morrow. Everybody is very pleased with him and he had a long conversation with Jessie last night after dinner.

I enclose herewith corrected proof, 64 pages, and an Unwin letter which came with the first batch. Something in the wording of his first para. makes me think that you had better watch his vagaries. I wonder if he is not meditating publishing the book suddenly and making trouble perhaps with Lloyds.

As to his remark[s] about the title, they are simply impertinent and I don't think they need be answered.

I don't remember anything about my agreement with F. U., not even the fact of signing it. I hope he has got no participation in translation rights. Please let me know, or else send me the agreement for inspection which I will return in 24 hours.

By a cable from John Quinn I hear that the first edition of A. of G. was 15,000 and that a further 5,000 are being printed, which is just exactly a fortnight after the date of publication.

I enclose a letter which got torn by accident, which speaks for itself. With reference to that you know my feeling is that I should like all my work placed in its entirety with some Film Co. if the thing can be done.[1]

I enclose also duly corrected "Author's Note" for Tales of Unrest, which please forward to Doubleday, who is anxious for it.

I am afraid it will be some time before I can see anybody, at any rate a stranger, here. I have had a very bad shake up and feel very weak and unwell now. My coming to town is put off indefinitely. I do not think I will be able to come with Jessie, unless her appointment with Sir Robert Jones is at the end of May.

I would very much like to see you. My health is very precarious indeed and I want to talk to you about the future and consult you upon my idea of dealing with part at least of the money earned in America; but I cannot

---

[1] This letter has not survived. For Conrad's interest in cinema, see Gene M. Moore's essay 'Conrad's "film-play" *Gaspar the Strong Man*' in Moore, ed., *Conrad on Film*, pp. 31–47.

write it in a letter. If you can spare me a day, do so my dear fellow, because my mind is not at ease.

Ever Yours

J Conrad.

To John Quinn
Text Telegram Berg; Unpublished

[30 April 1919][1]

Quinn 31 Nassau Street
Let Curle stand my Napoleonic novel shall be for you letter follows[2]

Conrad

To J. B. Pinker
Text Telegram Berg; Unpublished

[Wye, Kent]
[2 May 1919
3.15pm]

Bookishly L[on]d[o]n
Did you cable money to Rettinger* he left Barcelona 24th

Conrad

To [?]
Text TS Private collection; Unpublished.

Spring Grove, Wye, Kent
May 2[nd] 1919

You must forgive this dictated letter,[3] I am laid up with severe gout and cannot use the pen.

[1] Date stamp.
[2] On 10 April, Conrad had told Quinn that *The Arrow* would be dedicated to him. On the 28th, Quinn wired Conrad: 'First edition fifteen thousand Arrow Gold published April twelfth dedicated Curle. Letter directing dedication me received few days afterwards (Stop) Second edition five thousand dedicated me ready for press (Stop) While delighted your suggestion sure considering facts you will want Curle dedication stand. Please cable decision. Publishers holding presses awaiting your reply' (NYPL).
[3] Some clues hint at the identity of this unknown recipient, but they are far from conclusive. He (or she) took an interest in bibliography and had a connection with Cambridge. The earliest known owner of this letter was Grizel (1900–87), wife of Hubert Hartley, a master at Eton. She counted among her friends Sydney Carlyle Cockerell, Director of the Fitzwilliam Museum, to whom Conrad wrote a friendly letter on 19 August. Another possible bibliophile would be Montague Rhodes James, Provost of King's College from 1905 to 1918, subsequently Provost of Eton, an authority on mediaeval manuscripts and author of unforgettable ghost stories; as a Fellow of King's, he had been Ted Sanderson's tutor.

It would be the greatest pleasure for us both to see you here, but as to the reprints of which you speak there would be nothing to discuss. I gave my permission to Mr Shorter to reprint them out of purely friendly feeling connected with my early days when Mr Shorter made a most generous offer to publish in the "Illustrated London News" a novel by a then utterly unknown man. That the novel did not appear was my fault entirely because I did not finish it. I laid it aside for other work.

I was in hopes of being able to come to Cambridge with my boy to see Mr Harrison, of Trinity College,[1] but I cannot reasonably hope to be out of bed in time. I have been suffering from gout ever since February last. It has hindered me very much in my work, and as to leisure the only sort that I know is the forced sort when I am laid on my back.

With kindest regards

Joseph Conrad.

To Elbridge L. Adams

Text TS Doheny; Unpublished

[letterhead: Spring Grove]

3. 5. 19.

My dear Mr Adams[2]

It was very pleasant to hear from you again. I will tell you at once that our boy has come through this war alive and is now with us, having been discharged out of the army about a month ago. We are touched by your remembering that we had a son out there and by your feeling reference to it.

Your letter has made me feel ashamed again after the lapse of years for the utterly unnecessary heat in argument which I displayed that afternoon when you and I went for a drive in the Ford and discussed the question of individual liberty. I remember when I confessed it to my wife afterwards with much compunction how shocked she was, but you have been extremely good about it. Your candid letter was very pleasant reading for me, mainly because my point of view has become practically demonstrated to you. Pray do not believe that I am triumphing, for there is much to say for the other – I may call it – the ethically utilitarian attitude. In fact it is the undeniable strength of that attitude that makes it so exasperating to the objectors of my sort. The

---

[1] Ernest Harrison (1877–1943), a classicist, elected to a fellowship in 1900.

[2] Elbridge Lapham Adams (1866–1935?), journalist and book collector, brought out a study of *Joseph Conrad: The Man* in 1925; on a lighter note, he was editor of the *Century Anthology of Porcine Poetry* (1924). He became acquainted with Conrad in 1916 and was one of his hosts on the American tour in 1923.

foundation of my argument was really the feeling that there is more than one kind of utility, whether in the moral or in the material sphere.

Thank you very much for your friendly invitation, which I prize immensely, but I am afraid that my travelling days are over. My health has been rather bad for the last two years and shows no sign of improvement. Still, one never knows!

My wife thanks you for your kind message to her and sends her kindest regards.

> Believe me most sincerely yours
>
> Joseph Conrad

P. S. Many thanks for the press cutting. If you wait for the English edition it will be some time because the book cannot appear for some months yet on this side.[1]

To John Quinn
Text TS NYPL; Unpublished

> [letterhead: Spring Grove]
> Kent.
> 3. 5. 19.

My dear Quinn.

It was a curious imbroglio of which the fault was entirely mine, though I think Doubledays might have sent me revised slips of "Arrow" early enough to have them returned in time for correction.

The fact is that the dedication to you was a sudden thought insofar that for a long time I had determined to dedicate to you my Napoleonic novel, which is the next work I am to write after finishing "The Rescue", which now is awaiting its last pages. Then, while passing the first proofs of "Arrow" it occurred to me that I would not keep you waiting and that the "Arrow" was perhaps good enough to be inscribed to you. But in truth it is better as it is, for certainly the Napoleonic novel is bound to be a bigger thing in every way. "The Rescue" which is now awaiting its final pages has been destined ever since 1914 for the U. S. Ambassador in Vienna, I mean Mr Penfield, who was so kind and friendly in obtaining our release from Austria. His name will be gratefully remembered as long as there is one of the Conrad tribe alive.

It was very good of you to send me a cable. Within an hour of its receipt I cabled Doubleday to let Curle stand, which was really the only thing to

---

[1] Unwin published *The Arrow* on 6 August.

do. Your friendly attitude and comprehension of the situation assuaged my distress at that absurd complication.

My wife sends her best regards

Yours

Joseph Conrad.

I won't say anything more because I have been laid up with gout for more than a week now and I find even dictating a letter a strain on my poor muddled head.

To Captain Anthony Halsey

Text TS Lowens; Lowens (1977)

[letterhead: Spring Grove]
Kent
5. 5. 19

Dear Capt Halsey.[1]

Your note found me in bed with a bad attack of gout; bad enough to prevent me even dictating a letter. I have no doubt that my wife has attended to the water business.

I can assure you that everybody is very happy in your charming house. I haven't been outside the fences since I saw you, but if one must be a prisoner this certainly is a very charming spot to be imprisoned in. The young foliage of the grove is very pretty to look at just now.

My wife joins me in kind regards.

Very Sincerely yours

Joseph Conrad

To G. Jean-Aubry

Text TS Yale; Unpublished

[letterhead: Spring Grove]
Kent.
5. 5. 19.

My dear Aubry.

I am sending you here a set of booklets published lately by Wise. Perhaps you will like to have them and I have signed every one in order to enhance their value.

---

[1] Captain Anthony Halsey owned Spring Grove, the house the Conrads occupied for six months. As a second lieutenant in the *Philomel* during the Anglo-Boer War, he was twice mentioned in dispatches. From 1910 to 1912, when he retired, he was an inspecting officer in the Coastguard Division.

We were very sorry not to see you here the other week. Your postcard from Birmingham arrived yesterday. Are those lectures of yours going to be printed?[1] If so, please let me know in what periodical they are going to appear.

As we don't know what your engagements may be I suggest that you should drop us a line and come along to see us the first time you are at liberty to give us that pleasure. This house is only three minutes' walk from Wye station, so the question of road transportation does not arise. Meantime everybody in the house sends you their warm regards and I am

Yours as ever

J. Conrad.

PS. So glad you like my Poland paper.[2]

To T. J. Wise
Text TS BL Ashley 2953; Unpublished

[letterhead: Spring Grove]
Kent.
5. 5. 19.

Dear Mr Wise.

Thank you very much for the books and your letter accompanied by your portrait and the photograph of your library. I have signed the two copies you wished me to sign, and I return them here.

I am sorry to have been laid up again with an attack of gout and that is the reason why I am sending you this dictated letter. I can't write in a lying down position. However I am beginning to recover now, but I am afraid it will be a long time yet before I can walk more than from one room to another.

The only person likely to know where the "Anatole France" and "Alphonse Daudet" articles are to be found[3] is Mr Jean Aubry, who has done a very detailed bibliography of all my work.[4] Aubry is back from his lecturing tour in Holland and his address is – C/o J. & W. Chester, 11 Great Marlborough Street, W. 1.[5]

---

[1] These lectures formed the basis of Jean-Aubry's *French Music of Today*, trans. Edwin Evans (Kegan Paul, 1919).
[2] 'The Crime of Partition'.
[3] There were two pieces on Anatole France, one in the *Speaker*, 1904, the other in the *English Review*, 1908; the Daudet essay appeared in the *Outlook*, 1898. All three appeared as pamphlets under the imprint of Richard Clay, Wise's printer of choice.
[4] As Wise already knew, since Jean-Aubry had helped him to find fugitive pieces.
[5] Jean-Aubry's employers.

My warm thanks for the three inscribed booklets. They look most interesting. It was very kind of you to think of sending them to me. Believe me

very faithfully Yours

Joseph Conrad.

To J. B. Pinker
Text MS Berg; Unpublished

[Spring Grove?]

[early May 1919?][1]

Dearest Pinker

Please give B[orys] who is taking John to school a cheque for £10. I am sending you a set of Wise booklets for your collection.

I am feeling flattened out and look forward to seeing you on Thursday.

Ever Yours

J. C.

To J. B. Pinker
Text TS Berg; Unpublished

[letterhead: Spring Grove]

9. 5. 19.

My dear Pinker.

In reference to my last article for the Daily Mail it struck me after you went away that it had better not be paraded in the U. S. The loss in money would not be great and I don't want to risk hurting that public's feelings, which the article might do by the allusions to the reduction of the British Navy contained in the last paragraph or two. If you glance at it you will see what I mean. The proposal to reduce our Navy did come from the U. S., as well as some tall talk about displacing the British Merchant Service from its leading position as the goods-carrier of the world.[2]

---

[1] Three pieces of evidence suggest this dating: the stationery is watermarked THRONE DECKLE and the only other letter on this paper can be dated [23 April]; Conrad had recently had a new consignment of pamphlets from Wise; the letter to Pinker of 9 May shows that Pinker had just been to Spring Grove for a 'long talk', probably on Thursday the 8th.

[2] Conrad discusses, and dismisses, the call for naval disarmament in the opening paragraphs of the third section. The US Government wanted not to reduce the Royal Navy but to surpass it by building more capital ships. During the peace negotiations, Lloyd George fought the 'Naval Battle of Paris', an attempt to reverse these plans, which were anyway defeated by the Republican majority in Congress (J. Kenneth McDonald, 'Lloyd George and the Search for a Postwar Naval Policy, 1919' in A. J. P. Taylor, ed., *Lloyd George: Twelve Essays* (New York: Atheneum, 1971), pp. 192–4).

My mind has been set at rest by our long talk and if I were to feel just a little better than I do I could turn to my work with good effect. Unluckily I am rather worse than better to-day and will have to stay in bed on account of the very acute pain in the knee. I have had such set-backs before, but they are always disagreeable and depress one somewhat.

As far as it is arranged now Borys is proceeding to Cambridge on Monday. He will be in your office betwccn 12 and 1, and if you are not there pray, my dear Pinker, leave £20 in an open cheque for him. I don't think he will stay in Cambridge more than a day, though he may be detained there to interview one of the tutors who is in the position to give him good advice on the course of studies to pursue before he goes into residence.

Ever affect^ly yours

J. Conrad

To A. G. Ross

Text TS Leeds; Unpublished

[letterhead: Spring Grove]
Kent.
9. 5. 19.

Dear Sir,[1]

It gives me great pleasure to send you £1. 1. 0. for the testimonial for Mr. Edmund Gosse.[2]

Yours faithfully

Joseph Conrad.

A. G. Ross, Esq.

To J. C. Squire

Text TS Berg; Unpublished

[letterhead: Spring Grove]
Kent
9. 5. 19

Dear Mr Squire[3]

If I had not been laid up you would have had the end now in your hands. You have now the complete Part Five in your possession. Of the last Part (Six)

---

[1] Tentatively identified as Alexander Galt Ross (1860–1927), author of *Religion and the Modern Mind: Lectures Delivered before the Glasgow University Society of St Ninian* (1908).

[2] Conrad was one of the signatories to an 'Address from Men and Women of Letters' presented to Gosse along with a portrait bust by Sir William Goscombe John on 21 September, his seventieth birthday. A. G. Ross also signed this Address (*The Times*, 22 September, p. 13).

[3] John Collings Squire (1884–1958; knighted 1933), acting editor of the *New Statesman*, 1917–18, founded the *London Mercury* in 1919; he edited this literary magazine, loved and loathed for

24, 800 words are written and another 10, 000 will finish it – perhaps less. I have been in bed and in too much pain to be able to work, but I have been improving for the last two days and expect to tackle the thing to-morrow.

I shall at once send four chapters of the last part to Pinker to be clean-typed and forwarded to you for Greiffenhagen's reading. I am very glad he has got the balance of the story to illustrate. Will you kindly give him my appreciative regards.

Kindest regards

Yours

J. Conrad

To J. B. Pinker

Text MS Berg; Unpublished

[letterhead: Spring Grove]
Kent
10. 5. 19.

My dearest Pinker.

Thank you very much for the trouble you have taken in this matter.[1] I shall write at once to the Treasury asking for a permit to forward money to Warsaw. At the same time I will get in touch with the man in Paris in case the Treasury should think fit to refuse permission and then I suppose we will have to risk it with a messenger.

I am sending you Chapters I, II, III, IV, of Part Six, of "Rescue". Will you please have the usual two copies made and return me my corrected set? I had a note from Squire asking me for more copy in order that Greiffenhagen should read it and get on with future illustrations; so when the copies are made please send one direct to Land and Water. The other set, I presume, will be going at once to the U. S.[2]

To J. E. Hodgson

Text TS/MS Bodley Eng. c.4802; Unpublished

[letterhead: Spring Grove]
12. 5. 19.

Dear Mr Hodgson

I quite understand that those reprints must be dealt with carefully if high prices are to be maintained.

its traditional tastes, until 1934. He was also editor of the English Men of Letters Series and published a prodigious amount of his own poetry and essays. Between leaving the *New Statesman* and launching the *London Mercury*, he seems to have done some work for *Land and Water*, hence the present letter; see also the letter to Shanks of 28 June.

[1] See the letter of [6 July].

[2] Perhaps mutilated by an autograph hunter, the text ends here.

It is very good of you to offer to advise me about the sale of the five booklets in question. I send them on to you, signed, and I would be glad to hear what offer you are disposed to make for them.

The catalogue you speak of in your letter has not arrived. I hope you will send me your catalogues from time to time. I should like very much to see them, though I feel it is too late in the day for me to begin a collection of fine books.

> Yours faithfully
>
> Joseph Conrad.

PS On second thoughts I send you 2 more booklets (printed by Shorter). Pray include them in the estimate.

Seven altogether.

To G. Jean-Aubry
Text MS Yale; Unpublished

> [Spring Grove]
>
> 12 Mai. [1919][1]

Cher Aubry.

Nous serons très heureux de Vous voir le Samedi. Arrivez pour le lunch, le même train (11ʰ Char +) que pour Hamstreet seulement prenez Votre ticket pour Wye. La maison est a 3 minutes de marche de la station. Borys viendra a Votre rencontre.

Vous aurez votre exemplaire de Arrow quand vous arrivez. C'est rempli de coquilles. Enfin.

Amitiés

> Tout a Vous
>
> J. C.

Translation

Dear Aubry.

We will be very glad to see you on Saturday. Come for lunch, the same train (11 am Char +) as for Hamstreet, but get your ticket for Wye. The house is three minutes' walk from the station. Borys will come to meet you.

---

[1] The reference to Wye identifies the year.

You shall have your copy of Arrow when you arrive. It's full of misprints. So be it.

Friendly regards

Yours truly

J. C.

To Hugh Walpole

Text MS Texas; Unpublished

[Spring Grove]
12 May. 1919.

Dearest Fellow.

Here's the copy[1] according to promise. I've corrected some errors and misprints – but not all. They are too many. The correct text will be that of the first English edition of which you shall of course get a copy in due time.

I've been laid up, feeling very ill and dispirited. What I dread is a "break-up" and a lingering end. However I don't think it's for this time.

B[orys]'s gone to Cambridge this morning feeling very shy and doubtful of the future, but I fancy he will soon get over that sense of unworthiness which oppresses him now.

Jessie's dear love

Ever Yours

J. Conrad.

To Sir Sidney Colvin

Text MS Lubbock; Unpublished

[Spring Grove]
Wednesday [14 or 21? May 1919][2]

My dear Colvin.

I have been laid up so long and got so much behind with Rescue that I must stay at home and keep at work. Besides I have a swollen knee which must be kept quiet if it is to get better this side of Xmas. B[orys] will attend his mother and will be much more useful to her than a dead-lame husband.

I hope however to run up about 10th June and it will be to see you and for nothing else. My health generally is very unsatisfactory. It makes me savage, and misanthropical, and pessimistic and utterly odious to gods and men.

---

[1] The US edition of *The Arrow*.

[2] According to a letter to Pinker of 30 April, the appointment with Sir Robert Jones would be in May. A letter to Quinn of 26 May implies that the consultation took place on the 24th. Earlier in the month, Borys was busy taking John to school and being interviewed in Cambridge.

Therefore I am not anxious to show myself unless to those I can trust. The only sentiment that survives my (temporary) moral degradation is my deep affection for your wife and yourself. Nothing seems able to wither that.

My dear love to Lady Colvin (and in that you are included) and my thanks for your p. c which I did not deserve.

Ever Yours

J. Conrad

To J. B. Pinker
Text Telegram Berg; Unpublished

[Wye, Kent]
[19 May 1919
11. 55][1]

Bookishly L[on]don
Received cable from Anderson[2] about cinema Rights[3] have you heard from Her

Conrad

To Richard Tanner
Text TS Texas; Unpublished

[letterhead: Spring Grove]
20. 5. 19.

Dear Mr Tanner.[4]

In reply to your letter of the 18th inst. I can see the difficulty of inserting a promise into a formal agreement, but I must confess that I don't see why the extra-cottage should not have been included in the agreement to let the house for £250 a year. However I will be perfectly satisfied with a letter from Colonel Bell, as you suggest. Indeed, considering who I am dealing with, a verbal promise would have been enough.

---

[1] Date-stamp.

[2] Jane Anderson, who continued to take an interest in Conrad's doings. Her original telegram has not survived; for its sequel, see the note to Pinker of [23 May]. She was currently in the USA, hoping to succeed in Hollywood.

[3] Conrad sold the 'world cinema rights' for *Chance*, *Victory*, and *Lord Jim* to Lawrence Giffen of the Alice Kauser Agency on 20 May and would shortly sell his share of the rights to *Romance*: see Moore, ed, *Conrad on Film*, p. 45, n. 11. See also the letters to Pinker of 9 and 10 June.

[4] Richard Tanner, of Lenhall Farm, Bishopsbourne, was estate agent to Colonel Matthew Gerald Edward Bell, lord of the manor of Bishopsbourne and owner of Oswalds, the Conrads' final residence.

I will be glad to get the agreement in due course and then we will be able to arrange a date for the experts to examine the electric light installation. But that had better be done some time in September. However I hope to see Mrs Bell and perhaps the Colonel himself, and certainly you, between this and the date of our taking possession, and we will be able to arrange all those matters in the way most convenient to the Colonel and Mrs Bell.

Yours faithfully

Joseph Conrad.

To J. B. Pinker
Text MS Berg; Unpublished

[Spring Grove]
[c. 21 May 1919]¹

Dearest Pinker.

Do, pray, inquire into this. I answered W. H. S[mi]t[h]s telling them that those burlesque titles make me think that somebody has been pulling the enquirer's leg.[2] I also asked them to answer any communication they may receive from you.

Yours

J. C.

To G. P. Putnam's Sons Co.
Text TS Elstob; Unpublished

[letterhead: Spring Grove]
Kent
21. 5. 19

Dear Sirs.[3]

You have an exaggerated idea of my obscurity as an author. When a book of mine appears anybody who has got a pair of eyes and has the time to look at [the] daily paper will be able to find out the name of my publisher and

---

[1] Written on the recto of a letter from W. H. Smith, the booksellers, dated 20 May.

[2] On behalf of a customer, Smith's had asked if Conrad were the author of *The Baldheaded Man* and *The Waitress Bold* because they had had a request from America for thirty copies of each. *The Bald-headed Man* is a novel by Andrew Simpson (New York: Broadway Publishing (c. 1912)). The other title is a phantom.

[3] Although the original request came from G. H. Grubb, an employee, Conrad fired his broadside at the firm. Putnam's, a New York house, had published the first US edition of *Typhoon* in 1902.

the price of the book. Therefore I don't think it necessary to send you the information you require.

Yours faithfully

Joseph Conrad

To J. B. Pinker
Text MS Berg; Unpublished

[Spring Grove]
[23 May 1919]¹

My dear Pinker
    I've just got this. As I don't know anything of the present situation the decision must rest with you.² Pray let me know.

Ever Yours

J. C.

To J. B. Pinker
Text TS/MS Berg; Unpublished

[Spring Grove]
[c. 24 May 1919]³

Dearest Pinker.
    Thank you for your letter. The cable was a pleasant surprise. The Jane Anderson cable was a still greater surprise and you will know how to deal with it; but nothing would surprise me on her part, not even her ability to acquire the rights in some way or other.
    I do intend to carry out the plan I outlined to you and I am much interested in what you say about Frank Vernon.⁴ If, as you say, he is so friendly perhaps you could arrange that luncheon before very long. It occurs to me that a talk with him before I tackle the actual job may be of some help in settling my views as to how it is to be done. I am alluding now to the *Agent*.⁵ I have an instinct for what is dramatically effective; what I am not certain of is the nature of stage effects. If it was not for the consideration of encroaching on your time I would just as soon see F. V. here for the day, if he could be induced to come. Of course you must be present when we meet.

---

¹ Written on the back of a telegram from Jane Anderson received on this date.
² The telegram reads: 'Fifteen day extension option imperative please see that Pinker grants this immediately Dearest Love Jane Anderson' (Berg).
³ The period of the cables about film rights.
⁴ A producer, author, and translator. See Conrad's letter to him of 23 November.
⁵ Conrad began his adaptation of *The Secret Agent* in October 1919; it was staged in November 1922.

Are we to see you with Ralph here on Monday, as it was suggested, though I think not absolutely decided on when you were here?

Thank you for receiving B[orys] personally. He tells me that Dana had called you on the telephone as he wished to see you. I wonder what was the important matter? I hope it wasn't only to tell you that the play would be taken off in a fortnight.[1]

Please, when you write, tell me a little more of F. Vernon because though I have heard the name I know nothing precise about his activities in the theatrical world.

Do you know anything about another Joseph Conrad who has published a novel some time ago?[2] I never heard of him but there is no doubt that the novel exists, for I have heard of it from two different people. Has there been anything of the sort to your knowledge within the last, say, five or six years?

Ever affect^{ly} Yours

J. Conrad

PS. A certain notion (of the fiscal order) has occurred to me the other day; but I don't want to write about it. So you may see me in town next week for I fancy it is quite worth my taking your advice on it. This of course if you do *not* come with R[alph] on Monday in which case I could state it in five minutes here, for your consideration.

To Richard Curle
Text MS Indiana; Curle 41[3]

[letterhead: Spring Grove]
Kent.
25th May '19

My dear Curle.

Just a word of welcome – from a bed of sickness. I've had a most awful time – ever since Jan^y.

I've just finished the Rescue!

Of course my dear fellow you must come to see us as soon as you can spare the time. My poor wife has to contemplate the delightful prospect of another operation in about 3 months' time.

---

[1] Henry Dana and Marie Löhr were going to close *Victory* on 14 June.
[2] Supposedly the author of *The Bald-headed Man* and *The Waitress Bold*: see the letter of [c. 21 May].
[3] Curle omits 'Just a word . . . since Jan^y', 'Of course . . . the time', and 'All that . . . forgotten'.

I've here a set of privately prin^d booklets (of various things of mine) for you also a 1st Ed copy of Shadow Line and the complete first set corrected proofs of the new ed^{on} of Nostromo.[1] All that may prove to you that you have not been forgotten.

Au revoir then. Drop us a line.

Yours always

J. Conrad

To J. B. Pinker
Text TS Berg; Unpublished

[letterhead: Spring Grove]
Kent
25. 5. 19.

Dearest Pinker.

I finished "The Rescue" at one o'clock to-day. The final batch in my possession consists of Chapters VI, VII, VIII and IX; a little over fourteen thousand words which will be in your hands before one o'cl. on Wednesday. I have just written a note to Squire to set his mind at rest, sending a friendly message to Greiffenhagen and a few words of acknowledgement for Foster and Allison; for I do feel that in all this affair we have been treated very well by "Land & Water".

I am still too seedy to feel very much elated at the termination of a task which would never have been done without the support of your steady friendship and unwearied devotion to my affairs. I am so profoundly conscious of it that with the end of every book my thought turns naturally towards you first with affectionate regard.

Ever Yours

J. Conrad

To John Quinn
Text TS NYPL; Unpublished

[letterhead: Spring Grove]
Kent
26. 5. 19.

My dear Quinn.

Thank you very much for your friendly and interesting letter of April 28th. We are rejoiced to hear that the operation has apparently re-established

---

[1] This backlog of presentation copies was the consequence of Curle's long absence overseas.

your health. My wife, who has had already two operations was extremely interested and moved by the description of your feelings. She didn't say much to me about her own but I suppose she understood thoroughly what you said.[1] You will sympathise with her, my dear Quinn, when you hear that she has to live now for the next three months with the prospect of another ordeal of the same kind. The bones having failed to join thoroughly Sir Robert Jones has decided two days ago to perform another operation at the end of August. It's not a very pleasant prospect to live with, but Sir Robert Jones promises success definitely this time. I have been more or less seedy ever since January last and even at the present time I am not free from gout yet, not being able to do more than hobble painfully from one room to another. On the other hand Borys seems to be quite well now and the boy John though lanky and long for his age is strong enough, and he left us for school after the Easter holidays full of good resolutions about his work.

I am absolutely in accord with your opinion on the European situation, including in that, of course, the attitude and the action of the U. S.[2] It is a most horrible tangle which has never been faced with proper resolution. I can't say I feel happy about it. I am trying to keep my thoughts away from that moral and political chaos which is so disturbing to contemplate.

Yesterday I wrote the last words of "The Rescue". I would have loved to have dedicated that book to you, but it has been promised to Mr Penfield in gratitude for his exertions to liberate the Conrad tribe from captivity to

---

[1] Quinn's response to being told that the chances of his surviving the operation were at most 85 per cent was to think upon mortality: '"Terror" wasn't the feeling I had, nor fear. I wasn't afraid of the future or of my past – not for one thousandth part of a second ... Tourgenif* said somewhere ... that "death is the one irreparable thing". The feelings of a man who may be going to his death are really indescribable. I wasn't stupefied or my feelings benumbed ... I was thinking twenty things at one time and it was all inexpressible; there was so much to say that I said nothing ... So I know what the feeling is that you and the Missus have had hanging over you' (Quinn to Conrad, 28 April, TS carbon NYPL).

[2] 'In my opinion the armistice was the greatest blunder in all history. If the war was fought to end German militarism, the best way of ending German militarism would have been the destruction or capture or unconditional surrender of the German army, with only its broken remnants escaping across the Rhine. The greatest opportunity in all the world to inflict such a tremendous lesson in applied psychology upon the Germans was lost when the French and the English weakly, and I think, stupidly agreed to grant an armistice to the Germans on Wilson's ambiguous fourteen points. The politicians nearly lost the war ... Without any treaty of peace Germany cannot fight for ten or twenty years, but unless she is now permanently disarmed, not temporarily demobolized*, and unless there is a perpetual inspection ... of her forts, arsenals, munition plants and all other factories capable of making munitions ... in thirty or forty years she will re-arm those seventy million brutes in the heart of Europe, still worshipping only force' (*ibid.*). Quinn also wrote at length about the importance of granting Danzig (Gdańsk) to the Poles.

the Austrian philistines.[1] Thank you very much, my dear Quinn, for your friendly, wise and indulgent behaviour in the miserable imbroglio about the A. of G.[2] Your enlightened appreciation of that book has given me the greatest possible pleasure. The Napoleonic novel which I refer to mentally as "Quinn's book" will be a very different piece of work. It was destined for you long before I even began to write the "Arrow of Gold", and then, on a sudden impulse, I decided not to keep you waiting for that sign of my regard all that time. Curle was to get the next volume of short stories. However fates willed it otherwise and muddled up the whole affair most effectively. And, by the way, Curle has just returned from S. Africa and after dropping me a line from London has proceeded on a visit to his people in the North. I expect him in a few days here, when I shall tell him that the "Arrow" is dedicated to him; for he doesn't know anything about it yet. He is a little eccentric and a little trying, but his friendship is above suspicion and he is the most devoted of my "young braves". I do feel a real affection for him.

I am a little too tired with the rush of the last lap of "The Rescue" to write any more to-day. My wife sends you her warm regards and I am my dear Quinn

Affect^ly Yours

Joseph Conrad.

To J. B. Pinker
Text MS Colgate; Unpublished

[Spring Grove]
Tuesday. [27 May 1919][3]

Dearest Pinker.

I was glad to get your handwritten note. Thanks.

Herewith Chap. vi & vii part Six. of Rescue. Pray put them out to be clean-copied, for it is only right that Greiffenhagen should have some time to think out his illustrations. Tomorrow ev^g I shall post to you Chap viii and ix – which is the last.

Ever Affect^ly Yours

J. C.

---

[1] The Biblical Philistines were Samson's captors.
[2] 'It was awfully fine of you to think of dedicating the book to me. I appreciate the honor tremendously – more than I can say. I am especially pleased that you thought of dedicating a book which meant so much to you personally to me. But our friend Curle richly deserved it. I think he had prior claims to mine' (*ibid.*).
[3] Conrad sent on Chapter viii later that day. On the 25th, Conrad had written of having Chapters vi–ix still 'in my possession'.

To J. B. Pinker

Text MS Colgate; Unpublished

[Spring Grove]

27. 5. 19.

Dearest Pinker.

Herewith viii of Part Six *Rescue*. Tomorrow I will send you the ix and last.

———————

Thanks for original type of iii. iv. v p^t six received yesterday together with dupl^{te} copy of same which I shall return to you in a day or two for sending to the States.

———————

Yes. Jane seems slightly distracted.

———————

Please tell your (our) collicitor* on 'phone that I thank him for draft of will and that I haven't yet looked at it but shall do so directly R is off my mind for good.

Next thing is that I've to judge short stories for L & W. There are 13 of them in the house crying for notice.[1]

Ever Yours

J. C.

To T. Fisher Unwin

Text MS Rosenbach; Unpublished

[letterhead: Spring Grove]

27. 5. 19.

Dear Sir.

Thanks very much for the copy of Lynds book.[2] It was very kind of you to send it to me.

---

[1] The other judges were Arnold Bennett and S. Neville Foster, and their adjudications appeared in the 12 June issue of *Land and Water* (p. 12). The winners were Ethel Colburn Mayne and H. J. Jones; Conrad expressed his preference for the former. A Conrad letter clearly intended for Foster and dated 30 May 1919 was sold at auction in Marburg, Germany, on 19–20 June 1984, but it has once more gone out of sight. According to the catalogue, it reads in part: 'I return the stories which truly did not demand a great amount of thought but have caused me a good deal of perplexity. However I have affixed . . . consecutive No's to five of the stories. Of course I'll associate myself with any verdict You and Bennet[t] may agree upon . . . Pray send me proof of Part Six if it can be managed without inconvenience' (J. A. Stargardt, Catalogue no. 631).

[2] Unwin had recently published Robert Lynd's *Old and New Masters*, which has a dozen pages on Conrad.

As to the proofs of A of G. I would have been much distressed if you had not sent them to me. I devote particular care to the text of the English Edition always and it is to be considered the standard one.

Believe me

Very faithfully Yours

Joseph Conrad.

To Sir Sidney Colvin

Text MS Hofstra; J-A, 2, 221

[Spring Grove]

29 May 1919

My dear Colvin.

Thanks for your good letter. I shall certainly try to come up in the first fortnight of June.

I could send you a copy of *Arrow of Gold* US edition, but the correct text will be that of the 1st English edition which I have just passed for the press. But that won't come out till Oct*er*. The U. S. ed: text is faulty and I would like Lady Colvin and yourself to first see the *A of G* at its best.

On the 25th May (Rogation Sunday[1]) I wrote the last words of *The Rescue* which I began about 22 years ago![2] On the 28th I finished revising the final chapter, and now I am done with the thing till proofs of book-form begin to come in – next year some time.

I shall feel much honoured to be mentionned* in your article in the Scribners Mag.[3] It was very dear of you to send me the pages to see. Do you wish me to return them to you? I am delighted to have proof visual that you are at work on the material of your reminiscences in that informal manner. The tone is charming. Jess is just gone out for a drive. She's keeping her cheery serenity – but what a horrid prospect to live with! With my dear love to you both

Ever Yours

J. Conrad

---

[1] The fifth after Easter, the prelude to the three days of prayer and fasting preceding the feast of the Ascension.

[2] In March 1896.

[3] See the letter of [14 July]: these articles were published in 1920.

To J. B. Pinker

Text MS Berg; Unpublished

[Spring Grove]
Thursday. [29 May 1919][1]

My dear Pinker

Herewith the last pp of Rescue – almost good enough for book-form as they stand.

Give our warm regards to Mrs Pinker. We hope she is already improving. We hope to have good news tomorrow through Ralph who looks quite himself again.

Jessie has asked me for the quarter's pension (20) a little in advance. Pray send it to her. The prices are awful.

I hope to see you soon after Whit'tide.[2] Am better. Hope to goodness it will last.

Ever Yours

J. Conrad.

To G. Jean-Aubry

Text MS Yale; *L. fr.* 145

[Spring Grove]
30. 5. 19.

Très cher.

Je viens d'envoyer Votre addresse au Dr Tebb – le medecin que V[ou]S avez vu chez moi l'hiver passé a Londres. Il veut V[ou]S demander quelques conseils sur la meilleure manière de disposer de quelques lithographies de Rodin[3] (early manner) qu'il veut vendre a Londres ou à Paris. Je Vous serai infiniment obligé si V[ou]S lui indiquez la meilleure manière de s'y prendre.

Je suis un peu mieux. Je me repose – oui! Mais je ne sais pas comment ça se fait, je ne suis pas a mon aise ni mentalement ni moralement.

Tout à Vous

J. Conrad.[4]

---

[1] The day Conrad finished revising *The Rescue*.

[2] Whitsuntide: this year the ecclesiastical celebration of Pentecost would fall on Sunday, 8 June, and the secular holiday on the 9th.

[3] Redon, not Rodin: see the letter to Pinker of 2 September. Rodin never made prints.

[4] A telegram in the Jean-Aubry papers at Yale reads 'Expecting you thursday we presume by train to Wye if motoring adviseable* to start at ten regards Conrad': the date-stamp is blurred but appears to be 10 Ju[ne], and the message was received at Wye Post Office at 4.58 p.m.; 12 June was a Thursday.

Translation

Dear Friend.

I have just sent your address to Dr Tebb, the doctor you saw at my place in London last winter. He wants to ask you for some advice about the best way to dispose of some Rodin* lithographs (early manner) that he wishes to sell in London or Paris. I will be greatly obliged to you if you tell him the best way of bringing this about.

I am a little better. I relax – yes! But I do not know to what end; I am not at ease either mentally or morally.

Yours truly

J. Conrad.

To Hugh Walpole
Text MS Texas; J-A, 2, 222

Spring Grove
Wye
30. 5. 19

My dear Walpole.

I am delighted with your app[reciati]^{on} of A of G. and touched by the terms in which it is expressed.

You have put your critical finger on the spot. It is true that Mme Blunt-George scene is too long. But something may be said for it. Still it is a defect.

I'll be truly glad to see you here as soon as you can spare the time on your return to town.

On the 25 the last words of R were written – and on 28th I finished revising the last pages. And so that book begun 22 years ago passes out of my hands.

Glad to feel from your letter to Jessie that you have a great grip on your work and that your work has got such strong hold of you. This is a blessed state.

With great affection

Yours

J Conrad.

To J. B. Pinker
Text MS Berg; Unpublished

Spring Grove
Wye.
Kent
Wednesday [4 June 1919][1]

My dear Pinker

Thanks for the notes and the amount paid to B[orys] C[onrad]'s account. In the matter of the de luxe edition. D[oubleday] P[age] & Co. have in their hands corrected and with prefaces or notes:

Al.'s Folly (just arranged with Quinn to have the old preface printed)
Outcast. – new author's note.
T. of Unrest – new author's note.
The Nigger. – Original preface and author's note.

next to the *Nigger* should come *Lord Jim* and then *Youth*. Both these books should be printed from Dent's 5/- edition, which is correct as to text and has author's notes. You may send them copies direct, without further revision by me. – This gives them six vols, absolutely ready, to go on with at once.

Youth should be followed by *Typhoon* and I am writing today to Heinemann asking him to send me a copy for revision. I shall also write an author's note and you shall have the prepared vol after the holidays for transmission to Garden City. *Nostromo* comes next and for that we have the 5/- Dent's edition corrected and provided with an author's note. Therefore if you send them a copy of *N* together with a copy of *Typhoon* they will have 8 books ready for them in July. I asked D[oubleday] twice at what rate he meant to publish the de Luxe Ed^{on} but he did not tell me. Does he mean to have everything (up to *Chance*) out this year? That does not seem likely to me. However, to make all safe, will you be good enough to direct Meth: to send for revision copies of: *Mirror.* (6/- ed^{on}) and *Secret Agent, Set of Six, Under Western Eyes* (any edition).

Thanks my dear Pinker for your consent to act as trustee under my will. You have conveyed my intentions to the solicitor exactly. I have but a question to ask as to the effect of one clause about which I am in doubt. I hope to come up on the Thursday after the holiday and see you between 12 and 1 o'clock. I note what you say of Unwin's preliminary announcement of the

[1] On [29 May] Conrad promised a visit to London after the Whitsun holiday; here he is more specific.

pub^on of *Arrow*. The word "immediately" is in it and that is why I thought it better to advise you of it.

Ever Yours

J. Conrad.

To J. B. Pinker
Text MS Berg; Unpublished

[letterhead: Spring Grove]

Monday 9th. June '19

My dear Pinker.

I am again laid up. It's perfectly useless to hope to keep my app[oin]t[m]^ent with you on Wed:

As the matter of concluding with the Film people is important I am considerably worried. Have you anything to suggest? Perhaps a clerk from the Consulate could be sent down for the purpose?[1]

I am frightfully cast down.

B[orys] will arrive about noon on Wednesday bringing with him sec^ons III IV. V VI VII VIII IX of Pt Six Resc: typed copy marked for *US* in the same way as the previous batches – and this lot will complete *typed (corr^ed) Copy* for U. S. from which the serial is to be or has already begun to be printed.

As to galley slips D[oubleday] asks for, for his personal enjoyment I can't spare him my dup^te set which I intend to correct and use for setting up the book text.

Will you please either give or leave for B a ch: for £13. He will go on to Ripley and deposit John and then if Ralph cares to return here that way he would call for him sometime between 4. 30 and six at Bury[s] Court. It's very probable Cath: Willard will be in the car for the sake of the run but there will be plenty of room for Ralph['s] valise. Please consult the parties interested and tell B when you see him on Wed: if he is to call or not.

Ever affect^ly Your

J. Conrad

Curle has been here since Sat. He wishes to be remembered to you. The Fagans were here.[2] Between ourselves he's rather a fatuous person. I want to see F Vernon more than ever.

[1] A clerk from the United States Consulate to witness the signing of a film contract for *Romance*, the fourth of the novels bought by the Kauser Agency on behalf of Famous Players-Lasky. In the end, Conrad travelled to the United States Embassy for the settlement (Moore, ed., *Conrad on Film*, p. 45, nn. 10, 11; *MFJC*, p. 143).

[2] James Bernard Fagan and his wife Mary (née Grey). Born in Ireland in 1873, James Fagan was an actor–manager and copious playwright. In September 1918 he took over the Court Theatre, where his first productions were *The School for Scandal* and *The Lost Leader*.

To J. B. Pinker
Text MS Berg; Unpublished

[Spring Grove]

Tuesday *11 pm* [10 June 1919][1]

Dearest Pinker

I don't propose to acknowledge D[oubleday]'s letter to me in any way. – All this seems to me rather outrageous (and also silly) in the way he seems to threaten us with his partners' displeasure.[2] I must say I am disagreeably impressed. But You will know how to deal with the situation.

I am so much better today that I may venture to hope to be well enough to come up on Monday and sign at the consulate. Just let me know what you wish. Indeed my dear fellow I don't want to cause you more worry than I can help.

Ever Yours affect[ly]

J. C.

To Edmund Candler
Text MS Morgan; Candler xxxvii

[letterhead: Spring Grove]

14 June '19

My dear Candler.

Many thanks for the inscribed Copy. I have all your works except the *Vagabond* which, Hatchards tell me, is out of print, and the *Sepoy* which I am awaiting with impatience.[3]

I am getting better but still feel too broken up to leave the house. It is dear of you to promise us a visit. I am ashamed of myself not to have rushed over to see you directly you arrived. But I really could not put foot to the ground. Do let us know how you get on. One is still a little anxious. I own that for my own part I haven't yet got quite over the scare of the first news of your illness – You indomitable man.

On the 28 May I finished correcting the last pages of *Rescue*, and so that novel begun 22 years ago[4] has passed out of my hands – at last. The same evening I picked up *Siri Ram*[5] as I limped to bed and went on reading it through the still, very still, hours of the night to the end, marvelling and musing over the pages. It was a great experience.

---

[1] On the verso of a letter from Doubleday, 23 May.
[2] Doubleday wanted to lower the royalties on the collected edition.
[3] Candler's narrative of travel *A Vagabond in Asia* came out in 1900, and *The Sepoy* in 1919.
[4] 23.   [5] See the notes to the letter to Candler of 12 November 1918.

My wife joins me in warm regards to yourself and Your house.

Affectionately yours

J. Conrad.

To J. B. Pinker

Text MS Berg; Unpublished

[Spring Grove]

17. June '19

My dear Pinker.

I forgot yesterday to tell you that Capt Arthur Halsey R. N. (my landlord) wants the balance of his rent paid to his account in Drummond's Bank 49 Charing Cross. The amount is £*96. 12. 0* and it falls *due* on the *24 June*. Will you please do that for me?

As I took away from you the envelope on which you made a note of my request to pay £50 to my acc^t at the bank I venture to remind you of it here.

In the matter of the proceeds from the Film agreement I think I am right in assuming that the gross amount is £4. 400, of which Hueffer's share is £550 leaving £3. 850 of which (if my arithmetic is right) £770 belong to you and £3080 to me (on the *"one-fifth"* basis as agreed between us and covering everything, except book-rights and such serial rights whose proceeds do *not* reach the sum of £1000, for my lifetime).[1]

Assuming the above to be correct pray my dear Pinker invest in Gov^t bonds (at 80 I think you advised) 2250 and pay £500 into a deposit acc^t to the bank with only a fortnights withdrawal notice if possible – if not then a month. I will tell you when we meet why I reserve that sum but meantime pray believe it isn't for gambling on the stock exchange – or anywhere else. The balance of £330 please pay to my current acc^t as I want to have the disposal of that sum outside my current expenses.

I think this is enough worry to send you in one letter. Thanks for the copies of Mirror and Set of Six received this morning. I'll need Western Eyes – Sec^t Ag^t – very soon. I don't feel very much like writing these prefaces for D[oubleday]'s edition.[2] I hope you'll insist on £2000 for the extended edition. D's groans about the cost of production and the discount leave me

---

[1] The total for the film rights to *Romance, Lord Jim, Chance,* and *Victory* came to $22,500; of this, Ford received $2,500 for his share of *Romance* and Conrad the rest, less Pinker's commission (Moore, ed., *Conrad on Film*, p. 34).

[2] Nevertheless Conrad wrote Author's Notes to the books requested here as well as to those listed on [4 June]: *An Outcast* and *Tales of Unrest.*

cold. Indeed I've been making a small calculation and his figures strike me as absurd.

Jessie sends her love.

Ever Yours

J. Conrad.

To Richard Curle
Text MS Indiana; Curle 42

[Spring Grove]

Thursday. [19 June 1919][1]

Très cher Ami.

I have shown B[orys] your letter. He was getting too wretched at his unattached state[2] and no prospect of even some try in any direction. He has been immensely cheered, and, I assure you, he is properly appreciative of your friendly earnestness in the matter. So are his Mother and Father. We shall expect you next week as you suggest and then I'll tell you all about my business journey to town and of my arrangements as to the disposal of the money amounting to about £3080 *nett*.

I am glad to see the Arrow has pleased you. I am not at all sure of a good reception here. The sales in America are I understand a good deal better than Chance's or Victory's.[3]

I am considerably better. How long it will last no one can tell. Pink[er] told me he had seen you. He feels very friendly towards you.

Jessie's love

Ever Yours

J. Conrad

PS We shall be truly glad to see the Wedgwoods here any time they feel inclined to run out.

To Sir Sidney Colvin
Text MS Duke; Unpublished

[Spring Grove]

20th June '19

My dear Colvin.

Smitten by remorse at Lady Colvin's letter to Jessie I have this moment dispatched a copy of the *Arrow* (U. S.) to Lady Colvin. You'll have to wait for yours (U. K.) till early Sept*er*.

---

[1] Date from Curle: references to the film negotiations, Conrad's 'business journey' on the 16th, and Curle's visit 'next week' confirm this dating.

[2] Unattached to a job.   [3] Which had been vigorous.

I proceed to town on Monday and I should like to know if I may call soon after 4 o'clock and stay somewhat more than five minutes. Pray 'phone to Pinker 1809 Gerrard before noon on Monday.

If that is inconvenient then perhaps I may come on Tuesday soon after 3. I intend to start for home early in the afternoon.

Ever yours

J. C.

To Major Kenneth Campbell
Text MS Private collection; Unpublished

[Spring Grove]
21 June '19

My dear Capt Campbell[1]

Ever so many thanks for the parcel and your note. Your instructions are being attended to but it is too soon yet for a report.

I have still flying twinges and mild pain – spots in various parts of my anatomy. But I am so used to that that I consider myself in a fairly good state. Walking, which I have tried is not a success. It gives me an all-pervading pain in the ankle-joints which is not acute but is very disabling.

I am venturing on a journey to town on monday and even propose to spend one night there. A lot of little vexing affairs require my attendance but I shall try to take it all calmly – very calmly.

Ever your grateful

Joseph Conrad.

PS Don't you think it's about time you dropped the [Mr] to Conrad. Our friendship has now a good standing in mere years; and certainly in the depth of sentiment! Jessie sends her warm regards.

---

[1] Dr Kenneth Campbell had been an officer in the Royal Army Medical Corps and chief ophthalmic surgeon, Southern Command. Although Conrad addresses him here as Captain, Campbell was now a major. He had a practice in London and a country house in Wittersham, Kent, about twenty miles from Spring Grove. On 15 September 1919, Jessie Conrad wrote to Warrington Dawson: 'Conrad has been certainly much better since Major Campbell R.A.M.C. an old friend took him in hand. It is largely a faith cure between ourselves but none the less complete and comforting' (Randall, p. 197). Borys Conrad, however, told Randall that Campbell 'was *not* my father's physician . . . Any professional advice which he may have given would have been in consultation with Dr Fox, who was the family doctor at that time. My father would have been most punctilious on this point' (*ibid.*, p. 197, n. 1). Campbell died in 1943.

To Edmund Candler

Text MS Morgan; Candler xxxviii

[Spring Grove]
21 June '19

My dear Candler.

Ever so many thanks for Copy of Sepoy.

Everything you write is a matter of most sympathetic interest to me; and in the case of this book I must say I enjoyed it thoroughly in every way, in the facts, in the presentation and in the spirit of the writing itself.[1]

We are awaiting the word of your coming. But my dear fellow couldn't you stay the night? I would like a few quiet hours with you. You are liable to fly off [to] the ends of the world at any moment – and I am not getting any younger – and my affectionate regard for you is a sentiment of old standing. Do you realise how old it is? It isn't (to put it impressively) very far from a quarter of a century – well say one-fifth of a century not to make ourselves out older than absolutely necessary.

Ever Yours

J. Conrad

To Mr Roberts

Text MS Yale; Unpublished

[letterhead: Spring Grove]
Kent.
26 June '19

Dear M[r] Roberts[2]

Many thanks for your letter and the proof of review. It is a great satisfaction to me to see the *Arrow* widely appreciated.

I regret not to have anything to send you. As a matter of fact I am engaged for two more stories to the *Metropolitan Mag* and I'll have of course to complete my arrangement with them first of all. I have just finished a long

---

[1] In a series of sketches, Candler depicted the Indian soldiers he had met while serving as an official war correspondent in Mesopotamia.
[2] Without an envelope or any other indication of provenance, the identity of this recipient is uncertain. Since Conrad's novel was not published in Britain until August, his correspondent is likely to have been an editor with an American periodical.

novel and to tell you the truth I don't feel like writing anything at all just
now.
Believe me,

Sincerely yours

Joseph Conrad.

To Sir Sidney Colvin
Text MS Private collection; Unpublished

[Spring Grove]
Wye.
27. 6. 19

My dear Colvin.
Ever so many thanks for the Keats Letters.[1]
It has been good to breathe the atmosphere of friendship at 35 Pl^{ce} G^{ds}
Terr^{ce}.[2]
Apart from Gibbon in whose flat I stayed the night I saw no one in town.
It was exclusively a visit to your abode – almost a pilgrimage. For if one's
friendships are the gift of the Gods the place where such friends as you two
dwell must have something of the nature of a temple where one experiences
the blessing of unquestioning faith and a feeling of peace.
Our dear love

Ever Yours,

J. Conrad.

To Richard Curle
Text MS Indiana; Curle 43

[Spring Grove]
Friday. [27 June 1919][3]

Dear Richard.
You are very good. Both I and B[orys] agree absolutely with your view
that this matter should be negociated* personally and *not* by letter.
Please catch the 11 AM from Char + tomorrow (Sat.). We will meet you
at Ashford.

---

[1] Colvin's edition of *Letters of John Keats to His Family and Friends* (Macmillan, 1891).
[2] Palace Gardens Terrace, named after Kensington Palace.
[3] Presumably going by a postmark, Curle dates this as [28 June], a Saturday. Here Conrad
continues the agenda of [19 June].

Edmund Candler is coming by the same train to stay till Sunday.

Yours ever

JC.

To Edward Buxton Shanks

Text MS Indiana; Unpublished

[letterhead: Spring Grove]

Sat 28 June '19

Dear M[r] Shanks.[1]

I've just written to the Chief[2] – but it will all work out all right.

I have here my dup[ate] set of Pt VI up to galley *NINE* duly corrected. Therefore what you have got, incl[ing] galley NINE ending with the words "saved from himself" *is* corrected – and if they did not set up from that but from some uncorrected slips it is neither your fault nor mine. It is quite possible that the Chief in the press of business forgot to give the corr[d] slips (Part VI galleys one to Nine) to the printers. I did send that lot addressed to him in good time. Perhaps you will be able to lay hold of them. They must be somewhere in the office, unless the post failed to deliver.

The last instal[ent] extends about half way down galley FOUR and ends with the words "... no stratagem O Tuan?"

Therefore you have in hand (somewhere) about 4½ galleys duly corr[d] – enough for the next instal[t].

Meantime I shall correct all the galleys above NINE to the end and send them to you without delay.

Thanks for giving your earnest attention to this matter. M[aurice] G[reiffenhagen]'s last full-page with its remote suggestion of byzantine art is very good. Strange how one gets an impression of opulent, sultry colour from that 'black-and-white'.[3] If he meant it then it's quite a feat.

Kindest regards

Yours

J. Conrad

---

[1] Edward Richard Buxton Shanks (1892–1953) the poet, novelist, editor, and critic went to war in 1914 after a distinguished undergraduate career at Cambridge; in 1915 he was invalided out of the army and transferred to the War Office; from 1919 to 1922, he was assistant editor of the recently founded *London Mercury*; later he became a lecturer at the University of Liverpool and chief leader-writer for the London *Evening Standard*. His abundant bibliography includes *Queen of China and Other Poems* (1919), *Collected Poems* (1926), *Tom Tiddler's Ground* (1934), *Edgar Allan Poe* (1937), and *Rudyard Kipling* (1940).

[2] Foster, of *Land and Water*.

[3] Greiffenhagen had made his name by the exotic illustrations to Rider Haggard's romances.

PS The returned slips One to NINE were addressed to the Editor of L & W at 5. *Chan^y Lane*! So perhaps when you shifted they stuck there?

To G. Jean-Aubry
Text MS Yale; Unpublished

[Spring Grove]

Thursday. [3? July 1919][1]

My dear Aubry

We are very much grieved at the news of your illness. We hope it is nothing serious. Pray give us a line of news. We trust it will be news of improvement and that we shall soon have the pleasure of seeing Mrs Hardi[ng][2] and you here.

Kindest regards from everybody

Tout à Vous

J Conrad.

To Mary Pinker
Text MS Indiana; Unpublished

[Spring Grove]

5 July. '19

Dear Mrs Pinker,

It was very good of you to write and I am patting myself on the back for having found a specimen which you like.

I trust you have heard by this time from my wife's sister. Jessie wired to her on Thursday urging her to conclude, if at all possible, and advise you direct, at once. We understand perfectly well that Phillippa[3] must be placated without loss of time. Jessie went out on Friday to raid two villages but returned empty-handed, I am sorry to say.

Ralph's course is coming to an end on Thursday next and I understand he intends to travel home on that day. We shall all miss him very much. He is a dear boy. I don't think his residence here has profited him much, but, really, Wye as a teaching college is nothing short of a public scandal, and Ralph is not to be blamed in the matter of lost time.

Believe me, dear Mrs Pinker,

always Your very faithful servant

Joseph Conrad.

---

[1] No doubt on the strength of a postmark, Jean-Aubry noted the date as 6 July, which was a Sunday. Either Conrad confused the days of the week, or someone forgot to post the letter.
[2] The singer and patron, Louise Alvar Harding: see the letter to her of 3 November.
[3] A lonely pet belonging to Oenone, the Pinkers' daughter?

To J. B. Pinker
Text MS Private collection; Unpublished

[letterhead: Spring Grove]
Sunday. [6 July 1919]¹

My dear Pinker.

I drop you a line to tell you that I have heard from Warsaw and that the poor girl² has got the money all right.

Thanks are due to you for this, too, amongst the many other things you are doing for me So unweariedly.

Galsworthy's* are coming on the 9ᵗʰ· for the day. On Friday we are going to Essex to see the Hopes and we shall be back on Monday early to receive miss Capes³ who is coming for a couple of days.

I write you all this in view of the Vernon visit. Miss C would not be in the way of that.

Miss Hallowes will be back about the 20th. I should like to begin something then and, for preference, the *play*; should V. be at all encouraging.

Jessies love

Ever yours

J. Conrad

To Richard Curle
Text MS Indiana; Curle 44

[letterhead: Spring Grove]
7. July. '19.

My dear Curle.

Many thanks for your letter and for all the trouble you are taking about B[orys]'s future and my own affairs. The question of your health is very much in my mind. Do take care of Yourself as far as it lies in your power.

The letter from Your dealer in books reads eminently satisfactor[il]y. Pray give him his head on the U. S. road and we shall see what prize he pulls off.

On Fridʸ next we proceed to Essex.⁴ We will be back here on Sunday evening. Miss H. M. H. Capes arrives for a 2–3 days' stay on Monday afternoon. The next week-end is clear.

Ever Yours

J. C.

---

¹ Dated by the calendar of visits in the letter of 7 July.
² Very possibly his cousin Karola Zagórska (1885–1955), a singer, who visited the Conrads in 1916 and 1920. A letter to Pinker of 5 February 1920 refers to helping her financially when she was in poor health.
³ Harriet Mary Capes (1849–1936), a writer of books for children, was the dedicatee of *A Set of Six* and editor of *Wisdom and Beauty from Conrad* (1915).
⁴ The 11th.

The n° of Nth Am^{an} Review[1] awaits you here. It was concealed inside the damned armchair.

PS Jessie sends her love. Drop her a line if you are coming.

To Edward Garnett
Text MS Bryn Mawr; G. 287

[Spring Grove]
Kent
Monday 7th July '19

Dearest Edward.

It was the instinct (not the sense – the instinct) of what you have discerned with your unerring eye that kept me off the R. for 20 years or more.[2] That – and nothing else. My instinct was right. But all the same I cannot say I regret the impulse which made me take it up again. I am settling my affairs in this world and I should not have liked to leave behind me this evidence of having bitten off more than I could chew. A very vulgar vanity. Could anything be more legitimate?

The "innumerable multitude" for which I write falls naturally into two parts. One is composed of Edward Garnett and the other of the rest of mankind. To that last I can talk back. To Edward I cannot. And it is not my dear fellow that I have erected you into a fetish. There is nothing mystic in my attitude to you. There never has been. It is not vague dread that you inspired but an absolute confidence.[3]

I wouldn't like you to think my friendship importunate but I must remind you of your promise to come and see us in this house (which is odious). But perhaps sitting smoking together we could manage to forget where we are. Week-end, middle week, any time – and for as many days as you can spare.

---

[1] Whatever had attracted Conrad's or Curle's interest in a recent issue of the *North American Review*, it was nothing about themselves.

[2] In June 1896 Garnett wrote a detailed and encouraging commentary on 'The Rescuer', Part One (*Letters*, 1, pp. 283–7; *Portrait*, pp. 22–5). The very closeness of Garnett's attention, however, left Conrad alarmed as much as encouraged: 'Your commendation of part I plunges me simply into despair – because part II *must* be very different in theme if not in treatment and I am afraid this will make the book a strange and repulsive hybrid, fit only to be stoned, jumped upon, defiled and then held up to ridicule as a proof of my ineptitude' (*Letters*, 1, p. 296). When, in March 1898, Garnett read Part Two, again with a sympathetic but scrupulous eye, Conrad's first response was: 'Well. It isn't so bad as I expected if in every two pages only one and a half are too bad for anything . . . I've read your remarks. Gospel truth – except where you try to cheer me on. I shall certainly go on – that is if I can' (*Letters*, 2, pp. 46–7).

[3] On 4 June, Garnett had sent a substantial commentary on the serial version of *The Rescue*, framed with qualifications: 'I have rarely felt so uncertain about a work of art'; 'And I repeat I have rarely felt so uncertain in myself as to *my* impressions'; 'I must read the *whole* at one sitting to clarify my impression' (MS Texas; *Portrait*, pp. 138–9).

Only drop Jessie word of your coming – she sends you her love. After Monday next we shall be here all the time till the 25th of August.[1]
Ever Yours
J. Conrad.

The *Arrow* is to appear in Sepr I think. After Miss Hallowes left on her holiday I ceased to send you L & W from sheer compunction at throwing that thing, too, at your overwhelmed head. They will finish the R this month and the book-form is planned for the spring [of] 1920.

To Richard Curle
Text MS Indiana; Curle 45

[letterhead: Spring Grove]
Tuesday. [8 July 1919][2]

My dear Curle.
I opened the enclosed letter by mistake. Sorry.
I have yours of yesterday enclosing Knothe's to you.[3]
Of course he must be immensely busy. In this connection should he not see his way to place B[orys] under his own eye perhaps he could recommend him to some motor mf^g firm for employment or training – with premium or otherwise.[4] I feel that Knothe's word would give the boy some standing under any circumstances.
I've just written you to say we will be away this week-end. The *next* is clear and we hope to see you here say on Friday ev^g. (dinner) if that suits you.
Ever yours
J C.

To Sir Sidney Colvin
Text MS Yale; Unpublished

[Spring Grove]
11. 7. '19
9. A.M.

My dear Colvin
A thousand apologies for not having acknowledged the arrival of Your articles sooner.[5]

[1] Garnett arranged to come on 2 August (*Portrait*, p. 139).
[2] The day after Conrad sent word of his plans.
[3] Seeking a job for Borys, Curle had enlisted the aid of Colonel H. Knothe, DSO, MC, of the Metropolitan Carriage Works, Birmingham. Like Borys, he had served in the Mechanical Transport section of the RASC. See also the letter to Pinker of 21 August.
[4] With or without a fee for instruction on the job.
[5] Drafts of articles for *Scribner's Magazine*: see the letter of [14 July].

Will you let me keep them till Monday.

Our anxiety as to dear Lady Colvin is alleviated to a certain extent, but pray drop a word on a p-c *c/o G. F. W. Hope Esqre. The Dingle. Fingringhoe N^r Colchester* where we will be staying till Monday morning. We are leaving on this visit in an hour's time.

Our dear love to you both.

To Marguerite Ashley Dodd
Text MS Indiana; Unpublished

[letterhead: Spring Grove]
11th July '19

Dear Mrs Dodd[1]

My wife tells me that you have been looking for a copy of *Lord Jim*. I regret that I have no "1st Ed^on" to offer you but this recent reprint contains a corrected text and an "author's note" written specially for it.

Will you do me the honour to accept this inscribed copy[2] and believe me always

Your very faithful and Ob^d servant

J. Conrad

To Sir Sidney Colvin
Text MS Berg; J-A, 2, 223

[letterhead: Spring Grove]
Monday [14 July 1919][3]
11. a. m.

My dear Colvin.

Ever so many thanks for your p-c. with the good news. Jessie sends her dearest love and I kiss the hands of the Convalescent Lady who has such a large, such a preponderant place in our affections – in so many people's affections!

We returned from Essex at about 6 o'clock last evening. The whole household went to bed early. I waited till all sounds had died out, and then, with a mind refreshed and made receptive by a run of 120 miles (I am speaking

[1] Marguerite Augusta Ashley Dodd (née Edwards, 1851–1930) married George Ashley Dodd, a landowner and barrister, later High Sheriff of Kent, in 1870; they lived at Swinford Old Manor, near Ashford, formerly the residence of the Poet Laureate Alfred Austin.
[2] Like this letter, the inscribed copy is now in the Lilly Library.
[3] The Conrads returned from Essex on the 13th. The letter of 29 May and the use of Spring Grove stationery preclude dating this letter closer to the publication of Colvin's articles.

seriously) I sat down to read your two articles[1] – and it was a delightful (c'est le mot juste) experience. You are the most quietly effective of magicians. The masterly, slightly amused, serenity with which you evoke all these distinguished, glorious shades of the first article, by (as it were) a mere turn of the hand (a wonderful turn of the hand it is, too) is a joy to the discriminating reader. But the article on R. L. S. is an evocation of a personality; and the sustained force of feeling under the conversational phrases so admirably put together make of that short paper a great performance.[2]

I am infinitely touched my dear Colvin that you should have found me worthy to be mentioned on the same page with the brilliant and loveable friend of your youth. I regret only that I may appear in my admiration of the South Sea Vol: as not appreciative of RLS. as a "creator". Indeed my dear Colvin it is on that very ground that I admire the book. The islands may sink and the Pacific evaporate and even the terrestrial globe fly to pieces; but as long as one copy of the *South Seas* exists the King of Apamama* will live, for R. L. S. has breathed his humanity into that "weird and ominous" figure and made of him our fellow-man with loving touches of character and a marvellous insight into his power-loving and lonely soul.[3]

As to my own figures whose names your friendship remembers so well there can be no question here of greater or less. They are *other*. I am conceited enough to think that had they been offered to his notice R. L. S. would not have ignored them.[4] Liking or disliking, the generous great artist in prose would have recognised their existence.

Anch'io son pittore.[5]

Ever Yours

Joseph Conrad

---

[1] Colvin's 'Some Personal Recollections' appeared in the January–March 1920 issues of *Scribner's Magazine* (pp. 67, 69–82, 210–23, 338–54), and formed the basis of *Memories & Notes of Persons & Places, 1852–1912* (Arnold, 1922).

[2] The essay on Stevenson is the third of the Recollections; he had been a close friend of the Colvins, and Sir Sidney edited his letters.

[3] Colvin considers Stevenson's narrative of travel 'overloaded with information and the results of study', but adds: 'I ought to mention that a far better qualified judge, Mr Joseph Conrad, differs from me in this, and prefers *In the South Seas* to *Treasure Island*, principally for the sake of what he regards as a very masterpiece of native portraiture in the character of Tembinok, King of Apemama' (*Scribner's*, pp. 353–4). Stevenson devotes the whole fifth section of his book to this Gilbert Islands monarch, 'the last tyrant, the last erect vestige of a dead society'.

[4] Colvin expresses a fervent wish that Conrad and Stevenson might have met (*Scribner's*, p. 354). The magazine, but not the book, version, lists some memorable Conrad characters, all of them captains: Lingard, Beard, Whalley, MacWhirr, and Anthony.

[5] 'I, too, am a painter': Correggio's words on seeing Raphael's 'Santa Cecilia'; the incident is said to have happened around 1525.

To J. B. Pinker
Text MS Berg; Unpublished

[Spring Grove]
Mond. 14. 7. 19

Dearest Pinker.

Thanks for your letter received in Essex. I feel too remorseful for anything when I think of the constant calls I am making on your time and patience. Nevertheless I am lending you these letters from America. There is really no option as it is your indubitable right as the sole negotiator to know what is going on.

I have marked the material parts in red pencil and I propose to call on you to-morrow (Tuesday) about 12. 30. If you will lunch with me it will save you writing. The question is: am I to answer Quinn at all in so far as the Doubleday circus is concerned?

As to his suggestion about the Arrow I don't know where* to laugh or swear – something I must say.[1] But what? Fancy having such a proposal sprung on one!

Ever yours

J. Conrad

To Richard Curle
Text MS Indiana; Curle 46

[Spring Grove]
16. 7. '19

My dear Curle.

We shall expect you to come on Friday by the 4. 30 train from Char: +. Will you come on to Wye and walk up. We have to go out in the afternoon on unexpected business and *may* not be back in time for the car to meet you. It will run down later for your suit case. In any case we'll not be very late. $1/_2$ hour on the outside.

Infinite thanks for your letter. The invitation to the W[edgwoods] has been sent – as suggested.

Au revoir

Yours JC.

---

[1] For fuller details, see the letter of 31 July. On 19 June, Quinn had sent Conrad two letters under one cover: the first marked 'business', the second marked 'personal' (TSS NYPL). Together they occupy 17 typed pages. The 'personal' letter ends with a PS in which Quinn offers to dramatise *The Arrow of Gold*.

To J. B. Pinker

Text MS Berg; Unpublished

[letterhead: Spring Grove]

Thursday. [17 July 1919][1]

My dear Pinker

I was sorry not to see you but I had a talk with Eric and signed the agreement for the 2^d Ser: rights in Am:. Whatever the proceeds of this may be they must fall under our verbal agreement. A transaction of that kind is almost entirely the product directly or indirectly of your labours on my behalf.

I left with E. draft of the "s" letter. You will either amend it or cancel it altogether in the exercise of your discretion. Some sort of answer must be made eventually – but it could take the shape of mere thanks.

I have received your letter re the time of publication of the *Arrow*. Under the impression that Sept^{er} would be the month to which we would stick I have arranged for a couple of reviews (one of them by Colvin) to be ready for that time. Now they won't be ready – I fear.

Would you my dear Pinker ask Withers on 'phone for me whether the agreement for "Oswalds" (as amended in the sense of his remarks) is being expedited by Pemberton[2] – or is it still in his office? I am anxious to sign and be done with it since I've come to an agreement on all points with Bell's estate agent more than a fortnight ago.

Miss H[allowes] you may be interested to hear, returns on the 4th prox. On passing through town she is commissioned to buy a new typewriter the present one having given up after 14 years' service.

This looks like business. What it will turn out to be time will show. I am full of best intentions but I won't tackle Nap:[3] yet. The Prefaces will require my first attention. I am afraid there will be an interruption of *steady* work by Jessie's operation and also the move to the new house. It's no use beginning a big job till all that is over.

I have had 14 shots fired at me by Arbuthnot the photographer[4] – and still survive, as you see. The Am^{an} *Vanity Fair* pays for the performance.[5] I shall send some copies also to the aggrieved Garden City.

Yours ever

J. Conrad.

---

[1] Two days after the visit to Pinker's office to discuss the reply to Quinn dated 31 July.

[2] Withers was Conrad's solicitor, the senior partner in Withers, Benson, Birkett, and Davies; Pemberton acted for Colonel Bell.

[3] The long-postponed novel of the Napoleonic wars.

[4] Malcolm Arbuthnot, 43 New Bond St, London W1.

[5] Hugh Walpole's 'Joseph Conrad: A Pen Portrait by a Friendly Hand' appeared in the December issue of *Vanity Fair* (p. 39). The accompanying photograph was by Beresford, not Arbuthnot.

To Sir Sidney Colvin
Text MS Texas; Unpublished

[Spring Grove]

Monday. [21 July 1919][1]

My dear Colvin.

It appears that F. Unwin, having made arrangements with the Lloyds: Mag: Pinker took the veto off the proposed date of publication, and therefore the *Arrow* is to be published on the 6th after all.

I am ever so sorry the book is to be deprived of a send-off by You but perhaps by holding back the review in the *Observer* for a fortnight or so it may get your support yet when it will be most wanted; for I imagine the reception by the press will be pretty cool.

I am sending you a copy of the English edition.

With our dear love

Ever Yours

J Conrad

To Sir Sidney Colvin
Text MS Yale; Keating 281; J-A, 2, 229

[letterhead: Spring Grove]

Wednesday [30 July or 6 August 1919][2]

My dear Colvin

You will understand better how deeply I am moved by your letter when I tell you that during the "composition of that piece" I thought of you very often. I used to say to myself: "He will understand that" – after finishing certain bits. And as to the whole too, I must confess, I counted on you with some confidence. But I never expected that this work of my 60th year would find its way so straight into your heart – into your inextinguishably youthful heart! I own to feeling a little overwhelmed by the response. For you are generous without counting. You could be no other. Avarice is the vice of an age that you'll never, never reach.

You never suspected your close association with this book. And yet it is a fact that you are, not the first, but the only, man to whom I spoke of it some months before I put pen to paper. It was at Capel. You stood with back to the fire. But I did not lay a particular stress on my intentions and later I noticed that the circumstance had escaped your memory. And no wonder. I was very inarticulate that day – and on that subject too.

---

[1] Soon after the decision to bring publication of *The Arrow* forward to 6 August.

[2] On 21 July, Conrad promised to send Colvin the British version of *The Arrow*; he had already sent Lady Colvin the US edition, and Colvin had followed the serial version (letters of [14 or 21? May], 29 May, and 20 June). By the 7th, when Conrad made suggestions for the review, Colvin had evidently read the British text.

I can't give you an idea how worried I am over these corrections. A lot of course has been put right. I read the proofs innumerable times. Only the other week I sent six corrections more to Fisher Unwin. They were too late. And one of them is a grammatical blunder of the worst kind! Another is a *who* instead of *whom*. I had altered the construction of the phrase and forgot to insert the *m*. Horrible. The fact is between you and me (and Lady Colvin of course), that I have never been able to read *these* proofs in cold blood. Ridiculous! My dear (as. D. Rita would have said) there are some of these 42 year old episodes of which I cannot think now without a slight tightness of the chest[1] – un petit serrement de coeur. What a confession! Why, oh! why, didn't I send you the revise? I nearly did it. Then I felt ashamed of coming to worry you with a work that was emphatically my business.

Well, you have made me very happy. The first great joy I had out of that book was Lady Colvin's sympathy. Your good opinion rounds and completes that state of deep content which nothing but the praise of such friends as you both are can give. Our dearest love to you both.

Ever yours

Joseph Conrad

To John Quinn
Text TS/MS NYPL;[2] Unpublished

[letterhead: Spring Grove]
Kent.
31 July. '19

My dear Quinn.

Thanks for your two letters.[3] As you know I am always glad to hear from you and you cannot doubt that I appreciate greatly the real "good friend's"

---

[1] 1877 was the year of Conrad's mysterious activities in the Carlist cause. On the strength of his conversations with Conrad, Jean-Aubry assumed that *The Arrow* stuck close to autobiography (J-A, 1, pp. 43–5). With the exception of Jerry Allen (*The Thunder and the Sunshine, passim*), later biographers have been cautious (Baines) or downright sceptical (Van Marle, Karl, and Najder). The sceptics base their arguments on factual contradictions and a suspicious density of fictional tropes: see Jocelyn Baines, *Joseph Conrad: A Critical Biography* (Weidenfeld and Nicolson, 1960), pp. 51–7; Hans van Marle, 'Young Ulysses Ashore: On the Trail of Konrad Korzeniowski in Marseilles', *L'Époque Conradienne*, 2 (1976), 23–34; Karl, *Three Lives*, pp. 159–71; Najder, *Chronicle*, pp. 48–51, 429. In any case, Conrad had lived adventurously in Marseilles, and he felt himself gripped by the spirit if not the letter of those days. Cf. the comments on different kinds of truth in the letter of [9 or 16 August].

[2] Now in the Berg Collection, the TS draft that Conrad left with Eric Pinker on 15 July carries substantial revisions by Conrad and a few small changes by Eric's father. The NYPL text is a fair copy incorporating these amendments. The most notable change on the draft itself was the excision of these sentences from the beginning of the second paragraph: 'What surprises me is that Mr Doubleday should voluntarily assume the attitude of the suspected man! If the firm of Doubleday, Page do not think themselves above suspicion, I should like to know who will? I ask you – why anyone should?'

[3] The 'business' and 'personal' letters of 19 June. The business letter chiefly concerns a suggestion

interest you take in my fortunes. But frankly, you need not have pointed out to me the multiplicity of your occupations and the value of your time.[1] I am quite aware of the demands your position in the world makes upon you. That is why I am positively distressed that Mr. Doubleday should add to them by rushing to you with his complaints – a proceeding which strikes me as not very correct or dignified.

Mr. Doubleday knows that he is not, and cannot be suspect to me. Why, then, this exhibition of accounts, and display of exact figures and talking of the O. Henry transaction? I know the story of the O. Henry copyrights even to the amount paid to O. H's heir or heirs. Mr. Doubleday told me himself. The firm did not stand on its legal rights; and I appreciate their humane and honorable motives.[2] But my dear Quinn if everybody stood on this legal rights the world would be a still worse place for poor devils than it is. "Summa jus, summa injuris."[3]

As to figures you and I know very well that their positive value is just – nil. They are worth rather less than the paper than are written upon unless one is convinced of the perfect integrity of the man who has written them down. I am perfectly convinced of Mr. Doubleday's integrity. But I can't say that I am pleased at Mr. Doubleday complaining of my attitude and asking for assistance as though I were an impossible person. For that is what it amounts to. A man is entitled to a certain amount of privacy in his affairs. Mr. Doubleday also talks and even writes about his partners "discouragement". This looks

---

to expand the Collected Edition from 377 to 1,175 sets, which Doubleday had mooted and Quinn opposed. The personal letter is a stoic response to the news, passed on by Clement Shorter, that Conrad had sold the MS (actually TS) of *The Arrow* to T. J. Wise rather than offering it to Quinn.

[1] The letter is heavy with figures, including those for initial sales of *The Arrow* on which Conrad stood to make $6,800 whereas Doubleday would be out of pocket by $1,353 thanks to the cost of publicity. The other calculations compared projected royalties for the larger and smaller runs of the Collected Edition. Having relayed Doubleday's concerns at length, Quinn complains: 'the demands upon my time and strength sometimes become simply unbearable . . . I have to keep on repeating to myself: "Resist, Resist, Resist; No, No, No", and to hope that I will develop strength of will, and the patience to refuse, with as good a temper as I can command, the demands upon me from people who have no right to my time or strength or energy.' After more in the same vein, Quinn adds: 'Therefore I can't act as a buffer between Pinker and Doubleday Page & Company.'

[2] Perhaps to illustrate Doubleday's good nature, perhaps to demonstrate the firm's commercial abilities, Quinn cites the example of 'O. Henry' (William Sydney Porter, 1862–1910) whose collections of short stories sold by the million. Although Doubleday held all rights and had no obligation to pay royalties, he 'voluntarily compensated his widow (although she did not deserve it in my opinion) as though she had a contract'. Quinn starts this section of the letter: 'While there is no comparison between your work and that of O. Henry's, because humor always has a wider appeal than that of a serious artist, I know something of what they have done with O. Henry's works.'

[3] 'Summum jus, summa injuria': 'the highest justice does the greatest harm'. In the first century BCE, Cicero quoted this maxim as already proverbial (*De officiis*, 1, 33).

like, diplomatically speaking, "applying pressure" (to make me mend my ways, I suppose), or in plain Anglo-Saxon, "uttering a threat".[1] If it does not mean that, then what does it mean? That sort of thing will end by making me feel not "discouraged" but dissatisfied – profoundly so.

And the worst of it is, my dear Quinn, that all this is so completely unnecessary. Long before Mr. Doubleday's last visit here we had accepted the *377 copies-plan*. Pinker and I took exactly the same view of it as you do in your letter. I dismissed the matter from my mind as settled. Then Mr. Doubleday starts this new hare and asks me to join. But the transaction does not strike me as attractive. Why should this Mr. Wells (of whom I've never heard before) have 65% while I (who after all did write those books) am to have but 5% on the published price?[2]

With the fullest acknowledgement of your kind offer I don't think this a case for a buffer. A buffer is inserted between inimical forces to prevent damage. But my feelings towards Mr. Doubleday (the Man and the Firm) are very much the reverse of inimical. Doubleday thought fit to approach me in his own time, and I made no secret of it that I was pleased. On the other hand I was no obscure beginner then. I had made for myself a reputation of the most solid sort, because founded on the recognition of distinguished minds here and elsewhere. My position in English letters was unquestionable, my material position was so far from being unsatisfactory that had I been alone in the world I would have been content with it. For these results I owed no gratitude to any publisher, either in the way of material help or moral support in the past. (That never failed me – but it came from another quarter). I don't see any reason why I should not have perfect liberty to argue on any point, or object to any stipulation in any scheme or plan suggested by my publisher without giving offence. The exercise of a simple right does not imply antagonism (which would be stupid in this case) and does not call for a buffer.

With all deference to Mr. D's opinion I do not like the idea of a special set of "Sea"-books.[3] How would poor Thackeray have liked a set labelled

[1] 'In his talk on the telephone he [Doubleday] told me that he was very tired of being dealt with by Mr. Pinker on the assumption that he and his associates were not doing their best for Mr Conrad's interests. He was generally discouraged about the whole business, adding that, while he was keen on the Conrad thing, some of his thirteen partners were getting very tired of what they felt was lack of appreciation on Pinker's part for their efforts.'

[2] Doubleday had offered a 10 per cent royalty on the 377 sets priced at $120 each, yielding about $4,500; a larger set would earn Conrad about $7,500, a royalty of roughly 5 per cent. Although Doubleday stood to lose on the smaller edition and make very little ($450 net) on the larger, he had better prospects in view; Quinn quotes him as saying: 'it will leave us a new set of plates of a proper text and with proper introductions which will be of value to us and to him [Conrad] in our future trade editions.' Mr Wells seems to have been the wholesaler who would handle the edition.

[3] Doubleday had 'mentioned a set of Sea Stories in 5 or 6 volumes, which he thought might be sold in a special way'.

Mr. Thack's "Society Novels". He lived in society ("The Newcomes" could be described in a sense as a 'High-Life' novel). But it would be absurd to brand him as a "Society" writer. The sea is not my subject. Mankind is my subject and "imaginative rendering" of truth is my aim. The *Mirror* certainly is a book of prose inspired directly by the sea. The *Nigger* is a study of a group of seamen with a particular attention to their psychology – not to their adventures. *Youth* has been recognised for what it is too long for me to speak about it. *Typhoon*, it is generally admitted now, conveys much more than mere sea-effects. Those are the only works where the sea is in the foreground. It is often seen in the background of my other books just as "society" (and especially London society) is inevitably present in the foreground or in the background of Thackeray's novels – without making him a "Society" novelist. To be labelled insistently as a sea-writer will repel as many or more readers than it will attract, I fancy. That's why I am not enthusiastic about that scheme.

Pardon the long screed. The necessity was not of my seeking. The worst is that I haven't left myself time to speak adequately of your interesting suggestion of dramatising *The Arrow*. I am certain that Quinn's dramatisation of Conrad would be a great success of curiosity at the very least. Unluckily I am entangled in a negotiation about dramatic rights which prevents me returning you a definite answer at once. Personally I think the *Arrow*, which consists not of action but of shades of intimate emotions, not fit for the stage – less fit for the stage than any other of my books even. It is anything but dramatic in the 'Stage' sense. I am afraid you would find it a weary task after a little while.

But it is certainly an exciting suggestion. What does your friend mean by "melodramatic"?[1] That word is used so loosely! A melodrama is a play where the motives lack verisimilitude or else are not strong enough to justify a certain violence of action which thus becomes a mere fatuous display of false emotions. Violent action in itself does not make melodrama.

Kindest regards and warm thanks for Your friendly interest from my wife and boys. I am dear Quinn

always gratefully Yours
Joseph Conrad.

---

[1] Quinn had shown the scenario of his proposed adaptation of *The Arrow* to J. M. Kerrigan, formerly a member of the Abbey Theatre Company in Dublin: 'My artist friend said that the way I had sketched it was "too damned melodramatic", and I said that it was melodramatic and that that was why I thought it would go, but that it was not sentimental, and that it would catch the women for they would all applaud Rita's self-sacrifice, although very few of them are built that way themselves.'

To Richard Curle
Text MS Indiana; Curle 47[1]

[letterhead: Spring Grove]
Monday. 4 Augst 1919.
Dearest Curle.

Thanks for your good letter. To know of your readiness to stand by me at the critical time is a great comfort.

B[orys] had a most kind and promising answer from Col Knothe – making an appointement* in B'ham for the 14th. He answered it at once. But last night he got up suddenly a high temperature – and God only knows what may come of it. The Doctor has just left. We must wait & see. It may be a mere touch of malaria only. I am rather worried, the more so that John too has come back from school with a beastly cough and is quite out of sorts. I am keeping well – for me. Pray let us know how *You* get on – in health of body and mind. Gardiner[2] was here and talked of you with most intelligent appreciation. The doctors have ordered him to California – poor fellow. Jessie sends her love.

Ever Yours

J Conrad.

PS Pray remember me to your wife with the kindest regards. Jessie sends her love to Mother and Son.[3]
PPS. Arrow's publication day 6th Augs^t.

To Hugh Walpole
Text MS Texas; Unpublished

[letterhead: Spring Grove]
Tuesday. [5 August? 1919][4]
My dear Walpole.

We are expecting you then on Sat. It'll be good to see you again. It seems ages since I basked in the light of your countenance.

---

[1] Curle omits the PS and makes the PPS into a PS.
[2] Gordon Gardiner, whose health troubled him persistently.
[3] Cordelia and Adam Curle.
[4] The only visit to Spring Grove recorded in Walpole's diary was on the weekend of 9–10 August (Hart-Davis, *Walpole*, p. 187).

You'll find me very lazy, very stupid and mayhap snarly. You will want
Your most dulcet tones to "soothe the savage breast"[1] —
Of Yours ever
J. Conrad

Our love.
PPS *Let us know the train*

To Auguste Gilbert de Voisins
Text L. fr. 145
Spring Grove,
Wye,
nr Ashford, Kent.
6. 8. 19.

Monsieur le Comte Gilbert de Voisins,
St. Catherine's Lodge,
Hove. Sussex.

Cher Monsieur,[2]
Nous serons enchantés de vous voir chez nous la semaine prochaine lundi
ou mardi.
C'est que vous êtes loin à Brighton. En auto, la meilleure route serait par
Lewes, – Hawkhurst, – Tenterden, – Ashford. Wye est à trois milles et demi
d'Ashford, un peu à droite de la route Ashford-Canterbury. On peut faire
cela dans la matinée, en arrivant ici vers 1 heure pour le lunch.
En chemin de fer (par Londres), il y a un train de Charing Cross à onze
heures, qui arrive à Ashford (Kent), à 12. 51.
Je viendrai à votre rencontre. Nous nous reconnaitrons sans doute par des
signes particuliers. Mais si vous voulez, je mettrai une feuille verte quelconque
à ma boutonnière.
Voulez-vous, pouvez-vous passer la nuit chez nous? Envoyez-nous un petit
mot.
Bien à vous

---

[1] 'Music hath charms to soothe a savage breast' (William Congreve, *The Mourning Bride* (1697)).
[2] The son of a French officer and a Greek princess, Taglioni's grandson, and Hérédia's son-in-law, Comte Auguste Gilbert de Voisins (1877–1939) enjoyed a large fortune which enabled him to collect and travel as he pleased; he featured as a rider in Buffalo Bill's circus and made

Translation

Dear Sir,
We will be delighted to see you at our home next Monday or Tuesday.
You are some distance from Brighton. By car, the best route would be via
Lewes, – Hawkshurst, – Tenterden, – Ashford. Wye is three and a half miles
from Ashford, a little to the right of the Ashford-Canterbury road. You can
do that in the morning, arriving here for lunch about 1 o'clock.

By rail (from London) there is a train from Charing Cross at eleven o'clock,
which arrives in Ashford (Kent) at 12. 51.

I will come to meet you. We will no doubt recognise each other by distinguishing marks. But if you wish, I shall wear a sprig of something green in
my buttonhole.

Would you, can you spend the night with us? Drop us a line.

Yours truly

To J. B. Pinker
Text MS Berg; Unpublished

[Spring Grove]
6 Aug^t '19

My dear Pinker
This being the day of pub^{on} I wonder whether there will be any reviews.
Personally I feel neither elated nor hopeful. That does not mean I feel
discontented either with the work itself or with the material results. That would
be both stupid and ungrateful.

(This moment the doctor came in and told me that there is a good notice
in Mor^g Post¹).

Thanks for your two letters. I've sent on the Quinn reply as amended by
You. Garnett was here for 3 days. Some other people are coming for long
week-ends. That sort of thing must be stopped.

---

two expeditions to remote parts of China. He also wrote volumes of poetry and fiction; Conrad
owned four of them, including *Le Bar de la Fourche* (1909), a novel about prospecting for gold in
California.
1 The next day Conrad twice described this and other reviews as 'very poor'; unsigned, it is
available in *Critical Heritage*, pp. 314–16. Focusing on the novel's narrative obscurities, it is not
what Conrad would have called a 'selling review': 'Typical, particularly in its range and in
its concentration upon itself as shown in the extensions of its own researches, the novel has
something of the character of an experiment – a testing of how far the author's method can
be carried. And the risk involved is part of the fascination.'

I am writing to Withers to beg him to finish wrangling over the *Oswald's* agreement. It's about time it was signed and as it stands now it is fairly safe.

B[orys] is going to Birmingham on the 14th for personal interview with Col. Knothe. He won't settle down there till after Jessie's operation – say middle Sept^{er}.

That same Jessie calls for her pension (£20) which please send her this week together with the weeks money.

Ever yours

J. Conrad.

To André Ruyters
Text MS Yale; Unpublished

[letterhead: Spring Grove]

6. 8. '19.[1]

Dear Mr Ruyters

Thanks for your friendly letter. All the first part of the year I was ill and mostly in bed. I managed to do some work however, but I had no energy left for anything else.

Your intentions as to Lord Jim interest me very much. I fear You'll grow extremely weary of it long before the end. The other day I found that I could not read it myself to the end. It bored me.

As to the matter of double initials for signature of the *H of D* translation[2] n'en faites rien je Vous en prie. My regard for you and my interest in *your* work (not mine) has given me *all* the pleasure I derived from looking over your translation. I trust it implicitly. I am not conscious of having done anything to deserve having my initials coupled with yours in that connection. Whatever was done was done out of a friendly feeling and not for publicity. And, if you want another reason, I fear that it would put me in a difficult position in regard of my other translators. For I certainly would have no time to look at their translations. I have begun another novel – I am over sixty and but a sick man – I work very slowly – I have my own English text to revise for the limited edition which is now being prepared – I want some time to myself to do nothing – just do nothing. Car je suis las cher monsieur et ami – je suis las.[3]

Yours with the greatest regard

Joseph Conrad

---

[1] Misdated as 8 June in the Yale catalogue.   [2] The translation published in serial, 1924–5.
[3] 'For I'm lethargic, dear sir and friend – I am lethargic.'

To Sir Sidney Colvin
Text MS Yale; J-A, 2, 224

[Spring Grove]
7. 8. 19

Dearest Colvin.

You are a "real friend"!

The first notices (day of pub^{on} in M^g *Post*, *Dly Mail*, *Dly News*) are very poor, puzzle-headed hesitating, pronouncements; yet not inimical.[1] A very unsatisfactory send off.

Your question raises a delicate problem. A man of your savoir-faire, your sense of literary "convenances" and your homme du monde tact is best fit to judge how the autob^{al} note, if struck, may affect the work – and the man.

With all deference then I venture to suggest that the view of its being a study of a woman – *prise sur le vif* (*obviously*, you may say) and also the story of young, very young love told with a depth of emotion pointing to experience is what you perceive – what impresses you – in what consists the "quality" of the book. This said with your authority[2] will amount to a confession – a sufficient confession to a not particularly delicate world.

Perhaps you could also discover a "personal note of youth" both in the – so to speak – innocence and the completeness of this love affair – this emotional adventure fated to end as it ends in a world not meant for lovers and between these two beings both outside the organised scheme of society not because they are *declassés* in any sense but because of the origin of one and the deliberate renunciation of the other.

Pardon me if I have said too much. I rest in your affection and in Your comprehension which I never doubted.

Our deepest love to you both. Ever Your[s] in haste

J. Conrad.

PS Of course the plot cannot be told for there is none.

(Allègre is imagined from a glimpsed personality of no fame or position[3]).

---

[1] In the *Daily Mail* (p. 8), Hamilton Fyfe advised persistence with a novel whose characters were not initially fetching but would grow upon the reader. In the *Daily News* (p. 6), Robert Lynd dwelt upon Conrad's obliquity, the consequence (according to him) of a childhood spent among conspirators.

[2] Conrad is briefing Colvin for his upcoming review in the *Observer*.

[3] Franciszek Ziejka finds the original of this character in the portrait painter Louis-Gustave Ricard (1823–73) (Najder, *Chronicle*, p. 50).

To J. B. Pinker
Text MS Berg; J-A, 2, 225

[letterhead: Spring Grove]
7. 8. '19.

Dear Pinker.

I return here the lady's letter. I hope I am a modest person, but having dramatised the story myself and it having been performed in three English towns, in Paris and also (for a week) in Chicago;[1] and Bessie Carvill* being absolutely the first conscious woman-creation in the whole body of my work,[2] I can't find enough humility in me to proclaim my unbelief in it by letting an obscure writer (who does not even profess herself to be a dramatist!) attempt the same thing. Had the proposal come from a distinguished playwright, with a European reputation even, I would have declined it. One must have some pride in one's work. I don't trot out mine very much but I have it all the same. If there is a demand for One-act plays as the woman says (I don't believe it) then I can't admit either to myself or to the world that what I have done is so contemptible that, with my name to it, it stands no better chance than a casual adaptation by the first person that comes along, and with, apparently, no better qualifications for stage-work than I have.

All that it would be necessary to say in answer is that the lady is obviously not aware that Mr C. himself had dramatised the story in a one-act play, under the title *One Day More*, which has been performed in Europe and the U. S. and also published in the English Review and in a limited edition in London.

S. Colvin is determined to have a review of *A. of G.* in Observer next week. The "Day of Pub^{on}" notices in *M[orning] Post, D^{ly} Mail* and *Dly News* were very poor. Not inimical, you understand, but puzzled and hesitating. Just what I feared! An uncertain send off. And the worst of it is that at this season the public that is likely to ask for my book in libraries and book-shops is broken up, away on its holidays. The success of a novel is often made by tea-table and dinner-table talk. I think Unwin made a mistake in insisting on this date.

Yours ever

J. Conrad

---

[1] The known productions of *One Day More* are: Stage Society, London (1905), Théâtre des Arts, Paris (1909), Sunday Theatre Society, Chicago (1913 or '14), and Birmingham Repertory Theatre (1918).
[2] Among others, Bessie Carvil, of 'To-morrow' and *One Day More*, was preceded by Jewel, Aïssa, Amy Foster, and Nina Almayer.

To Edmund Candler

Text MS Morgan; Candler xxxix

[letterhead: Spring Grove]

8. 8. '19

My dear Candler

I really ought to have a nurse. I wrote you a letter more than a week ago and found it in my pocket yesterday. Then, in a fury, I tore it up without a moment's reflection. It's like a thing in a farce.

Luckily there was nothing deserving particular notice in that letter. I only thanked you for yours and expressed my satisfaction at the decent behaviour of the Indian Gov^t.[1]

_____

This novel appeared rather earlier than I expected. The reception has been rather uncertain. Very much what I expected. I don't think the stuff will interest you much. My interest in it is special and is not based on literary grounds. Now I rather regret having written it. This does not mean that I am ashamed of it as a piece of writing. But my sending you a copy is an act of friendship not of literary vanity. I suggest you should say nothing about it except just a word to let me know it has reached you.

Jessie joins me in kindest regards to yourself and all your house.

Affect^{ly} yours

J. Conrad

PS Shall we see You before You start for India?

To John Galsworthy

Text MS Forbes; J-A, 2, 226

[Spring Grove]

8. 8. '19.

Dearest Jack

Indubitably you have an inborn knowledge – la science profonde – of the right things to say at a given moment; at *any* moment I imagine – but certainly at the difficult period through which we have to live. The justness of all these things said in *Another Sheaf*[2] is what strikes one most, the more so that one cannot question your sincerity even if one questions your views – which I don't in the least. In all your French studies which I have seen you

[1] In offering Candler a post as Director of Publicity for the Punjab.

[2] A collection just published by Heinemann. Conrad refers to 'Impressions of France, 1916–17', 'The Land, 1917', 'The Land, 1918', 'The Drama in England and America', 'Speculations', and 'Grotesques'.

have all my sympathies. On the land question I am altogether with you. All you say about the stage seems to me undeniable – only I am less hopeful than you seem to be; but it is *Speculations* that appeal to my deeper feelings. In *Grotesques* I had the additional joy of that unique Galsworthian quality you put into your satires. Your Angel is simply "impayable" – quite beyond price; and the poor Dragoman[1] has a pathetic air of helpless intelligence and seems to be an extremely decent fellow one would like for a friend.

I got as far as this when the belated copies of The *A of G* arrived. I'll put this sheet of paper between the covers.

Never before was the act of publication so distasteful to me as on this occasion. Not that I shrink from what may be said. I can form a pretty good guess as to what will be said. The comforting thought is that, most likely, Fisher Unwin (who extorted the book from me in a truly Shylockian manner) will find himself cheated of his expectations. I expect from him a series of whining and impudent letters before very long. They'll be perfect of their kind, and moderately amusing.

We are only moderately well. B[orys] goes in a few days to Birmingham to see Col: Knothe the managing Director of the Oldbury Works. John begins to look better. Our dear love to you both.

Ever Yours

Joseph Conrad.

To Sir Sidney Colvin

Text MS Berg; J-A, 2, 224

[Spring Grove]
Sat: [9 or 16 August 1919][2]

Dearest Colvin

The Allègre affair I understand was a fact, of which I make an extended version.

The R[ita] of the Tremolino is by no means true except as to her actual existence. I mention it lightly the subject of the paper being the Tremolino and her fate.[3] *That* is literally true, just as the Rita of the Arrow is true fundamentally to the shore connections of that time.

Ever Yours

J Conrad

---

[1] 'An interpreter; strictly applied to a man who acts as a guide and interpreter in countries where Arabic, Turkish, or Persian is spoken' (*OED*). In 'Grotesques', a future fantasy set in 1947, a dragoman shows The Angel Æthereal around London.

[2] A successor to the letter of the 7th, which also refers to Henry Allègre, and written before the appearance of Colvin's review on the 24th.

[3] Doña Rita appears as 'a Carlist and of Basque blood' in 'The "Tremolino"', Sections 40–5 of *The Mirror of the Sea*. Introducing his World's Classics edition of *The Mirror*, Najder writes:

To J. B. Pinker

Text TS Berg; Unpublished

[letterhead: Spring Grove]

Aug: 12th [1919]^1

Will you please send a cheque for £16. 16. 0. the price of the new machine to Miss Hallowes here. There is also Borys' cheque for £8. due this month. Will you please make it out to me as I shall give him the money here. He leaves for Birmingham on Thursday morning and may be away for a couple of days.

Please debit my account with £5 commission on the fee of £50 paid me by the D[aily] M[ail] for the article in the Peace Number.^{2} I have used their cheque for paying Jessie's dressmaker's account, instead of sending it to you in a proper and businesslike manner. Pray take note that we have been paid for that item.

Would you order for me from Fisher Unwin 6 copies of the Arrow for presentation in France and other foreign parts?

I have seen the *Times* review, of course, and also one in the *Star* by James Douglas.^{3} There was also a full page article in the *Athenaeum*.^{4} All the reviews I have seen are distinctly friendly but I fear of not much use from the commercial point of view.

'Even 'The "Tremolino"'', the most insistently autobiographical piece, verily bristles with details either outright unrealistic or at best lifted from some other time and place' (Oxford University Press, 1988), p. xi.

^{1} Both stationery and references to recent work give the year.

^{2} 'Confidence' appeared on 30 June.

^{3} Walter de la Mare (1873–1956) reviewed *The Arrow* for the *TLS* (7 August, p. 422; *CH*, pp. 316–20). The review in the *Star*, a London evening newspaper edited by the novelist and belletrist James Douglas (1867–1940), is on p. 2 of the 8 August issue. According to de la Mare, the novel is rich in mystery and allure and its prose resonates; nevertheless the narrative method, especially of the conclusion, leaves 'it in a vital degree fragmentarily and insecurely told'. Douglas dwells on Rita, using her portrayal to show Conrad as a sardonic ironist who gives new life to the 'bleached bones' of romantic cliché. The final paragraph begins: 'Well, "The Arrow of Gold" is a masterpiece. Do not read it hastily, like a newspaper. Dream and idle over it. Taste its many flavours one by one. If you try to gulp it down it will annoy you and even bore you. And remember that it is a romantic comedy, not a bald, straight story. Rita is perhaps too literary to be taken quite seriously, but then she is a glamour, a wonder, a work of art.'

^{4} 8 August, p. 720, by Katherine Mansfield, who reviewed fiction for the *Athenaeum* every week as 'K. M.' Her witty review surmises that *The Arrow* must be by, as well as about, a young man, thus accounting for the 'flicker of dismay' she felt on first reading it. 'It is impossible not to believe that he has had this particular novel in the cellar for a considerable time – this sweet, sparkling, heady mixture in the strange-shaped bottle with the fantastic label. How does it stand being held up to the light, tasted, sipped, and compared with those dark foreign beverages with which he has made us so familiar?' Poorly, the review implies. The wine has not improved with cellaring. The plot culminates in 'a crisis so fantastical that we cannot but fancy Mr Conrad of to-day smiling at its stage horrors', and it revolves around an all-too-familiar mystery: 'the *femme fatale*, the woman of all times, the Old Enchantress, the idol before whom no man can do aught but worship, the Eternal Feminine, Donna* Rita, woman'.

Next week I will be sending you my doctor's account for the last six months, which may be a little heavy. Then there will be John's school account in due course.

I shall be bringing Jessie to town on the 28th for the appointment with Sir Robert Jones. We expect to be back the same day home, and that the operation, if there is any, will be fixed for the first week in October; but I will talk to you about that and many other things when we meet, which I hope will be soon. For the next week or so I shall try and get in touch with work. It will take some time because I have got myself deep into an idle mood, and besides the weather, too, makes one lazy.

Ever affect^{ly} Yours

J. Conrad.

To J. B. Pinker
Text TS/MS Berg; J-A, 2, 226[1]

Spring Grove,
Wye.
Kent.
14. 8. '19

My dear Pinker

Thanks for the cheques received this morning.

I had this morning also a whole batch of cuttings including a review by Holbrook Jackson in the *New Nation*, very enthusiastic,[2] and another in *Everyman* by Beresford who finds I am growing old;[3] a rather sudden conclusion to arrive at on the evidence of only one book; because, as far as I can remember, nobody found traces of senile decay in Victory or Shadow Line. However, a beginning of that sort of thing had to be made some time and I quite expected it to come on this occasion. I only wondered who would be the first to speak right out.

There is no denying the fact that there is a note of disappointment in almost every review;[4] but as far as I can judge it seems to arise more from

---

[1] Jean-Aubry omits the sentence beginning 'But I don't want to give D.'
[2] There was no such publication as the *New Nation* at that time. Holbrook Jackson (1874–1948) wrote for the *New Age*, but no review appeared there. The *Nation*'s is dated 6 September. Perhaps Conrad meant the unsigned review in the *New Statesman* of 16 August, available at the bookstalls a day or two in advance. The reviewer praises the 'endless prodigality of creation . . . the sign and guarantee of artistic greatness' (p. 497); the text is reprinted in *CH*, pp. 321–4.
[3] The popular novelist J[ohn] D[avys] Beresford (1873–1947) describes the novel as 'an allegory of youth wooing eternity', and adds that he 'missed something of that sudden, amazing magic which bewitches the pages of my favourite "Lord Jim". I wondered, now and again, if my author was not a little tired' (*Everyman*, 9 August, pp. 425–6).
[4] Even the *New Statesman* review calls the book 'something of a disappointment' (*CH*, p. 321).

the subject and its treatment, which somehow fail to satisfy the critical mind, than from any perception of failing powers in the writer. This is the penalty for having produced something unexpected, and I don't grumble at it. I only don't see why I should have Lord Jim thrown at my head at every turn. I couldn't go on writing Lord Jim all my life and I don't think you would have liked me to do so. I don't think that whatever has been written so far can affect the sales adversely. I remember that when Anatole France wrote his *Lys Rouge* (something that nobody expected him to write) the reception by the press was very much in the same note; yet my copy bought some time in the middle of the nineties is of the twenty-seventh edition.[1] I don't expect that sort of miracle for myself but I don't think that we need despair of a fair success with the public.

Have you any news from Garden City? In this connection I may tell you that I have a certain difficulty in beginning my Author's Note for the *Typhoon* volume. The volumes that have prefaces are – *Almayer, Outcast, Unrest, Nigger, Jim, Youth.*

Typhoon comes next in order to *Youth* but D[oubleday], with the six above has got enough for a start. When the *Typhoon* preface is done, there will be then two more books ready for the edition because *Nostromo*[2] which follows *Typhoon* is provided already with an Author's Note.

I am telling you this here for your information in case you should get some inaccurate statements or complaints from those people.

I suppose the whole thing is hung up for a time, but I hope that when it starts moving again you will let me know, so that I may get the others ready right away; which, just now I don't feel very much disposed to do at once. But I don't want to give D. the shadow of an excuse for groaning about delays caused by me.

Jessie sends her love to Mrs Pinker and yourself. One does not like to press for the promised visit in this very hot weather but how it would be* if you and Mrs Pinker came (say on Friday week) as far as Tonbridge Junc: and from there by car which we would send to meet your train. The[n] on Sat: you could return the same way. Jessie thinks that a mixed journey like this would be less irksome than either car or rail right through. And if you could bring your daughter with you it would be very charming and interesting to see her first under our roof. Pray tell Ralph that B[orys] will be away on

---

[1] Conrad read France's story of tormented passion in the year of publication, 1894 (*Letters*, 1, p. 169). Owen Knowles has detected many traces of this novel, especially in *Victory*: see 'Conrad, Anatole France, and the Early French Romantic Tradition: Some Influences', *Conradiana*, 11 (1979), 41–61, and Hervouet, *French Face, passim.*

[2] In the MS, Conrad put a number over each title, from 1 for *Typhoon* to 8 for *Nostromo.*

his Scotch call – so if he has any more amusing engagement we won't be
mortally offended. . . . Anyway it rests with you to allow him to squeeze you
in the car (which is only ample for 3) if you choose. Eric I suppose will be at
the post of duty but we hope he will be one of our first visitors in the new
(unfurnished) house.[1]

Ever Your

J. Conrad.

To Arthur Symons

Text MS Virginia; Hunter (1985, 3)

[letterhead: Spring Grove]

14. 8. '19

My dear Symons

You know what a brute I am to my friends. I ought to write you a yard of
apologies, but I prefer to throw myself on your mercy.

Herewith my latest bit of (pretty bad) prose. The reviews are friendly but
not very appreciative. No doubt *you* will understand what I am after in this
thing.

I have been mostly ailing. Jessie has the prospect of another operation
before her. We shall be in London in Sept and in Oct we are to move into
our new house near Canterbury.

With our love to you both.

Yours always,

J. Conrad.

To Alexander Robinson

Text TS Nielson; Unpublished

[Spring Grove]

Kent

August 15th. 1919.

Dear Mr Robinson.[2]

Many thanks for the set of photographs and the copy of the newspaper
notice you have been kind enough to make for me out of the Peterhead
paper.

---

[1] Oswalds.
[2] Alexander Robinson (1873–1948?) was indentured in Glasgow in 1888 and served as an apprentice in the *Loch Etive* from 16 November 1889 to 27 June 1891; he also sailed in the *Loch
Carron*. When he wrote to Conrad on 29 July 1919 (MS Indiana), he was living in Woodford,
Essex.

I had no memento of any kind of the Loch Etive for many years, till Mr Moxon (of Newcastle, N. S. W.) sent me the photograph of an oil painting of the ship which he has in his possession.[1] That was just before the war, and the painting is obviously very good, but the photograph you sent me is more of a real thing and I shall insert it together with the portrait of Capt. Stuart in my own copy of the Mirror of the Sea.[2] I think that the old Tweed should go in there too. I heard a lot about that ship from the Loch Etive's carpenter (Cummins, I think was his name) but I had no idea how she looked. She looks very fine; but what strikes one most in the photograph is the distance from the foremast to the bows. It seems most unusual.[3]

I am very glad you like the Mirror. It was written mainly for shore people but a sailor (of that time) would naturally understand best what I am trying to express there. Things have changed since, but old or new we need not be ashamed of the Service which had our best years. I suppose I am right in my surmise that you are the A. Robinson who was 2nd Officer of the *Earl of Shaftesbury*, some time in the middle of the eighties, lying in Penarth Dock ready to load. If so, then it is the last occasion on which we met on a dismal and damp afternoon in winter.[4] Let me express the hope that the world has used you well and assure you of an old shipmate's regard.

Believe me

very faithfully yours

Joseph Conrad.

To J. B. Pinker
Text TS Berg; Unpublished

[letterhead: Spring Grove]
Aug. 16th. 1919.

Dearest Pinker

Re Income Tax. I note that your letter gives the amount of last year's income after deduction of commission and expenses; but not, apparently, of

[1] The only surviving letter from Thomas F. Moxon is dated 13 March 1917 (MS Yale).
[2] Which includes 'Cobwebs and Gossamer', Conrad's memoir of 'Captain S–'. William Stuart (1832–94), master of the *Loch Etive*, was born in Peterhead, on the north-east coast of Scotland.
[3] For the *Tweed*, see the letter to A. T. Saunders of 26 January 1917. The *Loch Etive*'s carpenter was John Cumming (born 1847); another Peterhead man, he had also served in the *Tweed*.
[4] Conrad's five-day voyage as second mate of the *Falconhurst* took him from London to Penarth, near Cardiff, where he signed off on 2 January 1887. The *Earl of Shaftesbury* was docked there from 22 December 1886 to 10 January 1887. Conrad's other visit to Penarth was in the *Tilkhurst*, in May–June 1885. Alex Robinson was of course far too young to have been the man Conrad met there, and in any case, he seems never to have obtained his mate's certificate.

premiums of life insurance which I am entitled to deduct. Please send me note of what I pay to the Standard Life Company, so that I may fill in the form properly. I want to send my return on Tuesday evening.

Ever Yours

J. Conrad.

To Sydney Carlyle Cockerell
Text TS/MS V& A English MS RC/EE3; Meynell 324

[Spring Grove]

Kent.

August 19th. 1919.

Dear M[r] Cockerell.[1]

I return here the first volume with many thanks.[2] It is very curious reading, but somehow one cannot take it very seriously. What surprised me most was to discover how much there is of a mere society man in the writer, who takes himself and his feelings seriously only up to a certain point. A personality in antagonism to its proper sphere (I don't mean intellectual, I mean social) is always interesting; but with the best will in the world and with all sorts of sympathetic prepossessions I can't divest myself of the suspicion that all this is merely an attitude and nothing more, or at least very little more. All his indignations may be just, but one asks oneself how much they are justified in that particular individual.

Still I admit that he is, at least to me, always interesting. And what I admire most is the way he has managed to make his life so interesting to himself. I imagine that to that end he has sacrificed not only his fundamental convictions but his very instincts.

But there is nothing so easy as to be unjust to a man, so I'll say no more of this one for whom it is very difficult not to have a liking. Since, as I see, you want to be good to me, perhaps You'll send me the second vol:

It had* been very delightful to have even that tantalisingly short glimpse of you. I hope you will find time and inclination to come and see us in our

---

[1] After three years of selling coal, Sydney Carlyle Cockerell (1867–1962; knighted 1934) went to work for William Morris and the Kelmscott Press in 1892; thereafter, Cockerell's love of books and fine typography never waned. From 1908 to to 1937, he directed Cambridge University's Fitzwilliam Museum.

[2] The first volume of Wilfrid Scawen Blunt's *My Diaries: Being a Personal Narrative of Events, 1888–1914* (Secker, 1919). An English poet, horseman, traveller, Arabic scholar, landowner, and social celebrity, Blunt (1840–1922) had campaigned against British rule in Egypt, India, and Ireland, earning himself a term of imprisonment in the Irish cause.

new house before long. I'll let you know when the migration is achieved; but as you know, before this happens I have some anxious time before me. My wife sends her kindest regards.

Very sincerely Yours

Joseph Conrad.

To André Gide

Text MS Doucet; *L. fr.* 146

[letterhead: Spring Grove]

20. 8. '19

Cher Maître et Ami.

Je Vous envois l'Arrow of Gold – pour ce qu'il vaut – mais je n'ai pas la prétention de Vous le faire lire. C'est un envoi plutôt symbolique – une offrande a l'amitié qui m'est si précieuse et a cette admiration qui est devenue part intégrale de mon être intime.

La réception par la presse ici a été respectueuse. Par le public je ne sais pas et, en vérité, ça m'est bien égal. Et, a propos, Aubry a grande envie de traduire ce volume.[1] Qu'en dites-Vous? Il a très bien réussi avec les 4 contes de *Within the Tides* et ce volume là est bien dans ses moyens. J'ai lui ai promis de Vous en parler.

Mes félicitations pour la brillante re-naissance de La N. R. F.[2] Je suis fort impression[n]é par Votre Journal sans dates.[3] Comme tout ce qui vient de Vous c'est pour moi une joie – toujours un peu triste. Il me semble que joie un peu triste c'est presque la définition de la beauté en termes d'émotion. Peut-être.

Pensez quelquefois a moi avec amitié mon cher Gide. Voilà que je deviens sentimental . . . J'ai vu les annonces d'*Alm*^{er} *Folly* – et j'ai cru rêver. On ne sait pas ce que c'est, ni d'où ça vient, ni pourquoi ça existe. L'homme qui a écrit ça n'est pas precisement mort mais il est bien enterré. Cependant il encore tressaille – de temps en temps – le pauvre diable.

Je vais me mettre a l'oeuvre pour traiter de l'influence de Napoleon sur le bassin ouest de la Mediterranée – 2 vols avec notes, appendices et tables

---

[1] Jean-Aubry had probably visited Spring Grove on the 11th; Conrad's telegram of the 10th reads: 'No train 4.30 on Sunday will you come Monday morning Conrad' (Yale). Jean-Aubry's translation of *The Arrow* appeared in the *Revue des Deux Mondes*, 1926.

[2] The *Nouvelle Revue Française* had been suspended for the duration of the war. Publication resumed in June with a new editor, Jacques Rivière, who prefaced the issue with a manifesto promising fresh writers and fresh policies.

[3] The *Journal sans dates* had been serialised in the *NRF* before the war.

statistiques. Et cela sera un roman. J'ai l'idée que je ne finirai jamais cela. Cette pensée ne m'est pas désagréable. Il se trouvera toujours des imbeciles pour dire: il a voulu faire tellement grand qu'il en a crevé. Belle epitaphe. Pardonnez moi tous mes péchés (y compris the *Arrow of Gold*).

Tout à Vous

Joseph Conrad.

Translation

Cher Maître and Friend.

I am sending you *The Arrow of Gold* – for what it's worth – but I don't presume to make you read it. It is a purely symbolic gift – an offering to the friendship which is so precious to me and to that admiration which has become an integral part of my intimate being.

The reception by the press here has been respectable. By the public, I do not know and, in truth, it is all one to me. And, in this connection, Aubry is very eager to translate this volume. What do you think? He did very well with the 4 stories of *Within the Tides* and this volume is well within his range. I promised him that I would mention it to you.

My congratulations on the brilliant regeneration of the N. R. F. I am greatly impressed by your *Journal without Dates*. Like everything that comes from you, it is for me a joy – always mixed with a litle sadness. It seems to me that joy tinged with a little sadness comes close to being the definition of beauty in terms of emotion. Perhaps.

Think amiably of me sometimes, my dear Gide. There now, I am growing sentimental... I saw the advertisement for *Almayer's Folly* – and I thought I was dreaming. One doesn't know what it is; nor from where it comes, nor why it exists. The man who wrote that is not exactly dead but buried indeed. Nevertheless – from time to time – the poor devil still shudders.

I'm setting to work, writing about Napoleon's influence in the western basin of the Mediterranean – 2 vols with notes, appendices, and statistical tables. And that will be a novel. I have an idea that I'll never finish it. To me, that is not a disagreeable thought. One can always come up with some imbeciles who will say: he wanted to do something so big it killed him. A fine epitaph. Forgive all my sins (including *The Arrow of Gold*).

Yours truly

Joseph Conrad.

To J. B. Pinker
Text TS/MS Berg; Unpublished

[letterhead: Spring Grove]
August 21st. 1919

Dearest Pinker.

I want to tell you shortly of Borys's prospects of training and employment.

On the 14th of this month B. went to Birmingham to see Col. Knothe, who is the managing director now of the Metropolitan Carriage Works and Finance Company, which includes many firms of great standing and reputation, and apparently, from what K. told B has lately assimilated Vickers in that great combine.[1] Knothe is one of those men that leaving school at 15 or thereabouts manage to arrive at a very distinguished position by the time that they are 35 or so. His reception of B. was the friendliest possible, making him his guest at the hotel and making him dine with the managing director of Sunbeams,[2] the owners of some Welsh mines and other people of that sort. Afterwards K talked with the boy into the small hours of the morning on all sorts of matters connected with that business. The immediate personal arrangement which he proposed to him is as follows:— Generally, he advised B. to go in for metallurgy, which, he said, was the basis of all engineering enterprise. Practically he proposed to begin training him for a metal tester, so as to fit him for a post in the Oldbury Works, which are the nucleus of the combine. To that end he wishes B to give a month to the study of a certain chemical testing process, which he can acquire (sufficiently to give him an insight into method and principle) in about a month's time. Then K wants him to report himself at Oldbury Works at the beginning of October and begin his training in the mechanical part of the test and his practice in the chemical part of it, as one of the assistants in the chief-tester's department, which would imply no office work but actual shop and foundry experience for about 12 months. During that time B would have a nominal salary of £2 a month which would make him a member of the staff on the pay-sheet. At the end of that time K would be ready to give B. a post as junior tester at an approximate salary of £400. He warned B. however that being only a managing director[3] he could not guarantee this

---

[1] Forming the Metropolitan Vickers Company.
[2] The car makers.
[3] Colonel Knothe was a manager at the Metropolitan Carriage Works but not the managing director.

absolutely to him; but, as he said, what B would have learned would make him a more valuable person for any business of mechanical engineering, (such as motor or airplanes) to which, K said definitely, he would be able to introduce him should the Oldbury Works have no vacancies or should severe specialisation in metal testing not appeal to B sufficiently after a year's trial. He asked B. how much he thought he would have to live upon for the year and B. mentioned £300, which K. said would probably with care be enough. The living expenses are high in Birmingham and lodgings extremely difficult to find; and it may be necessary for B. at the beginning to take rooms & board in an hotel. However, we will manage that I daresay and taking it all around it seems to me that the trial is more than worth while.

B. of course is very anxious not to miss that chance. He has been enormously impressed by the talk of those men, the amazing magnitude of the operations and the enormous difficulty of the situation from the labour point of view.[1] That night in Birmingham – it appears that he and Knothe talked till 5 a. m. – opened his eyes to a lot of interesting things he had never suspected, both in the organisation and the technicalities of that industrial world which is trying to reconstruct itself on a colossal scale.

Thank you my dear old friend for your good letter. Indeed I did not want to encroach on your time to that extent; yet from the comfort and confidence your views and judgment have given me I can assure you that the time you have given to the writing of that letter has not been wasted.

Please give our united love to Mrs Pinker. We can see her point of view. It is unlucky that the month of Sept will be taken up by preparations to move and journeys to London. I rather dread the prospect. However J[essie] is making effective arrangements so as to make everything as easy as possible for me – while she is in the Nursing Home.

I have signed to-day the agreement for Oswalds – house, 2 cottg^{es}, 3 gardens – all complete – £250 a year. Two years certain and then on a year's notice.

I shall try to see you on the 28th prox^2 when we come up to see Sir R. J[ones]. We shall try to get back the same day.

Ever Yours

J. Conrad.

---

[1] I.e. the threat of strikes for higher pay.
[2] 28 August, not September.

To J. C. Squire

Text TS Berg; J-A, 2, 228

[letterhead: Spring Grove]
August 21st. 1919.

My dear Mr Squire.

Pardon this typewritten letter.

You are giving me most interesting news. My warmest wishes for success in every way in fame and fortune to your forthcoming venture.[1] May it command the respect of crowds, the affection of individuals and the loyal support of the young. As to the Old Gang (you call them The Illustrious I see – same thing) if you want to be good to them why, of course, you must not omit to put down my name too as contributor. What I could write that would be of any use to you I can't imagine at the moment. I don't know anything of the subjects you are going to treat but I am not likely to let ignorance stand in the way of my ambition.[2]

Please convey the expression of my profound gratitude to the writer of the *Arrow* review in the *N. S.* It has never been my lot to get recognition so finely expressed as in the opening paragraph of that review.[3]

I am sorry for the disappointment. Nothing would have been more dreary than a record of those adventures. All this gun-running was a very dull, if dangerous, business.[4] As to intrigues, if there were any, I didn't know anything of them. But in truth, the Carlist invasion was a very straightforward adventure conducted with inconceivable stupidity and a foredoomed failure from the first. There was indeed nothing great there worthy of anybody's passionate devotion.

But the undeserved appreciation of all those figures, which I have been moved to go and seek in that deep shadow in which from now on they shall rest undisturbed, is what touches me most. One does not undertake such a journey without misgivings. I hesitated for some sixteen years, and now it

---

[1] Squire's new magazine, the *London Mercury*.

[2] Conrad would contribute 'Stephen Crane: A Note without Dates' to the December issue; it is included in *Notes on Life and Letters*.

[3] 'Mr Conrad in the last few years has stepped into the place left vacant when Mr Hardy turned his attention away from the composition of novels. He has not only the prestige due to his own gifts, but also the mysterious incalculable prestige which attaches to the man who is admittedly first in any noble pursuit' (*New Statesman*, 16 August, in *CH*, p. 321).

[4] The reviewer finds 'it hard to resist the conclusion that Mr Conrad has exhumed a manuscript of earlier days, has seen in it things which again engaged his fancy and has worked over it enough to give many passages the impress of his finest quality, yet not enough to make it the equal of his latest works. The story is, in itself, a little unfortunate. We are promised gun-running and Carlist intrigues . . . But the gun-running turns out to be the merest and vaguest background' (*ibid.*, pp. 321–2).

has been done it would be the basest ingratitude in me to say that I regret the attempt. I have put my trust in the generosity of men and I have my reward. I am, dear Mr Squire, with the greatest regard

Yours

Joseph Conrad.

To Sir Sidney Colvin
Text MS Berg; Unpublished

[letterhead: Spring Grove]

23. 8. '19

Dearest Colvin

It seems incredible to me that you should have been able to think of the review in these days of agonising distress.[1] I don't know how to thank you sufficiently for this amazing proof of your friendship. My admiration for your firmness of mind is mingled with a profound almost remorseful sense of my unworthiness. I don't mind telling you now that your most alarming and totally unexpected news brought out in the course of an hour or so an incipient attack of gout – which after all did not turn out so bad as it looked at first, tho' I still have my left arm and hand in bandages and cotton wool. Jessie had been suffering considerably with her knee for a week, and I confess I restrained her first impulse to start for town immediately, not trusting myself to accompany her (it might have been a disabled foot instead of the hand) and B[orys] being then in Glasgow and not available to escort her. She was grieving bitterly at her helplessness. However the car was kept in readiness and we could have been in London in 3 hours if the next morning's wire had not been more reassuring. We have never suffered so acutely before from the sense of our uselessness to our friends. I feel very miserable (apart from being very seedy still) and poor Jessie is very much cast down by the way her affliction has been brought home to her deepest feelings.

I'll have to take her to London on the 28th. The appointement* is for 2. 30. The examination will no doubt leave a lot of pain behind it and I intend to take her home the same day for a couple of days in bed. Once she is packed in the car with rugs and cushions she will be able to support the journey back. But we'll come to your door (even if J. can not get out) at about 4 o'clock.

Our deepest love to your dear invalid and yourself.

Ever yours

J. Conrad

---

[1] Lady Colvin had been ill. Her husband's review would appear in the *Observer* on the 24th (p. 9). Colvin praises the scenes between Rita and Monsieur Georges, but considers the novel as a whole limited by 'autobiographical fact and reminiscence'.

<u>*24th*</u> I open the envelope to tell you of our great joy on receiving this morning a p-c from poor dear Lady Colvin herself. We thank her with the greatest regard and affection for the relief and happiness the sight of her handwriting has given to us.

To Richard Curle
Text MS Indiana; Curle 48[1]

[Spring Grove]

24. 8. '19.

Dear Curle.

I think I wrote you already of B[orys]'s reception by K[nothe]. It was most kind. The programme is for B to devote a month to the study of a certain chemical test (for metals) and then join the Oldbury works to learn metal-testing by actual practice – with the promise of a post at the end of 12 months – more or less.

Nothing could be more satisfactory.

B will try to get a coach in London so as to be near us when J[essie] is operated. Then at about 10 Oct he expects to proceed to Bir'gham.

Our warmest thanks for your interest and effective agency in this affair. I sent a copy of *A of G* to Mrs Iris[2] and Jessie wrote her a letter of thanks.

Have you seen this cutting? It has been reproduced in several provincial papers.

Jessie sends her love. B is now in Mull[3] – shooting. We shall be in London on the 28th for the examination but intend to go home the same day. Jess would like to put off oper^on (if any) till after we shifted houses. I'll keep you informed. We are most grateful to You my dear Richard for your friendly offer.

Ever your

J Conrad.

PS Our affect^te regards to your Wife and boy, and to the General and Mrs Wedgwood.

---

[1] Without the PS.   [2] Wedgwood.
[3] The Hebridean island.

To W. L. George

Text MS Yale; Unpublished

[letterhead: Spring Grove]

24. 8. '19

Dear M[r] George.[1]

I share fully your admiration for Bradshaw[2] tho' I think he goes too much into detail so that all sense of reality is lost and the book produces the effect of being a mere fairy-tale. It's impossible to believe that all this takes place every day! The more popular and picturesque treatment of the same subject in the A. B. C.[3] carries more conviction to my frivolous mind. As to the other works you mention I think we could get up a pretty quarrel over any one of them if we had nothing better to do.

I do feel indignant at what you say about the reception of your book by your political(?) friends.[4] God knows where you have pricked their inflated pedantry and caused it to hiss like an angry snake. But really people so full of ideas bearing on the regeneration of mankind and positively bursting with indignation, and compassion and self-importance, cannot be expected to pay any attention to common decency. And they don't. In one of the papers you mention I've seen a few weeks ago an instance (or an exhibition) of intellectual obscenity – which no idealism could excuse. Also there is a person going about in that region with a free hand in matters of literary criticism who is a palpable ass. I assure you that *my* friends haven't got the monopoly of stupidity.

I've never read Tchekow[5] but I've re-read the few lines on pp 15–16 of Typhoon, and, since you are so encouraging, I don't mind confessing that they seem to me all right. Charming little lot. What gave me serious concern however is that MacWhirr could not get a house like that nowadays for £45 or anything like it. It looks like a howling mistake on my part and some readers with no sense of chronology will be raising their eyebrows at the figure.

---

[1] Walter Lionel George (1882–1926) was born in Paris to British parents, studied at the Sorbonne, and served in the French army. When he moved to London he worked as a journalist and (during the war) a civil servant. A self-described 'conservative English radical' and feminist, he published books on social and political topics such as *France in the Twentieth Century* (1909), *The Intelligence of Women* (1916), and *The Story of Woman* (1925); his numerous works of fiction such as *A Bed of Roses* (1911) often reflect his involvement in the controversies of the day.

[2] Who published the compendium of all public train services in Britain and Ireland every month.

[3] The *ABC Railway Guide* was more selective, concentrating on services to and from London.

[4] His latest was *Eddies of the Day* (Cassell, 1919), a collection of essays, but the PS points to a work of fiction. Cassell brought out a new edition of the novel *The Making of an Englishman* in 1918 with a preface by George.

[5] Evidently, Conrad had not shared the enthusiasm of Edward and Constance Garnett; the latter had begun to publish her translations of Chekhov's stories.

I am glad you found some satisfaction in a part of your holiday at least. Our very best regards to the whole household.

Yours

J. Conrad

No. No. Don't say your people are mouthpieces. You don't make a drama with mere mouthpieces – and in the book one has a distinct sense of that. There is there a wealth of fascinating human detail a depth of shadows and a strenght* of rendering wherein dwells a great and sustained passion. So great that, I suppose, they thought a little levelling would do no harm. So they try to get a roller over your head. And in the last instance, whatever else that reception may mean, it also means *that you count*. There is no doubt of it in my mind.

To G. Jean-Aubry
Text MS Yale; Unpublished

[Spring Grove]
26. 8. '19

Cher Ami.

Voulez venir nous voir?

Nous serons a Londres le 28 pour Sir R. Jones mais nous avons l'intention de revenir le même jour. Le Samedi nous serons prêts a vous recevoir si Vous voulez venir par le 4. 30 de Char + a *Wye* car l'auto est en reparation.

Nous serons en famille (avec Miss H[allowes]) et nous aurons le temps pour une longue causerie.

Voulez-Vous nous dire un petit mot par le 'phone a Norfolk Hotel (*Gerrard 5508*) Surrey Street Strand ou nous arriverons vers une heure le Jeudi pour que ma femme puisse se reposer un peu avant d'aller a Cavendish Sq a 2. 30.

Je ne Vous demande pas de venir nous voir a l'hotel car c'est loin de tout – et puis l'occasion n'est pas bien gaie. J'espère repartir pour ici vers 4h 30 après une petite visite a Lady Colvin qui a été très malade.

J'ai écrit a Gide. Pas de réponse encore.

My wife's kindest regards

Affct^{ly} yours

J. Conrad.

Translation

Dear Friend.

Would you like to come to see us?

We'll be in London on the 28th for Sir Robert Jones but we intend to return the same day. We will be ready to receive you on Saturday if

You wish to come on the 4. 30 from Char + to *Wye* since the car is under repair.

We will be a family party (with Miss H) and have time for a long chat.

Would you care to give me a quick ring at the Norfolk Hotel (*Gerrard 5508*) Surrey Street Strand where we will be arriving around one o'clock on Thursday, so that my wife can rest a little before going to Cavendish Sq at 2. 30.

I am not asking you to come to see us at the hotel since it is a long way from everything – and then the occasion is not particularly cheerful. I hope to set out again for here around 4. 30 after a short visit to Lady Colvin who has been very ill.

I have written to Gide. No reply yet.

My wife's kindest regards

Affct^{ly} yours

J. Conrad.

To J. B. Pinker

Text MS Berg; Unpublished

[letterhead: Spring Grove]

27. 8. 19

Dearest Friend

Thanks for Your letter and assurances.

We are coming up to-morrow (Thursday) and I shall run in for a moment into your office about one o'clock.

Ever Yours

J. C.

To J. B. Pinker

Text MS Berg; Unpublished

[letterhead: The Norfolk Hotel
Surrey Street, Strand,
London W. C. 2]
[28 August 1919?][1]

My dear Pinker

We've arrived. I don't invade your office since we are to meet at one – but please bring with you – or else send me by the mess[eng]^{er} £10.

Ever Yours

J. C.

---

[1] While possibly dating from some other journey to town, this note fits the circumstances of the visit on the 28th.

To Richard Curle
Text MS Indiana; Curle 49

[Spring Grove]
30. 8. '19

My dear Curle.

Jessie has been considerably upset by the examination. She has been put to bed with a bad pulse for 3 days and asks me to thank you warmly for your good letter and tell you of the result at once.

Another operation is necessary. Sir R. Jones who is very confident as to ultimate success is going to the U. S. middle Sep^t and does not wish to operate till his return – that is about middle of Nov^{er} – as he has made up his mind to attend to the case himself throughout. He has asked me to bring Jessie to L'pool where he will be able to have her under his eye all the time.

From the domestic point of view the delay is not an unmixed evil as we'll be able to settle down (in a certain measure) in our new house before going to L'pool in Nov. But it is a beastly prospect to live with and a charming Xmas tide to look forward to for both of us.

We are glad to know You are having a good time. I will write to you again soon. Directly you come south again you must come to see us – here if before the 20th Sept. or in the new house about the 15 Oct. – the first visitor no doubt.

Jessie sends her love and thanks.

Ever Yours

J. Conrad

PS Remember us affect^{ly} to the Gen & Mrs Wedgwood. We hope that John[1] is making a good recovery.

To F. N. Doubleday
Text TS/MS Princeton; Unpublished

[letterhead: Spring Grove]
Kent.
Aug. 30th. 1919.

Dear Mr Doubleday.

I have been asked some time ago for some new photographs for publicity purposes. I am sending you to-day a couple of the latest, the product of a sitting for the *Vanity Fair* when something like a dozen negatives were taken.[2]

---

[1] The Wedgwoods' son.   [2] Cf. the letter of [17 July].

Those are my selection for myself and I shall ask the photographer to send you three others as soon as possible.

I am very glad that the original plan of 377 sets of the limited Edition is adhered to. It is much the safer proceeding and I cordially agree with your remarks on the subject, contained in your last letter to Pinker.

I am glad of the apparent popularity of the *Arrow* and I trust that your confident prophecy as to the good prospects of the *Rescue* will be realised to our mutual satisfaction and benefit.

I have now a complete set of galley slips of *Rescue*. They require much revision and pulling together, apart from the usual corrections. I have asked Pinker to transmit to you my very earnest request that twelve months should elapse between the publication of the *Arrow* (April 1919) and that of the *Rescue*. I feel that the *Arrow* must be given its full time.

The correct text and the Preface for the *Typhoon* volume, as planned for that edition including the *Typhoon* story, will reach you before long. Meanwhile I shall be dispatching to you further corrected texts and prefaces of the books up to and including *The Secret Agent* and also the *Mirror of the Sea*.

My wife who has the pleasant prospect of another operation in Novem^er wishes to be kindly remembered to you. As you may imagine I don't feel very happy just now.

Believe me

very cordially Yours

Joseph Conrad.

To J. B. Pinker
Text TS/MS Berg; Unpublished

[letterhead: Spring Grove]
Aug. 30th, 1919.

My dear Pinker.

You will think me a perfect nuisance. What I want to ask you is to have two copies of the Arrow of Gold specially bound for me in morocco bindings in the best modern style for presentation: one to Sir. R. Jones and the other to Miss Lithgow.[1] I really have no idea who is doing distinguished bindings nowadays or else I would not give you this additional trouble.

I enclose here account for another lot of furniture for which please send cheque to the dealer.

---

[1] An aunt of Colonel James Lithgow (1883–1952), Borys's former commanding officer?

Jessie had to go to bed for 3 days at least with a nasty fluttery heart – as the result of the journey and the examination. She sends her love.

Ever Yours

J. Conrad

To W. M. Parker
Text MS NLS Acc. 5892/6; Dryden

[Spring Grove]

2. 9. 19

Dear M[r] Parker[1]

I've just received your letter and I want to thank you for the friendly impulse which prompted you to write. The appreciation of a fellow-craftsman is always a great pleasure – and all the greater when expressed with sympathetic understanding of what one has tried to do.

This book,[2] I don't mind telling it to you, is very near my heart and I accept eagerly your profecy* of its taking a high place – some day.

Meantime the reception, though friendly, has been somewhat mixed. Believe me

very sincerely Yours

Joseph Conrad

To J. B. Pinker
Text TS/MS Berg; Unpublished

[letterhead: Spring Grove]

Sept. 2nd. 1919

Dearest Pinker.

Thank you very much for your letter. This time I really enclose the bill.

There is a matter which I am very tempted to undertake and want to consult you about. There is a collection of Odillon* Redon's lithographs (and a few original drawings) in series, amounting to 180 pieces.[3] It is an

---

[1] Glasgow-born, William Mathie Parker (1891–1973) published many books on Scottish literature; he also contributed frequently to the *Fortnightly Review*, *Glasgow Herald*, and *John O' London's* and wrote assiduously to well-known authors such as Conrad and Hardy in the hope of being granted 'personal sidelights'. Conrad first corresponded with him in November 1915: see *Letters*, 5, p. 532.

[2] *The Arrow*.

[3] For much of his artistic life, Odilon Redon (1840–1916) worked in dark tones, originally with charcoal drawings, then with lithographs. A quintessential Symbolist, he took his imagery from dreams and fantasies.

early collection and therefore in good states, several series rare, which poor Tebb[1] can hardly make up his mind to part with; but as far as I can see he will have to do so because he is reduced to great straits. He was a great friend of O. R. who stayed with him for a few weeks many years ago on his first visit to England. Tebb wants £300 for them, which I think even dealers could be induced to give as the worst of these plates fetch between 50 and 60 francs at sales in France. I talked over this matter with Jean Aubry, a later friend of O. R. too, and a man who knows all those matters thoroughly, and especially the present values of O. R.'s work. Aubry is also personally acquainted with several connoisseurs in this country who collect O. R. works. I went very thoroughly into the matter with him yesterday and he assures me that at the very worst all that collection could be disposed of at the average price of £2 a plate or drawing. The sales' catalogue's prices in America are of course much higher.

All this would take some little time to negotiate here and in that Aubry is ready to assist me, both for my own and Dr Tebb's sake. My idea is that I would like to take over the collection from Tebb, keep a couple of series, say, fifteen specimens for myself, and deal with the rest. I understand that there are amongst them a few etchings (about which the collectors are not very keen); but I like etchings and as far as I remember them – I saw them many years ago – they are very fine, though, of course, O. R. was not a great etcher. The fact of the matter is that I will have nothing whatever to put on the walls of the house and this opportunity seems very fascinating.

Do you think I could venture to do that? We had Tebb here for two days. To see that poor man with his little boy (he's spending his holidays with us) was simply heart-breaking. And a man of great worth and blameless life too.

Ever Yours

J. Conrad.

Have you seen the Dly Teleg: second notice, written magistrally by Courtney?[2] Upon my word, I think the book is making a little stir in the critical world.

---

[1] For Dr Tebb, see the letter to Pinker of [c. 1 April 1919], and for his collection, the letter to Jean-Aubry of 30 May.

[2] W[illiam] L[eonard] Courtney (1850–1928), literary editor of the *Daily Telegraph*, wrote what is not so much a review as a discussion of critical reactions to *The Arrow* (*CH*, pp. 324–5). Since the middle of the seventeenth century, usage has favoured 'magisterially' over 'magistrally'; the *OED*'s most recent citation for the latter comes from Hobbes, writing in 1656.

To John Galsworthy

Text MS Forbes; Unpublished

[Spring Grove]

3. 9. '19

Dearest Jack.

We have a man who apparently wishes to stay on and is prepared to run the light-plant as part of shover's¹ job.

Last week we went to town for the surgical examination. Sir R. J[ones] will operate again on his return from the U. S. in November; and he wants Jessie in L'pool, so as to have her under his eye.

Here's the prospect of a charming Christmas-tide for us both. However Sir R. J. seems very confident of ultimate success.

I have been doing nothing since last June but am trying now to pull myself together and start something. I don't suppose I'll succeed till we get into the new house – end [of] this month. And then there will be that L'pool journey hanging over us.

We hope You are both well and had a good quiet time. Indeed quiet is what I lack. Our dear love

Ever Yours

J. Conrad.

To J. E. Hodgson

Text MS Bodley Eng. c. 4802; Unpublished

[letterhead: Spring Grove]

Friday 4 [5]. 9. '19.²

Dear Mʳ Hodgson

I regret very much that an appointement* with the oculist in Maidstone to see to my younger boy's eyes will cause me to be away from home on Monday afternoon. This however is the sort of thing that cannot be put off.

I hope however that we may have better luck next time when you come down this way.³ We'll be presently moving to a house nearer Canterbury but not a very great distance from here.

Believe me

very faithfully yours

J. Conrad.

---

¹ Chauffeur's?   ² Friday was the 5th.
³ The envelope is addressed to Hodgson at the George Hotel, Rye.

To Major Gordon Gardiner
Text MS Harvard; Unpublished

[Spring Grove]
6. 9. '19[1]

My dear Gardiner

Just a line of warmest thanks for your letter on the Arrow. Your winged words went straight to my heart, and expanded it with a great pride and with a great gratitude.

Yours with deep affection
Joseph Conrad.

Love from Jessie. She will have to be operated [on] in November and Sir R. Jones wants me to bring her to L'pool so as to have her immediately under his eye.

She's bearing up wonderfully.

Borys wishes to be remembered to you.

To J. B. Pinker
Text MS Berg; Unpublished

[letterhead: Spring Grove]
6. 9. '19

My dear Pinker

Thanks for letters relating to the binding of books[2] and the question of prints – now given up.

For your visit here with Mr Vernon I would suggest Thurs: or Friday, as Tuesday, I suppose, would be too early for you to arrange and on Wed^{ay} Jessie (and as a matter of fact all of us) must go over to the new house for the measuring of floors and windows and so forth. It's the only day the Bells won't be at home this week and we must take advantage of it as the time is getting short.

I am sending you back the signed photos as requested.

I am writing an author's note for the Personal Record. It will be finished by Tuesday. I would like Dent to send the book to some of the papers at least. It would please me if the Auth^{rs} Note got some publicity, if only a little of it.

F[isher] U[nwin] does not seem to advertise much and from what I have seen the first edition (I wonder how many cop^{ies} he printed?) is not yet exhausted. He may however have been reprinting without saying anything about it.

---

[1] Catalogued at Harvard as 6 October, but the date is clear.
[2] Presentation copies? See the letters to Dent of 25 September and Pinker of 15 October.

I am sending You here Wither's* acc^t and the photographers bill. Will you also send B[orys] his £8 for *Sept.*

Looking forward immensely to seeing you soon.

Ever afft^{ly} yours

J. Conrad

Jessie sends her love.

To J. B. Pinker

Text MS Berg; Unpublished

[letterhead: Spring Grove]
Monday. [8 September 1919][1]

Dear Pinker.

This is the Note for A Personal Record.

Primarily for Dent's reprint it may go into the deluxe edition.

Pray have *two* copies made one for Dent and one for *US.* Send them to me please for revise before the[y] go to the publishers.

Also I want the original draft returned.

Ever Yours

JC.

To Rollo Walter Brown

Text TS Harvard; Unpublished

[letterhead: Spring Grove]
Kent.
Sept. 9th. 1919.

Dear Sir.[2]

Thank you very much for your friendly and pleasant letter. To hear on such good authority as yourself that one's work is becoming an influence in the artistic life of a great country is indeed most gratifying, though it gives one an increasing sense of responsibility in one's attitude to one's own productions.

---

[1] Conrad expected to finish the Note by Tuesday the 9th; on the 13th a clean copy was ready or close to ready for posting to Doubleday.

[2] When Rollo Walter Brown (1880–1956) wrote to Conrad, he was Professor of Rhetoric at Wabash College, Indiana; later he moved to Carleton College, Minnesota, and on to Harvard. In 1924 he gave up teaching in order to write full-time. Brown's works include *The Art of Writing English: A Book for College Classes* (1913) and *How the French Boy Learns to Write: A Study in the Teaching of the Mother Tongue* (1915).

As to the Preface of the *Nigger* I must confess that I don't think so well of it now as I used to do. But that bears only on the expression. My convictions in the main remain the same.

Therefore I am not ashamed of it and your idea of including it in that sort of anthology you contemplate pleases me very much.[1] I will leave it to you to negotiate the matter with my American publishers, conveying to you here only my personal authorisation to include that Preface, wholly or in part, in your forthcoming book. I feel confident that Messrs. Doubleday, & Page will try to meet your wishes – unless there is some particular reason to the contrary.

Kindest regards.

Yours faithfully

Joseph Conrad.

To F. N. Doubleday
Text TS Princeton; Unpublished

[letterhead: Spring Grove]

Sept. 13th. 1919.

My dear M[r] Doubleday.

Pinker came to lunch yesterday and brought me your note expressing your high opinion of *The Rescue*.

I am, of course, very delighted with your good opinion. It gave me the greater pleasure because I infer that the last third of the book has not disappointed you. I was naturally a bit anxious about it, there being, as you know almost exactly twenty years' interval between the old and the new. I doubted whether it would be in my power to recover the old mood, the old rhythms of the prose, and the intimate sense of the general effect I had wanted to produce then. I conclude from your kind note that I may lay those apprehensions aside.

Thank you for the friendly thought of sending me those encouraging words and for your good wishes, which my wife and I highly appreciate.

With our kindest regards

Yours very sincerely

Joseph Conrad.

Pardon this type. I've a painful wrist.

---

[1] Browne was compiling *The Writer's Art by Those Who Have Practiced It* (1921) for Harvard University Press; this anthology includes the Preface to *The Nigger*.

P. S. Just received: Proofs of *Note to my American Readers* and the *Preface* for the *Nigger*.[1] I can't tell you how much I appreciate this evident care for the correctness of the text on the part of your Book Dept. I shall return it by the next mail, duly corrected.

You shall also receive, probably by the same mail, clean copy of the new *Author's Note* for the *Personal Record*. That Note which should precede the original Preface, which is part of the book now, consists of about 2,700 words and will raise the number of words in the whole volume to just a little over 40,000, which, from a typographical point of view, is an advantage.

The Note is very intimate in tone, and is quite proper in a book of that sort.[2]

JC.

To W. M. Parker
Text TS NLS Acc. 5892/6; Dryden

[Spring Grove]
Kent.
Sept. 13th. 1919.

Dear Mr Parker.

The first thing that occurs to me on receipt of your letter is this:— that most of the newspapers of any standing in the U. K. have pronounced on the *Arrow of Gold* and that you may be losing your time in coming in with a study, however able, when the book, as things go now-a-days, is no longer an actuality. The monthlies and the quarterlies have their own contributors, even if they thought that the book deserves their especial notice; and generally in the serious order of criticism the acceptance of an article so purely literary would depend on the intrinsic value of what you wrote rather than on any special information.

Therefore, I very much doubt whether the sort of information which you have in your mind would help you really in your ambition to win the standing of a literary critic. That sort of success can only proceed from what the critic can find in himself to say about any work of art which, in its essence, is open to everybody's investigation and comment. The form in which you put your

---

[1] The Note 'To My Readers in America' explains the genesis of the Preface written to follow the final episode of *The Nigger* in the *New Review*. It first appeared in 1914, in the pamphlet *Joseph Conrad on the Art of Writing* and the Doubleday, Page edition of *The Nigger*. It reappears in the Doubleday collected editions.

[2] Accompanying the 'Familar Preface', this Author's Note dispels misconceptions both about Apollo Korzeniowski and about Conrad's decision to write in English, which he presents as inevitable.

request – which I do not consider presumptuous in the least – forces me to put these considerations before you.

Believe me that it is with the utmost friendliness that I ask whether you have really reflected upon what you are asking me to do? Even before my intimates I would feel reluctant to lay bare the springs of my activities and the sources of my inspiration. The very qualities that you recognise in this book, (in which some critics have perceived a restraint of emotional discretion) make it impossible for me to say anything that would be significant and touch upon the deeper motives which induced me to write *this* after so many other books. Mere facts, such as when it was begun and ended, under what conditions it was written of health or discomfort, freedom or worry of mind, would be of no use to you from a critical point of view; and I feel it would be a rather ridiculous proceeding for me to enlarge upon them. But if there ever comes the time for deeper disclosures to be made, you will see perfectly well, I think, that they cannot fittingly be made by anybody but myself.

Believe me

faithfully Yours,

J. Conrad.

To J. M. Dent
Text MS Yale; Unpublished

[Spring Grove]
17. 9. 19

Dear Mr Dent

I'll be in town on the 23d and could see you then at about 3. 30 if this suits you.

Cordially Yours

Joseph Conrad.

To J. B. Pinker
Text MS Berg; Unpublished

[letterhead: Spring Grove]
Wednes: [17 September 1919][1]

My dear Pinker

I send you John's school acct. Pray add to the amount £5 in accordance with the printed request. Mrs P[earce] took John at a reduction originally.

---

[1] The same day as the letter to Dent giving news of the visit.

Please when sending Jessie's weekly cheque add £25 to it so that she may settle all the small acc*ᵗˢ* and other expences* connected with our leaving this part of the country.

I'll be in town on the 23ᵈ and shall call on you a little before one o'clock.

Ever Yours

J Conrad.

To John Quinn

Text TS Texas; Unpublished

[letterhead: Spring Grove]

Sept. 18th. 1919.

My dear Quinn.

I imagine that H. Walpole does not want an introduction to you, who have been such a good friend to English Letters in the United States; but I suppose it will do him no harm if I mention to you that he is the most intimate of my younger friends. You have many tastes in common and he is very desirous to make your acquaintance.

I am always my dear Quinn

most Sincerely Yours

Joseph Conrad.

To Christopher Sandeman

Text MS Karl; Unpublished

[letterhead: Spring Grove]

19. 9. '19

My dear Sandeman.

This is a very interesting journal[1] and I read it with a particular pleasure derived both from the matter and from the expression of the writer's personality. It is perhaps a little bit too "intime"[2] – not in matter but in manner – for those editors. Strange beasts and not easily understandable. There are perfectly delightful passages, of things seen and things heard, rendered personally with remarkable effect. You certainly have an eye for the picturesque (you ought to "let yourself go" on that) in nature and man, and a fine feeling for the past.

As to exposing yourself to further rejections – Vous m'en demandez trop. I don't know what to say. I tell you They are strange beasts![3]

[1] A 93-page account of a journey across Spain on horseback which has survived along with the letter.
[2] Recalling Henri-Frédéric Amiel's *Fragments d'un journal intime* (1884)?
[3] The journal never found a publisher.

My wife sends her warm regards. Bon voyage. Do drop us a line on arrival at the palatial Casa.[1]

Yours affectionately

Joseph Conrad

To Hugh Walpole

Text MS Texas; Unpublished

[letterhead: Spring Grove]

19. 9. 19

Dearest Hugh.

Herewith the letter to Quinn. You had better know that my latest letter to him has been of a rather 'squashing' kind – of course perfectly friendly. But devil only knows how he has taken it. Those people's sensibilities are easily hurt.

I feel my approaching loneliness deeply. I shall try to hold on to the lifebuoy till you return, with (O Heavens!) or without (perhaps) an American wife.[2] You have been meditating on the brink so much that the slightest push may do it. The splash would be considerable! But before it comes we shall expect a good (and extended) notice – descriptive and analytical yet coloured in style and (preferably) impressionist in execution. However should You feel too agitated to do justice to the subject a cable to Conrad Bishopsbourne will do. But a notice we must have. I am too old and infirm to stand sudden shocks, now.

Well, as our peasants say (or used to say): "God be with you Brother". And keep us in your tenderest remembrance.

Jessie's love and the boy's greetings

Ever Yours

Joseph Conrad.

To Warrington Dawson

Text MS Duke; Randall 198

[Spring Grove]

22. 9. 19

Dearest Dawson.

I asked Jessie to write you at once. As to myself – well! But what is one to say? I am not either very well or very happy – I don't mean in my "domesticity".

---

[1] The family mansion in Jerez de la Frontera is called El Palacio.

[2] Much against his grain, Walpole had proposed to 'a ripping girl' in August 1918. Amiably she turned him down, and they remained friends. This overture to an Englishwoman was the only such gesture of his life (Hart-Davis, *Walpole*, pp. 174–5).

That is secure for all time. But I have la sensation du vide. Not perhaps le Vide Eternel, though after sixty one may well begin to grow aware of it a little, but of a certain inward emptiness. For 25 years I've been giving out all that was in me. But apart from that I have the feeling of approaching isolation. I don't say loneliness; I shall, I imagine, be always looked at now – but from a distance, as if set apart by my predestined temperament like some strange animal confined within a fence for public view. Through my fault – or is it simply Fate? – I have missed all along the chances of closer contacts. But why continue – except only just to say that I have been and am now missing you very much. I trust you won't think I am complaining of things or people. That *would* be outrageous on *my* part! But man, I suppose, is the only animal that is *never* satisfied, perhaps because he's the only one that does not live on bread alone.

Nothing has given me greater satisfaction than your good words about the Arrow. You were often in my thoughts while I wrote. It was unavoidable.

I need not protest to you that I tried to be scrupulously fair in my treatment of the Blunts.[1] The antagonism of feeling had of course to come out since it is the very foundation of the story's psychology.

Borys sends you his warm greetings. John can hardly remember you. He is now a tall schoolboy. Jessie's love.

Always with affection

Yours

J. Conrad.

To J. B. Pinker

Text MS Berg; Unpublished

[letterhead: Spring Grove]
23^{d}. 9. 19

Dearest Pinker.

Eric would have told you of our short interview. I wanted mainly just to see him. He looks well and is nice.

I take it I may come to you[2] on Wed: the 1st Oct. by the 4. 30 from Ashford. On Thursday I should like to run over and see John at school for an hour or so. On Friday I won't follow you *all* over the estate on your rounds but only over a part if I am allowed; and on Sat. You'll send me home to the new residence much improved and refreshed. I certainly want improving not

---

[1] Like Dawson, Blunt is a South Carolinian devoted to his mother and voluble on matters of race.

[2] To Burys Court, Pinker's house near Reigate, Surrey.

so much in my morals as in my manners which are more of an "idle and worthless member of the community".

Can you tell me something of the Corbett Smith who wrote the inclosed*. Is he "a reputable and serious citizen?" I'd like to know before answering him.[1]

Please pay in to Drummond's Bank acc^t of Capt A. Halsey. RN. £13 – of which part is one extra week's rent and part for a palatial chicken house we have bought from him.

I have asked Eric to send Miss H[allowes] salary for next quarter (ending Dec^{er}) at the rate of £20 per quar: She ought to get that small rise.[2]

Jessie and my love to you and your household.

Ever Yours

J. Conrad.

To Sir Sidney Colvin
Text MS Duke; Unpublished

[letterhead: Spring Grove]
24. 9. '19

My dearest Colvin.

I have read (before breakfast) your *Gambetta* a most excellent thing both as picture and appreciation of the man.[3] All the little touches are just right and "la lecture de cette petite piece est, par soi, extremement attrayante".

Pray do not hesitate to do as much more of these "vignettes" as You can think of. With or *without* revision they would make a delightful volume of glimpses and appreciations by a contemporary, conveyed with the charm and personal character of the living speech almost audible in the literary form. If I mention revision at all it is not to *improve* but to *enrich*: should memory recall some additional little touch.

Please très cher, look at the last line of the first paragraph of the quoted letter. (Sai*si*ssant)

Also in the note (p 8) the words " . . . course of the *next year* 1888 etc etc" – do not fit anywhere in the chronology of the article. The words *next year* referring

---

[1] Major Arthur Corbett-Smith (1879–1945), late of the Royal Field Artillery, was the author of *The Retreat from Mons by One Who Shared It* (1916), *The Marne – and After* (1917), and *The Seafarers* (1919); his 'Portrait Study' of Nelson came out in 1926.
[2] By 10 December, the salary was £25.
[3] Colvin's 'vignette' of Gambetta may be found in *Memories & Notes of Persons and Places 1852–1912* (1921), pp. 274–85. Comparing the public and private faces of the French statesman, Colvin recalls their first meeting in the winter of 1874–5; they discussed censorship and free expression. For Conrad's attitude to Gambetta, see the letter of [21 April 1917].

to the time G's letter was written (1877)[1] the year ought to be 1878. Is that so?

Jessie is made happy by my good report. She is resting to-day and as cheerful as usual.

Our dearest love to you both.

Ever yours

Joseph Conrad.

To Edward Garnett
Text MS Free; G. 289

[Spring Grove]
24 [25 or 26?]. 9. 19[2]

Dearest Edward.

My loving thanks for your letter.[3] I don't think there is a single remark You make that I don't understand both in the letter and in the spirit.

I have looked at once, here and there, at your marks and marginal notes in various numbers. I quite see. As it happened I came upon one par: which you condemn in toto but which I can't take out as it bears on the story itself — the plot. But I shall try to put it into other words.

Don't you know my dear Edward how stupid people are! They take delight in merest twaddle, they look out for and welcome the obvious. And they understand hardly anything which is not either one or the other.

Miss H[allowes] is looking out and preparing for dispatch to you the Nos you mention.[4]

Yes, the *A of G* is "swallowed down". The amount of reviewing was really greater than for *any* of my books, I think. People write to each other (and sometimes to me too) about it. Next thing to a "sensation". *The Church Times* (High) the *Guardian* (*Evan*[al]) and the *Methodist Times* (2 notices) are most

---

[1] Colvin reproduces a letter from him of that year.

[2] Since Conrad quotes from Garnett's letter dated the 25th, either Garnett's date or Conrad's is wrong.

[3] Garnett marked up an instalment of *The Rescue* and returned it to Conrad with a letter dated 25 September (MS Texas; *Portrait*, pp. 140–1). Garnett suggests trimming the dialogue, especially that of the European characters: 'You have, here, a habit of saying too much, of letting the characters express themselves too fully.' Following his critique, Garnett adds: 'What a damnable life, reading MS. & making comments. The only certainty one has is of shades of one's own imbecility.'

[4] A telegram to Pinker handed in at Wye, 10:45 a.m., 25 September, reads: 'Please try induce Land and Water give or sell me complete set of numbers containing Rescue important Conrad' (Berg).

sympathetic and – yes – almost intelligent.[1] I am not joking. Who would have thought it possible!!

Give my love to David.[2] I am glad he likes it. And just hint to him that I am not a musty old reactionary in my feelings. My misfortune is that I can't swallow *any* formula and thus am wearing the aspect of enemy to all mankind.

Jessie sends her dear love. She has been badly lamed by the surgical exam^{on}, and spends most of her time in bed. There must be another operation on R. Jones' return from US, about middle Nov^{er} and in Liverpool, as R. J. wants to have her there under his eye. Beastly prospect.

Ever Yours
J. Conrad

To J. M. Dent
Text TS Berg; Unpublished

[Spring Grove]
Sept. 25th. 1919.

Dear Mr Dent

I am sending you here the *Author's Note* to the *Personal Record*.[3] It is to be printed first, after the preliminary pages, before the *Familiar Preface*. Pray send me a proof. I should like this Note to secure a certain amount of publicity, you will see why when you read it. Let us hope that the book will have the chance of being taken notice of by the Press, at least as much as *Youth* or *Lord Jim*. In this connection, will you have the kindness to have one copy bound specially for me for a present to a lady who understands fine bindings.

---

[1] In a PS, Garnett had asked: 'What was the net effect of the *A of G* on the world? They swallowed it down, didn't they – not *quite* clear as to how they liked it?' The reviews in religious journals are *Church Times*, 29 August, p. 180; the *Guardian: The Church Newspaper* (not in fact Evangelical in tendency, but High Church – i.e. embracing rather than spurning 'Roman' rituals), 18 September, p. 935; the *Methodist Times* did not review *The Arrow*, but the *Methodist Recorder* did: 11 September, p. 11. All welcomed Conrad's novel, if anything, more warmly than the secular press. The *Guardian* lauded his prose, finding it of a much higher quality than English-born writers had achieved. The *Church Times* thought the 'elusive' portrayal of Rita was characteristic of 'the highest art'; the *Methodist Recorder* described Conrad as 'matchless in our time, matchless here', and while conceding that some readers accustomed only to mediocre fiction might be bored, asserted that others would be 'invigorated': 'The wiser man or woman will forswear the average, and determine to obtain the fellowship of this new spirit and new company.'

[2] Edward's son (1892–1981): under the pseudonym Leda Burke, David had just published his first novel, *Dope Darling: A Story of Cocaine*.

[3] Dent put out two new editions of *A Personal Record* in 1919, distinguished by the quality of paper and binding.

In the matter of the School Book[1] I wish you luck with your negotiations with my other publishers.

Believe me

Sincerely Yours

Joseph Conrad

To John Quinn

Text TS/MS NYPL; Unpublished

[letterhead: Spring Grove]
from tomorrow: Oswalds
Bishopsbourne
N^r Canterbury
Sept. 29th. 1919.

My dear Quinn.

About a week ago I gave a letter of introduction to you to Walpole and I hope you found him as nice a fellow as he really is.

My wife has been examined by Sir Robert Jones just before his departure for America, where he is now, and the operation has been put off till his return some time in the middle of November. Meantime she remains much crippled and suffering not a little pain at times, but she bears it well in her confidence that ultimately Sir R. Jones will make everything right for the rest of her life.

In the meantime we are about to move into a new house. The new address card has been sent to you already. The weather has gone to pieces and a gale of wind is blowing at the present moment, while the general strike of railways is putting a stormy complexion on the future.[2] We had neither letters nor papers for the last two days and God only knows when this will start on its way to you. The young lady in our local post-office is yawning her head off in complete idleness and every man in the Ashford railway-works, is walking about in his Sunday clothes and with a flower in his buttonhole. There is not a whistle, a rumble or a clank to be heard in the whole landscape. A profound peace broods over the land. But a dump of high-explosive shells looks a most peaceable thing in the world, too!

However we managed to get your namesake, John, in time to school and that is a blessing. Borys is with us, but he may be called any time

---

[1] Nothing came of this project, which caused some friction between Dent and Pinker: see the letter to Dent of 25 October.

[2] The strike began on Saturday the 26th. Very few trains were running, farmers came to Canterbury market by horse and cart, and food supplies were rationed.

by the Government to drive a lorry on the high roads. I am told that a transport officer has arrived in Ashford to take hold of road-traffic, but for the present he is lying low in the hope that things will right themselves without any need for strong measures. The most amazing thing is that, to me and to a few other people who are able to look at it dispassionately, the whole row rests on a clerical error, the word *definitive* being used in the Government declaration of a week ago instead of the word *definite* which was obviously meant.[1] The whole tenor of the document means that and nothing else, and yet it seems impossible to explain the mistake away. The misunderstanding serves the purposes of a few hot-heads too well for that.

I wonder how things will look by the time you read these lines. But its no use speculating upon events with which common sense has nothing to do. So I will turn to a point or two in your private letter of June 19th, which I have not had the industry or the energy to answer in my last.[2]

I was extremely pleased to receive your congratulations upon "The Rescue".

As to my Polish Article which you seem to like, I think that Paderewski's son-in-law was perhaps not wrong in his judgment as to it not being fit for popular propaganda. It appeared here in the Fortnightly Review and was much more noticed generally than anything of the sort I have ever written. I am also very satisfied with its publication in Collier's Weekly.[3]

I was much amused by your reference to Massingham, with his politics (the mildest-mannered man that ever patronised throat-cutting from humanitarian motives, and I must confess that when it comes to that I much prefer the actual fellow with the knife)[4] and to C. Shorter, with his nosing

---

[1] On behalf of the employers, Sir Auckland Geddes, President of the Board of Trade, had made a 'definitive offer' of wage increases. J. H. Thomas, leader of the National Union of Railwaymen, was eloquently sceptical about this offer, arguing that far from being firm, it was tentative and hedged about with conditions (*The Times*, 25 September, p. 11).

[2] The 'personal' letter, which runs to seven typed pages: Conrad's earlier reply was on 31 July.

[3] Concerning 'The Crime of Partition', Quinn wrote: 'I suggested to Paderewsky's son-in-law, who has been acting as Polish Consul here in New York, that it should be published in fifty or a hundred thousand copies, but he said he enjoyed it and while it had a beautiful style, it did not put the Polish case in simple enough language for the American people.' Publication in *Collier's Weekly* had been on 14 June.

[4] H. W. Massingham, editor of the London *Nation*, was a Liberal with some tolerance for revolutionary violence overseas but not at home. On his visit to Quinn, they had argued about Irish politics. The *Nation* advocated dominion status for Ireland while recognising the strength of Republican feeling and deploring the British government's coercive policies. See, for example 'Cant about Ireland', 12 April 1919, pp. 38–9, and 'The War against Ireland', 20 September, pp. 721–2.

amongst your MSS. What C. S. told you is perfectly correct.[1] I sold the typed first draft of A. of G. and also the incomplete MS of "Rescue" (completed in type) to Mr. Wise, because I wanted the money at once for a specific purpose.

I had the less hesitation in doing that because I considered that you had all my pen-and-ink MSS. and that you would care less for MSS. based on a type-written first draft, even if containing a large proportion of pen-and-ink work in it. And from that point of view I confess that I thought it possible that you had enough of my MSS. The fact is that you are now the possessor of every line of my pen-and-ink first drafts, Wise having only acquired the two mixed drafts of my two considerable works done in that manner, for which he paid rather more than I would have liked to ask you, precisely because of their mixed character.

Then from another point of view the matter stands thus: you are now the possessor of all my pre-war productions, including also "The Shadow Line" and the two short stories which were published during the war.[2] What Wise has got hold of are the publications after the war. Thus your collection, to which I often give a thought, has got a double character of completeness in so far that it is *all* pen-and-ink Conrad and *all* pre-war Conrad. And in that you can have no rival. Perhaps from those points of view, of completeness and unity of period, your collection is as good already as it can be. Personally I feel that I would prefer to have a smaller thing absolutely complete, both in time and kind, than a larger but not complete collection. But then I am no collector and cannot pretend to know how a collector would feel. I have a delicacy in suggesting any transaction to you now, but I think you ought to know that I have here in my possession 45 pages of MS. containing two complete pieces, both unpublished. One (15 pp.) a political note on Poland: the other (30 pp.) an Admiralty paper which the Admiralty did not make use of.[3] That paper is the very last piece I wrote completely in pen-and-ink before deciding to do henceforth my first drafts on the typewriter also.[4] I can't possibly guarantee that I will never go back to my former practice, but I may safely say that it is a most unlikely thing. With those two pieces your collection would be in its kind and period absolutely complete. Of course

[1] While Quinn argued with Massingham, C. K. Shorter 'nosed around' Quinn's flat, 'looking at books and diving into closets and cases'. Seeing the collection of Conrad MSS, Shorter gave Quinn the unwelcome news that Wise now owned the TS of *The Arrow*.
[2] 'The Tale' and 'The Warrior's Soul', collected posthumously in *Tales of Hearsay*.
[3] 'A Note on the Polish Problem' and 'The Unlighted Coast': both are in *Notes on Life and Letters*.
[4] With Miss Hallowes at the keyboard.

Wise would have those too, but I will hold them back till I hear whether you would care to add them to your collection or not.

My wife must have been alluding to a mixed draft of *Falk*, which she discovered some time ago at the bottom of a drawer. I don't know whether the pen-and-ink draft of *Falk* (I mean the story of that name) had been preserved. If it has been preserved then it must be in your collection.[1] If it is not in it then those 60 small pages of type, corrected, altered, and in many places altogether re-written (on versos of pages and between the lines) are the only remaining trace of *Falk*'s original composition. But in any case they belong to your period and notwithstanding their mixed character I am going to send them to you without of course any question of payment arising between us in that respect. Those 60 pp. are not the complete *Falk*. The preliminary pages are wanting. The text consists of the narrative proper beginning with the words "And was this Hermann a hero?" and goes on for about 8000 words, but we have been unable to find the concluding pages. Even in the case of you having a complete MS of *Falk* that lot is worth joining to it because the variations are extremely wide, amounting in places to complete change of text. After all these years I myself was surprised to see what a lot of work I put into that story.

I may just as well tell you (since you have been drawn into the discussion) that in consequence of Pinker's strong representations Mr Doubleday has reverted to the original plan of 377 sets for the de luxe Edition. This is in agreement with your own point of view in the matter which, as expressed in your letter, confirmed me in my opinion and stiffened my attitude.

I will also tell you (and that had perhaps better remain entre-nous) that I am thinking seriously of dramatising some of my own work, beginning perhaps with *The Secret Agent*. I don't talk about it at large. One or two intimates here, and a certain theatre man called Frank Vernon whom I found most intelligent and sympathetic, know of that project of mine. It is still only a project. I haven't been able to begin yet; but to-morrow we are going from here to our new house and then I shall have a try, say for a month or six weeks, and if I don't get on I shall drop it and devote myself to the Napoleonic novel, which for the present is hung up.

My wife sends her kindest regards and her thanks for your sympathetic interest in her fate. We do hope that your trouble is over by* good by now and your health secured permanently after this long period of suffering.

Always my dear Quinn

Most sincerely yours

Joseph Conrad

[1] Quinn purchased it in 1912 (*Letters*, 5, pp. 69, 73, 81).

To J. B. Pinker

Text TS/MS Berg;[1] Unpublished

[Spring Grove]

[September? 1919][2]

[...] new novel is quite enough for me just at present.

The preface for the *Typhoon* is finished and you shall have it, with the corrected text, in the course of this week for dispatch to America. It will be followed shortly by the prefaces and corrected texts of *The Secret Agent* and the *Mirror of the Sea.*

I hope you'll not think I am making a fuss about some new notion of mine. It will be within your recollection that I talked to you about that very point, anxiously enough at that, just because of my distrust of what D[oubleday] would do. I think you agreed that 12 months ought to elapse between the two publications. Anyway whether *The Arrow* is a success or a failure from a business point of view there would be no sense in throwing out another book right on top of it.

Ever Yours

J. Conrad

To T. J. Wise

Text TS BL Ashley 2953; Unpublished

[letterhead: Spring Grove]

Sept. 30th. 1919.

Dear Mr Wise,

Let me thank you for the Swinburne Bibliography[3] which I've read with the greatest interest. A most remarkable piece of loving industry and of cultivated capacity for such work.

The consequence of what Richard Curle told me I am sending you here a statement of eight complete items of various *Author's Notes,* and other papers written within the last eighteen months. I don't know whether you will care to have them and whether you will care to pay the price I want for

---

[1] A fragment.

[2] On 30 August, Conrad promised Doubleday an Author's Note for *Typhoon* 'before long' and expressed his wish to see a year's pause between publication of *The Arrow* and *The Rescue.* Conrad told Pinker on 10 December that Doubleday now had Author's Notes to *Typhoon* and *The Mirror.* Since the problem of spacing the novels was urgent, a September date looks more probable than anything later.

[3] Part One of *A Bibliography of the Writings in Prose and Verse of Algernon Charles Swinburne* printed for Wise in an edition of 125 copies; the second part appeared in 1920.

them – which is £10 a piece. They all contain as much pen-and-ink writing, nearly, as type and are the original first drafts with all the corrections and alterations, except such as may have been made in proof. Of each no more than two *clean* copies have been made for the printers in England and America, and these when sent back to me with the first proofs have been invariably destroyed by myself. Each is signed on first and last pages, is correctly dated and has its little history noted in a line or two in my handwriting.

I would reserve to myself the private publication (25 copies) of those that have not been already done by you or Mr Shorter;[1] in which case I would take care that you should have two copies of any such issue. I am telling you all this without assuming in the least that you would want these things. Personally I am indifferent whether they remain in England or go to the U. S. But as you have acquired the first drafts of all my post-war publications (after the *Shadow Line*; but that was written and published during the war) I thought I would mention their existence to you first.

The postal difficulties in consequence of the Railway strike prevent me from sending you the pages for inspection.

Believe me, dear Mr Wise

very faithfully yours

Joseph Conrad

from JC.

The MSS for disposal consist of the following complete items:-

4 Author's Notes for the following books:-

> OUTCAST OF THE ISLANDS.
> TALES OF UNREST
> TYPHOON & OTHER TALES
> A PERSONAL RECORD.

And the following four complete papers:-

> TRADITION
> THE CRIME OF PARTITION
> CONFIDENCE
> STEPHEN CRANE, A Note without Dates.

In all 89 pages first draft in type and pen-and-ink, averaging about 200 words a page.

---

[1] Of the titles listed at the end of the letter, 'Tradition' was printed as a pamphlet for Wise, and 'Confidence' 'for the Author' – but in reality also for Wise.

To J. B. Pinker

Text MS Berg; Unpublished

[letterhead: Spring Grove]
[early October? 1919][1]

Dearest Pinker.

I suppose that is what is wanted for the sort of advertising pamphlet they are preparing.

Ever Your

J. Conrad.

To T. J. Wise

Text MS BL Ashley 2953; Unpublished

[Spring Grove]
2 Oct. '19

My dear Mr Wise.

I assure you that my appreciation of your Swin[burn]^e bib^{phy} is perfectly sincere. The interest and judiciousness of extracts from correspondence and the other details you insert as to the history of MS and editions make it a very attractive reading.

Thanks for Ch: for £80. The eight items (as specified) are in an envelope addressed to You, and of course my wife and my secretary know that they are now your property. I feel reluctant to entrust them to the post as yet.

Very Sincerely Yours

Joseph Conrad.

To J. B. Pinker

Text MS Indiana; Unpublished

Oswalds
Bishopsbourne
Kent.
Tuesday. 7th Oct 1919.

My dear Old Friend

Many thanks to you both for the wire inviting me to B[urys] Court. We managed to make a start with the move last Friday. We slept in this house last night.

I would be very grateful if you let me come on Friday for a week-end off.

---

[1] '10/19' has been pencilled on the MS: if correct, this note dates from the very end of the Conrads' tenancy of Spring Grove. The origin of the pamphlet remains unknown.

I know you will like to hear that the first act of the S. A. is well advanced. I'll tell you all about this and other things when we meet.

Ever Yours

J. Conrad

To J. B. Pinker
Text MS Berg; Unpublished

Oswalds
Bishopsbourne
8. 10. '19.

My dear Pinker

Thanks for your wire. I shall start from Ashford by the 4. 30 pm on Friday. Please send *Miss L. Hallowes* a cheque for £7, money I borrowed from her to-day, addressing her at *11. Oakley Street Chelsea S.W.3*.

Will you also send B[orys]'s ch for £8 (for Oct), here.

I say no more as we'll see each other so soon.

Ever Yours

J. Conrad

PS If a letter arrives for me at your office please forward to Burys Court.

To G. Jean-Aubry
Text MS Yale; *L. fr.* 148

Oswalds
Bishopsbourne
Kent.
14. 10. 19

Mon cher Aubry.

Je viens de recevoir une lettre de Gide ou il me dit qu'une femme vient de s'emparer de *Arrow* pour le traduire.[1] Je vais protester de toutes mes forces. Il me jette en pature a un tas des femmes qui lui font des histoires (il le dit lui même). Tout ça m'ennuie.

Nous sommes campés ici pour un mois. Puis L'pool je suppose. Pouvez-Vous venir pour la journée – peut-être Samedi.[2] Je voudrai Vous causer un

---

[1] The translator was Mme Madeleine Octavie Maus: see the letter to Gide of 4 November and *Portrait*, pp. 145–9. Aubry did eventually translate *The Arrow*.

[2] On Wednesday the 15th, Conrad sent Jean-Aubry a telegram: 'Take 10.45 Victoria to Canterbury car will meet. Conrad' (Yale).

peu et Vous monttrer* la lettre de Gide. Il est impossible de Vous prier de passer la nuit. N'y a pas de chambre.
En hâte

Tout a Vous

JC.

Translation

My dear Aubry.

I have just now had a letter from Gide in which he says that a woman has just got hold of *The Arrow* for translation. I am going to protest with all my might. He throws me as bait to a gaggle of women who have made a fuss (he says it himself). All this annoys me.

We are camped here for a month. Then Liverpool, I suppose. Can you come for the day – perhaps Saturday. I should like to have a chat with you and show you Gide's letter. It is impossible to ask you for the night. No bedroom.
In haste.

Yours truly

JC.

To Mary Pinker
Text MS Lowens; Lowens (1986)

[letterhead: Oswalds]
14 Oct. '19.

Dear Mrs Pinker.

I must thank you for the charming peaceful days of ease under your roof.

J. B. P[inker] and I parted hastily in the Rway station as though we were truly glad to get rid of each other, and I don't know what happened to him since. I didn't look in at the office as I intended to do. I went off rather early to see John whom I found looking well and lively. I went away much reassured about the situation[1] which is nothing as bad as I thought. I need not tell you dear Mrs Pinker that the kindly feeling you manifest towards me and all mine is the most gratifying development of my long friendship with your husband. I wonder whether he really has an idea of the intense pleasure he gave me by these two drives?[2] He took me to the station through the lanes and it was all perfectly lovely – including the weather on both occasions.

---

[1] At his preparatory school.
[2] Probably in his four-in-hand carriage, of which Pinker was very proud.

It looks as if heaven itself had made up its mind to smile on his efforts to be good to me.

Believe me dear Mrs Pinker

most faithfully yours

Joseph Conrad

PS Jessie before going off to Canterbury this morning "on business" has instructed me to give you her love and her thanks for your kindness to me.

To Sir Sidney Colvin
Text MS Duke; Unpublished

Oswalds
Bishopsbourne
Kent.
15. 10. 19

My dear Colvin

Jessie wrote to Lady Colvin whose p-card must have crossed her letter. Yours to me did not reach my hands till yesterday having been discovered by B[orys] *under* a tray where it hid itself in the general desarroi of the move.

You must really give me the credit of not having had anything to do with the absurd quote-marks and the absurd apostrophe of the Oswalds on the change-of-address cards. I had nothing to do with the ordering of the same and I asked Miss H[allowes] to correct them before sending them out.

Pray don't believe the reports of the papers. There never has been a more sheepish-looking lot of strikers. I know a good many railway workers and have talked with many men of various grades. They had hardly anything to say for themselves, and wished the whole thing over as soon as possible. Labour troubles are nothing new in Eng^d (even before the days of the Unions). The 18th Centr^y was full of them – and now the men *have* something to lose. The rush back to work was a sight to see. Their relief was immense. And note that Ashford is a great R[ail]way centre with all the workshops of the S[outh] E[astern] Comp^y containing 10000 men or so.

We are camped in this new house with a few sticks of furniture – and not at home to anybody. But people understand the situation. There are no carpets, no curtains (as yet); the bare boards echo loudly our footsteps in the passages; the nakedness of the walls stares at us from all sides. I haven't got the heart to do anything till this horrid suspense of the impending operation is over. No! We are not fit for human companionship. However Lady Millais is sure to drop in and Lady Northcote[1] has signified her intention to see Jessie before going to town. Luckily my study is more or less completed and may serve for a drawing-room. Of course the above are Jessie's "grand friends". Of their sentiments towards myself I know nothing. My only lady is Lady Colvin. I kiss her hands dutifully and affectionately. I shall try to drop in at 35 P[alace] Gardens Terr: before long.

Ever yours

J. Conrad

Jessie's dear love.
PS Have begun a Play!!!
  1st Act nearly finished!!!!!!

To Richard Curle
Text MS Indiana; Curle 50

Oswalds
Bishopsbourne
Kent.
15. 10. 19

Dearest Richard

I just sent off a letter to you c/o Pink[er].

Now I know again your address I hasten to thank you for Your letter received today. You are a very good friend, and we are both very grateful to you for your promise to stand by us in L'pool. Your better news about yourself has cheered me up. We are camped here with a few sticks of furniture without curtains and carpets, and, in our state of horrid suspense, not caring to undertake anything more. Next spring I hope we will take steps to settle down to a comparatively civilized life.

Of course *you* may come if you care to run the risk. Let us know directly you return from Scotland.

All luck to you my dear fellow whenever you go and whatever you attempt. We'll discuss the pamph*ts* when we meet.

Jessie's love.

Ever Yours

Joseph Conrad

---

[1] Lady (Alice) Northcote (died 1934), widow of Henry Stafford, Baron Northcote, third Governor General of Australia. In 1919, she became a DBE (Dame of the British Empire) for her services to hospitals.

To Hugh R. Dent
Text TS Berg; J-A, 2, 230

Bishopsbourne
Kent.
Oct. 15th. 1919.

My dear Dent.

I am an author without a MS drawer. I never have anything unpublished by me, or else I would certainly let you have it.

I am sorry I cannot for the present let you have the Chronicle articles, or even their dates.[1] We have just come into this house and have not quite finished unpacking.

I can't let you have the typescript of "The Rescue" for I have none in my possession; but I have a printed text which I will send to you directly I can spare it, for your *own* reading – not for setting. I am actually looking it over and can't part with it for some little time.

For goodness sake don't give way utterly to the vice of "reading Conrad". I present this request of course very much against my inclination and only out of regard for your own person. I have heard a lady say that reading Conrad too much produced a "detestable effect" upon one. I don't know exactly what she meant by "detestable" but I feel it my duty to warn you. I suppose she was thinking of some kind of mental surfeit.

However continue to think kindly of me.

Yours

J. Conrad

To J. B. Pinker
Text TS/MS Berg; Unpublished

Oswalds
Bishopsbourne
Kent.
Oct. 15th. 1919.

My dear Pinker.

Here is the "Stephen Crane" which I call a "Note Without Dates". As you see it is very short and summary and much more personal than literary.

My idea is to send it to Squire for his "London Mercury", as he had asked me to contribute something not exactly to his first number but in general

---

[1] See the letter to J. M. Dent, 25 October.

to his periodical. I excused myself at the time on the ground of my general unfitness for that sort of thing, but I want to be friendly to S. and since this thing got itself written I think of giving it to him. I can't really ask payment for such a trifle. As to publication in the U. S., which you suggested, you will of course deal with it exactly as you think proper.[1]

My stay with you has refreshed me greatly. My love to all the members of the team. I spent all the morning in town buying a hat and an overcoat after which I proceeded to see John. Matters there are by no means bad. Those people make too much fuss over him. I tell you more when we meet.

Ever Yours

J Conrad

PS Regards to Eric.
? Have you heard from the binder of the 2 copies of A. of G.[2] The R. des Deux Mondes has an article on it in its 1st Oct. issue.[3] After copy has been taken (or copies) please send one on to Squire. I'll drop him a line to say its coming.

To J. C. Squire
Text TS Berg; Unpublished

Oswalds
Bishopsbourne
Kent.
Oct. 17th. 1919

My dear Mr Squire.

Forgive me for not answering your letter sooner. We were in the middle of a move when the strike raged all round us. "Raged" is only my exaggerated way of putting things. It was much more like a severe fit of stagnation; and all the fellows were walking about in their Sunday best looking sheepish and feeling very sick. The time of the Antonines was an easy going time, but perhaps even less stable than the time in which we live.[4] I don't think I could

---

[1] US publication was in the *Bookman*, February 1920, beginning the revival of Crane's name in North America.
[2] As requested on 30 August.   [3] See the letter to the reviewer, Louis Gillet, 25 October.
[4] In the third chapter of *The Decline and Fall of the Roman Empire* (1776), Edward Gibbon calls the years between the death of the tyrant Domitian in 96 CE and the accession of the blunderer Commodus in 176 CE 'the period in the history of the world during which the condition of the human race was most happy and prosperous'. The emperors were Nerva, Trajan, Hadrian,

prove my opinion to you in set terms but this is the feeling I have. However we shall see.

I have instructed Pinker to send you a typed copy of a little something about Stephen Crane which was suggested to me by the enquiry of a young journalist whom I have never seen but who writes to me sometimes.[1] I am having it forwarded to you as a mere sign of friendship and goodwill and *not* as a business transaction. It is, properly speaking, nothing at all; and if you don't want to print it pray throw it into the waste-paper basket in perfect assurance that you won't be hurting my feelings in the least. In fact I feel that I ought to apologise for intruding that scrap of a thing on your notice.

Pardon the type. I've a gouty wrist.

Best wishes for the L[ondon] M[ercury]. With great regards

Yours

Joseph Conrad

To Lewis Saul Benjamin
Text TS Lubbock; Unpublished

Oswalds
Bishopsbourne
Kent.
Oct. 25th. 1919.

My dear Sir.[2]

I am very much complimented by the invitation of your Committee and I enclose here the cheque for a guinea, begging you to convey my thanks for the conferred distinction.[3]

Antoninus Pius (whose reign, Gibbon observes, 'is marked by the rare advantage of furnishing very few materials for history'), Lucius Verus, and Marcus Aurelius. Yet the reign of the philosopher Marcus Aurelius and his co-emperor Lucius Verus was marred by rebellion in the frontier provinces and barbarian incursions into northern Italy; under the earlier Antonines, the follies of Rome itself were outrageous enough to provoke the *Satires* of Juvenal.

[1] Peter Ferguson Somerville (1877–1964)? See *Letters*, 5, pp. 546–7. Squire took the 'Note' for the *London Mercury*.

[2] Lewis Saul Benjamin (1874–1932). He and his wife, Helen Mira Benjamin, took the appropriate pseudonyms 'H. and L. Melville' to edit *Full Fathom Five*, published in April 1910; the selection includes one excerpt from 'Youth' and three from *The Nigger*. 'Lewis Melville' wrote the lives and edited the letters of many authors, among them Lady Mary Wortley Montagu, Tobias Smollett, Laurence Sterne, William Beckford, and William Cobbett. His two-volume biography of Thackeray appeared in 1899.

[3] Perhaps an invitation to the dinner at the Blackfriars Club on 26 November to honour Captain Bruce Bairnsfather, the military cartoonist. The club's membership consisted mostly of journalists, literary men, and graphic artists.

As to the pleasure of the dinner being achieved by me, that is another question. I am severely handicapped in my movements by attacks of gout (unconnected with any festivities) which I am afraid have become habitual with me. As to this year there is also the additional obstacle of my being engaged far away from London on the 26th of next November. But with invincible optimism I shall cherish the hope of better luck next year.

Believe me

very faithfully Yours

Joseph Conrad

L. S. Benjamin Esqr.

To J. M. Dent

Text TS/MS Berg; J-A, 2, 230

Oswalds,
Bishopsbourne,
Kent.
Oct 25th. 1919

Dear Mr Dent.

I called yesterday to ask you for one copy of *Nostromo* and one copy of *Shadow Line* which last I want to give to my boy in order to replace the one he lost with the rest of his belongings during the retreat of March 21st.[1] The copy of *Nostromo* is for Mrs Thorne, the daughter of Henry Arthur Jones, who wants to have the edition with the Author's Note, of the existence of which she was not aware.[2]

I saw J. B. P[inker] for a few minutes yesterday morning and in justice to him I must tell you that in the matter of the difference which has arisen between you he has been acting generally in accordance with my views. Personally I have a great dislike to have a collection of fragments of my prose in volume form, even when the object of it is educational. There is also the feeling that such an issue is, to a large extent, experimental (and an unwillingness to face the possibility of the experiment not turning out a complete success), without some good inducement of a material kind. I don't know the details of your negociation*, as I had hardly the time to exchange a few words on the subject with P. on whom I called in reference to quite a different matter, having nothing to do with publishing. But I thought I would just put my point of view before you shortly, as I understood that the difference bears upon the question of royalties.

[1] 1918.   [2] See the letter to Mrs Thorne of the 27th.

I suppose that the "Chronicle" articles about which you wrote me last week were those which appeared under the title of "Well Done". From a note in my possession I see that they appeared in August 1918.[1]

Some time ago the question of publishing a volume of my occasional work, such as articles on Daudet, Maupassant, France, H. James, the two Titanic articles, and a selection from several others was mooted between P. and myself.[2] The idea was rather new to me and at first not very attractive. But if it came to anything I should certainly like it to come out uniform with the novels published by you. How does the idea strike you – the publication being planned for the autumn, 1920? By that time I shall be deep in the work on the third novel of my contract with you. *The Rescue* by then will be about six months old as a published book, and a volume of that sort may be useful just to keep my name before the public, both in this country and in America. On the other hand that consideration is not of very great importance, and there may be perhaps an objection to include a volume of that character in your uniform set. My mind is not made up yet and I would be glad to know what views you have on the matter.

Of course anything of the sort would entail a certain amount of additional labour for the year 1920 which I am not very anxious to undertake.

Believe me

always Yours faithfully

Joseph Conrad

To Louis Gillet
Text L. fr. 148

Oswalds.
25 Oct. 1919.

Cher Monsieur,[3]

Laissez-moi vous serrer la main pour votre article dans la "Revue des Deux Mondes".[4]

---

[1] 22, 23, and 24 August.

[2] The origin of *Notes on Life and Letters*.

[3] For almost forty years, Louis Gillet (1876–1943) contributed regularly to the *Revue des Deux Mondes*; it was there that he reviewed *Suspense* as well as *The Arrow of Gold*. An art historian and student of English and German literature, he became curator of the Jacquemart-André collection at the Abbaye de Châalis, near Paris, in 1912, and a member of the Académie française in 1935. His close friendship with Romain Rolland (who portrayed him in his fiction as 'Olivier') was interrupted by a quarrel about the First World War, in which Gillet fought and suffered wounds. His other friends included Monet, Péguy, and Claudel; later, he befriended Joyce. Gillet replied to Conrad's letter on 5 November (MS Yale).

[4] 'Le Nouveau Roman de M. Conrad', 1 October, pp. 676–85. Because Conrad's characters often behave mysteriously and unpredictably, Gillet compares him with Dostoevsky, but finds

Que vous dire? Ce n'est pas souvent qu'un auteur d'un livre si personnel se trouve à pareille fête. Etre compris – ca arrive parfois – mais être compris d'une façon à la fois si subtile et si généreuse, c'est une rare expérience.

Pulvis et umbra[1] – tout cela! Mais dans le souffle chaud de votre sympathie j'ai senti de nouveau tressaillir en moi la vie invincible du souvenir.

Votre reconnaissant.

Translation

Dear Sir,

Allow me to shake your hand for your article in the *Revue des Deux Mondes*. What can one say to you? Not often does an author of such a personal book find himself at a feast like this. To be understood – that sometimes happens – but to be understood in a manner at once so subtle and so generous is a rare experience.

Pulvis et umbra – and all that. But in the warm breath of your sympathy I have again felt the invincible life of memory quiver within me.

Yours gratefully.

To Jenny Doris Thorne

Text MS Duke; Unpublished

Oswalds
Bishopsbourne
Kent.
27. 10. '19

Dear Mrs Thorne.[2]

The precious book[3] having been only defaced by me in obedience to your commands is leaving this house with all the ceremonies of registration.

---

in the latter's work a tendency to dramatise pathology and neurosis in contrast to Conrad's 'pur sentiment du tragique de la vie' (678). The mystery is especially dense around Rita, on whom the reviewer dwells at length: 'M. Conrad est trop artiste pour ne pas laisser autour de la délicieuse fille une large zone d'inexpliqué' (684).

[1] In *Odes*, 3, 7, Horace contrasts the constant renewal of the natural and heavenly worlds with the finality of our own deaths. When we have joined the illustrious dead, 'Pulvis et umbra sumus', 'we are dust and shadow'.

[2] Jenny Doris or Dora Thorne (née Jones, 1888–1947) was the daughter of the playwright Sir Henry Arthur Jones, whose *Life and Letters* she published in 1930. She moved in theatrical and literary circles when not in Cyprus, Morocco, Egypt, or Greece with her husband, a civil servant and judge. After her divorce in 1923, she wrote sketches for dailies and magazines and did volunteer work. Her autobiography, *What a Life!*, appeared in 1932.

[3] *The Arrow*: *Nostromo* went off to her on 2 November.

Thanks for your charming and kindly note. Pray give my affectionate regards to your father.[1]

Having spent with you under the same roof something like 127 minutes (comme le temps passe!) it is but natural I should subscribe myself ——

Always your most faithful friend and
servant

Joseph Conrad.

To J. M. Dent
Text TS Berg; Unpublished

Oswalds
Bishopsbourne
Kent.
Oct. 29th. 1919

My dear Dent.

I am forwarding your letter to Mr Pinker whom I expected on a visit here yesterday but who was prevented at the last moment.

In my last I begged you for one copy of *Nostromo* and one of the *Shadow Line*, which have not arrived yet, probably the fault of the P. O.

That vol. of my occasional pieces will have to be considered in all its bearings. I haven't even yet begun to make a selection. There will be not enough literary articles to give it a purely literary character. Other things will have to go in. But after all there is no hurry about that and the selection and preparation may give me mental relaxation while I am writing the Napoleonic novel.

I have not begun it yet for the state of suspense about the date and indeed the success of the operation hanging over our heads stands in the way of the intense concentration which I need for the beginning of a book. But I am thinking of it every day and the moments thus passed in self-communion cannot be called idle. Something of them will remain and will find its place when the actual work begins.

Kindest regards

Yours

J. Conrad

[1] Sir Henry (1851–1929) was a disciple of Ibsen, whose serious and comic plays alike confront the evasions and deficiencies of contemporary society.

To J. B. Pinker
Text TS/MS Berg; Unpublished

Oswalds
Bishopsbourne
Kent.
Oct. 30th. 1919.

Dear Pinker,

Thank you for your letter and the returned assessment paper.[1] I have written to the Surveyor's office in Ashford in the sense of your suggestion.

I am glad to hear that Vernon was interested. I have no doubt he will speak quite openly, for that is the way in which he can be helpful to me. Of course you have looked at the thing. I don't know whether I asked you specifically to do so, but that you should be sufficiently interested in my first big attempt for the stage seems to me a matter of course.

The enclosed corrected text of *One Day More* has been prepared by Miss H[allowes] and is now ready to go to America.[2]

We are comforted by your news of Mrs Pinker and we look forward very much to seeing you here next Tuesday.

Our love to your wife (not forgetting yourself).

Ever yours

J. Conrad

To Jenny Doris Thorne
Text MS Duke; J-A, 2, 231

[letterhead: Oswalds]
2. 11. 19.

Dear Mrs. Thorne.

I have signed the preface – since this copy is sent to you for the sake of the preface – or rather Author's Note, as I call it. I've also written a few words on the fly-leaf.[3]

I've been greatly delighted by your sympathetic appreciation of the *Arrow*.

You will easily understand that of this affair not everything could be set down. The inner truth of the scene in the locked room is only hinted at. And

---

[1] From the Inland Revenue.
[2] For the Doubleday edition of 377 copies, published in 1920.
[3] 'To Mrs Thorne in common friendship, for the man of the book, from the man who wrote the words in it, blindly – perhaps – but with a great devotion J. C 1919' (Duke).

as to the whole who could have rendered its ominous glow, its atmosphere of exaltation and misery?

Daignez me garder un bon souvenir.[1]

Bien à vous

J. Conrad

To Louise Alvar Harding

Text MS Morgan; J-A, 2, 232

[letterhead: Oswalds]
3 Nov '19

Dear Mrs Harding.[2]

I ought to have answered Your letter ages ago. I hope our friendly Aubry explained to you the reason of the delay. You need not have hesitated to write. You have expressed yourself charmingly and I can assure you that Your fine and understanding sympathy has given me the greatest pleasure.

Nothing could have been more flattering to my amour propre than your saying that "I knew how to lose my head – and how to keep it". The "Divine Madness" was so strong that I would have walked into a precipice, deliberately, with my eyes open, for its sake. And now it seems incredible; and yet it is the same old heart – for even at this distance of time I can't smile at it.

Believe me dear Mrs Harding

Your very faithful friend & servant

Joseph Conrad

To André Gide

Text MS Doucet; Vidan (1970)

[letterhead: Oswalds]
4 Nov. 19

Mon cher Gide

Votre discussion sur *Typhon* et *C des T* avec Ruyters[3] me demontre Votre extrême scrupulosité. Je n'en ai jamais douté.

---

[1] 'Please remember me kindly.'

[2] Louise ('Loulette') Alvar Harding (1883–1965) sang professionally as a soprano under the name Louise Alvar, touring with Maurice Ravel, among others. She was the daughter of Ernest Beckman, a writer and member of the Swedish Parliament, and a granddaughter of Anders Fredrik Beckman, Bishop of Skara. She and her husband, a wealthy English barrister, held a literary and musical salon at their house in Holland Park, Kensington; her circle included Manuel de Falla, Camille Saint-Saëns, Gian Francesco Malipiero, Albert Roussel, Salvador de Madariaga, T. S. Eliot, Hugo von Hofmannsthal, and Paul Valéry.

[3] Ruyters felt that Gide's translation of 'Typhoon' should be either re-done from scratch or given up entirely, lest it damage the reputations of author and translator. The strongly worded

Mais je pense que quand on est scrupuleux il faut l'être tout-à-fait. Si mes écritures ont un caractère prononcé c'est leur virilité – esprit allure, expression. Personne ne m'a denié ça. Et vous me jetez aux femmes! Vous dites Vous-même dans Votre lettre qu'au bout du compte une traduction est une interpretation. Eh bien, j'ai le désir d'être interprété par des esprits masculins. C'est tout naturel. Et je crois que j'ai le droit de le demander comme je me suis permis de faire au sujet de Arrow of Gold.

Vous avez jugé bon de repondre par un refus. C'est très bien; et je Vous assure que je ne Vous adresserais jamais plus au sujet de mes traductions. Mais franchement mon cher quand Joseph Conrad après beaucoup d'hesitation fait une prière motivée sur un sujet qui lui tient fort au coeur on ne lui repond pas sur ce ton. "Une dame *c'est emparée* du livre(!)" – et Vous, André Gide, Vous n'y pouvez rien! Vous auriez du dire "belle" dame et ça aurait été parfait. Tout a fait circa Louis-Phillipe.*[1] Voyons mon cher – Vous me parlez longuement de Vos difficultés, des difficultés de Ruyters, de Mme Rivière.[2] Vous m'en parlez comme a un homme qui doit y être fortement interessé, dont l'intelligence et le coeur sont engagés dans le succès de cette traduction; mais quand il s'agit de mon sentiment a moi Vous me parlez "d 'une dame qui s'est emparée . . . " Et cela doit etre assez pour moi! On dirait que Vous me prenez pour un sot.

Vous ne deignez* même pas me dire que Vous la jugez competente pour mener a bien cette traduction. Vous me dites seulement que M. Aubry la connait! Que ce que ça peut me faire? Evidement il connait beaucoup de personnes dont je n'ai jamais entendu parler.

Votre lettre que je viens de relire me remplit de malaise. Voulez-Vous me faire comprendre que Vous voudriez laisser tomber la traduction? Si c'est ça j'y consens. Seulement je Vous prie de me repondre definitivement par un Oui ou Non – comme ça doit entre hommes.

Bien à Vous

J. Conrad

correspondence on this issue ran from August to December 1918 (André Gide, André Ruyters, *Correspondance 1907–1950*, ed. Claude Martin, Victor Martin-Schmetz (Presses Universitaires de Lyon, 1990), pp. 192–205).

[1] The 'Citizen King' Louis-Philippe reigned from 1830 to 1848: Conrad makes Gide sound like a bourgeois character from Balzac, whose novels anatomise the failings of that era.

[2] Isabelle Rivière (died 1971): despite his fulminations here about female translators, Conrad had expressed some satisfaction with her work on *Victory*: 'Remerciez bien vivement Mme Rivière de ma part pour sa fidelité, son habilité son succès dans la tâche ingrate de traduction' (to Gide, 4 September 1916: *Letters*, 5, p. 649). Gide, on the other hand, found collaboration with her very trying (J. H. Stape, 'The Art of Fidelity: Conrad, Gide, and the Translation of *Victory*', *Journal of Modern Literature*, 17 (1990), 155–65).

Translation

My dear Gide

Your debate with Ruyters over 'Typhoon' and 'Heart of Darkness' reveals your extreme scrupulosity. I have never doubted it.

But I think that when one is scrupulous, one should be entirely so. If my writings have a pronounced character, it is their virility – of spirit, inclination, style. No one has denied me that. And you throw me to the women! In your letter, you yourself say that in the final reckoning, a translation is an interpretation. Very well, I want to be interpreted by masculine intelligences. It's perfectly natural. And I believe I have the right to ask for whatever I please concerning the *Arrow of Gold*.

You saw fit to answer me with a refusal. That is fine; and I assure you that I shall never again address you on the subject of my translations. But frankly, my dear fellow, when after much hesitation Joseph Conrad makes a reasonable request about something very close to his heart, one does not answer in this fashion: 'A lady has *got her hands on* the book (!)' – and you, André Gide, can do nothing about it. To complete the effect, you ought to have said 'lovely' lady. Quite as in the days of Louis-Philippe. Look here, dear fellow, you talk to me at length about your difficulties, about Ruyters' difficulties, about Mme Rivière's difficulties. You talk to me about it as if to a man who must be greatly concerned with this, whose heart and mind are bound up in the success of this translation; but when it comes to my feelings, you speak to me of 'a lady who has got her hands on . . . ' And that should suffice me! One would say you took me for an idiot.

You do not even deign to tell me that you judge her competent to make this translation succeed. You simply tell me that M. Aubry knows her. What good will that do me? Clearly he knows many people of whom I've never heard him speak.

Your letter, which I have just reread, fills me with discomfort. Do you want me to understand that you would like to let the translation go? If that is so, I consent. I only ask you to reply with a definite Yes or No – as is proper between men.

Yours

J. Conrad

To G. Jean-Aubry
Text TS Yale; Unpublished

[letterhead: Oswalds]
Nov. 7th. 1919.

My dear Aubry.

The long and the short of the matter is this:- there is a piano in a private house, 91 Onslow Gardens, S. W. 7. which Miss Hallowes knows as a good instrument. In fact it belongs to her uncle. Will you consent to see it for me within the next week, just dropping a note to the above address to E. Hallowes Esqre., the day before to announce your coming. Please don't let my request inconvenience you in any way, and just drop me a line to say that you are too busy. The matter is not very pressing.

I am afraid that I have quarrelled with Gide for good. The answer he sent to my request to let you translate A. of G. is not the sort of answer you send to a man whom you take seriously. I pointed it out to him and said distinctly that this sort of thing looked as if he were taking me for a fool. At the same time he bothers me with all his scruples about the style of the translations by all these women! Therefore I told him that his letter caused me a certain "malaise" and that if his recital of difficulties in conjunction with the slighting manner of his reply to my request meant that he wanted to let the affair of the translations drop I was prepared to consent to it. But I asked him to give me a clear answer by "oui ou non, comme cela se doit entre hommes".

I need not tell you that in all this I tried to appear more hurt than angry. The truth of the matter however is that the more I thought the letter over during this fortnight the more angry I felt myself to be. So I did not wait to consult you. After all, my very severe annoyance is quite justifiable.

I hope you have been pleased with the reception of your lecture. Perhaps you will manage to run down here once more before we leave and tell me all about it. At any rate we are sure to meet in London before very long. I am going to write to-morrow to Sir R. Jones and send him the radiograph of the joint which was taken the other day in Canterbury.

My wife's best regards.

Tout à Vous

J. Conrad

To J. B. Pinker

Text TS Berg; J-A, 2, 232

[letterhead: Oswalds]

Nov. 7th. '19

Dearest Pinker.

Thank you very much for your letter. I was glad to know of the magic properties of the coat which kept you warm in Tonbridge. I thought that was impossible. I was still more glad to hear from Eric, to whom I wired yesterday, that you are definitely better.

I think that I will ultimately avail myself of the introduction you send me for Mrs Rea.[1] My only trouble is that as a friend of Arnold Bennett she may be a person of distinction in her town and that I may find myself involved in social duties. The very thought makes me shiver in anticipation! Apart, of course, from the success of Jessie's operation all my thoughts and all my vital energies will be concentrated on the play which every day seems to me a bigger and a more difficult undertaking. I don't mean by this that I shirk working at it. I have indeed worked yesterday and this morning to some purpose on the second scene of Act Two. The trouble is now to keep it within proper bounds as to length – there is so much to say and so much must be left out that the choice perplexes one and checks one's work. This is bad enough, but the real trouble will come when Act Three is taken in hand. As to Act Four I daren't even think of it. To make an audience of comfortable, easy-going people sup on horrors is a pretty hopeless enterprise; but I have developed crazily the ambition of making them swallow their supper and think it fine too. This is the way my madness lies at present.

I heard from Vernon this morning. He has accepted our invitation for Sunday but will have to go back by the last train.

Our love to you both.

Yours ever

J. Conrad

PS Pardon type. I dictated without thinking and am too lazy to re-write now.

---

[1] Wife of the impresario Alec L. Rea (1878–1953), whose business often took him to Liverpool. The Reas had dined with the Bennetts on 29 October (Newman Flower, ed., *The Journals of Arnold Bennett: 1911–21* (Cassell, 1932), p. 277).

To Richard Curle
Text MS Indiana; Curle 51[1]

[letterhead: Oswalds]

11. 11. 19

Dearest Dick.

Thanks for your good letter. I am very pleased with what you say of your plans for settling down. It will be good for you I feel sure, and outside my household you are the person about whom I am most concerned both in thought and feelings.

Have you seen Wise – I wonder? If the thing goes through pray ask him to mark his envelopes *Private* when he writes to me on that matter. Like that the letter is certain not to [be] opened by anybody but myself. It's as well for you to know that too tho' indeed we've never had any great secrets between us – as yet.

I am going on with the play. Vernon was here yesterday.

Love.

Yours

J Conrad

P. S Have you the Rcv: des Deux Mondes with the article on A of G?

To J. B. Pinker
Text TS/MS Berg; J-A, 2, 233

[letterhead: Oswalds]

Nov. 11th. 1919

Dearest Pinker

I told Vernon on Sunday that I would finish the Second Act the next day, and I did so according to plan. I hope to correct it in the course of to-day and post it to you at the same time with the letter, though in another envelope. Perhaps you will glance at it before sending it to John St., Adelphi in the usual course.[2]

V. and I got on very well indeed discussing the text and contriving scenery, in which last V. displayed his wonderful ingenuity. There are no longer any material obstacles in the way of a most effective production. He has solved them all to my complete satisfaction. As to the play itself V.'s hopefulness is so great as to frighten me a little. Still, he is an experienced and notable producer – he ought to know! Personally, I cannot defend myself from the

[1] Curle omits the paragraph beginning 'Have you seen Wise'.
[2] For typing up a fair copy.

dread of the whole thing turning out repulsive to average minds and shocking to average feelings.

As I go on in my adaptation, stripping off the garment of artistic expression and consistent irony which clothes the story in the book, I perceive more clearly how it is bound to appear to the collected mind of the audience a merely horrible and sordid tale, giving a most unfavourable impression of both the writer himself and of his attitude to the moral aspect of the subject. In the book the tale, whatever its character, was at any rate not treated sordidly; neither in tone, nor in diction, nor yet in the suggested images. The peculiar light of my mental insight and of my humane feeling (for I have *that* too) gave to the narrative a sort of grim dignity. But on the stage all this falls off. Every rag of the drapery drops to the ground. It is a terribly searching thing – I mean the stage.

I will confess that I myself had no idea of what the story under the writing was till I came to grips with it in this process of dramatisation. Of course I can't stop now. Neither can I tamper with the truth of my conception by introducing into it any extraneous sentiment. It must remain what it is. Having arrived at that conclusion (which, at any rate, is honest) I have resolved that since the story is horrible I shall make it as horrible as I possibly can. If there is any salvation for it it may possibly be found just in *that*. But I have not many illusions on that score. There is very little chance of salvation. There will be very little glory or profit in this production. In fact I have a feeling that it will be to me rather damaging than otherwise.

I have, as usual, opened my heart to you. Don't trouble to answer my arguments. I only want you to know. I don't suppose for a moment you will think I am discouraged.

It is a great experience and I want it to be complete.

Love to you from us both.

                                                              Ever Yours

                                                                          J Conrad

Mauretania arrived yesterday at South'on. R. Jones must be on board. The time draws near. Don't think me ungrateful but I mean to avoid all social obligations in L'pool. The play'll take up my morning's* and the Nursing Home all my afternoons. In the evening I'll want to be quiet. I need that. Do thank Bennett warmly from me, but I do not think I'll write to Mrs Rea. I'll want B[orys] to go over soon and look up such lodgings as may be advertised from day to day.

To Richard Curle

Text MS Indiana; Curle 52

[letterhead: Oswalds]
12. 11. '19.
9. 30 am.

Dearest Richard.

Thanks for yours. I did not hear from Wise, but you may perhaps clinch that bargain in the sense of your letter – which is full of common-sense. The money is already spent.

I haven't the slightest recollection of the article *Books*. I am glad you found my *Anatole*.[1] Do keep a list of your discoveries in view of a Vol: by and bye.

I have finished Act Two of the play (2 scenes) and shall in a moment begin act Three. A great adventure!

In haste. Love.

Yours

J. C.

PS On second thoughts I'll drop a line to Wise. But you may drop a note to him too. Thanks dear Dick for all your kindly offices.

To William Reno Kane

Text MS Berg; Kane

[letterhead: Oswalds]
Nov. 12th. 1919.

Dear Mr Kane.[2]

Your letter which has been a fortnight on the road suggests rather a biggish job. I don't care to answer your request by a couple of fatuous paragraphs. And to describe the inception, the growth of a novel, and the problems which a writer faces every day in the pursuit of his aim, is a large undertaking if it is to be done seriously, and, as you suggest, for the benefit of other writers.

Personally, I doubt the benefit. The pursuit of imaginative literature dealing with humanity at large, or with any specialised portion of it, is a lonely task. All writing worthy of the name is temperamental; but creative work is

---

[1] 'Books', *Speaker*, 15 July 1904; 'Anatole France, "L'Île des Pingouins"', *English Review* (December 1908). Both appeared as pamphlets in 1920; although described on the title-page as 'for the Author', the real impresario was Wise. Both also appear in *Notes on Life and Letters*.

[2] William Reno Kane (1885–1971) conducted *The Editor: The Journal of Information for Literary Workers*, which continued on and off until 1941. From his office in Ridgewood, New Jersey, Kane was also the publisher of *1001 Places to Sell Manuscripts: The American Writer's Yearbook and Directory to Publications*.

the most temperamental of all. If one began the disclosures for which you ask one would go too far. There are things not fit for everybody to know. A certain amount of platitudes could be written pleasantly on that subject as on any other. But for that I have neither leisure, I can assure you, nor yet the inclination.

"A brief account of my experiences as a writer" – you say! Oh, yes, it can be made brief enough. Years of unremitting concentration upon the task, hours of meditation, days in which one didn't know whether the sun shone or not – not one man in a million would understand and take to heart the truth that lies under those words. The majority would smile. What a fuss over a mere story! A story which, when it is done, does not seem so very extraordinary after all! How ridiculous! . . . Here and there some reader gifted with a little imagination and humanity would comment to himself: "Poor devil!" . . . Hardly worth while to lay one's heart bare to all mankind for that.

I have come very near to that, though, in a little book called "A Personal Record" published nearly nine years ago, and which is to be found in both editions of my works published by Doubleday, Page & Co. It contains also the history (in some sort) of my first published book, a novel entitled "Almayer's Folly". A new edition with an additional Author's Note has just appeared here, two days ago. I am sending you a copy as a sign of goodwill and sympathy for the bravely flying Pegasus and the man who directs his course;[1] and in order that you should not imagine me a crabbed, sour curmudgeon. It would be nothing short of criminal in me to be that; for my work has enlisted much sympathetic response from the first. For the mass of mankind I have nothing but the most sympathetic affection. For the critics nothing but gratitude. Yes, indeed, I have been understood, more than I expected, more perhaps than my imperfections deserved. I say *imperfections* because it is there that the artist craves most for sympathy; because, if he is an artist at all, it is these that he feels most keenly. As to the writers my conviction is that, in the last instance, each of them must fight his battles alone. What could one say to them (each Craft and Art being a great mystery) that could be of use in their work. Unless perhaps by suggestion on the lines of general morality. But I have never been presumptuous enough to set up as a moral preacher – especially to my brethren of the pen.

Believe me

very faithfully Yours

Joseph Conrad

---

[1] *The Editor* had Pegasus as its colophon.

To H. M. Tomlinson
Text TS Private collection; Unpublished

[letterhead: Oswalds]
Nov. 12th. 1919.

My dear Tomlinson

Forgive me my negative, and the typed letter, and all my sins, mentionable and unmentionable, of which you may perchance be aware. I am no good at writing about other men's work; I have my mind very full of my own; and there is still another reason for my hedge-hoggish attitude to your friendly request. It does not imply any lack of sympathy for Bone, whose temperamental attitude I understand very well, and for his work which has many high qualities.[1]

My wife thanks you for your kind enquiries and sympathy. She is awaiting now another operation and a Christmas in a Nursing Home. Very sweet prospect for both of us. We all here accept your benediction with grateful hearts and earnestly hope that You and all yours are well and happy.

Yours most sincerely

J. Conrad

To G. Jean-Aubry
Text MS Yale; *L. fr.* 149

[letterhead: Oswalds]
13. 11. 19

Mon cher ami.

Merci mille fois.

Je viens d'écrire a M. Hallowes pour le prier de me dire son prix.

Ma femme est enchantée de Votre bonne opinion. Elle a eu toujours envie d'un Broadwood.[2] Nous allons essayer de le faire venir tout de suite car le chauffage de la maison ira son train pendant notre absence.

Je viens d'achever le 2ème Acte. Le 3ème est commencé.

Vernon est enthousiasmé. Pour moi c'est une grande aventure – et je vais la mener jusqu'au bout. Vedrenne[3] est decidé a mettre sur la scène cette horrible histoire. Elle est tout simplement atroce quand on la regarde mise

---

[1] David William Bone (1874–1959; knighted 1946) served as a senior commander with the Anchor Line and had written *The Brassbounder* (1910), an autobiographical novel. After reading it, Conrad advised Bone not to leave the sea, and described it to Galsworthy as 'the most suburban thing (I mean spiritually) I've ever read' (*Letters*, 4, pp. 356, 380).

[2] Grand piano.

[3] J[ohn] E[ugene] Vedrenne (1867–1930), currently manager of the Royalty Theatre. Before the war, Vedrenne had collaborated with Harley Granville-Barker on the three seasons at the Royal Court that transformed the landscape of British theatre with productions of such 'uncommercial' and uncompromising playwrights as Hauptmann and Shaw.

a nu pour le theatre – qui est une chose bien brutale. Votre approbation de la *Lettre à Gide* me fait plaisir.

Pouvez Vous venir dans le courant de la semaine prochaine passer la nuit? Love from all.

Tout à Vous

J Conrad

Merci pour les deux N^{os} de la Revue.[1] Excellent! Mon ami. Excellent! Il n'y a que vous pour un tour de force comme cela. Felicitations.

Translation

My dear Friend,
A thousand thanks.
I have just written to Mr Hallowes asking him to tell me his price.
My wife is delighted by your favourable opinion. She has always wanted a Broadwood. We're going to try to get it at once, since the heating in the house will be working during our absence.
I have just finished the 2nd Act. The 3rd is started.
Vernon has grown enthusiastic. It is a great adventure for me – and I am going to see it through to the end. Vedrenne has decided to put this horrible story on the stage. It is simply gruesome when one looks at it laid bare for the theatre – something truly brutal. Your approval of the *Letter to Gide* gives me pleasure.
Can you come for a night next week?
Love from all.

Yours truly

J Conrad

Thank you for the two numbers of the magazine. Excellent! my friend. Excellent! Only you could have managed a tour de force like that. Congratulations.

To J. B. Pinker
Text TS Berg; Unpublished

[letterhead: Oswalds]
Nov. 13th. 1919.

My dear Pinker.
The Second Act is at last really being posted to-night together with this letter. The corrections and re-typing have taken up more time than we thought.

---

[1] *The Chesterian*, edited by Jean-Aubry.

Apart from that I didn't give it all my time as I have already started the Third Act and hope to have it finished in a week from to-day.

— I have had the offer of a Broadwood piano, a grand, in excellent condition and a beautiful tone. It has been inspected for me by the Editor of the Chesterian, a professional singer and a concert pianiste.[1] The price would be something in the neighbourhood of £80, and Jean-Aubry tells me that at the price it is an excellent affair. I shall make arrangements for transporting and delivery here sometime in the course of next week. I shall ask you then to send a cheque if the transaction goes through within the limit of price as above. I would have waited till next year if I had not been assured that this occasion is not one to let go by if I mean to have a piano at all.

— A visit from Jack and Ada is announced here for Saturday next – and I still know nothing as yet of Jack's War Baby![2] I suppose I will have to sit up half the night on Friday. Jessie's report is extremely dismal, and I must see for myself.

— I have received a little book from Doubleday which treats of the Garden City miraculous garden, and of the Garden City authors in alphabetical order.[3] Therefore J. C. is first. It contains a lot of cheerful statements and says that *The Arrow* was a best seller for its period, that *Chance* is being continually re-printed, and that of the others of the set 200, 000 copies have been sold. Whether fancy or fact all this makes cheerful reading; and I don't see any reason why they should invent that sort of information. A very complete bibliography of Kipling is included in that Vol. and also of O. Henry. But not of my work.

We saw Ralph yesterday looking well and he gave us a good account of both his parents.

Ever affect^{ly} Yours

Joseph Conrad

PS Please send me £5 in notes for wages.

To T. J. Wise

Text MS BL Ashley 2953; Unpublished

[letterhead: Oswalds]

13. 11. '19

Dear Mr. Wise.

I have had a letter from our friend Curle which I have answered.

---

[1] The singer would be Mme Alvar.
[2] Galsworthy's *A Saint's Progress*, published 16 October; in this novel, a clergyman's daughter gives birth to an illegitimate child whose father has been killed in the war.
[3] The *Country Life Press*, 'Published for the Friends of Doubleday, Page', 1919.

In this connection I'll say that I am willing to agree to the publication of 10 booklets (2 copies of each being sent to me) for the sum of £200, which I need now for a special purpose. Otherwise I would not have considered the matter at all. I consent also to fiction being included. But on that you must come to an understanding with Curle. (2 stories).[1]

Pardon this hasty scrawl. I want to catch the post. Friendly regards

Yours

J. Conrad

To T. J. Wise
Text MS BL Ashley 2953; Unpublished

[letterhead: Oswalds]
13. 11. '19

Dear Mr Wise.

As our letters crossed I just drop you a line to say that I consider this matter as settled, since on reading yours carefully I do not see any points of difference between us.

If you have a list of papers made up by Curle with whom I left the selection I here agree formally to the choice he has made.

Believe me

Always faithfully Yours,

J. Conrad

To Eugene T. Sawyer
Text MS Stanford; Unpublished

[letterhead: Oswalds]
14. 11. 19

Dear Sir.[2]

Many thanks for your friendly and appreciative letter which has touched me deeply. I am most grateful to you for the kindly thought which prompted you to write to me. Such messages are a great reward.

Believe me,

Yours with the greatest regard

Joseph Conrad.

---

[1] The second series of Wise pamphlets included 'Prince Roman' and 'The Warrior's Soul'.
[2] Eugene Taylor Sawyer (1846–1924), an American, began writing sensational fiction in the 1870s; although he claimed to have originated the Nick Carter detective series, his former collaborators disputed the assertion. When Conrad wrote to him, Sawyer was living in San Jose, California.

To Edward Garnett

Text MS Colgate; G. 290

[letterhead: Oswalds]
Sunday. 16. 11. 19

Dearest Edward.

God (I don't know his address) is my witness that your two last letters (others too) have been put away amongst the "preciosa" of my study.
Miss H[allowes] is another witness – more accessible than the other. But why
protest so much? The very warmth of your criticism when we were walking up and down on the grass at Spring Grove (You remember) amazed
and touched me. That after all these years you should think my work
worth so much thought, so much feeling, so much interest gave me almost
a feeling of awe.[1] Such friendship gives to one's life a sense of continu-
ity, keeps off that dreadful suspicion of futility which dogs our footsteps
and as we grow older threads* on our very heels. It was a most unexpected experience and it – nothing else – makes the Rescue memorable
to me.

I scribbled 3 lines to you directly we got into this house but in the muddle
of the first days the envelope may not have been posted. Afterward I became
not so much busy as absorbed. I want to finish something before we move
from here to L'pool where Sir R. Jones is going to operate again on Jessie's
knee. A horrid prospect! She, as usual ever serene, sends you her dear love –
and has administered a scolding to me for not writing to you long before. In
her own obscure and penetrating manner she has understood many years
ago how much I owe to you.

I'll stop abruptly here. I have a gouty wrist – not fit to write with.
I shall let you know of our departure directly we get a date from the
Surgeon.

Ever unalterably Yours

J. Conrad.

PS I shall begin on Rescue in Jany and give it a month if necessary. All your
letters and marginal notes are religiously preserved for guidance.

---

[1] The most recent surviving letter dates from 13 October (MS Texas; *Portrait*, p. 142). Garnett
thought *The Rescue* 'gained on the second reading. I appreciated better the *immense feat* of
pulling off the subject at all! . . . I hope you didn't find my few comments unsympathetic &
hypercritical.'

To Sir Sidney Colvin
Text MS Lubbock; Unpublished

[letterhead: Oswalds]
18. 11. 19.

Dearest Colvin.

Thanks for your dear note. I am bad enough to be en robe-de-chambre all day but I've done some work.

It was unthinkable to disturb Lady Colvin. I do promise myself a good long talk next time I am in town.

Our united dear love to you both.

Ever Yours

J. Conrad.

To G. Jean-Aubry
Text MS Yale; Unpublished

[letterhead: Oswalds]
18. 11. 19

Cher Aubry.

Je pense que nous serons ici encore D^{che} prochain.[1] Nous serons enchantés de Vous voir. Envoyez nous un petit mot.

Amitiés de tout le monde

Tout à Vous

J. C.

Translation

Dear Aubry.

I think we shall still be here next Sunday. We will be delighted to see you. Do drop us a line.

Regards from everybody

Sincerely yours

J. C.

To J. B. Pinker
Text MS Berg; Unpublished

[letterhead: Oswalds]
Tuesday 18. 11. 19

My dear Pinker

I have concluded the piano deal and sent the cheque for £73–10. Please pay that amount to my acc^t in Lon^{on} West[minst]^{er} Bank.

---

[1] The 23rd.

The transportation will cost another £10 I guess. I'll send you the acc*.*

Eric would have told you of my visit. Since then I have progressed as far as the half of act III, having worked all the morning to-day, tho' I've a beastly gouty foot.

I do hope your throat is better. You want the Riviera cure badly, I think.

Borys will be going to L'pool on Thursday to start rooms-hunting, and also to discover something definite about Sir R. J[ones]. Pray send him £25 for his expenses.

Our love to you both.

Yours ever in the hope of better news

J. Conrad

To Gerald Cumberland

Text J-A, 2, 234

Oswalds.

Nov. 20, 1919.

Dear Mr. Cumberland,[1]

At the beginning I must say that I have not read the tales through as yet.[2] I am just now in a special mood which prevents me attaining that complete detachment from one's personality which would be necessary to answer your question: if I ever dare to answer it.

Perhaps if you were a youthful beginner it would have been somewhat easier. But you are not a beginner. You have written books, and, at your age, you ought surely to know the strength and character of the temperament behind your pen. And I suspect that you really do know all about yourself. I have not seen any criticisms – contemptuous or otherwise – of your volume of tales. I can see that they are mature productions, the expression of a personality already formed and obviously talented; but I can't form an opinion of its strength from these pages, nor yet gauge the force of the creative impulse that, if you go on, go on in that direction, would have to sustain you to the end of the road. I have no critical faculty. No man should trust me in that, because I don't trust myself. The case of my question to Mr. Jacques doesn't make a good precedent.[3] I had already then (though I did not know it myself) lived one of my lives. I was content with it; and had his verdict been different

---

[1] Gerald Cumberland was the pseudonym of Charles Frederick Kenyon (1881–1926), an author and musician who made his living as a dramatic and musical critic in Manchester and London. *Set Down in Malice*, a volume of reminiscences, appeared in 1918.

[2] *Tales of a Cruel Country* (1919), a collection set in war-time Greece.

[3] As Conrad remembers it in Section 1 of *A Personal Record*, he asked W. H. Jacques '"Would it bore you very much reading a[n] MS. in handwriting like mine?"'

I would have been perfectly content with it to this day. I had no conception of what a literary ambition may be and I don't know that I understand it even now. The very form of my question proves it sufficiently. I didn't ask him whether I should write. I didn't think of writing then. I really did not care what he might say. But I imagine that if he had said "No" I would have gone on and finished that piece of writing, simply because, in truth, I did not care.

And ever since I must confess that, in truth, I never did care what anybody said. It may appear a most brutal and ungrateful thing to come from a man who has been so well understood. When, after finishing *Almayer's Folly*, I hesitated at the parting of the ways, not at all from literary ambition but because of the strong hold my old life had still on me, I admit that it was Edward Garnett who tipped the balance. His words were: "You have the style, you have the temperament. Why not write another?" You will observe that he said nothing about the pursuit of literature. He simply said:- "Why not write another?" And I verily believe that I can do no better than pass on those words to you.

To Richard Curle
Text MS Indiana; Curle 53

[letterhead: Oswalds]
Saturday. [22 November 1919][1]

My dear Curle.

We are coming to London on Thursday on our way to L'pool for the operation which is fixed for Tuesday 2 of Dec.

I can't tell you where we will be staying. But I'll send you a wire on Wednesday. We shall proceed to L'pool on Sunday noon, as Jessie's room at the Nurs: Home wont be vacant till that day.

On Thurs: I'll be most likely lunching with Heinemann and having tea with an American. But we could meet in the evening. On Friday I lunch with Vernon (Vedrenne's partner) who is to be the producer of the play. I have just finished act III. I shan't touch the IV till the worry is over and we are settled down in L'pool.

Our love

Your

J. Conrad

[1] Curle's dating, confirmed by the travel arrangements.

PS The Archbishop's Wife¹ called yesterday. This is fame! Unfortunately Jessie was in bed and not well enough to see her.

PPS This is good news about the Travels being in the press.²

To R. B. Cunninghame Graham
Text MS Dartmouth; J-A, 2, 235; Watts 187

[letterhead: Oswalds]

22. II. 19

Dearest Don Roberto

I am just fresh from the second reading of your vol.³ My dear friend the track of Your unshod hor[s]es may be faint but it is imperishable.⁴

There is a tone, a deep vibration in these latest pages of Yours which has moved me profoundly.

In this great wealth of things grown precious with time it is hard to say on which the heart is set especially. Wonder goes with one as one turns the pages; in the Park or on the Pampa you have the gift of drawing the reader with You into the very core – the central, the imponderable – of your own expcrience; so that unless he be dead to all truth he looks at the lands of this earth (on which you have travelled so much) with your own eyes – the eyes of [a] wanderer, of a horseman and of a très noble gentilhomme.

Los Pingos – Bopicuá which of them, or of any one between, do I like best? When I read you I identify myself so completely with your words, your sensations and as it were the very soul of your vision that I'll never be able to answer that question to myself.

A Vous de Coeur

Joseph Conrad

---

¹ Edith Murdoch Davidson: her husband, Randall Thomas Davidson, became Archbishop in 1903. As the daughter of Archbishop Tait, she already knew her Canterbury.
² *Wanderings* appeared in 1920: for Conrad's reluctance to write an introduction, see the letter to Curle of 31 December.
³ *Brought Forward* (Duckworth, 1916): among the stories and sketches are 'Los Pingos' ('The Ponies') and 'Bopicuá'. Graham wrote to Conrad on 25 October promising a copy, praising *The Arrow*, and offering 'the biggest candle to be bought (if I were a Catholic) to La Virgen del Pilar' for a successful operation on Jessie Conrad's knee (MS Williams College; *Portrait*, p. 143).
⁴ Graham's preface to *Brought Forward* concludes: ''Tis meet and fitting to set free the horse or pen before death overtakes you ... I would have you know that hardly any of the horses that I rode had shoes on them, and thus the tracks are faint' (pp. x–xi).

To J. B. Pinker

Text TS Berg; Unpublished

[letterhead: Oswalds]

Nov. 22nd 1919.

Dearest Pinker.

We had word by wire yesterday that the operation is fixed for 2nd. of Dec. and so this period of almost intolerable suspense is drawing to a close. We propose to leave here on Thursday and spend Friday and Saturday in London. Jessie wants to see a few friends. As far as I know we shall start for Liverpool on Sunday noon, arriving there at 5. 20, taking Jessie straight to the Nursing Home, where a room for her will be vacant on that day. It's about time! She is pretty nearly at the end of her endurance; and, as a matter of fact, I too am no longer fit for anything but waiting for the day.

Did I tell you I finished Act Three on Thursday? Without being immensely bucked up by this progress I am fairly satisfied with it. What Vernon will think of it is another matter. I have just written to him asking him to arrange with you on the telephone to lunch with us two on Friday. I hope to bring with me the corrected First Draft of Act Three and I expect Miss H[allowes] will have it clean copied for you and Vernon the week after next. I won't begin Act Four till we are settled in Liverpool. I am really not fit to tackle it just now.

I suppose we will be in Liverpool six weeks. It is hardly safe to reckon on less. Plenty of time to finish the play and correct it and re-correct it and do all that can be done to it before it is thrown out to the beasts.

When he was last here Vernon in a most friendly manner offered to pay me a flying visit in Liverpool should I feel in need of advice or assistance. He said it would save me the trouble of writing to him. He is really a very good fellow and I owe you another candle (as they say in France) for bringing us together.

I wish I had heard from somebody that you are feeling definitely better. It was just like you, to write me an inspiriting letter while you were feeling seedy yourself. It came in good time and helped forward the end of that Third Act very much. I hope to talk several matters over, with you on Friday. Jessie sends her love to all your house.

Ever Yours

J. Conrad.

PS B[orys] meets great difficulty in finding rooms. We expect him back to-morrow.

To Frank Vernon
Text TS/MS Leeds; Unpublished

[letterhead: Oswalds]
Nov. 22nd. 1919.[1]

Dear M[r] Vernon.[2]

I expect you have read by this time the Second Act, which I am not concerned to defend as it stands. What I want to say is that I see and feel it like that, and have no conception of any other way. Of course that remark does not apply to the details of speech and visualisation. In that you will find me absolutely ready to accept suggestions. I have such confidence in your sympathetic understanding that I hardly feel the need of pointing out to you that it is a play in which a story is narrated, mainly. (There are plays which study the subject through mere characterisation of people involved, also plays where the story is told in action.) In this play the bulk of the story is narrated, not through an arbitrary whim of my own but in the logical development of the plan. The story is the story of the Verlocs. The first act begins it and presents visually the characters of those people. In fact it establishes them in the memory of the audience at that precise moment of their story. Through Acts Two and Three the story is narrated, not by mere mouthpieces invented for the purpose but by people who for various (and I hope perfectly clear) reasons are vitally concerned in what has happened. Act Four presents the end of the story, again visually, in the strict dramatic form of the consequent and final passions and emotions which can be watched in their ultimate workings to the very end.

Of course the story of Winnie Verloc could have been presented on the stage in a different way. I am quite aware of that; but having once adopted this conception it has made me its own, and any other way has become to me unthinkable. Not that I have renounced the dramatic form in the two – I may call – *narrative* Acts. On the contrary, I think I have kept the sense of the drama continuous through them. The people who talk about the Verlocs are not extraneous to the story. They are involved in it through their own emotions and desires of varying quality of strength, but, in any case, forming

---

[1] Mention of the plans for London and Liverpool confirms this date. Vernon's letter to Conrad of [4 November] (TS Berg; *Portrait*, pp. 144–5) taking issue with Conrad's belief that 'Everything depends on the actors' must be a reply to the present letter, and thus is wrongly dated. Conrad received Vernon's letter on 5 December: see the letter to Pinker of that date.

[2] Major Frank Vernon (1875–1940; until 1899, Frank Spicer), producer, author, and translator, was born in Bombay. After four years in the army, he returned in 1919 to the West End and resumed his collaboration with J. E. Vedrenne; later, he also produced plays in Paris.

a sufficient motive. At least so it seems to me. And that being done in my own way the rest depends on the actors. It is their interpretation that will make the whole thing either interesting or wearisome.

Since I sent to Pinker the more or less corrected draft of Act Two I have finished Act Three (Great Lady's Drawing-room) leaving the audience informed that *now*, within the next half hour or so, Mr Verloc, much shaken by the happenings of the morning, is going to face his wife, the only possession that a Secret Agent may call his own (everything else he has in the world including his life being from the nature of his occupation absolutely at the mercy of his employers' discretion.) He knows that prison for a couple of years is the safest place for him. But before he gains that refuge he must make a clean breast of the events to his wife and give her instructions for the future. This is the *moral* situation at the end of Act Three. *Visually* it ends on the fury and consternation of Mr Vladimir who holds the middle of the stage when the curtain falls. It is the best I could do for the moment; but I want to tell you that I would be ready to modify the last six pages or so if you deliberately come to the conclusion that from the theatrical point of view the ending of the Act is not sufficiently effective.

And in the last instance that too depends on the actors! Everything depends on the actors. That is why the stage has always frightened me.

In this connection I have a request to make. Would you find time to go to the Old Vic. in the first week of December and form an opinion of the girl who will be playing Lady Macbeth? She is only 20.[1] I have known her when she was still a child, before the war, but I have seen her on the stage only once (in 1917), in the part of Regina in *Ghosts*. In that part she was good; for me unexpectedly so; and in a way very difficult to define. But I certainly think that she *was* good. The quietness of her realisation was what impressed me most. Of course I have seen a good deal of her in private life, so to speak, and she was here last Sunday when I was moved by interest and curiosity to go over the part of Lady Macbeth twice with her, to see what she would do with it and also to offer my suggestions. She has got the physique for Mrs Verloc, and of course with her I would have the opportunity of impressing my conception of the part in a way I could not do with anybody else. She is very plastic yet and, as far as I can judge, very receptive. I won't

---

[1] Catherine Willard died in 1954. Her obituary in the *New York Times* gives 1900 as her date of birth; theatrical directories give 1895. She acted with the Old Vic company from September 1918 to May 1920; besides Lady Macbeth, she played Olivia, Beatrice, Katharina (the 'Shrew'), Gertrude, and the Chorus in *Henry V*. The part of Winnie Verloc eventually went to Miriam Lewes.

say anything more at present because this is a mere suggestion. But I hope you will find time to see her.

On Friday we will be all in London on our way to Liverpool where we must arrive on Sunday evening at the latest. The operation will take place on the 2nd. Dec^{cr}. Perhaps we could arrange a meeting with Pinker to make the third of the conclave. If you feel like it perhaps you will arrange with P on 'phone and lunch with us on Friday.

Yours sincerely

J. Conrad.

PS I won't begin act IV till we are in L'pool and the trouble is over. Just now I can't concentrate sufficiently.

To Edward Garnett

Text MS Texas; Unpublished

[letterhead: Oswalds]

23. II. 19.

My dear Garnett.

I was glad to get your letter. You don't say how your throat is. I hope you are better.

Jessie will be operated on the 2^d Dec. in L'pool. We shall be in London on Friday on our way there. I can't tell you where we are going to hang out for two days as I don't know myself yet. I'll drop you a line in a day or two. Perhaps we could meet.

Jessie sends her dear love.

Ever Yours

J. Conrad.

To André Gide

Text MS Doucet; Vidan (1970)

[letterhead: Oswalds]

24. II. 19.

Mon cher Gide.

Sans doute il y a de ma faute. Je n'ai qu'a Vous remercier de Votre lettre[1] et d'être parfaitement franc avec Vous. Eh bien, mon cher, je confesse que je

---

[1] Conrad wrote to Gide on the 4th and 24th; between these dates, Gide wrote twice, on the 10th and 21st (*Portrait*, pp. 145–9). In the first of his letters Gide agrees that the translation of *The Arrow* should be re-assigned to Jean-Aubry; in the second, he draws back, having learned that Mme Maus refused to give up her contract. Conrad's conciliatory tone suggests that he had not yet seen the second letter.

Vous serai infiniment reconnaissant si Vous pouviez donner le *Arrow* a Aubry. Je l'aurai là, sous la main. Je ne connais pas le français il est vrai, mais je le comprends et même je le sens assez bien. Et peut-être pourrai-je lui faire comprendre mieux de vive voix les nuances de ma pensée. Ce livre de ma 60ème année me tient fort au coeur. Vous qui comprenez tant de choses Vous saurez peut-être me pardonner cette faiblesse.

Dans deux jours nous quittons cette maison pour aller a Liverpool où ma femme aura a subir une nouvelle operation. Je suis dans un état de nervosité éxaspérant. Je suis en train de faire une pièce (adaptation de L'Agent Secret) mais en verité je ne sais pas ce que fais.

Je termine brusquement ici avec l'assurance de ma grande affection pour Vous.

Tout a Vous

J. Conrad

P. S. Nous serons absents 6 semaines. Ma femme se rapelle* a Votre bon souvenir.

Translation

My dear Gide

No doubt some of the fault is mine. I can only thank you for your letter and be perfectly frank with you. So, my dear fellow, I confess that I should be infinitely grateful if you could give the *Arrow* to Aubry. I shall have him here, under my hand. True I don't know French, but I understand it and even have the feel of it quite well. And perhaps I can give him a better idea of the nuances of my thinking *viva voce*. I hold this book of my sixtieth year very close to my heart. Perhaps you can forgive me this weakness.

We leave this house in two days to go to Liverpool, where my wife will have to undergo a new operation. I am in an exasperating state of nerves. I am in the middle of writing a play (adaptation of *The Secret Agent*) but truthfully, I don't know what I am doing.

Here I end abruptly, with the assurance of my great affection for you.

Yours

J. Conrad

P.S. We shall be away for six weeks. My wife sends her best wishes.

To William Rothenstein
Text MS Harvard; Unpublished

[letterhead: Oswalds]
24. 11. '19

My dear Will.

I am an abominable correspondent.

We were very glad to hear of you and of your plans. As to our plans: we are leaving here on Thursday on our way to L'pool where my wife will be operated [on] again on the 2^d Dec. A most horrid prospect for the merry season of Xmas.

My best wishes go with your John wherever he goes. Give him my love, especially, on this occasion of his entering on that Oxford life which I have no doubt is a very unique thing and very well worth having whether it turns out brilliant or not.

I've done not a stroke of *profitable* work since last July. I wrote some short prefaces for a limited edition (in America), and have been correcting the text. It's time to put my literary affairs in order. I confess I am getting just a little weary of paper and ink and all this business of scribbling.

I'll drop you a line after the operation. I think Jessie has written to dear Alice already. My love to you and all your House

Ever Yours

J. Conrad.

To Richard Curle
Text MS Indiana; Curle 55

[Oswalds?]
Wed^y [26 November? 1919][1]

Dearest Curle

We'll be at the Norfolk. Jessie arrives about 4 o'clock. If You come about 7. you will find me there too.

We are very very glad at your plans for settling down.[2] We'll have a good long talk.

Yours

J. C.

---

[1] Curle dates this as [26 December], which was a Friday. If his date is right, Conrad's letter to Mary Pinker of 24 December implies that the Conrads were now at home rather than about to pause in London. The following note to Jean-Aubry shows Conrad planning to meet Curle at the Norfolk on the evening of 27 November, a meeting suggested in the letter of the 22nd.

[2] 'I was then taking a house in Oxfordshire' (Curle's note).

To G. Jean-Aubry
Text MS Yale; Unpublished

[Oswalds]
[26? November 1919][1]
Nous serons a Norfolk Hotel Surrey St Jeudi soir. Voulez-Vous venir a 7[h]
et diner avec moi et Curle en garçon?

Tout à Vous

J. C.

Translation

We'll be at the Norfolk Hotel Surrey St on Thursday evening. Would you
like to come at 7 pm for a bachelor dinner with Curle and me?

Yours truly

J. C.

To J. B. Pinker
Text MS Berg; Unpublished

Norfolk Hotel
Surrey St Strand
London WC 2
Sunday. 30. 11. '19

Dearest Pinker.

I had a lot to say to you but somehow lost my opportunities.

Vernon has the III act since yesterday. I saw also Vedrenne.

Please send to Jessie in the usual way her weekly money to the Sefton Nur[g]
Home

70 Huskisson St.
Liverpool

Please pay in £100 to my acct at the bank and settle the enclosed bill for me.

This is all I'll worry You with just at present. I'll write to you on Tuesday
after the operation.

The address of the lodgings B[orys] found for us is

85. Kingsley Road
Princes Park
L'pool.

Our love

Ever Your

J Conrad.

---

[1] A card postmarked on the 27th, a Thursday, perhaps written the day before.

PS I will run up to town for a day, before you leave on your holiday.

To J. B Pinker
Text MS Berg; Unpublished

[85 Kingsley Road, Liverpool]
Wed^y 2 pm [2 or 3 December 1919]^1

Dearest Old Friend

Thanks for your note of this morning. I have just come from the Nurs^g Home. Jessie is in considerable pain but manages to look cheerful. She sends her best love to you and yours.

The operation was over at 11 am. Jones came down the stairs looking extremely pleased. It appears that the joint is perfectly stiff and all the trouble was caused by an ab[s]cess affecting part of the upper bone. That had to be cut away. Jones assured me that he had taken away everything that was looking in the least suspicious and that in all probability this is the end of Jessie's troubles. She will have to be watched for a few months lest another ab[s]cess should form but he assured me that it was not likely. If everything goes on as well as it looks we may be able to get away from here much sooner than we expected.

Life is rather impossible here. However we shall make the best of it. I will write you in a day or two.

Please my dear fellow ask D'day for as many sets of Coll^d Ed^{on} as you can get in reason – 3 – 4 or even six. I return the agreement duly signed.

I have been feeling beastly seedy in my tummy and am far from comfortable at this moment of writing.

Our love

Yours ever

J. Conrad

To J. B. Pinker
Text MS Berg; Unpublished

[85 Kingsley Road, Liverpool]
Friday evg [5 December 1919]^2

My dear Pinker

Jessie is getting on. It really looks as if her troubles were coming to an end. I and B[orys] are going to dine with Sir R. Jones on Sunday and he promised to talk over her prospects at length then.

---

^{1} At 11:30 a.m. on Tuesday the 2nd, Conrad wired Jean-Aubry with the news 'Operation performed successfully' (Yale). Anxious and ill, Conrad either headed this letter with the wrong day or postponed writing to Pinker until he felt stronger.

^{2} Dated by the progress of Jessie Conrad's recovery.

Meantime I am gouty. Was in bed yesterday. To-day I got up and found Vernon's letter (and act III) awaiting me downstairs.[1]

I see what he means. I wanted to do something out of the common. His line is pretty obvious. But he does not see that by conducting the development of Act II in 3 scenes (incorporating the Drawing Room) I will have to sacrifice certain effects of the last act.

However I am not quite fit just now to think the matter out, so I won't worry you with my views and arguments.

Jessie sends her love to Mrs Pinker and yourself in which I join.

Ever yours

J. Conrad

PS Don't think that I am scared off or discouraged or even disgusted. I simply feel that Vernon has given me food for anxious meditation. You'll hear from me soon; meantime please thank him warmly from me for his letter.

To Edward Garnett

Text MS Colgate; G. 291

85 Kingsley R^{d}

Princes Park

Liverpool

[8 December 1919][2]

Dearest Edward.

Now we can say for certain that the operation is a succes[s]; and we may hope that poor Jessie's troubles are nearing their end. She sends you her love.

My renewed thanks for your marginal notes and your letters about *The R.* I have started on the text now.

I'll drop You a line in a few days.

Ever Yours

J. Conrad.

To J. B. Pinker

Text MS Berg; Unpublished

[85 Kingsley Road, Liverpool]

10. 12. '19

My dearest Pinker.

Jessie's progress is so rapid that we *may* be ready to leave here about the 22^{d}.

---

[1] See *Portrait*, pp. 144–5.   [2] Dated by postmark.

If so we will take advantage of your kind offer to have John for a few days. Jessie will write to Mrs Pinker. I suppose it will be on the 18 or 20. We shall know soon for certain.

I have extended Miss Hallowes leave till after Xmas. Please send her the next quarter's salary (to March 1920) £25. to 11 Oakley St. Chelsea. She will start at once correcting the *Secret Agent* and the *Set of Six*, which are the next books for D'day.

What is he worrying about? He has got in hand with prefaces, complete: *A1. Folly – Outcast – T of Unrest Nigger Lord Jim Youth. Typhoon, Nostromo Mirror of the Sea. Personal Record.*

Let him publish that lot say at the rate of two a month. I'll let him have in Jany the prefaces of the *Sec. Agent* and *Mirror*. I can't do it before. If he can't wait let him do what he likes. Months ago I asked him when he was going to begin and at what rate he was going to publish. I must now work at Rescue text. There is a lot to be done. I'll take up the play on our return home. Here it is impossible.

Please transfer £200 to my acc^t to see me through the end of this year. Expenses here are rather heavy.

Pardon this disconnected scrawl. I'll run up to town to talk with you before long. Are you well? I dont know why I am anxious about Your health.

Yours ever

J. C

To Richard Curle
Text MS Indiana; Curle 54

85 Kingsley R^d
L'pool.
12. 12. 19

Dearest Richard.

I snatch a moment for this scrawl. Everything is going on so well that Jessie may be released from the Home about the 22^d – in which case we should spend only one day in London. I'll let you know the exact date.

Of course I feel happy. But as to doing anything it is impossible here. All the time is taken up in going up and down this dratted town for one thing or another and sitting with Jessie. My mind is a blank. I can't even look through the *R[escue]* proofs.

I won't call on your tried friendship to come over here. Jessie sends her love and her thanks for your sympathy. All this seems too good to be true and I have a dread of some beastly development. But every one assures me that this it isn't likely.[1] The wound itself is healing beautifully.

We shall want of course to see you on our passage through. Will you be in town?

Ever af'ctl^{ly} yours

J. C.

To Sir Robert Jones
Text TS copy Yale; Unpublished

85 Kingsley Rd
Princes Pk
L'pool
[12 December 1919][2]

Dear Sir Robert[3]

My friend, a distinguished man of letters, Mr Jean Aubry has arranged to come to L'pool and deliver a lecture on some French poets at the Royal Institution during my stay here.[4] He had fixed it for the 12th, – that is to-night. When I accepted your most kind invitation to the dinner I was under the impression that to-day was the 11th. My friend who arrived yesterday takes it for granted that I will attend his lecture and indeed I have promised to do so, of course, more than a month ago. I throw myself on your indulgence as to what I am to do in this difficulty. Can you let me off? Of course if you've made any arrangements as for instance Mr Watson[5] coming down here, on purpose, I shall have to throw Aubry over.

All this is my fault entirely and I am heartily ashamed to have to appeal to you in this way: but Aubry is an old friend and seems very anxious I should hear what he has to say. It is also an arrangement of old standing.

---

[1] 'This [time] it isn't likely'?
[2] On the surviving text, a copy made for J-A but not used there, Jean-Aubry wrote '10 dec. 1919'; the circumstance of the double commitment, however, points to the 12th as the proper date.
[3] Sir Robert Jones (1857–1933; knighted 1917, baronetcy 1926), an orthopaedic surgeon, was widely honoured at home and overseas. A native of North Wales, he practised in Liverpool, where he was consulting surgeon to all the large hospitals. He was also a consultant at St Thomas's Hospital, London, and a member of the War Office's Medical Advisory Board. From 1921 to 1925, he served as President of the British Orthopaedic Association. His monographs and textbooks on the surgery of joints, military orthopaedics, and general orthopaedics were widely used.
[4] Jean-Aubry was going to lecture on 'Verlaine et les musiciens'.
[5] Frederick Watson (1885–1935), the husband of Sir Robert's daughter Hilda. He wrote books for boys and once suggested a collaboration with Conrad: *Letters*, 5, pp. 69–70. Watson's *Life of Sir Robert Jones* appeared in 1934.

Pray forgive my stupidity and as the decision rests with you perhaps you will be good enough to phone a message for Mr Conrad to The Adelphi Hotel where I shall call in the afternoon.

If it was not for the feelings of that excellent fellow and devoted friend Jean Aubry, I would not have troubled you in this stupid way. But I am sure you will understand my difficulty.

Believe me, dear Sir Robert,

yours with greatest regard

Joseph Conrad.

To André Gide

Text MS Doucet; Vidan (1970)

[85 Kingsley Road, Liverpool]

15. 12. 19

Mon cher Gide

Je Vous écris encore de Liverpool mais nous allons rentrer chez nous à la fin de cette semaine. L'operation a parfaitement réussi et nous pouvons ésperer que la longue periode de souffrance est finie pour ma femme.

Merci de Vos deux bonnes lettres. Aubry est venu ici pour faire une conference et est resté deux jours. Il m'a montré la lettre de M. Gallimard[1] au sujet du titre du Vol des Contes *Within the Tides*. Les objections de M. Galli^d. a le publier sous le titre *Planteur de Malata* sont on ne peut plus justes. De même pour ses remarques sur l'alternative proposée par Aubry: *Entre Flot et Jusant*. Ceci est impossible comme M. G. le voit très bien.

Que pensez-Vous de: *En Marge des Marées?*[2] C'est ma suggestion a Aubry que j'ai prié de la présenter a M. Gallimard, qui sans doute Vous en parlera. Si l'alliteration ne Vous repugne pas trop ceci rend assez bien l'idée du titre anglais.

Pardonnez moi cet atroce gribouillage. J'ai le poignet goutteux. Quelle scie cette goutte! – Je ne sais pas comment Vous remercier de Votre indulgence et de Votre patiente amitié.

Tout à Vous

J. Conrad

---

[1] Gaston Gallimard (1881–1975), publisher of the *Nouvelle Revue Française*, had just established the Librairie Gallimard, which would become one of the most significant literary publishing houses in France.

[2] This was the title Gallimard accepted. *En marge des marées*: 'At the tides' edge'; *Entre flot et jusant*: 'Between ebb and flow'.

Mille amitiés de la part de ma femme. Elle espère de Vous voir chez nous bientôt. Elle s'en fait fête.

Translation

My dear Gide

I am still writing to you from Liverpool but we are going home at the end of this week. The operation has had an excellent outcome and we can hope that my wife's long period of suffering is over.

Thank you for your two good letters. Aubry has been here to give a lecture and stayed two days. He showed me the letter from M. Gallimard about the title of the volume of stories *Within the Tides*. M. Gallimard's objections to publishing it under the title *Planteur de Malata* are as fair as can be. Likewise his remarks on the alternative proposed by Aubry: *Entre Flot et Jusant*. This is impossible as M. G. well sees.

What do you think of: *En Marge des Marées*? This is my suggestion which I have asked Aubry to propose to M. Gallimard, who will no doubt tell you about it. If the alliteration does not repel you too much, this renders the idea of the English title quite well.

Excuse this horrible scrawl. I have a gouty wrist. What a bother this gout is! – I do not know how to thank you for your indulgence and your patient friendship.

Yours sincerely

J. Conrad

A thousand thanks on behalf of my wife. She hopes to see you soon at our house. She's overjoyed about it.

To Mary Pinker
Text MS Private collection; Unpublished

[letterhead: Oswalds]
24 Dec. '19

Dear Mrs Pinker

Our warmest thanks to Yourself and your children for your kindness to our child. I am writing in both our names because we are trying to keep Mrs Jessie lying down today and we won't even give her a pencil to play with. She certainly ought to rest completely for one whole day at least. She will be writing to you very soon, and meantime I am instructed to give you her love and assure you of her warm gratitude.

John is the only one of us in the privileged position of knowing *all* the family but Miss Pinker must not doubt of the prominent place she holds in our thoughts that at this season (and indeed at all seasons) turn affectionately to [the] Burys Court circle. May everything that is good, prosperous and happy attend you all in your united and individual lives unto the most remote future.

Believe me dear Mrs Pinker

always your most faithful friend and servant

Joseph Conrad.

To J. B. Pinker
Text MS Berg; Unpublished

[letterhead: Oswalds]
29 Dec. '19

Dearest Pinker.

I have been beastly seedy for days; not gout this time, but inflam[m]ation of the prostate with a swollen gland and a lot of pain in passing water. Quite a new sort of circus for me. I have to drug myself and be "very careful" – whatever that may mean. Anyhow a very depressing state of affairs; though I am assured that the affection* is *not* of a "virulent nature" and will pass off soon under the treatment. I wish it would make haste, then. The very acute stage is over by now, but the discomfort is still very great, and of course I feel horribly depressed. I have done nothing – you won't be very surprised to hear, but I shall get Miss H[allowes] back by next Monday and try to get hold of something. Prefaces for *Set of Six* and *Secret Agent* are the most urgent for U. S. and the corrections of *Rescue* for England.

I wonder how you are keeping? Shall we see you here soon? I mean very soon? It would be a great comfort. I am worrying myself generally without any reason that I could state. It is very silly no doubt. I have been confined indoors, so I haven't seen Tanner. Have you heard from him? Perhaps your visit here would settle or rather clear up the matter. I hope you've forgiven me for putting you in touch with that asinine personality. Ralph mustn't bear me a grudge either.

Jessie is ordered a course of massage and tonics. She is going on very well really, but of course *now*, the excitement is over, she feels rather shaky. I don't wonder at it. Tuesday the 2ᵈ of *this* month was the day of the operation, and to see her move about—it doesn't seem possible. She sends her dear love to Mrs Pinker and yourself and wants you to be the *first guest* here at the beginning of the new Era. My love to you all. Do drop me a line about yourself.

Ever Yours

J. Conrad.

PS Please send Tanner £62. 10 1ˢᵗ Quarter's rent. I enclose also the Po[w]ᵉʳ rate demand £19. A bill of Hatchards £8. 15

To Richard Curle
Text MS Indiana; Unpublished

[letterhead: Oswalds]
31. 12. '19

My dear Friend.

I let 24 hours pass over my first impulse; and now I am confirmed after careful thinking in my feeling that what you ask me to do is inadvisable from one point of view, and useless from another.

For as a counter move to your brother's megalomania it would miss its mark. The public would not know – and if it knew it would not care. It is a private affair. From the public point of view I really cannot write a preface to a book dedicated to myself. A move so open to misinterpretation (of the most obvious kind) can do no good to the book, or, on the face of it, be creditable to you and to me.[1]

I am so strongly convinced of this that I have no compunction whatever in saying *No*. It simply can't be done.

The thing to do, since your brother began the fuss, is for your publishers to insert short pars in the press, something to that effect: We have recei[ve]ᵈ a comm[unicati]ᵒⁿ from Mʳ J. Curle who is anxious that a work we are about to publish should not be ascribed mistakenly to his pen. We state here therefore that the volume we intend to issue in Janʸ (?) is not by Mʳ J Curle who has published some years ago a book of travels,[2] but by Mʳ Richard Curle critic and man of letters author of *Life is a Dream – Shadows out of the Crowd* etc . . . and of *Joseph Conrad: A Study* in our Men of Letters series.

Something like that. This is much more likely to get home than a preface where no allusion to your brother's outbreak could be made. Leaflets to that

---

[1] The work in question was *Wanderings*, which was already in press. Eventually, Conrad wrote a preface to another of Curle's books, *Into the East: Notes on Burma and Malaya* (1923).

[2] James Herbert Curle had published *The Gold Mines of the World* (1899) and *The Shadow-Show* (1912); his next book of travels was *This World of Ours* (1921).

effect could also be inserted in the copies of the 1st ed^{on} at no great cost, I suppose. In haste to catch post

Ever yours

J. Conrad.

To J. B. Pinker
Text MS Berg; Unpublished

[letterhead: Oswalds]

Wednesday. [31 December? 1919][1]

My dear Pinker.

Please send me £5 in notes as I have difficulty in cashing my cheques here. Also pray send B[orys] his £8 for Jan^y.

Ernest Dawson has left India for good.[2] He came here yesterday and stayed the night. Just the same good fellow only grey-headed now.

What with a gouty wrist and that other thing I am having a most miserable time.

Ever Yours

J. Conrad

To Sir Sidney Colvin
Text MS NYU; Unpublished

[London?]

Friday. [1917–1919?][3]

My dear Colvin.

How extremely kind of you to think of sending me the books. You are indeed a true friend. And what an interesting selection.

---

[1] The report on Conrad's health (see the letter to Pinker of the 29th) establishes the January referred to as that of 1920, but the 7th of that month seems late for the payment due to Borys Conrad.

[2] Major Ernest Dawson (1884–1960) met Conrad through W. E. Henley and H. G. Wells. Dawson contributed stories of life in Burma and Australia to *Blackwood's*; he had been serving in Burma as a magistrate and an officer in the Rangoon Volunteer Rifles.

[3] In the sale catalogue of letters from Conrad to the Colvins (Anderson Galleries, New York, 7 May 1928), this item appears between dated correspondence of 27 June and 11 July 1919; if the catalogue were accurate in its chronology, the date would thus be 4 July, the only intervening Friday, and the meeting proposed for 'Thursday' would be on the 10th. The circumstances, however, do not match those of early July. Conrad was unusually healthy then; his correspondence makes no mention of a gout attack, and he could travel at will. He saw the Colvins during his visit to London on 22 and 23 June. On Friday, 11 July, the Conrads left for a weekend with the Hopes. More probably, the present letter belongs to a period when Conrad was in London, short of reading material, and suffering from a gouty foot or leg. This combination of circumstances occurred in December 1917–February 1918 and again in February 1919. Cf the letter of 30 December 1917, written after a 'raid' on the Colvins' library.

I do hope I will be able to put on if only a Jeager* boot¹ on Thursday. I hate going out in a cloth gout-boot – it's too early-Victorian for a common mortal. It was well enough for Lord Palmerston.²

Our dear love to You both

Ever Your

J. Conrad

¹ A boot made of the heavy but breathable fabric devised by Gustav Jaeger, who gave his name to the 'Sanitary Woollen System'.
² Henry John Temple, third Viscount Palmerston (1784–1865), three times Foreign Secretary and twice Prime Minister.

SILENT CORRECTIONS TO THE TEXT

The following slips of the pen have been silently corrected.

Missing full stop supplied

1917: Tuesday [16 Jan.]: after 'in town'; Tuesday evg. [16 Jan.]: after 'pay the C⁰'; 17 Jan. (to Cunninghame Graham): after 'admiring affection'; 22 Jan. (to Hastings): after 'the happiest results'; 26 Jan.: after 'famous *Tweed*)', after 'edition was published', after 'Merchant Service'; [late Jan.] (to Pinker): after '"... be a volume"'; [1 Feb.]: after 'typography', after 'Horrid'; 11 Feb.: after 'you know'; [c. 12 Feb.] (1st of 2 to Pinker): after 'damnable in a way'; [14 Feb.] (to Dent): after '*two parts*', after '1. 11'; [22 Feb.] (to Dent): after 'what you like'; [24 Feb.] (to Pinker): after 'deserves investigation'; [24 Feb.] (to Leon): after 'abominably seedy'; 1 March: after '"... undying regard"', after 'affectionate regards'; 19 March (to Pinker): after 'T[elegraph])'; 27 March (to Dent): after 'finished writing it'; [28 March]: after 'the *Professor*'; 2 April (to Colvin): after '6. 30'; [11? April]: after 'are going on', after 'this week ready', after '(Hutchinson. 6/-)'; [April?]: after 'may be effective', after 'in great pain'; [8? May]: after 'could be done', after 'Chelsea'; [11 May]: after 'containing the story'; [15 May]: after 'decent performance'; 6 June (to Dent): after 'when that appears'; 2 Aug.: after 'love to you all'; [13 Aug.]: after 'highly successful'; 15 Aug.: after 'on 21ᵗ Sepʳ'; Friday [12 or 19 October?]: after 'for *any* hat'; [24 Oct.]: after '(... quarrelling violently)'; 27 Oct.: after 'with the knee'; 31 Oct.: after 'done me good'; 12 Nov.: after 'may be this week'; [17? Nov.]: after 'about 12–30'; 30 Nov.: after 'kindly attentions'; [30 Nov.]: after 'more of my money', after 'about everything'; [8 Dec.]: after '*my* invitation'; [12 Dec.?] (to Pinker): after 'his contract', after 'you to say', after 'even sorry'; [15 Dec.?]: after '"... gives up the play"'; [19 Dec.] (to Pinker): after 'here with us'; 31 Dec. (to Ada and John Galsworthy): after 'love to you both'; 31 Dec. (to the Sandersons): after 'love to you all'; Sat: [May–Dec.]: after 'reached me to-day'.

1918: 1 Jan. (to Galsworthy): after 'in your person'; [29 Jan.]: after 'put him off'; 12 Feb. (to Pinker): after 'to the house'; 19 Feb. (to Pinker): after 'his leave expenses'; [c. 28 Feb.]: after 'consented', after 'to the fees'; 4 March (to Pinker): after 'remember his name'; [6 March]: after 'the question', after

549

'in the morning', after 'is right'; 20 April: after 'when you write'; 28 April
(to Colvin): after '(... dated 23^d)'; [3 May]: after 'infinity of comp^lts', after
'Her love'; 9 May (to Walpole): after 'or thereabouts'; 15 May: after 'all these
matters'; 27 May: after 'about 12. 30', after '(... relinquished pension)', after
'have to say', after 'detain her'; 12 [June]: after 'for an account'; [13 June]:
after 'Part v'; 25 June: after 'four o'clock'; [5 July]: after 'any new develop^ts';
[6 July] (to Jessie Conrad): after 'to the Bank', after 'by 8. 30', after 'flying
about'; 17 July: after 'the 15 Aug^st'; [4 Aug.]: after 'poor Kitty'; [c. 8 Aug.]
(to Jessie Conrad): after 'for the journey'; [c. 8 Aug.] (to Pinker): after 'on
Monday'; [9 Aug.]: after 'for a moment'; [14 Aug.]: before 'But it occurred',
after 'of the two'; [1 Sept.]: after 'worse again'; 27 Sept.: after 'a few lines';
[11 Oct.]: after 'with many thanks'; 17 Oct. (to Roberts): after 'I apologise';
21 Oct. (to Colvin): after 'the 17th'; [23 Oct.] (to Pinker): after 'sends her
love'; [28 Oct.]: after 'recover completely'; 15 Nov.: after 'to me at once'; 19
Nov.: after 'fort brave homme'; [20 Nov.]: after 'Meth: Thanks'; [22? Nov.]:
after 'to Hampton', after 'now and then'; 27 Nov.: after 'fort de la chose';
[27 Nov.?]: after 'taken no notice'; 3 Dec.: after 'about the house'; 6 Dec.
(to Pinker): after 'in England'; 10 Dec. (to Pinker): after 'Sends her love';
16 Dec.: after 'to you both'.

1919: [15 Jan.]: after 'a small child'; 21 Jan.: After 'sends her love'; 8 Feb.:
after 'love to You'; [13 Feb.] (to Mackintosh): after 'mother's mind'; [13 Feb.]
(to Pinker): after '*The Con[n]oisseur?*)', after 'for £26. 10'; 15 Feb. (to Dent): after
'throes of Rescue'; 18 Feb.: after 'regis^ed post'; 26 Feb. (1st of 2 to Pinker): after
'considerable time'; 12 March: after 'sends her love'; 19 March: after 'sends
her love'; 20 March (to Pinker): after 'into F. U's clutches'; 3 April (to Pinker):
after 'for your visit'; [5 April]: after 'une depêche'; 14 April: after 'word from
you'; 10 May: after 'with a messenger'; 12 May (to Walpole): 'are too many';
[14 or 21? May]: after 'is very unsatisfactory'; 27 May (to Pinker): after 'the
IX and last'; 20 June: after 'early Sept^er'; 28 June: after 'the next instal^l';
[17 July]: after 'verbal agreement'; [21 July]: after 'English edition'; 31 July:
after 'wife and boys'; [5 Aug.?]: after 'see you again'; 7 Aug. (to Colvin): after
'love to you both'; 20 Aug.: after 'dans ses moyens'; 24 Aug. (to Curle): after
'Mrs Wedgwood'; 26 Aug.: after 'a 2. 30'; 27 Aug.: after 'about one o'clock';
30 Aug. (to Doubleday): after 'happy just now'; 6 Sept. (to Pinker): after
'Personal Record', after 'seeing you soon'; [8 Sept.]: after 'Personal Record',
after 'the deluxe edition', after 'for *US*'; [17 Sept.] (to Pinker): after 'part of
the country'; 19 Sept. (to Walpole): after 'tenderest remembrance'; 24 [25 or
26?] Sept.: after 'love to David'; [early Oct.?]: after 'they are preparing';
[7 Oct.]: after 'when we meet'; 15 Oct. (to Colvin): after 'and affectionately';

15 Oct. (to Pinker): after 'Oct. issue'; 17 Oct.: after 'a gouty wrist'; 11 Nov. (to Curle): after 'on that matter'; 13 Nov. (to Wise): after 'hasty scrawl'; 16 Nov.: after 'preserved for guidance'; [22 Nov.] (to Curle): after 'called yesterday'; 22 Nov. (to Cunninghame Graham): after 'moved me profoundly'; 24 Nov. (to Rothenstein): after 'to dear Alice already'; [26 Nov.?] (to Curle): after 'good long talk'; 30 Nov.: after 'just at present'; [2 or 3 Dec.]: after 'at 11 am'; [8 Dec.]: after 'in a few days'; 10 Dec.: after '*Personal Record*'; 12 Dec.: after 'the exact date'; 31 Dec.: after 'useless from another'.

Dittography
3 Jan. 1917: a second 'seems' after 'Who rules us'; [late Jan. 1917] (to Quinn): a second 'a' after 'is sixty-five if'; [23 June 1917]: an 'is' after 'She's'; [15 December 1917?]: a second 'as' after 'his I'd just'; 9 May [1918]: a second 'we' before 'will return here'; 23 Oct. 1918 (to Ruyters): a second 'un' after 'convient envoyez'; 30 Aug. 1919 (to Curle): a second 'a' after 'to live with and'; [17 Sept. 1919]: a second 'a' after 'took John at'.

Comma supplied
[7 or 14 March 1917]: after 'shall see them', after 'pièces de conviction'; 16 April 1918: after 'agreement with Dent'; 22 Sept. 1919: after 'I imagine'.

Question mark supplied
[4 Feb. 1917]: after '*this* point of view'; [14 Feb. 1917] (to Dent): after 'enclosed portrait'; [9? March 1917]: after 'in their relations'; [27 Nov. 1917]: after 'Chablis (white)'; 30 Jan. 1919: after 'flounderings anxiously'; [17 July 1919]: after 'is it still in his office'.

Dash supplied
19 March 1917 (to Dent): after 'two collectors'; [30 Nov. 1917]: after 'cheapest room'; 20 Aug. 1919: after 'plutôt symbolique', after 'pour moi une joie', after 'de la Mediterranée'; 29 Dec. 1919: after 'her move about'.

Bracket supplied
[17? Nov. 1917]: after 'by road'; 2 Oct. 1919: after 'as specified'.

Quotation mark supplied
22 Jan. 1917 (to Hastings): after 'enough but Samburan etc etc', after 'in his ship.'; [11? April 1917]: after 'Behind the Ger^{an} Veil'; 28 April 1918

(to Gide): before 'Grand Prix'; Nov. 27th 1918 (to Jean-Aubry) after 'regards'; 19 Feb. 1919: after 'Now'; 24 Sept. 1919 (to Colvin): after 'extremement attrayante'.

Capital letter supplied
1 Oct. 1917 (to Wharton): for 'Oct' in Conrad's dating.

The following slips have been silently corrected in typed or hand-copied letters.

11 June 1918: 'perfectly' for 'peorfectly'; 9 Sept. 1918 (to Colvin): 'serious' for 'serios'; (to Gardiner): 'repellent' for 'repallant'; 25 Sept. 1918 (to Pinker): comma added after 'And anyhow', after 'or wickedness'; 27 Sept. 1918: 'help of artifice' for 'help oa artifice', comma added after 'whether or no'; 7 Oct. 1918: 'consensus' for 'concensus', comma added after 'As I have said' 9 Oct. 1918: comma added after 'for a fortnight'; 25 Nov. 1918 (to Jean-Aubry): 'Çeci' changed to 'Ceci'; 6 Dec. 1918 (to Pinker): full stop added after 'in England', comma added after 'After all'; 12 Dec. 1918: question mark added after 'in the tropics'; 30 Jan. 1919: comma added after 'am not frightened'; 27 Feb. 1919: a second 'her' deleted after 'Marie Lohr any day'; 1 March 1919: 'Miscellanea' for 'Miscellania'; 19 Aug. 1919: comma added after 'may be just'; 21 Aug. 1919 (to Pinker): 'nucleus' for 'nucleous'; (16 Squire): comma added after 'some sixteen years'; 30 Aug. 1919 (to Doubleday): 'prophecy' for 'prophesy'; 11 Nov. 1919 (to Pinker): comma added after 'with the letter', after 'my adaptation', after 'in the book'; 22 Nov. 1919 (to Vemon): bracket added after 'told in action'.

CORRIGENDA FOR VOLUMES 4-5

Volume Four
Page 108, n. 4: for '*New*' read '*News*'.

Volume 5
vii: Index of names, 708.
xvii: Hunter (1985, 2): 'Letters from Conrad, II'.
xxii–xxiii (1915): *Within the Tides* published in US 15 January; in UK, 24 February. *Victory* published in US c. 27 March; in UK, 24 September.
xxix: for 'Janko' read 'Yanko'; for '*górali*' read '*górale*'.
xlviii (Mackintosh biography): for 'Dunbar' read 'Duncan'.
l and 147, n. 3: Eric Pinker died in 1973.
liv and 697, n. 1: Shorter born 1857.
lvii and 562: Grace Willard born 1877.
35: no [letterhead].
83, n. 3: insert 'in' after 'home'.
163, 190, 202, 206, 480, 494, 519, 531, 660: superfluous 'c' before cedilla.
186: for 'previous' read 'precious'; after 'before you leap', insert 'I say this wholly affectionately and more than half-seriously'.
213: for 'devoré' read 'devoué'.
227: after 'opportunity of joining' add 'in'.
276 (Harrison): replace with MS text, p. 161.
325: for 'many, mostly' read 'many. Mostly'.
345: '*re-arrangement*' with hyphen, not dash.
360, n. 4: for 'Pinter' read 'Pinker'.
378: first line should begin 'ranged from'.
391–2 (Curle): MS Private collection; delete commas after 'Well', 'see', 'sincerity', 'insight', 'jeers', 'After all', 'Yours ever'; 'Standard' and 'Times' not underlined; for 'twopenny' read 'two-penny'; after 'terrifically busy' insert new paragraph 'Love from us all'.
405, n. 3: replace 'two' with 'three'.
417, n. 2: for 'Scupinelli' read 'Scapanelli'.
427–8: MS Private collection; [letterhead: Capel House]; for 'thoughts . . . sit' read 'thought . . . sits'; MS punctuation is 'of being idle of being useless, with a sort of absurd anxiety as though'; MS ends 'Believe me very sincerely yours Joseph Conrad'.

433, n. 2: replace 'Conrad' with 'Conrad's'.

438–9 (Wedgwood): MS Private collection; [letterhead: Capel House]; for 'volume of short' read 'vol. of short'; for 'attempt on' read 'attempt at'; after 'offer some' add 'little'; for 'publication' read 'publications'; for 'stands it all.' read 'stands it all!'; MS signed 'Joseph Conrad'.

455, n. 2: the *Metropolitan Magazine* offered $2,000 for 'The Planter' (Paul R. Reynolds to J. B. Pinker, 3 February 1915 (TS Berg)).

461, n. 2: the contract was with Fiction Pictures, Inc. (Paul R. Reynolds to J. B. Pinker, 12 January, 16, 19 March 1915 (TSS Berg)).

463, n. 1: replace '34' with '37'.

527 (Symons): published in Hunter (1985, 3) as 28 October 1919; 1915 dating is right.

539 (Colvin): for 'One cannot' read 'One can't'.

556–7 (Curle): MS Private collection; delete commas after 'Richard', 'make of it'; remove hyphens from 'week-end' and 'to-morrow'; replace 'The value' with '*The* value'; remove apostrophe from 'afraid won't'; close up 'so far'; add 'both' after 'love to you'.

558, n. 1: replace 'Marshall' with 'Marshal'.

579 (Thomas): for '12 Ap '16' read '12 Ap 16.'; for 'Believe me' read 'Believe [me]'.

671, n. 5: Flight Commander Bertram Denison Kilner.

695 (Gardiner): insert N-dash before 'or at any rate'.

(Index I): delete 'Harrison, 276'; 'Penfield, Frederick' should read 'Penfield, Frederic'.

(Index II): add 'Millais, John, 608'; to 'Conrad: Works', add "The Partner", 311, *A Personal Record*, 161, *Suspense*, 126'; insert 'Neel, Philippe, 649'; replace 'Wicker' with 'Wicken'; join Salisbury entries under 'Salisbury, Marquis of'; in 'Zajączkowski, Albertyna', change 'ski' to 'ska'.

INDEXES

In Index I, which identifies recipients, only the first page of each letter is cited. Letters to more than one person are indexed under each name and marked [††].

In Index II, an index of names, run-on pagination may cover more than one letter. References to ships are consolidated under 'Ships'; to newspapers and magazines, under 'Periodicals'; to London and its localities, under 'London'; to the war and its campaigns, under 'First World War'. For the last category, see also 'Ships' and individual entries for countries (e.g., France, Germany, Poland), government departments (e.g., War Office, Foreign Office), naval, military, and aeronautical units (e.g., Army Service Corps, Royal Naval Reserve). References to works by Conrad, uniform editions, and selections from his writing appear under his name.

INDEX I. RECIPIENTS

INDEX II. GENERAL